P9-CFE-526

Michael Suchanick:
Multi-Linguist
Kung Fu Artist*
Karaoke King
Is Welcome Here

Your life. You can
bring it with you.
Learn more about
Michael and tell us
more about you
visit pwc.com/bringit

*connectedthinking

PRICEWATERHOUSECOOPERS

Michael Suchanick:
Multi-Linguist
Kung Fu Artist*
Karaoke King
Is Welcome Here

Your life. You can
bring it with you.
Learn more about
Michael and tell us
more about you
visit pwc.com/bringit

*connectedthinking

PRICEWATERHOUSECOOPERS 🄿

SPECIAL ADVERTISING SECTION

ACHIEVEMENT STARTS WHEN
YOU HARNESS THE POWER
OF MANY PERSPECTIVES.

WE KNOW GREATNESS IS OFTEN THE PRODUCT OF PEOPLE BRINGING FRESH PERSPECTIVES TO THE TABLE.

That's why Northrop Grumman is committed to the internships and educational programs that support fresh thinking and diversity in our organization. By partnering with organizations like the Society of Hispanic Professional Engineers and offering company-wide mentoring, we're fostering a breadth of perspectives to power our world-class aerospace and defense projects. Perspectives like yours.

Achievement never ends.

NORTHROP GRUMMAN

DEFINING THE FUTURE™

www.careers.northropgrumman.com

Community
Values
Tradition
Opportunity
Family

You deserve a career with a purpose. This human-service career has the potential to be your lifelong passion because you'll be giving generations of children the opportunity to reach their full potential as responsible adults.

Visit www.scouting.org for information on employment opportunities in Scouting.

BOY SCOUTS OF AMERICA®

OUR GOALS ARE GLOBAL.
ARE YOURS?

ADM

Archer Daniels Midland Company is a world leader in agricultural processing and fermentation technology. The agriculture industry is full of opportunities. It's more than just corn and soybeans. When you advance your career at ADM, you become a part of global solutions that feed the world, develop renewable resources and unlock nature's potential. With over 26,000 employees across the globe, we welcome a broad mix of attitudes, approaches, perceptions and backgrounds. **Make your goals our goals.**

FOR MORE INFORMATION, VISIT US
ONLINE AT WWW.ADMWORLD.COM

The Vault/INROADS Guide to Diversity Internship,
Co-op and Entry-Level Programs
is made possible through the generous support
of the following sponsors:

Abercrombie & Fitch

ARROW ELECTRONICS, INC.

The Vault/INROADS Guide to Diversity Internship,
Co-op and Entry-Level Programs
is made possible through the generous support
of the following sponsors:

Exelon.

FirstEnergy
Foundation

 imagination at work

Hallmark
Cards

HCA

Limitedbrands

 LOCKHEED MARTIN

L'ORÉAL
WORLD LEADER IN BEAUTY PRODUCTS

North Carolina Office of State Personnel

NORTHROP GRUMMAN
DEFINING THE FUTURE™

 Northwestern Mutual
FINANCIAL NETWORK®

OSRAM
SYLVANIA

PRICEWATERHOUSE COOPERS

Protective
Doing the right thing is smart business.℠

The Vault/INROADS Guide to Diversity Internship, Co-op and Entry-Level Programs is made possible through the generous support of the following sponsors:

Rockwell Collins

Schering-Plough

STATE FARM
Auto Life Fire
INSURANCE

SunTrust

TeneT

TEREX

TOYOTA

TXU

UnitedHealthcare
It just makes sense.

WAL★MART
where successful careers begin

Weyerhaeuser

Wyeth

The media's watching Vault!
Here's a sampling of our coverage.

"For those hoping to climb the ladder of success, [Vault's] insights are priceless."
– *Money magazine*

"The best place on the web to prepare for a job search."
– *Fortune*

"[Vault guides] make for excellent starting points for job hunters and should be purchased by academic libraries for their career sections [and] university career centers."
– *Library Journal*

"The granddaddy of worker sites."
– *US News and World Report*

"A killer app."
– *The New York Times*

One of Forbes' 33 "Favorite Sites"
– *Forbes*

"To get the unvarnished scoop, check out Vault."
– *Smart Money Magazine*

"Vault has a wealth of information about major employers and job-searching strategies as well as comments from workers about their experiences at specific companies."
– *The Washington Post*

"Vault has become the go-to source for career preparation."
– *Crain's New York*

"Vault [provides] the skinny on working conditions at all kinds of companies from current and former employees."
– *USA Today*

CIT is a leading commercial and consumer finance company and a leader in the financial industry. We are committed to the development of our employees and invite you to explore the opportunities we have available. Whether you are just beginning your career or are a seasoned professional, there are a variety of current opportunities that could be right for you. We offer competitive salaries and comprehensive benefits as well as programs for educational assistance, Work/Life and internal training. For more information about a career at CIT, visit us at www.cit.com.

I CIT Drive
Livingston, NJ 07039

THE VAULT/INROADS GUIDE TO

DIVERSITY INTERNSHIP, CO-OP AND ENTRY-LEVEL PROGRAMS

Our *differences*
make our community stronger.

We embrace all the things that
make us different. We support
an environment that respects
every person's heritage . . .
every person's dreams.

Exelon®

THE VAULT/INROADS GUIDE TO

DIVERSITY INTERNSHIP, CO-OP AND ENTRY-LEVEL PROGRAMS

VAULT EDITORS

For information about permission to reproduce selections from this book, contact Vault Inc.150 W. 22nd St. New York, New York 10011-1772, (212) 366-4212.

Library of Congress CIP Data is available.

ISBN 1-58131-439-6

Printed in the United States of America

Acknowledgments

Acknowledgments from Vault

We are extremely grateful to Vault's entire staff for all their help in the editorial, production and marketing processes. Vault would also like to acknowledge the support of our investors, clients, employees, family, and friends. Thank you!

Acknowledgments from INROADS

INROADS would like to thank the entire staff of Vault for their work in completing this very useful resource. In addition, a warm thank you goes to our former CEO, Charles I. Story, for his vision in leading this effort, Wilson Martinez del Rio, Tanza Pride, Jacquelyne Bailey, Tina Marie Bradley, Javona Braxton, Tracy Gray, Samatha Johnson, INROADS managing directors and their staff, and all of our corporate sponsors who so willingly donated time, funding, and efforts to support this publication.

Special thanks also from Vault and INROADS to the committee members who helped finalize the survey: Rod Adams of PricewaterhouseCoopers, Jen Carmody of Deloitte & Touche USA LLP, Betty Granata of GE, Joelle Hayes of United Technologies Corporation, Tamara Hilliard of IBM, Ann Nowak of Liberty Mutual Insurance Company, Tracey Sumner of MetLife and Shaneen Tatum of Lockheed Martin.

We are proud to be an employer that embraces inclusiveness and diversity.

Limitedbrands

BATH & BODY WORKS / C.O. BIGELOW / EXPRESS / HENRI BENDEL
THE LIMITED / VICTORIA'S SECRET / WHITE BARN CANDLE CO.

We are proud to be an equal opportunity employer.

Table of Contents

UNLEASH YOUR POTENTIAL

TEREX, the third largest equipment manufacturer in the world, strives to recruit, employ and develop highly talented and motivated individuals.

We believe that having a diverse group of employees stimulates ideas and creative thinking, a key to both our success and yours.

For more information about TEREX internships and career opportunities, please visit us at www.terex.com.

THE STRENGTH OF MANY. THE POWER OF ONE.

TEREX is an Equal Opportunity Employer / Affirmative Action Employer M/F/D/V

FOUND:
A job where the paycheck is only half the reward.

Do you want more out of your job than just a paycheck? Do you want to be challenged and learn new things? Do you want your talents to be recognized? Put your career in a position to grow at State Farm,® a Fortune 500® company. With a variety of jobs and placement opportunities all across the U.S., go ahead and reward yourself and your career. Join the State Farm team.

LIKE A GOOD NEIGHBOR, STATE FARM IS THERE.®

Like you, we have some distinctive characteristics of our own.*

For the fifth year in a row, PricewaterhouseCoopers was voted the #1 ideal employer in our profession in the Universum Undergraduate Survey of business students.

visit pwc.com/lookhere

unleash your
potential

... we have. GE's Evolution Series locomotive generates 16 cylinders' worth of power with only 12 cylinders, cutting emissions up to 40 percent as compared to our prior models. In addition, it was the first locomotive that met the new U.S. Environmental Protection Agency emissions standards. We call this ecomagination. At GE we invite you to unleash your ecomagination through a career in engineering, finance, manufacturing, sales and marketing, human resources, or information technology.

ecomagination℠
to learn more visit us at gecareers.com
an equal opportunity employer

imagination at work

A diversified technology, financial services, media company.

Introduction

Vault is proud to partner with INROADS, a top nonprofit organization that trains and develops talented minority youth for professional careers in business and industry, on the second annual edition of the *Vault/INROADS Guide to Diversity Internship, Co-op & Entry-Level Programs*. Vault and INROADS make ideal partners to bring students, young professionals and educators the most recent, accurate and up-to-date information on corporate diversity planning, representation, strategies and programs.

For this second annual Guide, 167 top companies and organizations shared their actions and goals in the crucial area of corporate diversity in self-reported profiles. By participating in the Guide, companies are not endorsing Vault or INROADS, and there is no requirement that they be, have been or plan to be an INROADS partner. Rather, they are expressing their commitment to, and appreciation of, the importance of diversity in the 21st century workplace.

We thank all the participants in the second annual *Vault/INROADS Guide to Diversity Internship, Co-op & Entry-Level Programs* and we hope that its readers will find it instructive and useful in evaluating potential employers and partners.

The Editors
Vault, Inc.

Letter from Charles H. Cornelius

Welcome to the second edition of the *Vault/INROADS Guide to Diversity Internship, Co-Op and Entry-Level Programs*. INROADS is honored to again partner with Vault, the premier career resource publisher, to create this valuable tool. Designed to benefit both students and corporations, this book is composed of companies who have developed effective programs to build and maintain diverse, high-quality workforces. Through attracting, recruiting, developing, rewarding and retaining efforts, these companies demonstrate that an active commitment to diversity is a priority in their corporate mission and goals. These efforts are as important to us as they are to you.

Our mission at INROADS is to develop and place talented minority youth with our partnering corporations who strive to build and maintain a diverse workforce. We have been perfecting this service for 36 years. With over 100,000 students who have been involved with our training and placement, we take pride in both the astute leaders produced, and in the profound partnerships we have built with the largest companies in the world.

Having recently joined INROADS as president and CEO, I spent much of the beginning of my tenure visiting with numerous clients and talking with them about the growing need for diversity. It is astounding to report that although the challenges with diversity differ from those of 1970, when INROADS began, the nation's leading corporations' demand for talent is increasing dramatically and becoming more important than ever. Companies know that their success depends on whether diversity is linked to their business strategies.

Many of the companies featured in this book have aligned their strategies by partnering with INROADS. This Guide is an opportunity to display their commitment to diversifying their current and future leaders. We are pleased to partner with many of these corporations who seek to become more inclusive and retain diverse talent at all levels.

For companies who are not INROADS corporate sponsors, we encourage you to develop a customized and strategic plan for the future of your workforce with us. For students and recent college graduates, we invite you to consider all of the great opportunities that lie inside this resource. Diversity is an opportunity for us all. Let's move forward and take it to the next level.

Sincerely,

Charles H. Cornelius
President & CEO
INROADS, Inc.
Next Level Opportunity

Letter from Chris Simmons

PricewaterhouseCoopers (PwC) is honored to be a part of this publication. Our commitment to diversity is not complex. Our focus is on empowering all of our people to be their best—to enable them to develop their talent and skills and take their careers as far as they are able. We understand that when people are inspired, when they feel welcome, when they feel an attachment to an organization, that's when they perform at their best. We believe that's just common sense…and good business.

We know that talented people come in all colors and from all backgrounds, and in this competitive employment environment, we can't afford to overlook any potential source of talent. We also understand that in order to attract the best and the brightest students, we must be known as an employer of choice. So developing a successful diversity strategy has proven a smart investment in our future workforce.

We also take great pride in knowing that we're doing the right thing for our people. Our ultimate goal is to be a distinctive organization, one with an empowered, diverse, talented and high-performing workforce. Partnering with INROADS is one way to ensure fulfillment of this goal. Our commitment to diversity will continue not only to be reflected in our beliefs, but in our ongoing actions. Our continued support of the work of INROADS is an example of that action.

We applaud Vault and INROADS for bringing this information together for both students and corporations who strive to make a difference in shaping America's workforce.

Sincerely,

Chris Simmons
Chief Diversity Officer
PricewaterhouseCoopers

How to Use this Guide

Over the past few years, most U.S. companies have devoted increasing resources to diversity initiatives as well as to the management and administration of these efforts. Nearly all have developed their own unique cultural approach and methods of administration. The *Vault/INROADS Guide to Diversity Internship, Co-op and Entry-Level Programs* was developed to provide students with the essential objective information necessary to meaningfully evaluate corporate diversity initiatives and programs. We hope that the information contained within this Guide will enable students to match their interests and career objectives with an appropriate company.

The Guide format presents the same information for all companies in a user-friendly way, addressing the degree to which several widely-recognized "best practices" are being incorporated into the company's diversity program.

The complete survey sent to the company is printed in the Guide. In cases where a company did not respond to a question, the unanswered question is not reprinted in their profile; it is simply left out. For questions where companies had the option of choosing one or more options to answer a question, we listed the choices the company chose; to see which answers the company did not choose, you can refer to the full text of the survey.

We encourage you to use the information in the Guide as a springboard to ask constructive questions and open a dialogue that will empower you to define your relationship with the company. In the case of students evaluating potential employers, it may be whether the company's efforts measure up to your personal goals and developmental needs.

The survey upon which the *Vault/INROADS Guide to Diversity Internship, Co-op and Entry-Level Programs* is based was finalized by the efforts of a committee composed of representatives from top companies in fall 2004. Participants included Steve Canale of GE, Shannon Thrasher-Bynes of IBM, Carin Kaiser of Kraft, Shaneen Tatum of Lockheed Martin, Kim Washington-Barr of PricewaterhouseCoopers, Tamara Hilliard of IBM, Joelle Hayes of United Technologies Corporation, Tracey Sumner of MetLife, Ann Nowak of Liberty Mutual Insurance Company and Jen Carmody of Deloitte & Touche USA LLP.

Definitions

The survey refers to full-time or permanent exempt employees in the U.S. Entry-level college graduate hires are new full-time, professional or white-collar hires made directly from undergraduate institutions. The survey also covers interns, who typically work during the summer months, and co-ops, who typically work for more extended periods of time during the school year.

For this survey, diversity is defined as male and female minorities and white women but does not include gay and lesbian employees.

For this survey, minorities are defined as those whose ethnic background is other than White/Caucasian (e.g., African-American/Black, Latino/Hispanic, Asian and Native American).

Firm Contact Info

This section contains basic information, including the contact person for diversity hiring. Offices and revenue, also in this section, give a sense of the size of the company.

Recruitment

Here's where you find out how to get hired at the company of your choice. This section contains useful information on schools at which the company recruits (for new hires) as well as other outreach efforts, including participation in conferences, career panels and scholarship programs. Similar info is available for professional hires, as well as insight on whether the company uses women and/or minority-owned executive search firms to make hires.

Internships and Co-ops

Internships and co-op programs are a key way to be hired by any top company. This section describes the type of internships and co-op programs (there may be more than one) offered by the company, as well as contact information.

Scholarships

Many companies offer special scholarship programs for qualified minority students. You'll find the details, including the amount, the deadline to apply and contact information in this section for companies that offer scholarships.

Affinity Groups

If you're thinking of joining a company you may wish to join an affinity group or employee network, which is an internal organization that addresses the needs and interests of specific minority groups, and other employee groups.

Entry-Level Programs/Full-Time Opportunities/Training Programs

Looking for a place to work after graduation that may differ from the place where you did your internship? This section gives an overview of the type of entry-level positions at the company, including training and any kind of educational perks, like tuition reimbursement.

Strategic Plan and Diversity Leadership

Once a company has committed to work at being more diverse, there are various ways in which the company can advance that commitment. It may be helpful for the reader to pay attention to what steps the company's management has taken to communicate its diversity commitment widely and to develop a clear action plan for progress. Is diversity progress a goal that has been set with company-wide responsibility and accountability? Do diversity leaders have a voice on management issues? You can begin to explore some of those issues in this section.

The Stats

Find out how large your potential employer is, and see its revenue growth. Companies may choose to add additional information on minority and male/female demographics if they choose.

Retention and Professional Development

This section covers retention rates of women and minorities, as well as the steps the company is taking to reduce attrition.

Diversity Mission Statement

Many companies have a kind of guiding credo that shapes their approach to employment diversity issues; you'll find it in this section (if the company has one).

Additional Information

This section of the diversity profile is comprised of a narrative composed by the company. There were no requirements regarding what had to be addressed (although we admit to having made a few suggestions). For example, some companies chose to list diversity awards. This section offers a great place for the company to elaborate on some of its answers to the survey questions and discuss things they are doing that we may have failed to cover.

In conclusion, we hope that this book assists you in identifying companies that are a good match to your diversity values and needs. Remember: although you can get a quick impression by flipping through these pages and looking at diversity program overviews, and yes/no responses, the most important factor is the commitment of the company to diversity goals. We hope you find what you're looking for in the *Vault/INROADS Guide to Diversity Internship, Co-op and Entry-Level Programs*.

Survey Invitation Letter from Vault and INROADS

Dear Employer,

We are writing to invite you to participate in an exciting project and to ask for your involvement in the second edition of the *Vault/INROADS Guide to Diversity Internship, Co-op & Entry-Level Programs*, an effective means to explore corporate performance in the critical area of diversity.

INROADS, a nonprofit organization that trains and develops talented minority youth for professional careers in business and industry, and Vault Inc., a premier source of employment information for MBAs, JDs, college students and grad students, have partnered to develop the attached Corporate Diversity Survey. We finalized this year's survey with the advice and assistance of a committee of representatives from top employers (GE, IBM, Deloitte, United Technologies Corporation, Lockheed Martin, Liberty Mutual, MetLife and PricewaterhouseCoopers—all among the INROADS Top 10 in terms of number of interns). We are requesting that all firms listed below complete the survey, which we believe represents the best way to stimulate diversity progress and achieve a measure of consistency in how diversity information is reported.

Vault compiles all of the completed surveys into a directory called the *Vault/INROADS Guide to Diversity Internship, Co-op & Entry-Level Programs*. The Guide's purpose is to educate the business and career center communities, as well as interested students and recent graduates, on the commitment and types of diversity programs in place at approximately 600 major corporations (see list below). The objectives of publishing the Guide are:

- To provide a consistent profile of current corporate diversity planning, implementation and representation;

- To identify the best practices for the design and implementation of diversity initiatives in companies; and

- To outline the strategies, programs, and metrics that top companies use to increase the recruitment, retention and promotion of minority and women employees.

This guide differs from some of Vault's other publications, such as the *Vault Guide to the Top 100 Law Firms* and the *Vault Guide to the Top 50 Banking Employers*, in two significant ways:

- **There are no rankings.** Rather, Vault is simply gathering and presenting information about each company's diversity efforts. Firm profiles will appear in alphabetical order.

- **All information is self-reported by each firm.** Each employer's data will be published virtually as submitted, with only minor editing from Vault for clarity and length, and <u>all edits will be reviewed and approved by the employer prior to publication.</u>

The *Vault/INROADS Guide to Diversity Internship, Co-op & Entry-Level Programs* will be distributed in print and electronic form free of charge to every firm that submits a completed survey, to 10,000 current and recent INROADS interns, and to the career center offices at approximately 500 colleges and universities in the United States. This is our second edition. Please let Marcy Lerner know if you would like to see last year's edition.

We hope that you will join us in this effort by completing and returning the attached survey in a timely manner.

If you have any questions, please direct them to Vault VP of Content, Marcy Lerner, at (212) 366-3724 or mlerner@vault.com, or INROADS New Media Manager, Tanza Pride, at TPride@INROADS.org.

Best regards,

Charles Cornelius
President & CEO
INROADS
www.INROADS.org

Samer Hamadeh
Co-founder & CEO
Vault
www.vault.com

Vault/INROADS Diversity Survey

Survey Introduction

Thank you for taking the Vault/INROADS Diversity Survey (2006 edition). Following are a few pointers on completing the survey. If you have any questions about the survey or how to answer a question, please contact Marcy Lerner, Vault VP of Content, at marcy@staff.vault.com or at (212) 366-3724, or Tanza Pride, INROADS New Media Manager, at tpride@INROADS.org. We thank you for your understanding and welcome comments and feedback as we seek to improve the survey for future editions.

The Process

Participation is entirely free of charge. We ask that a representative or group of representatives from your firm complete the attached questionnaire (in MS Word format) within the next five weeks. Please note that each firm should complete and return only one questionnaire. Do not handwrite or PDF survey responses.

Distribution

The *Vault/INROADS Guide to Diversity Internship, Co-op and Entry-Level Programs* (15,000 total print copies) will be distributed free of charge to every employer that submits a completed survey, to over 10,000 former and current INROADS interns, and to the undergraduate career office of approximately 500 colleges and universities in the United States. The guide will also be sold through college and university bookstores and on the Internet. Excerpts from the Guide will also be available free at www.vault.com. At no additional charge, moreover, the entire Guide will be available to Vault Gold subscribers and to the 500-plus colleges and universities worldwide that have subscribed to the Vault Online Career Library (1,000,000 total PDF copies).

Instructions

1. You may opt to skip any question. If you skip a question, we will not publish the question in your completed entry.

2. The survey covers only U.S. internship, co-op and entry-level hiring, although we do ask for your worldwide locations, employee numbers and revenue figures.

3. The survey refers to full-time exempt employees in the U.S.

   - Entry-level college graduate hires are new full-time, professional or white-collar hires made directly from undergraduate institutions.
   - Exempt employees are employees who are not temporary, hourly or contract.

4. Under section I, Diversity Team Leader/Diversity Campus Recruiting Team Leader, please list the person or persons heading the diversity recruiting efforts at your organization.

5. Under section I, Office Locations, feel free to list the exact locations or supply the number of locations, to list your headquarters plus the number of offices, or to use any other method you prefer of listing locations.

6. Under section XII, Additional Information, points you may wish to address in the narrative include:

- More detail on diversity scholarships for interns, co-ops or entry-level college hires
- More detail on part-time/flex-time programs
- More detail on the workings of your diversity committee
- The names of minority associations with which you have relationships
- A list and description of diversity awards and honors
- Any financial support or service donated to minority public interest organizations and the names of such organizations.

We very much appreciate your participation and look forward to your response.

Vault/INROADS Diversity Survey

I. Firm Info

Contact Person: _____ Title: _____

Diversity Team Leader/Diversity Campus Recruiting Team Leader: (name & title):

_____

Firm Name: _____

Address: _____

City: _____ State: _____ Zip: _____

Phone: _____ Fax: _____ E-mail: _____

Office Locations (worldwide): _____

_____

Career web site address _____

II. Recruitment of Interns, Co-ops and Entry-Level College Graduate Hires

1. Does your firm annually recruit at any of the following types of institutions? (Check all that apply and list the schools).

☐ Ivy League schools: _____

☐ Other private schools: _____

☐ Public state schools: _____

☐ Historically Black Colleges and Universities (HBCUs): _____

☐ Hispanic Serving Institutions (HSIs): _____

☐ Native American Tribal Universities: _____

☐ Other predominantly minority and/or women's colleges: _____

2. Of the schools that you listed above, do you have any special outreach efforts directed to encourage <u>minority students</u> to consider your firm?

☐ Hold a reception for minority students

☐ Conferences.   Please list: _____

☐ Advertise in minority student association publication(s)

☐ Participate in/host minority student job fair(s)

☐ Sponsor minority student association events

☐ Firm's employees participate on career panels at school

☐ Outreach to leadership of minority student organizations

☐ Scholarships or intern/fellowships for minority students

☐ Other. Please specify: _____

3. What activities does the firm undertake to attract minority and women employees?

☐ Partner programs with women and minority associations

☐ Conferences. Please list: _____

☐ Participate at minority job fairs

☐ Seek referrals from other employees

☐ Utilize online job services

☐ Other. Please specify: _____

(a) Do you use executive recruiting/search firms to seek to identify new diversity hires? Yes ☐ No ☐

(b) If yes, list all women- and/or minority-owned executive search/recruiting firms to which the firm paid a fee for placement services in the past 12 months: _____

_____

II. Internships and Co-ops

For the following section, please repeat this template as necessary for all of your U.S.-based internships and co-ops, including those aimed at minority undergraduate students and non-minority undergraduate students (i.e., INROADS)

Name of internship/co-op program: _____

Deadline for application: _____

Number of interns in the program in summer 2005 (internship) or 2005 (co-op): _____

Pay ($US) _____ (indicate if by week, by month, or for entire program)

Length of the program (in weeks): _____

Percentage of interns/co-ops in the program who receive offers of full-time employment

_____

Web site for internship/co-op information

_____

Please describe the internship program or co-op, including departments hiring, intern/co-op responsibilities, qualifications for the program and any other details you feel are relevant.

IV. Scholarships

For the following section, please repeat this template as necessary if you have more than one scholarship aimed at minority undergraduate students.

Name of scholarship program: _____

Deadline for application for the scholarship program: _____

Scholarship award amount ($US) _____ (indicate if by week, by month, or for entire scholarship)

Web site or other contact information for scholarship

_____

Please describe the scholarship program, including basic requirements, eligibility, length of program and any other details you feel are relevant.

V. Affinity Groups

For the following section, please repeat this template as necessary if you have more than one affinity group at your organization.

Name of affinity group/employee network

Please describe the affinity group/employee network, including its purpose, how often it meets, web site, etc.

VI. Entry-Level Programs/Full-Time Opportunities/Training Programs

For the following section, please repeat this template as necessary if you have more than one full-time, entry-level program, training program or management/leadership program at your organization.

Name of program: _____

Length of program _____

Geographic location(s) of program _____

Please describe the training/training component of this program _____

Please describe any other educational components of this program (i.e., tuition reimbursement)

_____

VII. Strategic Plan and Diversity Leadership

How does the firm's leadership communicate the importance of diversity to everyone at the firm? (e.g., e-mails, web site, newsletters, meetings, etc.)

1. Who has primary responsibility for leading diversity initiatives at your firm? Name of person and his/her title:

_____

2. (a) Does your firm currently have a diversity committee? Yes ☐ No ☐

If yes, please describe how the committee is structured, how often it meets, etc.

_____

(b) If yes, does the committee's representation include one or more members of the firm's management/executive committee (or the equivalent)? Yes ☐ No ☐

(c) If yes, how many executives are on the committee, and in 2005, what was the total number of hours collectively spent by the committee in furtherance of the firm's diversity initiatives? How many employees are on the committee, and how often does the committee convene in furtherance of the firm's diversity initiatives?

Total Executives on Committee: _____

3. Does the committee and/or diversity leader establish and set goals or objectives consistent with management's priorities?

Yes ☐ No ☐ Partially (explain): ☐ _____

Please elaborate, if you wish.

4. Has the firm undertaken a formal or informal diversity program or set of initiatives aimed at increasing the diversity of the firm?

Yes, formal ☐ Yes, informal ☐ No ☐

Please elaborate, if you wish.

5. (a) How often does the firm's management review the firm's diversity progress/results?

☐ Monthly

☐ Quarterly

☐ Twice a year

☐ Annually

☐ Does not review/measure progress/results

☐ Other, please specify_____

(b) How is the firm's diversity committee and/or firm management held accountable for achieving results?

_____

VIII. The Stats

(Numbers requested are firm totals for U.S. and international offices on 12/31/04 and on 12/31/05.)

	Total in the U.S.		Total outside the U.S.		Total worldwide	
	2005/2004		2005/2004		2005/2004	
1. Number of employees						
2. Revenue						

Please elaborate on your firm's demographic profile, including the percentage of minorities in the U.S., number of minorities in the U.S., percentage of male/female employees, percentage of minorities and/or women on the executive team, and any other figures you may wish to reveal.

IX. Retention and Professional Development

1. How do 2005 minority and female attrition rates generally compare to those experienced in the prior year period?

☐ Higher than in prior years

☐ Lower than in prior years

☐ About the same as in prior years

☐ Please elaborate if you wish.

2. Please identify the specific steps you are taking to reduce the attrition rate of minority and women employees. (It is suggested that you elaborate on this issue in the final question of this survey.)

☐ Develop and/or support internal employee affinity groups (e.g., minority or women networks within the firm)

☐ Increase/review compensation relative to competition

☐ Increase/improve current work/life programs

☐ Adopt dispute resolution process

☐ Succession plan includes emphasis on diversity

☐ Work with minority and women employees to develop career advancement plans

☐ Review work assignments and hours billed to key client matters to make sure minority and women employees are not being excluded

☐ Strengthen mentoring program for all employees, including minorities and women

☐ Professional skills development program, including minority and women employees

☐ Other. Please specify

XI. Diversity Mission Statement

Please state your organization's diversity mission statement if applicable.

XII. Additional Information

In a narrative of 500 words or less, please provide any additional information regarding your firm's diversity initiatives that you wish to share. See instructions for details and suggestions.

Firms invited to participate in the Vault/INROADS Diversity Survey

3M

84 Lumber Company

A.G. Edwards, Inc.

AAA Automotive Club

Abbott Laboratories

Abercrombie & Fitch

ABN AMRO Holding N.V.

Accenture

Advance Auto Parts

Advanced Micro Devices (AMD)

AdvancePCS

AES

Aetna Inc.

Affiliated Computer Services

Aflac

AGCO

Agilent Technologies, Inc.

AIG

Air Products & Chemicals, Inc.

AK Steel Holdings

Albertsons

Alcoa, Inc.

Allegheny Energy, Inc.

Allergan, Inc.

Allied Waste Industries

Allmerica Financial

Allstate Insurance Company

Alltel

Altria Group, Inc.

Amazon.com

Amerada Hess

Ameren Corporation

American Airlines, Inc.

American Axle & Mfg.

American Cancer Society

American Cast Iron Pipe Co.

American Electric Power (AEP)

American Express Company

American Family Insurance

American Financial Grp.

American Greetings

American Home Products

American Red Cross, The

American Standard

AmerisourceBergen

Ametek

Amgen

AMR

AmSouth Bancorporation

Anadarko Petroleum Corporation

Anheuser-Busch Companies, Inc.

Aon Corporation

Apache

Apple Computer

Applied Materials, Inc.

Applied Signal Technology, Inc.

Aramark

Archer Daniels Midland Company

Armstrong Holdings

Arrow Electronics, Inc.

ArvinMeritor

Asbury Automotive Group

Asea Brown Boveri Inc.

Ashland Inc

AstraZeneca PLC

AT & T

AT&T Wireless Services

Aurora Health Care

Autoliv

Automatic Data Processing (ADP)

AutoNation

Auto-Owners Insurance

AutoZone

Avaya Inc.

Avery Dennison

Avnet

Avon Products

BAE Systems

Baker Hughes

Ball

BancWest Corporation

Bank of America

Bank of New York

Barclays Capital

Barnes & Noble

BASF Corporation

Baxter International

Baystate Medical Center

Bayer CropScience

BB&T Corporation

BE&K, Inc

Becton, Dickinson, and Company

Bed Bath & Beyond

Bell Atlantic

BellSouth

Berkshire Hathaway

Best Buy

Big Lots

BJC Health System

BJs Wholesale Club

Black & Decker

Blackwell Sanders Pepper Martin LLP

Blue Cross and Blue Shield Association

Boeing Company, The

Boise Cascade

Bonneville Power Administration

Borders Group

Boston Scientific Corporation

Boy Scouts of America

BP p.l.c.

Briggs & Stratton

Brinker International

Brinks

Bristol Myers Squibb

Brunswick

Bunzl Distribution

Burlington Northern Santa Fe Railway Co.

Burlington Resources

C. R. Bard, Inc.

C.H. Robinson Worldwide

Cablevision Systems

Caesars Entertainment

Calpine

Campbell Soup Company

Cap Gemini Ernst & Young

Capital One Financial Corporation

Cardinal Health Inc

Caremark Rx

CarMax

Caterpillar

CDW Computer Centers, Inc.

Cendant Corporation

CenterPoint Energy, Inc.

Centex Homes

Central Parking Corporation

Cerner Corporation

Charles Schwab

Charter Communications

ChevronTexaco

CHS

Chubb Corporation, The

Cigna

Cinergy Corporation

Cintas Corporation

Circuit City Stores

Cisco Systems

CIT

Citigroup Inc.

City National

Clarian Health

Clear Channel Communications

Cleveland Clinical Foundation

Clorox Company, The

CNA Insurance

CNF

Coca-Cola

Coca-Cola Bottling Company

Coca-Cola Enterprises

Colgate-Palmolive

Collins & Aikman

Colorado Springs Utilities

Columbia St. Mary's Hospitals & Clinics

Comcast Cable Communications, LLC

Comerica, Inc.

Compass Bancshares, Inc.

Computer Associates Internation

Computer Sciences Corporation

ConAgra Foods, Inc.

ConocoPhillips

Conseco

Consolidated Edison Company of New York

Constellation Energy

Consumers Energy Corporation

Continental Airlines

Convergys Corporation

Cooper Tire & Rubber

Coors Brewing Company (Adolph Coors)

Corn Products International Inc

Corning Incorporated

Costco Companies

Countrywide Financial

Coventry Health Care

Cox Enterprises

CPC International Inc.

Credit Suisse

Crown Holdings

CSX Corporation, Inc.

Cummins

CVS

D&K Healthcare Resources Inc

D.R. Horton

DaimlerChrysler Corporation

Dana Corporation

Danaher

Darden Restaurants

Daymon Worldwide, Inc.

Dean Foods

Dell

Deloitte & Touche USA LLP

Delphi Automotive

Delphi Corporation

Delta Air Lines

Deluxe Corporation

DENTSPLY International

Deutsche Financial

Devon Energy Corporation

Dial Corporation

Dillards

Dole Foods

Dollar General

Dominion

Domino's Pizza, Inc.

Donaldson Company

Dover

Dow Chemical Company

DTE Energy

Duke Energy Corporation

Duke Realty Corporation

Dun & Bradstreet

DuPont

Dynegy Inc.

E.W. Scripps Company, The

Eastman Chemical

Eastman Kodak Company

Eaton Corporation

EBay Inc.

Echostar Communications Corp.

Ecolab, Inc.

Edison International

El Paso Corporation

El Paso Electric

Electronic Data Systems

Eli Lilly

EMC Corporation

Emcor Group

Emerson Electric

Energy East

Engelhard

Entergy Corporation

Enterprise Products Partners

Enterprise Rent-A-Car Company

Equitable Life Assurance Society of the

Equity Office Properties Trust

Erie Insurance Group

Ernst & Young LLP

Estee Lauder

Exelon Corporation

Express Scripts

ExxonMobil Corporation

Family Dollar Stores

Fannie Mae

Farmland Industries

Federal Aviation Administration

Federal Reserve Bank of NY

Federal-Mogul Corporation

Federated Department Stores

FedEx

Fidelity Investments

Fidelity National Financial

Fifth Third Bancorp

First American Corp.

First Data Corporation

FirstEnergy Corporation

First National Bancshares, Inc.

Fisher Scientific

Fluor

FMC Corporation

Foot Locker Inc

Ford Motor

Fortune Brands, Inc.

FPL Group, Inc.

Frank Russell & Company

Freeport-McMoRan Copper & Gold Inc.

Gannett Corporation

Gap Inc.

Gateway

GE

GEICO

General Dynamics Land Systems

General Growth Companies

General Mills Inc.

General Motors Corporation

Genuine Parts

Georgia-Pacific Corporation

Gillette

GlaxoSmithKline plc

Golden West Financial Corporation

Goldman Sachs & Co.

Goodrich Corporation

Goodyear Tire & Rubber

Graybar Electric

Great Plains Energy, Inc.

Group 1 Automotive

Guardian Life of America

Guradian Life Insurance Company of Ameri

H&R Block

H.J Heinz

Halliburton

Hallmark Cards, Inc.

Harley-Davidson

Harleysville Group, Inc.

Harrahs Entertainment

Hartford Financial Services Group Inc, T

HCA, Hospital Corporation of America

HDR, Inc.

Health Insurance Plan of Greater New York

Health Net

Hearst Corporation

Henry Schein

Hershey Company, The

Hewlett-Packard

Hibernia

Hilton Hotels

Hitachi

Home Depot

Honeywell International Inc.

Hormel Foods

Host Marriott

Household International

HSBC

Hughes Supply

Humana Health Plans

Huntington Bancshares

IAC/InterActiveCorp

IKON Office Solutions

Illinois Tool Works

IMS Health Incorporated

ING Americas

Ingram Industries

Intel Corp.

International Business Machines Corporation

International Council of Shopping Center

International Paper

International Steel Group

Interpublic Group of Companies

Interstate Bakeries

ITT Industries, Inc.

J.C. Penney Company, Inc.

Jabil Circuit

Jacobs Engineering Grp.

JEA

Jefferson-Pilot

JM Family Enterprises

Jo-Ann Stores Inc

John Deere

John Hancock

Johnson & Johnson

Johnson Controls Inc.

Jones Apparel Group

JPMorgan Chase

Kaiser Permanente

KB Home

Kellogg Company

Kelly Services

Kerr McGee Corporation

Key Bank

KeySpan

Kiewit Corporation

Kimberly-Clark

Kinder Morgan Energy

Kindred Healthcare

Kmart Holding

Knight Ridder

Kohl's Corporation

KPMG LLP

Kraft Foods

Kroger Company

L-3 Communications

Laidlaw International

Land OLakes Inc.

LandAmerica Financial

Lear Corporation

Leggett & Platt

Lehman Brothers

Lennar

Level 3 Communications, Inc.

Levi Strauss

Lexmark International

Liberty Mutual Insurance Company

Limited Brands

Lincoln Financial Group

Liz Claiborne, Inc.

Lockheed Martin Corporation

Loews Corporation

Longs Drug Stores

L'Oreal USA

Lowes Companies, Inc.

Lucent Technologies

Lyondell Chemical

Manpower

Marathon Oil

Marriott International, Inc.

Marsh Inc.

Marshall & Ilsley Corporation

Masco

Massachusetts Mutual Life

Mattel Inc.

Maxtor

Mayo Foundation

Maytag

MBNA Corporation

McDonald's Corporation

McGraw-Hill

McKesson Corporation	Nextel Communications, Inc.	Pacific Life Insurance Company
MeadWestvaco Corporation	Nike Inc.	PacifiCare Health Sys.
Medco Health Solutions	NiSource	Parker Hannifin Corp.
Medtronic, Inc.	Nissan Motor Corporation	Pathmark Stores
Mellon Financial	Nokia	Pearson Education
Merck	Nordstrom, Inc.	Pepco Holdings
Merrill Lynch & Co Inc	Norfolk Southern	Pepsi Bottling (PBG)
METLIFE	Nortel Networks Corporation	Pepsi North America
MGIC Investment Corporation	North Carolina Office of State Personnel	PepsiAmericas
MGM Mirage	Northeast Utilities	PepsiCo Inc.
Michelin North America	Northern Trust Company (The)	Performance Food Group
Microsoft	Northrop Grumman Corporation	PETsMART Inc
Middle Tennessee State University	Northwest Airlines	Pfizer Inc
Minnesota Mutual Life Insurance	Northwestern Mutual Financial Network	PG&E Corp.
Mirant		Phelps Dodge Corporation
Mohawk Industries	NTL	Philip Morris Companies, Inc.
Monsanto Company	Nucor	Phillips-Van Heusen
MONY-Mutual of New York	NVR	Pinnacle West Capital
Moodys Corporation	Occidental Petroleum	Pitney Bowes
Motorola	Office Depot, Inc.	Plains All American Pipeline
Murphy Oil	OGE Energy	PNC Financial Services Group, Inc.
Mutual of Omaha Insurance	Ohio State University Hospitals	PPG Industries
Nash Finch	Old Republic Intl.	PPL Corporation
National City Corporation	Olin Corporation	Praxair
National Fuel Gas	OM Group	Premcor
Nationwide	Omaha Public Schools	PricewaterhouseCoopers
Navistar Corporation	Omnicare	Principal Financial Group
NBC Universal	Omnicom Group	Procter & Gamble Company, The
NCR Corp	Oracle	Progress Energy
NetBank	OSRAM SYLVANIA	Progressive
New York Life Insurance Company	Owens & Minor	Protective Life Corporation
New York Times	Owens Corning	Prudential Financial
Newell Rubbermaid	Owens-Illinois	PSEG
Newmont Mining	Oxford Health Plans, Inc.	Publix Super Markets
	Paccar	

Pulte Homes Inc.

Qualcomm Incorporated

Quest Diagnostics

Qwest Communications International Inc.

R. J. Reynolds Tobacco Holdings, Inc.

R.J. Reynolds Tobacco

R.R. Donnelley

RadioShack Corporation

Raytheon

Reebok International

Regions Financial Corporation

Reliant Energy

Rite Aid

Robert Half International Inc.

Roche Pharmaceuticals

Rockwell Automation Inc.

Rockwell Collins

Rohm & Haas

Ross Stores

Roundys

Royal Bank Of Canada

Royal Dutch/Shell group of Companies

Russell Corporation

Ryder Systems, Inc.

Ryland Group Inc., The

Safeco Corp.

Safeway, Inc.

Saks Incorporated

Sanmina-SCI

Sara Lee Corporation

SBC Communications, Inc.

SC Johnson & Son

SCANA

Schering-Plough Corporation

Schlumberger

Science Applications International Corp.

Sealed Air

Sears Roebuck

SEI Investments

Sempra Energy

ServiceMaster

Shaw Group

Shell Oil Company

Shell Trading

Sherwin-Williams Co.

Siemens

Simmons Company

SLM Corporation

Smith International

Smithfield Foods

Smurfit-Stone Container Corporation

Sodexho

Solectron Corporation

Sonic Automotive

Southern Company

SouthTrust Corporation

Southwest Airlines

Southwest Gas Corporation

Spartan Stores

Sprint Nextel Corporation

SPX

St. Paul Travelers Companies, Inc., The

Staples, Inc.

Starbucks Coffee Company

Starwood Hotels & Resorts Worldwide

State Farm Insurance

State Street Corporation

Steelcase Inc.

Storage Technology Corporation

Stryker

Sun MicroSystems

Sunoco Inc

SunTrust Banks, Inc.

SUNY Upstate Med Univ

SUPERVALU Inc

Symbol Technologies, Inc.

Synovus Financial Corp.

Sysco

T. Rowe Price

Target Corporation

Teachers Insurance & Annuity (TIAA-CREF)

Tech Data Corporation

TECO Energy

Telephone & Data Sys.

Temple-Inland

Tenet Healthcare Corporation

Tenneco Automotive

Terex Corporation

Tesoro Petroleum

Texas Instruments

Textron

Thrivent Financial for Lutherans

Time Warner, Inc.

Timken

TJX Companies, The

Toyota Motor Company

Toys 'R' Us

TransMontaigne

Travelers Corporation (The)

Triad Hospitals

Tribune Company

Turner Corporation (The)

TXU

Tyco International

Tyson Foods

UAL

UBS AG

Unilever USA

Union Bank of California

Union Pacific Corporation

Union Planters Corporation

UNISYS

United Auto Group

United Defense Industries Inc

United HealthCare Corp.

United Parcel Service (UPS)

United Rentals, Inc

United Stationers

United Technologies Corporation

UnitedHealth Group Company

Universal Health Services

University Hospitals/Cleveland

Unocal

UnumProvident

US Airways

US Bancorp

USAA

USG Corporation

U.S. Steel Corporation

USX

Valero Energy Corporation

Verizon Communications

Verizon Wireless

VF Corporation

Viacom

Visteon

Vulcan Materials Co.

W.R. Berkley

W.W. Grainger, Inc.

Wachovia Corporation

Walgreens

Wal-Mart Stores, Inc.

Walt Disney

Washington Mutual Savings Bank

Waste Management Inc

WellChoice

Wellpoint Health Networks Inc.

Wells Fargo & Company

Wesco International

Western & Southern Financial

Weyerhaeuser

Whirlpool Corporation

Williams Companies, The

Winn-Dixie Stores

Wisconsin Energy

Wisconsin Public Service Corporation

Wyeth Pharmaceuticals

Xcel Energy

Xerox Corporation

YMCA of the USA

York International

Yum! Brands, Inc.

Zions Bancorporation

Zurich North America

We're privileged to help build the future.
One inspired mind at a time.

Children are eager to learn. And the men and women of Lockheed Martin are eager to help. That's why we support educational initiatives that help children reach their greatest potential – from one-on-one mentoring to broad-based programs designed to excite students about math and science. We also provide grants and local programs for students of all grades – from elementary school to universities. At Lockheed Martin, we're serious about education. Because we believe that giving back is the very best way forward.

LOCKHEED MARTIN
We never forget who we're working for™

www.lockheedmartin.com

DIVERSITY
PROFILES

84 Lumber Company

1019 Route 519
Eighty Four, PA 15330
Phone: (800) 664-1984

Locations

500 offices in 40 states in the US

Diversity Leadership

Position currently being filled.

Employment Contact

Angeles Valenciano
Director of Diversity & Inclusion
1019 Route 519
Eighty Four, PA 15330
Phone: (800) 664-1984 Ext. 2180
www.84lumber.com/About84/careers.asp

Recruiting

Please list the schools/types of schools at which you recruit.

• Private schools
• Public state schools
• Historically Black Colleges and Universities (HBCUs)
• Other predominantly minority and/or women's colleges

Do you have any special outreach efforts directed to encourage minority students to consider your firm?

• Hold a reception for minority students
• Advertise in minority student association publication(s)
• Participate in/host minority student job fair(s)
• Sponsor minority student association events
• Firm's employees participate on career panels at schools
• Outreach to leadership of minority student organizations
• Scholarships or intern/fellowships for minority students

What activities does the firm undertake to attract minority and women employees?

• Partner programs with women and minority associations
• Participate at minority job fairs
• Seek referrals from other employees
• Utilize online job services

Do you use executive recruiting/search firms to seek to identify new diversity hires?

No.

Internships and Co-ops

Select Intern Program

Deadline for application: May 1st
Number of interns in the program in summer 2005 (internship) or 2005 (co-op): 2006 is the first year

Pay: $7.42-$9.42 per hour

Length of the program: 12 weeks

Percentage of interns/co-ops in the program who receive offers of full-time employment: New program/no data yet

The internship program is an elite opportunity for freshmen interested in recurring summer internships. Interns will learn all aspects of 84 Lumber over three summer internships. They will also gradually focus on an area of interest with the ultimate goal of full-time employment upon graduation and fast-track to leadership.

Corporate Internships

Deadline for application: May 1st

Number of interns in the program in summer 2005 (internship) or 2005 (co-op): 2006 is the first year

Pay: Varies by department

Length of the program: Flexible

Percentage of interns/co-ops in the program who receive offers of full-time employment: New program/no data yet

Internships are available for all majors at our corporate headquarters in Eighty Four, Penn.

Scholarships

School of Business & Public Administration

Scholarship award amount: $1,000

The scholarship is awarded to the University of D.C. to be given to two students.

Entry-Level Programs/Full-Time Opportunities/Training Programs

84 Lumber Manager Trainee

Length of program: Six to 12 months

Geographic location(s) of program: U.S. nationwide

Paid training includes OJT, Self-Study CD, Early Development Program, and Team Headquarters Training.

84 Lumber Inventory Manager

Length of program: Six to 12 months

Geographic location(s) of program: Corporate headquarters, Eighty Four, Penn.

Paid training includes OJT, Self-Study CD, Early Development Program, and Team Headquarters Training.

Strategic Plan and Diversity Leadership

How does the firm's leadership communicate the importance of diversity to everyone at the firm?

The firm communicates the importance of diversity by using our inter-company web site, e-mails and holding meetings.

Who has primary responsibility for leading diversity initiatives at your firm?

The manager of diversity initiatives position is being filled.

Does your firm currently have a diversity committee?

No, we are in the process of starting one.

Has the firm undertaken a formal or informal diversity program or set of initiatives aimed at increasing the diversity of the firm?

Yes, formal.

How often does the firm's management review the firm's diversity progress/results?

Monthly.

How is the firm's diversity committee and/or firm management held accountable for achieving results?

Results are calculated and are then shared with the senior management team at weekly meetings.

The Stats

Employees

2006: 9,584
2005: 8,850
2004: 8,500

Revenue

2005: $3.9 billion
2004: $3.4 billion

Retention and Professional Development

How do 2005 minority and female attrition rates generally compare to those experienced in the prior year period?

Lower than in prior years.

Please identify the specific steps you are taking to reduce the attrition rate of minority and women employees.

- Adopt dispute resolution process.
- Work with minority and women employees to develop career advancement plans.
- Professional skills development program, including minority and women employees.

Diversity Mission Statement

In addition to 84 Lumber's success through teamwork, we strive to have the best associates and improve our standing as an employer of choice. We hire talented, dedicated, go-getters, and we embrace their different cultural backgrounds, skills, talents, abilities, and experiences. At 84 Lumber Company we understand that diversity brings us many benefits.

Abercrombie & Fitch

BRANDS
www.abercrombie.com/diversity

Abercrombie & Fitch

6301 Fitch Path
New Albany, OH 43054
Phone: (614) 283-6500
www.abercrombie.com/careers

Diversity Leadership

Todd Corley
VP Diversity & Inclusion
6301 Fitch Path
New Albany, OH 43054
Phone: (614) 283-6500
www.abercrombie.com/diversity

Recruiting

Please list the schools/types of schools at which you recruit.

- Ivy League schools
- Other private schools
- Public state schools
- Historically Black Colleges and Universities (HBCUs)
- Hispanic Serving Institutions (HSIs)
- Other predominantly minority and/or women's colleges

Do you have any special outreach efforts directed to encourage minority students to consider your firm?

- Hold a reception for minority students
- *Conferences:* National Black MBA Association
- Advertise in minority student association publication(s)
- Participate in/host minority student job fair(s)
- Sponsor minority student association events
- Firm's employees participate on career panels at schools
- Outreach to leadership of minority student organizations
- Scholarships or intern/fellowships for minority students

What activities does the firm undertake to attract minority and women employees?

- Partner programs with women and minority associations
- Conferences
- Participate at minority job fairs
- Utilize online job services

Internships and Co-ops

INROADS

Length of the program: 10 weeks

Scholarships

UNCF/Abercrombie & Fitch Scholarship Program

Scholarship award amount: $3,000

Web site or other contact information for scholarship: Please contact UNCF (United Negro College Fund) at www.UNCF.org for additional details.

Applicants should have a minimum GPA of 3.0 and be enrolled in a four-year institution.

Hispanic Scholarship Fund/Abercrombie & Fitch Scholarship Program

Scholarship award amount: $3,000

Web site or other contact information for scholarship: Please contact UNCF at www.UNCF.org for additional details.

Applicants should have a minimum GPA of 3.0 and be enrolled in a four-year institution.

Asian Pacific Islander American Scholarship Fund/Abercrombie & Fitch Scholarship Program

Scholarship award amount: TBD

Web site or other contact information for scholarship: Please contact APIASF at www.APIASF.org for additional details.

Entry-Level Programs/Full-Time Opportunities/Training Programs

Manager in Training (MIT) Program

Length of program: 90 days (approximately)

Geographic location(s) of program: Various

A bachelor's degree is required.

Strategic Plan and Diversity Leadership

How does the firm's leadership communicate the importance of diversity to everyone at the firm?

The firm communicates diversity initiatives through e-mails, our web site, newsletters, district-wide meetings and all-store conference calls.

How often does the firm's management review the firm's diversity progress/results?

Weekly, via conference calls with all store recruiters, in which we review diversity scorecard data on applications and hires, offers made, etc. The firm also has a diversity committee, formed in the second quarter in 2006, with nine executives on the committee.

Diversity Mission Statement

At Abercrombie & Fitch, we are committed to increasing and leveraging the diversity of our associates and management across the organization. We support those differences through a culture of inclusion, so that we understand our customers, enhance organizational effectiveness, capitalize on the talents of our workforce and represent the communities in which we do business.

Additional Information

In order to keep our associates, customers, vendors and the broader community informed of our progress and efforts in creating a world-class organization, which is focused on our people, we created a section on diversity and inclusion on our web site (which is accessible from the home page) that openly lists our strategic partners, inclusion initiatives and efforts in the communities in which we do business.

Accenture

1345 Avenue of the Americas New York, NY 10105 Phone: (917) 452-4400 www.accenture.com www.uscareers.accenture.com **Locations** More than 110 offices in 48 countries.	**Diversity Leadership** Felix J. Martinez U.S. Diversity Recruiting 161 N. Clark Chicago, IL 60601 Phone: (312) 693-2616 Fax: (312) 652-2616 E-mail: felix.j.martinez@accenture.com

Recruiting

Please list the schools/types of schools at which you recruit.

Accenture recruits at public, private and Ivy-league schools. Highlighted below are the historically black colleges and universities and the hispanic serving institutions where Accenture recruits:

- Ivy League schools
- Other private schools
- Public state schools
- *Historically Black Colleges and Universities (HBCUs):* Howard, Morehouse, Spelman, FAMU, NC A&T, Prairie View A&M, Clark Atlanta, North Carolina A&T
- *Hispanic Serving Institutions (HSIs):* UPR - Rio Piedras, UPR - Mayaguez

Do you have any special outreach efforts directed to encourage minority students to consider your firm?

- *Hold a reception for minority students:* Diversity-focused open house in Atlanta, New York, Chicago and Washington, D.C., and hold receptions at all our targeted schools
- *Conferences:* National Black MBA Association, National Society of Black Engineers, National Society of Hispanic MBAs, Society of Hispanic Professional Engineers, Society of Women Engineers, Women for Hire, Women in Technology
- Advertise in minority student association publication(s)
- *Participate in/host minority student job fair(s):* National Black MBA Association, National Society of Black Engineers, National Society of Hispanic MBAs, Society of Hispanic Professional Engineers, Society of Women Engineers, Women for Hire, Women in Technology.
- Sponsor minority student association events
- Firm's employees participate on career panels at schools
- Outreach to leadership of minority student organizations
- Scholarships or intern/fellowships for minority students
- *Other:* Accenture has created several programs aimed at attracting and retaining ethnic minority and women employees, including Accenture's Women's Networking Forum, Accenture Student Empowerment Program and Student Leadership Conference.

What activities does the firm undertake to attract minority and women employees?

- *Partner programs with women and minority associations:* Catalyst, INROADS, National Black MBA Association, National Society of Black Engineers, National Society of Hispanic MBAs, Society of Hispanic Professional Engineers, Society of Women Engineers

- *Conferences:* National Black MBA Association, National Society of Black Engineers, National Society of Hispanic MBAs, Society of Hispanic Professional Engineers, Society of Women Engineers, Women for Hire, Women in Technology
- *Participate at minority job fairs:* National Black MBA Association, National Society of Black Engineers, National Society of Hispanic MBAs, Society of Hispanic Professional Engineers, Society of Women Engineers, Women for Hire, Women in Technology
- Seek referrals from other employees.
- Utilize online job services
- *Other:* Accenture hosts exclusive Open House & Networking Events for minority and women employees

Do you use executive recruiting/search firms to seek to identify new diversity hires?

Yes.

Internships and Co-ops

Accenture Internship Program

Deadline for application: Applications are due in the early winter time frame

Pay: Accenture offers market-competitive wages for interns.

Length of the program: They last for a period of at least 10 weeks—typically from late May/early June and ending in mid-August/early September.

Percentage of interns/co-ops in the program who receive offers of full-time employment: Approximately 90-95 percent of interns receive offers for employment.

Web site for internship/co-op information: campusconnection.accenture.com

Aside from our overall internship program, Accenture has been a strong supporter of INROADS interns since the organization began in 1970 in Chicago, and was one of the original 17 corporate sponsors. We also have a limited number of internships available through the National Action Council for Minorities in Engineering (NACME) and the Accenture On-Campus Internship program. Interesting fact: Accenture partner Andrew Jackson from the Cleveland office was the first inductee into the INROADS Alumni Hall of Fame.

We also provide internship opportunities to students participating in our Accenture Student Empowerment Program and Accenture's Women's Networking Forum.

Intern analysts participate in a variety of roles, including those of an actual full-time analyst. As an intern, you may participate in client or internal engagements with an emphasis on the planning, design and installation of management information systems. Assignments may include:

- Defining user requirements
- Programming
- Coding and testing applications
- Analyzing, designing and implementing business process improvements
- Project administration
- Researching work on a proposal
- Developing an array of technology-based solutions to improve business performance—from interactive, virtual technologies to object-oriented, client/server and Internet applications
- Developing training and human performance management programs

Additionally, all interns attend a three-day leadership conference during the summer. The agenda for the conference includes team building exercises, meeting our executives, diversity presentations, networking opportunities, motivational speakers and a showcase of our clients.

Scholarships

Accenture is committed to providing financial support for a variety of programs at institutions of higher education. We are also very serious about the advancement of minorities. We believe that there are tremendous opportunities for bright, hardworking individuals who wish to apply their skills to the advantage of businesses on a global scale. We also believe that education helps individuals reach their maximum potential.

At Accenture, we have made a commitment to help support meritorious minority students in pursuit of their dreams. That's why we have established a series of scholarship programs:

Accenture Scholarship Program For Minorities

Deadline: Applications are due in the month of February each year.
Award amount: Scholarship awards of $2,000 are awarded to outstanding students for undergraduate study.
Web site: http://careers3.accenture.com/Careers/US/DiversityInclusion/Scholarships/Scholarships_Minorities.htm

The Accenture Scholarship Program for Minorities was created to encourage minorities to pursue degrees in engineering, computer science and a variety of programs related to information systems and decision or management sciences. Scholarships of $2,000 are awarded to outstanding students for undergraduate study. Scholarship recipients are selected solely on merit, based on academic achievement, leadership, participation in school and community activities, work experience, statement of education and career goals, personal essay and an outside appraisal. This scholarship program is administered by Scholarship Management Services, a department of Scholarship America.

Accenture American Indian Scholarship Fund

Deadline: Applications are due during the May/June time frame each year.
Award amount: Accenture awards three types of scholarships ranging in amounts of $1,000 to $20,000.
Web site: http://careers3.accenture.com/Careers/US/DiversityInclusion/Scholarships/aigc

Accenture awards three types of scholarships to high-achieving American Indian and Alaskan Native students seeking degrees and careers in the professional, teaching, social services, high technology or business fields:

Accenture Scholars: Three undergraduate scholarships of $20,000 each will be awarded to high school seniors pursuing a four-year undergraduate program at a U.S. university or college.

Accenture Fellows: Two graduate scholarships of $15,000 each will be awarded to undergraduate students pursuing an advanced degree at a U.S. accredited university or college.

Finalist Scholarships: Two undergraduate scholarships of $1,000 per year for four years and one graduate scholarship of $2,500 per year for two years will be awarded to candidates for the Accenture Scholars and Fellows scholarships.

In addition to the funding, scholarship recipients are eligible for summer internships with Accenture, as first-year graduate students or junior-year undergraduate students. Applicants will be evaluated based on academic excellence, demonstrated leadership ability, commitment to preserving American Indian culture and communities, and proof of enrollment in a federally recognized American Indian/Alaskan Native tribe.

Thurgood Marshall Scholarship Fund

Deadline: Application deadlines vary
Award amount: Accenture awards $2,500 for each semester
Web site: http://www.thurgoodmarshallfund.org/scholarships/scholarships.htm

This program awards scholarships directly to students at participating member schools. The Thurgood Marshall Fund is a 501(c)(3) organization, which provides scholarship money to HBCUs for the purpose of helping students complete their education.

In the fiscal year 2005, Accenture awarded 12 scholarships at $2,500 to deserving students for each semester. Additionally, in November of fiscal year 2006 Accenture will be part of the Thurgood Marshal Leadership Institute, which offers opportunity for students to meet with corporate sponsors.

Thurgood Marshall has 47 member schools. All TMSF Scholarships are awarded through the 47 member schools. Students interested in a TMSF scholarship should contact a scholarship coordinator at any member college or university and apply through the school.

Affinity Groups

Through a national networking program, Accenture provides the structure and guidance necessary to develop, maintain and grow the following local networking groups in each office location:

- African-American
- American Indian
- Asian-American
- Gay and Lesbian
- Hispanic American/Latino
- Multicultural
- Women
- Work/Life Strategy
- Military

These groups provide individuals who share a common purpose an opportunity to come together to discuss specific issues related to workplace diversity, such as:

- Present members with networking opportunities
- Foster a means for individuals with similar backgrounds to discuss similar challenges and opportunities
- Offer professional direction
- Promote diversity throughout the company
- Support national and local recruiting activities
- Provide employees with heritage packets that highlight various cultural celebrations throughout the year

Accenture currently has 32 U.S. offices with active local office diversity programs. In locations that lack critical mass of the demographic groups above, or where the location does not have formalized interest groups, multicultural groups have been put in place.

Entry-Level Programs/Full-Time Opportunities/Training Programs

Accenture professionals are encouraged to understand the value in differences. Diversity training programs are available to all Accenture employees to raise their awareness of cultural diversity and help them more fully appreciate the differences in everyone.

Here are just some of the diversity training programs Accenture offers:

Appreciating Gender Differences: This three-hour instructor-led course heightens the awareness of gender differences and demonstrates the importance of appreciating and valuing the dynamics between men and women. This helps create an inclusive workplace, which increases team innovation and productivity. The course is available to all U.S. people at Accenture.

Cultural Awareness Guides: These information briefs (available for individual study) provide information to help Accenture employees increase their cultural awareness and provide insight on work styles and behaviors across specific cultures, including appropriate salutations, communications etiquette, preferred modes of communication, meeting styles and respect.

The Diversity Principle: This one-hour course is designed to empower each individual to have a positive impact on Accenture through diversity awareness. Employees learn how they can create a work environment rich in diversity that celebrates the valuable contributions of every team member. The presentation defines diversity at Accenture, establishes diversity as a key company priority and demonstrates how negative stereotypes and related situations can contribute to a nonproductive working environment.

The Diversity Principle In Motion: Presented in a group setting, this workshop takes a further in-depth examination of people's perceptions and behaviors regarding individuals who are different from them. It helps participants recognize inappropriate behaviors related to differences in the workplace and become fully aware of the vehicles in place to address these behaviors; presents Accenture's commitment to the diversity initiatives; and makes participants aware of relevant Accenture policies related to diversity.

Accenture also offers other training resources for teams to use at a local or organizational level.

Diversity Ice Breakers are fun, education activities that teams and communities can use to demonstrate the importance of diversity at Accenture.

Mentoring Toolkit: Accenture has developed a "mentoring toolkit" to help individuals foster their own mentoring relationships on a formal or informal and ongoing basis. These mentoring relationships are in addition to mentoring activities established through our two national programs, the Mentoring Program for Women and the Minority Mentoring Program.

Strategic Plan and Diversity Leadership

How does the firm's leadership communicate the importance of diversity to everyone at the firm?

Accenture communicates regularly with employees on our global inclusion program. Some of the vehicles we leverage are:

- Executive memos
- Internal web site
- Local memos
- U.S.-wide newsletter
- Networking meetings
- Conference calls

Who has primary responsibility for leading diversity initiatives at your firm?

Accenture's commitment to diversity comes right from the top, with our Chief Diversity Officer Kedrick Adkins reporting directly to our Chief Executive Officer Bill Green. Kedrick's role encompasses creating and implementing a broad strategy for diversity within Accenture, including the following:

- Develop a strategy to increase and effectively manage diversity among all of our global workforces.
- Implement training programs to increase our awareness of and sensitivity to diversity issues.
- Create appropriate internal and external communication.
- Increase diversity among our supplier base.
- Monitor and measure performance against plan objectives.

Does your firm currently have a diversity committee?

Yes.

If yes, please describe how the committee is structured.

Accenture's diversity initiatives are led by three primary groups:

U.S. Diversity Advisory Council
The U.S. Diversity Advisory Council is a group of leadership partners with representation from several of the operating units and capability groups. The Diversity Advisory Council confirms priorities, helps set strategic direction and takes a leadership role in implementing key initiatives.

U.S. Women's Steering Group

The U.S. Women's Steering Group is comprised of a committee of Accenture female partners. The U.S. Women's Steering Group manages, implements and leads different women's initiatives across the U.S.

Workforce Diversity Leads

Within each of the Accenture entities there is a lead dedicated to ensuring that diversity is embraced by all Accenture people.

If yes, does the committee's representation include one or more members of the firm's management/executive committee (or the equivalent)?

Yes.

Does the committee and/or diversity leader establish and set goals or objectives consistent with management's priorities?

Yes. Accenture's diversity efforts continue to align with the company's top global priorities of engaging senior leadership, improving retention of senior executive women and focusing on the U.S. minority pipeline.

Has the firm undertaken a formal or informal diversity program or set of initiatives aimed at increasing the diversity of the firm?

Yes, formal.

Here are some of the key initiatives for this year:

Leading a Diverse Workforce: This is a new program designed for senior executives to focus on the complexities of a global work environment and the actions we can take to promote inclusiveness.

Global Inclusion Advisory Council: To further expand the infrastructure of our global network, we are assembling key senior executives from around the world to serve on an advisory council. The council's mission is to further ensure the integration of global inclusion concepts into each area of our business from both a geographic and operating group perspective.

International Women's Day: For the second consecutive year, Accenture hosted the global women's event on March 8, 2006—universally known as International Women's Day. A series of events around the world brought together thousands of Accenture clients and professionals to focus on the advancement of women in the workforce and included local panels, workshops and a global web cast featuring top women business leaders. The development of women and our commitment to attract, retain and advance them has become part of Accenture's culture and is a key factor in the future success of our organization.

How often does the firm's management review the firm's diversity progress/results?

Quarterly.

The Stats

Employees

2006: 133,000 (as of July)
2004: More than 126,000 (as of November)

Revenue

2005: $15.55 billion (fiscal year ended Aug. 31, 2005)
2004: $13.67 billion (fiscal year ended Aug. 31, 2004)

Retention and Professional Development

Please identify the specific steps you are taking to reduce the attrition rate of minority and women employees.

- Develop and/or support internal employee affinity groups (e.g., minority or women networks within the firm)
- Increase/improve current work/life programs
- Work with minority and women employees to develop career advancement plans
- Strengthen mentoring program for all employees, including minorities and women
- Professional skills development program, including minority and women employees

Diversity Mission Statement

Accenture is a global management consulting, technology services and outsourcing company. With more than 126,000 people in 48 countries, we bring together the unique experiences and perspectives of a diverse workforce to deliver cutting-edge technologies and solutions to companies around the world to help them become high-performance businesses. Accenture strives to attract and retain the best people and provide an environment where they can all develop professionally and build a rewarding career. As a result, we have an environment rich in diversity that acknowledges each individual's uniqueness, values his or her skills and contributions, and promotes respect, personal achievement and stewardship. Learn more about our diversity efforts at http://diversity.accenture.com.

Additional Information

Accenture is committed to helping build tomorrow's leaders. We sponsor various workshops and forums for minorities and women to help foster their growth and development. The events also serve as an excellent opportunity for college students of similar backgrounds to get to know each other and learn more about a career in consulting.

Here are three of Accenture's key programs:

Accenture Student Empowerment Program

This three-year program is targeted toward diverse, rising sophomores with majors in business, computer science and engineering. Participating students will:

- Shadow Accenture personnel for a day at a local office.
- Attend networking lunches to help establish a mentoring relationship.
- Participate in the End of Year Forum to understand how to meet long-term career goals.
- Attend the Leadership Conference the summer following their second mentoring year.
- Gain valuable exposure to the business world, explore the consulting career path and understand what companies are looking for.

Accenture Student Leadership Conference

This three-day conference is held for a limited number of outstanding seniors at our education center in St. Charles, Ill. (near Chicago). This helps participants further develop and refine leadership skills and experience the same learning environment as full-time employees.

Accenture's Women's Networking Forum

This program is a series of one-day networking events at Accenture local offices for top female students in their junior or senior year. Selected women will attend a one-day event at the local Accenture office closest to their university and:

- Network and build relationships with top Accenture female employees, along with top women from other universities.
- Gain valuable exposure to the business world and build leadership skills to use in any business setting.
- Get a realistic preview of what it's like to be an Accenture employee.
- Explore career paths within Accenture and understand what we are seeking in future employees.
- Learn how to successfully overcome challenges women face in the workplace.

In 2005, Accenture made *Working Mother* magazine's list of "100 Best Companies for Working Mothers," ranked as one of 25 notable companies in diversity by *DiversityInc* and was named as a "Top 10 Employer" for African-Americans by *Black Collegian Magazine.*

Aetna Inc.

<table>
<tr><td>

151 Farmington Avenue
Hartford, CT 06156
Phone: (860) 273-0123
Fax: (860) 273-3971
www.aetna.com

</td><td>

Diversity Leadership
Caroline Wilke
University Relations Lead
151 Farmington Avenue, RSAA
Hartford, CT 06156
Phone: (860) 273-7831
Fax: (860) 273-1757
E-mail: wilkec@aetna.com

</td></tr>
</table>

Recruiting

Please list the schools/types of schools at which you recruit.

• Ivy League schools
• Other private schools
• Public state schools
• Historically Black Colleges and Universities (HBCUs)
• Hispanic Serving Institutions (HSIs)
• Native American Tribal Universities
• Other predominantly minority and/or women's colleges

Do you have any special outreach efforts directed to encourage minority students to consider your firm?

• Hold a reception for minority students
• *Conferences:* NSHMBA, ALPFA, NABA, NBMBAA
• Advertise in minority student association publication(s)
• Participate in/host minority student job fair(s)
• Sponsor minority student association events
• Outreach to leadership of minority student organizations

What activities does the firm undertake to attract minority and women employees?

• Partner programs with women and minority associations
• Participate at minority job fairs
• Seek referrals from other employees
• Utilize online job services

Do you use executive recruiting/search firms to seek to identify new diversity hires?

Yes.

Internships and Co-ops

Aetna's Summer Internship Program

> *Deadline for application:* We post new dates every year
>
> *Number of interns in the program in summer 2005 (internship) or 2005 (co-op):* 123 Interns, 15 Co-ops
>
> *Pay:* $10-18 per hour
>
> *Length of the program:* 12-14 weeks
>
> *Web site for internship/co-op information:* www.aetna.com/working

Aetna's internship and cooperative education (co-op) programs offer college students the experience of a lifetime. As an intern or co-op participant, you'll have the opportunity to use your creativity and fresh perspectives in a health care company that thrives on change. You'll work—and make a difference.

You'll be able to formally integrate your academic knowledge and explore your career interests through productive and exciting work assignments.

Affinity Groups

Aetna African-American Employee Network (AAEN)

Mission: To provide opportunities for members to develop and enhance their professionalism through programs, workshops and network opportunities, and to develop a strong partnership between Aetna and AAEN that supports strategic business initiatives.

Aetna Hispanic Network (AHN)

Mission: To support Aetna's diversity initiatives and programs by assisting with Aetna's strategic goals in Hispanic emerging markets, and providing AHN members with professional and career development.

Aetna Network of Gay, Lesbian, Bisexual and Transgender Employees (Angle)

Mission: To contribute to Aetna's business and diversity strategies by providing networking support to our members and resources to the corporation.

Aetna Women's Network (AWN)

Mission: To bring women together to help develop the "new Aetna" by offering skill development tools, breaking down geographic and functional barriers to career growth, and developing leadership and exposure.

Aetna Working Mothers' Network (AWMN)

Mission: To bring working parents together to help support, develop and retain talent for Aetna.

Asian-American Network (AsiANet)

Mission: To support Aetna's diversity initiatives and programs, assist Aetna in achieving its goals in the global and Asian-American markets, and assist network members with their personal and career development.

Entry-Level Programs/Full-Time Opportunities/Training Programs

Aetna's Actuarial Training Program

Aetna's Actuarial Training Program, which includes a Student Program and an Intern Program, provides participants with the experience, training and support necessary to become a future financial leader within the company. The program offers a challenging and supportive environment in which the actuarial student can attain fellowship and grow professionally.

Actuaries are considered the financial engineers and the leading professionals in finding ways to manage risk. They lay the foundation for long-term success by designing and pricing new products, as well as ensuring that existing products are financially sound. They also ensure that the company's reserves are sufficient to meet its future obligations.

What's Required?

- 3.0 GPA or above is desired with a concentration in actuarial science, mathematics, statistics or economics.
- Demonstrated ability to successfully complete actuarial exams.
- Strong analytical, critical thinking and communication skills.
- Demonstrated leadership and initiative.

Leadership Development Program

The Aetna Information Services (AIS) Leadership Development Program (LDP) is a three-year, fast-track program whose purpose is to recruit, hire and develop talented new graduates into the future technology leadership at Aetna. This is more than just a job —it's a career path.

LDP participants contribute to a series of challenging projects and technical assignments within Aetna Information Services and other selected Aetna business areas in our Pennsylvania and Connecticut offices. These assignments last approximately eight months each, with one rotation outside the participant's home office location expected.

Rotational stops may include assignments in the following disciplines:

- Infrastructure and Networking
- Application Development
- IT Architecture
- Software Testing
- Database Management
- Project Management
- Strategic Planning

LDP participants are trained, coached and evaluated to achieve optimum performance. Participants are assigned a carefully selected career mentor, who provides development opportunities and guidance through career-related experiences. LDP participants also attend formal leadership and skills training, and have the opportunity to participate in various networking events and activities. Participants work with the program manager to find the right full-time leadership opportunity within AIS upon completion of the program.

Preferred Qualifications:

- BS or BA in computer science or management information systems; other business majors are also considered
- 3.3 GPA
- Demonstrated strong communication, analytical, team, interpersonal and problem-solving skills
- Previous intern/co-op work experience

Technical Development Program (Tracks I & II)

The Aetna Information Services (AIS) Technical Development Program (TDP) Tracks I and II guide recent undergraduates through two potential tracks of achievement and career progression.

TDP Track I

TDP Track I participants are hired as full-time employees in either our Pennsylvania or Connecticut office within a specific technology division. Track I opportunities include:

- Software Testing
- Application Development
- Project Planning
- Data Warehousing and Data Mining
- IT Architecture
- User and Infrastructure Support

TDP Track II

TDP Track II participants are hired into a full-time position in either our Pennsylvania or Connecticut office. This three-year rotational program includes approximately one year in each of the three major disciplines of the Software Delivery Lifecycle. The three major disciplines are:

- Application Development Ore Testing
- Project Support

At the end of the rotations, participants work with the program manager to find the right full-time opportunity within one of the three disciplines.

Both TDP programs are complemented by a one-year training curriculum specifically designed for new college graduates. Participants are invited to various networking events for opportunities to meet with management and other TDP program participants, and are assigned a career mentor who provides development opportunities and guidance through career-related experiences.

Preferred Qualifications:

- BS or BA in computer science, computer engineering, management information systems; other business majors are also considered
- Demonstrated strong communication, analytical, team, interpersonal and problem-solving skills
- 3.0 GPA
- Previous intern/co-op work experience

The E.E. Cammack Group School

The E.E. Cammack Group School is a premier one-year, fast-track training program where talented recent graduates are recruited, hired and developed into future Aetna sales leaders.

Strategic Plan and Diversity Leadership

How does the firm's leadership communicate the importance of diversity to everyone at the firm?

A combination of e-mails, web site, newsletter, meetings and we have just produced our first annual company-wide diversity report.

Who has primary responsibility for leading diversity initiatives at your firm?

Raymond Arroyo, head of Aetna's Office of Diversity.

Does your firm currently have a diversity committee?

Yes, several. Two high level company-wide councils mentioned below, as well as various diversity councils within business segments.

The Aetna Diversity Board

A newly formed group of 17 executives, chaired by our CEO and president to:

- Provide governance, resources and visibility
- Drive actions and increase accountability
- Monitor enterprise-wide programs (review workforce representation and supplier diversity progress on quarterly basis)
- Evaluate results and impact
- Report progress during quarterly meetings and to entire organization

Aetna Diversity Alliance

Mission Statement:

We are a multidisciplinary team that leverages and integrates each other's resources to maximize Aetna's diversity-related presence and reach, internally and externally. Our goal is to help Aetna earn the distinction, financially and by reputation, of being the preferred benefits company for all of our constituents.

If yes, does the committee's representation include one or more members of the firm's management/executive committee (or the equivalent)?

Yes.

How many employees are on the committee, and how often does the committee convene in furtherance of the firm's diversity initiatives?

The Aetna Diversity Board has 18 executive members and the Aetna Diversity Alliance has 23 in a combination of executives and middle management.

Does the committee and/or diversity leader establish and set goals or objectives consistent with management's priorities?

Yes.

Has the firm undertaken a formal or informal diversity program or set of initiatives aimed at increasing the diversity of the firm?

Yes, formal.

How often does the firm's management review the firm's diversity progress/results?

Quarterly.

How is the firm's diversity committee and/or firm management held accountable for achieving results?

Each business segment has diversity milestone objectives appropriate to that business consisting of workforce representation goals, workplace environment and culture, and supplier diversity targets, and is built into the business scorecard. Aetna uses a diversity index to measure inclusive culture through responses to employee survey questions regarding inclusion and supervisory behavior. Scorecard achievements are directly tied to executive compensation.

Retention and Professional Development

How do 2005 minority and female attrition rates generally compare to those experienced in the prior year period?

About the same as in prior years.

Please identify the specific steps you are taking to reduce the attrition rate of minority and women employees.

- Develop and/or support internal employee affinity groups (e.g., minority or women networks within the firm)
- Increase/review compensation relative to competition
- Increase/improve current work/life programs
- Adopt dispute resolution process
- Succession plan includes emphasis on diversity
- Work with minority and women employees to develop career advancement plans
- Professional skills development program, including minority and women employees

The Stats

Employees

2005: 27,677
2004: 26,848

Revenue

2005: $22.5 billion
2004: $19.5 billion

Diversity Mission Statement

We foster an inclusive work environment through collaboration and partnerships to increase employee engagement, strengthen business relationships, encourage innovation, influence multicultural markets and ultimately enhance Aetna's business results.

Additional Information

Diversity is a brand imperative that helps to bring Aetna's health and related benefits to the attention of the fastest-growing segments of the U.S. population—the African-American and Hispanic/Latino markets, as well as the Asian market. In addition, Aetna's ongoing commitment to diversity builds greater competency among Aetna's employees. As a result, diversity is an important element of Aetna's strategic initiatives.

We deliver on Aetna's brand promise by valuing and respecting the strengths and differences among our employees, customers and communities because they reflect our continued future success. Our customers, suppliers and strategic partners are increasingly diverse and multicultural. We must be positioned to understand, interface, relate to and meet their needs. Our challenge is to seek out and use our diversity in ways that bring new and richer perspectives to our jobs and to our business.

We are currently concentrating on the following:

- Recognizing diversity as a business imperative in increasing our business opportunities and partnerships with key external markets, communities and suppliers.
- Creating a work environment that engages, enables and empowers people to do their best work.
- Focusing specifically on recruitment, retention and development of diverse talent at all levels in the organization.
- Establishing and supporting programs that increase the understanding and appreciation of cultural differences through the Aetna Foundation and charitable giving.
- Providing diversity education to all employees.

Aflac

1932 Wynnton Road
Columbus, GA 31999
Phone: (706) 660-7445
Fax: (706) 660-7253
www.aflac.com

Locations
Columbus, GA

Employment Contact
Keyla Cabret
University Relations Coordinator
1932 Wynnton Road
Columbus, GA 31999
Phone: (706) 660-7445
Fax: (706) 660-7253
E-mail: kcabret@aflac.com

Recruiting

Please list the schools/types of schools at which you recruit.

• Public state schools
• Historically Black Colleges and Universities (HBCUs)

What activities does the firm undertake to attract minority and women employees?

• Participate at minority job fairs
• Seek referrals from other employees

Do you use executive recruiting/search firms to seek to identify new diversity hires?

No.

Internships and Co-ops

Aflac Internship/Co-op Program

Number of interns in the program in summer 2005 (internship) or 2005 (co-op): 20
Pay: $8-12.50 hourly
Length of the program (in weeks): Nine to 10 weeks
Web site for internship/co-op information: www.aflac.com

Principal Duties and Responsibilities:

• Performs assigned duties, under direction of experienced personnel, to gain knowledge and experience in preparation for a professional opportunity within the information technology, actuarial, sales support and administration, communications, accounting, finance, human resources, or other assigned business unit.

• Provides assistance on specific projects, including analysis of departmental business practices or procedures, case studies, data analysis, time-defined projects, or ad hoc project of some facet of the industry/department structure or process.

• Receives training and performs duties to become familiar with division functions, operations, management skills or style, and company policies and practices affecting each phase of business; observes experienced workers to acquire knowledge of methods, procedures and standards required for performance of departmental duties.

Education and Experience:

• Must be currently enrolled in a university pursuing a bachelor's or master's degree in the specific field required by the participating division, such as information technology, business administration, accounting, finance, communications, journalism, broadcasting or marketing.

• Minimum 3.0 GPA.

Strategic Plan and Diversity Leadership

How does the firm's leadership communicate the importance of diversity to everyone at the firm?

E-mails, memos, web site, online newsletters, meetings and campus celebrations.

Who has primary responsibility for leading diversity initiatives at your firm?

Brenda J. Mullins, second vice president, diversity/human resources.

Does your firm currently have a diversity committee?

Yes.

If yes, please describe how the committee is structured, how often it meets, etc.

In 2001, the Aflac Diversity Council was established. The council is composed of employees throughout the company with various backgrounds and job levels. The council supports professional development and networking opportunities for employees. The committee typically meets for one hour once a month, however there are occasions where the council will meet more frequently to plan diversity-related events.

If yes, does the committee's representation include one or more members of the firm's management/executive committee (or the equivalent)?

Yes.

If yes, how many executives are on the committee, and in 2005, what was the total number of hours collectively spent by the committee in furtherance of the firm's diversity initiatives? How many employees are on the committee, and how often does the committee convene in furtherance of the firm's diversity initiatives?

There are a total of 20 council members; one corporate officer; five members of management (managers and supervisors), and 14 non-management members.

Does the committee and/or diversity leader establish and set goals or objectives consistent with management's priorities?

Yes.

Aflac's Diversity Council's main objectives are to: serve as a source of information to strengthen Aflac's ability to attract, retain and develop a diverse workforce; support and enhance Aflac's community involvement; serve as sources for information that can enhance expanding consumer markets; and serve as liaisons to senior management.

Has the firm undertaken a formal or informal diversity program or set of initiatives aimed at increasing the diversity of the firm?

Yes, formal.

How often does the firm's management review the firm's diversity progress/results?

Monthly.

How is the firm's diversity committee and/or firm management held accountable for achieving results?

Management is held accountable for the development and success of corporate objectives and initiatives, including diversity initiatives. Management is evaluated and rated by method of the performance evaluation.

Diversity Mission Statement

The Aflac Diversity Council develops, supports and implements diversity-related initiatives that help Aflac better achieve its business objectives.

Additional Information

Aflac's diversity commitment is evidenced by its embracing culture. Fifty years ago, Aflac was founded on the philosophy of treating everyone with care, respect, dignity and fairness—which we continue to champion. With an ever-growing workforce and customer base, Aflac relies on the diverse talents of its Columbus employees. Valuing individuals' unique contributions enhances the satisfaction and performance of our employees, improves our products and services, and enriches the Columbus community.

Aflac's demographics reaffirm our commitment to diversity. In 2000, 35 percent of Aflac's workforce was minority. Today, minorities make up 42 percent of the workforce. Minorities in management positions at Aflac have increased from 20 percent in 2000 to 25 percent in 2005. We have minority women who serve as senior vice presidents of major departments within our organization.

Aflac's Diversity Council, which includes employees of different job levels, ethnicities, cultures, tenure and ages, develops and supports diversity-related initiatives. Each year, the council sponsors Celebrate Our Diversity Day, dedicated to workplace diversity. On this day, employees learn about other cultures by sampling foods from around the world and enjoying exhibits and performances. In 2005, to celebrate Aflac's 50th anniversary, this event expanded into a week. The celebration included generational diversity day, military day, working parents' day and women's day, and culminated in a cultural diversity day.

Aflac is a significant local contributor to the United Negro College Fund and works with the Metro-Columbus Urban League. The company has donated millions of dollars to organizations such as the MLK Memorial Fund and the Smithsonian for the development of the African-American Museum of History and Culture to be located in Washington, D.C.

Aflac is committed to purchasing goods and services from women and minority vendors. We identify, establish and evaluate relationships with minority- and women-owned businesses. Over the last few years, Aflac's supplier diversity initiatives have grown significantly: In 2002, Aflac spent a total of $5.4 million with minority- and women-owned suppliers (three percent of corporate spending). By the end of 2005, Aflac spent $29.5 million with minority and women-owned suppliers (8.8 percent of corporate spending).

Aflac's Minority Mentoring Program, which focuses on our sales force, assists minority sales representatives in developing competencies and practical knowledge. Aflac's Diversity Development Grant increases the number of minority agent recruits and sales in certain cities. Special funding and dedicated consultants assist grant winners in implementing effective multicultural strategies. As of 2004, this program had resulted in 102 Hispanic and African-American agent recruits.

Aflac has learned many valuable lessons about diversity.

While Aflac is grateful to have received many diversity awards, the true measure of our diversity success is in the lives of the people we touch. By listening to our employees, we have discovered valuable ideas and received feedback that has made considerable differences in our community and organization. Key examples are our employee opinion surveys. These surveys allow us to communicate with each employee. We receive firsthand feedback on our environment, leadership and processes we need to continue or make more efficient for employees. Management uses the survey results to develop plans of action to continue to make Aflac an employer of choice and one that embraces diversity.

Agilent Technologies, Inc.

5301 Stevens Creek Blvd.
Santa Clara, CA 95051
Phone: (408) 345-8830
Fax: (734) 533-6779
E-mail: nury_plumley@agilent.com
www.jobs.agilent.com

Locations

US: Alabama • Arizona • California •
Colorado • Connecticut • Delaware •
District of Columbia • Florida • Illinois •
Indiana • Louisana • Maryland •
Massachusetts • Minnesota •
Missouri • New Jersey • New Mexico •
New York • North Carolina • Ohio •
Oregon • Pennsylvania • Texas • Vermont
• Washington • Wisconsin

ASIA PACIFIC: Australia • China • India
Japan • Korea • Malaysia • Singapore •
Taiwan • Thailand

EUROPE: Austria • Belgium • France •
Germany • Ireland • Israel • Italy •
Netherlands • Russia • Spain •
Switzerland • United Kingdom

Diversity Leadership

Nury Plumley
Diversity Recruiting Program Manager
5301 Stevens Creek Blvd.
Santa Clara, CA 95051
Phone: (408) 345-8830
Fax: (734) 533-6779
E-mail: nury_plumley@agilent.com

Recruiting

Please list the schools/types of schools at which you recruit.

• *Ivy League schools:* Cornell
• *Other private schools:* Stanford University, Santa Clara University, Duke
• *Public state schools:* UC Berkeley, UC Santa Barbara, UC Davis, CalPoly, San Luis Obispo, Colorado State, University of Colorado at Boulder, PENN State, Sonoma State, Purdue, University of Michigan, University of Illinois
• *Historically Black Colleges and Universities (HBCUs):* NCA&T, Howard
• *Hispanic Serving Institutions (HSIs):* New Mexico State

Do you have any special outreach efforts directed to encourage minority students to consider your firm?

• *Conferences:* CGSM, SWE, NSBE, SHPE
• Advertise in minority student association publication(s) (sometimes)
• Participate in/host minority student job fair(s)
• Sponsor minority student association events
• Firm's employees participate on career panels at schools

• Outreach to leadership of minority student organizations
• Scholarships or intern/fellowships for minority students

What activities does the firm undertake to attract minority and women employees?

• Partner programs with women and minority associations
• *Conferences:* SWE, WITI
• Participate at minority job fairs
• Seek referrals from other employees
• Utilize online job services

Do you use executive recruiting/search firms to seek to identify new diversity hires?

No (very rarely).

Internships and Co-ops

INROADS is one of our sourcing channels for the U.S. Internship Program. Students from INROADS are incorporated into the company-wide Internship Program.

> *Deadline for application:* Applications for the U.S. Internship Program are accepted throughout the year. Most of our offers for internship assignments are presented to candidates during the months of January through May, and often into June.
> *Pay:* Varies, based on year in school and physical work location.
> *Length of the program:* Varies. Minimum length is 10 weeks, but some assignments could last as long as six months.
> *Percentage of interns/co-ops in the program who receive offers of full-time employment:* Rate of eligible interns who receive offers from Agilent is approximately 70 percent. Eligible interns are those who are scheduled to graduate and who have received favorable performance evaluations by their managers.
> *Web site for internship/co-op information:* http://www.jobs.agilent.com/students/

Agilent's U.S. Internship Program is designed for those who really want to contribute and gain practical experience in their area of interest. The goal of this program is to hire students into regular jobs after graduation. To qualify, a student must:

• Have completed his/her freshman year in college
• Have strong academic achievement in a technical or business curriculum pursuing a BS, BA, MS, MBA or PhD

• Be majoring in:
      Electrical engineering
      Mechanical engineering
      Industrial engineering
      Computer science
      Computer engineering
      Chemical engineering
      Chemistry
      Bio science
      Materials science
      Physics
      Management information systems
      Computer information systems
      Information technology
      Masters in business administration

Affinity Groups

Asian Employee Network (AEN) — Bay Area

Mission:

To help create a company in which all members of a diverse, global workforce can contribute to their highest potential in meeting the business needs of Agilent, its partners and customers. We seek to actively involve Asian-American employees in this ongoing process. AEN has an executive sponsor, an internal web site, and monthly and quarterly events. The group also hosts some events with other similar network groups from other local companies.

Bay Area Women's Network (BAWN)

Mission:

• To exemplify and celebrate the strength, citizenship and diversity of Agilent's women.
• To promote professional development and personal/life skills development for Agilent women.
• To advocate for the growth and development of women leaders within Agilent.

BAWN is an employee network group that works to achieve its mission statement via public forums, video viewings, roundtable discussions, communications programs and attending events of interest together. While we are focused on issues that impact women, our forums provide skills and knowledge development for all Agilent employees. Having men join our organization and participate in our forums encourages an open dialogue and better learning for all. The group has an internal web site and quarterly events.

Black Employee Network Forum (BEF) — Bay Area

Mission:

• To be at the forefront of helping Agilent meet its high-performance, high-growth goals.
• To assist Bay Area African-Americans in assuming leadership roles within Agilent.
• To assist Bay Area African-American employees in achieving their personal and professional development goals.
• To promote a sense of belonging and unity within the Agilent environment.
• The BEF has monthly meetings and an executive sponsor.

Gay & Lesbian Employee Network (GLEN) — Sonoma County

Agilent Technologies' GLEN vision is an outgrowth of Agilent Technologies' organizational values and corporate objectives.

Agilent Technologies is a safe and pleasant work environment, free of harassment and discrimination where all employees, regardless of their sexual orientation, are recognized for their individual achievements, gain a sense of satisfaction and accomplishment, are rewarded and promoted equally, and receive equal opportunities and benefits.

Agilent Technologies is a supportive environment for gay, lesbian, bisexual and transgender employees. At work, they feel comfortable to be open about their sexual orientation, and employees treat their families like they treat all other employees' families.

GLEN has quarterly meetings and an executive sponsor.

(East) Indian Employee Network Group (INET) — Bay Area

INET envisions Agilent to be an organization that helps attract and retain a diverse workforce, including people from different nations. The network of employees of Indian origin is organized to:

• Support, develop and grow as members of this organization to achieve their full professional potential.

• Offer a competitive advantage for Agilent through a diverse perspective on future challenges.
• Bring together employees of Indian origin in order to make meaningful contributions to Agilent by increasing knowledge of a global and multicultural marketplace.
• Make Agilent a diverse and a better place to work for everyone.
• INET has monthly meetings and occasional forums.

Management of Development and Advancement (MDA) — Sonoma County

Mission:

To lead diversity initiatives across all Sonoma County Employee Network Groups and increase management's understanding of diversity as a critical and necessary factor for Agilent's long-term business success. The vision is to achieve strategic alignment and cooperation across all Sonoma County Employee Network Groups and foster an environment where all employees feel valued.

Women's Leadership Development (WLD) — Sonoma County

To provide a forum that gives women opportunities to practice leadership skills by coordinating various projects, such as educating girls about careers in technology and science, professional skills development workshops and resolving workplace issues related to women.

The Physical Informational Emotional (PIE) Networking Group — Colorado

To provide information and support for all employees, and to help them enhance their physical and emotional capabilities by offering opportunities to:

• Increase functionality, productivity and happiness.
• Improve personal development.
• Maximize their contributions to Agilent's success.
• PIE is a great example of a successful grassroots effort.
• PIE formed in May 1989 as a result of a group of nonmanagement people who felt there was a need for a networking group for employees with physical and/or emotional disabilities.
• Diversity is a critical area of focus for Agilent. In partnership with Agilent's Diversity Made Real Program, PIE's goals include informing and supporting all employees experiencing physical and/or emotional limitations.

Others:

• Abilities Network
• La Voz (Hispanic Network Group)
• Native American Employee Network
• Northern Colorado Diversity Team
• Celebrating Our Differences Group
• Spokane Inclusivity Taskforce

Entry-Level Programs/Full-Time Opportunities/Training Programs

Agilent has a year-long global Next Generation Leadership Program, which has two strategic corporate programs designed to accelerate the readiness of Agilent's leadership pipeline by identifying and developing a pool of top talent capable of managing world-class emerging, growth and mature businesses. Participants in this program are nominated by management and selected by their respective businesses, and as such the programs are not open for general enrollment:

LEAD is a strategic leadership development process designed to accelerate the readiness of high potential operating managers and individual contributors for integrating manager or expanded leadership roles.

AIM is a strategic leadership development process designed to accelerate the readiness of high potential integrating managers for senior or expanded leadership roles.

Program objectives and benefits: increase leadership effectiveness, gain self and strategic business insights, establish global network, expand circle of influence and develop strategic business skills.

Program components include: 360-degree assessment, workshops, global leadership forums, leadership in action series, coaching, mentoring, networking and business project teamwork.

Both programs feature a proven accelerated development process which provides: 1) opportunities to build leadership skills and confidence in own abilities through involvement in action learning with peers in high potential cross-functional, cross-business and cross-geographic teams, networking and virtual learning events, 2) a feedback-rich environment based on Agilent's Leadership Framework, and 3) alignment with a continuous leadership pipeline.

Strategic Plan and Diversity Leadership

How does the firm's leadership communicate the importance of diversity to everyone at the firm?

Agilent has several means to communicate the importance of diversity to everyone at the firm: internal web site, internal newsgram (INFOSPARK), coffee talks, forums, brown bags, employee network group sessions and more.

Who has primary responsibility for leading diversity initiatives at your firm?

Nury Plumley, global staffing campus and diversity program manager. We also have a diversity council led by the Sr. VP of HR and one of the executive team—the Sr. VP of one of our businesses.

Does your firm currently have a diversity committee?

Yes.

If yes, does the committee's representation include one or more members of the firm's management/executive committee (or the equivalent)?

Yes.

If yes, how many executives are on the committee, and in 2005, what was the total number of hours collectively spent by the committee in furtherance of the firm's diversity initiatives? How many employees are on the committee, and how often does the committee convene in furtherance of the firm's diversity initiatives?

> *Total Executives on Committee:* Two

Does the committee and/or diversity leader establish and set goals or objectives consistent with management's priorities?

Yes.

Has the firm undertaken a formal or informal diversity program or set of initiatives aimed at increasing the diversity of the firm?

Yes, formal and informal. Agilent has, since its inception, included diversity initiatives in its overall staffing plans; currently we are also developing a formal Diversity Recruiting and Sourcing Program.

How often does the firm's management review the firm's diversity progress/results?

Monthly—with diversity responsibility.
Quarterly—executives review quarterly.

Retention and Professional Development

How do 2005 minority and female attrition rates generally compare to those experienced in the prior year period?

About the same as in prior years.

Please identify the specific steps you are taking to reduce the attrition rate of minority and women employees.

• Develop and/or support internal employee affinity groups (e.g., minority or women networks within the firm)
• Work with minority and women employees to develop career advancement plans (some mentoring)
• Strengthen mentoring program for all employees, including minorities and women
• Professional skills development program, including minority and women employees

Diversity Mission Statement

Harness Global Diversity as Agilent's competitive advantage

At Agilent, we believe that our global competitiveness will be accomplished not only by designing, manufacturing, marketing and selling superior products, but also by leveraging the diversity of our customers, stakeholders, employees and partners all around the world.

Our success is achieved through:

• An environment that enables all to develop and contribute to their full potential
• Leaders that engage, focus, mobilize and leverage all cultures
• Strategies that direct our diverse, collective intelligence to solve urgent business challenges
• Excellent resources and tools that enable our people to excel
• Systems and processes that align and support our vision for success

Additional Information

At Agilent, we recognize the business value of integrating diversity and inclusion into our normal business practices. While we still maintain a distinct Diversity Compliance/AA program, beyond that, diversity and inclusion is everyone's responsibility and thus, you will find aspects of it throughout the company. For example, there is a diversity component in the staffing organization where we work to increase the diversity of our pipeline; there is a diversity component to our corporate affairs activities where we work in diverse communities around the world with our Agilent After School Initiative; and there is a diversity component in our global leadership and learning function where we have tools and resources to help our employees, managers and leaders work more effectively across cultural boundaries. Also, within each business there is the focus on how to unleash and focus the diverse ideas of all of our global population to contribute to innovation and business success for our company.

A statement from our CEO:

Agilent's inclusive environment and workforce, and our acceptance of diverse ideas, help us achieve global success in several ways: we attract and retain top talent; we create an environment of diversity of thought and insight, which will only improve our ability to be innovative in everything we do. The bottom line is that diversity and inclusion give us a powerful business advantage, and we want to make sure they remain a part of our business philosophy, planning and practice.

Bill Sullivan, President and CEO

Air Products and Chemicals, Inc.

7201 Hamilton Boulevard
Allentown, PA 18195-1501
Phone: (610) 481-4911
Fax: (610) 481-5900
E-mail: info@airproducts.com

Diversity Leadership

Stacy Halliday
Recruiter, Engineering and IT
7201 Hamilton Blvd.
Allentown, PA 18195
E-mail: hallidsb@airproducts.com
www.airproducts.com/careers

Recruiting

Please list the schools/types of schools at which you recruit.

• Ivy League schools
• Other private schools
• Public state schools

Do you have any special outreach efforts directed to encourage minority students to consider your firm?

• Hold a reception for minority students
• *Conferences*: NSBE, SWE, Consortium
• Participate in/host minority student job fair(s)
• Sponsor minority student association events
• Scholarships or intern/fellowships for minority students

What activities does the firm undertake to attract minority and women employees?

• Partner programs with women and minority associations
• Participate at minority job fairs

Do you use executive recruiting/search firms to seek to identify new diversity hires?

No.

Internships and Co-ops

INROADS, GEM, Air Products

Deadline for application: Varies based on assignment
Pay: Varies based on experience
Length of the program: 10-26 weeks
Percentage of interns/co-ops in the program who receive offers of full-time employment: Approximately 67 percent of the interns who are returning to school for their senior years
Web site for internship/co-op information: www.airproducts.com/Careers/NorthAmerica/UniversityRecruiting/Co-OpInternProgram.htm

Affinity Groups

Employee networks are part of an overall diversity program intended to make Air Products a more inclusive, creative, responsive and efficient organization—one that recognizes and captures all the potential of its people.

Air Products has six employee networks:

• All Asian Americans at Air Products Network
• Ethnically Diverse Employee Network
• Gay and Lesbian Empowered Employees
• HOLA (Hispanic Organization of Latinos and Amigos)
• Parents Association
• Women in Business

Web site for more information:

www.airproducts.com/Careers/NorthAmerica/Diversity/EmployeeNetworks.htm

Entry-Level Programs/Full-Time Opportunities/Training Programs

Career Development Program

The Career Development Program (CDP) is a strategic investment in the future of Air Products. Since this program began in 1959, it has provided a steady flow of talent, including BS and MS engineers, PhD engineers and scientists, BS and MS information technology (IT) specialists, and financial and commercial MBAs into our company.

In this program, participants are given an opportunity to develop their skills and interests through various positions in different areas of the company. This normally involves the completion of three different assignments during the first two to three years of employment. Every individual is encouraged to take an active role in influencing his or her career path.

Over the years, many past and current leaders of Air Products, including our current CEO John P. Jones, have joined the company through the CDP. We're looking for people who will help shape the future of Air Products.

Engineering Development Program

The Engineering Development Program (EDP) is designed for entry-level chemical and mechanical engineers (zero to two years of experience). The program provides entry-level chemical and mechanical engineers with experience in various areas of the company in various types of positions. While on the program, participants are able to develop their engineering and professional skills while achieving a better understanding of their interests and strengths.

The program consists of five rotations that include different locations and assignments with durations of 10 to 24 months. Typical assignments for chemical engineers on the program may include manufacturing, environmental health and safety, operations, process, production, project, research and start-up roles. Typical assignments for mechanical engineers on the program may include manufacturing, safety, operations, maintenance, reliability and design roles.

Program Requirements

Academic Record: Air Products hires candidates with outstanding academic records. A baseline GPA is one of the factors we consider, in addition to work experience and activity involvement.

Disciplines: Recent graduates or rising seniors who have received or are pursing a BS or MS in the following majors will be considered:

• Chemical Engineering
• Mechanical Engineering

Assignment Descriptions

Air Products offers you a world of engineering opportunities in our Career Development Program (CDP) and Engineering Development Programs (EDP). Numerous engineering positions are available in both our world headquarters in the Lehigh Valley, Pennsylvania area and in our many field locations throughout the United States. Typical engineering roles are:

- **Design Engineers:** Responsible for the design, analysis, specification and troubleshooting of mechanical equipment for use by various operating groups. Typical equipment items are valves, piping, pressure vessels, heat exchangers and packaged process units. Other specialty items, such as blend panels, burners, food freezers and gas cabinets, are also within the scope of design engineers.

- **Machinery Engineers:** Involved with the design, application, selection and long-term operation of compressors, turbines, pumps and expanded systems, including auxiliaries, such as lubrication and seal systems, heat exchangers, piping, and instrumentation and control systems.

- **Maintenance Engineers:** Provide a variety of support services to our production facilities. Preventive and predictive maintenance programs, troubleshooting, work order systems, planning and scheduling, lubrication programs and work sampling are among their responsibilities.

- **Manufacturing and Operations Engineers:** Involved in all phases of manufacturing and plant operations. Assignments for chemical and mechanical engineers are found in Air Products' maintenance, process, production, project engineering and quality assurance functions. Their assignments are either at our corporate headquarters or domestic plants.

- **Process Engineers:** Responsible for optimum process design and improvement of our facilities. This includes not only the development of a thermodynamically efficient process, but also the economic design of each piece of equipment. Process engineers apply engineering principles to the design, development and operation of chemical and gas separation plants across a wide range of businesses: specialty chemicals, cryogenic air separation, high-temperature process for the production of hydrogen and carbon monoxide, electronic specialty gases (ESG), liquefied natural gas (LNG) and hydrocarbon separation processes.

- **Process Control Engineers:** Ensure that the production plants we build can be monitored and controlled to optimum efficiency. Depending on its size and complexity, a plant may employ a simple PLC (programmable logic controller) or more sophisticated DCS (distributed control system), each of which must be configured to perform appropriate control and monitor display functions. Advanced control applications such as MPC (model predictive control) also fall within their realm of responsibility.

- **Process Systems Engineers:** Responsible for developing P&IDs (process and instrumentation diagrams) that provide the definitive scope of equipment, valves, flowmeters, safety devices, etc., for a new facility. They also ensure that all start-up, shutdown and other operational and maintenance requirements are included in the facility's design.

- **Product Development Engineers:** Responsible for the technical, economic and business aspects of new market development from conception through commercialization and, ultimately, to customer acceptance. They become involved in equipment design and testing, process development, economic and market studies, and sales and profit forecasts.

- **Production Engineers:** Responsible for monitoring the production process to ensure sound operation and the efficient use of raw materials and energy. Their work typically includes resolving technical operating problems to minimize production costs and to improve on-stream time.

- **Project Engineers:** Manage and coordinate the efforts of our various engineering groups and other departments in the design and construction of a facility. As a project engineer, you must be both a capable engineer and administrator, using critical path methods and computer cost controls as tools in taking the facility or equipment from the contract signing to start-up.

- **Project Development Engineers:** Responsible for capital cost estimates and profitability analyses for major capital expenditures. They are involved throughout the project cycle, coordinating all engineering input for the initial bid to the customer, preparing a detailed project budget and managing final execution of the project's cost.

- **Research and Development Engineers:** Support a broad spectrum of research activities from long-range fundamental programs to more market-driven applied R&D efforts. Significant resources of the company are committed to numerous areas, including cryogenic and noncryogenic gas separation technologies, wastewater treatment, liquid natural gas processing, polymers, industrial and specialty chemicals and environmental controls.

- **Safety Engineers:** Ensure that we are applying the highest degree of technology to maximize safety in the laboratory and field environments. Responsibilities include leading HazOp reviews for specific projects, developing fault trees for safety-relief scenarios and analyzing incidents for root cause failures.

- **Start-Up Engineers:** Responsible for the start-up and commissioning of all new production facilities. They inspect all equipment, perform operational readiness inspections, commission equipment and conduct performance testing of the entire facility.

The Information Technology Career Development Program

Program Overview

The Information Technology Career Development Program (CDP) is designed for entry-level IT specialists (zero to two years of experience) joining Air Products. The program provides entry-level IT specialists with experience in various areas of the company in various types of positions. While in the program, participants are able to develop their technical and professional skills while achieving a better understanding of their interests and strengths.

The program consists of three rotations that include different assignments with durations of approximately 10 months. Typical assignments for IT specialists on the program may include business process, e-business, infrastructure, data and regional execution services.

Program Requirements

Academic Record: Air Products hires candidates with outstanding academic records. A baseline GPA is one of the factors we consider in addition to work experience and activity involvement.

Disciplines: Recent graduates or rising seniors who have received, or are pursuing, a BS or MS in the following areas will be considered:

- Assignment Descriptions
- Computer Engineering
- Computer Science
- Information Systems
- Information Technology
- Management Sciences and Information Systems

Air Products' Global Information Technology Group is dedicated to serving the company's worldwide businesses, and plays a key role in achieving strategic objectives. IT products and services cover the spectrum of business functions, allowing participants of the IT Career Development Program to gain a broad knowledge of company activities. Typical roles for IT CDP participants are discussed below.

IT Business Process Services incorporates the application development and support activities for our global gases and chemicals businesses and provides liaison and support to the enterprise business process activities, as well as applied engineering, modeling and computer aided engineering services for engineering. Business Process Services consist of four primary process groups with three supporting centers of expertise: offering and customer relationship management (CRM), supply chain management (SCM), asset creation and improvement, and enabling processes. The centers of expertise include the ERP/SAP (enterprise resource planning/systems and applications in data processing) program management office, decision sciences, and application delivery services across the global IT organization.

E-Business IT Services includes such diverse activities as APDirect™, our online ordering system, as well as solutions services, value-added services, web business, business-to-business applications, application technical standards, and systems integrity support and testing—all with a global focus and all aimed at enhancing the way business is done. By understanding the needs and capabilities of its customers, Air Products is creating applications that deliver value, strengthen businesses and ultimately strengthen the industries in which it participates. For several years in a row, Air Products E-Business initiatives have been recognized by *InternetWeek* as one of the top 100 E-business programs in the U.S.

IT Infrastructure Services is responsible for global telecommunications and network services, the service operations center and the client server organizations. Consolidated infrastructure services standardize the desktop, the server environment and mainframe services, and provide focused, rapid advancement in telecommunications and data networks. IT Infrastructure Services organization provides an ideal opportunity to develop and apply in-depth technical knowledge across a variety of technologies.

IT Planning, Business Relationship and Data Services include the office of the chief information technologist, who is responsible for planning the IT architecture, managing the introduction of new computer technology into Air Products and creating the architecture design for new applications. In addition, this office runs projects to evaluate and introduce step-out computer technology, which has a high potential to deliver business value to Air Products. IT Planning, Business Relationship and Data Services also includes data resource management services, decision support services, IT strategy development, operational planning, budgeting and forecasting, IT work portfolio and process management, change management, communications and resource management, and strategic alliance management. Knowledge management services is also a part of this function and addresses the expanding requirements for best practices sharing, team collaboration and self-help through an effective, responsive Intranet.

IT Country Clusters and Regional Execution provides development and business analysis resources as well as functional leadership of IT personnel in key global regions including Asia, Latin America, Eastern Europe and South Africa for all gases, chemicals and corporate functions in those geographies.

Web site for more information:

www.airproducts.com/Careers/NorthAmerica/UniversityRecruiting/WelcomeAndOverview.htm

Strategic Plan and Diversity Leadership

Who has primary responsibility for leading diversity initiatives at your firm?

Victoria Boyd, director of diversity.

Does your firm currently have a diversity committee?

Yes.

If yes, does the committee's representation include one or more members of the firm's management/executive committee (or the equivalent)?

Yes.

Does the committee and/or diversity leader establish and set goals or objectives consistent with management's priorities?

Yes.

Has the firm undertaken a formal or informal diversity program or set of initiatives aimed at increasing the diversity of the firm?

Yes, formal.

How often does the firm's management review the firm's diversity progress/results?

Quarterly.

Allergan, Inc.

2525 Dupont Dr.
Irvine, CA 92612
Phone: (800) 347-4500

Employment Contact
Allergan, Inc.
2525 Dupont Dr.
Irvine, CA 92612
Phone: (714) 246-5398
www.allergan.com/site/careers

Recruiting

Please list the schools/types of schools at which you recruit.

Public state schools: UCI, UCLA, UCSD, CSULG, CSUF, Pepperdine

Do you have any special outreach efforts directed to encourage minority students to consider your firm?

Other: Via the on-campus college minority clubs/groups

What activities does the firm undertake to attract minority and women employees?

Utilize online job services

Do you use executive recruiting/search firms to seek to identify new diversity hires?

Yes.

Strategic Plan and Diversity Leadership

Who has primary responsibility for leading diversity initiatives at your firm?

Senior Director, HR.

Does your firm currently have a diversity committee?

No.

Does the committee and/or diversity leader establish and set goals or objectives consistent with management's priorities?

Yes.

Has the firm undertaken a formal or informal diversity program or set of initiatives aimed at increasing the diversity of the firm?

Yes, informal.

How often does the firm's management review the firm's diversity progress/results?

Twice a year.

Retention and Professional Development

How do 2005 minority and female attrition rates generally compare to those experienced in the prior year period?

About the same as in prior years.

Please identify the specific steps you are taking to reduce the attrition rate of minority and women employees.

• Increase/review compensation relative to competition
• Increase/improve current work/life programs

Allstate Insurance Company

2775 Sanders Road
Northbrook, IL 60062
www.allstate.com

Locations

Nationwide

Employment Contact

Devon Carter
HR Professional
2775 Sanders Rd Suite A1
Northbrook, IL 60062
E-mail: dcaad@allstate.com

Recruiting

Please list the schools/types of schools at which you recruit.

• Ivy League schools
• Other private schools
• Public state schools
• Historically Black Colleges and Universities (HBCUs)
• Hispanic Serving Institutions (HSIs)

Do you have any special outreach efforts directed to encourage minority students to consider your firm?

• Advertise in minority student association publication(s)
• Participate in/host minority student job fair(s)
• Sponsor minority student association events
• Firm's employees participate on career panels at schools

What activities does the firm undertake to attract minority and women employees?

• Partner programs with women and minority associations
• Participate at minority job fairs
• Seek referrals from other employees

Do you use executive recruiting/search firms to seek to identify new diversity hires?

Yes.

Internships and Co-ops

Allstate Internship Program

Deadline for application: Rolling
Number of interns in the program in summer 2005 (internship) or 2005 (co-op): 116
Pay: Weekly
Length of the program: 12 weeks
Percentage of interns/co-ops in the program who receive offers of full-time employment: 20 percent for 2005
Web site for internship/co-op information: www.allstate.jobs

Scholarships

Education Support Programs

Allstate continues to see excellent results through its partnership with the ConSern Education Program. This program assists employees or members of their families with securing educational funding for private (K-12), undergraduate and professional education.

In 2005, 3,191 employees used the ConSern program for education loans or assistance, receiving $140,446 in the form of educational loans. Also, the program had awarded free scholarships to four of our employees.

Entry-Level Programs/Full-time Opportunities/Training Programs

Learning & Development

A high-performance work environment requires continuous learning. Allstate invested more than $14.8 million in 2005, helping employees cultivate new skills leading to new job opportunities through a variety of programs:

The Learning Resource Network (LRN)—an e-learning platform for interpersonal, technical and leadership development courses —available 24/7 at virtually every employee's workstation. The LRN total usage for 2005 was 1,297,941 hours with over 568,000 courses completed.

Professional education programs that offer industry and professional designations, as well as tuition reimbursement for undergraduate and graduate degree programs.

Onsite open enrollment undergraduate and MBA programs at the corporate headquarters in Northbrook, as well as online undergraduate and graduate degree programs supported by tuition reimbursement and available to all eligible employees through the University of Phoenix.

Workshops

The other 50 percent of Allstate's job-related education is accounted by instructor-led workshops. In addition to its corporate headquarters, instructional facilities are located in all regional offices, call centers, processing centers and other facilities. Allstate facilitators, as well as outside vendors, provide a full range of topic coverage and a variety of viewpoints within the workshops.

Strategic Plan and Diversity Leadership

How does the firm's leadership communicate the importance of diversity to everyone at the firm?

For Allstate's corporate culture, a commitment to communication is fundamental, and it begins at the top. Edward M. Liddy, Allstate chairman and CEO, describes a deceptively simple modus operandi: "At Allstate, we invest in truthful communication in a multitude of ways, through our people and through our processes. The result is a culture in which people are free to express their opinions, challenge the status quo and help guide the company with a sound moral compass."

Liddy believes that open, honest, two-way communication is the bedrock of ethical standards. "How much time you invest in communication is equally important," he notes. "An independent study showed that Allstate annually devotes an estimated two million man-hours to communication in all forms—face-to-face, electronic and print. These hours not only reflect corporate and departmental communications, but also local communication efforts throughout the company by individual units and offices that dedicate resources to communication."

Methods of Communicating Diversity Issues

The flow of information from Allstate's senior management to all employees is ongoing, and it is accomplished through a multitude of vehicles and media:

• Quarterly communication meetings hosted by Ed Liddy.

• Town hall meetings conducted by Ed Liddy and fellow senior leaders.

• *Allstate NOW*—This popular company communications vehicle has been published continually since the 1970s, and is now an online publication directed to all employees and agents. *Allstate NOW* features news, information and interviews designed to inform and align employees and agencies behind company strategies and key initiatives, and also to foster pride in working for Allstate. The site recorded more than 1.2 million visits in 2004, which attests to its popularity and value as a communications source.

• "Helping Hands" volunteer opportunities—This ongoing schedule of events is posted prominently near each cafeteria.

• Broadcast Bulletins: From weekly *Allstate NOW* broadcast e-mails—providing employees with updates on everything from company and industry news, upcoming programs, events and volunteer opportunities—to voice mail broadcasts communicating messages around safety security and stability, Allstate believes in using all mediums to communicate thoroughly, honestly and frequently with employees.

• Intranet web site.

• Company management and department leaders disseminate information on an ongoing basis via departmental/group meetings, e-mail and video messages, memoranda and publication articles.

• External company communications

• These include press releases and media/trade publication articles, as well as speeches delivered by company leaders to a variety of audiences.

Liddy is convinced of the value of employee communications in fostering understanding, enthusiasm and a sense of belonging. "I believe that when employees are well-informed and understand the business and their roles," he notes, "it shows in their performance—and in their commitment to the company and its standards."

Liddy is a champion for diversity and uses all of the above venues to discuss the importance of diversity and work/life.

Who has primary responsibility for leading diversity initiatives at your firm?

Anise Wiley-Little, AVP and chief diversity officer.

Does your firm currently have a diversity committee?

Yes, Allstate currently has a diversity committee. In 2005, Allstate formed a corporate diversity council to further expand on the company's commitment and great strides with regard to diversity and to ensure that Allstate continues to meet the changing demographic needs of both customers and employees.

The diversity council will strive to assess all the diversity initiatives throughout the company with a futuristic focus on three long-term initiatives that will strengthen our unified approach to diversity and the measurement behind it.

Allstate also has a Diversity & Work/Life team dedicated to improving diversity and work/life, meeting affirmative action goals, ergonomics, equal pay and external recognition. The team is comprised of six full-time staff members reporting in to a director.

If yes, does the committee's representation include one or more members of the firm's management/executive committee (or the equivalent)?

Yes, the committee's representation does include one or more members of the firm's management/executive committee (or the equivalent). The diversity council consists of 14 senior-level decision makers—including representatives from the diversity team, supplier diversity, marketing, corporate relations, selection and leadership—dedicated to integrating diversity within Allstate business strategy. Chairman and CEO Ed Liddy is the executive sponsor of the council.

Does the committee and/or diversity leader establish and set goals or objectives consistent with management's priorities?

Yes. The mission of the corporate diversity council is to identify, recommend and champion the implementation of strategies and initiatives to effectively drive high performance for all, maximizing productivity of Allstate's workforce. At Allstate, managing diversity is a strategy for leveraging differences in the workplace and marketplace to gain a competitive advantage.

Has the firm undertaken a formal or informal diversity program or set of initiatives aimed at increasing the diversity of the firm?

The firm has undertaken a formal diversity program or set of initiatives aimed at increasing its diversity.

For many years, Allstate has been a recognized diversity leader in the marketplace and in the workplace. The company's diversity strategy has proven to be a sound business practice that has contributed to Allstate's growth and profitability goals.

A core component of the diversity strategy at Allstate continues to be effective education for all employees. Since its inception, the diversity education program has reached more than 40,000 employees delivering a message that focuses on inclusion and managing personal behavior in order to maximize performance.

In 2003, Allstate introduced a new diversity curriculum that includes updated material and a new format utilizing classroom and online training. This training is called Diversity—Allstate's Competitive Edge (ACE) and it is required for all employees. In 2005, 2,347 employees completed this training.

In 2004, Allstate rolled out a new leader's diversity training curriculum, "Creating an Environment for Success." This facilitated workshop is required for new managers with direct reports. As part of Allstate's diversity initiative, workshop participants develop specific actions to increase their effectiveness through self-assessment, shared best practices, and an increased understanding of the importance of differences and their implications on management/leadership style. This course is also available as an optional refresher for existing managers with direct reports who have previously completed other diversity training. In 2005, 260 participants completed this course.

Additionally in 2005, 651 employees completed the Diversity & Work/Life course on the Learning Resource Network (LRN) as a part of the Allstate Management Curriculum.

A diversity video is also used in training. In this video, Ed Liddy, chairman, president and CEO, Tom Wilson, president, Allstate Protection and Casey Sylla, president, Allstate Financial share their vision of diversity.

How often does the firm's management review the firm's diversity progress/results?

The firm's management reviews the firm's diversity progress/results annually.

How is the firm's diversity committee and/or firm management held accountable for achieving results?

Measurement is a key to understanding the overall effectiveness of our Diversity and Work/Life strategy.

In 2004, we launched a new employee retention survey to help us better understand the factors that engage and retain our employees. Its purpose is to collect and centrally retain data from existing employees about what impacts their decision to join, stay or leave the company. The survey, which is available on the Internet, is conducted with new employees at 90 days and at the one-, three- and five-year anniversary dates—points in time that are high risk for turnover.

Allstate conducts workforce assessments on an annual basis for all its major business units/shared service areas to provide leadership with information to aid in making decisions regarding human capital strategies. The assessments include information on new hires, turnover and performance ratings, as well as a summary of survey results. Assessment data are analyzed for differences by demographics, such as gender, ethnicity, job level, age and tenure.

Allstate also has an enhanced employee feedback system that includes an annual survey (QLMS—Quality, Leadership, Measurement, System) to collect data on the work environment and the effectiveness of leadership. The data helps us to shape leadership actions and enhance existing programs.

Beginning in 2001, we included questions in the survey to assess the impact of elder care on our employee population. Survey results indicate this is a growing area of concern for employees. Our ongoing strategy is to ask a random sampling of Diversity & Work/Life questions to continue to assess the issues and challenges faced by employees.

The Stats

Employees

2005: 37,219 (U.S.); 2,844 (Outside the U.S.)

Retention and Professional Development

Please identify the specific steps you are taking to reduce the attrition rate of minority and women employees.

• Develop and/or support internal employee affinity groups (e.g., minority or women networks within the firm)
• Increase/review compensation relative to competition
• Increase/improve current work/life programs
• Adopt dispute resolution process
• Succession plan includes emphasis on diversity
• Work with minority and women employees to develop career advancement plans
• Review work assignments and hours billed to key client matters
• Strengthen mentoring program for all employees, including minorities and women
• Professional skills development program, including minority and women employees

Diversity Mission Statement

The Diversity, Inclusion & Work/Life team partners with business clients to create an effective work environment to drive a high performance culture that enables higher productivity, higher morale, more innovation and risk taking, and a better work environment. Our policies, procedures, programs and interventions are designed to promote inclusion, work/life balance, dignity and respect, commitment to affirmative action and leveraging differences to maximize innovation and creativity.

American Airlines, Inc.

4333 Amon Carter Blvd. Fort Worth, TX 76155 Phone: (817) 963-1234 www.aacareers.com	**Locations** **Dallas/Fort Worth, TX (HQ)**

Recruiting

Please list the schools/types of schools at which you recruit.

- Ivy League schools
- Other private schools
- Public state schools
- Historically Black Colleges and Universities (HBCUs)
- Hispanic Serving Institutions (HSIs)

Do you have any special outreach efforts directed to encourage minority students to consider your firm?

- *Conferences:* NSHMBA, NBMBAA, SHPE, NSBE, BDPA, ALPFA, NABA
- Participate in/host minority student job fair(s)
- Sponsor minority student association events
- Firm's employees participate on career panels at schools
- Outreach to leadership of minority student organizations
- *Other*: INROADS

What activities does the firm undertake to attract minority and women employees?

- Partner programs with women and minority associations
- *Conferences*: WAI, NAWMBA
- Participate at minority job fairs
- Seek referrals from other employees

Do you use executive recruiting/search firms to seek to identify new diversity hires?

No.

Internships and Co-ops

INROADS

Number of interns in the program in summer 2005 (internship) or 2005 (co-op): 2
Length of the program: 8-12 weeks

Monster DLP

Number of interns in the program in summer 2005 (internship) or 2005 (co-op): 2
Length of the program: 8-12 weeks

Affinity Groups

- African-American Employee Resource Group
- Asian Cultural Association
- Caribbean Employees
- Christian Resource Group
- Employees with Disabilities
- Gay, Lesbian, Transgender and Bisexual Employees
- Indian Employees
- Jewish Resource Group
- Latin Employee Resource Group
- Muslim Resource Group
- Native American Employee Resource Group
- Women in AAviation
- Work and Family Balance
- 40 Plus/Senior Employees

Strategic Plan and Diversity Leadership

How does the firm's leadership communicate the importance of diversity to everyone at the firm?

American Airlines communicates diversity initiatives through e-mails, the firm web site, newsletters and meetings.

Who has primary responsibility for leading diversity initiatives at your firm?

Debra Hunter Johnson, VP, Diversity and Corporate Leadership.

Does your firm currently have a diversity committee?

Yes.

If yes, please describe how the committee is structured, how often it meets, etc.

The committee is composed of the ERG (Employee Resource Group), as well as leadership and executive officers.

If yes, does the committee's representation include one or more members of the firm's management/executive committee (or the equivalent)?

Yes.

How many employees are on the committee, and how often does the committee convene in furtherance of the firm's diversity initiatives?

There is one employee for each Employee Resource Group.

Total Executives on Committee: 14

Does the committee and/or diversity leader establish and set goals or objectives consistent with management's priorities?

Yes.

Retention and Professional Development

How do 2005 minority and female attrition rates generally compare to those experienced in the prior year period?

About the same as in prior years.

Please identify the specific steps you are taking to reduce the attrition rate of minority and women employees.

- Develop and/or support internal employee affinity groups (e.g., minority or women networks within the firm)
- Increase/improve current work/life programs
- Succession plan includes emphasis on diversity

Diversity Mission Statement

At American Airlines, we are committed to diversity. With diversity comes opportunities for success, which is good for our employees, our customers, our communities and ultimately our business.

We also do more than state our commitment to diversity. Our commitment is displayed in numerous ways and frequently sets the standard for other companies.

Our many achievements include:

- First major commercial airline to hire a female pilot
- First U.S. airline to provide a Spanish and Portuguese language onboard magazine, *Nexos*
- First airline to create a targeted sales team focused specifically on ethnic and GLBT markets
- Award winning Diversified Supplier Program
- Ongoing employee and company involvement in diverse community affairs and charitable organizations
- 14 employee resource groups and a Diversity Advisory Council that take active roles in business solutions

Employee resource groups are an important part of AMR's efforts to foster an inclusive work environment. Through our employee resource groups, we've created opportunities for employees to have a voice in business, support each other and share their unique perspectives, cultures and experiences with other employees.

Together, we create the team that delivers the best air travel service in the world. Our employees are proud to be part of American Airlines.

American Cancer Society

1599 Clifton Road
Atlanta, GA 30329
www.cancer.org

Locations
All 50 states and Washington, D.C.

Diversity Leadership
Ree Stanley
Chief Diversity Officer

Employment Contact
Recruitment Department
1599 Clifton Road
Atlanta, GA 30329
Phone: (404) 320-3333
Fax: (404) 982-3677
E-mail: acs.jobs3@cancer.org

Recruiting

Please list the schools at which your firm recruits.

• Ivy League schools
• Other private schools
• Public state schools
• Historically Black Colleges and Universities (HBCUs)
• Hispanic Serving Institutions (HSIs)
• Native American Tribal Universities
• Other predominantly minority and/or women's colleges

Do you have any special outreach efforts directed to encourage minority students to consider your firm?

• *Conferences:* NAACP, NUL
• Participate in/host minority student job fair(s)

What activities does the firm undertake to attract minority and women employees?

• Conferences: NAACP, NUL
• Participate at minority job fairs
• Seek referrals from other employees
• Utilize online job services
• *Other:* Advertise in *Diversity* magazine

Do you use executive recruiting/search firms to seek to identify new diversity hires?

No.

Internships and Co-ops

INTERNSHIPS at the AMERICAN CANCER SOCIETY

Deadline for application: Varies; we have fall, spring, summer and year-long internships

Number of interns in the program in summer 2005 (internship) or 2005 (co-op): Over 25 summer 2005 internships

Pay: Varies by location (range $375-$562.50 per week)

Length of the program: Eight to 10 weeks (some one-year internships)

Percentage of interns/co-ops in the program who receive offers of full-time employment: About two percent

Web site for internship/co-op information: www.cancer.org

Entry-Level Programs/Full-Time Opportunities/Training Programs

Various full-time opportunities are available nationwide.

Strategic Plan and Diversity Leadership

Who has primary responsibility for leading diversity initiatives at your firm?

The chief diversity officer.

Does your firm currently have a diversity committee?

Yes.

If yes, please describe how the committee is structured, how often it meets, etc.

We have 13 divisions and HR representatives from each division meet quarterly to discuss initiatives and progress with the COO of ACS.

If yes, does the committee's representation include one or more members of the firm's management/executive committee (or the equivalent)?

Yes.

If yes, how many executives are on the committee, and in 2005, what was the total number of hours collectively spent by the committee in furtherance of the firm's diversity initiatives?

Total Executives on Committee: Two. Hours unknown.

Does the committee and/or diversity leader establish and set goals or objectives consistent with management's priorities?

Yes. We have a diversity staff of five employees whose focus is on diversity strategies in employment, volunteerism, and communicating our message to diverse populations.

Has the firm undertaken a formal or informal diversity program or set of initiatives aimed at increasing the diversity of the firm?

Yes, formal.

How often does the firm's management review the firm's diversity progress/results?

Quarterly.

How is the firm's diversity committee and/or firm management held accountable for achieving results?

Diversity initiatives are part of every VP's performance objectives.

The Stats

Employees

2005 (U.S.): 7,000
2005 (worldwide): 7,000

Retention and Professional Development

How do 2005 minority and female attrition rates generally compare to those experienced in the prior year period?

About the same as in prior years.

Please identify the specific steps you are taking to reduce the attrition rate of minority and women employees.

• Increase/improve current work/life programs
• Adopt dispute resolution process
• Succession plan includes emphasis on diversity
• Strengthen mentoring program for all employees, including minorities and women
• Professional skills development program, including minority and women employees

Diversity Mission Statement

We know too well that cancer does not discriminate. It reaches across all populations to claim thousands of diverse lives each year. This unequivocal truth is the compass that guides our fight against cancer. To continue making progress toward our goals, we must have a professional and volunteer staff as diverse as the millions of people who are touched by cancer each year.

The American Cancer Society is committed to waging war against the disease. Through research, education, advocacy and service, we are winning battles and saving lives. Our volunteers, staff and supporters make every victory possible—by discovering scientific breakthroughs, by building public awareness and educating the public, by raising money to support the services we provide to thousands of cancer patients and survivors, and by ensuring that cancer is a top priority with our nation's lawmakers.

Our ability to value each other's differences is vital to our mission. At the heart of the Society's diversity plan is the belief that we can meet our organizational goals if we leverage diversity as an organizational resource. Creating an inclusive environment where all people are appreciated and have opportunities to learn will prepare our greatest asset—our people—to continue meeting and exceeding our lifesaving goals in the future.

American Electric Power (AEP)

1 Riverside Plaza
Columbus, OH 43215-2372
Phone: (614) 716-1000
Fax: (614) 716-1823
www.AEP.com/careers

Locations

Arkansas • Indiana • Kentucky •
Louisiana • Michigan • Ohio • Oklahoma •
Tennessee • Texas • Virginia • West
Virginia

Diversity Leadership

Mary Cofer
Director, Diversity/Culture

Employment Contact

Peggy Sibila Buck
Senior College Relations Coordinator
1 Riverside Plaza
Columbus, OH 43215
Phone: (614) 716-1856
Fax: (614) 716-4800
E-mail: psbuck@AEP.com
www.AEP.com/careers

Recruiting

Please list the schools/types of schools at which you recruit.

- Other private schools
- Public state schools
- Historically Black Colleges and Universities (HBCUs)
- Hispanic Serving Institutions (HSIs)
- Other predominantly minority and/or women's colleges

Do you have any special outreach efforts directed to encourage minority students to consider your firm?

- *Conferences*: Black Engineer of the Year, AABE, NSBE, etc.
- Participate in/host minority student job fair(s)
- Sponsor minority student association events
- Firm's employees participate on career panels at schools
- Outreach to leadership of minority student organizations
- Scholarships or intern/fellowships for minority students

What activities does the firm undertake to attract minority and women employees?

- Partner programs with women and minority associations
- Conferences
- Participate at minority job fairs
- Seek referrals from other employees
- Utilize online job services

Do you use executive recruiting/search firms to seek to identify new diversity hires?

Yes.

Internships and Co-ops

Length of the program: 12 weeks

Percentage of interns/co-ops in the program who receive offers of full-time employment: 25-85 percent

Web site for internship/co-op information: www.AEP.com/careers

Co-op Requirements:

- Must be in sophomore year at college (a minimum of 50 credit hours) and preferably have completed at least one core class
- Are available to co-op for a minimum of two non-consecutive terms
- Are willing to rotate to different work sites to expand knowledge and experience with differing projects
- 3.0 GPA or better preferred
- Preferably U.S. citizens or permanent residents

Internship Requirement:

- Must be in junior or senior year of college
- Work one or two sessions, typically only during the summer
- 3.0 GPA or better preferred
- Preferably U.S. citizens or permanent residents

Scholarships

AEP scholarships are awarded annually on a competitive basis to children of AEP employees who are high school seniors planning to pursue a baccalaureate degree. AEP does not offer college scholarships to our customers or their children. However, AEP does have a long history of support for K-12 education, as well as for colleges and universities, including grants for teachers and workshops. Read more about it on our web site at www.aep.com under the "About Us" tab.

Entry-Level Programs/Full-Time Opportunities/Training Programs

(Full-time) Associates (MBA)

- MBA graduates
- Prefer one to five years of related experience
- Are willing to rotate to different work assignments for a more complete understanding of the business for a duration of approximately one to two years

(Full-time) Associates (Engineering)

- Hold a bachelor's degree in engineering from an ABET accredited school/program
- Prefer one to three years of related experience
- Are willing to rotate to different work assignments for a more complete understanding of the business for a duration of approximately one to two years

(Full-time) Analysts

- Must have completed their undergraduate degree in a business-related area
- Prefer one to three years of related experience
- Are willing to rotate to different work assignments for a more complete understanding of the business for a duration of approximately one-two years

Strategic Plan and Diversity Leadership

How does the firm's leadership communicate the importance of diversity to everyone at the firm?

The firm communicates diversity information through e-mails, the company web site, newsletters, meetings and mandatory training.

Who has primary responsibility for leading diversity initiatives at your firm?

Mary Cofer, director personnel services and EEO. (Please contact her for diversity-related specifics.)

Does your firm currently have a diversity committee?

Yes.

The Stats

Employees
2005: 19,600
2004: 20,000
Revenue
2005: $11.9 billion
2004: $14.7 billion

Diversity Mission Statement

AEP is committed to providing and fostering an inclusive business environment that leverages the unique talents, perspectives and experiences of each employee.

Additional Information

Our Commitment to Diversity

Like fingerprints, every human being is different. Beyond obvious differences such as race, gender, age, height and weight, there are more subtle dissimilarities: personality, motivation, education, work ethic and goals.

At AEP, we recognize and respect the differences among those who contribute to the success of our company: our investors, our shareholders, our customers and our employees. We know that together, we make up one, great organization—a company that produces a product that allows each and every one of us to pursue success in life, in business and in everything that we do.

Recently, we launched a series of diversity initiatives under the theme "Everyone Counts." These initiatives are ongoing and dedicated to the philosophy that each of us has something valuable to contribute to the good of the organization. We encourage different points of view, all working together toward AEP's common goals. We value unique thinking within the context of teamwork.

We understand that to truly succeed, all of us must stretch beyond our own personal comfort zones of the familiar and embrace the similarities and differences of others who contribute to the success of our company.

Are you one?

One you can look up to and learn from. A leader in paving the way and making a difference for others. A company that always gets it right.

American Express has a very simple philosophy about winning: it's all about having the best talent and fostering an atmosphere where top performers feel inspired, encouraged and rewarded.

That's why we're a global leader in diversified financial services, and one of the most recognized and respected brand names in the world.

Extraordinary people work here and build exceptional careers.

Find out how you can become one of them.

www.americanexpress.com/jobs
American Express is an equal opportunity employer.

American Express Company

200 Vesey Street Mail Drop 01-35-01 New York, NY 10285 www.americanexpress.com	**Diversity Leadership** Linda S. Hassan Director, Talent Acquisition and Diversity Recruitment 200 Vesey Street Mail Drop 01-35-01 New York, NY 10285 www.americanexpress.com/campus

Recruiting

Please list the schools/types of schools at which you recruit.

• Ivy League Schools
• Private Schools
• Public State Schools
• *Historically Black Colleges and Universities (HBCUs):* Clark Atlanta University, Morehouse College, Spelman
• Other predominantly minority and/or women's colleges

Do you have any special outreach efforts directed to encourage minority students to consider your firm?

• Hold a reception for minority students
• *Conferences*: National Black MBA Association, National Society of Hispanic MBAs, National Association of Black Accountants, National Association of Asian American Professionals
• Advertise in minority student association publication(s)
• Participate in/host minority student job fair(s)
• Sponsor minority student association events
• Firm's employees participate on career panels at schools
• Outreach to leadership of minority student organizations
• Scholarships or intern/fellowships for minority students

What activities does the firm undertake to attract minority and women employees?

• Partner programs with women and minority associations
• *Conferences*: Please see conferences listed above
• Participate at minority job fairs
• Seek referrals from other employees
• Utilize online job services

Do you use executive recruiting/search firms to seek to identify new diversity hires?

No.

Internships and Co-ops

Summer Internship Program

Length of the program: 10-12 weeks
Percentage of interns/co-ops in the program who receive offers of full-time employment: Varies year to year
Web site for internship/co-op information: www.americanexpress.com/campus

Marketing BA summer interns at American Express are responsible for contributing to strategy development and value-added benefits for targeted customer segments, including both current and prospective customers. Focus may include new customer segments as well as established customer bases.

Individuals have specific goals that directly support key business unit metrics and have the authority and accountability to manage critical projects that drive results for both our customers and shareholders.

American Express is a leader in the financial services arena and is considered one of the premier marketing companies. With over 150 years of history, the Amex blue box is one of the most recognizable logos in the world. The American Express Campus Internship Program is best in class and offers a realistic job preview, project ownership, opportunity to impact the bottom line, exposure to executives, networking and fun!

Potential Responsibilities:

• Support American Express' strategic relationship with service establishments and/or partners
• Assist in the conceptualization of creative marketing strategies and campaigns
• Demonstrate strategic thought leadership to drive results and maintain the integrity of the Amex brand
• Increase profitability and success of business through effective, targeted marketing strategies
• Identify new and underserved market segments to drive business growth
• Manage analytics associated with evaluating Cost/Benefit and profitability of marketing initiatives, establishing appropriate metrics for success and demonstrating result
• Work with cross-functional partners to leverage organizational synergies to execute programs from concept through launch

Relevant Background:

• Undergraduate degree, marketing concentration preferred
• Experience in consulting, marketing, business analysis, or general management
• Experience in one of our target industries (charge/credit card, finance, retail, travel, services, interactive), which can be utilized in the development of strategy
• Full lifecycle project management experience

Valued Skills:

• Strong customer focus and fully developed project management skills
• Ability to conceptualize and sell ideas internally
• Strong negotiation, communication and presentation skills
• Team player/individual contributor with a desire to function in a flexible, changing environment
• Strong analytics
• Demonstrated ability to drive results

Affinity Groups

• Black Employee Network
• Association of Hispanics Organized to Raise Awareness
• Chai—Jewish Employee Network
• Disabilities Awareness Network
• PRIDE Network (Lesbian, Gay, Bisexual, Transgendered Employee Network)

• SALT (Christian Employee Network)
• WIN (Women's Interest Network)
• NATION (Native American, Tribal and Indigenous Organizational Network)

In support of American Express' corporate policy "to establish a work environment that encourages and supports each person to reach his or her full potential—regardless of any non-work-related factor such as age, race, gender, sexual orientation, religion, disabilities or other differences," 49 employee network chapters have been formed within the company. They are initiated and driven by employees. While separately they may each represent a different segment of the population, they all share common goals. The intent of employee networks is not to highlight differences but to enlighten and make us more sensitive to the unique workplace issues confronting persons of different backgrounds. It is for this reason that networks must be open to all employees so that the knowledge of each group can be shared with all colleagues.

Employee networks sponsor programs that enhance professional and personal growth. Participants engage in educational activities, including job fairs and cultural events; act as liaisons to management and to the community; participate in outreach and volunteer programs; support employee recruitment and retention initiatives; and enhance marketing efforts in targeted communities. Participation in networks also offers employees a supportive environment in which to expand their skills and develop leadership capabilities.

Entry-Level Programs/Full-Time Opportunities/Training Programs

Full-Time Opportunities: Marketing

Training Programs: Global Finance Undergraduate Development Program
Geographic location(s) of program: 1. Marketing—New York only; 2. Finance—New York, Phoenix, Salt Lake City

We look at our campus hires as future leaders within the organization. Professional development and training are critical to achieving these goals. Marketing analysts create a development plan and work with their leader to participate in a number of training and development courses including valuing diversity and practicing inclusion, personal presence, situational self-leadership, and project management. In addition to the course listed above, participants in the Global Finance Development Program take classes to enhance their accounting, audit and analytical skills.

Strategic Plan and Diversity Leadership

How does the firm's leadership communicate the importance of diversity to everyone at the firm?

American Express leadership communicates the importance of diversity via corporate communications, company Intranet, web site, meetings, new hire orientation and training programs.

Who has primary responsibility for leading diversity initiatives at your firm?

Henry Hernandez, vice president and chief diversity officer.

Does your firm currently have a diversity committee?

Yes, the committee meets quarterly.

If yes, does the committee's representation include one or more members of the firm's management/executive committee (or the equivalent)?

Yes.

Does the committee and/or diversity leader establish and set goals or objectives consistent with management's priorities?

Yes, the committee's goals are established based on American Express' overall diversity goals and objectives.

Has the firm undertaken a formal or informal diversity program or set of initiatives aimed at increasing the diversity of the firm?

Yes, formal.

How often does the firm's management review the firm's diversity progress/results?

Quarterly.

The Stats

Employees

2005: 77,500 (worldwide)

Revenue

2005: $29 billion

Retention and Professional Development

How do 2005 minority and female attrition rates generally compare to those experienced in the prior year period?

About the same as in prior years.

Please identify the specific steps you are taking to reduce the attrition rate of minority and women employees.

• Develop and/or support internal employee affinity groups (e.g., minority or women networks within the firm)
• Increase/improve current work/life programs
• Succession plan includes emphasis on diversity
• Work with minority and women employees to develop career advancement plans
• Review work assignments and hours billed to key client matters to make sure minority and women employees are not being excluded
• Strengthen mentoring program for all employees, including minorities and women

Diversity Mission Statement

Diversity & Global Inclusion Vision is to be the premium provider of solutions that leverage diverse talent in creating an inclusive work environment and competitive advantage in the global marketplace.

American Express' employees around the world represent many age groups, ethnicities, family structures, races, religions, sexual orientations, nationalities, and levels of mental and physical ability. While all American Express employees possess essential core competencies, we also speak many languages, come from a wide array of cultures, and comprise diverse educational backgrounds and life experiences. When it comes to the broad horizon of human experience, diversity encompasses all facets of imagination and innovation.

Additional Information

Diversity is absolutely critical to the success of American Express, from a business and value standpoint. We must cultivate an environment in which people want and are able to contribute to their fullest potential because employees are examining the values of the institution and the values of their leaders. People are looking for companies and institutions that have strong values. Diversity is a business imperative and is central to the success of the company.

Ken Chenault, CEO, American Express

Raise the roof on your career

...and discover a place where everyone's ideas matter.

There are so many different people at American Family Insurance and they all have one thing in common: they're crucial to our success. That's why we're committed to creating an environment of encouragement, empowerment, and inclusion.

Raise the roof on your expectations and discover all a career can be with an internship at American Family Insurance.

As a leader in insurance and investment services, we offer the training, technology, and pay-for-performance your talent deserves in an inclusive, stable, empowered environment you'll love.

We currently have internships in all fields including claims, marketing, IT and many more.

There are a lot of reasons to consider American Family Insurance as you map out your career and future. We'd like to share some of our most notable successes with you:

June 2006, Ranked #36, "100 Best Places to Work in IT," *Computerworld*

December 2004, "Top 500 Technology Innovator," *Information Week*

So, if you're excited by new challenges, welcome change, and want your work to have impact, why not and reach all of your goals as a valued member of our family? We're looking for more great people—like you! EOE.

Expect more, because American Family delivers more.

www.americanfamilyinsurance.jobs

AMERICAN FAMILY
INSURANCE ®

All your protection under one roof ®

American Family Mutual Insurance Company & its Subsidiaries Home Office-Madison, WI 53783

American Family Insurance

6000 American Pkwy.
Madison, WI 53783
Phone: (608) 249-2111
Fax: (608) 243-4921
www.americanfamilyinsurance.jobs

Locations

17 States

Diversity Leadership

Jeff Close
Staffing Manager
6000 American Parkway
Madison, WI 53783-0001
Phone: (608) 249-2111

Employment Contact

Teresita Torrence
Strategic Staffing Specialist
6000 American Parkway
Madison, WI 53783-0001
Phone: (608) 249-2111
Fax: (608) 243-6529
E-mail: ttorrenc@amfam.com

Recruiting

Please list the schools/types of schools at which you recruit.

- *Private schools:* Edgewood College in Madison and all other private Wisconsin colleges
- *Public state schools:* University of Wisconsin-Madison and University of Wisconsin System Schools, Madison Area Technical College and Technical Colleges throughout Wisconsin, Hertzing College, Northern Illinois University, University of Illinois, Illinois State University, Drake University, Iowa State University, Northern Iowa University

Do you have any special outreach efforts directed to encourage minority students to consider your firm?

- *Conferences:* NEON—National Economic Opportunity Network, MSLC—Multicultural Student Leadership Conference
- Advertise in minority student association publication(s)
- Participate in/host minority student job fair(s)
- Sponsor minority student association events
- Firm's employees participate on career panels at schools
- Outreach to leadership of minority student organizations
- Scholarships or intern/fellowships for minority students

What activities does the firm undertake to attract minority and women employees?

- Partner programs with women and minority associations
- Participate at minority job fairs
- Seek referrals from other employees
- Utilize online job services

Do you use executive recruiting/search firms to seek to identify new diversity hires?

Yes.

If yes, list all women- and/or minority-owned executive search/recruiting firms to which the firm paid a fee for placement services in the past 12 months:

Consultis, New Directions and several other firms.

Internships and Co-ops

I/S Summer Internship Program

Deadline for application: March 1st
Number of interns in the program in summer 2005 (internship) or 2005 (co-op): Approximately 10 interns
Pay: $16.50 per hour (2006)
Length of the program: 12 weeks
Percentage of interns/co-ops in the program who receive offers of full-time employment: About 10 percent
Web site for internship/co-op information: www.americanfamilyinsurance.jobs

Those who intern in applications development work side-by-side with a mentor and other full-time technologists to provide application planning, design, development, enhancements and maintenance. We work with a variety of web, client server and mainframe development tools. We provide professional and technical services for the development and ongoing support of both our end users and the I/S Division. In this developmental position, interns gain experience as they program, test and debug applications and subroutines under the leadership of our mentor and senior technologists. Other possible opportunities may be available in base technology support areas such as database administration, networking, security, peripheral components, customer support, desktop platforms, server support and end user computing.

Actuarial Internship Program

Deadline for application: March 1st
Number of interns in the program in summer 2005 (internship) or 2005 (co-op): About five interns
Pay: $18.50 an hour (2006)
Length of the program: 12 weeks. There may be opportunities to work part time during the school year and over the semester breaks as well.
Percentage of interns/co-ops in the program who receive offers of full-time employment: About 25 percent
Web site or other contact information for scholarship: www.americanfamilyinsurance.jobs

The American Family Property/Casualty and Life/Health actuarial summer internship programs are designed to involve students in a variety of actuarial activities, including assistance in modeling projects and development of rate indications. These activities will provide students with valuable experience in the type of work they could be involved with in their future career.

Requirements:

• Pursuit of a bachelor's degree in actuarial science, math or a related field such as risk management, statistics or computer science.
• Depending on the position, there may be a requirement that the candidate has sat for at least one of the actuarial exams.
• The candidate should be at least in their second year of school at a university.
• Depending on the position, courses in interest theory and/or actuarial mathematics may be required.
• Experience with Microsoft Office and programming languages such as Visual Basic is considered a plus.

INROADS

Deadline for application: Ongoing
Number of interns in the program in summer 2005 (internship) or2005 (co-op): 6 interns
Pay: Hourly rate varies depending on year in school

Length of the program: 12 weeks in the summer. There may be opportunities to work part time during the school year and to work over the semester break as well.

Web site for internship/co-op information: www.americanfamilyinsurance.jobs

INROADS interns at American Family are placed in paid positions related to their majors or career goals. We strive to match their interests and skills with the needs of our internal divisions. Most INROADS interns work at American Family during summers between academic sessions. But in some cases these summer opportunities can turn into a continuous engagement during the school year based on manager needs and intern availability.

Corporate Internship Program

Deadline for application: Ongoing

Number of interns in the program in summer 2005 (internship) or 2005 (co-op): 77 interns (summer 2005)

Pay: Hourly rate varies depending on year in school

Length of the program: 12 weeks in the summer. There may be opportunities to work part time during the school year and to work over the semester break as well.

Percentage of interns/co-ops in the program who receive offers of full-time employment: four percent overall

Web site for internship/co-op information: www.americanfamilyinsurance.jobs

All of the above programs fall under the umbrella of the corporate internship program at American Family Insurance. In addition to matching students to positions aligned with their majors and career goals, each student is assigned a mentor, provided meaningful work, opportunities to interact with fellow interns, a performance appraisal and the opportunity to provide feedback on their internship experience with American Family.

Entry-Level Programs/Full-Time Opportunities/Training Programs

EXCEL Claims Training Program

Length of program: Six weeks

Geographic location(s) of program: Training takes place at our corporate headquarters in Madison and thoughout our 17 operating states.

Please describe the training/training component of this program: Classroom training, hands-on training in our education center, and on-the-job training and mentoring.

Strategic Plan and Diversity Leadership

How does the firm's leadership communicate the importance of diversity to everyone at the firm?

All new employees participate in a diversity workshop. New managers receive more in-depth training. There are numerous e-mails, presentations, etc., promoting diversity throughout the year.

Does your firm currently have a diversity committee?

Yes.

If yes, please describe how the committee is structured, how often it meets, etc.

Committees are located at our major offices. The teams consist of HR representatives, employees and managers.

If yes, does the committee's representation include one or more members of the firm's management/executive committee (or the equivalent)?

No.

Does the committee and/or diversity leader establish and set goals or objectives consistent with management's priorities?

Yes. At the core of our diversity efforts is the PEOPLE Plan. To us, "PEOPLE" stands for "Partnership in Equal Opportunity Producing Leadership Excellence." Included within the PEOPLE Plan are initiatives that enrich and support not only our employees but also the communities we serve. These initiatives include internships, educational programs, scholarships, neighborhood and community involvement activities, support of emerging market development and active participation in cultural celebrations.

Has the firm undertaken a formal or informal diversity program or set of initiatives aimed at increasing the diversity of the firm?

Yes, formal and informal. The firm's goal is for our workforce to reflect the population of the communities in which we do business. On a less formal level, the strategic staffing area of HR has developed a community outreach program to offer job seeking and career planning services to our local minority communities.

How often does the firm's management review the firm's diversity progress/results?

Quarterly.

How is the firm's diversity committee and/or firm management held accountable for achieving results?

It has become part of our management's annual performance plan.

Retention and Professional Development

Please identify the specific steps you are taking to reduce the attrition rate of minority and women employees.

- Increase/review compensation relative to competition
- Increase/improve current work/life programs
- Succession plan includes emphasis on diversity
- Strengthen mentoring program for all employees, including minorities and women
- Professional skills development program, including minority and women employees
- *Other*: The advancement of women and minorities is a major corporate goal

Diversity Mission Statement

American Family Insurance is dedicated to fostering a culture that is welcoming, diverse and inclusive—a culture that supports our goal of attracting and retaining "the best and the brightest."

Additional Information

We promote a culture of diversity and inclusion through ongoing efforts that include a variety of initiatives designed to promote awareness and understanding of the value that inclusion and diversity bring to us all.

Our commitment to inclusion and diversity enables our employees to contribute to our business in a way that enhances their performance and helps them provide world-class service to our diverse customers. And by ensuring that inclusion and diversity are woven throughout our culture and business practices, we are creating the foundation for future success.

We strive to build the most talented workforce possible—one that mirrors the communities we serve. We believe it is motivating for employees to work in an inclusive environment where they feel respected and valued for their individuality. That's why we embrace and celebrate our unique differences and similarities.

At American Family, inclusion and diversity are a part of our very foundation. From a strong foundation, there are no limits to what we can achieve.

American Family Insurance is an equal opportunity employer.

American Red Cross, The

2025 E Street, NW
Washington, DC 20006
Phone: (202) 303-8819
Fax: (202) 303-0200
www.redcross.org

Diversity Leadership

Mori Taheripour
Vice President of Corporate Diversity
2025 E Street, NW
Washington, DC 20006
Phone: (202) 303-8819
Fax: (202) 303-0200
E-mail: taheripourm@usa.redcross.org

Recruiting

What activities does the firm undertake to attract minority and women employees?

- Partner programs with women and minority associations
- *Conferences:* National Urban League, National Minority Supplier Development Council, Congressional Black Caucus, U.S. Pan Asian Chamber of Commerce, NAFEO
- Participate at minority job fairs
- Seek referrals from other employees
- Utilize online job services

Internships and Co-ops

Presidential Internship

Deadline for application: March 1, 2007
Pay: $400 per week
Length of the program: 10 weeks
Web site for internship/co-op information: www.redcross.org

Scholarships

The Presidential Intern Program brings diverse undergraduate and graduate college students into the Red Cross in key professional areas by providing paid internships. The relationships fostered between the interns and Red Cross often results in future employees, donors and volunteers.

Entry-Level Programs/Full-Time Opportunities/Training Programs

STAR TRACK III

Length of program: Two years
Geographic location(s) of program: National in scope

StarTrack III is a two-year, self-directed executive development program sponsored and funded by the national headquarters. The program's goal is to develop a diverse, highly qualified pool of up to 30 high-potential candidates who are competitive for chapter executive vacancies in the top 150 chapters within six years of entering the program. Participants, with the guidance of experienced coaches, create and execute a competency-based individual development plan that includes chapter-based experiential activities and training, both internal and external to the American Red Cross.

Participation in Star Track III will necessitate periodic, program-sponsored travel throughout the United States, ranging from one day for various meetings, to up to four weeks for interim assignments. The cumulative time commitment away from the office is a minimum of seven weeks spread over the 24-month program.

Specific program components include:

Individual Development Plan—Using feedback from a 360-degree assessment process, participants compare their current mastery of skills and competencies with those required of a high-performing chapter executive, to create an individual development plan. This plan forms the road map for self-directed learning activities during the program.

Coaching—An experienced chapter executive will be matched with the participant to assist in creating the individual development plan. This coach will work with the participant for the duration of the program, checking progress and assessing competency development through regularly scheduled telephone conversations and meetings.

Individual Chapter-Based Assignments—A four-week interim chapter executive assignment and a one-week audit services team chapter assignment are arranged for each participant during the program. These two "hands-on" assignments have been consistently rated the most valuable aspects of StarTrack by past participants.

Workshops—Three group workshops will be conducted during program. A three-day workshop in April 2002 will introduce participants and coaches to StarTrack Program III, their roles and responsibilities, coaching models, strategies for forming and maintaining a coaching relationship, the results of the participant's 360-degree assessment and creation of the individual development plan. A two-day workshop, to be held midway through the two-year program in April 2003, will be designed and developed to meet the evolving needs of participants. Includes meeting with coaches to complete the 12-month progress assessment. A final workshop is held in the last month of the program involving both participants and coaches to assess participants' competency development during the program.

Panel Review Team Interview—Participants attend a panel review team interview at the 18th-month mark of the program to demonstrate and receive feedback on their competency mastery. Interviews are conducted by teams of two experienced chapter executives and one chapter chair, who use real-life scenarios to objectively assess participants on their mastery of critical chapter executive competencies and provide constructive feedback.

Strategic Plan and Diversity Leadership

How does the firm's leadership communicate the importance of diversity to everyone at the firm?

The corporate diversity department works closely with communications and marketing and their staff, using broadcast e-mails, internal and external web sites, the *Diversity Works* newsletter and various other media to promote the strategy and plans for increasing the diversity of the organization.

Who has primary responsibility for leading diversity initiatives at your firm?

Mori Taheripour., VP of corporate diversity.

Does your firm currently have a diversity committee?

Yes.

If yes, please describe how the committee is structured, how often it meets, etc.

The National Diversity Council is composed of volunteer leaders from any Red Cross Chapter or Blood Region, appointed by the National Board of Governors, and charged to provide advice to the board on diversity matters. Each member serves a one- to three-year term, with the potential to be reappointed for an additional term. The council meet three times per year.

If yes, does the committee's representation include one or more members of the firm's management/executive committee?

Yes.

Total Executives on Committee: One

Does the committee and/or diversity leader establish and set goals or objectives consistent with management's priorities?

Yes, diversity strategy and goals are set as a component of the corporate business planning process.

Has the firm undertaken a formal or informal diversity program or set of initiatives aimed at increasing the diversity of the firm? Yes, formal.

The overall focus of the corporate diversity department is to increase the diversity of Red Cross staff and volunteers and to ensure the organization increasingly represents the diverse communities its serves. Specifically, we pursue explicit market segment approaches to the African-American, Asian Pacific Islander and Hispanic/Latino communities, as well as our Youth and Young Adult and Supplier Diversity programs.

How often does the firm's management review the firm's diversity progress/results?

Annually.

How is the firm's diversity committee and/or firm management held accountable for achieving results?

The president and CEO sets performance goals, including diversity goals for her direct reports and evaluates their performance against all of these goals in determining merit increases.

The Stats

Red Cross headquarters demographic profile: approximately 80/20 majority/minority; 60/40 female/male; 2/12 minorities/majorities on the executive team.

Employees

2005: 30,000

Revenue

2005: $3 billion

Retention and Professional Development

How do 2005 minority and female attrition rates generally compare to those experienced in the prior year period?

About the same as in prior years.

Please identify the specific steps you are taking to reduce the attrition rate of minority and women employees.

•Develop and/or support internal employee affinity groups (e.g., minority or women networks within the firm)

•Adopt dispute resolution process

•Succession plan includes emphasis on diversity

Diversity Mission Statement

By 2008, every household in America will be involved with the Red Cross as volunteers, employees, blood donors, financial donors, customers and/or suppliers, assuring that we are representative of America and recognized for our commitment to diversity and inclusiveness.

Additional Information

All great organizations are built on great foundations. The American Red Cross is built on a foundation based on diversity—positive leadership throughout all its operations, making it an inclusive organization fostering inclusive service to all Americans and our international neighbors in need.

The Red Cross has a solid foundation of commitment to diversity and we are building upon it every day. Valuing the diversity among people—diversity of thinking, backgrounds and culture—helps the Red Cross better meet the needs of the communities we serve. The diversity among Red Cross workers is vital to developing and delivering life-saving services to the American public. Drawing upon those similarities and learning about the differences enhances our human experience and helps make us one of the most relied upon and recognized humanitarian organizations in the world.

Through our national network of Red Cross units in every community in the country, we build relationships and run programs working towards our goals:

• To integrate diversity into every Red Cross unit's strategic and business planning processes
• To increase understanding of how diversity impacts the mission of the American Red Cross
• To help units use diversity as a strategy to enhance their regular business activities

To achieve the broadest possible success from our organizational investment in diversity, the Red Cross has established programs, both locally and nationally. We also have diversity consultants who are trained in the use of our Strategic & Tactical Model for Diversity Business Planning. The Red Cross also established partnerships with organizations that share our diversity goals and help us reach diverse audiences. The programs, consultants and partnerships are what help us work towards realizing our full potential and strive towards the total diversity of our people, programs and services.

COMMITMENT

At Anadarko Petroleum Corporation, our commitment to excellence runs deep.

We are committed to developing the youth of today into leaders for tomorrow.

We award scholarships to promising college students, provide internships, sponsor organizations that help develop our youth and volunteer our time to mentoring young students in at-risk schools in math, science, reading and free enterprise.

We believe in the value of education, and that's why we're proud to support the INROADS program.

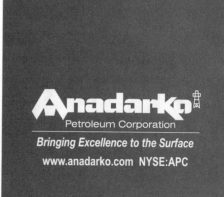

Anadarko
Petroleum Corporation

Bringing Excellence to the Surface
www.anadarko.com NYSE:APC

Anadarko Petroleum Corporation

1201 Lake Robbins Drive
The Woodlands, TX 77380
www.anadarko.com

Locations

US
UK

Employment contact
E-mail: employment@anadarko.com

Diversity Mission Statement

Anadarko's vision for employment is to create the premier, diversified employment culture incorporating the industry's best practices, effective sourcing vehicles, efficient processes and strong networking relationships to maintain Anadarko's competitive human capital advantage.

In an effort to continue our diversity program and ensure that the best available candidates are secured and retained for future company growth, we plan to take a three-pronged approach.

1. Strategically impact our mid-career hiring with an aggressive program that is designed to fill the gaps in our competencies and has a positive impact on our demographics from a diversity perspective.

2. Enhance our selection of universities in our college hiring practices to give us a diverse population of employees with the different technical skill sets and business acumen we need for the future.

3. Continue to leverage and more effectively utilize the INROADS program for internships, with the goal to convert INROADS students to full-time employment with Anadarko.

Anheuser-Busch Companies, Inc.

1 Busch Place
St. Louis, MO 63118
Phone: (314) 577-2000
Fax: (314) 577-2900
Toll Free: (800) 342-5283
www.anheuser-busch.com

Locations

St. Louis (corporate office)
Offices worldwide

Diversity Leadership

Arturo Corral
Director of Diversity

Employment Contact

Alene Becker
Senior Director
Phone: (314) 577-3971
Fax: (314) 577-0719
E-mail: alene.becker@anheuser-busch.com

Recruiting

Please list the schools/types of schools at which you recruit.

• Public state schools
• Historically Black Colleges and Universities (HBCUs)
• Hispanic Serving Institutions (HSIs)

Do you have any special outreach efforts directed to encourage minority students to consider your firm?

• Participate in/host minority student job fair(s)
• Firm's employees participate on career panels at schools
• Outreach to leadership of minority student organizations
• Scholarships or intern/fellowships for minority students

What activities does the firm undertake to attract minority and women employees?

• Participate at minority job fairs
• Seek referrals from other employees
• Utilize online job services

Do you use executive recruiting/search firms to seek to identify new diversity hires?

Yes.

Internships and Co-ops

INROADS

Pay: Varies
Length of the program: Varies
Web site for internship/co-op information: www.buschjobs.com

Scholarships

Hispanic Scholarship Fund and Urban Scholarship Fund

Scholarship award amount: Varies

Web site or other contact information for scholarship: www.anheuser-busch.com

Entry-Level Programs/Full-Time Opportunities/Training Programs

The company has a wide variety of training programs available to all employees.

Strategic Plan and Diversity Leadership

How does the firm's leadership communicate the importance of diversity to everyone at the firm?

We have communication meetings across the country where diversity is one of the many topics discussed with employees. Also, a diversity page is now available through our company's Intranet.

Who has primary responsibility for leading diversity initiatives at your firm?

Arturo Corral, director of diversity.

Does your firm currently have a diversity committee?

Yes.

Please describe how the committee is structured, how often it meets, etc.

We have a corporate committee that is structured by representation across business units with human resource generalists and specialists. This group meets on a monthly basis and is lead by the diversity team.

Does the committee's representation include one or more members of the firm's management/executive committee (or the equivalent)?

Yes, the committee includes a number of executives.

How many executives are on the committee, and in 2005, what was the total number of hours collectively spent by the committee in furtherance of the firm's diversity initiatives? How many employees are on the committee, and how often does the committee convene in furtherance of the firm's diversity initiatives?

There are about 12 members total and the total time devoted, including planning, meeting and follow-up is approximately 10-20 hours per month.

Does the committee and/or diversity leader establish and set goals or objectives consistent with management's priorities?

Yes. The committee aligns its activities to goals and objectives of HR as well as the company's vision and mission.

Diversity Mission Statement

A diversified workforce is made up of individuals with a variety of backgrounds and ethnic make-up and experiences which translate into different perspectives.

Applied Materials, Inc.

3050 Bowers Avenue
Santa Clara, CA 95054
www.appliedmaterials.com

Locations

Countries:
US • India • Israel • Japan

Continents:
Asia • Europe

Employment Contact

Beth Trout
Program Manager, Global Staffing
9700 US HWY 290 E
Austin, TX 78724
Phone: (512) 272-3594
Fax: (512) 272-0918
E-mail: Beth_Trout@amat.com
www.appliedmaterials.com/careers/index.html

Recruiting

Please list the schools/types of schools at which you recruit.

- *Ivy League schools:* Cornell
- *Other private schools:* Stanford, MIT, Cal Tech
- *Public state schools:* Berkeley, University of Texas-Austin, Texas A&M, University of Illinois, Purdue University, Georgia Tech, Arizona State University, University of Texas-El Paso, Michigan State University

Do you have any special outreach efforts directed to encourage minority students to consider your firm?

- Participate in/host minority student job fair(s)
- Outreach to leadership of minority student organizations

What activities does the firm undertake to attract minority and women employees?

- Partner programs with women and minority associations
- *Conferences:* SWE, NSBE, NABA and SHPE
- Participate at minority job fairs
- Seek referrals from other employees
- Utilize online job services

Do you use executive recruiting/search firms to seek to identify new diversity hires?

No.

Internships and Co-ops

College Programs Intern/Co-Op Program

Deadline for application: Open
Pay: Pay is by the hour and varies
Length of the program: Varies
Percentage of interns/co-ops in the program who receive offers of full-time employment: 30-40 percent
Web site for internship/co-op information: www.appliedmaterials.com/careers/college_intern.html

Applied Materials offers various internship and co-op programs designed to provide students with hands-on experience, an opportunity to develop skills in an area of interest and the ability to gain knowledge about the company and the semiconductor industry while enhancing their education. Paid internships and co-ops are offered throughout the company in multiple divisions, and vary in both duration and location.

Students seeking an internship or co-op assignment must:

• Be enrolled in a degree-seeking program
• Be enrolled in a minimum nine-hour class load or three-quarters of the full-time load during the fall and spring semesters (Course requirements do not apply to summer internships or co-op assignments.)
• Possess a 2.5 GPA or above on a 4.0 scale and a 4.0 on a 5.0 scale
• Students who wish to be considered for a co-op assignment must register through their university co-op office

Affinity Groups

LEAD (Leadership Encouraging Achievement through Diversity

LEAD provides the opportunity for the corporation and its African-American employee base in Austin to team up to create a general sense of community and emphasize corporate citizenship among all employees, ultimately reinforcing Applied Materials' standing as an employer of choice.

HIP (Hispanics in Partnership)

HIP's mission is to create networking opportunities for employees, to cultivate leadership and to promote career growth, thus enabling a corporate partnership for diversity. The group's members aim to serve as role models by promoting educational opportunities within the Hispanic population, while also encouraging all AMAT employees to participate in the opportunities provided by Hispanics in Partnership.

WPDN (Womens Professional Development Network)

The mission of the Austin WPDN is to inspire and enable a community of women to reach their full potential while strengthening Applied Materials' goal to be an employer of choice.

Entry-Level Programs/Full-Time Opportunities/Training Programs

Global College Hire Program

Length of program: Varies
Geographic location(s) of program: U.S., Europe and Asia

Global College Program

Applied Materials' Global College Program (GCP) is a specialized full-time paid opportunity for new college graduates. It is designed to train and develop new graduates in all fields, enabling them to make a significant contribution to the company while learning information valuable in their full-time position.

The GCP leverages the success of the new college graduates to meet the changing business needs globally. The program is designed to aid in the assimilation of all new college hires in the company globally and provide training and assimilation resources for all hires from support to business to engineering. Whether the new hire is a financial analyst in Santa Clara, a planner in Austin or a support engineer in Europe or Asia—or any other position in any other location—this program will provide the tools to enable the new college hire to make an impact quickly. Customized training and assignments, along with activities designed to provide networking, team building and technical learning are incorporated into the program.

Training

This new hire program includes training courses and project assignments designed to help with the transition from academia to the corporate environment. The assignments can involve a variety of functional areas relevant to the background and job position of the new college graduate. Networking, leadership and team building opportunities are available to provide the global college hires with valuable contacts and skills. Each employee will receive a customized training plan. Participants will receive technical and professional development training specific to their full-time employment or general to Applied Materials' culture.

To learn more about the program, visit our web site: http://www.appliedmaterials.com/careers/global_college_program.html

Applied Signal Technology, Inc.

400 W. California Ave.
Sunnyvale, CA 94086
Phone: (408) 749-1888
Fax: (408) 738-1928
www.appsig.com

Locations

California • Maryland • Oregon • Texas •
Utah

Diversity Leadership

Diane Cusano
Human Resources Department Manager

Employment Contact

Todd Penns
www.appsig.com

Recruiting

Please list the schools/types of schools at which you recruit.

Public state schools

Do you have any special outreach efforts directed to encourage minority students to consider your firm?

Advertise in minority student association publication(s)

What activities does the firm undertake to attract minority and women employees?

Advertising in the following magazines: *Graduating Engineer: Black and Hispanic, Diversity Careers, Working Women*

Do you use executive recruiting/search firms to seek to identify new diversity hires?

No.

Strategic Plan and Diversity Leadership

Who has primary responsibility for leading diversity initiatives at your firm?

Diane Cusano, department manager human resources.

Does your firm currently have a diversity committee?

No.

The Stats

	TOTAL (U.S. & WORLDWIDE)	
	2005	2004
Number of employees	673	508
Revenue	$156.1 million	$142.8 million

DEMOGRAPHIC PROFILE				
	TOTAL EMPLOYEES	MALE EMPLOYEES	FEMALE EMPLOYEES	MINORITY EMPLOYEES
West Coast	564	72%	26.5%	25%
East Coast	109	70%	29%	13%

If you believe
in the power
of potential,
you're in.

You're
in great
company.

ARAMARK

Aramark Tower
1101 Market St.
Philadelphia, PA 19107
www.ARAMARK.com

Locations

Headquartered in Philadelphia, ARAMARK has approximately 242,500 employees serving clients in 20 countries.

Employment Contact

Kristina Creed
Manager of College Relations
1101 Market Street
Philadelphia, PA 19107
Phone: (630) 271-2041
Fax: (630) 271-5335
E-mail: creed-kristina@aramark.com

Recruiting

Please list the schools/types of schools at which you recruit.

- Public state schools
- Other private schools
- Historically Black Colleges and Universities (HBCUs)
- Hispanic Serving Institutions (HSIs)
- Native American Tribal Universities

Do you have any special outreach efforts directed to encourage minority students to consider your firm?

- Participate in/host minority student job fair(s)
- Sponsor minority student association events
- Outreach to leadership of minority student organizations

What activities does the firm undertake to attract minority and women employees?

- *Conferences:* National Society of Minorities in Hospitality, National Black MBA, National Hispanic MBA, Thurgood Marshall Scholarship Fund
- Seek referrals from other employees
- Utilize online job services

Do you use executive recruiting/search firms to seek to identify new diversity hires?

Yes.

Internships and Co-ops

ARAMARK is a great place to start your career. As part of the ARAMARK team, you will get a chance to learn hands-on from the best in the business. These individuals are interested in developing you as a person and as a professional.

A variety of internship opportunities are available in the following areas:

- Accounting
- Engineering
- Facilities management

- Food and beverage
- Human resources
- IT
- Lodging
- Sales

To apply, please visit our web site at www.ARAMARK.com.

Entry-Level Programs/Full-Time Opportunities/Training Programs

Pathways To Leadership

Length of program: Depends on line of business (six-13 weeks)
Geographic location(s) of program: Nationwide

Strategic Plan and Diversity Leadership

How does the firm's leadership communicate the importance of diversity to everyone at the firm?

The firm's leadership communicates diversity intitiatives through its web site, e-mails, newsletters and extensive online and in-person training programs.

Who has primary responsibility for leading diversity initiatives at your firm?

VP of diversity.

Does your firm currently have a diversity committee?

Yes.

If yes, does the committee's representation include one or more members of the firm's management/executive committee (or the equivalent)?

Yes.

The Stats

	TOTAL IN THE U.S.		TOTAL OUTSIDE THE U.S		TOTAL WORLDWIDE	
	2005	2004	2005	2004	2005	2004
Number of employees	170,000	178500	70,000	64,000	240,000	242,500
Revenue	$8.68 billion	$8.36 billion	$2.28 billion	$1.83 billion	$10.96 billion	$10.19 billion

Diversity Mission Statement

Kaleidoscope, ARAMARK's Commitment to Diversity

ARAMARK understands that a mosaic of backgrounds, styles, perspectives, values and beliefs adds value to our workforce, our workplaces and our business partners.

We are comprised of unique individuals who, together, make the company what it is and what it can be in the future. Only when all individuals contribute fully can the strength and vision of ARAMARK be realized.

Our Principles for Valuing Diversity

1. Because we are committed to being a company where the best people want to work, we champion a comprehensive diversity initiative.

2. Because we thrive on growth, we recruit, retain and develop a diverse workforce.

3. Because we succeed through performance, we create an environment that allows all employees to contribute to their fullest potential.

OUR GOALS ARE GLOBAL.
ARE YOURS?

Archer Daniels Midland Company is a world leader in agricultural processing and fermentation technology. The agriculture industry is full of opportunities. It's more than just corn and soybeans. When you advance your career at ADM, you become a part of global solutions that feed the world, develop renewable resources and unlock nature's potential. With over 26,000 employees across the globe, we welcome a broad mix of attitudes, approaches, perceptions and backgrounds. **Make your goals our goals.**

FOR MORE INFORMATION, VISIT US
ONLINE AT WWW.ADMWORLD.COM

Archer Daniels Midland Company

P.O. Box 1470 Decatur, IL 62525 Phone: (800) 637-5843 Ext.4814 or Ext. 5249 Fax: (217) 451-4383 www.adm.com	**Diversity Leadership** John Taylor Director, Corporate and Supplier Diversity Jessica Heckman University Relations Coordinator **Employment Contact** www.admworld.com/naen/careers/college.asp careers.admworld.com

Recruiting

Please list the schools/types of schools at which you recruit.

- *Ivy League schools:* University of Chicago, Tufts, Emory
- *Other private schools:* Rose-Hulman Institute of Technology, Millikin University, Bradley University, Illinois Weslyan University, Illinois College, Culver-Stockton College, University of Dayton
- *Public state schools:* University of Illinois, Illinois State University, Southern Illinois University, Eastern Illinois University, Western Illinois University, University of Missouri Columbia, Texas A&M, University of Missouri Rolla, Iowa State, Kansas State, Purdue University, Oklahoma State, University of Iowa, University of Nebraska, University of Minnesota, University of North Dakota, North Dakota State, South Dakota School of Mines, Florida State University, Florida A&M, Ohio State University, Michigan Tech University, University of Michigan, University of Wisconsin, New Mexico State, Northern Iowa University, Vincennes University, Montana State University, University of Idaho, Michigan State University
- *Historically Black Colleges and Universities (HBCUs):* North Carolina A&T, Clark Atlanta University
- *Hispanic Serving Institutions (HSIs):* New Mexico State, Texas A&M

Do you have any special outreach efforts that are directed to encourage minority students to consider your firm?

- Hold a reception for minority students
- Conferences
- Advertise in minority student association publication(s)
- *Participate in/host minority student job fair(s):* Bradley Morris Inc., Advancing Minorities Interest in Engineering (AMIE), Minorities in Agriculture, Natural Resources and Related Sciences (MANRRS), Society for Women Engineers, Women for Hire, National Society of Black Engineers, Urban League Diversity Job Fair, National Association of Black Accountants, Kappa Alpha Psi Diversity Job Fair, Institute of Food Technologist, Congressional Black Caucus, National Black MBA Association, Latinos for Hire, Society of Women Engineers
- Sponsor minority student association events
- Firm's employees participate on career panels at schools
- Outreach to leadership of minority student organizations
- Scholarships or intern/fellowships for minority students

What activities does the firm undertake to attract minority and women employees?

- Partner programs with women and minority associations
- Conferences
- Participate at minority job fairs

• Seek referrals from other employees
• Utilize online job services
• *Other:* Bradley Morris Inc., Advancing Minorities Interest in Engineering (AMIE), Minorities in Agriculture, Natural Resources and Related Sciences (MANRRS), Society for Women Engineers, Women for Hire, National Society of Black Engineers, Urban League Diversity Job Fair, National Association of Black Accountants, Kappa Alpha Psi Diversity Job Fair, Institute of Food Technologist, Congressional Black Caucus, National Black MBA Association, Latinos for Hire, Society of Women Engineers

Do you use executive recruiting/search firms to seek to identify new diversity hires?

Yes.

Internships and Co-ops

ADM Internship Program

> *Deadline for application:* We will accept students until April, but complete most recruiting by the end of fall semester.
> *Pay:* Monthly salary dependent upon division where intern works
> *Length of the program:* 10-12 weeks
> *Percentage of interns/co-ops in the program who receive offers of full-time employment:* 65 percent
> *Web site for internship/co-op information:* www.admworld.com

An internship with ADM allows students to work in a variety of different areas within the company: accounting, internal audit, engineering, IT, elevator management, grain terminal operations management, commodity trading and other specialty areas.

Students can find themselves in a variety of different locations across the Midwest. They can range from working in a manufacturing environment to a country grain elevator or even in a corporate setting. Our program promotes the development of the student while providing a training ground for potential employees. Our internship provides many benefits including a monthly salary, housing arrangements and a structured orientation and wrap-up ceremony. Students are required to have a minimum GPA of 2.8, be of junior status and be legally authorized to work in the United States.

Our co-op program is new in existence and mirrors our summer internship program. Of course, the major difference is the amount of time the student works for us. Most students have the opportunity to work from May to December and will return to school at the beginning of their spring semester.

Scholarships

ADM offers scholarships to the following universities:

• Atlanta University Center, Consortium
• Florida A & M University
• Iowa State University
• Kansas State University
• Michigan Technological University
• New Mexico State University
• North Carolina A & T State University
• Ohio State University
• Oklahoma State University
• Purdue University
• Texas A & M University
• University of Illinois at Urbana-Champaign
• University of Missouri – Columbia
• University of Missouri – Rolla

• University of Nebraska – Lincoln
• University of North Dakota

Kansas State ADM Scholarship

The recipient of this scholarship will be a student properly enrolled in the College of Agriculture at Kansas State University from a diverse background pursing a degree in grain science, agriculture economics/agricultural engineering or food science (at Kansas State University). Successful applicants will have 60 hours of college credit with a GPA of 3.0/4.0 or better. Each scholarship award is valued at $10,000. There may be additional qualification criteria and interested students should contact the College Relations Department at ADM for full details.

Illinois State ADM Scholarship

The recipient of this scholarship will be a minority student who is interested in the food and agribusiness industries and enrolled in the Department of Agriculture at Illinois State University. In addition, applicants must be U.S. citizens and classified as new beginning freshmen or new transfer students with a transfer degree who have applied for and have been admitted to the fall term with a major and sequence offered by the Department of Agriculture. Each scholarship is valued at $5,000 per year (at $2,500 per semester following certification of qualification) and is renewable for up to eight consecutive semesters (four semesters for transfer students). The total potential value of the scholarship is $20,000. Each scholarship recipient is required to maintain at least a 2.8 cumulative GPA. There may be additional qualification criteria and interested students should contact the College Relations Department at ADM for full details.

Affinity Groups

ADMWIN; ADM Women's Initiative Network

The ADM Women's Initiative Network (WIN) exists to facilitate the professional development of women at ADM, while helping them reach their individual goals and potential. One part networking, one part professional development, one part mentoring, WIN draws on the most important resource we have: each other. Working together, with the support of top ADM management, we'll help enhance the positive impact of women in our company through recruitment, retention and development efforts.

Entry-Level Programs/Full-Time Opportunities/Training Programs

Training Program for Engineering (referred to as a Production Assistant)

Recent engineer graduates are assigned to a production unit where they gain firsthand exposure to leadership of employees, equipment troubleshooting and dealing with the myriad of challenges faced routinely in a facility that operates around the clock, 365 days a year. The experience begins with on-the-job training through observation and typically progresses to full responsibility for a work group working rotating shifts during the first year. Production assistants experience a very "hands-on" environment and are placed at one of our processing facilities through the United States, primarily within the Midwest.

Training Program for Commodity Trading (referred to as a Commodity Trader Trainee)

The position of commodity trader trainee is one of buying and selling commodities in the cash market, as well as making and coordinating arrangements for the transportation of the product. Our commodity traders learn the fundamentals of the business by embarking on an intense two-month training curriculum, which involves thorough classroom and on-site learning. Training occurs at our corporate headquarters, river terminals, country elevators and processing plants.

Training Program for Grain Terminal Operations Management (referred to as a Grain Terminal Operations Management Trainee)

This is a three-stage position. The employees will each be stationed at one of approximately 50 elevators across the Midwest, United States. The trainees then moves into stage two of their training program and will be relocated to a different elevator/terminal for further training. Stage three of this program is the continuous career advancement. Positions in stage three will include supervisors, superintendents, multiple location management, middle management and corporate careers.

Retention and Professional Development

Please identify the specific steps you are taking to reduce the attrition rate of minority and women employees.
• Develop and/or support internal employee affinity groups (e.g., minority or women networks within the firm)
• Increase/improve current work/life programs

Diversity Mission Statement

ADM remains committed to unlocking the potential of all of its people. To this end, we seek to recruit talent wherever it exists. This is an inclusive policy that recognizes the need for concerted efforts to tap into a diverse pool of human resources as we continue to serve and thrive in an increasingly diverse society. In this way, we can provide our suppliers, customers, shareholders and global community with maximum value now and into the future.

We interpret diversity in its broadest sense. While we are, of course, an equal opportunity employer, ADM also welcomes a broad mix of attitudes, approaches, perceptions and backgrounds.

Additional Information

Supplier Diversity

ADM places a high priority on its commitment to supplier diversity, in which we have significantly expanded our utilization of minority-owned, women-owned, disabled veteran-owned and HUBZone-located enterprises to provide products and services to ADM. We work with such groups as the National Minority Supplier Development Council (NMSDC) and the Women's Business Enterprise National Council (WBENC) in order to meet this commitment.

Arrow Electronics, Inc....

A global provider of products, services and solutions to industrial and commercial users of electronic components and computer products

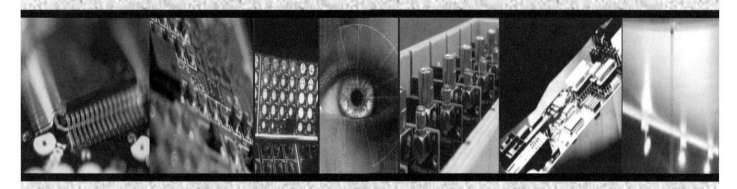

Real Careers for Real People.

Arrow Electronics, Inc.

50 Marcus Drive
Melville, NY 11747-4210
Phone: (631) 847-2000
www.arrow.com

Locations

270 worldwide

Diversity Leadership

Sherry Snipes
Compliance & Diversity Manager
50 Marcus Dr.
Melville, NY 11552
Phone: (631) 847-2000
Fax: (631) 847- 2551
E-mail: ssnipes@arrow.com
www.arrow.com/careers

Recruiting

Please list the schools/types of schools at which you recruit.

- *Public state schools:* Stony Brook University, Baruch College, Texas A & M, New York Institute of Technology
- *Other private schools:* Hofstra University, St. Johns University, C.W. Post University
- *Historically Black Colleges and Universities (HBCUs):* HBCU.com

Do you have any special outreach efforts directed to encourage minority students to consider your firm?

Outreach to leadership of minority student organizations

What activities does the firm undertake to attract minority and women employees?

- Partner programs with women and minority associations
- Participate at minority job fairs
- Seek referrals from other employees
- Utilize online job services

Do you use executive recruiting/search firms to seek to identify new diversity hires?

Yes.

Internships and Co-ops

Corporate Internship Program

Deadline for application: Varies by open position
Pay: Varies by position
Length of the program: 12 weeks
Percentage of interns/co-ops in the program who receive offers of full-time employment: 25 percent

Internships vary by department. Internships are historically available in corporate legal, corporate finance/accounting, human resources and corporate communications.

Strategic Plan and Diversity Leadership

Who has primary responsibility for leading diversity initiatives at your firm?

Compliance and diversity manager.

Does your firm currently have a diversity committee?

Yes. The Diversity Steering Committee is a cross-functional, diverse team of employees from across the U.S. who meet monthly to design and drive the diversity strategy for the organization.

If yes, does the committee's representation include one or more members of the firm's management/executive committee (or the equivalent)?

Yes.

How many employees are on the committee, and how often does the committee convene in furtherance of the firm's diversity initiatives?

> *Total Executives on Committee:* Two

Does the committee and/or diversity leader establish and set goals or objectives consistent with management's priorities?

Yes.

Has the firm undertaken a formal or informal diversity program or set of initiatives aimed at increasing the diversity of the firm?

Yes.

How often does the firm's management review the firm's diversity progress/results?

Annually.

The Stats

Employees

2005: 11,400

Revenue

2005: $11.2 billion

Diversity Mission Statement

Arrow Electronics strives to foster and grow a diverse and inclusive environment that encourages an open exchange of ideas, where each individual is valued, respected and enabled to reach his or her potential. We firmly believe that embracing and learning from individual differences is a strength that will give Arrow a sustained, competitive advantage with customers and suppliers, and enable innovation for Arrow's continued success.

Aurora Health Care

2920 W. Dakota Avenue
Milwaukee, WI 53234-3910
www.Aurorahealthcare.org

Locations

Aurora Health Care is a health care provider in Wisconsin. Our corporate office is located in Milwaukee.

Diversity Leadership

Rhonda Taylor-Parris
Director, Workforce Planning
2920 W. Dakota Avenue
Milwaukee, WI 53234-3910
Phone: (414) 647-3346
Fax: (414) 647-4878
E-mail: Rhonda.Taylor-Parris@Aurora.org

Recruiting

Please list the schools/types of schools at which you recruit.

- Private schools
- Public state schools

Do you have any special outreach efforts directed to encourage minority students to consider your firm?

- Participate in/host minority student job fair(s)
- Firm's employees participate on career panels at schools
- Scholarships or intern/fellowships for minority students

What activities does the firm undertake to attract minority and women employees?

- Participate at minority job fairs
- Seek referrals from other employees
- Utilize online job services

Do you use executive recruiting/search firms to seek to identify new diversity hires?

Yes.

Internships and Co-ops

INROADS-Wisconsin

Deadline for application: Based on the INROADS program requirements
Number of interns in the program in summer 2005 (internship) or 2005 (co-op): 26 interns in summer 2005
Pay: Pay is bi-weekly; rate depends on field and standing in school (range: $10.30—$18.75)
Length of the program: 10-week minimum commitment
Percentage of interns/co-ops in the program who receive offers of full-time employment: Over 50 percent receive offers
Web site for internship/co-op information: www.inroads.org

Internships are offered in the following career fields:

- Business: finance, accounting, HR, marketing
- Information Service/Technology: MIS, IS, IT, computer science
- Engineering: biomedical engineering
- Medical: pre-med, physical therapy, occupational therapy, athletic training
- Nursing, pharmacy

All students must meet all INROADS program qualifications. (Many students who attend school in state work throughout the school year.)

Scholarships

Jestene McCord INROADS Intern Scholarship

Deadline for application for the scholarship program: Mid-July
Scholarship award amount: $1,000/per year awarded

This scholarship is only offered to returning Aurora INROADS interns who meet the requirements and are nominated for it.

Stanley Kritzik Innovation and Technology Scholarship

Deadline for application for the scholarship program: None
Scholarship award amount: $1,000/per year awarded

This scholarship is only offered to Information Technology Aurora INROADS interns who meet the requirements.

Aurora Health Care INROADS Intern Book Scholarship

Deadline for application for the scholarship program: None
Scholarship award amount: 10 $200 scholarships awarded per year

This scholarship is offered to 10 Aurora INROADS interns who meet the requirements.

Entry-Level Programs/Full-Time Opportunities/Training Programs

Aurora Leadership Academy

Length of program: 15 months
Geographic location(s) of program: Milwaukee, WI

This program prepares employees with high potential for first line management positions. Employees are nominated by their immediate supervisor and are paired up with a leader that serves as a mentor.

Strategic Plan and Diversity Leadership

How does the firm's leadership communicate the importance of diversity to everyone at the firm?

The importance of diversity and Aurora's commitment to diversity is captured in our values. Aurora's values consist of accountability, teamwork and respect, setting the standard for service, continually improving our quality, controlling our costs, and "The

INROADS®

Power of Diversity." We communicate the commitment to diversity in our management bulletin, *Aurora Today* (employee newsletter), and the Aurora Diversity Plan.

Who has primary responsibility for leading diversity initiatives at your firm?

Rhonda Taylor-Parris, director of workforce planning.

Does your firm currently have a diversity committee?

Yes.

Please describe how the committee is structured, how often it meets, etc.

The committee consists of Aurora's seven senior leaders and they meet on a quarterly basis.

Does the committee's representation include one or more members of the firm's management/executive committee (or the equivalent)?

Yes.

How many employees are on the committee, and how often does the committee convene in furtherance of the firm's diversity initiatives?

The committee members consist of Aurora's seven senior leaders and they meet on a quarterly basis. Meetings are held more frequently if needed.

Total Executives on Committee: Seven

Does the committee and/or diversity leader establish and set goals or objectives consistent with management's priorities?

Yes. Goals and objectives are set annually and added to the annual strategic plan. Departments throughout the organization draft their business plans according to the goals and objectives set forth in the strategic plan.

Has the firm undertaken a formal or informal diversity program or set of initiatives aimed at increasing the diversity of the firm?

Yes, formal. Diversity education modules are placed on our internal diversity web site for managers to facilitate with their staff. The diversity modules are resources that provide an opportunity for employees to learn more about diversity and provide a forum for the expression of concerns and the sharing of experiences. Aurora also provides classes in the "Managing Diversity Education Series" for managers to learn how to effectively manage in a diverse environment.

How often does the firm's management review the firm's diversity progress/results?

Quarterly.

How is the firm's diversity committee and/or firm management held accountable for achieving results?

Employee's attitudes around diversity are captured in an annual survey that Aurora conducts. The results of the survey determine our diversity index, which is what leaders are held accountable for improving/maintaining. Achievement of outcomes is included in the incentive and merit increases as a part of the annual performance review process.

The Stats

Employees

2005: 25,000
2004: 25,000

Revenue

2004: $2.5 billion

Retention and Professional Development

Please identify the specific steps you are taking to reduce the attrition rate of minority and women employees.

The attrition for rate of minority and women employees is not a critical issue for us.

Diversity Mission Statement

In order to provide the best health care and achieve the desired health outcomes for all that we serve, a diverse and culturally competent workforce is essential.

Avaya Inc.

211 Mt. Airy Rd.
Basking Ridge, NJ 07920
www.avaya.com

Locations

Basking Ridge (HQ)
Avaya has multiple locations throughout the United States and over 90 locations worldwide.

Diversity Leadership
Lyn Grabau
University Relations Manager
211 Mt. Airy Rd.
Basking Ridge, NJ 07920
Phone: (303) 538-4144
Fax: (303) 538-4144
E-mail: grabau@avaya.com
www.avaya.com/careers

Recruiting

Please list the schools/types of schools at which you recruit.

• Ivy League schools
• Other private schools
• Public state schools

What activities does the firm undertake to attract minority and women employees?

Utilize online job services

Do you use executive recruiting/search firms to seek to identify new diversity hires?

Yes.

If yes, list all women- and/or minority-owned executive search/recruiting firms to which the firm paid a fee for placement services in the past 12 months:

We only use firms for executive hiring.

Affinity Groups

4A—Asian/Pacific Americans at Avaya

The charter of the 4A organization is to support Avaya's efforts to achieve the goal of a diverse workforce and to address concerns related to Asian/Pacific American employees. In addition, 4A provides several opportunities for networking and mentoring: we host employment candidates during their interviews, provide mentoring to those new employees who request it, and represent 4A concerns to upper management.

Members of 4A-Avaya come together and work together for these purposes:

• To advance the educational and professional development of APAs
• To promote the importance of diversity in the workplace
• To educate Avaya employees on the rich heritage, diverse cultures and valued traditions of APAs
• To recognize and publicize the achievements and accomplishments of APAs
• To serve as a resource to promote Avaya's objectives and mission

- To foster the advancement of APAs in the business through mentorship, professional development and education
- To build a supportive network to communicate issues for APAs in business
- To create opportunities for personal and professional growth
- To be a positive presence within the business and throughout the communities in which we work

EQUAL! Home

Company Without Closets...

The SAFE Place to Work and Grow

EQUAL! is an educational and support group that addresses workplace environment issues affecting employees who are gay, lesbian, bisexual or transgendered, or who have family, friends or colleagues who are gay, lesbian, bisexual or transgendered. Our mission is to advocate a work environment that is inclusive and supportive of gay, lesbian, bisexual and transgendered employees—enabling all employees to perform to their fullest potential. EQUAL! is a resource serving our customers, shareholders, colleagues, families and the global community in which we work and live. EQUAL! commits to advancing change that will help people respect and value differences, thus allowing employees to achieve Avaya's vision.

HISPA—The Hispanic Association of Avaya

HISPA-Avaya is a nonprofit organization that serves many different purposes professionally and socially.

HISPA provides:

- The opportunity to mentor others
- The opportunity to utilize a very valuable network
- Exposure beyond your local sphere of influence
- The chance to be part of "Una segunda familia"

NOVA—Natives Offering Value at Avaya

NOVA stands for Natives Offering Value at Avaya. NOVA is an organization open to all employees committed to the career advancement, educational needs and general understanding of Native Americans and equality of all employees. By developing our Native American resources as employees, business partners and customers, we support Avaya in leveraging diversity as a competitive advantage. As we move to strengthen corporate diversity, we aid in achieving global business results.

Other Affinity Groups

- ABL — Alliance of Black Leaders at Avaya
- IDEAL — Individuals with Disabilities Enabling Advocacy Link
- WAVE — Women at Avaya Valuing Excellence

Entry-Level Programs/Full-Time Opportunities/Training Programs

We have tuition reimbursement and Avaya University, which provides in-house training at all levels.

Strategic Plan and Diversity Leadership

How does the firm's leadership communicate the importance of diversity to everyone at the firm?

The firm communicates the importance of diversity through e-mails and the company web site.

Has the firm undertaken a formal or informal diversity program or set of initiatives aimed at increasing the diversity of the firm?

Yes, informal.

How often does the firm's management review the firm's diversity progress/results?

Annually.

Diversity Mission Statement

Our value as a company is realized by recognizing the value of each individual. Our strategic intent is to create a culture of unity and global community, where every employee feels included, supported and respected.

We align around common business objectives—revenue, cost, people and process—and within that framework, we acknowledge and support diverse groups. We are a global company in every sense—geographically, strategically and culturally. We embrace diversity as a competitive advantage. Harmonizing and leveraging the diversity of our people will realize our full potential. In the spirit of global community, our diversity will unite us, and it will enhance the quality of our work and our work lives.

Barclays Capital

200 Park Avenue
New York, NY 10166
Phone: (212) 412-4000
Fax: (212) 412-6795
Barclayscapital.com/campusrecruitment

Locations

London (HQ)

Additional offices in:

Europe, Middle East and Africa:
Amsterdam, Birmingham, Dubai, Dublin,
Frankfurt, Geneva, Johannesburg, Lisbon,
Lugano, Madrid, Manchester, Milan,
Munich, Paris, Reading, Zurich

Americas:
Boston, Calgary, Chicago, Los Angeles,
Mexico City, Miami, New York, San
Francisco, São Paulo, Washington, D.C.,
Whippany

Asia Pacific:
Bangkok, Beijing, Hong Kong, Jakarta,
Kuala Lumpur, Labuan, Mumbai, Seoul,
Shanghai, Singapore, Sydney, Taipei,
Tokyo

Diversity Leadership

Mark Kurman
Head of Diversity, Americas

Tara Udut
Head of Campus Recruiting, Americas

Employment Contact

Tara Udut
Head of Campus Recruiting, Americas

Recruiting

Please list the schools/types of schools at which you recruit.

• Ivy League schools
• Other private schools
• Public state schools
• Historically Black Colleges and Universities (HBCUs)
• Hispanic Serving Institutions (HSIs)
• Other predominantly minority and/or women's colleges

Active partners with Sponsors for Educational Opportunity Program, INROADS and Toigo.

Do you have any special outreach efforts directed to encourage minority students to consider your firm?

• Hold a reception for minority students
• Conferences
• Advertise in minority student association publication(s)
• Sponsor minority student association events

INROADS

• Firm's professionals participate on career panels at schools
• Outreach to leadership of minority student organizations
• Scholarships or intern/fellowships for minority students
• Contest/Challenge
• Outreach to sororities, fraternities and other minority student clubs

What activities does the firm undertake to attract women and minorities?

• Partner programs with women and minority banking associations
• Conferences
• Seek referrals from other professionals
• Utilize online job services

Do you use executive recruiting/search firms to seek to identify new diversity hires?

Yes.

Affinity Groups

We have four active employee forums in the Americas and two in the U.K., with several others being formed in the U.K.

Americas

• Barclays Cultural Alliance—Ethnicity networking group
• GLBT Network—Gay and lesbian networking group
• Women's Leadership Forum—Women's networking group
• Disability Champions Network—Disability networking group

U.K.

• Women's Internal Network—Women's networking group
• GLBT Network—Gay and lesbian networking group

Purpose

Employee forums are open to all employees and are recognized by the firm for their support of business and diversity goals.

Strategic Plan and Diversity Leadership

How does the firm's leadership communicate the importance of diversity to everyone at the firm?

Erin Mansfield, managing director, U.S. compliance and chairperson of the U.S. diversity committee, is one of the primary communicators of our commitment to diversity. She and Michael Evans, head of global HR (see below), are responsible for ensuring that diversity is part of Barclays Capital's culture and that it is incorporated in the day-to-day business activities at the firm.

The importance of diversity is further communicated through our diversity committee, employee forums and sponsorships. Employees can access information via the diversity web site, e-mails and monthly diversity and employee forum group meetings.

Who has primary responsibility for leading overall diversity initiatives at your firm?

Michael Evans, as the head of global human resources, leads the primary business group responsible for supporting and facilitating all the efforts of the individuals in diversity initiatives throughout the firm.

Tara Udut, head of campus recruiting, Americas, and her group work with regional campus recruiting committees as well as targeted campus teams to ensure that diversity is an important business consideration. Each team has an executive charged with ensuring specific focus on diverse student representation.

Pamela Sinclair, director, HR—front office and Jamie Garstad, director, HR—infrastructure. As heads of our client relationship teams, Ms. Sinclair and Ms. Garstad have responsibility for ensuring that diversity-related recruiting initiatives are integrated in the experienced hire arena. They regularly reinforce our commitment to diversity with our search partners and review how their performance contributes to furthering our diversity agenda.

Does your firm currently have a diversity committee?

Yes.

If yes, does the committee's representation include one or more members of the firm's management/executive committee (or the equivalent)?

Yes, the committee consists of senior representation from all areas of the firm.

If yes, how many executives are on the committee, and how often did the committee convene in furtherance of the firm's diversity initiatives in 2005?

> *Total Executives on Committee:* 11 senior managers
> *Number of diversity meetings annually:* 12, once a month

Does the committee(s) and/or diversity leader establish and set goals or objectives consistent with management's priorities?

Yes, we use a model that focuses our initiatives along three key work streams—recruit, develop and retain—with a designated senior manager responsible for progress along each stream.

Has the firm undertaken a formal or informal diversity program or set of initiatives aimed at increasing the diversity of the firm?

Yes, formal. To reiterate, a broad range of staff are committed to initiatives within each of three major work streams.

Diversity Mission Statement

At Barclays Capital we are committed to providing creative and innovative solutions for our clients and the attraction and retention of world-class professionals enables us to fulfill that commitment. We actively promote diversity to sustain continued business success and therefore we:

Seek to build a workforce that reflects the communities in which we live and work so that we are best able to meet the needs of our clients.

Strive to ensure that the talents of all our employees are fully utilized and that no job applicant or employee will receive less favorable treatment on the grounds of race, religion, gender, age, physical ability, sexual orientation or nationality.

Aim to provide our employees with a working environment that encourages dignity and respect, and is free from discrimination and harassment.

Aspire to be an employer that has a reputation for fairness, integrity, innovation and creativity in order to attract and retain clients as well as potential and existing employees.

Diversity is a business imperative and we are committed to being an organization that values diversity and promotes the inclusion of all people who share the firm's aspirations and performance expectations.

Additional Information

Barclays Capital supports the National Black MBA Association Metro-Chapter, Toigo, Sponsors for Educational Opportunity and INROADS.

The National Black MBA is a business organization that leads in the creation of economic and intellectual wealth from the African-American community. One of the main operating principles of the NBMBA is to establish and maintain an effective information and communication network. Additionally, the NBMBA enhances the membership's professional and career development goals that link black business professionals.

Toigo is the only graduate-level program with a specialized focus on leadership development and career services for minority MBAs pursuing careers in finance. Each year this organization selects the best and brightest minority business school students to become Toigo Fellows and assists them in joining the top firms on Wall Street.

INROADS is a program whose mission to develop and place talented students of color in business and industry to prepare them for corporate and community leadership.

Sponsors for Educational Opportunity is a program that places outstanding college students of color in substantive internships that are designed to lead to full-time jobs with Wall Street firms.

We make things
brighter.

healthier.
stronger.
safer.
cleaner.
fresher.
faster.
better.

Especially careers.

BASF makes the products you buy better, too. The colors that wake up your make-up. Performance plastics that make your bicycle helmet hard on knocks. Indigo that makes your blue jeans blue. And through our highly personalized Professional Development Program (PDP), your career can go much further.

The Professional Development Program is your guide through the diverse world of BASF. It provides you with the opportunity to gain an understanding of BASF from different perspectives, and to apply your expertise through real-world rotational assignments.

BASF Is Proud To Be An Equal Opportunity Employer.

www.basf.com/careers

WE DON'T MAKE THE PRODUCTS YOU BUY.
WE MAKE THE PRODUCTS YOU BUY BETTER.

BASF Corporation

100 Campus Dr.
Florham Park, NJ 07932
Phone: (973) 245-6000
Toll Free: (800) 526-1072
www.basf.com/careers

Locations

Florham Park, NJ (US HQ)
Ludwigshafen, Germany (Global HQ)

Diversity Leadership

Ingrid Abreu
Manager, Management Development &
Diversity

Employment Contact

Catharina King
Recruitment Specialist
University Recruiting

Recruiting

Please list the schools/types of schools at which you recruit.

• Ivy League schools
• Other private schools
• Public state schools

Do you have any special outreach efforts directed to encourage minority students to consider your firm?

• Hold a reception for minority students
• *Conferences:* SWE, NSBE, SHPE, NSHMBA, Reaching out
• Participate in/host minority student job fair(s)
• Sponsor minority student association events
• Firm's employees participate on career panels at schools
• *Scholarships or intern/fellowships for minority students:* TMSF, Jackie Robinson Foundation
• *Other:* Monster Diversity Leadership Program sponsor

What activities does the firm undertake to attract minority and women employees?

• Partner programs with women and minority associations
• Conferences
• Participate at minority job fairs
• Seek referrals from other employees
• Utilize online job services

Internships and Co-ops

Internship

Deadline for application: On going
Number of interns in the program in summer 2006 (internship) or 2006 (co-op): 17 interns
Pay: Competitive
Length of the program: 12 weeks
Percentage of interns/co-ops in the program who receive offers of full-time employment: 80 percent

Web site for internship/co-op information: www.basf.com/careers

MBA Internship Professional Development Program

The BASF MBA Internship Program provides MBA graduates with the opportunity to apply their education and background to challenging assignments, develop technical and managerial expertise, network at senior levels throughout BASF and explore possible careers with the company. Individual assignments in your field of expertise will be designed and planned to enhance your career development and deliver immediate value to BASF.

The program focuses on financial management and consists of assignments in business groups, financial functions and logistics. Projects include preparing operational plans, break-even analysis, acquisitions and divestitures. A technical undergraduate degree is desirable but not necessary.

Requirements:

- First-year MBA students only
- Demonstrated academic achievement: GPA 3.0+
- International perspective required, international experience preferred
- Three to five years work experience prior to MBA/international experience preferred
- Undergraduate finance or technical degree preferred (e.g., chemistry, engineering, etc.)
- Bilingual preferred, German fluency preferred
- Intercultural orientation, business acumen
- Authorization to work in the U.S. without restriction

Logistics/Customer Care Internship

The qualified candidate will be responsible for the management of customer orders through the entire order fulfillment process. The intern will ensure complete customer satisfaction through timely, thorough follow-through—keeping the customer apprised of their account status. The interns will function in a team environment while retaining the ability to empower themselves to perform their specific job functions and make decisions that are in the best interests of the customer and BASF. Additional responsibilities include, but are not limited to, assisting in the resolution of outstanding credit issues, non-conformances and various supply chain-related projects. This position will interface with various functions within the business, such as marketing, sales and logistics, at all levels of the organization.

Requirements:

- Knowledge of MS Office
- Must be a self-starter and able to make key decisions in a fast-paced dynamic work environment
- Action-oriented, with good problem solving and analytical skills
- Excellent communication skills
- Demonstrated academic achievement
- A desire to advance career within the business
- Rising seniors only
- Authorization to work in the U.S. without restriction

Desired Skills:

- A bachelor's degree in supply chain, business, logistics or finance preferred
- Experience in customer service account management or internal sales preferred
- Bilingual (French, German and/or Spanish) a plus
- APICS certified a plus (production and inventory management)
- Knowledge of SAP preferred

Chemical Engineering Internship Professional Development Program

We offer junior chemical engineering students the opportunity to spend a summer working at a North American BASF site or at BASF AG's international headquarters in Ludwigshafen, Germany, where the company operates the world's largest integrated chemical complex. Interns will partake in various chemical engineering projects/practical assignments and an opportunity to apply what you've learned in school. Competitive salary, round-trip travel to Ludwigshafen, Germany (if selected for the Germany program).

Requirements:

• Excellent communication skills
• Outstanding work ethic
• Demonstrated academic achievement
• College juniors only (rising seniors)
• German language skills preferred for those interested in the Germany program
• Mobile-minded
• International orientation (a plus)
• Bilingual (a plus)

Accounting Internship Professional Development Program

We offer rising seniors the opportunity to spend a summer working at BASF's North American headquarters site in Florham Park, N.J., in the corporate financial planning and controlling department. Interns will receive exposure to various corporate level accounting functions, which include monthly financial closings, accounting procedure reviews, accounting research, financial statement development and financial system integrations.

Requirements:

• Excellent communication skills
• Outstanding work ethic
• Demonstrated academic achievement: GPA 3.0+
• College juniors only (rising seniors)
• Authorization to work in the U.S. without restrictions

Affinity Groups

• African-American Employee Group (AAEG)
• Women and Business Issues (W&BI)
• Gay Lesbian Bisexual Transgender and Friends (GLBT&F)
• Latin American Employee Group (LAEG)

Groups of BASF employees are committed to a long-term strategy that contributes to the overall values and goals of the corporation. They each define their mission, which supports BASF's overall strategy. They convene frequently and use different means for communication, including e-mails and feature stories/events on their web sites, hosted in the BASF intranet.

Entry-Level Programs/Full-Time Opportunities/Training Programs

MBA Professional Development Program

The Professional Development Program (PDP) provides MBA graduates with the opportunity to apply their education and background to challenging assignments, develop technical and managerial expertise, network at senior levels throughout BASF and explore possible career tracks with the company. Two domestic six-month assignments in your field of expertise will be designed for your first year in the program. In the second year, PDP participants will be required to participate in a minimum of a three-month assignment in Germany and an additional nine-month international assignment with the sponsoring group. These assignments will be designed and planned to enhance your career development and deliver immediate value to BASF.

Requirements:

- Must be willing to relocate—various job locations within the United States
- International perspective required, international experience preferred
- Three to five years work experience prior to MBA/international experience preferred
- Undergraduate finance or technical degree preferred (e.g., chemistry, engineering, etc.)
- Bilingual preferred, German fluency preferred
- Intercultural orientation, business acumen

Accounting Professional Development Program

BASF Corporation's Professional Development Program for accountants is a high-profile, fast-track program for accounting graduates who demonstrate strong potential. The program's goal is to develop future accounting managers and business controllers for a world-class chemical company, BASF Corporation—The Chemical Company.

The 18-month program consists of training assignments in each of the following accounting areas:

- Accounting services
- Corporate accounting
- Business/managerial accounting
- Corporate financial planning and analysis
- Site accounting (a four-month assignment at a major production facility either in Geismar, La.; Freeport, TX or Wyandotte, Mich.)

Upon successful completion of the program, the incumbent will, based upon existing opportunities at that time, be eligible for a two-year assignment within one of the above accounting functions. Subsequent to that, opportunities for advancement will be based upon performance and will include not only the above area but also other opportunities within BASF Corporation.

During the course of the program the incumbent will be exposed to a wide array of technical and personal growth opportunities. Additionally, the incumbent will be expected to pursue an MBA degree and/or CPA. We seek bright, geographically mobile, well-rounded individuals who are searching for an excellent entrance opportunity into private sector accounting.

Requirements:

- Excellent communication skills
- Outstanding work ethic
- Demonstrated academic achievement
- College seniors only
- Authorization to work in the U.S. without restrictions

Logistics/Customer Care Representative

Qualified candidates will be responsible for the management of customer orders through the entire order fulfillment process. The customer care representatives will ensure complete customer satisfaction through timely, thorough follow-through—keeping the customer apprised of their account status. Customer care representatives will function in a team environment while retaining the ability to empower themselves to perform their specific job functions and make decisions that are in the best interests of the customer and BASF. Additional responsibilities include, but are not limited to, assisting in the resolution of outstanding credit issues, non-conformances and various supply chain related projects. This position will interface with various functions within the business, such as marketing, sales and logistics, at all levels of the organization.

BASF Corporation offers a comprehensive program of employee benefits, including insurance coverage for medical, dental, life and long-term disability, and employee savings (401k) and pension plans.

Requirements:

- Knowledge of MS Office
- Must be a self-starter and able to make key decisions in a fast-paced dynamic work environment
- Action-oriented, with good problem solving and analytical skills
- Excellent communication skills
- Demonstrated academic achievement
- A desire to advance career within the business
- College seniors only
- Authorization to work in the U.S. without restrictions

Desired Skills:

- A bachelor's degree in supply chain, business, logistics or finance preferred
- Experience in customer service account management or internal sales preferred
- Bilingual (French, German and/or Spanish a plus)
- APICS certified a plus (production and inventory management)
- Knowledge of SAP preferred

Chemical Engineering Professional Development Program

This comprehensive program provides new college graduates with the opportunity to gain an understanding of BASF from different perspectives and to apply their expertise through real world assignments. PDP participants explore career options and develop technical and professional decision-making skills, while fulfilling specific business needs through two nine-month rotational assignments at different sites. PDP participants gain valuable exposure to BASF culture and values, and have the opportunity to live and work in a wide range of locations, including some of our major sites in Louisiana, Michigan, New Jersey, North Carolina, South Carolina and Texas.

The program may consist of assignments in the following areas:

- Manufacturing/operations
- Corporate engineering (process/project)
- Ecology and safety
- Maintenance
- Research and development

BASF Corporation offers a comprehensive program of employee benefits, including insurance coverage for medical, dental, life and long-term disability, and employee savings—401(k)—and pension plans.

Requirements:

- Excellent communication skills
- Outstanding work ethic
- Demonstrated academic achievement
- College seniors only
- Chemical engineering degree required
- Mobile-minded
- International orientation (a plus)
- Bilingual (a plus)
- Authorization to work in the U.S. without restrictions

Strategic Plan and Diversity Leadership

How does the firm's leadership communicate the importance of diversity to everyone at the firm?

The firm communicates diversity initiatives by sending quarterly communications to the senior management team and spotlighting stories on the BASF Intranet.

Who has primary responsibility for leading diversity initiatives at your firm?

Ingrid Abreu, manager, management development and diversity.

Does your firm currently have a diversity committee?

Yes. The diversity team (DT) is comprised of 11 members who review diversity related information and make recommendations to the HR leadership committee. The team meets once a month virtually and once a year in person.

If yes, does the committee's representation include one or more members of the firm's management/executive committee?

Yes.

If yes, how many executives are on the committee, and in 2005, what was the total number of hours collectively spent by the committee in furtherance of the firm's diversity initiatives? How many employees are on the committee, and how often does the committee convene in furtherance of the firm's diversity initiatives?

The BASF diversity team has been designed to include representatives from a wide cross-section of the corporation. The team is comprised of 11 members from various sites in the North American region. We have taken years of service and experience levels into consideration in the composition of the team. Members represent a variety of communities: manufacturing and engineering, sales and marketing, purchasing, customer service, finance, research and development, human resources, PMU and legal. Each team member serves at least two years. We have two executive women on the team and we meet once a month for an hour via virtual teleconference and also for two days in person for our annual diversity strategy meeting.

> *Total Executives on Committee:* Two

Does the committee and/or diversity leader establish and set goals or objectives consistent with management's priorities?

Yes.

Has the firm undertaken a formal or informal diversity program or set of initiatives aimed at increasing the diversity of the firm?

Yes, informal.

How often does the firm's management review the firm's diversity progress/results?

Quarterly.

The Stats

	2005 STATS	
	U.S.	WORLDWIDE
Number of employees	10,000	81,000
Revenue	$11.3 billion	$50.4 billion

Diversity Mission Statement

Vision

At BASF NAFTA, we value the differences in our workforce as they are key to the success of our business and to the achievement of our status as partner of choice. Consistent with our values, BASF has an inclusive environment that promotes respect and dignity for all in the workplace.

Resources

Diversity alliance consists of the diversity team (cross-functional group from various sites and backgrounds), employee groups (African-American Employees Group—AAEG; Women & Business Issues—W&BI; Gay Lesbian, Bisexual, Transgender & Friends—GLBT&F and Latin American Employee Group—LAEG) and extended alliance members that represent other HR functions including staffing, etc.

2006 Strategy

Focus on recruitment and retention, talent development and community outreach.

Goals

• To attract diverse candidates to work at BASF
• To maximize the development of the diverse talent in BASF
• To strengthen BASF's visibility and presence in the diverse communities we serve

Bayer Corporation celebrates and embraces diversity in the workforce through our commitment to leadership, education and career development. We strive to foster an environment that encourages our employees to value and express differing ideas and beliefs and one that

Diversity. Alive.

empowers them to reach their full potential. We take pride in our efforts to be an employer of choice dedicated to attracting, recruiting and retaining the best and brightest people in the world.

HealthCare   CropScience   MaterialScience   BayerUS.com

Bayer CropScience

2 T.W. Alexander Drive
Research Triangle Park, NC 27709
Phone: (866) 992-2937
www.bayerjobs.com

Diversity Leadership

Summer Busto
Manager, Talent Acquisition & Domestic
Relocation
P.O. Box 12014
Research Triangle Park, NC 27709
Phone: (919) 549-2437
E-mail: summer.busto@bayercropscience.com

Recruiting

Please list the schools/types fo schools at which you recruit.

Public state schools

Do you have any special outreach efforts directed to encourage minority students to consider your firm?

Other: INROADS Program

What activities does the firm undertake to attract minority and women employees?

• Seek referrals from other employees
• Utilize online job services

Do you use executive recruiting/search firms to seek to identify new diversity hires?

No.

Internships and Co-ops

INROADS

Length of the program: 14 weeks
Web site for internship/co-op information: www.bayerjobs.com

We hire interns in various departments based on need and availability of projects. Since 2004 we've had interns in O&I, supply chain, marketing, HR, government regulatory affairs and accounts payable.

The Stats

Revenue

2005: $7.396 billion

Baystate Medical Center

759 Chestnut Street
Springfield, MA 01199
Phone: (413) 794-5655
Fax: (413) 794-8274
www.baystatehealth.com/jobs

Diversity Leadership
The director of recruitment is responsible for all recruitment initiatives.

Employment Contact
Fran Del Padre
E-mail: fran.delpadre@bhs.org

Recruiting

Please list the schools/types of schools at which you recruit.

- Public state schools
- Other private schools
- Hispanic Serving Institutions (HSIs)
- Other predominantly minority and/or women's colleges

Do you have any special outreach efforts directed to encourage minority students to consider your firm?

- Conferences
- Sponsor minority student association events
- Firm's employees participate on career panels at schools
- Outreach to leadership of minority student organizations
- Scholarships or intern/fellowships for minority students

What activities does the firm undertake to attract minority and women employees?

- Partner programs with women and minority associations
- Conferences
- Participate at minority job fairs
- Seek referrals from other employees
- Utilize online job services

Do you use executive recruiting/search firms to seek to identify new diversity hires?

Yes.

Internships and Co-ops

INROADS; Clinical Externships

Number of interns in the program in summer 2005: 10 internships, four externships
Pay: $11.50-$16 per hour, based on program and year in school
Length of the program: INROADS, eight-10 weeks. Externships depends on specialty
Percentage of interns/co-ops in the program who receive offers of full-time employment: 100 percent of the INROADS students who have successfully completed the program have been offered full-time employment.

We are a major medical center and teaching hospital that offers internships with the INROADS program. We offer internships for nursing and pre-med students, as well as other clinical and nonclinical specialities. The INROADS program runs for 10 weeks in the summer and prepares students to become registered nurses in a variety of specialty areas. The internship offers a progressive program throughout the students' four years of college. When the students graduate, they are fully prepared to become registered nurses. Our students become per diem employees and as such may take advantage of any Baystate services offered to other per diem employees. They may also take advantage of our forgivable loan program for nurses. During their senior year of nursing they may take advantage of early signing bonuses for nursing positions.

Strategic Plan and Diversity Leadership

How does the firm's leadership communicate the importance of diversity to everyone at the firm?

Our monthly news publication publishes articles; our internal web site offers information about educational programs and updates; global e-mails go out to management alerting them to information that they can share with their staffs; in-services are provided; diversity is part of our annual "Knowledge Refreshers" for staff.

Who has primary responsibility for leading diversity initiatives at your firm?

Senior VP of Human Resources, Paula S. Dennison.

Does your firm currently have a diversity committee?

Yes.

If yes, please describe how the committee is structured, how often it meets, etc.

Made up of staff and management employee representatives from spiritual services, interpreter services, staff development, professional and organizational development, staff RNs and nursing managers.

If yes, does the committee's representation include one or more members of the firm's management/executive committee (or the equivalent)?

Yes.

If yes, how many executives are on the committee, and in 2005, what was the total number of hours collectively spent by the committee in furtherance of the firm's diversity initiatives?

54 hours.

If yes, how many employees are on the committee, and how often does the committee convene in furtherance of the firm's diversity initiatives?

The committee has regularly scheduled meetings.

Does the committee and/or diversity leader establish and set goals or objectives consistent with management's priorities?

Yes.

Has the firm undertaken a formal or informal diversity program or set of initiatives aimed at increasing the diversity of the firm?

Yes, formal. Affirmative action, recruitment processes; JCAHO initiatives; magnet hospital initiatives; and our internal customer service program.

The Stats

Employees

2005: 6,170 (U.S.)

Revenue

2005: $1.3 billion (U.S.)

Number minorities: 1,313
Minorities: 21.3 percent
Minority executives: 7.3 percent
Males: 20.4 percent
Females: 79.6 percent
Female executives (from supervisor level through CEO): 66.8 percent

Retention and Professional Development

How do 2005 minority and female attrition rates generally compare to those experienced in the prior year period?

Higher than in 2004.

2005: 25.85 percent minority
2004: 24 percent minority

Please identify the specific steps you are taking to reduce the attrition rate of minority and women employees.

- Increase/review compensation relative to competition
- Increase/improve current work/life programs
- *Adopt dispute resolution process:* In place for 22 years
- Work with minority and women employees to develop career advancement plans
- Professional skills development program, including minority and women employees

Additional Information

We are very much involved with community outreach, which includes collaborative efforts for minority students from grammar school through senior year in high school. We have a department that is solely responsible for collaborating with school systems as well as working closely with community groups such as the Urban League, etc. We have grown our INROADS internship program over the past several years and hope to increase our commitment in the future. We offer "career ladders" for the majority of our staff nurses (which are predominately women) as well as recognition for clinical certifications and tuition reimbursement to support further education. Our "work/life" department continually reviews its programs and has expanded its services offered to employees.

Black & Decker

701 E. Joppa Rd.
Towson, MD 21286
Phone: (410) 716-3900
Fax: (410) 716-2933
Toll Free: (800) 544-6986
www.bdk.com
www.bdksales.com

Locations

Towson, MD (HQ)
Campbellsville, KY • Charlotte, NC • Chesterfield, MI • Danbury, CT • Decatur, AR • Denison, TX • Ft. Lauderdale, FL • Fort Mill, SC • Hopkinsville, KY • Jackson, TN • Lake Forest, CA • Mira Loma, CA • Montpelier, IN • Reading, PA • Rialto, CA • Shelbyville, KY • Shelton, CT • Tampa, FL

Additional Information

Black & Decker was founded in 1910, when Duncan Black and Alonzo Decker invested $1,200 to operate a machine shop. Their first designs included a vest pocket adding machine and a candy dipping machine. Since that time, Black & Decker has grown to be a leading global manufacturer and marketer of quality power tools and accessories, hardware and home improvement products and technology-based fastening systems. Our products and services are marketed in more than 100 nations, and we have manufacturing operations in 11 countries. Throughout our businesses, we have established a reputation for product innovation, quality, end-user focus, design and value. Our strong brand names and new product development capabilities enjoy worldwide recognition, and our global distribution is unsurpassed in our industries.

In 2005, Black & Decker had annual sales of over $6 billion and the company employs approximately 25,000 people around the world. The corporate headquarters is located in Towson, Md.

Black & Decker is made up of three business segments:

Power Tools—headquartered in Towson, Md. Product categories include: corded and cordless power tools and equipment, outdoor tools, home products, accessories and product service. Major brand names include: Black & Decker, DeWalt, Firestorm, Workmate, Porter-Cable and Delta.

Home and Hardware Improvement—headquartered in Lake Forest, Calif. Product categories include: security hardware, commercial and residential door locksets, door hardware and plumbing products. Major product categories are: Kwikset, Baldwin, Weiser and Price Pfister.

Fastening and Assembly Systems—headquartered in Shelton, Conn. Product categories include: assembly systems, specialty screws, metal and plastic fasteners, self-piercing riveting systems and platform-management services. Major brand names include Emhart Teknologies, Autoset, Gripco, Heli-Coil and Ultra-Grip.

Our Commitment to Diversity

We are committed to developing a culture and environment in which all employees are respected and their differences are fully utilized toward meeting our organization's goals. This will allow us to provide a stimulating, challenging and satisfying environment for our employees and to improve returns to our investors through increased innovation and creativity, and consistent improvement in the quality and profitability of our businesses. Our policies, practices and accountabilities reflect our belief that inclusion is a core value that will allow us to achieve higher levels of customer and employee satisfaction.

One of the ways in which we are working to achieve our diversity and inclusion objectives is through the Workplace Advisory Council that has been established in our power tools and accessories business. The mission of the council is to provide advice and recommendations on workplace issues directly to our business heads.

For more information on career opportunities with Black & Decker, please visit our web site at www.bdk.com.

IS THERE A FUEL MORE EFFICIENT THAN TEAMWORK?

FLYING SOLO MAY HOLD A CERTAIN ALLURE, but you always understood the value of teamwork. So does Boeing. Here, teams composed of accomplished professionals with differing backgrounds, ideas and perspectives are developing an amazing array of sophisticated technologies. We're on a journey to amazing destinations and we want you to help take us there. As the world's largest aerospace company, our diverse projects and programs can turn your childhood dreams into today's opportunities. You'll be joining an organization known for its support of learning both on and off the job, and one that has also been honored as higher education's top corporate sponsor. The job categories below include some of the key skills we are seeking.

- Aeronautical Engineering
- Aerospace Engineering
- Business/Finance
- Chemical Engineering
- Civil Engineering
- Electrical Engineering
- Electromagnetic Engineering
- Embedded Software Engineering
- Industrial Engineering
- Manufacturing Engineering

- Material Science Engineering
- Mechanical Engineering
- Optics
- Payloads
- Physics/Math
- Propulsion
- Reliability Maintainability Testability Engineering
- Software Engineering
- Structures
- Systems Engineering

To view a comprehensive listing of all available positions, please visit: boeing.com/collegecareers.
Security clearance requirements are indicated in the position listings. U.S. citizenship is necessary for all positions requiring a security clearance.

Boeing is an equal opportunity employer supporting diversity in the workplace.

Apply at: *boeing.com/collegecareers*

Forever New Frontiers

Boeing Company, The

100 North Riverside Chicago, IL. 60606 Phone: (312) 544-2000 www.boeing.com/collegecareers	**Employment Contact** Kara Yarnot Senior Manager, College & Diversity Programs

Recruiting

Please list the schools/types of schools at which you recruit.

- Ivy League schools
- Other private schools
- Public state schools
- Historically Black Colleges and Universities (HBCUs)
- Hispanic Serving Institutions (HSIs)
- Native American Tribal Universities
- Other predominantly minority and/or women's colleges

Do you have any special outreach efforts directed to encourage minority students to consider your firm?

- Hold a reception for minority students
- *Conferences:* National Society of Black Engineers, Society of Hispanic Professional Engineers, National Association of Asian-American Professionals, Hispanic Engineer National Achievement Awards Conference, Society of Women Engineers, Women of Color in Technology
- Advertise in minority student association publication(s)
- Participate in/host minority student job fair(s)
- Sponsor minority student association events
- Firm's employees participate on career panels at schools
- Outreach to leadership of minority student organizations
- Scholarships or intern/fellowships for minority students

What activities does the firm undertake to attract minority and women employees?

- Partner programs with women and minority associations
- *Conferences:* See above list
- Participate at minority job fairs
- Seek referrals from other employees
- Utilize online job services

Internships and Co-ops

Deadline for application: Positions are posted from September through April
Number of interns in the program in summer 2005 (internship) or 2005 (co-op): 1,000 interns and co-ops
Length of the program: 12-14 weeks for internships; six months for co-ops
Percentage of interns/co-ops in the program who receive offers of full-time employment: 50-60 percent
Web site for internship/co-op information: www.boeing.com/collegecareers

Scholarships

Scholarship money is given to selected universities and the universities select the scholarship recipients on Boeing's behalf.

Affinity Groups

- Boeing Asian-American Association
- Boeing Black Employees Association
- Boeing Employee Association for Sexual Minorities
- Boeing Hispanic Employees Network
- Boeing Employee Association for Gays and Lesbians
- Boeing Employee Ability Awareness Association

Retention and Professional Development

Please identify the specific steps you are taking to reduce the attrition rate of minority and women employees.

- Develop and/or support internal employee affinity groups (e.g., minority or women networks within the firm)
- Increase/review compensation relative to competition
- Increase/improve current work/life programs
- Adopt dispute resolution process
- Succession plan includes emphasis on diversity
- Work with minority and women employees to develop career advancement plans
- Review work assignments and hours billed to key client matters to make sure minority and women employees are not being excluded
- Strengthen mentoring program for all employees, including minorities and women
- Professional skills development program, including minority and women employees

Bonneville Power Administration

905 NE 11th Avenue
Portland, OR 97208
Phone: (503) 230-3000
www.bpa.gov

Locations

Portland OR (HQ)
Various jobs located in:
Idaho • Montana • Oregon • Washington

Employment Contact

www.jobs.bpa.gov

Recruiting

Please list the schools/types of schools at which you recruit.

• Ivy League schools
• Other private schools
• Public state schools
• Historically Black Colleges and Universities (HBCUs)
• Hispanic Serving Institutions (HSIs)
• Native American Tribal Universities
• Other predominantly minority and/or women's colleges

Do you have any special outreach efforts directed to encourage minority students to consider your firm?

• Advertise in minority student association publication(s)
• Participate in/host minority student job fair(s)
• Sponsor minority student association events
• Firm's employees participate on career panels at schools
• Outreach to leadership of minority student organizations
• Scholarships or intern/fellowships for minority students

What activities does the firm undertake to attract minority and women employees?

• Partner programs with women and minority associations
• Participate at minority job fairs
• Seek referrals from other employees
• Utilize online job services

Do you use executive recruiting/search firms to seek to identify new diversity hires?

Yes.

Internships and Co-ops

STEP (Student Temporary Employee Program) and SCEP (Student Career Experience Program)

Deadline for application: Rolling

Pay: Range is from $10 to $25 per hour, dependingdent on the type of position.

Length of the program: STEP participants generally work in one-year increments but could work during the summer only. For SCEP, if program requirements are met and FTE (manpower authorization) and budget are available, a participant can be eligible for a permanent position upon graduation.

Percentage of interns/co-ops in the program who receive offers of full-time employment: SCEP participants only are eligible for possible conversion to full-time employment. At the end of Fiscal Year 2004, 43 students were offered full-time career positions.

Web site for internship/co-op information: www.jobs.bpa.gov (Click on "student" and you will get info on our two programs.)

Any organization within BPA can recruit students if they have the FTE and the budget to fund the position.

Entry-Level Programs/Full-Time Opportunities/Training Programs

High Voltage Power System Electrician, Line Worker and Substation Operator Apprentice Program

Length of program: Three and a half to four years

Geographic location(s) of program: Washington, Oregon, Montana and Idaho

Intensive classroom study, homework and on-the-job-training. End-of-Step presentations, exams and reviews are required every six months and if successful, the apprentice will be promoted to the next step of the apprenticeship program, and finally to journeyman.

Pay starts out at $20.91 per hour. To join the company as a SCEP, you must meet all the student eligibility requirements, and be enrolled in a two-year college in a course of study leading to a degree or certificate related to the electric utility industry, such as electrical theory, electronics, industrial arts or industrial technology. Watch for the vacancy announcements on our web site each fall for complete details.

Strategic Plan and Diversity Leadership

Who has primary responsibility for leading diversity initiatives at your firm?

Godfrey Beckett, manager diversity and EEO.

Does your firm currently have a diversity committee?

Yes.

If yes, does the committee's representation include one or more members of the firm's management/executive committee (or the equivalent)?

Yes.

Does the committee and/or diversity leader establish and set goals or objectives consistent with management's priorities?

Yes.

Has the firm undertaken a formal or informal diversity program or set of initiatives aimed at increasing the diversity of the firm?

Yes, formal and informal.

The Stats

As of August 2006 we have 3,035 government employees at BPA.

Diversity Mission Statement

The office of human resources, diversity and EEO provides leadership and serves as a principal advisor to the senior vice president, employee and business resources, the BPA administrator and chief executive officer and executive committee members on the impact and use of policies, proposals and programs related to human capital management, diversity management, equal employment opportunity and achievement of a high performing organization.

Office staff develops, facilitates, administers, and oversees and evaluates effective strategies, programs, policies and reports that support the BPA mission through:

• Strategic agency-wide human capital management program, which includes alignment of BPA mission and people; measurement of management accountability and organizational improvements; and, semi-annual reports to DOE headquarters
• Human resources, diversity and equal employment opportunity policy development, evaluation and oversight
• Legislative proposal development and analysis
• Labor relations, including technical assistance to, and coordination of, the Partnership Council
• EEO Title VI and VII compliance and resolution programs, which includes affirmative employment planning and reporting
• Alternative dispute resolution programs
• Diversity management strategy and program support, including technical assistance to, and support of, the Pluralism Council
• Workforce statistics and analysis

Borders Group

100 Phoenix Dr.
Ann Arbor, MI 48108
Phone: (734) 477-1100
Fax: (734) 477-1965
www.bordersgroupinc.com

Locations

Ann Arbor, MI

Diversity Leadership

Suzann Trevisan
Senior Manager, Diversity Programs
100 Phoenix Drive
Ann Arbor, MI 48108
Phone: (800) 243-7510
Fax: (734) 477-1127

Recruiting

Please list the schools/types of schools at which you recruit.

Public state schools

Do you have any special outreach efforts directed to encourage minority students to consider your firm?

Participate in/host minority student job fair(s)

What activities does the firm undertake to attract minority and women employees?

• Participate at minority job fairs
• Seek referrals from other employees
• Utilize online job services

Do you use executive recruiting/search firms to seek to identify new diversity hires?

Yes.

Internships and Co-ops

Borders Group Summer Intern Program

Deadline for application: January 1st
Length of the program: 12 weeks
Percentage of interns/co-ops in the program who receive offers of full-time employment: It depends on the year.
Web site for internship/co-op information: www.bordersgroupinc.com

We continue to build upon the success of our Summer Internship Training Program. The program is intended to provide meaningful work experience to rising college seniors who would then become candidates for our College Graduate Training Program after graduation. Interns are placed in positions in finance, marketing/merchandising, information technology and human resources for a 12- to 14-week summer experience with Borders Group. In addition, our summer interns participate in an informative and interactive training program that is designed to help prepare them for their career.

Affinity Groups

- African-American Employee Action Group
- Women's Employee Action Group
- GLBT Employee Action Group

Employee action groups are a vehicle to better understand and support the complexity of varying employee and customer cultures and backgrounds. EAGs represent the diversity of and within a unique constituency, and are employee-driven teams composed of individuals at varying levels and with different functions. The purpose of the employee action groups is to explore and construct meaning on a range of issues that support diversity efforts in the workplace, marketplace, and the local community. These groups meet on a monthly basis.

Entry-Level Programs/Full-Time Opportunities/Training Programs

College Grad Training Program

Length of program: Six months
Geographic location(s) of program: Ann Arbor, MI

We have had great success with our College Graduate Training Program. The goal of the program is to hire and develop college graduates in order to build a strong foundation of future leaders within Borders. College grads are placed in meaningful roles throughout our organization in the following functional areas: finance, marketing/merchandising, information technology, operations and human resources. In addition, participants go through an informative and interactive training program that is designed to help prepare them for success at Borders. The College Graduate Training Program consists of the following elements:

- *Mentorship Guidance:* College grads are partnered with a mentor who is an experienced team member.

- *Cross-Functional College Grad Team Project:* College grads work together in cross-functional group projects that provide the company with predetermined deliverables at the end of the training period.

- *Operational Activities:* College grads spend time training in our stores and distribution centers in order to see how our internal customers operate.

- *Professional Development Series:* College grads participate in a number of training sessions that are designed to build their professional skills.

- *Functional Learning Lessons:* College grads participate in a number of meetings with departmental leaders who share more specific information on how Borders operates.

Strategic Plan and Diversity Leadership

How does the firm's leadership communicate the importance of diversity to everyone at the firm?

The firm uses its web site, electronic newsletters, *Quarterly Scoop* newsletter, Intranet, meetings and training programs to showcase the importance of diversity.

Who has primary responsibility for leading diversity initiatives at your firm?

Dan Smith, senior vice president of HR and Suzann Trevisan, senior manager diversity programs.

Does your firm currently have a diversity committee?

Yes. The committee meets monthly. Borders Group has developed a diversity task force to focus on building strategic initiatives that drive diversity awareness throughout the organization. The task force establishes the focus for diversity efforts throughout our business units, and develops strategies with the help of advisory committees made up of employees from the corporate offices, the field and the distribution facilities. Using various methods like those listed below, the diversity task force and the advisory committees have improved our overall business and nurtured Borders Group's commitment to diversity. The diversity task force focuses on the areas of employee awareness, customer outreach, supplier diversity and recruiting/retention.

If yes, does the committee's representation include one or more members of the firm's management/executive committee (or the equivalent)?

Yes.

How many employees are on the committee, and how often does the committee convene in furtherance of the firm's diversity initiatives?

> *Total Executives on Committee:* One executive and five directors/senior managers

The DTF Leaders provide formal updates to our Executive Team twice a year.

Does the committee and/or diversity leader establish and set goals or objectives consistent with management's priorities?

Yes.

Has the firm undertaken a formal or informal diversity program or set of initiatives aimed at increasing the diversity of the firm?

Yes, formal.

How often does the firm's management review the firm's diversity progress/results?

Monthly.

Retention and Professional Development

Please identify the specific steps you are taking to reduce the attrition rate of minority and women employees.

- Develop and/or support internal employee affinity groups (e.g., minority or women networks within the firm)
- Increase/improve current work/life programs
- Succession plan includes emphasis on diversity
- Work with minority and women employees to develop career advancement plans
- Professional skills development program, including minority and women employees
- *Other:* We have our Pacesetters Programs at the corporate level and in the field which are specifically dedicated to employee development. Both divisions of the program place an emphasis on minority recruitment and retention initiatives.

Diversity Mission Statement

At Borders Group, diversity is who we are. Our commitment to diversity extends to progressive policies, which uphold the right to personal dignity and fairness.

Every person has the right to be treated with respect and dignity, regardless of race, religion, color, creed, national origin, age, gender, gender identity, sexual orientation, disability, veteran or military status, marital status or citizenship status, and other categories protected by applicable federal, state and local laws.

Borders Group supports the individualism of each employee and encourages all who wish to grow to explore their talents and seek expanded opportunities. This deep-rooted enthusiasm for diversity of people and perspectives extends far beyond the walls of our stores. It reaches from our corporate office into our stores, distribution centers and into every community we serve around the world.

151

Community
Values
Tradition
Opportunity
Family

You deserve a career with a purpose. This human-service career has the potential to be your lifelong passion because you'll be giving generations of children the opportunity to reach their full potential as responsible adults.

Visit www.scouting.org for information on employment opportunities in Scouting.

BOY SCOUTS OF AMERICA®

Boy Scouts of America

P. O. Box 152079
1325 W. Walnut Hill Lane
Irving, TX 75015-2079
Phone: (972) 580-2118
Fax: (972) 580-2549
www.scouting.org

Diversity Leadership

Carolyn Altemus
Director, Diversity and Executive Recruiting
E-mail: caltemus@netbsa.org
LearningforLife.org/career

Recruiting

Please list the schools/types of schools at which you recruit.

• Private schools
• Public state schools
• Historically Black Colleges and Universities (HBCUs)
• Hispanic Serving Institutions (HSIs)
• Native American Tribal Universities
• *Other predominantly minority and/or women's colleges:* Asian Serving Universities

Do you have any special outreach efforts directed to encourage minority students to consider your firm?

• *Conferences:* LULAC, HACU, Asian Inc., NCLR, Alpha Phi Alpha, Professional Women, NACE, Job Choices Diversity Edition
• Advertise in minority student association publication(s)
• Participate in/host minority student job fair(s)
• Sponsor minority student association events
• Firm's employees participate on career panels at schools
• Outreach to leadership of minority student organizations
• Scholarships or intern/fellowships for minority students
• *Other:* Internship Mentoring Program

What activities does the firm undertake to attract minority and women employees?

• Participate at minority job fairs
• Seek referrals from other employees
• Utilize online job services
• *Other:* Internal ads in *Scoutreach Newsletter,* Black EOE publication, *Hispanic Network Magazine,* Job Choices Diversity Edition, Hispanic Career World

Do you use executive recruiting/search firms to seek to identify new diversity hires?

No.

Internships and Co-ops

Local Council Internship Model

Deadline for application: Varies by location

Number of interns in the program in summer 2005 (internship) or 2005 (co-op): Varies by location

Pay: Pay varies by location

Length of the program: Semester

Percentage of interns/co-ops in the program who receive offers of full-time employment: Approximately 70 percent or more

Web site for internship/co-op information: Each local council has its own internship program

The local council college internship program is designed to be a unique, educational work and interpersonal relationship program especially and specifically designed to increase practical knowledge of the role and responsibilities of professional scouting. Students can receive academic credit for their internship from their college or university, and your local council receives another opportunity to extend scouting's relationships and mission.

A local council internship program for college students provides an opportunity to develop a pool of qualified entry-level professionals and the ability to focus on serving an increasingly diverse population.

Scholarships

Each local council has its own procedure and options.

Entry-Level Programs/Full-Time Opportunities/Training Programs

Professional Development I, II, III

Length of program: One to two weeks

Geographic location(s) of program: Texas and regionally by area

The Boy Scouts of America realizes that in order for employees to grow and be productive, people need opportunities to learn. The fact that more than 75 percent of the BSA's professionals receive training each year is a testimony to the commitment by local councils and the national organization. Training courses, with set periods of time to acquire specific information, are part of our overall plan of development.

Professional scouters receive continuous instruction through formal as well as informal training. The BSA fosters an environment of continuous learning to nurture the collective creativity and skills that will benefit both professionals and the organization. We share knowledge, ideas and experience to create a workforce that is involved in decision making and an inclusive work environment that ensures the success of scouting in the local area.

BSA is committed to the training and development of individuals because we fully recognize the benefits of mutual growth and development.

Strategic Plan and Diversity Leadership

How does the firm's leadership communicate the importance of diversity to everyone at the firm?

The chief scout executive of the Boy Scouts of America continually emphases the strategic need to increase and retain a diverse workforce as well as membership in the organization; we continually communicate the importance of diversity through BSA's "Who Are We" web page, monthly diversity newsletters, and editorials and advertising in internal and external publications; we've established diversity committees who will review, educate, govern and enforce the need to increase and retain diverse employees, members, and volunteers.

Who has primary responsibility for leading diversity initiatives at your firm?

Carolyn Altemus, director, diversity and executive recruiting.

Does your firm currently have a diversity committee?

Yes.

If yes, please describe how the committee is structured, how often it meets, etc.

The Communications Committee meets monthly; the Workforce Committee meets annually; and the Training Committee meeting quarterly. Each committee is lead by an advisor and is made up of employees of all levels, ethnicities and genders.

If yes, does the committee's representation include one or more members of the firm's management/executive committee (or the equivalent)?

Yes.

If yes, how many executives are on the committee, and in 2005, what was the total number of hours collectively spent by the committee in furtherance of the firm's diversity initiatives? How many employees are on the committee, and how often does the committee convene in furtherance of the firm's diversity initiatives?

The Communications Committee meets about 175 hours yearly, and there are 30 employees on the committee. The Training Committee meets about 120 hours per year, and there are 10 employees on the committee.

Does the committee and/or diversity leader establish and set goals or objectives consistent with management's priorities?

Yes.

Has the firm undertaken a formal or informal diversity program or set of initiatives aimed at increasing the diversity of the firm?

Yes, formal.

Boy Scouts of America established strategies and goals to recruit and retain the number of minorities and women executives.

How often does the firm's management review the firm's diversity progress/results?

Quarterly.

How is the firm's diversity committee and/or firm management held accountable for achieving results?

Critical achievements are assigned to Diversity Committees and their performance in serving on the committee is reviewed annually as part of their yearly performance evaluation.

Retention and Professional Development

How do 2005 minority and female attrition rates generally compare to those experienced in the prior year period?

Higher than in prior years—for all categories except African-American men.

Please identify the specific steps you are taking to reduce the attrition rate of minority and women employees.

• Increase/improve current work/life programs

• Succession plan includes emphasis on diversity
• Work with minority and women employees to develop career advancement plans
• Strengthen mentoring program
• Increase professional skills development programs

Diversity Mission Statement

More than 90 years ago, the Boy Scouts of America (BSA) was founded on the premise of teaching boys moral and ethical values through an outdoor program that challenges them and teaches them respect for nature, one another and themselves. Scouting has always represented the best in community, leadership and service.

The Boy Scouts of America has selected its leaders using the highest standards because strong leaders and positive role models are so important to the healthy development of youth. Today, the organization still stands firm that their leaders exemplify the values outlined in the Scout Oath and Law.

On June 28, 2000, the United States Supreme Court reaffirmed the Boy Scouts of America's standing as a private organization with the right to set its own membership and leadership standards.

The BSA respects the rights of people and groups who hold values that differ from those encompassed in the Scout Oath and Law, and the BSA makes no effort to deny the rights of those whose views differ to hold their attitudes or opinions.

Scouts and scouters come from all walks of life and are exposed to diversity in scouting that they may not otherwise experience. The Boy Scouts of America aims to allow youth to live and learn as children and enjoy scouting without immersing them in the politics of the day.

We hope that our supporters will continue to value the Boy Scouts of America's respect for diversity and the positive impact scouting has on young people's lives. We realize that not every individual or organization subscribes to the same beliefs that the BSA does, but we hope that all Americans can be as respectful of our beliefs as we are of theirs, and support the overall good scouting does in American communities.

BP p.l.c.

BP North America
4101 Winfield Road
Warrenville, IL 60555
Phone: (630) 821-3000
www.bp.com/careers/us

Locations

London, UK (HQ)
Warrenville, IL (North America HQ)
Houston, TX (Exploration HQ)

Recruiting

Please list the schools/types of schools at which you recruit.

- Ivy League schools
- Other private schools
- Public state schools
- Historically Black Colleges and Universities (HBCUs)
- Hispanic Serving Institutions (HSIs)
- Native American Tribal Universities
- Other predominantly minority and/or women's colleges

Do you have any special outreach efforts directed to encourage minority students to consider your firm?

- Hold a reception for minority students
- Conferences
- Advertise in minority student association publication(s)
- Participate in/host minority student job fair(s)
- Sponsor minority student association events
- Firm's employees participate on career panels at schools
- Outreach to leadership of minority student organizations
- Scholarships or intern/fellowships for minority students

What activities does the firm undertake to attract minority and women employees?

- Partner programs with women and minority associations
- Participate at minority job fairs
- Seek referrals from other employees
- Utilize online job services
- Other, please specify

Do you use executive recruiting/search firms to seek to identify new diversity hires?

Yes.

The Stats

Employees

2005: 96,200
2004: 102,900

Revenue

2005: $262 billion
2004: $285 billion

Retention and Professional Development

Please identify the specific steps you are taking to reduce the attrition rate of minority and women employees.

- Develop and/or support internal employee affinity groups (e.g., minority or women networks within the firm)
- Increase/review compensation relative to competition
- Increase/improve current work/life programs
- Adopt dispute resolution process
- Succession plan includes emphasis on diversity
- Work with minority and women employees to develop career advancement plans
- Review work assignments and hours billed to key client matters to make sure minority and women employees are not being excluded
- Strengthen mentoring program for all employees, including minorities and women
- Professional skills development program, including minority and women employees

Diversity Mission Statement

Diversity & Inclusion at BP

BP's diversity and inclusion plan focuses on talent and inclusion. As a global company, we are competing for resources and markets in many parts of the world. We are also competing for the best available talent worldwide: people with ideas, passion and the ability to grasp and conquer the challenges we face in the various regions where we currently operate or seek to operate.

We seek to attract and retain the best talent available: men and women regardless of background, age, religion, ethnic origin, nationality, disability or sexual orientation. This will enable us to achieve world-class business results through the creation of an environment where every individual is given equal access to development and advancement, and can realize her or his full potential.

To achieve this aspiration, we are taking immediate, real actions targeted towards developing a practical and sustainable approach to diversity and inclusion on a global basis.

The HR team is conducting reviews of our people management processes to ensure they are fair, robust and powerful enactments of our commitment to meritocracy. To support these efforts, we seek to include diversity in every selection committee. Furthermore we have insisted upon diverse candidate slates from our external search partners. Finally, to ensure delivery, we measure the results.

Underpinning this strategic focus, we emphasize the importance of communication and monitoring.

Brinker International

6820 LBJ Freeway
Dallas, TX 75240
Phone: (972) 770-9824
www.brinkerjobs.com

Locations

Dallas, TX (HQ)
Global operations

Diversity Leadership

Mark King
Senior Manager, Diversity & Inclusion
6820 LBJ Freeway
Dallas, TX 75240
Phone: (972) 770-9824
E-mail: mark.king@brinker.com

Employment Contact

Annette Green
Director, Recruiting—Home Office

Martin Riggs
Director, Recruiting—Field

Recruiting

Please list the schools/types of schools at which you recruit.

Recruiting takes place but under no formalized program.

Do you have any special outreach efforts directed to encourage minority students to consider your firm?

• Hold a reception for minority students
• Advertise in minority student association publication(s)
• Participate in/host minority student job fair(s)
• Sponsor minority student association events
• Outreach to leadership of minority student organizations
• Scholarships or intern/fellowships for minority students

What activities does the firm undertake to attract minority and women employees?

• Partner programs with women and minority associations
• *Conferences:* National Society of Minorities in Hospitality; Professional Women Leadership
• Participate at minority job fairs
• Seek referrals from other employees
• Utilize online job services

Do you use executive recruiting/search firms to seek to identify new diversity hires?

Yes.

Internships and Co-ops

INROADS

Deadline for application: January

Number of interns in the program in summer 2005 (internship) or 2005 (co-op): Four

Pay: $10 per hour

Length of the program: 10 weeks

Percentage of interns/co-ops in the program who receive offers of full-time employment: 25 percent (one out of four)

Strategic Plan and Diversity Leadership

How does the firm's leadership communicate the importance of diversity to everyone at the firm?

Comprehensive approach to communications. Diversity messaging is aligned with quarterly employee meetings; key brand meetings; diversity e-mails; company newsletters; diversity section on Intranet and external web site; leadership talks (open forums), etc.

Who has primary responsibility for leading diversity initiatives at your firm?

Mark King, senior manager, Office of Diversity & Inclusion.

Does your firm currently have a diversity committee?

Yes.

If yes, please describe how the committee is structured, how often it meets, etc.

The team is strategically comprised of senior leadership representatives from home office and brands. The team meets quarterly or more frequently as needed. Meetings are facilitated by the Office of Diversity & Inclusion.

If yes, does the committee's representation include one or more members of the firm's management/executive committee (or the equivalent)?

Yes.

If yes, how many executives are on the committee, and in 2005, what was the total number of hours collectively spent by the committee in furtherance of the firm's diversity initiatives? How many employees are on the committee, and how often does the committee convene in furtherance of the firm's diversity initiatives?

Total Executives on the Committee: 56 percent are executives

• Number of hours spent advancing diversity unknown (work is done within and outside of meetings)
• Total of nine employees on the committee
• Quarterly meetings minimum; can meet more frequently as needed

Does the committee and/or diversity leader establish and set goals or objectives consistent with management's priorities?

Yes. Collaborative approach; goals are set from recommendations by the Office of Diversity & Inclusion and senior leadership vision and expectations.

Has the firm undertaken a formal or informal diversity program or set of initiatives aimed at increasing the diversity of the firm?

Yes, formal diversity initiative in place.

How often does the firm's management review the firm's diversity progress/results?

Quarterly.

How is the firm's diversity committee and/or firm management held accountable for achieving results?

All officers have diversity goals included in performance management structure.

33 percent female—Brinker senior leadership team.

The Stats

Employees

2005: 120,000

Revenue

2005: $3.9 billion

Retention and Professional Development

How do 2005 minority and female attrition rates generally compare to those experienced in the prior year period?

About the same as in prior years.

Please identify the specific steps you are taking to reduce the attrition rate of minority and women employees.

• Increase/improve current work/life programs
• Succession plan includes emphasis on diversity
• Work with minority and women employees to develop career advancement plans
• Professional skills development program, including minority and women employees

Diversity Mission Statement

We believe in celebrating the differences that make a good company great and in leveraging individual strengths to create an innovative, inclusive and unified team.

Life. Enhanced.

New Breakthroughs, New Opportunities.

If you're looking for an exciting place to work with a future full of opportunities, consider Bristol-Myers Squibb.

In just over three years, we have introduced several major medicines to treat serious diseases, including cancer, mental illness, HIV, chronic hepatitis B, and rheumatoid arthritis. And we have a robust pipeline of investigational medicines in full development.

Help us fulfill our mission **to extend and enhance human life**. You'll not only help enrich the lives of others, but also have the opportunity for a rewarding career with personal and professional advancement in a high-caliber, team-oriented environment.

Please see our website at
www.bms.com/career
for a complete listing of opportunities

BMS offers opportunities for MBA students and graduates to join Summer and Full-Time Associate Programs in the following areas: Marketing, Finance, Information Management, Human Resources and Technical Operations.

Undergraduate-level students and other advanced-degree graduates may also pursue internship, co-op and permanent job opportunities in many business divisions and functions across BMS and its family of companies.

 **Bristol-Myers Squibb**

Bristol-Myers Squibb
P.O. Box 4000, Princeton, NJ 08543-4000

Bristol-Myers Squibb is an equal opportunity employer.

©2006 Bristol-Myers Squibb Company   ZN-K0112 07/06

Bristol-Myers Squibb

345 Park Avenue
New York, NY 10154-0037
Phone: (212) 546-4000
www.bms.com

The Stats

Employees

2005: 42,000

Revenue

2005: $19.2 billion

Additional Information

Different perspectives make it possible. At Bristol-Myers Squibb, we're a diverse team of talented and creative people—each with a different perspective. We value each person's unique contributions and inspire each other to develop the innovative solutions that extend and enhance the lives of our patients around the world.

Flexibility makes it possible. At Bristol-Myers Squibb, our people find fulfillment in their work, extending and enhancing the lives of patients around the world. And they have fulfilling lives at home, too. Bristol-Myers Squibb offers a flexible range of work/life programs that help our employees at each stage of their lives. We're proud to be ranked in the top 100 of *Working Mother* magazine's "Best Companies for Working Mothers."

Opportunities make your growth possible. Ask yourself—how far do you want to go? At Bristol-Myers Squibb, we're determined to be the company where our employees can achieve their career goals. We offer a range of opportunities to help you get there. It's simple. Your growth helps us to better extend and enhance the lives of patients around the world.

Bunzl Distribution

701 Emerson Road Suite 500
St. Louis, MO 63141
Phone: (314) 997-5959
Fax: (314) 228-0002
www.bunzldistribution.com

Locations

United States:
Atlanta, GA • California • Dallas, TX • Denver, CO • Kansas City, MO • North Brunswick, NJ • Philadelphia, PA • St. Louis, MO • Denver, CO

International:
Canada • Mexico • UK

Diversity Leadership

Monique Bowens
Employment Administrator
701 Emerson Road Suite 500
St. Louis, MO 63141
Phone: (314) 997-5959
Fax: (314) 228-0002
E-mail: monique.bowens@bunzlusa.com

Recruiting

Do you have any special outreach efforts directed to encourage minority students to consider your firm?

• Participate in/host minority student job fair(s)
• Sponsor minority student association events
• Outreach to leadership of minority student organizations
• Scholarships or intern/fellowships for minority students

What activities does the firm undertake to attract minority and women employees?

• Participate at minority job fairs
• Seek referrals from other employees

Do you use executive recruiting/search firms to seek to identify new diversity hires?

Yes.

If yes, list all women- and/or minority-owned executive search/recruiting firms to which the firm paid a fee for placement services in the past 12 months:

We haven't placed any candidates as of yet.

Internships and Co-ops

INROADS

Length of the program: Summer, winter and spring breaks
Percentage of interns/co-ops in the program who receive offers of full-time employment: 100 percent

Entry-Level Programs/Full-Time Opportunities/Training Programs

Management Trainee Program (i.e Sales, Sales Management, Warehouse, Distribution, Logistics, Procurement)

Length of program: Six to 12 months
Geographic location(s) of program: Worldwide

We customize and diversify our business in all segments with highly skilled and self-driven candidates in the above core areas. Also, we make sure our candidates understand our entire business scope. We offer tuition reimbursement for undergraduate and graduate degrees. Also, we offer four-year scholarships for all Bunzl employee dependents.

Strategic Plan and Diversity Leadership

How does the firm's leadership communicate the importance of diversity to everyone at the firm?

We conduct diversity training along with communicating the diversity initiatives to the employees through our Intranet.

Who has primary responsibility for leading diversity initiatives at your firm?

Robin Pokoik, VP, HR and benefits.

Does your firm currently have a diversity committee?

No.

Has the firm undertaken a formal or informal diversity program or set of initiatives aimed at increasing the diversity of the firm?

We are in the process of creating a diversity program within our organization.

Burlington Northern Santa Fe Railway Company

2500 Lou Menk Drive
Fort Worth, TX 76131-2828
Phone: (817) 352-6008
Fax: (817) 352-7108
www.bnsf.com

Locations

Fort Worth, TX (corporate office)
Operations in a total of 26 states and 2 Canadian provinces.

Diversity Leadership

Pamela Sherlock
Director Staffing

Employment Contact

Susan Hutchison
E-mail: susan.hutchison@BNSF.com

Recruiting

Please list the schools/types of schools at which you recruit.

• Private schools
• Public state schools
• Historically Black Colleges and Universities (HBCUs)

Do you have any special outreach efforts directed to encourage minority students to consider your firm?

• *Conferences:* NSBE, NSHBA, NBMBA, NACE (local, regional and national)
• Participate in/host minority student job fair(s)
• Outreach to leadership of minority student organizations
• Scholarships or intern/fellowships for minority students

What activities does the firm undertake to attract minority and women employees?

• *Conferences:* NSBE, NSHBA, NBMBA, NACE
• *Other:* BOLD Initiative

Do you use executive recruiting/search firms to seek to identify new diversity hires?
No.

Internships and Co-ops

BNSF Railway

> ***Deadline for application:*** Early spring
> ***Pay:*** Varies
> ***Length of the program:*** Varies; typically eight to 10 weeks
> ***Web site for internship/co-op information:*** www.bnsf.com/jobs

The BNSF internship program gives college students practical, on-the-job experience in a business environment.

Candidates for internships are typically full-time students currently enrolled at a college or university who are pursuing an under-graduate degree or a graduate degree in a field of study that supports BNSF's business objectives. BNSF recruits candidates from college campuses, minority student referral programs, the Internet, employee referrals and unsolicited resumes.

Interns are assigned to a department that will then direct the intern's activities on specific projects and work assignments.

BNSF departments that seek interns include: accounting/finance, corporate audit services, engineering, human resources, marketing, mechanical, safety, technology services, transportation/operations and other support departments. While most assignments are at BNSF's corporate headquarters (Fort Worth, Texas), some interns are placed in field locations across the BNSF system. Field assignments are predominantly for the Transportation/Operations, Engineering and Mechanical Departments.

The program includes an orientation with an overview of corporate policies and appropriate conduct. Interns participate in several key activities throughout their program, including:

- Presentations by various department leaders
- Midterm and final activity status reports prepared by the intern
- Intern team presentations at the end of the program
- Midterm and final performance evaluations by supervisors
- Exposure to some BNSF management trainee program activities
- Networking opportunities

Scholarships

BNSF Diversity Scholarships

Deadline for application for the scholarship program: Students apply through their universities by March of each year. *Scholarship award amount:* Honored recipients receive $5,000 (payable in two annual installments of $2,500 for students' junior and senior years).

Five scholarships are established at four predesignated universities. Students must have at least a 3.0 GPA, be well-rounded and pass a skills assessment exam. A facility review panel recommends the top two to three sophomore students. Students all receive two summer internships with BNSF.

Affinity Groups

- Native American
- Hispanic
- Women's
- African-American
- Asian-American

The purpose of each group is to promote the professional and personal development of its members. All groups meet at least monthly and all have internal web sites.

Entry-Level Programs/Full-Time Opportunities/Training Programs

BNSF Railway Management Trainee Program

BNSF recruits candidates from college campuses, the Internet, BNSF's former interns and internal job postings. As part of the selection process, a potential candidate visits BNSF's corporate headquarters to participate in panel interviews and a comprehen-

sive skills assessment. Candidates for the program must be team players who value diversity and who drive for results. They should also have a good scholastic record, a history of leadership roles in school or the community, previous internship experience, ability to analyze problems logically, excellent oral and written communication skills.

> *Length of program:* Six to 12 months
> *Geographic location(s) of program:* Across BNSF system, with large number at corporate headquarters

Management trainees receive cross-functional, departmental training during their six—or 12-month training period, as well as exposure to all departments through an initial one—month corporate orientation. Each trainee can request a BNSF mentor for career and personal guidance. The training itself is tailored to the individual and monitored by the sponsoring business group and Human Resources Department.

Strategic Plan and Diversity Leadership

How does the firm's leadership communicate the importance of diversity to everyone at the firm?

BNSF communicates through internal diversity conferences, diversity councils, affinity groups, newsletters, departmental meetings, awareness training sessions and various written forms of communication.

Who has primary responsibility for leading diversity initiatives at your firm?

Ed McFalls, assistant vice president, human resources and diversity.

Does your firm currently have a diversity committee?

Yes.

There are two types of diversity committees:

> Executive Diversity Council—consists of BNSF's CEO, six direct reports and the AVP of human resources and diversity. Group meets quarterly to review diversity successes and opportunities. In 2004, this group spent at least eight hours as a council, but they address initiatives throughout the year during weekly executive meetings.

> There are 16 regional diversity councils (across our system)—consisting of both union and management employees that are responsible for resolving diversity tensions in their respective locations. In 2004, each council spent approximately 36 hours furthering diversity initiatives (monthly meetings of approximately three hours each).

If yes, does the committee's representation include one or more members of the firm's management/executive committee (or the equivalent)?

Yes.

Does the committee and/or diversity leader establish and set goals or objectives consistent with management's priorities?

Yes. Each committee's goals are established based upon BNSF's overall diversity strategy.

Has the firm undertaken a formal or informal diversity program or set of initiatives aimed at increasing the diversity of the firm?

Yes, formal. BNSF developed diversity strategies that addresses executive/leadership support, recruiting and enhancing talent, community involvement and continual education and awareness.

How often does the firm's management review the firm's diversity progress/results?

> Quarterly: CEO & Senior VPs perform a detailed review quarterly.
> Annually: VP and AVP are provided an overview/update at annual management meeting.

The Stats

Employees

2005: 120,000 (worldwide)

Revenue

2005: $3.9 billion

Diversity Mission Statement

We view diversity as a business necessity, a business opportunity and a moral imperative. To achieve diversity, BNSF has undertaken strategies and actions that recognize, accept, value and utilize the differences and similarities among all applicants, employees, customers, suppliers and the community.

To advance our vision, we have a diversity business purpose. Embracing diversity helps BNSF to: recruit, hire and promote the best diverse talent; create a collaborative workforce that functions as a team; understand and market to a diverse customer base; procure from a diverse supplier base; and provide quality service that meets our customers' needs and requirements.

Additional Information

By design, BNSF's diversity definition is simple: respecting and valuing the differences and similarities of people. Too often, diversity is defined by the traditional terms of race, gender, age, religion and culture. At BNSF, we have expanded the definition to include diversity of mind, experience, education, skills and thought.

BNSF affinity groups share a vision to advance the personal and professional development of their members, expose their members to increased leadership opportunities, provide support and networking for members, participate in community service, and work with corporate diversity to achieve other BNSF people initiatives, including employee recruitment and retention. Nevertheless, they are unique when they address the particular needs of their group. Currently, there are five active affinity groups at BNSF: BNSF Asian-American Network, Hispanic Leadership Council, African-American Networking Group; Women's Network and the Council of Native Americans.

Hundreds of BNSF people throughout the railway have volunteered for regional diversity councils, and work tirelessly to educate co-workers about different cultures and backgrounds. They are also responsible for identifying and resolving local diversity tensions, before formal resolutions have to be implemented. They host diversity celebrations such as Martin Luther King, Jr. Day, Veteran's Day, Cinco de Mayo and Women's Month, among others. Lastly, they promote community advocacy initiatives by getting involved with the communities in which they live and work.

BNSF has hosted annual diversity forums and summits to bring together 200 to 300 employees and the leadership team to share ideas and identify ways for BNSF to enhance its diversity efforts. Invitees include a broad representation of BNSF departments and are randomly selected to allow opportunity for more BNSF people to participate in the conferences. At each event, participants have the opportunity to talk with BNSF leaders, brainstorm ideas on how to make BNSF a more diverse community, listen to experts' insights and perspectives on success in corporate America, network with employees from throughout the company, and participate in experiential learning.

BNSF offers a variety of alternative work arrangements on a limited basis, informally administered by each department, for certain positions including traditional flex-time, daily flex-time, compressed workweek and telecommuting/working from home.

Campbell Soup Company

1 Campbell Place
Camden, NJ 08103-1701
Phone: (856) 342-4800 Ext. 2225
www.campbellsoupcompany.com

Diversity Mission Statement

Campbell Soup Company is a global manufacturer and marketer of high quality, branded convenience food products. With sales exceeding $7 billion, Campbell Soup Company is the world's largest manufacturer and marketer of soup, and a leading producer of sauces, juice beverages, biscuits and confectionery products.

At Campbell, we define diversity as the vast array of human differences and similarities, inclusive of everyone. In order to compete and succeed in a changing marketplace we must cultivate and embrace a diverse employee population that fuels our growth and enriches our global culture.

As part of our Campbell's Vision, "Together We Will Do Extraordinary Things in the Workplace and Marketplace," our commitment to building and strengthening teams has the greatest focus of our leadership. We must have diverse perspectives, talents and teams to meet this business challenge. You won't find a better place for your talent, ideas and experience than at Campbell Soup Company.

Campbell Soup Company is an equal opportunity employer by choice, and supports the principles of hiring a diverse workforce. EEO/AA/D/V

Visit our web site at http://careers.campbellsoupcompany.com

Capital One Financial Corporation

1680 Capital One Dr.
McLean, VA 22012
Phone: (703) 720-1000
www.capitalone.com/careers

Locations

US:
California • Florida • Massachusetts •
Texas • Virginia • Washington, D.C.

International:
Canada • UK

Diversity Leadership

Rob Keeling
Vice President of Diversity

Employment Contact

Vicki Mirandah
Director of Diversity
Phone: (804) 284-2158
E-mail: vicki.mirandah@capitalone.com
www.capitalone.com/careers

Recruiting

Please list the schools/types of schools at which you recruit.

• *Ivy League schools:* Cornell, Harvard, University of Pennsylvania
• *Other private schools:* Duke, Notre Dame, University of Richmond, Rensselaer, Carnegie Mellon
• *Public state schools:* University of Virginia, Virginia Tech, Georgia Tech, University of Texas, University of Michigan, University of Maryland, Penn State, Ohio State, Rutgers, University of Illinois, N.C. State, Purdue, William & Mary, University of Florida, University of Wisconsin, University of Minnesota and James Madison University
• *Other predominantly minority and/or women's colleges:* Wellesley

Do you have any special outreach efforts directed to encourage minority students to consider your firm?

• Advertise in minority student association publication(s)
• Sponsor minority student association events
• Firm's employees participate on career panels at schools

What activities does the firm undertake to attract minority and women employees?

• *Conferences:* Simmon's School of Management Leadership Conference, Linkage Women in Leadership
• *Participate at minority job fairs:* NAACP, NSBE, NBMBAA, NSHMBA, National Association of Women MBAs, Reaching Out, MBA, MEAC/SWAC job fair, SWE
• Seek referrals from other employees
• Utilize online job services

Do you use executive recruiting/search firms to seek to identify new diversity hires?

No.

Internships and Co-ops

Capital One Summer Intern Program

Deadline for application: March 10th

Pay: $23 per hour

Length of the program: 11 weeks

Percentage of interns/co-ops in the program who receive offers of full-time employment: 90 percent

Web site for internship/co-op information: www.capitalone.com/careers/campusrecruiting.shtml

If you're looking to put your education to the test in real business situations, beef up your resume, add to your skills and have fun too, then our Summer Intern Program may be perfect for you! As an intern, you'll get involved in and be responsible for challenging projects that can have a significant impact on our business—no making coffee or picking up dry-cleaning here! Your projects will typically be team-oriented, and you'll gain new skills in a positive learning environment. Other great benefits of our intern program include an executive speaker series, team building events and an intern-specific training class.

Affinity Groups

Five associate networks:

• African-American Network,
• Asian Pacific Network,
• Hispanic Network,
• LGBT (lesbian, gay, bisexual and transgender) Network,
• Women's Network

Capital One's associate networks were created to support Capital One's growing diverse population. These networks provide support in the form of programs, resources and tools that enable Capital One's diverse associates to achieve their full potential in an environment that values the differences we bring to the workplace.

The networks also support the organization's diversity strategy. Their objectives are closely linked to Capital One's goals of recruiting, retaining and developing diverse talent, and leveraging their differences to contribute to the success of the organization.

Diversity Mission Statement

At Capital One, diversity means finding associates with different backgrounds, life and work experiences, beliefs and communication styles. Diversity means seeking and embracing our differences because of the richness those differences add to our lives and the many advantages they provide to our business.

Rich Fairbank
Chairman and Chief Executive Officer

Charter Communications

12405 Powerscourt
St. Louis, MO 63116
www.chartercom.com

Locations

USA

Employment Contact

Heather Reynolds
Senior Recruiting Generalist
12405 Powerscourt
St. Louis, MO 63131
Phone: (314) 543-2552
Fax: (314) 543-2385
E-mail: heather.reynolds@chartercom.com
www.chartercom.com/aboutus/careers/
careers.aspx

Recruiting

Please list the schools/types of schools at which you recruit.

• Private schools
• Public state schools
• Historically Black Colleges and Universities (HBCUs)
• Hispanic Serving Institutions (HSIs)
• Other predominantly minority and/or women's colleges

Do you have any special outreach efforts directed to encourage minority students to consider your firm?

• *Conferences:* NAMIC, WICT, NAACP
• Advertise in minority student association publication(s)
• Participate in/host minority student job fair(s)
• Sponsor minority student association events
• Firm's employees participate on career panels at schools
• Outreach to leadership of minority student organizations
• Scholarships or intern/fellowships for minority students

What activities does the firm undertake to attract minority and women employees?

• Partner programs with women and minority associations
• *Conferences:* NAMIC, WICT, NAACP
• Participate at minority job fairs
• Seek referrals from other employees
• Utilize online job services

Do you use executive recruiting/search firms to seek to identify new diversity hires?

Yes.

Internships and Co-ops

Emma Bowen Foundation

Deadline for application: Potential interns apply to the Emma Bowen Foundation directly

Number of interns in the program in summer 2005 (internship) or 2005 (co-op): Two to three interns

Length of the program: Three to six months

Percentage of interns/co-ops in the program who receive offers of full-time employment: 85 percent

Web site for internship/co-op information: www.emmabowenfoundation.com

Strategic Plan and Diversity Leadership

How does the firm's leadership communicate the importance of diversity to everyone at the firm?

The firm's leadership communicates diversity's importance through membership drives with NAMIC, WICT and other e-mails, newsletters and outreach opportunities within the community.

Who has primary responsibility for leading diversity initiatives at your firm?

Sandra Young, vice president of corporate human resources; Heather Reynolds, senior recruiting generalist and Lamont Orange, vice president enterprise security.

Does your firm currently have a diversity committee?

Yes, we have a strong presence in NAMIC and WICT, where we have several members throughout the organization involved in.

If yes, please describe how the committee is structured, how often it meets, etc.

NAMIC and WICT, both meet monthly.

If yes, does the committee's representation include one or more members of the firm's management/executive committee (or the equivalent)?

Yes.

If yes, how many executives are on the committee, and in 2005, what was the total number of hours collectively spent by the committee in furtherance of the firm's diversity initiatives? How many employees are on the committee, and how often does the committee convene in furtherance of the firm's diversity initiatives?

Yes, several. Exact number unknown since membership is by division.

The Stats

Employees

2005: 16,000

Retention and Professional Development

How do 2005 minority and female attrition rates generally compare to those experienced in the prior year period?

Lower than in prior years.

Please identify the specific steps you are taking to reduce the attrition rate of minority and women employees.

• Develop and/or support internal employee affinity groups (e.g., minority or women networks within the firm)
• Increase/review compensation relative to competition
• Succession plan includes emphasis on diversity
• Work with minority and women employees to develop career advancement plans
• Professional skills development program, including minority and women employees

Diversity Mission Statement

It takes all kinds of people to bring it all together.

Cintas Corporation

6800 Cintas Blvd
Cincinnati, OH 45262
Phone: (513) 459-1200

Locations

Throughout North America

Diversity Leadership

Marsha Thornton

Employment Contact

Rick Johnson
www.Cintas.com/careers

Recruiting

Please list the schools/types of schools at which you recruit.

• Ivy League schools
• Other private schools
• Public state schools
• Historically Black Colleges and Universities (HBCUs)
• Hispanic Serving Institutions (HSIs)
• Native American Tribal Universities
• Other predominantly minority and/or women's colleges

Do you have any special outreach efforts directed to encourage minority students to consider your firm?

• Hold a reception for minority students
• Advertise in minority student association publication(s)
• Participate in/host minority student job fair(s)
• Sponsor minority student association events
• Firm's employees participate on career panels at schools
• Outreach to leadership of minority student organizations
• Scholarships or intern/fellowships for minority students

What activities does the firm undertake to attract minority and women employees?

• Partner programs with women and minority associations
• Participate at minority job fairs
• Seek referrals from other employees
• Utilize online job services

Do you use executive recruiting/search firms to seek to identify new diversity hires?

No.

Entry-Level Programs/Full-Time Opportunities/Training Programs

Management Trainee

Length of program: 24 months
Geographic location(s) of program: Nationwide

Citigroup Inc.

399 Park Avenue New York, NY 10043 Phone: (800) 285-3000 www.oncampus.citigroup.com **Locations** National and international locations	**Diversity Leader** Gina Deperino Assistant Vice President, Corporate College Relations

Recruiting

Please list the schools/types of schools at which you recruit.

Citigroup Inc. and its subsidiaries and their affiliates (collectively, "Citigroup") recruit at a number of schools both within the United States and internationally. At these schools our businesses host presentations, on-campus interviews and/or participate in career fairs. Please check with your career services department to inquire about Citigroup's involvement on your campus.

Do you have any special outreach efforts directed to encourage minority students to consider your firm?

Citigroup is engaged in a variety of outreach efforts directed toward minority students. The level of engagement ranges from sponsoring student receptions, attending diversity conferences and career fairs, supporting programming toward financial education, participating on panels, offering scholarships to qualifying interns/fellows and outreach to the leadership of minority student organizations.

What activities does the firm undertake to attract minority and women employees?

Citigroup's ability to attract and retain diverse undergraduate, graduate, and professional talent is fundamental to our success. To recruit the best talent, we continue to strengthen our partnerships with organizations such as NSHMBA, NBMBAA, The Robert Toigo Foundation, Consortium for Graduate Studies (CGSM), National Association of Women MBAs, Reaching Out MBA and Global MBA.

Do you use executive recruiting/search firms to seek to identify new diversity hires?

No.

Internships and Co-ops

INROADS

Deadline for application: The deadline is established by INROADS.
Number of interns in the program in summer 2005 (internship) or 2005 (co-op): 65 INROADS interns participated in Citigroup's 2005 summer internship program.
Pay: $12 to $18 per hour
Length of the program: 10 weeks
Percentage of interns/co-ops in the program who receive offers of full-time employment: In 2005, 10 INROADS interns in the U.S. and Mexico received and accepted Citigroup's offer of full-time employment.

Scholarships

Citigroup/INROADS Scholarship

Scholarship award amount: Citigroup awards eight scholarships ranging from $1,250 to $2,500 to outstanding INROADS interns in select regions. Scholarship criteria are determined by the INROADS staff in that location.

Web site or other contact information for scholarship: www.inroads.org

Affinity Groups

Citigroup's employee networks are employee initiated groups open to all employees to provide an opportunity to share common experiences and build awareness of diverse cultures and communities. Citigroup employee networks exist in 12 cities in the U.K. and the U.S. In 2005, five new networks were formed, bringing our total to 26. Another 18 groups are now in formation. Recognized U.S. groups include: African Heritage, Asian Pacific Heritage, Hispanic, Pride (a group focused on the lesbian, gay, bisexual, and transgender communities), Women, and Working Parents. In the U.K., Pride, Women, Working Parents and a multicultural network called Roots have been recognized.

Entry-Level Programs/Full-Time Opportunities/Training Programs

Citibank North America Management Associate Program

Length of program: Two years
Geographic location(s) of program: New York tri-state area

Two year rotation through various retail banking functions.

Technology Leadership Program (TLP)

Length of program: Two years
Geographic location(s) of program: New York

The program is designed to bring technical and leadership talent into the IT organization and to accelerate the development of the participants through the program elements. The program lasts two years and includes four rotational assignments with project and people management, as well as periods of high-intensity classroom training, self-instruction and exposure to different senior managers and operating styles, which enhances the leadership development experience.

Global Transaction Services Analyst Program

Length of program: Two years
Geographic location(s) of program: New York

Classes are taught by a combination of Citigroup professionals and public accounting and business school professionals.
In addition, there is a four to five week training program in New York: two weeks of accounting, one week of finance and one to two weeks of overview of Citigroup businesses.

Additional information regarding the program:

- Accounting, finance and general business concepts taught
- Computer training: financial modeling utilizing Excel and word processing
- Each analyst is assigned an analyst buddy as well as a junior and senior mentor

INROADS®

Finance Analyst Program

> **Length of program:** Two years
> **Geographic location(s) of program:** New York

The analyst training program is approximately 10 weeks in duration and focuses on the specific skill sets and knowledge needed to succeed at Citigroup. This program offers classes in financial accounting, corporate finance, analytics, cash flow modeling, risk and credit analysis, and capital markets. Additionally, the training provides an understanding of the industry groups with whom analysts will work. Classes are taught by a combination of world-class consultants, university professors and banking professionals. Additionally, all analysts are assigned junior and senior mentors.

Strategic Plan and Diversity Leadership

How does the firm's leadership communicate the importance of diversity to everyone at the firm?

• Company Intranet
• E-mail
• Newsletter
• Diversity Annual Report
• Employee Cultural Heritage Month Programs

Who has primary responsibility for leading diversity initiatives at your firm?

Ana Duarte McCarthy, chief diversity officer, global workforce diversity and college relations

Does your firm currently have a diversity committee?

Yes, Citigroup's diversity operating council, which formed in 2000, is comprised of senior diversity and human resources leaders from core businesses and regions. The council meets bi-weekly to review progress against our strategy, share best practices, and align policies globally.

If yes, does the committee's representation include one or more members of the firm's management/executive committee (or the equivalent)?

No.

Does the committee and/or diversity leader establish and set goals or objectives consistent with management's priorities?

Yes.

Has the firm undertaken a formal or informal diversity program or set of initiatives aimed at increasing the diversity of the firm?

Yes, formal.

How often does the firm's management review the firm's diversity progress/results?

Quarterly.

How is the firm's diversity committee and/or firm management held accountable for achieving results?

Since 2002, Citigroup businesses and managers have been required to develop annual diversity plans and, through quarterly reviews, have been held accountable for progress against these plans. These reviews culminate in an annual review of our franchise efforts with Citigroup Inc.'s full board of directors. In total, 162 diversity reviews were conducted in our businesses in 2005.

The Stats

Employees

2005/2004: Approx. 300,0000 (worldwide - same for both years)

Revenue

2005: $83.6 billion (worldwide)
2004: $79.6 billion - 2004 (worldwide)

Retention and Professional Development

How do 2005 minority and female attrition rates generally compare to those experienced in the prior year period?

About the same as in prior years.

Please identify the specific steps you are taking to reduce the attrition rate of minority and women employees.

• Develop and/or support internal employee affinity groups (e.g., minority or women networks within the firm)
• Increase/improve current work/life programs
• Adopt dispute resolution process
• Succession plan includes emphasis on diversity
• Strengthen mentoring program for all employees, including minorities and women
• Professional skills development program, including minority and women employees

Diversity Mission Statement

Employer of choice

Citigroup values a work environment where diversity is embraced, where people are promoted on their merits and where people treat each other with respect and dignity. Around the world, we are committed to being a company where the best people want to work, where opportunities to develop are widely available, where innovation and an entrepreneurial spirit are valued and where employees are encouraged to fulfill their professional and personal goals.

Service provider of choice

Citigroup strives to deliver products and services to our clients that reflect both our global reach and our deep local roots in every market where we operate. The diversity of our employees enables us to better understand our clients, while the breadth of our product offerings allows us to serve them better.

Business partner of choice

Citigroup works to create mutually beneficial business relationships with minorities, women, disabled veterans, and other people with disabilities. We recognize that working with a wide range of professionals, suppliers, and consultants strengthens the communities we serve while creating value for our shareholders.

Neighbor of choice

Citigroup believes it has a responsibility to make a difference in the neighborhoods in which we live and work around the world. We reach out to and form relationships with nonprofit organizations, civic groups, educational institutions, and local governments representing the diverse nature of these communities.

Clorox Company, The

1221 Broadway
Oakland, CA 94612
Phone: (510) 271-7000
www.thecloroxcompany.com

Locations

Oakland, California (HQ)

Various global locations

Employment Contact

Eva Breilein
Manager, Talent Acquisition and Diversity
1221 Broadway
Oakland, CA 94612
Phone: (510) 271-7332
Fax: (510) 271-6593
E-mail: eva.breilein@clorox.com

Recruiting

Please list the schools/types of schools at which you recruit.

• Ivy League schools
• Public state schools

Do you have any special outreach efforts directed to encourage minority students to consider your firm?

Conferences: NSHMBA, SWE

What activities does the firm undertake to attract minority and women employees?

• Partner programs with women and minority associations
• *Conferences:* NSHMBA, SWE, NABA
• Seek referrals from other employees

Do you use executive recruiting/search firms to seek to identify new diversity hires?

Yes.

Internships and Co-ops

INROADS

Deadline for application: April for summer internship
Number of interns in the program in summer 2005 (internship) or 2005 (co-op): 11
Pay: $14-$18 per hour depending on level
Length of the program: Eight to 12 weeks

The Clorox Company offers three different internship programs: there are eight to 10 interns hired for marketing, eight to 10 hired for research and development and 10-12 INROADS interns hired for various other functions (i.e. human resources, product supply, information services and finance and accounting). Interns work closely with full-time professionals on a variety of projects. Marketing looks for associate marketing managers and associate marketing intelligence managers for interns. To intern in marketing, a business administration degree with a marketing focus and other marketing internships are pluses. Other qualifications include demonstrated outstanding leadership/results orientation skills, and strong analytical/problem solving abilities.

Research and development looks for process core technology, corporate packaging and consumer applied technology interns. To intern with research and development, students must have completed their junior year with a minimum 3.0 GPA. Recommended majors include a bachelor of science in either packaging sciences, engineering or chemical engineering. INROADS interns must have a cumulative GPA of 2.8 or better as a sophomore or junior at a four-year school with at least two summers remaining prior to graduation. Prefer degrees in: business, engineering, information and computer sciences, sales and marketing.

Affinity Groups

Affinity groups for Hispanics, Asians, African-Americans, women and GLBT are to be created this fiscal year.

Entry-Level Programs/Full-Time Opportunities/Training Programs

Diamond Leadership Foundation

Length of program: Depending on the module, three to seven days
Geographic location(s) of program: General offices, Oakland, CA

Strategic Plan and Diversity Leadership

How does the firm's leadership communicate the importance of diversity to everyone at the firm?

Web site, newsletters, meetings, diversity and inclusion task force.

Who has primary responsibility for leading diversity initiatives at your firm?

Bill Ingham, director, talent acquisition and diversity.

Does your firm currently have a diversity committee?

Yes. The firm has a steering committee consisting of three members of the executive committee who meet semi-annually. The firm also has a diversity and inclusion task force of 25 cross-functional leaders who meet quarterly.

If yes, does the committee's representation include one or more members of the firm's management/executive committee (or the equivalent)?

Yes.

Does the committee and/or diversity leader establish and set goals or objectives consistent with management's priorities?

Yes, business and organizational effectiveness goals.

Has the firm undertaken a formal or informal diversity program or set of initiatives aimed at increasing the diversity of the firm?

Yes, formal.

How often does the firm's management review the firm's diversity progress/results?

Quarterly.

How is the firm's diversity committee and/or firm management held accountable for achieving results?

It is tied to their compensation.

Retention and Professional Development

Please identify the specific steps you are taking to reduce the attrition rate of minority and women employees.

• Develop and/or support internal employee affinity groups (e.g., minority or women networks within the firm)
• Increase/improve current work/life programs
• Succession plan includes emphasis on diversity
• Work with minority and women employees to develop career advancement plans
• Strengthen mentoring program for all employees, including minorities and women
• Professional skills development program, including minority and women employees

Columbia St. Mary's Hospitals & Clinics

4425 N. Port Washington Road
Glendale, WI 53212
Phone: (414) 326-2661
Fax: (414) 291-1427
www.columbia-stmarys.org

Locations

City of Milwaukee, Ozaukee County,
Glendale

Diversity Leadership

Cynthia R. Stewart
Director, Diversity Resources & Language
Services
4425 N. Port Washington Road
Glendale, WI 53204
Phone: (414) 326-2661
Fax: (414) 291-1427
E-mail: cstewart@columbia-stmarys.org

Brenda Buchanan
Manager, Community Career Development
INROADS Coordinator
4425 N. Port Washington Road
Glendale, WI 53204
Phone: (414) 326-2655
Fax: (414) 291-1427

Internships and Co-ops

INROADS

Deadline for application: Spring 2006
Number of interns in the program in summer 2005 (internship) or 2005 (co-op): 11 interns
Pay: $11.20 per hour
Length of the program: 10 weeks
Percentage of interns/co-ops in the program who receive offers of full-time employment: 90 percent

Qualifications for the program vary.

Scholarships

Estil Strawn Scholarship Program

Deadline for application for the scholarship program: May 15, 2006
Scholarship award amount: $1,000; $500 book scholarship
Web site or other contact information for scholarship: Only open to company employees/interns

To apply, you must be an employee in good standing, be studying in a field that would fit within a health care environment and have successfully completed an application process including an interview.

Strategic Plan and Diversity Leadership

How does the firm's leadership communicate the importance of diversity to everyone at the firm?

The firm communicates the importance of diversity through e-mails, leadership meetings, education sessions for staff and leadership, the diversity scorecard and our newsletter.

Who has primary responsibility for leading diversity initiatives at your firm?

The director of diversity resources.

If yes, please describe how the committee is structured.

The council meets monthly. Two committees report to the council and they meet as necessary, usually one or more times per month. The council is made up of individuals from all levels of the organization, including executive leadership and is headed by an executive leader.

If yes, how many executives are on the committee, and in 2005, what was the total number of hours collectively spent by the committee in furtherance of the firm's diversity initiatives? How many employees are on the committee, and how often does the committee convene in furtherance of the firm's diversity initiatives?

Total Executives on Committee: Three

• Total Hours: 50 (meeting time/strategizing)
• Total Members: 13

The Stats

2005 STATS				
TOTAL EMPLOYEES	MINORITIES	FEMALE	FEMALE EXECUTIVES	MINORITY
5,600	21 percent	83.9 percent	60 percent	7 percent

Diversity Mission Statement

The Columbia Saint Mary's Diversity Resources Council promotes the unique perspectives provided by distinctions of age, culture, ethnicity, family status, gender, physical/cognitive ability, race, religion, sexual orientation and socio-economic status.

The council exists to support the overall vision and mission of CSM by advocating an inclusive environment that both respects and leverages the rich diversity of our employees, physicians, patients and surrounding community.

Our purpose is:

• To identify strategies and accountabilities related to diversity for CSM
• To educate the organization on how diversity is integral to achieving our mission
• To provide educational opportunities to continuously build cultural competence at all levels
• To strengthen the organization through valuing and promoting a diverse workforces

Additional Information

The organization has a position dedicated to targeting youth at the high school and college level to provide coaching, mentoring, internships, etc. The goal is to increase interest in health care and to provide growth opportunities for students.

Our scorecard is designed to build accountability across the organization and at all levels.

We have a strong language services program with an emphasis on education and service to populations with limited or no English speaking abilities. We are also working to build programs or processes to hire more bilingual staff in positions at all levels in the organization and to utilize bilingual employees who have the skills necessary to serve as interpreters and translators.

We maintain affiliations and programs with community organizations to build community strength. We also own several clinics (medical and dental) that provide outreach to uninsured and underinsured persons and the homeless.

Comcast Cable Communications, LLC

1500 Market Street
Philadelphia, PA 19102
Phone: (215) 981-7783
Fax: (215) 981-8501
www.comcast.com

Locations

Philadelphia, PA (HQ)
Locations in 42 states

Employment Contact

Mary Pennington
Senior Director Recruitment & Career
Development
E-mail:
Mary_Pennington@cable.comcast.com

Recruiting

Please list the schools/types of schools at which you recruit.

• Ivy League schools
• Other private schools
• Public state schools
• Historically Black Colleges and Universities (HBCUs)
• Hispanic Serving Institutions (HSIs): This is being implemented in 2006.
• Native American Tribal Universities
• Other predominantly minority and/or women's colleges

Do you have any special outreach efforts directed to encourage minority students to consider your firm?

• Hold a reception for minority students
• Conferences
• Advertise in minority student association publication(s)
• Participate in/host minority student job fair(s)
• Sponsor minority student association events
• Firm's employees participate on career panels at school
• Outreach to leadership of minority student organizations
• Scholarships or intern/fellowships for minority students
• *Other:* Comcast recruitment efforts are not only national, but regional in scope. Recruiters for specific locations will develop partnerships with local colleges and universities and may become involved in any of the above activities on a regional or local level.

What activities does the firm undertake to attract minority and women employees?

• Partner programs with women and minority associations
• *Conferences:* NABA, National Society for Black Engineers, and other regional and local conferences through out the country.
• Participate at minority job fairs
• Seek referrals from other employees
• Utilize online job services
• *Other:* Internship programs such as Emma Bowen Internship Program, specific to attracting minorities groups.

Internships and Co-ops

> **Pay:** $450-$560 per week for internships
> **Length of the program:** 12 weeks if summer. If it is a co-op per terms of institution's co-op program.
> **Web site for internship/co-op information:** www.comcast.com

Comcast offers part-time and full-time summer employment to students enrolled in, or who have recently graduated from, college or graduate degree programs. In partnership with the Philadelphia Youth Network and WorkReady, Philadelphia, Comcast will also offer opportunities to high school students who are employed by these organizations. The Summer Internship Program affords students a solid introduction to the workforce through on-the-job learning and mentoring by Comcast leaders. At the same time, Comcast is able to further its commitment to diversity and community investment, while benefiting from the energy and knowledge of our summer interns. Summer internship programs afford us the ability to build lasting relationships with students, learning institutions and community organizations that will assist Comcast in building its next generation of Comcasters.

Departments hiring include:

HR, IT, accounts payable, marketing, real estate, finance, Comcast programming, investor relations, public affairs, and corporate communications.

Qualifications for the program:

Must be a full-time student

Affinity Groups

Senior Women's Group

The purpose of the group is to provide senior level women at Comcast an environment in which to enhance business acumen and business savvy, share information and feedback among peers and leverage each other as resources, advocates and sounding boards. In order to strengthen the relationships at the highest levels, the group is focused on the vice president level and above in cable and senior director level and above in corporate. Events are held each quarter and while the purpose of the group is primarily focused on bringing together the company's most senior women leaders, the goal also is to leverage this group for insight regarding leadership development opportunities for the next generation of women leaders.

Entry-Level Programs/Full-time Opportunities/Training Programs

Entry-level training program in engineering, Associate Electrical Engineering Program

Comcast offers other entry-level opportunities in the following departments: accounting, administration, customer service, human resources, and marketing.

> **Length of program:** One to two years
> **Geographic location(s) of program:** Philadelphia, PA

Associate Electrical Engineering Program—the individual is assigned to the VP of engineering. They have exposure to various aspects of field operations, engineering, plant operations, plant upgrades, testing of equipment, and vendor negotiations.

Strategic Plan and Diversity Leadership

How does the firm's leadership communicate the importance of diversity to everyone at the firm?

The firm communicates diversity initiatives through: Diversity training, the Intranet and part of interview training. In addition, the Diversity Committee provides quarterly reports. There is a Monthly Leadership Link communication by executive officers to senior leadership throughout the company and diversity is promoted in leadership development programs. Diversity initiatives are also incorporated into annual goals for senior leaders.

Who has primary responsibility for leading diversity initiatives at your firm?

David L. Cohen, executive vice president, Comcast Corporation.

Payne Brown, vice president of outreach strategies, Comcast Corporation.

Charisse Lillie, vice president of human resources, Comcast Corporation and senior vice president, human resources, Comcast Cable Communications.

Does your firm currently have a diversity committee?

Yes, in the last few years, Comcast has established two committees as part of its commitment to diversity. The first committee is the Diversity Council. The council is responsible for meeting quarterly and reviewing the Company's overall progress in terms of 1) employee diversity, 2) diversity programming, and 3) supplier diversity. The council takes a critical look at progress in these three areas of the business and discusses and outlines means of holding executives in all markets accountable for reaching certain milestones.

The second committee committed to diversity in the workplace is the Diversity Communications Committee. The mission of this committee is to identify field best practices as it relates to diversity in programming, suppliers and among employees. This group meets quarterly to share with each other progress being made in local markets relative to our outreach efforts. Another important responsibility of this group is to identify internal talent worthy of nomination for various industry publications and awards. It is important to note that Comcast does not "put itself out there" relative to bragging about its own. One of the tasks of this committee is to identify the diverse talent in the workforce and look for opportunities to showcase this talent through publications, panel discussions, speaking engagements and industry awards.

If yes, does the committee's representation include one or more members of the firm's management/executive committee (or the equivalent)?

Yes.

If yes, how many executives are on the committee, and in 2005, what was the total number of hours collectively spent by the committee in furtherance of the firm's diversity initiatives?

Total Executives on Committee: 12 on the Diversity Council, 10 on the Diversity Communications Committee.

How many employees are on the committee, and how often does the committee convene in furtherance of the firm's diversity initiatives?

Diversity Council: 12 employees on the committee
The Diversity Communications Committee: 18 employees that make up the committee.

Each group meets quarterly and additional meetings are held as needed.

Does the committee and/or diversity leader establish and set goals or objectives consistent with management's priorities?

Yes, the key focus is in areas of programming, corporate communication, recruitment, retention outreach, and supplier diversity.

Has the firm undertaken a formal or informal diversity program or set of initiatives aimed at increasing the diversity of the firm?

Yes, there is a formal program for supplier diversity, programming and recruitment and outreach initiatives.

How is the firm's diversity committee and/or firm management held accountable for achieving results?

Diversity goals are tied into the management achievement component of objectives for all leadership. This is ultimately tied into the bonus.

The Stats

Minorities Overall: 40 percent
Women: 37 percent

TOTAL NUMBER OF EMPLOYEES		TOTAL REVENUE	
2006 (through end of Q2)	2005 (through end of Q2)	2005	2004
66,690	60,528	$22,255 billion	20,307 billion

Retention and Professional Development

Please identify the specific steps you are taking to reduce the attrition rate of minority and women employees.
• Develop and/or support internal employee affinity groups (e.g., minority or women networks within the firm)
• Increase/review compensation relative to competition
• Increase/improve current work/life programs
• Adopt dispute resolution process
• Succession plan includes emphasis on diversity
• Work with minority and women employees to develop career advancement plans
• Strengthen mentoring program for all employees, including minorities and women
• Professional skills development program, including minority and women employees

Diversity Mission Statement

Keeping Cultures, Communities, and Customers Connected

Respecting the individuality and dignity of others by appreciating their differences and similarities is a tradition deeply rooted in the Comcast credo. Our commitment to diversity is woven into every aspect of our business and reflected through our workforce, our suppliers, and our social responsibility. We know that to complete the big picture, we must focus on the many diverse pieces that it comprises.

To learn about the culture at Comcast Cable, you need only read our credo. Developed by our own employees, representing all levels throughout the organization, the credo gives us focus and direction in an ever-changing, high-growth environment. We will be the company to look to first for the communications products and services that connect people to what's important in their lives.

Comcast Promise

• We will entertain, inform and empower our customers while enriching our communities.
• To keep this promise, we will commit to:
• An ongoing introduction of new communications products and services
• Consistent financial results that define the industry's best
• An enjoyable work environment that allows people to grow personally as well as professionally
• A belief that consistent, professional and respectful customer service is everybody's job

Comcast Touchstones

Our company, reputation and true success are founded on the following core values:

• *Ethics:* we will be true to the highest standards of honesty, fairness and integrity
• *Quality:* we will commit ourselves to excellence in our products and personal relationships
• *Flexibility:* we will maintain our ability to adapt to an ever-changing world
• *Diversity:* we will respect and reflect the customers, communities, and cultures we serve
• *Employee Focus:* we will invest in people with the belief that our company can only be as strong as its work force
• *Enthusiasm:* we will work with an unbridled passion for our business

Additional Information

Diversity comes in many forms—race and gender are ones that easily come to mind; however, there is also diversity of interests, skills and talents, personalities—all of which comprise diversity at Comcast. Diversity is key to the success or our organization. Diversity is, in fact, one of the Comcast Touchstones—a part of our credo which defines who we are as a company. Simply stated "we will respect and reflect the customers, communities and cultures we serve."

To support this, we are involved in a number of recruiting initiatives that allow us to build upon our current success. As an organization, we work with over 100 organizations to ensure that we are attracting and retaining a diverse workforce. Nationally, we have participated in events sponsored by the National Society for Black Engineers, the National Black MBA Association, the National Hispanic MBA Association, among others. Comcast is an active participate in the Emma Bowen Internship Program, targeted to helping minority students gain experience in the field of telecommunications. Over the past two years, Comcast has increased student placements by over 100 percent. Students work in locations throughout the country, and are invited to spend several days at the Philadelphia headquarters, meeting with Comcast's senior executives. More recently, through the work of Comcast's Diversity Council, we have strengthened our partnerships with organizations including La Raza, LULAC, and the National Hispanic Chamber of Commerce.

Many of our diversity initiatives are driven at the local and regional level, and include on-going efforts to partner with associations and community organizations to identify diverse talent for our organization. We have funded student scholarships for members of professional associations. Working through our public affairs and community investments teams, Comcast connects with the community through support of organizations including local chapters of the NAACP, Urban League, Boys and Girls Clubs, and the YWCA.

Another of the Comcast Touchstones is Employee Focus—we invest in people with the belief that our company can only be as strong as its work force. We support continuous development of our workforce, including involvement in professional associations. Our employees are actively involved in groups including the National Association of Multicultural Ethnicity in Communications and Women in Cable and Telecommunications. Our employees have been recognized and received awards including "Women to Watch" from Women in Cable and Telecommunications, "50 Most Important Hispanics" by *Hispanic Engineer & Information Technology Magazine*, "Top 50 Most Influential Minorities in Cable" by *CableWorld* magazine, and "Distinguished Achiever Award" from the National Women of Color.

Whether it is individual employees or the company as a whole, Comcast is honored to be regularly recognized by local publications and national associations for our diversity efforts. Our diversity initiatives, our efforts in the community, and our commitment to our employees are all keys to this success.

ConAgra Foods, Inc.

1 ConAgra Dr.
Omaha, NE 68102-5001
Phone: (402) 595-4000
Fax: (402) 595-4707
www.conagrafoods.com

Locations

Various

Employment Contact

Staffing Support Team, College Recruiting
One ConAgra Drive 1-252
Omaha, NE 68102
Phone: (402) 595-4000
Fax: (402) 595-4707
www.conagrafoods.com

Recruiting

Please list the schools/types of schools at which you recruit.

- *Other private schools:* Too numerous to list
- *Public state schools:* Too numerous to list
- *Historically Black Colleges and Universities (HBCUs):* Xavier New Orleans, NCA&T, Howard
- *Hispanic Serving Institutions (HSIs):* UTEP

Do you have any special outreach efforts directed to encourage minority students to consider your firm?

- *Conferences:* Black MBA, Hispanic MBA, NHBA, Women's MBA, INROADS, MANRRS, Urban League, etc
- Participate in/host minority student job fair(s)
- Sponsor minority student association events
- Firm's employees participate on career panels at schools
- Outreach to leadership of minority student organizations
- Scholarships or intern/fellowships for minority students

What activities does the firm undertake to attract minority and women employees?

- Partner programs with women and minority associations
- *Conferences:* See above
- Participate at minority job fairs
- Seek referrals from other employees
- Utilize online job services

Internships and Co-ops

INROADS

Deadline for application: April
Pay: Varies
Length of the program: Varies
Web site for internship/co-op information: www.conagrafoods.com

Strategic Plan and Diversity Leadership

Who has primary responsibility for leading diversity initiatives at your firm?

Vivian Ayuso, diversity director.

Does your firm currently have a diversity committee?

Yes.

If yes, does the committee's representation include one or more members of the firm's management/executive committee (or the equivalent)?

Yes.

Does the committee and/or diversity leader establish and set goals or objectives consistent with management's priorities?

Yes.

Has the firm undertaken a formal or informal diversity program or set of initiatives aimed at increasing the diversity of the firm?

Yes, formal.

The Stats

Employees

2005: 40,000

Revenue

2005: $14 billion

Retention and Professional Development

How do 2005 minority and female attrition rates generally compare to those experienced in the prior year period?

About the same as in prior years.

Please identify the specific steps you are taking to reduce the attrition rate of minority and women employees.

- Develop and/or support internal employee affinity groups (e.g., minority or women networks within the firm)
- Increase/review compensation relative to competition
- Increase/improve current work/life programs
- Succession plan includes emphasis on diversity
- Strengthen mentoring program for all employees, including minorities and women
- Professional skills development program, including minority and women employees

Consolidated Edison Company of New York

4 Irving Place
New York, NY 10003
Phone: (212) 460-4314
Fax: (646) 654-2679
www.coned.com

Diversity Leadership

Joan Jacobs
Director, Equal Employment Opportunity
Affairs (EEOA)

Timothy Indiveri
Section Manager, Recruitment

Employment Contact

Matteo Dobrini
Senior Analyst

Recruiting

Please list the schools/types of schools at which you recruit.

• *Ivy League schools:* Columbia University, Cornell University, University of Pennsylvania
• *Other private schools:* Boston University, Clark Atlanta University, Cooper Union, Drexel University, Fordham University, Lafayette College, Lehigh University, Manhattan College, Marist College, New York Institute of Technology, New York University, Pace University, Polytechnic University, Rensselaer Polytechnic Institute, Stevens Institute of Technology, St. John's University
• *Public state schools:* Baruch College, City College of New York, Florida A&M University, Morgan State University, New Jersey Institute of Technology, Rutgers University, SUNY Albany, SUNY Maritime, University of Buffalo
• *Historically Black Colleges and Universities (HBCUs):* Clark Atlanta University, Florida A&M University, Morgan State University
• *Hispanic Serving Institutions (HSIs):* City College of New York
• *Other predominantly minority and/or women's colleges:* Boston University, Columbia University, Cornell University, University of Pennsylvania, Drexel University, Florida A&M University, New Jersey Institute of Technology, Rensselear Polytechnic Institute, Rutgers University

Do you have any special outreach efforts directed to encourage minority students to consider your firm?

• *Conferences:* American Association of Blacks in Energy (AABE), ASPIRA (Latino Youth), Asian-American Business Development Center (AABDC), African-American Female Executives (AAFE), Asian Women in Business (AWIB); One Hundred Black Men, Inc.
• Advertise in minority student association publication(s)
• Participate in/host minority student job fair(s)
• Sponsor minority student association events
• Firm's employees participate on career panels at schools
• Outreach to leadership of minority student organizations
• Scholarships or intern/fellowships for minority students

What activities does the firm undertake to attract minority and women employees?

• *Partner programs with women and minority associations:* NEW, AABE, Seedco, Society of Women Engineers, Society of Hispanic Professional Engineers
• Participate at minority job fairs

• Seek referrals from other employees
• Utilize online job services

Do you use executive recruiting/search firms to seek to identify new diversity hires?

Yes.

If yes, list all women- and/or minority-owned executive search/recruiting firms to which the firm paid a fee for placement services in the past 12 months:

Buckner & Associate, Regional Alliance for Small Contractors' Clearinghouse.

Internships and Co-ops

High School Weekly Co-op Program

Number of interns in the program in summer 2005 (internship) or 2005 (co-op): 15
Web site for internship/co-op information: www.coned.com

Con Edison continues to provide New York City high school students with a variety of work experiences that add another dimension to the technical skills they learn in the classroom. Through the High School Weekly Co-op program, students benefit from career development information, teamwork experiences and skills development.

In 2005, 15 students, including 13 minorities (86.7 percent) and two women (13.3 percent), were participants. 14 of the co-op students were employed by Brooklyn/Queens Electric Operations and held positions that were engineering-/computer-related, and three held manual labor positions at the Hudson Avenue Generating Station. In the past five years, 83 students have participated in the program, of whom 60 (72.3 percent) were minorities, and 11 (13.3 percent) were women.

Co-op Intern Program

Number of interns in the program in summer 2005 (internship) or 2005 (co-op): 62
Web site for internship/co-op information: www.coned.com

The Co-op Intern program invites college students, many of whom had previously worked for the company as summer interns, to supplement their studies with hands-on work during the school year.

In 2005, of this program's 62 participants, 36 were minorities (58.1 percent), and 15 were women (24.2 percent). In the past five years, 254 students have participated in the program, including 147 minorities (57.9 percent) and 68 women (26.8 percent).

Summer Intern Program

Number of interns in the program in summer 2005 (internship) or 2005 (co-op): 59
Web site for internship/co-op information: www.coned.com

Con Edison's Summer Intern Program provides high school and college students with work experiences that help them bring textbook knowledge to real-world settings and gain an understanding of the way we work at Con Edison. With this program, Con Edison identifies students who demonstrate high energy, strong intellect, and a genuine thirst for learning and who, upon graduation from college, may qualify as candidates for the company's Growth Opportunities for Leadership Development (GOLD) program. Students must be involved in the study of engineering, environmental science or business, such as accounting or finance.

In 2005, 59 interns participated in the program; 31 were minorities (52.5 percent), and 17 were women (28.8 percent). Since 2000, 54.9 percent of all participants were minorities and 35.4 were women.

Scholarships

Con Edison Scholarship Program

Deadline for application for the scholarship program: November 12
Scholarship award amount: $2,500 per student for 10 students—for entire scholarship
Web site or other contact information for scholarship: For Con Edison employees only—internal web site

The Scholarship & Recognition Program, a nonprofit organization, administers this program.

Thurgood Marshall Scholarship Fund (TMSF)

Scholarship award amount: $15,000 per student for three students—for entire scholarship

The TMSF is the only national organization that awards four-year merit scholarships, programmatic and capacity building support to 45 historically black public colleges and universities and the students who attend them. Con Edison supports this fund and the two scholarships are named for Con Edison and are for minority students majoring in the physical sciences and/or engineering.

The United Negro College Fund (UNCF)

Scholarship award amount: $5,000 per student for four students—for entire scholarship

The UNCF is the nation's oldest and most successful higher education assistance organization. The Con Edison Scholarship is awarded to students who are majoring in the fields of accounting, computer science, electrical, mechanical or nuclear engineering. This program fosters long-term relationships among the corporation, the students and the participating institutions. It increases student interest in the corporation and ultimately enlarges the pool of prospective minority employees.

The Hundred Year Association of New York

Scholarship award amount: $3,000 per student for two students—for entire scholarship

This program offers scholarships to the sons and daughters of career city employees. Con Edison has participated in this program since 1994. The selection committee receives 150 applications from diverse high school seniors each year and selections are based on scholastic achievement, leadership, commitment and community service.

CUNY Program for the Retention of Engineering Students (PRES)

This program was established in 1987 to provide academic support and guidance to underrepresented minorities and women in the engineering field, thereby reducing attrition. PRES currently serves more than 550 students and continues to effectively increase the performance of minority engineering students. Con Edison supports this program with an annual grant of $10,000.

Affinity Groups

American Association of Blacks in Energy (AABE)

AABE is a national association of energy professionals founded and dedicated to ensure the input of African-Americans and other minorities into the discussions and developments of energy policies regulations, R&D technologies and environmental issues.

http://aabe-nymac.org/home.html

Improve Continuously Committee (ICC)

This newly formed Con Edison group represents lesbians, gays, bisexual and transgender (LGBT) employees. ICC meets on a monthly basis to discuss providing opportunities for employee networks and mentoring. They also raise diversity awareness, share experiences and promote personal and professional growth.

Entry-Level Programs/Full-Time Opportunities/Training Programs

Growth Opportunities for Leadership Development (GOLD)

Length of program: 18 months
Geographic location(s) of program: New York

This program develops high-caliber college graduates for positions of increasing responsibility and leadership within the company during the course of an 18-month period. Through a series of practical, rotational job assignments, mentoring, and senior-management guidance, GOLD program participants tackle challenging supervisory and project-based jobs that provide valuable work experience insight into Con Edison's practices and operations. Upon successful completion of the program, participants are poised to advance into Con Edison's management ranks. In the past five years, we have hired 63 GOLD associates who had previously participated in the co-op and/or summer intern programs.

The program continues to be successful in recruiting and retaining minorities and women. In 2005, it enabled 59 college graduates, 31 of whom were minorities (52.5 percent) and 17 of whom were women (28.8 percent), to begin careers at Con Edison. In the past five years, 257 GOLD associates have participated in the program, including 141 minorities and 91 women.

Over the past five years, 75.5 percent of our GOLD program employees have remained with the company. Significantly, 74.5 percent of the minority participants and 72.5 percent of the women participants are continuing their careers at Con Edison. Such retention rates are solid signs of a successful program.

Tools for Employees Advancing into Management (TEAM)

Length of program: Approximately 12 months
Geographic location(s) of program: New York

The TEAM Program is a developmental experience designed to provide recently promoted union employees with the tools necessary to make a successful transition into a management role. The program's goal is to develop the participants into quality supervisors or individual contributors.

Tuition Aid Program

Length of program: As long as the employee is going to college
Geographic location(s) of program: New York

The Tuition Aid program continues to be a noteworthy feature of Con Edison's benefit package. The program offers reimbursement to eligible employees who pursue courses or programs that maintain or improve their present career skills. Upon the successful completion of a degree, the employee is provided with up to 100 percent reimbursement of tuition costs.

In 2005, 446 employees participated in the program; more than half of the participants were minorities, and 27.4 percent were women.

Strategic Plan and Diversity Leadership

How does the firm's leadership communicate the importance of diversity to everyone at the firm?

Con Edison's commitment to diversity is reaffirmed in the chairman's annual message that is mailed to every employee in the company. Following is that message:

Chairman's Message

TO: All Employees
FROM: Kevin Burke, Chairman of the Board
DATE: June 30, 2006
SUBJECT: Reaffirmation of Our Commitment to Equal Employment Opportunity and Affirmative Action

At Con Edison, we have long supported the principles of equal employment opportunity and affirmative action. We acknowledge and reaffirm that these values are integral to the foundation of our society, our workplaces, and our communities. Con Edison's commitment to these principles is reflected in our diverse employees—one of our greatest strengths.

We recognize that our company's success depends on how effectively we develop and utilize the talents of the men and women who make up our workforce. Therefore, we remain dedicated to maintaining an environment that is free of discrimination, and a workplace where all employees are afforded the opportunity to develop, perform, and reach their full potential without regard to race, color, religion, gender, age, national origin, gender identity, marital status, sexual orientation, citizenship, disability, orVietnam-Era, special disabled and/or other qualified veteran status.

Our commitment to these principles is set forth in further detail in Corporate Policy Statements 500-4 (EEO Policy), 500-12 (Employment of Individuals with Disabilities and Veterans' Policy), and 500-14 (Sexual Harassment Policy), which complement our standards of business conduct. I encourage you to read these policies, as it is every employee's job to do his or her share to maintain a workplace that is free of discrimination, harassment, and retaliation. Fulfilling this obligation means that we must promptly report any such behavior to the corporate EEOA office, an immediate supervisor or one with higher authority or your Human Resources representative. You may also report violations using the EEO complaint line, (212) 460-1065, or the complaint form on the EEO web site (http://intranet/eeo). All complaints will be promptly investigated, and employees who are found to have violated our EEO polices are subject to discipline, up to and including termination.

Con Edison stands behind its EEO policies. By sustaining and enhancing our outstanding diversity record, we will provide the best service to our customers and achieve our full potential as a responsible company.

In addition to the chairman's message, Con Edison sends out occasional e-mails to remind employees about the importance of diversity to all of us. We also post diversity messages on our elevator screens and bulletin boards at all our company locations. Finally, we encourage all employees to visit our internal EEOA website, which contains information regarding the importance of diversity.

Who has primary responsibility for leading diversity initiatives at your firm?

Joan Jacobs, director, Equal Employment Opportunity Affairs (EEOA).

Does your firm currently have a diversity committee?

No.

Does the diversity leader establish and set goals or objectives consistent with management's priorities?

Yes.

Has the firm undertaken a formal or informal diversity program or set of initiatives aimed at increasing the diversity of the firm?

Yes, formal.

How often does the firm's management review the firm's diversity progress/results?

Monthly.

How is the firm's diversity firm management held accountable for achieving results?

It is reflected in the diversity director's performance review.

The Stats

Employees

2005: 13,145
2004: 12,672

Revenue

2005: $8.1 billion
2004: $8.0 billion

Minority Employees

Minorities: 5,289 (40.2 percent)
Women: 2,032 (15.5 percent)

Retention and Professional Development

How do 2005 minority and female attrition rates generally compare to those experienced in the prior year period?

About the same as in prior years.

Please identify the specific steps you are taking to reduce the attrition rate of minority and women employees.

• Develop and/or support internal employee affinity groups
• Succession plan includes emphasis on diversity
• Work with minority and women employees to develop career advancement plans
• Strengthen mentoring program for all employees, including minorities and women
• Professional skills development program, including minority and women employees

Diversity Mission Statement

As our industry and our workforce continue to evolve in the new marketplace, we face challenges in maintaining and expanding our role as an industry leader and an employer of choice. To that end, our diverse workforce will continue to be one of our greatest strengths.

Con Edison has a longstanding commitment to the principles of equal employment opportunity and affirmative action, not just because it is a good business practice, but also because it is the right thing to do. Indeed, our company's success is tied to how effectively we develop and maximize the potential of our most valuable resources—the men and women of Con Edison.

At Con Edison, employment and personnel decisions, including hiring, job assignments, promotions and compensation are based on ability and merit, without regard for race, color, religion, gender, age, national origin, disability, marital status, sexual orientation, citizenship or military service status. In today's business world, workplace diversity and business accomplishment go hand in hand and we regard Con Edison's commitment to diversity as a key element in our company's ongoing success.

Our equal employment opportunity (EEO) policies set forth our commitment to these principles. Maintaining a workplace free of discrimination is an integral part of each employee's job. Each of us must contribute to a safe, productive and harmonious work environment, and we must respect every individual's dignity and well-being.

Our compliance with these policies is one of our most effective means of attracting and retaining highly qualified employees, providing the best service to our customers, and achieving our full potential as a responsible, concerned and competitive company.

Additional Information

The company's Recruitment office continued to strengthen its relationship with Nontraditional Employment for Women (NEW), an organization that works to train and secure employment for women in trades. In 2005, The Con Edison Learning Center, which is the size of a small community college, where skilled, professional instructors conduct courses in leadership and management development, and in highly specialized fields ranging from electric systems to environmental compliance, provided hands-on training for 88 women enrolled with NEW, who learned basic electricity, carpentry, plumbing, and math, and who were provided with an introduction to transmission and distribution systems. Since 2000, Con Edison has recruited 46 women from NEW. As hiring opportunities arise, NEW graduates will continue to be considered for employment opportunities.

In 2005, the Recruitment office re-established a partnership with Access for Women, a program sponsored by the New York City College of Technology. Access for Women serves women preparing for two-year and four-year degrees in such nontraditional technical fields as construction, building trades, and engineering technologies. Graduates of the program will be considered for employment opportunities.

Con Edison participated in several job fairs in 2005 that enabled us to meet a diverse pool of qualified potential applicants. These included job fairs sponsored by the New York State Department of Labor, New York City Housing Authority, NEW, and Women for Hire. Con Edison also participated in job fairs, such as the Career Forum for Women and Minorities, sponsored by Careers Conference of America; Careers and the Disabled Diversity Job Fair, sponsored by the Association of Higher Education and Disability (AHEAD); the CUNY Big Apple Job Fair, sponsored by The College Opportunity to Prepare for Employment (COPE) program of the City University of New York; and the Parks Opportunity Program (POP), sponsored by the New York City Department of Parks and Recreation. All participants in POP are provided placement services to learn skills through paid full-time seasonal intern assignments in the Department of Parks and Recreation's administrative and maintenance departments.

In addition, Con Edison attended career fairs held at colleges sponsored by organizations that advocate for diversity, including the Society of Women Engineers, at Cornell University; the National Society of Black Engineers, at Drexel University; the National Society of Black Engineers and the Society of Hispanic Professional Engineers, at Rensselaer Polytechnic Institute; and the Professional Advancement of Black Chemists and Chemical Engineers, at Florida A&M University. Con Edison also participated in career fairs at historically black universities, including Atlanta University, Florida A & M University, and Morgan State University. In 2005, Con Edison placed various print ads in ethnic newspapers, including El Diario, African Abroad, Chinese World, and Sing Tao.

Additional information regarding item VI: Con Edison offers a variety of programs geared to assist all employees, including minorities and women, in mastering their job functions, advancing their careers, and furthering their education. Classes and presentations are held at Con Edison's Learning Center, a multimillion-dollar facility, devoted to providing employees with practical training and personal development courses.

Whether it is training new customer service representatives or upgrading the skills of field workers, The Learning Center staff works closely with operating departments to develop training programs that enable us to maintain our system, run more effective operations, improve customer service, and nurture employee leadership skills. Courses are provided in electric, gas, and steam systems; customer operations; environment, health, and safety information technology; and leadership. Additionally, Strategic Issues Seminars are designed to help employees gain the leadership skills necessary to run the Con Edison of tomorrow. These seminars are held frequently and cover a wide-range of topics. Con Edison is also a corporate member of the Institute for Management Studies and the American Management Association, where employees can find classes and seminars covering many different topics. The company also provides Web-based, self-study programs that employees are able to take at their convenience. The programs offered at The Learning Center are available to all employees and are particularly useful to individuals who may need to advance their skill level or want to try a new career path.

Con Edison has received the following corporate and individual awards in the past three years:

2005

- *Diversity Inc's* "Top 50 Best Companies for Minorities"
- "The LATINA Style Top 50"
- New York Urban League "Champions of Diversity"
- *Black Enterprise's* "Top 40 Companies for Diversity"

2004

- *Fortune* magazine's "50 Best Companies for Minorities"
- *Hispanic* magazine's Corporate 100 List
- "The LATINA Style Top 50"
- *DiversityInc's* "Top 50 Companies for Diversity"
- Asian American Business Development Center's "Outstanding 50 Asian Americans in Business"
- Leadership Institute for African American Female Executives
- Top 10 Queens Women in Business
- *The Network Journal* magazine's "25 Influential Black Women in Business"

2003

- *Fortune* magazine's "50 Best Companies for Minorities"
- "The LATINA Style Top 50"
- *Hispanic* magazine's "Corporate 100"
- Westchester County Press Award—for our commitment to hiring minorities and women
- Women's Enterprise Development Center Award
- American Society of Mechanical Engineers "Charles T. Main Gold Medal"
- YWCA's Academy of Women Achievers
- YMCA's Black Achievers program

The following are organizations with diversity initiative programs that received Con Edison support in 2005:

- 100 Hispanic Women, Inc.
- Abyssinian Development Corporation
- African American Men of Westchester
- Agudath Israel of America
- American Association of Blacks in Energy
- American Civil Rights Education Services
- Asia Society
- Asian American Business Development Center
- Asian American Federation of New York
- Asian American Legal Defense and Education Fund
- Asian Americans for Equality, Inc.
- Asian Professional Extension, Inc.
- Asian Women in Business
- Asociación Puertorriqueña & Hermanos, Inc.
- ASPIRA of New York, Inc.
- Associated Black Charities
- Association of Minority Enterprises of New York
- AYUDA for the Arts
- Ballet Hispanico of New York
- Barnard College
- Black Agency Executives
- Brooklyn Chinese-American Association, Inc.
- Caribbean American Chamber of Commerce and Industry, Inc.

- Casita Maria, Inc.
- Catalyst
- Chinese-American Planning Council, Inc.
- Coalition of Asian Pacific Americans
- Committee for Hispanic Children and Families, Inc.
- Congressional Black Caucus Foundation, Inc.
- Council of Jewish Organizations of Flatbush, Inc.
- Dominican American National Roundtable
- Dominican Foundation
- Dominican Women's Development Center, Inc.
- El Carnaval del Boulevard
- El Museo del Barrio
- Foundation for Ethnic Understanding, Inc.
- Girl Scout Council of Greater New York, Inc.
- GRADS Foundation, Inc.
- Hispanic Federation of New York City, Inc.
- Hong Kong Dragon Boat Festival in New York, Inc.
- Institute for the Puerto Rican/Hispanic Elderly
- Instituto Arte Teatral Internacional, Inc.
- Jewish Children's Museum
- Jewish Community Relations Council of New York, Inc.
- Jewish Museum
- Korean-American Counseling Center, Inc.
- Latino Civic Association, Inc.
- Latino Commission on AIDS
- Latino Gerontological Center
- Latino Job Service Employer Committee
- League of Women Voters of the City of New York
- League of Women Voters of Westchester
- Lewis H. Latimer Fund, Inc.
- Martin Luther King Jr. Concert Series, Inc.
- Metropolitan Jewish Geriatric Foundation
- Museum of Chinese in the Americas
- Musica de Camara, Inc.
- NAACP
- NAACP ACT-SO Coalition of NYC Branches
- NAACP Legal Defense and Education Fund
- National Action Council for Minorities in Engineering
- National Council of Jewish Women, Inc.
- National Hispanic Business Group
- National Puerto Rican Forum, Inc.
- National Urban Fellows, Inc.
- New York Coalition of 100 Black Women
- New York State Assembly/Senate Puerto Rican/Hispanic Task Force
- New York State Association of Black and Puerto Rican Legislators, Inc.
- New York Women's Agenda
- Nontraditional Employment for Women
- One Hundred Black Men, Inc.
- Organization of Chinese Americans—Westchester & Hudson Valley Chapter
- Professional Women in Construction
- Promesa Foundation
- Puerto Rican Bar Association Scholarship Fund, Inc.
- Puerto Rican Family Institute, Inc.

- Puerto Rican Legal Defense and Education Fund
- Puerto Rican Traveling Theatre Company
- Queens Women's Network
- Redhawk Indian Arts Council
- Regional Aid for Interim Needs, Inc.
- Repertorio Español
- Russian Ethnic Bilingual Educational and Cultural Association
- San Juan Fiesta/Archdiocese of NY - Office of Hispanic Affairs
- Sociedad Puertorriqueña de Queens, Inc.
- Society of Hispanic Professional Engineers
- Society of the Educational Arts, Inc./SEA
- Teatro Circulo, Ltd.
- Thalia Spanish Theatre, Inc.
- Tomchei Torah Chaim Birnbaum
- Trey Whitfield Foundation Inc.
- UJA-Federation of New York
- United Negro College Fund
- West Indian-American Day Carnival Association, Inc.
- Wien House (YWHA)
- Women in Communications and Energy
- Women's City Club of New York, Inc.
- Women's Research and Education Fund
- YWCA

Convergys Corporation

201 E. 4th St.
Cincinnati, OH 45202
Phone: (513) 723-7000
Fax: (513) 421-8624
Toll Free: (800) 344-3000
www.convergys.com/turnyourfutureon

Locations

National and global locations

Diversity Leadership

Anthony Jones
Diversity Director

Employment Contact

Jim Hartman
Director of Human Resources
201 East 4th Street
Cincinnati, OH 45201
Phone: (513) 784-5670
E-mail: jim.hartman@convergys.com
www.convergys.com/careers_selection.html

Recruiting

Please list the schools/types of schools at which you recruit.

We recruit at the following schools:

Bowling Green State University, Brigham Young University, Carnegie Mellon University, Florida A&M, Florida International University, Florida State University, Georgia Tech, Miami University of Ohio, Northern Kentucky University, Ohio State University, Ohio University, Purdue University, University of Central Florida, University of Cincinnati, University of Dayton, University of Illinois, University of Michigan, University of Utah, Xavier University

Do you have any special outreach efforts directed to encourage minority students to consider your firm?

• Hold a reception for minority students
• Conferences
• Advertise in minority student association publication(s)
• Participate in/host minority student job fair(s)
• Sponsor minority student association events
• Firm's employees participate on career panels at schools
• Outreach to leadership of minority student organizations
• Scholarships or intern/fellowships for minority students
• *Other:* Host a Women in Technology Conference, sit on affiliate boards (BDPA for example)

What activities does the firm undertake to attract minority and women employees?

• Partner programs with women and minority associations
• Conferences
• Participate at minority job fairs
• Seek referrals from other employees
• Utilize online job services
• *Other:* Host a Women in Technology Conference

Internships and Co-ops

Convergys Internships In Various Resource Units

Deadline for application: March 15th

Number of interns in the program in summer 2006 (internship) or 2006 (co-op): 60

Pay: $9-$18 per hour

Length of the program: 12 weeks

Percentage of interns/co-ops in the program who receive offers of full-time employment: 70 percent

Web site for internship/co-op information: www.convergys.com

Convergys supports full-time summer internships and part-time year round internships in various locations, with Jacksonville and Orlando, Florida, Cincinnati, Ohio, and Itasca, Illinois being the primary locations of hiring activity. We focus on IT/IS, accounting/finance, business, marketing and human resources as disciplines of choice for the majority of our college hiring (full-time or interns). We also support the INROADS program as a national account.

Scholarships

Scholarships are offered at the following schools through the university scholarship program:

Bowling Green State University, Brigham Young University, Carnegie Mellon university, Florida A&M, Florida State University, Georgia Tech, Miami University of Ohio, Ohio State University, Purdue University, University of Central Florida, University of Cincinnati, University of Illinois, University of Michigan, University of Utah and Xavier University.

Please do not contact Convergys. We also offer scholarships to selected INROADS interns throughout Convergys.

We also offer the Convergys Academic Achievement Recognition Program described below:

Convergys Academic Achievement Recognition Program: Academic Year 2005 - 2006

Purpose of Program

To acknowledge and reward academically successful students who have chosen a field of study related to Convergys' business and its industry. Scholarships will be granted to students enrolled at selected universities based on specific criteria. Each university will select a qualified candidate(s) to be approved by Convergys.

This award is specifically designed to acknowledge students that excel in academic life and who have also demonstrated a unique ability to reach out to others through personal initiatives.

Convergys will seek to communicate with all scholarship recipients to facilitate dialogue regarding possible intern or full-time employment opportunities as such positions arise.

Objectives/Summary

Convergys is seeking to award academically-based scholarships in order to:

• Recognize academic achievement
• Assist in positioning Convergys as an employer of choice
• Assist in the recruitment of academically successful candidates for hiring needs.

Appropriate designees of the educational facility will select the award recipients, with final review by Convergys-appointed designees. Payment of the awards will be sent directly to the attending university for the purpose of tuition and tuition-related expenses.

Recipients may renew the scholarship according to the "renewal application" criteria outlined in the "evaluation criteria" section of this document.

Although commitment to a paid summer internship will not be required, nor availability of internships guaranteed, Convergys will make every effort to publicize internship opportunities and work toward offering internships to those that show interest.

Offers of full-time employment for scholarship recipients upon graduation (with or without Convergys internship experience) will be a goal of Convergys hiring managers. Convergys will collaborate with the appropriate university representatives to ensure the integrity of the selection process, providing unbiased review of applicants presented. Upon selection of scholarship recipients, the Convergys corporate public relations office will prepare appropriate internal and external communication of said awards.

Convergys reserves the right to discontinue this program at its sole discretion.

Affinity Groups

Global Women's Network

Convergys has a Global network for women that meets quarterly and various local site chapters that meet monthly or quarterly.

Strategic Plan and Diversity Leadership

How does the firm's leadership communicate the importance of diversity to everyone at the firm?

The firm's leadership showcases the importance of diversity using the following measures: company corporate communications, organizational development, community action teams and office of diversity communications such as e-mail, company Intranet, desk-drops and the web.

Who has primary responsibility for leading diversity initiatives at your firm?

Office of Diversity: Anthony Jones, director of diversity.

Does your firm currently have a diversity committee?

Yes.

If yes, please describe how the committee is structured, how often it meets, etc.

The Diversity Steering Committee is comprised of most of the senior officers (CEO, CFO, etc.) and meets annually. The Business Unit Diversity Council is comprised of representative from the business unit, chaired by business unit leader and meets once per month. The Corporate Diversity Council is comprised of representatives from corporate, chaired by the senior vice president and human resources and meets once per month.

If yes, does the committee's representation include one or more members of the firm's management/executive committee (or the equivalent)?

Yes.

Does the committee and/or diversity leader establish and set goals or objectives consistent with management's priorities?

Yes.

Has the firm undertaken a formal or informal diversity program or set of initiatives aimed at increasing the diversity of the firm?

Yes, formal.

The Stats

Employees (worldwide)

2005: 66,000
2004: 66,000

Revenue

2005: $2.6 billion
2004: $2.5 billion

Retention and Professional Development

Please identify the specific steps you are taking to reduce the attrition rate of minority and women employees.

• Develop and/or support internal employee affinity groups (e.g., minority or women networks within the firm)
• Increase/review compensation relative to competition
• Increase/improve current work/life programs
• Adopt dispute resolution process
• Succession plan includes emphasis on diversity
• Work with minority and women employees to develop career advancement plans
• Review work assignments and hours billed to key client matters to make sure minority and women employees are not being excluded
• Strengthen mentoring program for all employees, including minorities and women
• Professional skills development program, including minority and women employees

Diversity Mission Statement

Diversity Principles

Through Convergys' diversity initiatives, we will establish and maintain an environment that:

• Values individual differences
• Fosters consistent, mutual respect and open communication of ideas
• Attracts, develops, supports, and retains a diverse workforce with the ability to compete in the global market
• Increases our competitive advantage by leveraging the knowledge, skills, and unique talents of our employees
• Enhances career opportunities for all employees by working to develop each employee to his or her full potential
• Provides a richer, more fertile climate for creative thinking and innovation
• Is recognized by employees, clients, and the community as a fair and rewarding place to work

Additional Information

With diversity, Convergys takes an all-company, all-employee approach. From the CEO and his direct reports, to the customer service agents on the phone, we all have responsibilities and accountabilities to ourselves, our teams, our clients, and their customers. Our Office of Diversity is aligned with our business units' objectives as they pertain to client satisfaction and employee satisfaction and continually partners with our executives to maintain maximum alignment with business unit initiatives. Our approach is internal education, awareness and programs of choice, and our external message is clear, and concise: "Diversity at Convergys is viewed as a continuous process. Cultivating a systemic approach to diversity ensures that we look at our employees, systems, policies, practices, and behaviors to capitalize on our success. Our unique differences are the lifeline of our company."

Credit Suisse

11 Madison Avenue, 10th Floor
New York, NY 10010
Phone: (212) 325-2000
www.credit-suisse.com

Diversity Leadership

Tanji Dewberry
Assistant Vice President
Head of Diversity Recruiting
11 Madison Avenue, 10th Floor
New York, NY 10010
Phone: (212) 538-2594
E-mail: tanji.dewberry@credit-suisse.com
www.credit-suisse.com

Recruiting

Please list the schools/types of schools at which you recruit.

• Ivy League schools
• Public state schools
• Private schools
• Historically Black Colleges and Universities (HBCUs)
• Hispanic Serving Institutions (HSIs)
• *Other predominantly minority and/or women's colleges:* Host women's events at both Columbia and Barnard

Do you have any special outreach efforts that are directed to encourage minority students to consider your firm?

• Hold receptions for minority students
• Advertise in minority student association publication(s)
• Participate in/host minority student job fair(s)
• Sponsor minority student association events
• Firm's professionals participate on career panels at schools
• Outreach to leadership of minority student organizations
• Scholarships or intern/fellowships for minority students

What activities does the firm undertake to attract women and minorities?

• Partner programs with women and minority banking associations
• Conferences
• Participate at minority job fairs
• Seek referrals from other professionals
• Utilize online job services
• *Other:* Market jobs to alumni networks of educational nonprofits, i.e., LEAD, Prep for Prep, Albert G. Oliver Program, and A Better Chance; Host financial services boot camp for freshman and sophomores

Internships and Co-ops

Summer Analyst: Investment Banking

Credit Suisse Overview

As one of the world's leading banks, Credit Suisse provides its clients with investment banking, private banking and asset management services worldwide. Credit Suisse offers advisory services, comprehensive solutions and innovative products to companies, institutional clients and high-net-worth private clients globally, as well as retail clients in Switzerland. Credit Suisse is active in over 50 countries and employs approximately 40,000 people. Credit Suisse's parent company, Credit Suisse Group, is a leading global financial services company headquartered in Zurich. Credit Suisse Group's registered shares (CSGN) are listed in Switzerland and, in the form of American Depositary Shares (CSR), in New York.

Investment Banking

Credit Suisse offers a broad range of investment banking and securities products and services to meet the needs of institutional clients, companies and government bodies.

Private Banking

Credit Suisse provides expert advice and a comprehensive range of investment products and services tailored to the complex needs of high-net-worth individuals globally as well as private and business clients in Switzerland.

Asset Management

Credit Suisse serves clients by offering products across the full range of investment classes, from equities, fixed income and multiple-asset class products to alternative investments.

Program Structure

Our 10-week Summer Analyst Program for rising college seniors gives you outstanding exposure to business and the financial services industry.

Whether you're working alongside a full-time analyst or staffed as the only analyst on a deal team, our summer program gives you the tools you'll need to jump start your career in finance and investment banking. Responsibilities may include analyzing companies using financial modeling and valuation techniques, examining the impact of a transaction on a client's capital structure and analyzing the consequences of a merger or acquisition.

Summer analysts will be placed directly into an industry or product group. As a summer program participant, you will have the opportunity to work on deals in your group, gaining hands-on experience and working on all aspects of advising and transacting business for our clients. Summer analysts are formally reviewed at the mid and end points of the summer, and offers are made on the last day of the program, enabling you to return to school with a full-time position secured.

Our U.S. regional breadth offers unique opportunities to execute transactions from conception to close, which differentiates Credit Suisse from our competitors.

Training

You will attend a brief company orientation and a seven-day training program and then start work in your group for the summer, receiving further training while on the job.

Your learning experience will continue through the summer speaker series, where you'll hear from senior employees across the divisions. In addition, you'll participate in networking events and firmwide events that will help ensure that you are exposed to all the areas within the bank and understand the big picture of a global investment bank. You'll also enjoy interacting with the other summer analysts and full-time employees at a variety of social events throughout the summer.

To help you determine your strengths and plan your career, summer analysts are matched with mentors within investment banking, who provide advice and guidance throughout the summer.

Qualifications

Interested candidates must be between their junior and senior years at a four-year college or university. Credit Suisse is noted for the diversity of its employees, but seeks candidates with a common set of abilities—highly motivated and creative individuals who have demonstrated academic achievement, specifically in finance and accounting, and have the ability to work independently and as a member of a team. We look for intelligent, driven and hardworking candidates with consistent leadership involvement in school activities and athletics, and a solid interest in the financial sector.

Summer Analyst: Fixed Income or Equity Sales and Trading

Program Structure

The Credit Suisse Securities division offers two separate, 10-week summer programs—one in equity sales and trading and one in fixed income sales and trading. If chosen for a first-round interview, students will interview for BOTH the equity sales and trading and the fixed income sales and trading programs—please only submit your resume once for these programs. Second-round interviews are held separately and will be equity-specific or fixed income-specific. This will be determined based on your first-round interviews. In both programs, you'll spend one week in training, followed by three three-week rotations on either fixed income or equity desks.

• Sales Rotation—You'll spend three weeks working within one sales product area. In Equity, this rotation will give you the chance to work with the coverage sales, institutional sales, international sales, automated execution systems, prime services, convertible sales or derivative sales teams. In fixed income, you'll work with the corporate, structured products, interest rates, structuring, global foreign exchange, emerging markets, CDO group or derivatives sales teams.

• Trading Rotation—You'll spend three weeks working within one trading product area. In equity, it will include the cash trading, derivative trading, program trading, international sales trading and exchange traded funds teams. In fixed income, these groups include the corporate, structured products, interest rates, global foreign exchange, emerging markets or interest rate products trading teams.

• Sales or Trading Rotation—You'll spend your final three weeks on one of the above-mentioned sales or trading desks in either fixed income or equity.

These programs are a great way to become familiar with the sales and trading arena, as well as the overall investment process, gaining a broad and varied view of several potential career paths.

Training and Content

Both programs provide summer analysts with the foundation necessary for a successful summer experience. They begin with an intense one-week training period in New York, where all summer analysts participate in a capital markets overview, several desk overviews and a library tour. You'll be trained on Bloomberg and learn Credit Suisse technology systems and databases. You'll tour the NYSE, and you'll meet with traders and salespeople from all of the various products.

After your first week of training, you'll hit the ground running, working to support a variety of desks within fixed income or equity. Your learning experience will continue through the summer speaker series, where you'll hear from senior employees across the divisions. In addition, you'll participate in networking events, community service and firmwide events that will help ensure that you are exposed to all the areas within the bank and understand the big picture of a global investment bank.

To help you determine your strengths and plan your career, summer analysts are matched with junior and senior mentors within your program's division, who provide advice and guidance throughout the summer. You'll also enjoy networking with the other summer analysts and full-time employees at a variety of social events throughout the summer.

Qualifications

Must be a rising senior (graduating in December 2007 or May 2008) and a bachelor degree candidate from a four-year college or university. Credit Suisse is noted for the diversity of its employees, but seeks candidates with a common set of abilities—highly motivated and creative individuals who have demonstrated academic achievement and have the ability to work independently and as a member of a team. Strength in verbal and written communication and computer literacy is essential. We look for intelligent, driven and hardworking students with consistent leadership involvement in school activities and athletics, and proven interest in the financial arena.

Summer Analyst: Equity Research Associate

If you're a dynamic undergraduate looking for an intense and valuable introduction to the equity research arena, the Equity Research Summer Analyst Program may be for you. By working with one of our top-ranked senior research analysts, you'll gain an in-depth understanding of company analysis as well as the overall investment process. You will also have exposure to other divisions at Credit Suisse, including Credit Suisse global sales force, equity traders and institutional clients.

We offer our summer analysts a solid one-week training program to provide you with the skills to join one of our outstanding research teams. Throughout the summer, you may work on projects involving financial analysis and investigative research. Equity research summer analysts also have the opportunity to learn financial modeling and forecasting skills and to help produce research reports. In order to fully understand equity research's role at Credit Suisse, every summer intern will spend time with equity salespeople and equity traders. In addition to your day-to-day responsibilities, you'll be assigned an industry-specific project to work on throughout the summer.

Qualifications

Credit Suisse is noted for the diversity of its employees, but seeks candidates with a common set of abilities—highly motivated and creative individuals who have demonstrated academic achievement, specifically in finance, marketing and accounting courses and have the ability to work independently and as a member of a team. Strength in verbal and written communication, and computer literacy is essential to all that we do. Candidates must be juniors.

HOLT Summer Analyst

The HOLT division of Credit Suisse is offering a summer internship program, based in Chicago, for undergraduate students interested in learning and applying advanced business strategy analysis and buy-side valuation methodologies.

Through theoretical and applied research, HOLT has developed a framework that better explains the dynamic relationship between corporate financial performance and stock market pricing. HOLT's central premise is that the stock market sets prices based on cash flows, not traditional accounting measures of corporate performance.

As a summer analyst you will gain exposure to multiple global industries, interact with numerous areas of the bank, engage in strategic initiatives for key clients around the globe, carry out in-depth analysis of the factors underlying corporate financial performance and valuation, enhance your ability to structure and present persuasive analyses, and gain financial analysis skills of leading investment management and management consulting firms.

Training

The summer training program begins with an intense two-week training period where summer analysts participate in a capital markets overview, valuation review, a research product overview and a condensed version of the HOLT University training program.

Responsibilities

HOLT is seeking summer analysts for several different teams. As such, responsibilities will include some but not all of the following:

• Study and utilize the most advanced corporate strategy and valuation frameworks, including our proprietary CFROI® methodology to model and analyze corporate actions.
• Become proficient using the HOLT ValueSearch software to develop buy and sell recommendations, the same software used by more than 700 institutional money managers worldwide.
• Gain introduction to a suite of proprietary investment products and use those products to provide key investment insights to internal and external clients (i.e., buy-side clients, Credit Suisse Fixed Income, Credit Suisse Investment Banking).
• Work with HOLT sales to assist in the development of sales strategies utilizing HOLT's custom solutions and capabilities.

• Interact with some of the top analyst teams on Wall Street in a number of different industries.
• Conduct detailed analysis, from an aggregate sector or country perspective down to company specific, utilizing our proprietary database of over 18,000 companies in 55 countries.
• Identify key corporate performance and valuation issues and the underlying drivers behind a firms' warranted value.
• Identify and test ideas to improve HOLT's analysis of both individual companies and broad-scale valuation trends.
• Participate in project teams to develop new products and methodologies serving a range of internal and external client needs.
• Develop and communicate market insights.
• Understand valuation issues and propose improvements to the HOLT valuation model through a meaningful contribution to the HOLT Framework Committee & Meetings, making periodic presentations to HOLT team members.

Qualifications

• Pursuing a degree in finance, economics or a five-year accounting program
• Keen interest in stock and bond market valuation
• Excellent analytic skills
• Strong verbal and written communication skills, interpersonal skills (individual interaction as well as presentations to large groups), and computer literacy
• Working knowledge of statistics, econometrics and financial modeling
• Self-motivated and team-oriented.

Summer Analyst: Real Estate Finance and Securitization

Program Structure

The real estate finance and securitization group's (REFS's) main product areas fall into the broad categories of real estate and real estate-related financial products—commercial mortgage-backed securities, for example. This group has a balance sheet of over $11.5 billion and operates in a principal capacity as well as providing investment banking services to corporate clients, institutions and publicly traded real estate companies.

REFS is organized into several operating teams:

• Origination Group—Organized on a geographic basis in both the New York and Los Angeles offices, origination teams invest in debt and equity and combination financing for office, industrial, retail, hotel and multifamily, single tenant and other property types. Loans can be made for "whole loan" sale, securitization or balance sheet purposes.

• Investment Banking—Provides advisory services for companies and institutions regarding their real estate activities. The work involves sale mandates, securitization, mergers and acquisitions, and other transactions.
• Structured Finance—Focuses on securitization transactions and other "financially engineered" exits for REFS's investments.
• Trading—Encompasses several units involving whole loans, commercial mortgage-backed securities (CMBS) and derivatives.

As a summer analyst, you will develop your understanding of the field by working on a variety of transactions. Summer analyst positions are located in New York.

Training and Content

The Fixed Income Dedicated Summer Program begins with an intense one-week training period in New York, where summer analysts participate in a capital markets overview, a bond math review and a library tour. You'll be trained on Bloomberg and learn Credit Suisse technology systems and databases. You'll tour the NYSE, and you'll meet with traders and salespeople from all of the various products.

Your learning experience will continue through the summer speaker series, where you'll hear from senior employees across the divisions. In addition, you'll participate in networking events, a community service project, and firmwide events that will help ensure that you are exposed to all the areas within the bank and understand the big picture of a global investment bank.

To help you determine your strengths and plan your career, summer analysts are matched with junior and senior mentors within fixed income, who provide advice and guidance throughout the summer.

Qualifications

Must be a degree candidate from a four-year college or university, who will be between junior and senior year. Candidates must also be highly motivated and creative individuals who have demonstrated academic achievement, specifically in finance, marketing and accounting courses, and have the ability to work independently and as a member of a team. Strength in verbal and written communication, and computer literacy is essential. We look for intelligent, driven and hardworking students with consistent leadership involvement in school activities and athletics, and proven interest in the financial sector arena.

Summer Analyst: Fixed Income Research

Program Structure

The experience, knowledge and commitment to serving the interests of our clients make Credit Suisse's fixed income and economics research one of the most innovative and insightful in the industry. Credit Suisse is particularly known for its excellence in global macroeconomics, strategy and foreign exchange, in both developed and emerging markets. In addition, the firm has preeminent U.S. high grade and securitized asset research.

By working with one of our widely respected senior research analysts in emerging markets, structured products, or credit research, you'll become knowledgeable about a research group and learn the fundamentals of research analysis. You will also gain exposure to other divisions of Credit Suisse including: our sales force, fixed income traders, investment bankers and institutional clients.

Training and Content

The Fixed Income Research Program provides summer analysts with the foundation necessary for a successful summer experience. It begins with an intense one-week training period in New York where summer analysts participate in a capital markets overview, a bond math review and a library tour. You'll be trained on Bloomberg and learn Credit Suisse technology systems and databases. You'll tour the NYSE, and you'll meet with traders and salespeople from all of the various products.

After your first week of training, you'll hit the ground running, working to support a variety of desks within the fixed income division. Your learning experience will continue through the summer speaker series, where you'll hear from senior employees across the divisions. In addition, you'll participate in networking events, community service and firmwide events that will help ensure that you are exposed to all the areas within the bank and understand the big picture of a global investment bank.

To help you determine your strengths and plan your career, summer analysts are matched with junior and senior mentors within fixed income, who provide advice and guidance throughout the summer. You'll also enjoy networking with the other summer analysts and full-time employees at a variety of social events throughout the summer.

Qualifications

Must be a degree candidate from a four-year college or university. Credit Suisse is noted for the diversity of its employees, but seeks candidates with a common set of abilities—highly-motivated and creative individuals who have demonstrated academic achievement, specifically in finance, marketing and accounting courses, and have the ability to work independently and as a member of a team. Strength in verbal and written communication, and computer literacy is essential to all that we do. We look for intelligent, driven and hardworking students with consistent leadership involvement in school activities and athletics, and proven interest in the financial sector arena. We look for a background in business, quantitative or economic-related fields of work or study, strong quantitative, research, writing and communication skills, and a basic understanding of capital markets and statistics. Some language skills are required for certain research groups.

Summer Analyst: Asset Finance Capital Markets

Asset finance capital markets summer analysts are investment bankers within the fixed income division (FID). As a member of the asset finance group, you will work within a team to help develop funding strategies for our clients. You'll also act as a liaison between our clients and the capital markets division, and execute transactions backed by a variety of asset classes, including auto loans, credit card receivables, home equity loans and student loans. Our clients cover many different industries and range from specialty finance firms to Fortune 500 companies.

During the 10-week program, summer analysts will have the opportunity to participate in all aspects of transaction execution: working with the client, performing due diligence, communicating with the FID trading floor and managing the accountants, rating agencies and attorneys. They will also help perform any cash flow or financial analyses involved in completing the transaction. Finally, summer analysts will support the ongoing effort to build and strengthen client relationships by preparing marketing materials to pitch the ABS product to new clients as well as presenting new ideas to current clients. Summer analyst positions are located in New York.

Training and Content

The Fixed Income Dedicated Summer Program begins with an intense one-week training period in New York where summer analysts participate in a capital markets overview, a bond math review and a library tour. You'll be trained on Bloomberg and learn Credit Suisse technology systems and databases. You'll tour the NYSE and you'll meet with traders and salespeople from all of the various products.

Your learning experience will continue through the summer speaker series, where you'll hear from senior employees across the divisions. In addition, you'll participate in networking events, a community service project and firmwide events that will help ensure that you are exposed to all the areas within the bank and understand the big picture of a global investment bank.

To help you determine your strengths and plan your career, summer analysts are matched with junior and senior mentors within fixed income, who provide advice and guidance throughout the summer.

Qualifications

Must be a degree candidate from a four-year college or university, who will be between junior and senior year. Credit Suisse is noted for the diversity of its employees, but seeks candidates with a common set of abilities—highly motivated and creative individuals who have demonstrated academic achievement, specifically in finance, marketing and accounting courses and have the ability to work independently and as a member of a team. Strength in verbal and written communication, and computer literacy is essential to all that we do. We look for intelligent, driven and hardworking students with consistent leadership involvement in school activities and athletics, and proven interest in the financial sector arena.

Application (All Positions)

In addition to applying through career services all interested candidates **MUST** complete an application on the Credit Suisse web site—www.credit-suisse.com/standout—for consideration.

Scholarships

Douglas L. Paul for Achievement

Deadline for application for the scholarship program: December
Scholarship award amount: $5,000

Credit Suisse will offer $5,000 scholarships to a number of college sophomores of African, Latino and Native American descent. Recipients of the scholarships will be selected based on their academic excellence, leadership abilities and interest in the financial services industry. In addition to monetary resources, students who receive the scholarship will have the opportunity to participate in our Wall Street Summer Immersion Program in New York. This unique 10-week placement provides students with an educational opportunity to learn about the various areas of an investment bank, with rotations in equities, fixed income and investment banking. For more information, please visit our web site at www.credit-suisse.com/standout.

Strategic Plan and Diversity Leadership

How does the firm's leadership communicate the importance of diversity to everyone at the firm?

Credit Suisse utilizes a variety of communication methods to convey the importance of diversity, including newsletters, marketing brochures, e-mail memorandums, meetings and a web site on the company Intranet.

Who has primary responsibility for leading diversity initiatives at your firm?

Angie Casciato, Managing Director, Global Head of Diversity and Inclusion

Does your firm currently have a diversity committee?

Yes.

If yes, does the committee's representation include one or more members of the firm's management/executive committee (or the equivalent)?

Yes.

If yes, how many executives are on the committee, and in 2005, what was the total number of hours collectively spent by the committee in furtherance of the firm's diversity initiatives? How many employees are on the committee, and how often does the committee convene in furtherance of the firm's diversity initiatives?

Total Executives on Committee: 13

Number of diversity meetings annually: Four to six

Does the committee and/or diversity leader establish and set goals or objectives consistent with managment's priorities?

Yes.

Has the firm undertaken a formal or informal diversity program or set of initiatives aimed at increasing the diversity of the firm?

Yes, formal.

How often does the firm's management review the firm's diversity progress/results?

Quarterly.

The Stats

Revenue (Worldwide)

2005: $ 49,600 million

Diversity Mission Statement

Credit Suisse's Global Diversity Inclusion Mission is to create an inclusive culture whereby:

• Employees' differences are valued and leveraged for the benefit of the business.
• Employees are able to realize their full potential.
• Employees are treated with dignity and respect.

Has the firm undertaken a formal or informal diversity program or set of initiatives aimed at increasing the diversity of the firm?

Yes, formal.

How often does the firm's management review the firm's diversity progress/results?

Quarterly.

The Stats

Revenue (Worldwide)

2005: $ 49,600 million

Diversity Mission Statement

Credit Suisse's Global Diversity Inclusion Mission is to create an inclusive culture whereby:

• Employees' differences are valued and leveraged for the benefit of the business.
• Employees are able to realize their full potential.
• Employees are treated with dignity and respect.

Additional Information

Credit Suisse is dedicated to attracting, developing and retaining the best people in the industry. We bring together individuals of different genders, races, ages, nationalities, religions, sexual orientations and disabilities to create a world-class team of financial service professionals.

At the core of the Credit Suisse philosophy of inclusion is the firm's Global Dignity at Work Policy—a set of conduct guidelines that apply to all employees worldwide. This policy ensures that diversity, inclusiveness and dignity in the workplace are everyone's responsibility. These enduring values are part of the very fabric of our business. They shape the way we hire, develop and promote employees, and they guide us in the way we treat one another.

CSX Corporation, Inc.

500 Water St., 15th Fl.
Jacksonville, FL 32202
Phone: (904) 359-3100
Fax: (904) 359-2459
www.CSX.com

Locations

All US/Largest Railroad in the Eastern
US/operate east of the Mississippi River
with 10 Operating Divisions in
Jacksonville, FL (HQ); including:

Albany, NY • Atlanta, GA • Baltimore,
MD • Chicago, IL • Cleveland, OH •
Florence, SC • Huntington, WVA •
Louisville, KY • Nashville, TN

Diversity Leadership

Susan O. Hamilton
AVP Diversity and EEOC
500 Water Street
Jacksonville, FL 32202
Phone: (904) 366-4092
Fax: (904) 359-3728
E-mail: Susan_Hamilton@csx.com

Recruiting

Please list the schools/types of schools at which you recruit.

We recruit at approximately 25 different colleges and universities, including several historically black schools, and have a booth every year at both the national black and national Hispanic MBA expositions (only railroad).

Do you have any special outreach efforts directed to encourage minority students to consider your firm?

• Hold a reception for minority students
• Conferences
• Advertise in minority student association publication(s)
• Participate in/host minority student job fair(s)
• Firm's employees participate on career panels at schools
• Outreach to leadership of minority student organizations
• Scholarships or intern/fellowships for minority students

What activities does the firm undertake to attract minority and women employees?

• Partner programs with women and minority associations
• Conferences
• Participate at minority job fairs
• Seek referrals from other employees
• Utilize online job services

Do you use executive recruiting/search firms to seek to identify new diversity hires?

Yes.

Internships and Co-ops

INROADS Interns

Deadline for application: April

Number of interns in the program in summer 2005 (internship) or 2005 (co-op): 25, half of which are returning interns.

Pay: We pay a $40,000 fee and a base rate of pay by department to each intern.

Length of the program: Two to three months depending on return dates for school.

We have hired 17 INROADS interns permanently over the past three years out of 29 interns.

Affinity Groups

- African-American
- Hispanic
- Working parents
- Employees caring for elderly parents
- Young professionals
- Military
- Gay/lesbian
- Women's network

Entry-Level Programs/Full-Time Opportunities/Training Programs

Management Training Program

Length of program: January/July and July/December

Geographic location(s) of program: Headquarters-based with some travel to field locations, assignments

Rotations through the company with orientations periodically.

Open to graduates, MBA graduates, successful internal candidates—we have a corporate tuition reimbursement program available to all management employees, not just new hires.

Strategic Plan and Diversity Leadership

How does the firm's leadership communicate the importance of diversity to everyone at the firm?

The CEO and his five direct reports have diversity goals in their overall performance management program. Diversity goals cascade within their organizations. Diversity is one of our core competencies.

Who has primary responsibility for leading diversity initiatives at your firm?

Susan Hamilton, senior vice president, AVP-Diversity and EEOC, reporting to Senior Vice President Bob Haulter, who reports to the CEO.

Does your firm currently have a diversity committee?

Yes. Global Diversity Council meets monthly, and there are 15 satellite diversity councils, including most operating divisions.

If yes, does the committee's representation include one or more members of the firm's management/executive committee (or the equivalent)?

Yes.

If yes, how many executives are on the committee, and in 2005, what was the total number of hours collectively spent by the committee in furtherance of the firm's diversity initiatives? How many employees are on the committee, and how often does the committee convene in furtherance of the firm's diversity initiatives?

There are 60 members, each spending a minimum of two to five hours per month.

> *Total Executives on Committee:* One senior vice president, one vice president, three division managers, one state vice president, three assistant vice presidents

Does the committee and/or diversity leader establish and set goals or objectives consistent with management's priorities?

Yes.

Has the firm undertaken a formal or informal diversity program or set of initiatives aimed at increasing the diversity of the firm?

Yes, formal.

How often does the firm's management review the firm's diversity progress/results?

Quarterly.

How is the firm's diversity committee and/or firm management held accountable for achieving results?

We report periodically to the board of directors. We have shared performance goals and shared competencies.

The Stats

Employees
2005: 2005
2004: 34,000

Revenue
2004: $8 billion

Retention and Professional Development

How do 2005 minority and female attrition rates generally compare to those experienced in the prior year period?

About the same as in prior years.

Please identify the specific steps you are taking to reduce the attrition rate of minority and women employees.

• Develop and/or support internal employee affinity groups (e.g., minority or women networks within the firm)
• Increase/review compensation relative to competition
• Increase/improve current work/life programs
• Adopt dispute resolution process

- Succession plan includes emphasis on diversity
- Work with minority and women employees to develop career advancement plans
- Review work assignments and hours billed to key client matters to make sure minority and women employees are not being excluded
- Strengthen mentoring program for all employees, including minorities and women
- Professional skills development program, including minority and women employees
- *Other:* Expanding our formal coaching/mentoring program to various field locations

Diversity Mission Statement

To embrace and value the differences of all CSX employees, while blending them into one team.

DaimlerChrysler Corporation

1000 Chrysler Dr.
Auburn Hills, MI 48326-2766
Phone: (248) 576-5741
Fax: (248) 576-4742
www.daimlerchrysler.com

Additional Information

DaimlerChrysler Corporation's Chrysler Group is a North American-based unit of DaimlerChrysler AG. At the Chrysler Group, we design, manufacture and sell vehicles under the Chrysler, Jeep® and Dodge brand names. Through our fourth brand, Mopar®, we offer original equipment and performance quality parts.

The Chrysler Group's strategy is to grow product leadership by constantly building innovative and segment-defining vehicles, and to continue to improve operating performance by leveraging the technology, purchasing and production synergies made possible by DaimlerChrysler's global reach.

DaimlerChrysler is committed to fostering an inclusive work environment where all employees are treated with dignity and respect. Our company policies and standards of conduct reinforce this commitment. In doing so, we recognize the value that diverse perspectives bring to business success in enabling innovation and robust decision making.

As stated in our corporate diversity statement and through the leadership commitment to diversity, DaimlerChrysler Corporation is proud of and committed to our diversity initiatives that create and maintain an inclusive work environment, which encourages and values teamwork. One of the greatest strengths of our company is its diversity. We value our employees for their different talents, backgrounds, cultures, experiences and lifestyles, and strive to achieve the diversity in our workplace that reflects the diversity of our customers and the communities in which we do business. Further, we are committed to encouraging diversity among our dealers, suppliers and partners throughout the business enterprise.

As such, DaimlerChrysler Corporation has a diversity council, consisting of the company's top management, which provides leadership on corporate actions and programs fostering diversity. Furthermore, DaimlerChrysler supports a rich community of diverse employee resource groups that are initiated and chartered by employees. These self-organized groups provide support and networking opportunities, such as mentoring, working in the community, career development and assisting in other activities that promote cultural awareness.

Additionally, DaimlerChrysler offers a number of programs that help employees to better balance their work and personal lives. Some examples of these programs include a resource and referral program, discounted child care and home services providers, a no-cost employee assistance program and flexible work arrangements.

From our cadres of diverse designers, engineers and staff to the men and women on the factory floor to our network of dealers and suppliers, we're dedicated to creating the best cars and trucks possible. To find out about more about DaimlerChrysler and career opportunities throughout its facilities, visit us at www.careers.chrysler-group.com.

Daymon Worldwide, Inc.

200 Fairfield Ave.
Stamford, CT 06902
Phone: (203) 352-7500
www.daymon.com

Locations

China • Czech Republic • England •
Germany • Hong Kong • Indonesia •
Japan • Malaysia • New Zealand •
Portugal • Singapore • South Africa •
South Korea • Taiwan • plus 30+ states
in the US

Diversity Leadership

Clint Sollenberger
Director of Talent Management
Daymon Worldwide
700 Fairfield Ave
Stamford, CT 06902
Phone: (203) 352-7500
Fax: (203) 352-7947

Recruiting

Please list the schools/types of schools at which you recruit.

- Ivy League schools
- Public state schools
- Other private schools
- Historically Black Colleges and Universities (HBCUs)

Do you have any special outreach efforts directed to encourage minority students to consider your firm?

- Scholarships or intern/fellowships for minority students
- *Other:* Seek referrals from current Daymon employees

What activities does the firm undertake to attract minority and women employees?

Partner programs with women and minority associations.

Do you use executive recruiting/search firms to seek to identify new diversity hires?

Yes.

Internships and Co-ops

INROADS

Deadline for application: March/April
Number of interns in the program in summer 2005 (internship) or 2005 (co-op): 11 interns
Length of the program: Eight to 12 weeks
Percentage of interns/co-ops in the program who receive offers of full-time employment: 75-100 percent (depending on performance and fit)

The goal of Daymon's internship program is to expose interns to as much of the business as possible and to help them find an area that piques their interest. The internship positions are project-based and can be found in our field locations, HR, finance, IT and many other departments in the organization, including the executive branch. Candidates for our program must possess the following competencies to be successful in this role: strategic agility, drive for results, priority setting, interpersonal savvy, customer focus, business acumen, informing and personal learning.

Entry-Level Programs/Full-Time Opportunities/Training Programs

Management Development Program

Length of program: One year
Geographic location(s) of program: Throughout the country

Three-month rotations in different areas of the business.

Strategic Plan and Diversity Leadership

How does the firm's leadership communicate the importance of diversity to everyone at the firm?

• Communication with senior management to incorporate into business units
• Regular articles in company's daily online news publication and quarterly newsletter
• Company-wide quarterly conference calls
• New associate orientations

Who has primary responsibility for leading diversity initiatives at your firm?

Kelly Bruce, general manager.

Does your firm currently have a diversity committee?

Yes.

If yes, please describe how the committee is structured, how often it meets, etc.

The council is comprised of a chair, a vice chair, a vice president liaison, 13 members and numerous project participants throughout the company. The executive sponsors of the council are the company's president and human resources vice president. Currently, the council members are located in three countries, and so meetings are held via conference call once a month. Subcommittees are formed for each project, and those teams meet on a calendar determined by each project lead. Projects are defined and then the appropriate research is conducted to provide a recommendation to the company with regard to the specific initiative. The executive sponsors review the recommendations and present them to the officer group for consideration.

If yes, does the committee's representation include one or more members of the firm's management/executive committee (or the equivalent)?

Yes.

If yes, how many executives are on the committee?

Total Executives on Committee: Four—two executive sponsors, one vice president liaison and one member who is a vice president.

Does the committee and/or diversity leader establish and set goals or objectives consistent with management's priorities?

Yes.

Has the firm undertaken a formal or informal diversity program or set of initiatives aimed at increasing the diversity of the firm?

Yes, formal: Diversity Metrics or Measures.

How often does the firm's management review the firm's diversity progress/results?

Quarterly.

The Stats

U.S. Employees

2005: 1,446
2004: 1558

Worldwide Employees

2005: 10,700
2004: 11,000

Retention and Professional Development

How do 2005 minority and female attrition rates generally compare to those experienced in the prior year period?

About the same as in previous years.

Please identify the specific steps you are taking to reduce the attrition rate of minority and women employees.

• Develop and/or support internal employee affinity groups (e.g., minority or women networks within the firm)
• Succession plan includes emphasis on diversity
• Strengthen mentoring program for all employees, including minorities and women
• Professional skills development program, including minority and women employees

Diversity Mission Statement

Daymon Worldwide is a global company working in diverse markets and with diverse customers. Our company's motto of "Noble, Profitable and Fun" states our first value as being noble. Our company's greatest asset has always been—and will always be—our associates. Continuing to respect and support the diversity of our associates will increase the value of our company and will always be our greatest opportunity for growth as a business and as individuals. Our commitment to our associates and principals also extends to the communities where we conduct business and we strive to be a responsible and contributing member.

Deloitte & Touche USA LLP

1633 Broadway
New York, NY 10019-6754
Phone: (212) 489-1600
Fax: (212) 489-1687

Locations

See web site for complete listing of all
office locations.

Employment Contact

Kaplan Mobray
U.S. Diversity Recruiting Leader
1633 Broadway
New York, NY 10019
Phone: (212) 492-4680
Fax: (212) 653-4059
E-mail: kmobray@deloitte.com
www.deloitte.com/careers

Recruiting

Please list the schools/types of schools at which you recruit.

• Ivy League schools
• Other private schools
• Public state schools
• Historically Black Colleges and Universities (HBCUs)
• Hispanic Serving Institutions (HSIs)
• Native American Tribal Universities
• Other predominantly minority and/or women's colleges

We actively recruit at over 250 colleges and universities across the United States including many HBCUs and HSIs.

Do you have any special outreach efforts directed to encourage minority students to consider your firm?

• Hold a reception for minority students
• *Conferences:* NABA, ALPFA, NBMBA, NSHMBA, ReachingOUT MBA, NSBE, SHPE, CGSM
• Advertise in minority student association publication(s)
• Participate in/host minority student job fair(s)
• Sponsor minority student association events
• Firm's employees participate on career panels at schools
• Outreach to leadership of minority student organizations
• *Scholarships or intern/fellowships for minority students:* INROADS, Jackie Robinson Foundation, Thurgood Marshall Foundation, Future Leaders Apprentice Program
• *Other:* Southeast Case Study Program in conjunction with HBCUs, host Diversity and Professional Development Forums, Monster Diversity Leadership Program

What activities does the firm undertake to attract minority and women employees?

• *Partner programs with women and minority associations:* INROADS, HACE, ALPFA, NABA, Consortium of Graduate Studies in Management (CGSM)
• *Conferences:* NABA, ALPFA, NSHMBA, NBMBAA, NSBE, NAWMBA, ReachingOut MBA, SHPE, CGSM
• Participate at minority job fairs
• Seek referrals from other employees
• Utilize online job services

• *Other:* Deloitte National Leadership Conference (takes place in July). Over 450 students attend this three-day leadership and networking program. See web site for more details: http://careers.deloitte.com/students_internships.aspx

Do you use executive recruiting/search firms to seek to identify new diversity hires?
Yes.

Internships and Co-ops

Consulting Summer Scholars

The overall internship program takes place during winter and summer.

> *Deadline for application:* Ongoing/varies
> *Number of interns in the program in summer 2005 (internship) or 2005 (co-op):* 2,000 interns
> *Pay:* Varies by program and location
> *Length of the program:* 10-12 weeks
> *Percentage of interns/co-ops in the program who receive offers of full-time employment:* 90 percent
> *Web site for internship/co-op information:* http://careers.deloitte.com/students_internships.aspx

Departments:

• Deloitte & Touche LLP—audit and enterprise risk services (summer and winter internship opportunities)
• Deloitte Consulting LLP—Summer Scholars Program; systems analysts, business analysts and human capital analysts
• Deloitte Financial Advisory Services LLP—summer intern opportunities available within forensic and dispute services
• Deloitte Tax LLP—summer and winter intern opportunities available in over 10 tax specialty areas
• Deloitte Services LP—intern and co-op opportunities available year-round within office services and technology, human resources, and clients and markets

Qualifications/Responsibilities:

• Strong analytical skills
• Team player
• Demonstrated leadership in extra-curricular activities
• Mature interpersonal relationship and communication skills
• Strong performance in major field of study

Our goal is to provide our interns with a meaningful and hands-on experience giving them insight into a career in professional services. You will play a pivotal role with responsibilities that range from analyzing client issues and interviewing key personnel to developing recommendations and preparing presentations. You will be part of an active collaborative engagement team providing our clients with solutions that are practical as well as visionary. Your internship will enhance your teaming and networking skills as you will participate in a number of team-building activities and office-wide meetings.

Please see our career site for specific job description information: http://careers.deloitte.com/students_internships.aspx

Scholarships

Deloitte Future Leaders Apprentice Program

> *Deadline for application for the scholarship program:* Ongoing
> *Scholarship award amount:* Ranges from $2,500-$10,000 for entire award

The Deloitte Future Leaders Apprentice Program (FLAP) is a pre-packaged entry-level leadership development program and recruiting tool to attract high potential campus and experienced minority candidates to the organization. The program consists of three components: mentorship, scholarship award and customized leadership and professional development training. Candidates will also gain exposure to senior leadership at the Deloitte U.S. firms via informal and formally scheduled networking opportunities. We also provide scholarships through specific colleges/universities and organizations, including ALPFA and NABA.

Affinity Groups

- BEN—Black Employee Network
- AAA—Asian-America Alliance
- HNET—Association of Hispanic and Latino Employees
- GLOBE—Gay, Lesbian, Bisexual Employees
- International BRG—International Network
- DPN—Deloitte Parenting Networking
- WIN—Women's Initiative

For all Affinity Groups:

- Open to all people, in all businesses
- Key driver in delivering our diversity and inclusion initiative
- Part of the larger strategy to create a more inclusive culture by promoting a sense of community around a core identity
- Influencing themselves, influencing the organization, influencing the community
- Professional development
- Foster career advancement through coaching and mentoring
- Enhance effectiveness of employees at work
- Increase interaction across functional areas and work groups
- Recruitment and retention
- Provide feedback mechanisms
- Targeted recruiting efforts
- Community service
- Help direct community involvement strategy
- Increase activities/projects of interest
- Professional networks
- Attendance and sponsorship of professional associations tied to business resource group (e.g. ALPFA & NABA)

Entry-Level Programs/Full-Time Opportunities/Training Programs

Efficacy Development: Maximizing Your Professional and Personal Development

Length of program: One-and-a-half days
Geographic location(s) of program: Held in conjunction with key professional association conferences (i.e., NABA, ALPFA, NBMBA), thus in various parts of the United States

The seminar will allow participants to develop:

- An awareness of obstacles that can impede peak performance
- Sharpened skills and explore the use of feedback for continuous professional improvement
- Effective networking strategies for career management

Breakthrough Leadership Program (BLP)

Length of Program: Eight-month program
Geographic location(s) of the program: Held in various locations across the United States

Comprehensive minority leadership development program for top-performing managers and senior managers from all of our businesses. BLP components include face-to-face training, various self-assessments, 360-degree feedback and one-on-one coaching.

Howard University School of Business Center for Accounting Leadership Development Program for African-Americans/Blacks

Length of Program: One-week program
Geographic location(s) of the program: Held at Howard University

Participants receive support for the CPA exam and informal networking opportunities with key leaders from the profession and industry.

Ellen P. Gabriel Fellows Program

Geographic location(s) of the program: Held in various locations across the United States

Participants are senior managers who work on special projects of strategic significance for the organization, attend a leadership development seminar facilitated by Columbia University and visit the Institute for the Future in Silicon Valley.

Strategic Plan and Diversity Leadership

How does the firm's leadership communicate the importance of diversity to everyone at the firm?

- Briefings by management, both Deloitte & Touche USA LLP CEO and individual-function-specific subsidiary CEOs to respective audiences/employees
- Creation of the "Think Tank" committee by National Diversity Center and chaired by the U.S. managing partner. This is comprised of 12 members chosen by business leadership program (one-year term). The scope of the issues to be addressed focus on enhancing a more inclusive environment that supports our strategic choice of "Where the Best Choose to Be."
- Identify and discuss merits of key organizational issues, provides forward thinking with provocative, proactive, thoughtful, solutions and recommendations that will positively impact our business
- U.S. managing partner on regional office visits
- Intranet diversity site, national Intranet news stories and Intranet news stories on individual function/business sites
- Recruitment marketing that delivers a consistent message of our brand and message
- Direct communications (e-mail and in person) to business resource groups (affinity groups), as well as, from employees groups to employees via local events
- New hire orientation on-boarding
- E-brochures or fliers on diversity and specific programs
- National partner/principal/director meeting

Who has primary responsibility for leading diversity initiatives at your firm?

Redia Anderson Banks, chief diversity officer, principal, diversity and inclusion initiative.

Does your firm currently have a diversity committee?

Yes.

If yes, please describe how the committee is structured, how often it meets, etc.

The national diversity and inclusion council is composed of representatives from each geographic region and business unit. The council meets face-to-face on a quarterly basis and in between these meetings via conference calls.

If yes, does the committee's representation include one or more members of the firm's management/executive committee?

Yes.

If yes, how many executives are on the committee, and in 2005, what was the total number of hours collectively spent by the committee in furtherance of the firm's diversity initiatives? How many employees are on the committee, and how often does the committee convene in furtherance of the firm's diversity initiatives?

All representatives on the council are partners/principals/directors. Each representative is responsible for executing his or her respective D&I plan, which is in alignment with the overall organization's D&I strategy. There are 14 members on the council plus four members from the National Diversity Center.

Does the committee and/or diversity leader establish and set goals or objectives consistent with management's priorities?

Yes, the organization's diversity and inclusion strategy is in alignment with our people strategy, which is one of the organization's strategic choices.

Has the firm undertaken a formal or informal diversity program or set of initiatives aimed at increasing the diversity of the firm?

Yes, formal.

How often does the firm's management review the firm's diversity progress/results?

Quarterly.

How is the firm's diversity committee and/or firm management held accountable for achieving results?

Each regional and business unit has a D&I scorecard with specific goals/objectives and metrics for measuring success, which is monitored on a quarterly basis. As part of the individual's performance review, it is a factor considered.

The Stats

Number of employees (employees, partners and principals)

Total in the U.S. 2005/2004: 33,000

Revenue

Total in the U.S. 2005/2004: $7.81 billion

2005 U.S. DEMOGRAPHIC PROFILE (INCLUDES PARTNERS/PRINCIPALS AND EMPLOYEES)				
MINORITY REPRESENTATION	WOMEN REPRESENTATION	MINORITY HIRES	WOMEN HIRES	2005 BOARD OF DIRECTORS
29.3 percent	45.1 percent	39.2 percent	46.2 percent	27.3 percent women, nine percent minority representation

Retention and Professional Development

How do 2005 minority and female attrition rates generally compare to those experienced in the prior year period?

Lower than in prior years.

Please identify the specific steps you are taking to reduce the attrition rate of minority and women employees.

• Develop and/or support internal employee affinity groups (e.g., minority or women networks within the firm)
• Increase/review compensation relative to competition
• Increase/improve current work/life programs
• Adopt dispute resolution process
• Succession plan includes emphasis on diversity
• Work with minority and women employees to develop career advancement plans
• *Other:* Review work assignments and hours billed to key client matters to make sure minority and women employees are not being excluded
• Strengthen mentoring program for all employees, including minorities and women
• Professional skills development program, including minority and women employees
• Other

Diversity Mission Statement

Our mission is to help our people and our clients benefit from a strong and active commitment to diversity and inclusion in the workplace and global marketplace.

Additional Information

With businesses like ours, which are so inextricably linked to the attraction, development and retention of intellectual capital, an inclusive and inviting culture is absolutely essential to our success. How so? Great talent in all parts of our businesses drives our growth, profitability and marketplace success.

For us, there is simply no better way to attract, retain and develop the best and brightest talent than with a culture that is widely recognized for encouraging personal and professional growth, inviting different perspectives and valuing individual contributions. Over the past year, that is exactly where our diversity and inclusion efforts have been centered.

Our diversity and inclusion initiative supports Deloitte & Touche USA LLP and its subsidiaries (U.S. firms) people strategy to develop, deploy, and connect our people. We have three overarching goals: talent pipeline management: Create a robust and diverse talent pipeline to successfully position the U.S. firms for a long and profitable future.

• In 2005 we saw representation and recruitment numbers go up and attrition numbers go down.
• We admitted and promoted more minority candidates to the partnerships and director level than ever before.
• We increased the percentage of minority new hires.

Professional development: create opportunities for all of our people to increase their knowledge and skills.

• Launched breakthrough leadership program, a comprehensive minority development program for high-potential, top-performing managers and senior managers from all our business.
• Continued to provide the efficacy development seminar: Maximizing Your Professional and Personal Development.
• Launched our new e-learning course: Diversity & Inclusion: Bottom Line Impact.

Culture/inclusion: continue to foster an inclusive culture with policies, practices, and behaviors that value all of our people.

• Business resource groups: More than 50 chapters in local offices across the U.S. firms
• Asian BRG (ABRG)
• Black Employee Network (BEN)
• Deloitte Parents Network (DPN)
• Gay, Lesbian, or Bisexual Employees (GLOBE)
• Hispanic/Latino Network (Hnet)
• International BRG (IBRG)
•Women's Initiative (WIN)

DENTSPLY International

World Headquarters
Susquehanna Commerce Center
221 W. Philadelphia Street
P. O. Box 872
York, PA 17405 - 0872
Phone: (800) 877-0020

Locations
22

Diversity Leadership
Ernest H. White
Manager
Corporate Diversity and Sales Staffing
DENTSPLY International Inc.
www.dentsply.com/careers

Recruiting

Please list the schools/types of schools at which you recruit.

- Other private schools
- Public state schools
- Historically Black Colleges and Universities (HBCUs)
- Other predominantly minority and/or women's colleges

Do you have any special outreach efforts directed to encourage minority students to consider your firm?

- Hold a reception for minority students
- Participate in/host minority student job fair(s)
- Firm's employees participate on career panels at schools
- Outreach to leadership of minority student organizations

What activities does the firm undertake to attract minority and women employees?

- Partner programs with women and minority associations
- Seek referrals from other employees
- Utilize online job services

Do you use executive recruiting/search firms to seek to identify new diversity hires?

Yes.

Strategic Plan and Diversity Leadership

Who has primary responsibility for leading diversity initiatives at your firm?

Ernest H. White

Does your firm currently have a diversity committee?

Yes.

If yes, does the committee's representation include one or more members of the firm's management/executive committee (or the equivalent)?

Yes.

How often does the firm's management review the firm's diversity progress/results?

Quarterly.

The Stats

Employees

2005: 3,600 (U.S. Employees)
2005: 3,800 (Employees outside the U.S.)
2005: 7,200 (Worldwide Employees)

Revenue

2005: $1,715.13 million

Retention and Professional Development

How do 2005 minority and female attrition rates generally compare to those experienced in the prior year period?

About the same as in prior years.

Please identify the specific steps you are taking to reduce the attrition rate of minority and women employees.

• Develop and/or support internal employee affinity groups (e.g., minority or women networks within the firm)
• Increase/review compensation relative to competition
• Increase/improve current work/life programs
• Adopt dispute resolution process
• Succession plan includes emphasis on diversity
• Work with minority and women employees to develop career advancement plans
• Review work assignments and hours billed to key client matters to make sure minority and women employees are not being excluded
• Strengthen mentoring program for all employees, including minorities and women
• Professional skills development program, including minority and women employees

Diversity Mission Statement

As the global leader in our industry we understand the significance and importance of setting the industry standard in all that we do. This includes fostering an environment that puts our differences to work in the marketplace and in our communities. Our Employee CARE Program is designed to be a sequential program that, when fully engaged, drives the recruitment, development and retention of talent—supporting an environment that values and benefits from the differences our employees bring to the workplace to fully participate in our business success.

Dominion

Dominion
120 Tredegar Street
Richmond VA 23219

Locations

Richmond (HQ)
Cleveland, OH • Houston, TX • New Orleans, LA • Oklahoma City, OK • Pittsburgh, PA

Diversity Leadership

Teri Taylor
HR Consultant—Diversity

Employment Contact

Lucy Rothnie
College Recruiter
POB 26532
Richmond, VA 23261-6532
Phone: (804) 771-6208
Fax: (804) 771-4843
E-mail: lucy_rothnie@dom.com
www.dom.com/jobs/index.jsp

Recruiting

Please list the schools/types of schools at which you recruit.

• Private schools
• Public state schools
• Historically Black Colleges and Universities (HBCUs)

Do you have any special outreach efforts directed to encourage minority students to consider your firm?

Dominion actively participates in the career fairs of many HBCUs and the student chapters of professional organizations such as the National Society of Black Engineers and the Society of Women Engineers. Building stronger relationships with HBCUs is a priority for our company and we support many, either directly or through our support of the United Negro College Fund. Dominion is also a supporter of the annual Black Engineer of the Year Award conference where, in 2005, one of our executives won the Black Engineer of the Year Award in Career Achievement. For the past three years, an annual survey by *U.S. Black Engineer & Information Technology Magazine* has named Dominion as one of the private-sector organizations considered most supportive of the nation's historically black engineering schools.

Internships and Co-ops

Dominion Internship/Co-op Program

Pay: Amount varies based on assignment

Length of program: Generally, 10-12 weeks during the summer. Students may also have the option to work during breaks in the regular school year.

Percentage of interns/co-ops in the programs who receive offers of full-time employment: Currently, 40 percent of students eligible to graduate in 2006 have accepted full-time positions with Dominion.

Web site for internship/co-op information: www.dom.com/jobs/intern.jsp

Dominion's intern program engages college or college-bound students for paid work sessions that involve projects or assignments closely related to the student's area of study. Work experiences generally are not required for college credit, nor required to satisfy degree or graduation requirements.

Work sessions are structured, supervised, professional and relate to the student's area of study. These experiences allow students to sharpen their skills, develop a network of contacts, assess their strengths and test classroom theories in real world settings.

In addition to working during school semesters or summer breaks, intern opportunities may include working during other school breaks or on a part-time basis while attending school, if the company has opportunities available.

Students must maintain a GPA of 2.5/4.0 or above and must be currently enrolled in and attending a four-year university.

Scholarships

Dominion Diversity Scholarship Program

Deadline for application for the scholarship program: February 15th of each year
Scholarship award amount: Currently $2,000 per year, in additional to salary during summer work sessions
Web site or other contact information for scholarship: www.dom.com/jobs/dsp.jsp

The Diversity Scholarship Program (DSP) was initially offered in 1988 as part of the company's commitment to equal opportunity and affirmative action. The DSP served as a recruiting tool to motivate minorities to pursue careers in engineering and other professions. Dominion is proud to continue to offer this unique opportunity and to expand the program to be more inclusive. The focus of the scholarship has changed from strictly seeking minority applicants to seeking candidates from more diverse backgrounds. Acceptance of the scholarship will require that the student agree to a 10-week work session during each summer of their eligibility. Interested students are encouraged to visit our diversity scholarship web page at www.dom.com/jobs/dsp.jsp, where they can learn more about the program, and watch interviews with current interns and co-op students.

At the time of application, students must satisfy the following requirements:

• All applicants must currently have a 3.5 GPA or above on a 4.0 scale.
• All applicants must be enrolled or accepted for enrollment as a full-time student for the current academic year.
• At the time of applying, college applicants must be either a freshman or sophomore in a four-year program at an accredited institution. (If a student is pursuing a degree program that requires more than five years to complete, participation will be evaluated on a case-by-case basis.)
• Current high school applicants must have applied for admission as a full-time student at an accredited college or university. (Currently, preference is given to students pursuing degrees in engineering, geology, petrotechnology or related degrees.)
• Applicants must be eligible to work in the U.S.

Strategic Plan and Diversity Leadership

How does the firm's leadership communicate the importance of diversity to everyone at the firm?

Dominion's leadership communicates the importance of diversity using a variety of methods. Our internal newsmagazine *Connect* regularly features articles that discuss various aspects of diversity at Dominion. Recent topics have included generations in the workplace, supplier diversity at Dominion, the impact of our community relationships on our workforce diversity commitment, and Dominion's overall diversity strategy. Our employee diversity councils publish newsletters and regularly update bulletin boards at our various locations with diversity-related news. The diversity and staffing team supports our leadership team with diversity-related data and research designed to assist them with meeting their business goals.

We also utilize our internal and external web pages to communicate specifics about our diversity initiatives. Our online multicultural calendar (www.dom.com/about/education/culture/index.jsp) features multicultural holiday information while highlighting some of our talented Dominion employees.

Who has primary responsibility for leading diversity initiatives at your firm?

Anne M. Grier, vice president of human resources.

Does your firm currently have a diversity committee?

Yes, Dominion has diversity councils at two levels. First, we have our Executive Diversity Council consisting of vice presidents, senior vice presidents, directors and key contributors from each line of business and key business areas including:

• Finance
• Supplier diversity
• Corporate communications
• Human resources
• External affairs

The Executive Diversity Council meets quarterly and is charged with the development and evaluation of Dominion's diversity strategic initiatives. The work of the Executive Diversity Council is important to our President and CEO, Tom Farrell, who has established his expectation for the council.

Secondly, we have employee diversity councils in several of our business locations. Those councils consist of 15-20 employees from diverse backgrounds and work areas, union represented and nonunion represented, management and nonmanagement. The employee diversity councils meet monthly and support the work of the executive council through grassroots diversity-related activities. Participation is voluntary and each employee council has an executive sponsor who sits on the executive diversity council.

If yes, does the committee's representation include one or more members of the firm's management/executive committee (or the equivalent)?

Yes.

If yes, how many executives are on the committee, and in 2005, what was the total number of hours collectively spent by the committee in furtherance of the firm's diversity initiatives? How many employees are on the committee, and how often does the committee convene in furtherance of the firm's diversity initiatives?

Total executives on committee: 15 of the 19 members are company executives

Does the committee and/or diversity leader establish and set goals or objectives consistent with management's priorities?

Yes.

Has the firm undertaken a formal or informal diversity of set of initiatives aimed at increasing the diversity of the firm?

Yes.

Dominion's workforce diversity strategy focuses on four key areas:

• Visible leadership
• Recruitment and retention
• Communication and education
• Measurement and accountability

We believe that success in each of these areas is critical to our ability to manage diversity effectively. Each focus area has a series of supporting initiatives. Recently updated, our diversity strategy has been communicated to all members of the organization through a series of articles in our internal newsmagazine, *Connect*.

How often does the firm's management review the firm's diversity progress/results?

Quarterly.

Retention and Professional Development

How do minority and female attrition rates generally compare to those experienced in the prior year period?

About the same.

Please identify the specific steps you are taking to reduce the attrition rate of minority and women employees.

• Increase/review compensation relative to competition
• Increase/improve current work/life programs
• Succession plan includes emphasis on diversity
• Work with minority and women employees to develop career advancement plans
• Strengthen mentoring program for all employees, including minority and women employees

Diversity Mission Statement

Dominion's Philosophy

Valuing people creates and reinforces an inclusive, creative and productive environment in which each employee feels accepted, respected and believes it is possible to achieve his/her fullest potential.

Additional Information

Dominion recognizes the value of the diversity of its employees and considers it one of our organizational strengths. We consider diversity beyond those human characteristics that are easily seen to include those factors which are not so readily apparent: disability, education, ethnic background, sexual orientation, socioeconomic status, geographic region, to name a few.

Dominion is committed to creating and reinforcing an inclusive, creative and productive environment in which each employee feels accepted, respected and believes it is possible to achieve his/her fullest potential. We also believe in shared goals and a common vision, which guide the efforts of all employees.

Dominion's strategy for workforce diversity focuses on four key areas:

• Visible leadership
• Recruitment and retention
• Communication and education
• Measurement and accountability

Each is critical to our ability to achieve the inclusive environment that we aspire to. Our Executive Diversity Council has primary responsibility for the corporate strategy.

It is the responsibility of each subsidiary and the Dominion Services Company to adopt action plans reflecting these principles and to incorporate diversity initiatives into ongoing business plans. This sound business practice will assist us in maintaining our position as an industry leader.

Successfully managing the diversity of our workforce is not the responsibility of one person or one area. Each employee's contribution to these efforts is essential to our success in this area.

Domino's Pizza, Inc.

Domino's Pizza, Inc.
30 Frank Lloyd Wright Drive
Ann Arbor, MI 48106
Phone: (734) 930-3030

Locations

Ann Arbor, MI (HQ)
Atlanta, GA • Baltimore, MD • Los
Angeles, CA • Phoenix, AZ

Employment Contact

Jodi Royse
30 Frank Lloyd Wright Drive
Ann Arbor, MI 48336
Phone: (734) 930-3039
Fax: (866) 268-9119
E-mail: roysej@dominos.com
www.dominos.com

Recruiting

Please list the schools/types of schools at which you recruit.

- Private schools
- Public state schools
- Historically Black Colleges and Universities (HBCUs)
- Hispanic Serving Institutions (HSIs)

Do you have any special outreach efforts directed to encourage minority students to consider your firm?

- Advertise in minority student association publication(s)
- Participate in/host minority student job fair(s)
- Sponsor minority student association events
- Firm's employees participate on career panels at schools
- Outreach to leadership of minority student organizations

What activities does the firm undertake to attract minority and women employees?

- Participate at minority job fairs
- Seek referrals from other employees
- Utilize online job services

Do you use executive recruiting/search firms to seek to identify new diversity hires?

No.

Internships and Co-ops

Deadline for application: April 1st
Number of interns in the program in summer 2005 (internship): 20
Pay: $12
Length of the program: 16 weeks
Percentage of interns/co-ops in the program who receive offers of full-time employment: 60 percent
Web site for internship/co-op information: www.dominos.com

The Domino's Pizza Summer Internship Program is designed with the following objectives for students:

- Gain business experience in chosen field
- Have an opportunity to use their skills and expand their current skills
- Expand knowledge of a particular field of expertise
- Explore career options at Domino's
- Build their personal network

Not only does the Summer Internship Program at Domino's allow students to build on their professional skills, the program also includes a variety of activities to enhance their professional career, including lunch and learns with all executives (including the CEO), interviewing and resume building workshops, company sponsored events (NASCAR racing, rock-climbing and other fun events), etiquette education dinners, etc.

The Summer Internship Program includes opportunities in the following disciplines:

- Marketing
- Human resources
- Information services
- Accounting
- Finance
- Communications
- Management
- Supply chain management

Affinity Groups

It has been proven that company performance is strongly linked to the ability to successfully attract, retain and develop a diverse team member population. Team member forums are a venue to accomplish this; therefore Domino's Pizza supports the formation and operation of team member forums as well as welcomes and values the ideas and contributions of all team members.

Team member forums are groups of employees with common interests or backgrounds that share insights, different perspectives and contribute to each other's professional development as well as the company's mission.

Key focus areas for employee forums:

- Employee development—provide personal and professional development and informal networking opportunities to team members.

- Workplace Insight—as subcommittees of the diversity team, provide viewpoints on company policies and workplace issues to aid our expansion into traditionally under-represented communities in ways such as recruiting, employment practices and policies and marketing.

Entry-Level Programs/Full-Time Opportunities/Training Programs

Domino's Pizza Leadership Development Program

Length of program: 12-18 months
Geographic location(s) of program: Nationwide

Domino's Pizza recognizes that to be "best in class" and maintain our position as the world leader in the pizza delivery industry, we need to have exceptional leaders. To prepare and develop future leaders, a development program, known as "Project People Pipeline" was established.

The purpose of the people pipeline is to:

- Recruit and select early-career, high-potential team members

- Establish a rotational development program
- Provide broad organizational, business and leadership training
- Prepare for future leadership positions within Domino's Pizza
- Ensure workplace readiness, cross-functional knowledge and advanced leadership training to team members, who will provide immediate value to the company

During the program, the candidate will be fully integrated into new positions in a series of rotational assignments. Company-sponsored relocation to various business sites will be required in conjunction with completing various assignments. The assignments may include positions in the following areas of the business:

- Corporate store operations
- Finance and accounting
- Human resources
- Information services
- Marketing
- Public relations/communications
- Distribution/purchasing
- International
- Legal

Job responsibilities and objectives are established for each assignment and the candidate receives performance evaluations upon completion of each assignment. Typical position assignments are approximately six months in duration. The candidate will complete four to five various position assignments while in the people pipeline.

In addition to completing assignments, the candidate is also provided with leadership and organizational training defined in a customized plan known as a "Learning Map." Mentors are assigned to aid in the development of the candidate. In addition the candidate will complete leadership assessments during the program.

Each People Pipeline Program candidate graduates from the program once he/she has successfully completed all assignments and courses identified in the learning map, in approximately 18 to 24 months. The leadership team and PeopleFirst then work together to identify a permanent position for the candidate upon completion of the program that utilizes the skills, talents, interests and experiences gained throughout the program.

Strategic Plan and Diversity Leadership

How does the firm's leadership communicate the importance of diversity to everyone at the firm?

Company web site, company meetings and targeted events.

Who has primary responsibility for leading diversity initiatives at your firm?

Alexandra Rozema, talent management director.

Does your firm currently have a diversity committee?

Yes.

If yes, please describe how the committee is structured, how often it meets, etc.

The diversity committee is made up of members of the executive team who meet quarterly to review progress on diversity initiatives in the organization.

If yes, does the committee's representation include one or more members of the firm's management/executive committee (or the equivalent)?

Yes.

If yes, how many executives are on the committee, and in 2005, what was the total number of hours collectively spent by the committee in furtherance of the firm's diversity initiatives? How many employees are on the committee, and how often does the committee convene in furtherance of the firm's diversity initiatives?

Eleven executives are in the committee and in 2005 the total hours spent furthering Domino's diversity initiatives was 30. Subgroups of the committee meet monthly—this included over 40 team members in 2005.

Does the committee and/or diversity leader establish and set goals or objectives consistent with management's priorities?

Yes.

Has the firm undertaken a formal or informal diversity program or set of initiatives aimed at increasing the diversity of the firm?

Yes, formal.

How often does the firm's management review the firm's diversity progress/results?

Quarterly.

How is the firm's diversity committee and/or firm management held accountable for achieving results?

These objectives are part of the business plan and measured through our performance appraisal process.

The Stats

	TOTAL IN THE U.S.		TOTAL OUTSIDE THE U.S		TOTAL WORLDWIDE	
	2006	2005	2006	2005	2006	2005
Number of employees	13,500	13,300	250	230	13,750	13,530
Revenue	$1.38 billion	$1.33 billion	$129.6 million	$117 million	$1.51 billion	$1.4 billion

Breakdown of revenue:

Domestic franchise: $161.9 million
Domestic company-owned stores: $401.0 million
Domestic distribution: $819.1 million
International: $129.6 million

Retention and Professional Development

How do 2005 minority and female attrition rates generally compare to those experienced in the prior year period?

About the same as in prior years.

Please identify the specific steps you are taking to reduce the attrition rate of minority and women employees.

• Develop and/or support internal employee affinity groups (e.g., minority or women networks within the firm)
• Increase/improve current work/life programs
• Succession plan includes emphasis on diversity
• Professional skills development program, including minority and women employees

Diversity Mission Statement

Domino's Pizza is committed to an inclusive culture that values the contributions of our customers, team members, suppliers, and neighbors.

Duke Energy Corporation

526 S. Church St
Charlotte, NC 28202-1803
Phone: (704) 594-6200
Fax: (704) 382-3814
www.duke-energy.com/careers/welcome/

Locations
US:
Charlotte, NC • Cincinnati, OH • Houston, TX • Denver, CO
International:
Australia • Canada

Diversity Leadership
Richard T. Williams
Vice President of Talent Management and Diversity

Employment Contact
Lynetta Chisolm
Director of Staffing and Recruiting
400 S. Tryon Street
Charlotte, NC 28201
Phone: (704) 382-3412
Fax: (704) 260-5352
E-mail: lschisol@duke_energy.com
www.duke-energy.com/careers/recruiting

Recruiting

Please list the schools/types of schools at which you recruit.

- Ivy League schools
- Other private schools
- Public state schools
- Historically Black Colleges and Universities (HBCUs)

Do you have any special outreach efforts directed to encourage minority students to consider your firm?

- Hold a reception for minority students
- Advertise in minority student association publication(s)
- Participate in/host minority student job fair(s)
- Sponsor minority student association events
- Firm's employees participate on career panels at schools
- Outreach to leadership of minority student organizations
- Scholarships or intern/fellowships for minority students

What activities does the firm undertake to attract minority and women employees?

- Partner programs with women and minority associations
- *Conferences:* NSBE, SWE, NABA, SHPE, ALPFA
- Participate at minority job fairs
- Seek referrals from other employees
- *Other:* Strategies vary from year to year based on needs, but may include attendance at conferences for networking purposes and the possible use of online services

Do you use executive recruiting/search firms to seek to identify new diversity hires?

Yes.

Internships and Co-ops

Co-op/Internship Program

Deadline for application: Currently we have no set deadlines, but post jobs at the schools when needed

Number of interns in the program in summer 2005 (internship) or 2005 (co-op): 18 interns; 187 co-op

Pay: Hourly, based on degree major and completed coursework

Length of the program: Approximately 12 weeks

Percentage of interns/co-ops in the program who receive offers of full-time employment: 10 percent

INROADS

Deadline for application: Determined by INROADS.

Pay: Hourly, based on degree major and completed coursework. Students are paid bi-weekly

Length of the program: Approximately 12 weeks

Percentage of interns/co-ops in the program who receive offers of full-time employment: Not applicable at this time. For Charlotte, it depends on the number of opportunities, we use our interns/co-ops as a pipeline for our openings, but we look at all of our interns as a recruiting tool.

Web site for internship/co-op information: www.duke-energy.com

INROADS internships are designed to provide students with an opportunity to work in a variety of departments to gain a broad experience, or a specific area aligned with their career interests and goals. Our INROADS recruiting needs are primarily focused on students pursuing undergraduate degrees in accounting, finance, electrical, mechanical and chemical engineering. On occasion, a limited number of co-op/intern opportunities may be available for business and information technology majors.

Next Level

Deadline for application: Open

Pay: Hourly-based on degree major and completed coursework

Length of the program: Approximately 10 weeks

Web site for internship/co-op information: www.duke-energy.com

The Next Level is an internship program targeted towards students of color in the Greater Cincinnati area. This summer internship experience is designed to provide students with an opportunity to work in a variety of departments to gain broad experience and to prepare them for life in corporate America. Students pursuing undergraduate degrees in accounting, finance, electrical, mechanical and chemical engineering are highly desired; however, business and information technology majors are eligible for this program.

Scholarships

Minority Professional Association Scholars: Awarded 12 renewable scholarships in 2005.

Helping Orient Minorities in Engineering (HOME): Awarded three full scholarships at North Carolina A&T University.

National Association of Black Accountants (NABA): Awarded three scholarships to accounting students.

Affinity Groups

Employee Resource Groups

Employee resource groups have been in existence at Duke Energy for at least 10 years, and include the following ERGs whose mission is to increase employees' personal and professional success through collaborative initiatives. Through networking and development activities, the groups benefit from interaction with executive sponsors and mentors, as well as access to information about professional development opportunities and career advancement.

The Collaborative for Positive Change (CPC)

The mission of the CPC is to establish and maintain a support system that focuses on the empowerment of African-American employees while contributing to the achievement of the company's goals. Its vision is to work as a consulting group that is the focal point for African-Americans and will unify, support and empower others to grow and reach their ultimate potential.

The Leadership Development Network (LDN)

Creates an environment where employees interested in developing leadership skills can interact with other employees to build their skills and abilities.

The Minority Professional Association (MPA)

Provides an open environment for development and networking opportunities to facilitate individual and collective growth of African-Americans at Duke Energy and in the community.

The Business Women's Network (BWN)

Supports Duke Energy's commitment to women's leadership development, provides employees an opportunity to engage in conversation with senior leaders concerning leadership skills specific to women's shared experiences and professional development needs, and enables employees to acquire and develop those skills.

Women In Nuclear (WIN)

Provides a network through which female employees in the nuclear field can exchange knowledge about nuclear technologies and issues, while furthering their professional development.

The mission of the Women's Network is to motivate and support all women; as well as heighten awareness about women's issues in order to remove barriers and be recognized as a valued force within the company.

The Hispanic Heritage Network

The mission of the Hispanic Heritage Network is to promote and preserve the Hispanic culture while helping the company achieve its goals of leading a workforce that is truly balanced and a reflection of the people we serve; with this, we will lead in energizing the social, cultural and economic development of our community. Its vision is to help the company shape its future by improving its services and communications, and by creating a dynamic relationship with the growing Hispanic/Latino community, attracting new talent who exhibit the drive, professional capabilities and desire to become part of the Duke Energy family.

The North American Young Generation in Nuclear

This group is dedicated to supporting young professionals in the nuclear industry.

Strategic Plan and Diversity Leadership

How does the firm's leadership communicate the importance of diversity to everyone at the firm?

Work with the human resources staffing group and the consultants in the business units.

Who has primary responsibility for leading diversity initiatives at your firm?

Richard Williams, vice president of talent management and diversity.

Does your firm currently have a diversity committee?

Yes.

If yes, please describe how the committee is structured, how often it meets, etc.

Diversity council meets bi-monthly; please see the Additional Information section for more details.

If yes, does the committee's representation include one or more members of the firm's management/executive committee (or the equivalent)?

Yes.

How many employees are on the committee, and how often does the committee convene in furtherance of the firm's diversity initiatives?

Total Executives on Committee: Approximately 25

Does the committee and/or diversity leader establish and set goals or objectives consistent with management's priorities?

Yes.

Has the firm undertaken a formal or informal diversity program or set of initiatives aimed at increasing the diversity of the firm?

Yes, formal.

How often does the firm's management review the firm's diversity progress/results?

Quarterly.

The Stats

Employees

2005: 23,500

Revenue

2005: $17 billion

Retention and Professional Development

How do 2005 minority and female attrition rates generally compare to those experienced in the prior year period?

About the same as in prior years.

Please identify the specific steps you are taking to reduce the attrition rate of minority and women employees.

- Develop and/or support internal employee affinity groups
- Increase/review compensation relative to competition
- Increase/improve current work/life programs
- Adopt dispute resolution process
- Succession plan includes emphasis on diversity
- Work with minority and women employees to develop career advancement plans
- Review work assignments and hours billed to key client matters to make sure minority and women employees are not being excluded
- Strengthen mentoring program for all employees, including minorities and women
- Professional skills development program, including minority and women employees
- *Note*: Our turnover is fairly typical for the utility industry and relatively low for all employee groups

Diversity Mission Statement

Build a high-performance organization with a strong focus on diversity, inclusion and employee development.

Additional Information

The purpose of the Diversity Council is to provide a collaborative approach to diversity and inclusion strategies and initiatives. This council serves as a partner to the diversity team in establishing corporate diversity and inclusion strategy throughout the enterprise. The council is accountable to the executive sponsors.

Accountabilities:

- Reviews, supports and guides the development of strategies and operational plans for enterprise diversity strategy
- Reviews and analyzes enterprise measures and emerging workforce trends
- Evaluates the implementation of plan initiatives
- Each member serves as advocate and role model for diversity and inclusion
- Provides a forum for continuous education on matters related to diversity and inclusion
- Since talent management, staffing and workforce planning strategies are crucial to the success of diversity and inclusion strategies, the Diversity Council also provides oversight for these areas
- Provides an annual report to the sponsors
- Others, as agreed upon by the council

Organizational Roles:

- The vice president of diversity and talent management and diversity chairs the council.
- The director, diversity strategies serves as secretary.
- At least one member from each business unit serves as a member of the council and, of course, serves as an advocate within the business unit. Members serve two-year terms, with staggered rotation. Members are appointed by the chair in consultation with the sponsors.
- Ex officio members may be appointed.

Membership Criteria:

- Leadership within a business unit is desirable.
- Demonstrated interest and commitment to diversity and inclusion.
- Willingness to lead by example and to be a role model for diversity and inclusion.

Operating Expectations:

- The Diversity Council meets bi-monthly.
- An agenda and supporting documentation will be provided to members at least five days prior to the scheduled meeting.
- Meetings may involve speakers, educational awareness sessions and other professional development related to diversity and inclusion.
- Members are responsible on an ongoing basis to communicate opportunities, general information or considerations for future agenda items.

Decision Rights:

- Final decisions around issues that the committee is unable to resolve will rest with the chair in consultation with the sponsors. In line with the principles of inclusion, decisions will be made only after all viewpoints are completely heard and considered.
- Decisions made by the Diversity Council are for implementation at the enterprise level with recommendations for use by the business units.

Duke Realty Corporation

600 E. 96th Street, Suite 100
Indianapolis, IN 46240
Phone: (317) 808-6000
Fax: (317) 808-6794
www.dukerealty.com

Locations

Indianapolis (HQ)

Atlanta, GA • Chicago, IL • Cincinnati, OH • Cleveland, OH • Columbus, OH • Dallas, TX • Minneapolis, MN • Nashville, TN • Orlando, FL • Raleigh, NC • St. Louis, MO • Tampa, FL • Weston, VA

Employment Contact

Jenny E. Bean
Assistant Vice President HR

Ginny Jackson
Staffing Manager

Apply online at www.dukerealty.com

Recruiting

Please list the schools/types of schools at which you recruit.

- *Other private schools:* Spelman, Clark Atlanta, Morehouse, Vanderbilt
- *Public state schools:* Indiana University, Purdue University, Indiana-Purdue University (IUPUI), Georgia Tech, Florida State, Georgia State, Emory
- *Historically Black Colleges and Universities (HBCUs):* Spelman, Clark Atlanta, Morehouse

Do you have any special outreach efforts directed to encourage minority students to consider your firm?

- Hold a reception for minority students
- *Conferences:* AUC Job Fair
- Advertise in minority student association publication(s)
- Participate in/host minority student job fairs
- Firm's associates participate on career panels at schools

What activities does the firm undertake to attract minority and women employees?

- Partner programs with women and minority associations
- *Conferences:* AUC, Black Expo, career forum for minorities and women
- Participate at minority job fairs
- Seek referrals from other associates
- *Utilize online job services:* Other media outlets—iHispano.com
- *Other:* Participants in Project REAP; Participants in INROADS in Indianapolis, Chicago and Atlanta

Internships and Co-ops

The Duke Realty Internship Program (INROADS and Non-INROADS)

Number of interns in the program in summer 2005 (internship) or 2005 (co-op): 24 interns (nine INROADS and 15 non-INROADS)

Pay: $12-$16 per hour

Length of program: 12 weeks

Percentage of interns/co-ops in the program who receive offers of full-time employment: We have a conversion rate of over 95 percent

Web site for internship/co-op information: www.Dukerealty.com

The Duke Internship Program is designed to be a multi-summer internship program with the ultimate goal of hiring interns into a full-time position upon graduation. The interns will have one to four summers of in-house training with us prior to being offered a full-time position. During these summers, interns will learn about our company culture, delivery system and the long-term benefits of employment at Duke, with the expectation that their contributions and productivity are successively higher each summer.

PROJECT REAP (Real Estate Associate Program)

Number of interns in the program in summer 2005 (internship) or 2005 (co-op): One associate a year

Pay: $40-$45k per year

Length of program: 12-month program

Percentage of interns/co-ops in the program who receive offers of full-time employment: Conversion rate of 100 percent

Web site for internship/co-op information: www.reap.org

REAP is an industry-backed, market driven program with a five year track record. REAP finds, trains and places talented dedicated minority professionals with leading commercial real estate firms. The internship lasts for 12 months with the goal of converting interns into full-time associates.

Entry-Level Programs/Full-Time Opportunities/Training Programs

Duke has two formal training programs available to interns and associates.

Career Development Training

Duke offers a variety of career development training courses to support associates in developing their work skills. Courses are available for interns and associates in all of our markets. Typical courses include:

• Personality Types in the Workplace
• Communication Between the Genders
• Dealing with Difficult People
• Effective Interviewing
• Stress Management

ElementK

Computer-based training is available for all interns and associates. This online training solution provides training for select Microsoft products, sexual harassment and diversity training.

In addition, associates participate in departmental training.

Strategic Plan and Diversity Leadership

How does the firm's leadership communicate the importance of diversity to everyone at the firm?

Quarterly associate conference calls, company newsletters, annual performance reviews, (including the CEO's annual review), e-mails, financial support for diversity council and other sponsored diversity activities, career development courses, quarterly diversity training activities and a diversity CD that new hires must review during their first few months at Duke.

Who has primary responsibility for leading diversity initiatives at your firm?

Denny Oklak, CEO and president, and his executive team.

Does your firm currently have a diversity committee?

Yes.

Duke Realty Corporation Diversity Council

It is the mission of the Duke Realty Corporation Diversity Council to educate, increase awareness and be advocates for diversity at Duke. The Diversity Council leads the company in recognizing the value of respect and inclusiveness, fosters Duke's core values and promotes the understanding and appreciation of our differences and similarities. In so doing, we strive to develop and nurture a strong, diverse workforce in order to produce exceptional customer satisfaction and shareholder value.

The Diversity Council is made up of 24 associates from every level (entry to executive) and from each of our 13 locations nationwide. The Diversity Council meets two to three times per year in person and via conference calls every other month.

The Diversity Council also provides diversity training to over 1,100 associates on a quarterly basis.

If yes, does the committee's representation include one or more members of the firm's management/executive committee (or the equivalent)?

Yes.

If yes, how many executives are on the committee, and in 2005, what was the total number of hours collectively spent by the committee in furtherance of the firm's diversity initiatives? How many associates are on the committee, and how often does the committee convene in furtherance of the firm's diversity initiatives?

There are four executive/management associates on the diversity council. Over 150 hours per year are spent on furthering the diversity initiatives.

Total Executives on Committee: Four

Does the committee and/or diversity leader establish and set goals or objectives consistent with management's priorities?

Yes. Annually, corporate goals are set for management. These goals include increasing minority hires and decreasing minority turnover. Throughout the last few years, diversity was put on associates' reviews, a minority vendor program was rolled out and associate satisfaction was measured with several questions pertaining to diversity at Duke. In addition, each intern has a career development plan in place.

Has the firm undertaken a formal or informal diversity program or set of initiatives aimed at increasing the diversity of the firm?

Yes, formal. Our diversity council was created to assist the company in furthering its diversity goals and initiatives. One major accomplishment that the council achieved was to propose to Duke's management committee that they add a diversity component on all associate performance review forms.

How often does the firm's management review the firm's diversity progress/results?

Quarterly.

How is the firm's diversity committee and/or firm management held accountable for achieving results?

It is on both the CEO's performance review and all employee performance reviews.

The Stats

Employees
2005: 1,065
2004: 1,078

Revenue
2005: $8 billion
2004: $7.7 billion

Retention and Professional Development

How do 2005 minority and female attrition rates generally compare to those experienced in the prior year period?

About the same as in prior years. There was a decrease in turnover between 2004 and 2005.

Please identify the specific steps you are taking to reduce the attrition rate of minority and women employees.

• Increase/review compensation relative to competition
• Increase/improve current work/life programs
• Succession plan includes emphasis on diversity
• Strengthen mentoring program for all associates, including minorities and women
• Professional skills development program, including minority and women associates
• *Other:* Associate opinion survey—including diversity questions

Diversity Mission Statement

Company Statement

Diversity is an important strategic issue at Duke Realty Corporation involving our associates, our customers and our shareholders. As our workforce and customer base continues to become more diverse, our challenge is to understand and value our individual differences and similarities, and those of our customers and prospective customers. Our behaviors and actions must demonstrate and confirm our respect for each other and each other's contributions.

Diversity involves developing organizational processes that are inclusionary rather than exclusionary, and which create an environment for company contributions by everyone.

Our expectation is that by responding in a positive and proactive way to these diversity issues, we will be better prepared for our long-term future through continued commitment of our associates, ongoing and successful relationships with existing and potential customers and continued investment from existing and prospective shareholders.

The company, recognizing the very broad nature of the term "diversity," offers the following examples of the many dimensions of diversity:

• Age and experience
• Culture (individual, group, global)
• Economic status

- Education and training
- Gender and sexual orientation
- Marital and family status
- Personal style
- Disabilities
- Race, nationality and ethnicity
- Religion
- Veteran and active armed service status

To reinforce this commitment in our daily work, all company activities, policies, practices and procedures are to be carried out in accordance with this policy. Each associate is personally responsible and accountable for ensuring that her/his actions and behaviors reflect this policy.

Diversity Council Statement

It is the mission of the Duke Realty Corporation Diversity Council to educate, increase awareness and be advocates for diversity at Duke. The Diversity Council will lead the company in recognizing the value of respect and inclusiveness, will foster Duke's core values and will promote the understanding and appreciation of our differences and similarities. In so doing, we strive to develop and nurture a strong, diverse workforce in order to produce exceptional customer satisfaction and shareholder value.

Additional Information

Duke's commitment to diversity in the workplace is paramount to the company's ability to attract and retain associates. The Duke Diversity Council was created to cultivate an environment in which all associates feel valued and have the opportunity to grow. This environment of inclusiveness helps make Duke an attractive culture for today's best and brightest.

To be able to attract and retain minority associates, the company offers a variety of diverse benefits. Here are just a few:

Adoption

Any full-time associate with at least 90 days' service receives 10 days' paid leave upon adopting a child. Duke offers an adoption assistance plan, which will reimburse any full-time associates, with at least six months of service, for certain qualifying adoption expenses up to $7,500 per adoption.

EAP

Duke realizes that in today's world, balancing work and home can be a real test of an associate's time and energy. All associates and their immediate family, including spouses and dependent children, are immediately eligible to participate in Duke's Employee Assistance Program (EAP) and work/life benefit. The EAP is a free benefit, which provides confidential consultation and short-term counseling for most of the problems that can hinder happiness and effectiveness at work and home. Examples include, but are not limited to: marital difficulties, financial or legal problems, parenting concerns and other stress-related issues. Prenatal kits, child safety kits and elder care kits are also available at no cost.

Tuition Reimbursement

Duke reimburses associates (with at least six months of service) for 100 percent of the cost of tuition, registration fees and books with a maximum of $3,000 per year. Many Duke associates have been able to achieve their goal of receiving a degree with the aid of the Tuition Reimbursement Program since Duke started offering it in 1998.

Health Insurance for Part-time Associates

Duke offers medical coverage to any part-time associate who has had at least three consecutive years of prior full-time service. In addition, there are additional paid benefits for part-time associates.

Employer Assisted Housing

The employer assisted housing program helps Duke associates realize the dream of home ownership. Any associate with at least six months' service and an annual salary of $57,000 or less (excluding bonus) may receive up to a $3,000 forgivable loan to use toward the purchase of their first home. Duke has been able to assist 70 associates with the purchase of their first home since the program began in 2001.

Career Resource Library

The Duke human resources department maintains the career resource library, which contains many different resources for Duke associates to use when situations, needs or interests arise.

Currently, the library contains over 300 different resources, some of which are the most popular titles in business today. Topics such as leadership, diversity, personal growth, time management and organization, business writing, communication and career development are available, as well as many others. Duke has also just added "How to Speak Spanish" CDs to the library for associates to use.

Community Days

All associates receive two paid community days each year to use in volunteering for charitable community activities.

In 2004, 287 associates at Duke utilized at least one Community Day. Volunteer activities have been performed for the following organizations:

- United Way
- Habitat for Humanity
- Big Brothers Big Sisters
- Cancer Society
- Juvenile Diabetes Foundation
- Race for the Cure
- Arthritis Foundation

Duke is committed to diversity and we show our commitment in various ways. Whether it's volunteer support or financial support, diversity at Duke is making a difference.

Over the last several years, Duke associates have received various honors in appreciation for their commitment. Associates were honored with the following awards:

INROADS

- Board member of the year—three years in a row
- Business coordinator of the year—two years
- Business advisor of the year
- Highest conversion rate
- Rainmaker of the year—two years

Finalist for Mayor's Diversity Award

Duke also supports various diverse organizations/associations. The following is a list of some of the organizations we support and participate in:

- INROADS in three cities
- Project REAP
- Asian Alliance
- Regional Black MBA
- CREW—Commercial Real Estate for Women

Along with the various honors, Duke contributes associates' time and company funding for various organizations and associations.

Here is a small list:

• United Way in all 13 of our markets
• Big Brother Big Sisters
• Habitat for Humanity
• American Cancer Society
• American Diabetes Association

DuPont

1007 N. Market Street
Wilmington, DE 19898
Phone: (302) 774-1000
Fax: (302) 999-4399
www1.dupont.com/dupontglobal/corp/careers/index.html

Diversity Leadership
Sandra Lewis
Manager of Diversity and WorkLife

Employment Contact
Shannon Freeze-Flory
Manager of Recruitment and Selection
1007 N. Market Street
Room D 6156
Wilmington, DE 19898
Phone: (302) 774-2112

Recruiting

Please list the schools/types of schools at which you recruit.

- Ivy League schools
- Other private schools
- Public state schools
- Historically Black Colleges and Universities (HBCUs)
- Hispanic Serving Institutions (HSIs)

Do you have any special outreach efforts directed to encourage minority students to consider your firm?

- Hold a reception for minority students
- *Conferences:* SWE, NSBE, SHPE, AISES, NSHMBA, NOBCCHE, Consortium, NABA, WEPAN
- Participate in/host minority student job fair(s)
- Sponsor minority student association events
- Firm's employees participate on career panels at schools
- Outreach to leadership of minority student organizations
- *Scholarships or intern/fellowships for minority students*: GEM, NACME

What activities does the firm undertake to attract minority and women employees?

- Partner programs with women and minority associations
- *Conferences:* SWE, NSBE, SHPE, AISES, NSHMBA, NOBCCHE, Consortium, NABA, WEPAN
- Participate at minority job fairs
- Seek referrals from other employees
- Utilize online job services

Do you use executive recruiting/search firms to seek to identify new diversity hires?

No.

Internships and Co-ops

Engineering Co-op/Intern Program

Deadline for application: Ongoing posting on the Web. We have three main terms in spring, summer and fall.
Pay: Pay is competitive, based on student's education level and degree.
Length of the program (in weeks): We offer terms of varying length, based on business need and student availability during the school year. Some students work the 12-16 weeks in the summer. We also have students who work six-month terms (spring/summer or summer/fall).
Percentage of interns/co-ops in the program who receive offers of full-time employment: About 50 percent
Web site for internship/co-op information: www1.dupont.com/dupontglobal/corp/careers/univ_internships.html

Our co-op/internship program is a key part of DuPont's engineer recruiting strategy. The program provides an excellent pool of motivated, diverse and well-prepared employees for DuPont. Assignments are located throughout the U.S. Minimum qualifications:

• Legal right to work in the United States without restrictions
• Attending an ABET accredited engineering school
• 3.3 minimum GPA preferred (3.0 as absolute minimum)
• Completed freshman year
• Prior work or volunteer experience
• Demonstrated leadership capability

Finance MBA Development Program

Deadline of Application: April, 2006
Pay: Monthly pay in the $5,000-6,000 range
Length of program: 12-14 weeks
Percentage of Interns/co-ops in the program who receive full time offers of employment: 90 percent

MBA interns are placed throughout the finance areas in the businesses and in corporate finance. They are primarily functioning as business analysts. We attract MBAs from top U.S. business schools. We seek prior financial experience.

Sourcing & Logistics Co-op Program

Deadline for application: Recruit throughout the year based on need. There are two sessions for co-ops: May/June to December and January to June.
Number of co-ops in the program in: 12-24 at any given time
Pay: Pay is competitive, based on student's education level and degree
Length of the program: Approximately six months (24 weeks)
Percentage of interns/co-ops in the program who receive offers of full-time employment: Approximately 50 percent
Web site for internship/co-op information: www1.dupont.com/dupontglobal/corp/careers/univ_internships.html

The Sourcing & Logistics Co-op Program is a key part of our recruiting strategy. The program provides an excellent pool of motivated, diverse and well-prepared employees for DuPont. Assignments are located in Wilmington, Delaware.

Requirements for the Sourcing & Logistics Co-op Program:

• Currently enrolled as a full-time, undergraduate student at an accredited college or university
• BA/BS candidates—a specific major is not relevant although some preference will be given to candidates studying supply chain management, logistics, engineering, operations management, transportation or business administration
• Minimum GPA: 2.8
• Ability to relocate to Wilmington, Delaware, for the duration of the co-op/internship program

- Legal right to work in the United States without restrictions
- Only those candidates who are able to complete the entire assignment will be considered

In addition to these requirements, candidates must possess the following qualifications:

Business knowledge: Ability to learn about DuPont's various businesses and their unique purchasing agreements

Computer skills: Experience with MS Office (Word, Excel, Access, PowerPoint). Candidates must be able to work with the Internet and learn internal DuPont systems and tools

Resourcefulness: Candidates must be able to identify leveraging opportunities (the advantage of having businesses buy supplies and services collectively versus individually)

Implementation: The ability to handle multiple priority assignments, as well as the ability to work independently with minimal supervision

Networking skills: Candidates must have the ability to network with different internal and external groups and contacts, and be capable of working in a team environment.

Scholarships

We no longer give scholarships directly, however we provide funding through third parties (e.g., NACME, UNCF).

Affinity Groups

Corporate Black Employees Network (CBEN)

Web site: www1.lvs.dupont.com/networks/cben

The purpose of CBEN is to link the individual sites' networks into a unified network.

CBEN strives to:

- Recognize, strengthen and support all black networks throughout the corporation
- Create an atmosphere of nurturing and mentoring for all black employees
- Partner with DuPont leadership in addressing issues affection black employees
- Communicate information to all black employees in a timely manner
- Encourage two-way communications among networks (sharing of best practices)
- Provide a more cohesive, concentrated and formalized effort to shape organizational decisions
- Seek alignment and agreement to identify and implement initiatives affecting the greater whole
- Help the corporate leadership understand issues affecting black employees
- Serve as an agent for positive change within the DuPont Corporation, wholly-owned subsidiaries and associated joint ventures

By doing these things, we build a strong, united community ready to address issues and challenges to ensure that we can contribute to our fullest potential in the work environment and achieve business success.

DuPont Women's Network (DWN)

Web site: http://cdcrs58.lvs.dupont.com/DWN/default.htm

DWN's mission is to foster development of DuPont women (and DuPont as a whole) through the leveraging of tools and ideas; to enable retention and personal and business growth; and to improve the capability of the corporate intellectual asset base.

Hispanic Network (HISNET)

Web site: www1.lvs.dupont.com/networks/hisnet/

The mission of the Hispanic Network is to promote an environment across the corporation that empowers Hispanics to perform at their maximum potential, and to recognize and value the contribution of Hispanic employees.

The Hispanic Network works toward accomplishing the following goals:

- Inclusion of Hispanics in all aspects of the businesses
- Empowerment of all Hispanics to contribute, learn, grow and advance
- Recognition of Hispanic employees for their accomplishments and contributions
- Fair and respectful treatment of Hispanic employees
- A corporate work environment that welcomes and supports Hispanic employees

DuPont Asian Group (DPAG)

Web site: http://dpag.es.dupont.com/

The purpose of DPAG is to:

- Promote a corporate environment that fully values and maximizes contributions of Asian-Americans
- Encourage and support DuPont Asian-Americans in achieving business success and personal growth

Bisexuals, Gays, Lesbians, Transgendered and Allies at DuPont Network (BGLAD)

Web site: www.dupontbglad.com/

BGLAD's mission is to help DuPont attract, utilize and retain talented bisexual, gay, lesbian and transgendered people by:

- Using its collective power to eliminate homophobia and heterosexism within DuPont businesses
- Serving as a resource regarding bisexual, gay, lesbian and transgender issues, and as a point of contact between DuPont and the community at large
- Partnering with human resources to address mental, emotional and physical health issues, and to help design compensation and benefit plans accordingly
- Providing opportunities to discuss and advance issues, to expand the network and increase the visibility of its members
- Ensuring a safe, healthy and supportive environment in the workplace that empowers bisexual, gay, lesbian and transgendered employees to be open and authentic about themselves
- Partnering with DuPont businesses to identify and capitalize on the bisexual, gay, lesbian and transgendered market

DuPont Part-Time Network (DPTEN)

The Global DuPont Part-time Employees Network was started to provide a community of support and information for all DuPont employees and businesses currently in or considering part-time roles. Our members are global, both men and women, working both full- and part-time schedules.

DPTEN strives to maximize DuPont employee professional contribution, maximize personal life balance satisfaction and maximize DuPont sustainable business results through valued employees.

DPTEN's purpose:

- To establish a community for full-service DuPont employees working part-time or any interested supportive DuPont employee working full time
- To provide a "voice" from this diverse work group
- To define benefit/value of the part-time employee

There are both corporately sponsored and site sponsored affinity networks in DuPont. Corporately sponsored networks receive funding support for initiatives and activities that are driven through DuPont corporate headquarters. However, site and business units maintain autonomy in their support of local networks.

The networks conduct biannual conferences. BGLAD, DPAG and HISNET included marketing segments during their last conference. Some networks conducted marketing surveys and used the information gathered to conduct sessions where conference participants helped business marketing managers identify opportunities for businesses covering automotive paints and refinishes, Corian® and Zodiaq® surfaces, and Solae™ products. The CBEN network identified an area that provided future opportunity for the Crop Protection business, and CBEN collected funds during its last conference to help villagers in underdeveloped countries.

Entry-Level Programs/Full-Time Opportunities/Training Programs

Field Engineering Program

> *Length of program:* Four years minimum (Two assignment minimum)
> *Geographic location(s) of program:* U.S.-based program; locations throughout country
> *Web site:* www1.dupont.com/dupontglobal/corp/careers/univ_fieldprograms_engineering.html

Series of rotational assignments providing developmental experience in roles such as engineering, business, operations leadership, sales/marketing, R&D and Six Sigma. Strong emphasis on career development via tools, training and coaching throughout the year. Required participation in annual development meeting that offers training (soft & hard skills), presentations on business initiatives and programs, networking opportunities (with peers, technical leaders and management), and exposure to senior leadership via keynote presentation(s). Six Sigma training required.

Tuition reimbursement supported via corporate program. Support for professional engineering society conferences and educational opportunities.

Finance Field Program

> *Length of program:* Two to three rotational assignments/four to six years
> *Geographic location(s) of program:* United States

Training would be aimed at providing:
- Three diverse work experiences
- DFU Courses: Ethics, DuPont Accounting, Internal Controls, etc.
- Support of certifications such as CPA, CIA and continuing education

Marketing Leadership Development Program

> *Length of program:* Three years
> *Geographic location(s) of program:* Start in Wilmington, Delaware (for U.S. hires), rotate within U.S. and potentially move to one of our global markets.
> *Web site:* www1.dupont.com/dupontglobal/corp/careers/univ_fieldprograms_marketing.html

This is a development program comprised of many elements that could be considered training. For example, we have developed a performance assessment process unique to the program to ensure that our participants get the feedback they need to develop into potential business leaders. With regard to formal training, we have scheduled formal training, which includes:

- Six Sigma training in the first year
- LEAD II training (middle manager training in DuPont) the second year
- At each of our semiannual meetings, we include topical training. Examples include: Myers Briggs, "Strengthfinders," "The First 90 Days," etc.

We offer tuition assistance to those foreign students localized outside the U.S. Additionally, DuPont offers tuition reimbursement for preapproved and agreed-upon educational development opportunities.

DuPont Corporate IT Field Program

Length of program: Field members are required to complete three to five assignments from 18-30 months in length. On average, members are part of the program for six to eight years.

Geographic location(s) of program: Primarily within the contiguous states where DuPont is located, including Wilmington, Delaware.

Web site: www1.dupont.com/dupontglobal/corp/careers/paths_infotech.html

- Basic training and orientation for new employees
- DuPont targeted development discussion training
- Other training and education based upon developmental gaps identified for each assignment

For qualified candidates, there is a tuition reimbursement program.

DuPont Human Resources Field Program

Length of program: Based upon the series of rotational development assignments designed for the individual, a participant may be associated with the program from three to five years.

Geographic location(s) of program: The program is focused within the United States. The rotational design entails relocation to DuPont sites throughout the U.S. and corporate headquarters located in Wilmington, Delaware. Participants gain global business experience and an understanding of human resources policies and strategies associated with a global workforce. Opportunities to work on global teams and interact with employees around the world are provided to participants.

The DuPont human resources field program provides participants with early career development opportunities through a series of rotational assignments. Each rotational assignment is designed to give the individuals the opportunity to foster their skills in a variety of HR functional areas. Upon completion of the program, individuals will have a strong foundation on which to build an exciting career as an HR leader at DuPont. Program benefits include:

- Exposure to many of the businesses within the DuPont portfolio
- Extensive contact with senior-level HR and business leaders across the company
- A support network of fellow program participants that will be beneficial to the individual throughout his or her career
- Meaningful assignments designed to engage individual development goals and career objectives
- Biannual development workshops created specifically for program participants

Individual development is the foundation upon which the human resources field program is founded. The program has a listing of training programs that each individual is required to attend. Six Sigma training and certification is also required. Biannual development workshops designed specifically for program participants are also held. Individual development/training is identified through personal targeted development plans. As with all employees at DuPont, program participants may participate in our Assistance for Lifelong Learning (tuition refund) program.

Strategic Plan and Diversity Leadership

Who has primary responsibility for leading diversity initiatives at your firm?

Willie C. Martin, vice president for diversity and work/life; Sandra Lewis, manager, diversity and work/life.

Does your firm currently have a diversity committee?

No.

Does the committee and/or diversity leader establish and set goals or objectives consistent with management's priorities?

Yes.

Has the firm undertaken a formal or informal diversity program or set of initiatives aimed at increasing the diversity of the firm?

Yes, formal.

How often does the firm's management review the firm's diversity progress/results?

Monthly. Ongoing reviews vary according to drivers/processes.

How is the firm's diversity committee and/or firm management held accountable for achieving results?

Management is held accountable for achieving results in several different ways, including the annual assignment of critical operating tasks and as part of managers' normal performance. Managers are held accountable by leadership, which reviews succession plans at every level of the organization. The CEO and a representative from the diversity area review succession plans for directors and all levels above. DuPont's corporately sponsored affinity networks hold conferences biannually. The conferences are a forum for employees to meet, review past performance and set new expectations for the coming years. During these conferences, leadership is also held directly accountable by employees.

The Stats

	TOTAL IN THE U.S.		TOTAL OUTSIDE THE U.S		TOTAL WORLDWIDE	
	2005	2004	2005	2004	2005	2004
Number of employees	12,199	12,891	34,000	53,000	60,000	81,000
Revenue	N/A	N/A	N/A	N/A	$27.1 billion	N/A

Retention and Professional Development

How do 2005 minority and female attrition rates generally compare to those experienced in the prior year period?

Lower than in prior years.

Please identify the specific steps you are taking to reduce the attrition rate of minority and women employees.

• Develop and/or support internal employee affinity groups (e.g., minority or women networks within the firm)
• Increase/review compensation relative to competition
• Increase/improve current work/life programs
• Adopt dispute resolution process
• Succession plan includes emphasis on diversity
• Work with minority and women employees to develop career advancement plans
• Strengthen mentoring program for all employees, including minorities and women
• Professional skills development program, including minority and women employees

Diversity Mission Statement

To foster an inclusive environment in a way that unleashes the potential of people and enables winning businesses to deliver significant shareholder value.

Additional Information

DuPont believes in the power of our networks (affinity groups) and the role they play in helping employees realize their full potential and achieve business success. The six corporately sponsored networks (i.e., (CBEN), (DWN), (HISNET), (DPAG), (BGLAD) and (DPTEN) are critical to the success of the DuPont diversity strategic imperatives. The networks assist in recruiting, retention, representation, community relations, marketing and communications initiatives. They serve as sounding boards for the organization and are partners in helping DuPont achieve its diversity vision by improving performance feedback, employee development and retention and marketing strategies to diverse customers. The networks provide a diverse perspective and, in some cases, drive company policy. Additionally, they are role models of inclusive organizations, as all networks are open to anyone who wants to join in support of their objectives.

The networks are helping DuPont gain a global competitive advantage. For example, the DuPont Asian Network hosted a "Glimpse of Asia/Business Expo" during Asian Heritage Month 2004 to build cultural awareness as DuPont moves into emerging markets. The exposition was so successful that the Hispanic Network soon followed with an exposition as well. These events are examples of how diverse groups of employees have contributed to business success by helping leadership understand that as DuPont moves into new markets, and subsequently cultures, the appreciation for diversity within the business context is key to success.

Beginning as early as 1985, the results of several work/life surveys determined work balance issues were not only a concern for women, but also for men as well. DuPont concluded that work/life balance was a "mainstream business issue." Other work/life surveys have helped us gather information to implement programs that assist employees in becoming more productive. Follow-up surveys proved a direct correlation between work/life supports and happy, healthy employees. Feedback indicated that those employees that had used our work/life programs or knew about our work/life programs felt more supported and less stressed. It also indicated that employees were more productive and more likely to go the "extra mile" for the company's success.

Our current work/life offerings include:

- Paid adoption leave
- Adoption assistance
- Dependent care spending accounts
- Dependent care reimbursement for overnight travel
- Family leave
- Flexible work practices
- Just in time care (back-up dependent care program)
- LifeWorks (resource and referral service)
- Work/life committees/teams

Awards and Recognition (involving treatment of people)

- DuPont was named among the 50 Best Employers in Argentina by *Apertura*.
- DuPont was named Corporation of the Year by the Minority Supplier Council.
- DuPont was inducted into the *Working Mother* Hall of Fame.
- Ellen Kullman was named to *Fortune*'s 50 Most Powerful Women in Business.
- The Louisiana Chemical Association recognized DuPont Pontchartrain as The Best in Louisiana.
- DuPont Argentina was named among the 60 best companies to work for in Argentina, according to the 2005 Great Place to Work® survey.
- DuPont ranked 26th in the 2005 Harris Interactive Reputation Quotient (RQ) survey.
- *La Tribune de Genève* named DuPont as a most "important" employer in Geneva.

- DuPont was selected as one of the 100 Best Companies for Working Mothers in the United States by *Working Mother* magzine (2005).
- The National Safety Council selected DuPont as the recipient of the 2006 Green Cross for Safety Medallion for corporate excellence in safety (2005).
- *Fortune* ranked DuPont 188th on the Global 500 rankings, their annual list of the world's largest corporations (2005).
- *The Scientist* magazine named Pioneer among the Best Places to Work for Scientists in Industry (2005).
- DuPont Argentina was ranked among the Top 10 Companies to Work For in Argentina in a list published by The Great Place to Work Institute (2005).
- DuPont Mexico was named a Best Place to Work in a survey published by the Mexican business magazine *EXPANSION* and The Great Place To Work Institute (2005).
- The DuPont Sabine River Works in Orange, Texas, was voted Best Place to Work in Orange County (2005).
- The National Association for Female Executives (NAFE) named DuPont one of the Top 30 Companies for Executive Women (2005).

Dynegy Inc.

1000 Louisiana St., Ste. 5800
Houston, TX 77002
Phone: (713) 507-6400
Toll Free: (877) 396-3499
www.dynegy.com

Diversity Mission Statement

Dynegy Inc. provides electricity, natural gas and natural gas liquids to markets and customers throughout the United States. Through its energy businesses, Power Generation and Natural Gas Liquids, the company owns and operates a diverse portfolio of assets. The company also strives to achieve diversity in its human capital assets, recognizing that diversity encompasses a great many factors such as ethnicity/race, gender, sexual orientation, language, religion, work status, and social and economic status. One of the company's goals is to promote and maintain an inclusive environment free from discrimination.

EchoStar Communications Corp.

9601 S. Meridian Blvd.
Englewood, CO 80112

Locations

Over 150 globally

Employment Contact

Laurie Musgrave
Manager, College Recruiting
9601 S. Meridian Blvd.
Englewood, CO 80112
Careers web site:
www.dishnetwork.com/careers
College Recruiting/Internship web site:
www.dishnetwork.com/college

Internships and Co-ops

EchoStar hosts one of the most competitive and comprehensive summer internship programs in the nation. If you have a thirst for adventure and the desire to prove yourself, consider joining EchoStar as a summer intern. EchoStar Communications Corp. is the parent company of DISH Network, and hires over 60 interns each summer for positions throughout the company, including: accounting, internal audit and tax, customer service support, engineering/R&D, finance, human resources, information technology, legal, marketing, operations, public relations, sales, and training and development.

The summer-long program allows college and graduate students to interact with other interns from across the country while working with managers and executives on projects that receive wide exposure and have a lasting impact on the company. Our interns work to both enhance their education and open themselves up to the many full-time opportunities that EchoStar has to offer. In addition to working on substantial projects, interns participate in field trips, training and other enrichment activities, such as executive team presentations, tours of our operations centers and digital broadcast centers, and social events like baseball games and hikes.

EchoStar offers exciting and challenging summer internship opportunities to:

- Students studying business, IT, engineering, liberal arts and other related areas (bachelor's and master's), with at least one more quarter of school left after the summer of their internship, and no more than two years of college or graduate school remaining
- Students who demonstrate intelligence, drive and energy through a track record of extracurricular involvement, service, leadership, prior experience, honors and other achievements
- Students with exceptional communication, technical, analytical and problem-solving skills
- Students who pass our rigorous screening process, including assessment exams

An internship at EchoStar is much more than a summer job—it is an experience that will provide a lifetime of benefits!

Ecolab, Inc.

Ecolab Center
370 N. Wabasha Street
St. Paul, Minnesota 55102-2233
Telephone: (651)293-2233
Fax: (651)293-2092

Locations

St. Paul, MN (HQ)
Ecolab has offices in more than 180
countries worldwide.

Diversity Leadership

Stephanie Jax
Manager, College Relations
370 N. Wabasha St.
St. Paul, MN 54022
Phone: (651) 293-4515
Fax: (651) 225-3304
E-mail: stephanie.jax@ecolab.com
www.ecolab.com/careers

Recruiting

Please list the schools/types of schools at which you recruit.

- *Public state schools:* University of Wisconsin-Madison, University of Wisconsin-Eau Claire, University of Minnesota, University of North Dakota, Michigan State University, Penn State, Purdue, Cal Poly Pomona, University of Houston, Florida State, University of IL-Champaign/Urbana, Iowa State, Ohio State
- *Historically Black Colleges and Universities (HBCUs):* Morgan State University, UNC, North Carolina A&T
- *Other predominantly minority and/or women's colleges:* College of St. Catherine's

Do you have any special outreach efforts directed to encourage minority students to consider your firm?

- Hold a reception for minority students
- *Conferences:* National Black MBA Association, National Society for Minorities in Hospitality
- Participate in/host minority student job fair(s)
- Sponsor minority student association events
- Firm's employees participate on career panels at schools
- Outreach to leadership of minority student organizations

What activities does the firm undertake to attract minority and women employees?

- Partner programs with women and minority associations
- *Conferences:* St. Kate's conferences, Woman's Food Service Forum
- Participate at minority job fairs
- Seek referrals from other employees

Do you use executive recruiting/search firms to seek to identify new diversity hires?

Yes.

Internships and Co-ops

Territory manager-in-training intern

Deadline for application: May 1
Number of interns in the program in summer 2005 (internship) or 2005 (co-op): Eight
Pay: $12 per hour
Length of the program: 10-12 weeks
Percentage of interns/co-ops in the program who receive offers of full-time employment: 100 percent
Web site for internship/co-op information: www.ecolab.com/careeers/collegerelations

As an Ecolab summer intern, you will develop your skills from the following:

- Work alongside a successful territory manager to learn customers' operations, understand their cleaning challenges and devise solutions to meet their needs.
- Gain exposure to the entire hospitality industry, including hotels, restaurants, hospitals, schools and dining facilities. You will also work with a wide customer base, including large corporate chains as well as independent, single-unit organizations.
- Learn how to successfully prospect to find new leads, set up new accounts and generate new business for the territory.
- Receive training on how to provide excellent customer service by troubleshooting Ecolab dish machines, laundry equipment and dispensing systems.
- Work closely with the district sales manager to perfect your sales, presentation and professional skills.
- Work for 10 weeks as part of an intern class to share feedback, resources and experiences.

Successful Ecolab interns will possess or show the following:

- Currently enrolled as a junior or senior undergraduate student
- Experience within the foodservice and/or hospitality industry is preferred
- Well-developed interpersonal and customer relations skills
- Organizational skills
- Strong mechanical aptitude
- Ability to lift and/or carry 50 pounds and an acceptable motor vehicle record

The objective of the internship program is to give you a hands-on, advanced-level overview of Ecolab and the institutional sales division. You will gain valuable sales and service experience by selling to and servicing our customers on a daily basis with an experienced salesperson. You will also be considered for long-term career opportunities within Ecolab through exposure to additional roles within the organization.

Undergraduate Finance Intern

Deadline for application: Early March
Number of interns in the program in summer 2005 (internship) or 2005 (co-op): 13
Pay: $16 per hour
Length of the program: 10-12 weeks
Percentage of interns/co-ops in the program who receive offers of full-time employment: 70 percent
Web site for internship/co-op information: www.ecolab.com/careers/college relations

Responsibilities could include:

- Provide management with financial analysis.
- Assess the performance of a business unit.
- Identify areas of opportunity and risk.
- Assist in the preparation of annual financial plans.
- Produce management reports.
- Perform regular month-end general ledger maintenance and reconciliations.
- Assist in special projects.

Requirements:

- Pursuing a B.A. or B.S. degree in a finance, accounting or a business related major
- Excellent analytical skills
- Strong communication skills
- Demonstrated project management skills
- Ability to work as a member of a team
- Well developed organizational skills
- Extensive PC spreadsheet skills

Information Technology Intern

Deadline for application: Early March

Number of interns in the program in summer 2005 (internship) or 2005 (co-op): Six

Pay: $16 per hour

Length of the program: 10-12 weeks

Percentage of interns/co-ops in the program who receive offers of full-time employment: 85 percent

Web site for internship/co-op information: www.ecolab.com/careers/collegerelations

Job duties and projects you could get involved in as an information technology intern at Ecolab include:

- Design and develop software products and tools.
- Create and modify applications to provide vital system statistics to various parts of the technology organization.
- Create custom web interface designs and change web site process.
- Develop large content management systems, including data repositories, web-based data access and UI system.
- Write system requirements and maintenance documentation.
- Software testing in multiple phases of the development cycle for initiatives across multiple organizations.
- Researching current industry software tools and technologies.

Qualifications:

- Pursuing a bachelor's degree in MIS, business or related field
- Demonstrated track record in project management
- Must be able to work independently and as part of a team on multiple overlapping projects
- Self-motivation and strong communication and interpersonal skills
- Analysis skills and attention to details for coding, testing/troubleshooting and for building and configuring applications

Food & Beverage Intern

Number of interns in the program in summer 2005 (internship) or 2005 (co-op): Three

Pay: $15 per hour

Length of the program: 10-12 weeks

Percentage of interns/co-ops in the program who receive offers of full-time employment: 70 percent

Web site for internship/co-op information: www.ecolab.com/careers

R&D Intern

Deadline for application: Varies

Number of interns in the program in summer 2005 (internship) or 2005 (co-op): 10

Length of the program: 10-12 weeks

Web site for internship/co-op information: www.ecolab.com/careers

Affinity Groups

EcoMondo

EcoMondo is an inclusive business and social network that supports Ecolab's growth through the integration and promotion of global talent diversity, global talent mobility and the creation of professional opportunities for associates with international interests.

E3

E3: Empowered, engaged, energized is a women's group that focuses on mentoring, leadership development and community outreach.

EcoEssence

EcoEssence is an African-American network that encourages interaction with, and growth and understanding of the various ethnic minority cultures that are represented at Ecolab.

Entry-Level Programs/Full-Time Opportunities/Training Programs

Territory manager-in-training

Length of program: Six months
Geographic location(s) of program: U.S.

Intensive 10-day training session at the world headquarters in St. Paul, Minn. All new hires attend this training session. Tuition reimbursement is offered for all positions.

Undergraduate Finance Development Program

Length of program: Two years
Geographic location(s) of program: St. Paul, MN

This is a two-year program where the associates hold two to three positions. They begin their first term with our CareerStart, on-boarding program.
Monthly development session, bimonthly update meetings and tuition reimbursement.

Operation Analyst- Engineering

Geographic location(s) of program: U.S.

Tuition reimbursement available.

Strategic Plan and Diversity Leadership

How does the firm's leadership communicate the importance of diversity to everyone at the firm?

• Ecolab Express: the employee web site
• Corporate diversity brochure
• Affinity group meeting notices

Who has primary responsibility for leading diversity initiatives at your firm?

Diana Lewis, senior vice president of human resources.

Does your firm currently have a diversity committee?

Yes.

If yes, does the committee's representation include one or more members of the firm's management/executive committee (or the equivalent)?

Yes.

Has the firm undertaken a formal or informal diversity program or set of initiatives aimed at increasing the diversity of the firm?

Yes, formal.

How often does the firm's management review the firm's diversity progress/results?

Monthly.

The Stats

	TOTAL IN THE U.S.		TOTAL OUTSIDE THE U.S		TOTAL WORLDWIDE	
	2005	**2004**	**2005**	**2004**	**2005**	**2004**
Number of employees	12,700	N/A	9,300	N/A	22,000	21,000
Revenue	51% of worldwide	51% of worldwide	49% of worldwide	49% of worldwide	$4.5 billion	$4.2 billion

Retention and Professional Development

How do 2005 minority and female attrition rates generally compare to those experienced in the prior year period?

Lower than in prior years.

Please identify the specific steps you are taking to reduce the attrition rate of minority and women employees.

• Develop and/or support internal employee affinity groups (e.g., minority or women networks within the firm)
• Work with minority and women employees to develop career advancement plans
• Strengthen mentoring program for all employees, including minorities and women
• Professional skills development program, including minority and women employees
• *Other:* CareerStart on-boarding process, individual development plans, Ecolab University training facilities/sessions

Diversity Mission Statement

We are committed to a culture that fully leverages our people's talents by promoting an environment where all people can make a difference, be heard, be supported, be developed and be rewarded for their contributions.

Additional Information

Ecolab associates possess shared expectations, which include a workplace built on respect, mutual values, trust and goodwill. Diversity is a core tenet that enables us to achieve a more rewarding professional atmosphere for all of our associates around the globe. At Ecolab, we believe that the success of our associates and the success of the company go hand in hand.

We support our diversity efforts by recruiting and hiring the best people of all backgrounds to represent our company. Some programs in which we participate include:

• National Black MBA
• INROADS, which develops and places talented minority youth in business and industry
• National Association of Minorities in Hospitality
• College of St. Catherine, Center for Sales Innovation for Female Sales Professionals

Erie Insurance Group

100 Erie Insurance Place
Erie, PA 16530
Phone: (814) 870-2000
Fax: (814) 461-2694
www.erieinsurance.com

Locations

Illinois • Indiana • Maryland • North Carolina • New York • Ohio • Pennsylvania • Tennessee • Virginia • Wisconsin • West Virginia

Employment Contact

Ann K. Scott
Vice President-Employment
E-mail: Ann.Scott@ErieInsurance.com

Recruiting

Please list the schools/types of schools at which you recruit.

• Private schools
• Public state schools
• Historically Black Colleges and Universities (HBCUs)

We recruit at the following schools: Penn State University (University Park), Penn State Behrend (Erie), Gannon University, Edinboro University of PA, Allegheny College, University of Pittsburgh, Ohio State University, Slippery Rock University, Clarion University, Indiana University of PA, Thiel College, Westminster College, Robert Morris College, Howard University, Central State University, Cheyney University of PA, Mercyhurst College, Grove City

Do you have any special outreach efforts directed to encourage minority students to consider your firm?

• Hold a reception for minority students
• Participate in/host minority student job fair(s)
• Firm's employees participate on career panels at schools
• Outreach to leadership of minority student organizations

What activities does the firm undertake to attract minority and women employees?

• Seek referrals from other employees
• Utilize online job services
• *Other:* Sponsorship of diverse community organizations and events

Internships and Co-ops

Future Focus — Actuarial & IT Internship Program

Deadline for application: March
Pay: Varies according to the work performed—generally between $11 and $16 per hour
Length of the program: Varies according to student schedule and department need; most are full-time from May to August; opportunities may exist to continue part-time through the school year for local students

Percentage of interns/co-ops in the program who receive offers of full-time employment: 45 percent

Web site for internship/co-op information: www.erieinsurance.com

About the Internship

The Erie Insurance Group Future Focus internship is available to students whose permanent residence is within approximately 250 miles of Erie's home office or who would like to begin a career in the Erie, Penn. community. Applications are accepted from students who are completing their sophomore or junior year. Qualifications include a major in IT or computer science for the IT internship, and in math or actuarial science for the actuarial internship. A minimum cumulative GPA of 3.0 is also required. For an IT internship, completion of the first class in COBOL is preferred. For an actuarial internship, passing at least one actuarial exam is preferred. Several interns are hired each year for this paid internship program. Relocation assistance is available if needed.

About the Special Features

The internship includes orientation to the company and the insurance industry through:

• A variety of challenging assignments in a stimulating work environment
• A personal mentor
• A welcome event for the interns and their mentors and supervisors
• Educational programs and round table lunches with company management
• Planned social events and opportunities for a wide variety of recreational activities will round out the interns' experience in Pennsylvania's scenic city on the lake

To apply, contact:

Melissa DiGiacomo, Employment Specialist
Employment Department
Erie Insurance Group
100 Erie Insurance Place
Erie, PA 16530
Phone: (814) 870-4035
Fax: (814) 461-2893
E-mail: Melissa.DiGiacomo@ErieInsurance.com

Entry-Level Programs/Full-Time Opportunities/Training Programs

ERIE University Claims Adjuster Training Program

Length of program: Four months
Geographic location(s) of program: Erie Insurance field claims office service territories; locations vary according to the needs of the company at the time of the training class

ERIE University is an exciting, dynamic training program that prepares bright, independent, hard-working candidates for careers in insurance claims. Training consists of a combination of fieldwork at the branch of initial hire and travel to our state-of-the art facility in Erie, Penn., for classroom training in an intense, supportive learning environment. Training lasts for approximately four months and covers a variety of topics, such as overview of the insurance industry and Erie Insurance; ERIE's service philosophy and standards; ERIE's product lines; claims, marketing, underwriting and other functions and procedures; field/home office interactions; product and policy information and other related topics.

Trainees attend classes taught by insurance experts both on company time and after hours. They also independently complete a variety of assigned projects and handle claims hands-on in the field. Trainees are also assigned a mentor who is a senior claims representative. Insurance training through the Insurance Institute of America is also included.

The ERIE University program leads to a career path in insurance that could eventually lead to management opportunities. Adjusters start in the position of claims adjuster I. With experience and additional education, they may advance to claims adjuster II and III. Then to claims examiner, claims supervisor, claims manager, etc.

We are seeking college graduates (BS/BA, any major) with some work experience beyond graduation who are willing to enroll in extensive training and commit to the challenging and rewarding career of claims adjusting. Insurance knowledge is not required.

Before entering ERIE University, candidates must commit to locating to an assigned territory as determined by the company's needs. Assigned territories will be in areas that report to the hiring office. For example, our Indianapolis branch serves the entire southern portion of the state of Indiana from Illinois east to Ohio and from the Kentucky border north to approximately Lafayette and Muncie. Our Rochester branch serves the entire state of New York. Candidates should be enthusiastic about relocating anywhere within their branch's service area.

A valid drivers license, good driving record and acceptable credit history are required—motor vehicle, credit, and criminal history reports will be ordered. College degrees will also be verified.

Good communication, interpersonal, analytical and organizational skills are required, along with independence and self-motivation.

Strategic Plan and Diversity Leadership

How does the firm's leadership communicate the importance of diversity to everyone at the firm?

Our commitment to diversity is incorporated into all of our communications both internally and externally. Our message of equal professional service is incorporated into all of our management and employee training.

Who has primary responsibility for leading diversity initiatives at your firm?

Michael Krahe, executive vice president, leadership and development.

Does your firm currently have a diversity committee?

No.

Does the committee and/or diversity leader establish and set goals or objectives consistent with management's priorities?

Yes.

Has the firm undertaken a formal or informal diversity program or set of initiatives aimed at increasing the diversity of the firm?

Yes, informal.

The Stats

Revenue

2005/2006: $1,125 billion (U.S.)

(Erie Insurance Group has U.S. operations only)

Retention and Professional Development

How do 2005 minority and female attrition rates generally compare to those experienced in the prior year period?

About the same as in prior years.

Please identify the specific steps you are taking to reduce the attrition rate of minority and women employees.

• Strengthen mentoring program for all employees, including minorities and women
• Professional skills development program, including minority and women employees

The positive effect of beginning your career with Ernst & Young is too great to measure.

A great start can take you further. At Ernst & Young we've created an environment that's conducive to personal and professional growth and success. And what we're offering is an opportunity to learn from some of the best talent in the industry. Become a benchmark for success. Visit us on the Web at ey.com/us/careers, or look for us on campus.

FORTUNE®
100 BEST COMPANIES TO WORK FOR 2005

Audit • Tax • Transaction Advisory Services

Quality In Everything We Do

Ernst & Young LLP

5 Times Square
New York, NY 10036
Phone: (212) 773-3000
Fax: (212) 773-6350
www.ey.com

Locations

Offices in 140 countries worldwide.

Diversity Leadership

Gioia Pisano
Associate Director, Office of Minority
Recruiting
99 Wood Avenue South
Iselin, NJ 08830
Phone: (732) 516-4243
Fax: (732) 516-4277
E-mail: gioia.pisano@ey.com

Recruiting

Please list the schools/types of schools at which you recruit.

• Ivy League schools
• Other private schools
• Public state schools
• Historically Black Colleges and Universities (HBCUs)
• Hispanic Serving Institutions (HSIs)
• Other predominantly minority and/or women's colleges

Do you have any special outreach efforts directed to encourage minority students to consider your firm?

• Hold a reception for minority students
• *Conferences:* National Association of Black Accountants (NABA), Association of Latino Professionals in Finance and Accounting (ALPFA), Hispanic Student Business Association (HSBA), National Association of Asian American Professionals (NAAAP)
• Advertise in minority student association publication(s)
• Participate in/host minority student job fair(s)
• Sponsor minority student association events
• Firm's employees participate on career panels at schools
• Outreach to leadership of minority student organizations
• Scholarships or intern/fellowships for minority students
• *Other:* Accounting Career Awareness Program with high school students and various universities
• *Other:* see below

The Your Master Plan (YMP) program was developed by Ernst & Young in collaboration with the University of Notre Dame, and the University of Virginia. The innovative Masters of Accounting program, which is fully funded by the firm, is primarily for non-accounting business majors. Over the past seven years, we have attracted over 1,000 students to the profession—and over 40 percent of these students were ethnic minorities.

What activities does the firm undertake to attract minority and women employees?

• Partner programs with women and minority associations
• *Conferences:* National Association of Black Accountants (NABA), Association of Latino Professionals in Finance and Accounting (ALPFA), Hispanic Student Business Association (HSBA)
• Participate at minority job fairs

• Seek referrals from other employees
• Utilize online job services
• INROADS

Do you use executive recruiting/search firms to seek to identify new diversity hires?

Yes.

Internships and Co-ops

An Ernst & Young internship is a great way to find out what a career here is all about.

Interns get an inside look at the people, methods and technologies of a large international firm. Get a sense of our environment. See how we carry out assignments. Understand the value we place on quality and integrity.

Interns may assist with research, help conduct audits, work on marketing strategies and assist in capital-sourcing efforts. Interns also may assist with tax planning engagements or learn about audit processes, then apply audit concepts—like internal control, cash, accounts payable and current liabilities—to real-life situations.

Interns also get the chance to attend EY's international Intern Leadership Conference, held in Orlando every August. This event helps thousands of interns from around the world experience the firm's teaming culture, learn leadership skills and network with future colleagues. Plus, it's a lot of fun.

Ernst & Young strongly supports INROADS and continues to increase its commitment each year.

To find out more about our internship program, go to ey.com/us/careers.

Scholarships

Ernst & Young and the Ernst & Young Foundation have committed more than $6 million since 1996 to fund programs and minority scholarships for undergraduate and graduate degree candidates who are majoring in disciplines related to the firm's service areas, such as accounting, information technology, computer science, taxation and finance. Scholarships are distributed through Universities and National Organizations.

In addition to providing scholarships to students, we also fund a Masters of Accounting program through the Your Master Plan (YMP) program which was developed by Ernst & Young in collaboration with the University of Notre Dame, and the University of Virginia. The innovative Masters of Accounting program, which is fully funded by the firm, is primarily for non-accounting business majors. Over the past seven years, we have attracted over 1,000 students to the profession—and over 40 percent of these students were ethnic minorities.

Affinity Groups

Professionals all over the country have taken part in initiatives through affinity groups or People Resource Networks—to foster diversity and underscore our commitment to provide an open, flexible and supportive workplace that values the contributions of all our people. Our People Resource Networks are action-oriented groups designed to provide an opportunity for minority professionals to network internally and externally with professionals in the same field, to create informal mentoring relationships and strengthen leadership skills through their involvement. We have specific people resource networks for:

• African-Americans
• Asian/Pacific Islanders
• Hispanics
• Gay, Lesbian, Bisexual and Transgender (GLBT)
• Women

Entry-Level Programs/Full-Time Opportunities/Training Programs

At Ernst & Young, our commitment to development starts day one at the firm with orientation, and continues throughout one's professional career. Our four-pronged approach includes:

Learning: Expand one's knowledge—through instructor-led courses and technology-enabled learning.
Experiences: Build your resume—with stretch assignments, role changes and opportunities to expand responsibilities.
Relationships: Forge important connections now—and for life—through networking, mentoring and counseling relationships.
Feedback: Gain insights—through performance feedback, goal-setting, development plans and self-assessment.

The personal and professional growth of our people is at the heart of our People First culture. Because the services we offer are only as good as our people's skills, knowledge and abilities.

Strategic Plan and Diversity Leadership

The firm has a strong commitment to diversity that starts at the top—John Ferraro our vice-chair of Client Services chairs the firm's Ethnicity Diversity Task Force. This task force, along with the firm's offices of diversity strategy and development and minority recruitment work along parallel paths to help Ernst & Young achieve its human resources goal, "To be the employer of choice among professional services firms for all people."

The Ethnicity Diversity Task Force includes partners and directors representing Ernst & Young's practices and geographic areas. The Ethnicity Diversity Task Force is charged with translating the firmwide vision for inclusiveness into action-oriented goals. The task force also develops strategy and examines initiatives to enhance the development and advancement of minorities in the firm. The task force meets regularly with our geographic areas and national business units to examine needed initiatives, holding their meetings in different area locations throughout North America, and take ownership to make sure that those initiatives get launched successfully.

The office of diversity strategy and development concentrates on the creation of strategies supporting awareness, communication, leadership accountability and career development. Much focus is placed on education, mentoring and networking, which fully supports the firm's People First culture and its commitment to creating lifelong relationships with its people by providing them with the opportunities and tools they need to succeed within the firm and beyond.

The information below highlights some of the firm's key initiatives around the development of our minority professionals:

Area/BU Diversity Frameworks

To focus on the firm's career development activities, diversity frameworks at the area level have been created to support the firm's national strategies. Each business unit leader leads the Area/BU Diversity Frameworks. Each BU commits an Area/BU diversity coordinator, an advisory council of Area/BU leaders, and subcommittees that focus on minority recruitment, career development, business development and communications. This group serves as the area's nucleus in initiating, championing and implementing change initiatives that will assist in creating a truly inclusive environment.

Minority Leadership Conference

The Ernst & Young Minority Leadership Conference, held every 18 months, brings together all of the firm's minority partners, principals, executive directors and directors—as well as the firm's senior leadership, including the entire executive board—to increase partners, principals, executive directors and directors' leadership and accountability leading to enhanced awareness of inclusiveness as a key element of the firm's strategy stronger commitment to the execution of key diversity drivers, and increased results and behavior change. It also provides an opportunity to increase minority partners, principals, executive director and directors' involvement in their business units' diversity initiatives, to continue dialogue around increasing minority representation in the firm's leadership and to network with minority partners, principals and directors and with senior firm leadership, as well as to continue the discovery of integrating diversity into the firm leadership culture and the People First environment.

Inclusiveness Learning Curriculum

The Inclusiveness Learning Curriculum sets a foundation for the success of the People First strategy by promoting the development of an "inclusive" leadership culture that respects individual talents and allows people to fully contribute to the success of the firm. Inclusiveness: An awareness workshop is an integral part of the inclusiveness curriculum. The workshop expands the learner's awareness of inclusiveness through facilitated discussions and activities. This curriculum is being used and delivered within the context of the firmwide and geography-based efforts that are currently in place. In addition, in a continued effort to cascade the message to all professionals, A Seat at the Table was developed as a two-and-a-half-hour session designed to raise awareness of the firm's commitment to inclusiveness. It will be deployed at a local level to staff, seniors and CBS equivalents.

Career Watch

In most business units, a standing leadership team or Career Watch Committee helps ensure that high-potential minorities and women are assigned to top clients, sales opportunities and projects, and are receiving the development opportunities they need to grow and excel. In other cases, individuals' development paths are studied to ensure there are no barriers to mentoring or access to opportunities for growth. Efforts like these help ensure that our best performers continue to develop and that any needs women and minorities might have are factored into their individual plans for growth.

Ethnicity Initiatives: Executive Mentoring Program and Learning Partnerships

Ernst & Young supports a formal mentoring program, the Executive Mentoring Program (EMP) that creates mentoring relationships by pairing high potential minority partners with Americas executive board members and an external coach to ensure that the firm fully capitalizes on the talent available in its leadership ranks.

In 2002, Ernst & Young launched a formal, year-long mentoring program called Learning Partnerships, which targets ethnic minorities as mentees and introduces a structured approach to mentoring and development, provides minority professionals with greater access to senior leaders, facilitates mentoring relationships and supports the creation of informal relationships across industries.

How often does the firm's management review the firm's diversity progress/results?

Quarterly.

The Stats

Countries Worldwide: 140
U.S. Locations: 95

Employees

107,000 (worldwide)
25,000 (U.S.)

Revenue

$16.9 billion for fiscal year ended June 30, 2005 (worldwide)

Retention and Professional Development

How do 2005 minority and female attrition rates generally compare to those experienced in the prior year period?

Lower than in prior years.

We are proud that our effort and culture have contributed to higher retention of our minority and women professionals when compared to prior years.

Please identify the specific steps you are taking to reduce the attrition rate of minority and women employees.

- Develop and/or support internal employee affinity groups (e.g., minority or women networks within the firm)
- Increase/improve current work/life programs
- Adopt dispute resolution process
- Succession plan includes emphasis on diversity
- Work with minority and women employees to develop career advancement plans
- Review work assignments and hours billed to key client matters to make sure minority and women employees are not being excluded
- Strengthen mentoring program for all employees, including minorities and women
- Professional skills development program, including minority and women employees

Exxon Mobil Corporation

5959 Las Colinas Boulevard
Irving, TX 75039-2298
Phone: (972) 444-1000

Additional Information

ExxonMobil is the industry leader in each of its core businesses and has an unmatched array of proprietary technologies aimed at increasing the productivity of its assets and employees. The company conducts business in almost 200 countries and territories around the globe and has established a new definition for world-class scale and efficiency.

ExxonMobil's policy is to provide equal employment opportunities in compliance with all applicable laws and regulations to individuals who are qualified to perform job requirements. We are committed to promoting a highly-productive work environment that treats all employees with respect, values diverse perspectives, encourages individual growth and achievement, and rewards people based on their performance. We have built a diverse global workforce that is focused on producing superior business results.

ExxonMobil closely monitors its diversity performance and continuously strives for improvement. We are committed to improving the gender balance in our company and to promoting leadership opportunities for women globally. In the United States, ExxonMobil's focus is on increasing the representation of women and minorities, including African-Americans, Hispanics, Asians and Native Americans. We support networks for female, African-American and Hispanic employees that provide mentoring, coaching and strategies to enhance personal and professional development. These organizations foster open and honest communications with all levels of management on relevant diversity and inclusion issues. Each of our networks is sponsored by a senior manager, who assists with aligning the group's objectives with ExxonMobil's business needs. Employee network groups also contribute time and energy to community efforts by participating in volunteer activities such as Junior Achievement, Habitat for Humanity and the United Negro College Fund Walk-a-Thon.

In addition, ExxonMobil is committed to being the employer of choice for its diverse group of highly-qualified employees by providing workplace flexibility and employee assistance programs. Some of these programs include adjustable work hours, adaptable work place, personal time, adoption assistance and dependent care assistance. Supervisors are expected and encouraged to foster an environment in which work gets done and reasonable flexibility is accommodated.

To find out more about ExxonMobil and career opportunities, visit www.exxonmobil.com/careers.

Fannie Mae

3900 Wisconsin Avenue, NW
Washington, DC 22066
Phone: (202) 752-3900
www.fanniemae.com/careers

Locations

Atlanta, GA • Chicago, IL • Dallas, TX •
Pasadena, CA • Philadelphia, PA •
Washington, DC
Plus 54 partnership offices across the US.

Diversity Leadership

Emmanuel Bailey
VP, Chief Diversity Officer

Phil Hendrickson
Diversity Sourcing Manager

Caitlin Howard
Campus Recruiter
3900 Wisconsin Ave. NW
Washington, DC 20016
Phone: (202) 752-3900

Recruiting

Please list the schools/types of schools at which you recruit.

• Ivy League schools
• Public state schools
• Historically Black Colleges and Universities (HBCUs)
• Hispanic Serving Institutions (HSIs)

Do you have any special outreach efforts directed to encourage minority students to consider your firm?

• *Conferences:* NSHMBA, NBMBAA
• Participate in/host minority student job fair(s)
• Firm's employees participate on career panels at schools
• Scholarships or intern/fellowships for minority students

What activities does the firm undertake to attract minority and women employees?

• Conferences
• Participate at minority job fairs
• Seek referrals from other employees
• Utilize online job services

Do you use executive recruiting/search firms to seek to identify new diversity hires?

Yes.

Internships and Co-ops

D.C. Public High School Program

Deadline for application: June 1
Number of interns in the program in summer 2006 (internship) or 2006 (co-op): 10
Pay: Minimum wage
Length of the program : Eight weeks

Percentage of interns/co-ops in the program who receive offers of full-time employment: None; it is for work experience in corporate.

Drexel Co-op Program

Deadline for Application: July 1st and January 1st
Number of interns in the program: Four (two fall, two spring)
Length of program: Six months
Percentage of co-ops in the program who receive offers for full-time employment: 20 percent

Scholarships

MBA Scholarship

Deadline for application for the scholarship program: February 15th
Scholarship award amount: $2,000

Seeking MBA intern interested in housing finance and minority home ownership; first-year MBA with strong finance skills; strong academic performance; recommendation from professor and personal recommendation.

Affinity Groups

Fannie Mae has several affinity groups all intended to foster a culture in which employees recognize and appreciate the diversity of their coworkers; the groups are employee-led and are encouraged to raise any issues and concerns to leadership. The employee networks include groups for those who identify themselves as the following:

• African-American
• Asian Pacific
• Catholic
• Christian Salt and Light
• Corporate Alumni
• Foreign National
• Hispanic
• Hindu
• Jewish
• Gay/Lesbian/Bisexual/Transgender
• Muslim
• Parents and Guardians with Children with Special Needs
• Single Parent
• Women

Entry-Level Programs/Full-Time Opportunities/Training Programs

Analyst Program

Length of program: 24 months
Geographic location(s) of program: Primarily D.C. or Bethesda, MD

The program lasts for one week, plus on-going training.

Internal Audit

Length of program: Full-time opportunities (MBA only)
Geographic location(s) of program: Washington, D.C.

This program provides on-the-job training and mentoring from internal audit and staff leaders.

Research Analyst Program

Length of program: Three month apprenticeship.
Geographic location(s) of program: Washington, D.C.

Applicants typically have a liberal arts background and 10 weeks training.

Enterprise Management System Program

Length of program: 24 months
Geographic location(s) of program: Reston, VA and Urbana, MD

This program provides one week of training.

Controllers

Length of program: Full-time opportunities
Geographic location(s) of program: Washington, D.C.

This program provides on-the-job training and mentoring from finance staff and leaders and one week of training.

Strategic Plan and Diversity Leadership

How does the firm's leadership communicate the importance of diversity to everyone at the firm?

We have an office of diversity and they are responsible for many programs that promote a diverse work environment. Fannie Mae is very committed to minority home ownership challenges and our business is providing liquidity to the mortgage finance market so that more lenders can offer loans to potential home buyers. We set minority home ownership goals each year. Every employee of Fannie Mae appreciates and contributes to that mission every day in the work they do.

Who has primary responsibility for leading diversity initiatives at your firm?

Emmanuel Bailey, VP and chief diversity officer.

Does your firm currently have a diversity committee?

Yes.

If yes, does the committee's representation include one or more members of the firm's management/executive committee (or the equivalent)?

Yes.

Does the committee and/or diversity leader establish and set goals or objectives consistent with management's priorities?

Yes. Diversity is one of 10 core commitments essential to our success.

Has the firm undertaken a formal or informal diversity program or set of initiatives aimed at increasing the diversity of the firm?

Yes, formal. We have an office of diversity whose primary mission is to foster a diverse culture and environment through policies, programs, thought leadership and partnerships. Our recruiting efforts are very focused on diversity efforts and we partner with many constituents, both internally and externally, to be successful in attracting a diverse workforce to Fannie Mae.

How often does the firm's management review the firm's diversity progress/results?

Quarterly.

The Stats

Employees

2006: 5,800 (U.S.)

Retention and Professional Development

How do 2006 minority and female attrition rates generally compare to those experienced in the prior year?

About the same as in prior years.

Please identify the specific steps you are taking to reduce the attrition rate of minority and women employees.

• Develop and/or support internal employee affinity groups (e.g., minority or women networks within the firm)
• Increase/improve current work/life programs
• Succession plan includes emphasis on diversity
• Strengthen mentoring program for all employees, including minorities and women
• Professional skills development program, including minority and women employees
• *Other:* training class on diversity

Diversity Mission Statement

As a corporation, Fannie Mae is guided by a set of values that permeates the way we conduct our business. Honesty, integrity and respect for others must be central to everything we do. Just as they are at the core of the way we do business, these values are permanent.

In keeping with these values, our corporate philosophy on diversity is based on respect for one another and recognition that each person brings his or her own unique attributes to the corporation. We are committed to providing equal opportunity for all employees to reach their full potential; it is a fundamental value, and it makes good business sense. Fannie Mae will be most successful in meeting its public mission and our corporate goals when we fully capitalize on the skills, talents and potential of all our employees.

Fannie Mae's approach to diversity is based on a two-tiered business rationale driven by our mission to tear down barriers, lower costs and increase the opportunities for home ownership and rental housing for all Americans. By this we mean that we designed the program to create opportunities for all employees internally, which in turn empowers employees to create opportunities for all Americans externally. The reason we do this is simple: it makes good business sense because it enables us to fulfill our mission. We must reflect the diversity of the society we serve in order to understand and address their home buying needs.

FedEx

942 S. Shady Grove Road
Memphis, TN 38120
Phone: (901) 818-7500
Fax: (901) 395-2000
www.fedex.com

Diversity Leadership

Linda Carter
Manager Corporate Human Resources Support
FedEx Express
3660 Hacks Cross Road
Bldg F, 3rd Floor
Memphis, TN 38125
Phone: (901) 434-6182
Fax: (901) 434-6356
E-mail: lfcarter@fedex.com

Recruiting

Please list the schools/types of schools at which you recruit.

- Ivy League schools
- Other private schools
- Public state schools
- Historically Black Colleges and Universities (HBCUs)

Do you have any special outreach efforts directed to encourage minority students to consider your firm?

- Advertise in minority student association publication(s)
- Participate in/host minority student job fair(s)
- Sponsor minority student association events
- Firm's employees participate on career panels at schools
- Outreach to leadership of minority student organizations
- Scholarships or intern/fellowships for minority students

What activities does the firm undertake to attract minority and women employees?

- Partner programs with women and minority associations
- Participate at minority job fairs
- Seek referrals from other employees
- Utilize online job services

Do you use executive recruiting/search firms to seek to identify new diversity hires?

No.

Internships and Co-ops

FedEx Express

Deadline for application: None
Number of interns in the program in summer 2005 (internship) or 2005 (co-op): 64 total

Pay: $2,700 per month

Length of the program: 10-12 weeks

Percentage of interns/co-ops in the program who receive offers of full-time employment: 14 percent in 2005

Departments that hire interns: Finance, legal, air operations, engineering, international and customer service. Participants must be in undergraduate or graduate school.

Affinity Groups

Asian Network Group

The purpose of the Asian Network Group is to promote cultural awareness, education and information regarding Asians at FedEx to ensure inclusion of all employees. The group meets monthly and sponsors/co-sponsors at least one corporate diversity forum with CCA annually. Interested persons are able to access group information via the diversity web site home page on the company's intranet.

African-American Network Group

The purpose of the African-American Network Group is to promote cultural awareness, education and information regarding African-Americans at FedEx to ensure inclusion of all employees.

The group meets monthly and sponsors/co-sponsors at least one corporate diversity forum with CCA annually. Interested persons are able to access group information via the diversity web site home page on the company's intranet.

Hispanic Network Group

The purpose of the Hispanic Network Group is to promote cultural awareness, education and information regarding Hispanics at FedEx to ensure inclusion of all employees. The group meets monthly and sponsors/co-sponsors at least one corporate diversity forum with CCA annually. Interested persons are able to access group information via the diversity web site homepage on the company's intranet.

Women's Network Group

The purpose of the Women's Network Group is to promote cultural awareness, education and information regarding women's issues at FedEx to ensure inclusion of all employees. The group meets monthly and quarterly and sponsors/co-sponsors at least one corporate diversity forum with CCA annually. Interested persons are able to access group information via the diversity web site home page on the company's intranet.

Each network group operates as a separate entity. Each group has a chairperson and other group officer positions as needed.

Strategic Plan and Diversity Leadership

How does the firm's leadership communicate the importance of diversity to everyone at the firm?

The firm's leadership communicates diversity information via e-mails, the company's web site, a quarterly diversity newsletter, forums for affinity groups, meetings, etc.

Who has primary responsibility for leading diversity initiatives at your firm?

Linda Carter, manager, corporate human resources support, affirmative action and diversity.

Does your firm currently have a diversity committee?

Yes.

If yes, please describe how the committee is structured, how often it meets, etc.

The VP Diversity Committee is made up of 12 FedEx Express executives and they meet bimonthly. Each operating company has its own diversity committee, including FedEx corporate.

How many employees are on the committee, and how often does the committee convene in furtherance of the firm's diversity initiatives?

Total Executives on Committee: 12

Bimonthly meetings; approximately 2.5 hours in length. Additional hours spent via communication media and attendance at various diversity functions which aim to:

- Develop strategies that attract, promote and retain diverse talent at all levels of the corporation
- Create the best work environment for diverse groups through programs, services and benefits enhancements
- Educate and raise awareness about diversity at FedEx
- Support the use of diverse suppliers
- Promote FedEx as a neighbor and employer of choice by enhancing its image through community outreach programs and internal and external communication strategies
- Support the development and implementation of marketing strategies aimed at diverse customers
- Develop corporate diversity strategies, programs and goals and ensure that the corporation accomplishes its diversity objectives

How is the firm's diversity committee and/or firm management held accountable for achieving results?

Each FedEx operating company has a diversity committee and/or diversity officer.

The Stats

	TOTAL IN THE U.S.	
	2005	2004
Number of employees	215,838	195,838
Revenue	$29,363 million	$24,710 million

Note: Fiscal year is June through May. Revenues and number of employees are reported for fiscal years FY04, year ended May 2004, and FY05, year ended May 2005.

DEMOGRAPHIC PROFILE			
	MALE EMPLOYEES	FEMALE EMPLOYEES	MINORITY EMPLOYEES
2004	71.39%	28.61%	43.36%
2005	71.42%	28.58%	43.30%

Retention and Professional Development

Please identify the specific steps you are taking to reduce the attrition rate of minority and women employees.

- Develop and/or support internal employee affinity groups (e.g., minority or women networks within the firm)
- Increase/review compensation relative to competition
- Increase/improve current work/life programs
- Adopt dispute resolution process
- Succession plan includes emphasis on diversity
- Work with minority and women employees to develop career advancement plans
- Professional skills development program, including minority and women employees

Diversity Mission Statement

Our diverse workforce, supplier base and supporting culture enable FedEx to better serve our customers and compete more effectively in the global marketplace. We value the contributions and perspectives of all employees regardless of race, gender, culture, religion, age, nationality, disability or sexual orientation. We will strive in our workplace practices to deal with our employees, customers and suppliers in a fair and ethical manner.

Additional Information

We continue to be viewed as innovators and trendsetters in the business world and are often asked to share our progressive systems, programs and philosophies that have earned us our reputation as an employer of choice. FedEx has earned recognition as one of the World's Most Admired Companies (*Fortune* magazine). Other national awards include:

- 50 Best Companies for Minorities to Work — *Fortune* magazine
- America's Most Admired Companies—*Fortune* magazine
- World's Most Admired Companies—*Fortune* magazine
- 100 Best Companies for Working Mothers—*Working Mother* magazine
- 50 Best Companies in America for Asians, Blacks and Hispanics—*Fortune* magazine
- 20 Better Places to Work—*Mother Jones Magazine*
- Outstanding Corporate Support Award—National Minority Business Council
- Award for Excellence in Corporate Community Services—Points of Light Foundation
- The Top 100 Companies Providing the Most Opportunities for Hispanics—*Hispanic Magazine*
- Diversity 100 Recognition Award—*Next Step Magazine*

Fidelity Investments

82 Devonshire St
Boston, MA 02109
Phone: (617) 563-7000
www.fidelity.com/jobs

Locations

Boston, MA (HQ)

Eight regional centers in the US and Canada and investor centers in more than 91 US cities.

Internal sites include: Canada, France, Germany, Hong Kong, India, Ireland, Japan and the UK

Employment Contact

Kim DiNicola
College Relations Director
Fidelity Investments
82 Devonshire Street
Boston, MA 02109
Phone: (617) 563-8537
Fax: (617) 385-1457
E-mail: kim.dinicola@fmr.com
www.fidelitycareers.com

Recruiting

Please list the schools/types of schools at which you recruit.

- Ivy League schools
- Other private schools
- Public state schools
- Other predominantly minority and/or women's colleges

Do you have any special outreach efforts directed to encourage minority students to consider your firm?

- Advertise in minority student association publication(s)
- Participate in/host minority student job fair(s)
- Firm's employees participate on career panels at schools

What activities does the firm undertake to attract minority and women employees?

- Partner programs with women and minority associations
- Participate at minority job fairs
- Seek referrals from other employees
- Utilize online job services

Do you use executive recruiting/search firms to seek to identify new diversity hires?

Yes.

Internships and Co-ops

Fidelity Intern/Co-op Program

Deadline for application: April

Number of interns in the program in summer 2005 (internship) or 2005 (co-op): 490 intern and co-ops company-wide

Length of the program: 12 weeks

Percentage of interns/co-ops in the program who receive offers of full-time employment : Six percent

Web site for internship/co-op information: www.fidelitycareers.com

Qualifications for the Fidelity Intern/Co-op Program vary depending on the assignment.

The Stats

	TOTAL IN THE U.S.		TOTAL OUTSIDE THE U.S		TOTAL WORLDWIDE	
	2005	2004	2005	2004	2005	2004
Number of employees	37,000	30,000	3,000	3,000	40,000	33,000

Fifth Third Bancorp

38 Fountain Sq. Plaza
Fifth Third Center
Cincinnati, OH 45263
Phone: (513) 579-5300
Fax: (513) 534-0629
Toll Free: (800) 972-3030
www.53.com

Locations

Florida • Indiana • Illinois • Kentucky •
Michigan • Ohio • Pennsylvania •
Tennessee • West Virginia

Employment Contact

Vickie McMullen
Campus Relations Leader
38 Fountain Square Plaza
Cincinnati, OH 45263
Phone: (513) 534-6264
Fax: (513) 534-4950
E-mail: vickie.mcmullen@53.com
www.53.com

Recruiting

Please list the schools/types of schools at which you recruit.

• *Other private schools:* Xavier University (Ohio) and the University of Dayton (Ohio)
• *Public state schools:* University of Cincinnati, Ohio State University, Northern Kentucky University, Michigan State University, University of Illinois, Miami University of Ohio, Case Western Reserve University and other regional universities.
• *Historically Black Colleges and Universities (HBCUs):* Wilberforce University, Florida A&M University

Do you have any special outreach efforts directed to encourage minority students to consider your firm?

• A reception for minority students
• *Conferences:* National Black MBA Association, National Society of Hispanic MBAs
• Sponsor minority student association events
• Firm's employees participate on career panels at schools
• Outreach to leadership of minority student organizations
• *Other:* Participate in the INROADS program

What activities does the firm undertake to attract minority and women employees?

• Partner programs with women and minority associations
• Participate at minority job fairs
• Seek referrals from other employees
• Utilize online job services

Do you use executive recruiting/search firms to seek to identify new diversity hires?

Yes.

If yes, list all women- and/or minority-owned executive search/recruiting firms to which the firm paid a fee for placement services in the past 12 months:

We use majority-owned firms, but demand diverse slates of candidates.

Internships and Co-ops

Deadline for applications to internship/co-op program: We follow campus deadlines for applications for co-ops and interns.

Number of interns in the program in summer 2005 (internship) or 2005 (co-op): 10 total

Pay: $12-$14 an hour

Length of the program: Eight weeks

Percentage of interns/co-ops in the program who receive offers of full-time employment: 80 percent

A college recruiting web site is being developed that will provide internship/co-op information.

Co-op and internship opportunities currently exist in: audit, operations, IT, finance, tax, treasury management and the asset management group.

Applicants must have a GPA of 3.0 or above and a major in accounting, finance, IT, business administration or marketing. For the operations internship, a specialization in operations is desired. Additional desired characteristics include strong analytical skills, ability to work in a team environment, good PC skills and good oral and written communication skills.

Affinity Groups

• Women's Network (Cincinnati, Cleveland, Columbus, Toledo, Detroit)
• African-American Network (Cleveland, Chicago and Detroit)
• Hispanic Network (Chicago)

The affinity groups' purpose is to act as support networks, and to encourage and provide opportunities for professional development through mentors, seminars and networking. Meetings are held once a month.

Entry-Level Programs/Full-Time Opportunities/Training Programs

IT Leadership Program, Operations Associate Program, Retail Associate Program, Commercial Associate Program, EFT Associate Program

Length of program: Varies from six to 18 months

Geographic location(s) of program: Most Fifth Third Bank locations (the exception being Operations Associates Program—in Cincinnati only)

These programs demonstrate business practices, operations and procedures in each department rotation, acquiring the knowledge and skills and experience required for assuming a permanent role. All programs provide classroom and on-the-job training.

Fifth Third Bank offers classroom and online professional development courses for knowledge and skill development.

Tuition reimbursement is offered as a benefit for all employees.

Strategic Plan and Diversity Leadership

How does the firm's leadership communicate the importance of diversity to everyone at the firm?

The firm's leadership communicates diversity through its web site, company newsletters and the diversity board.

Who has primary responsibility for leading diversity initiatives at your firm?

Ann Lazarus-Barnes, VP and director of diversity.

Does your firm currently have a diversity committee?

Yes. The board meets on a bimonthly basis and is divided into four key committees.

If yes, does the committee's representation include one or more members of the firm's management/executive committee (or the equivalent)?

Yes.

If yes, how many executives are on the committee, and in 2005, what was the total number of hours collectively spent by the committee in furtherance of the firm's diversity initiatives?

Total Executives on Committee: 10

Does the committee and/or diversity leader establish and set goals or objectives consistent with management's priorities?

Yes. The purpose of the board is to insure strategic success on diversity priorities.

Has the firm undertaken a formal or informal diversity program or set of initiatives aimed at increasing the diversity of the firm?

Yes, formal.

How often does the firm's management review the firm's diversity progress/results?

Quarterly.

How is the firm's diversity committee and/or firm management held accountable for achieving results?

Each EVP and affiliate president is responsible for achieving success as laid out by the diversity plan. The plan has one objective affecting compensation.

Retention and Professional Development

How do 2005 minority and female attrition rates generally compare to those experienced in the prior year period?

About the same as in prior years.

Please identify the specific steps you are taking to reduce the attrition rate of minority and women employees.

• Develop and/or support internal employee affinity groups (e.g., minority or women networks within the firm)
• Increase/review compensation relative to competition
• Increase/improve current work/life programs
• Succession plan includes emphasis on diversity
• Work with minority and women employees to develop career advancement plans

Diversity Mission Statement

Fifth Third Bank has a strong commitment to respect each individual and value every employee's personal contribution to the business. At Fifth Third Bank, we create an environment where everyone can be fully engaged, leaving no one out. We value diversity as an asset and will provide an environment where all individuals can maximize their potential for development.

Additional Information

All affiliates and lines of business have diversity plans. These plans have clear and measurable goals and focus on key initiatives to support long-term results, particularly in the key areas of recruitment, retention, advancement and promotion. Each line of business and affiliate has its own plan so that there is a common level of expectation and performance.

Powered by
Diversity

As a leading energy company,
our success comes from the knowledge and
ingenuity of our diverse group of employees. And
right now, we're looking to expand our workforce
– adding new, highly competent and enthusiastic
men and women to help drive our growth.

See how you can be part of the energy to build our
future. Visit us online at www.firstenergycorp.com.

FirstEnergy Corporation

76 South Main St.
Akron OH 44308
Phone: 330-761-7897
www.firstenergycorp.com

Locations

Various locations throughout Ohio,
Pennsylvania and New Jersey

Diversity Leadership

Deb Sergi
Director of Talent Management

Employment Contact

Peggy Breetz
Resourcing and Compliance Manager
Valencia Woodard
Supervisor Talent Acquisition

Recruiting

Please list the schools/types of schools at which you recruit.

• Public state schools
• Historically Black Colleges and Universities (HBCUs)

Do you have any special outreach efforts directed to encourage minority students to consider your firm?

• Advertise in minority student association publication(s)
• Participate in/host minority student job fair(s)
• Sponsor minority student association events

What activities does the firm undertake to attract minority and women employees?

• Partner programs with women and minority associations
• Participate at minority job fairs
• Seek referrals from other employees
• Utilize online job services

Do you use executive recruiting/search firms to seek to identify new diversity hires?

Yes.

Internships and Co-ops

Co-op/Internship Professional Development Program

Deadline for application: We offer various co-op/internship opportunities year round
Number of interns in the program in summer 2005 (internship) or 2005 (co-op): Approximately 200 students
Pay: $12- $22. Compensation is dependent on the student's major, number of quarters/semesters completed, and number of previous work sessions at FirstEnergy. Relocation is provided to students who meet company qualifications.
Length of the program: There are three sessions per year, each lasting 12 weeks or four months.
Percentage of interns/co-ops in the program who receive offers of full-time employment: 51 percent of eligible students converted to full-time employees upon graduation.
Web site for internship/co-op information: www.firstenergycorp.com/employment

The FirstEnergy Co-op/Internship Professional Development Program requires students who are enrolled in a major applicable to FirstEnergy's business (such as engineering, computer/IT, finance, and management) to attain a 2.5 grade point average or above. The largest business units employing co-ops/interns includes engineering, finance, IT, supply chain and rates. Business units provide work experience that is related to the students' majors. We sponsor students through INROADS.

FirstEnergy also participates in the Third Frontier Internship Program, sponsored by Governor Bob Taft in 2002. This project is the state of Ohio's largest-ever commitment to expanding Ohio's high-tech research capabilities, and promoting innovation and company formation that will create high-paying jobs for generations to come. Students who are Ohio residents attending an Ohio college/university enrolled in a high-tech curriculum containing mathematics, science and engineering are eligible for the Third Frontier Program once they complete their second year in school. The program reimburses FirstEnergy up to $3,000 per student.

Affinity Groups

Young Women's Professional Group

Entry-Level Programs/Full-Time Opportunities/Training Programs

Interesting development sessions are provided and designed to help students improve their skills in areas that are important for success at FirstEnegy, such as personal productivity, effective business writing, and communications and more.

New Supervisor Leadership Program

Length of program: 23 days over a seven-week period
Geographic location(s) of program: Ohio

Strategic Plan and Diversity Leadership

How does the firm's leadership communicate the importance of diversity to everyone at the firm?

The strategic vision statement on the corporate web site includes the following statement that expresses FirstEnergy's commitment to diversity:

FirstEnergy is a leading regional energy provider, recognized for operational excellence and customer service; the choice for long-term growth, investment value and financial strength; and a company committed to safety and driven by the leadership, skills, diversity and character of its employees.

Who has primary responsibility for leading diversity initiatives at your firm?

Debbie Sergi, director of talent management.

Does your firm currently have a diversity committee?

Yes.

FirstEnergy has a Workforce Planning and Diversity Committee. This committee is comprised of vice presidents from various business units that meet monthly.

If yes, does the committee's representation include one or more members of the firm's management/executive committee (or the equivalent)?

Yes.

If yes, how many executives are on the committee, and in 2005, what was the total number of hours collectively spent by the committee in furtherance of the firm's diversity initiatives? How many employees are on the committee, and how often does the committee convene in furtherance of the firm's diversity initiatives?

Total Executives on Committee: 11

Does the committee and/or diversity leader establish and set goals or objectives consistent with management's priorities?

Yes.

Has the firm undertaken a formal or informal diversity program or set of initiatives aimed at increasing the diversity of the firm?

Yes, informal.

How often does the firm's management review the firm's diversity progress/results?

Quarterly.

The Stats

	TOTAL IN THE U.S.	
	2005	2004
Number of employees	14,586	15,245
Revenue	$11,989 (dollars in millions)	$12,060 (dollars in millions)

WORKFORCE PERCENTAGES, YEAR END DECEMBER 2005		
MINORITIES	MALE	FEMALE
9.89 %	78.96 %	21.04%

Retention and Professional Development

How do 2005 minority and female attrition rates generally compare to those experienced in the prior year period?

Lower than in prior years.

Please identify the specific steps you are taking to reduce the attrition rate of minority and women employees.

• Develop and/or support internal employee affinity groups (e.g., minority or women networks within the firm)
• Increase/review compensation relative to competition
• Increase/improve current work/life programs
• Adopt dispute resolution process
• Succession plan includes emphasis on diversity
• Professional skills development program, including minority and women employees

Interns and co-ops participate in a coaching relationship where students are mentored by experienced employees who help them better understand FirstEnergy and its career opportunities, while also providing guidance and support throughout the students' work experiences. New hires at FirstEnergy are provided with and individual or "buddy" who can assist them in becoming acclimated to FirstEnergy, their individual department and business unit, and their specific work or reporting location. By doing so, a personal connection between the organization and the new employee is established from the first day, which also assists the onboarding process.

Additional Information

FirstEnergy has established the Young Women's Professional group to allow greater networking and identify women issues. We continually participate in salary surveys to ensure that employees are paid competitively and have a team that is reviewing our work/life programs for enhancements. Additionally, FirstEnergy has a dispute resolution program and internal harassment/discrimination process that all employees can utilize without fear of retaliation. FirstEnergy provides numerous professional skills development programs across the company for all employees.

FPL Group, Inc.

700 Universe Blvd.
Juno Beach, FL 33408
Phone: (561) 694-4000
Fax: (561) 694-4620
www.fplgroup.com/

Locations

Various cities in Florida and other cities in
the US

Diversity Leadership

Yolanda Cornell
Manager of EEO and Diversity

Employment Contact

Maritza Castano
College Recruiter
9520 W. Flagler St.
Miami, FL 33174
Phone: (305) 552-3348
Fax: (305) 552-3999
E-mail: maritza_castano@fpl.com

Recruiting

Please list the schools/types of schools at which you recruit.

• Ivy League schools
• Other private schools
• Public state schools
• Historically Black Colleges and Universities (HBCUs)

Do you have any special outreach efforts directed to encourage minority students to consider your firm?

• *Conferences:* SWE, NSBE, NSHMBA, NSBMBA
• Sponsor minority student association events

What activities does the firm undertake to attract minority and women employees?

• Conferences (see above)
• Seek referrals from other employees

Do you use executive recruiting/search firms to seek to identify new diversity hires?

No.

Internships and Co-ops

Internship Program

Number of interns in the program in summer 2006 (internship) or 2006 (co-op): 157
Pay: $870-$1,672 biweekly
Length of the program: Approximately 12 weeks
Web site for internship/co-op information: www.fpl.com

Interns are hired throughout the company in various different business units. Approximately 90 percent of the interns are in the engineering field. Qualifications usually entail working towards a relevant degree in the area of the internship and successful completion of a screening interview.

Entry-Level Programs/Full-Time Opportunities/Training Programs

Full-time new hires

Geographic location(s) of program: Various cities in Southeast Florida

The company provides tuition reimbursement for graduate and undergraduate degrees as well as on-the-job training.

Strategic Plan and Diversity Leadership

Who has primary responsibility for leading diversity initiatives at your firm?

Yolanda Cornell, manager of EEO and diversity.

Does the committee and/or diversity leader establish and set goals or objectives consistent with management's priorities?

Yes.

Has the firm undertaken a formal or informal diversity program or set of initiatives aimed at increasing the diversity of the firm?

Yes, formal. We have a team of diversity professionals whose main goal is to concentrate on minority recruiting and meet the guidelines of hiring minorities.

The Stats

Employees
2005: 14,805 (U.S.)
Revenue
2005: $10.522 million (U.S.)
2004: $9.630 million (U.S.)

Retention and Professional Development

How do 2005 minority and female attrition rates generally compare to those experienced in the prior year period?

About the same as in prior years.

Please identify the specific steps you are taking to reduce the attrition rate of minority and women employees.

• Increase/improve current work/life programs
• Succession plan includes emphasis on diversity
• Work with minority and women employees to develop career advancement plans

• Professional skills development program, including minority and women employees

Diversity Mission Statement

We will foster an inclusive business environment that values and leverages the diverse talents, perspectives and ideas of all employees.

GEICO

One GEICO Plaza
Washington, DC 20076
Phone: (301) 986-3000

Locations

Washington, DC (HQ)
Buffalo, NY • Coralville, IA • Dallas, TX •
Fredericksburg, VA • Honolulu, HI •
Lakeland, FL • Macon, GA • San Diego,
CA • Tucson, AZ • Virginia Beach, VA •
Woodbury, NY

Diversity Leadership

Thea Jenkins
Director of Minority Recruiting

Employment Contact

Shannon Smedstad
College Relations Manager
One GEICO Plaza
Washington, DC 20076
Phone: (301) 986-2802
Fax: (301) 986-3092
E-mail: DConcampus@geico.com
Career web site addresses:
www.geico.com/careers
www.geico.com/oncampus

Recruiting

Please list the schools/types of schools at which you recruit.

• Private schools
• Public state schools
• Historically Black Colleges and Universities (HBCUs)
• Hispanic Serving Institutions (HSIs)

Visit our complete list of schools online at www.geico.com/oncampus/schools.

Do you have any special outreach efforts directed to encourage minority students to consider your firm?

• Hold a reception for minority students
• Advertise in minority student association publication(s)
• Participate in/host minority student job fair(s)
• Sponsor minority student association events
• Firm's employees participate on career panels at schools
• Outreach to leadership of minority student organizations
• Scholarships or intern/fellowships for minority students

What activities does the firm undertake to attract minority and women employees?

• Partner programs with women and minority associations
• Participate at minority job fairs
• Seek referrals from other employees
• Utilize online job services

Do you use executive recruiting/search firms to seek to identify new diversity hires?

Yes.

Scholarships

GEICO Achievement Award Program

Deadline for application for the scholarship program: Varies

Scholarship award amount: GEICO offers $50,000 in scholarships every year to students from across the country. Our scholarship awards range from $500 to $5,000 each.

Web site or other contact information for scholarship: The scholarship program is available through various target schools.

Applicants will be sophomores or juniors majoring in business, information technology, mathematics or related degree programs, and possess at least a 3.0 overall GPA. Candidates will have demonstrated leadership skills within his or her campus and/or community, and possess a financial need.

Entry-Level Programs/Full-Time Opportunities/Training Programs

Emerging Leaders Management Development Program (Operations Management & Information Technology tracks)

Length of program: Two-and-a-half to three years

Geographic location(s) of program: The Operations Management track is available in New York, Virginia, Georgia, Florida, Texas, Arizona and California. The Information Technology track is available in our D.C. office only.

The Emerging Leaders Management Development program looks for graduates from top schools who are ready for a commitment to a dynamic organization and who can keep pace with our vigorous environment. Participants in the operations track rotate through every discipline of our business, including sales, customer service and claims. Information technology track participants rotate through various IT areas and work on special projects.

All participants attend management meetings and seminars, receive mentoring from directors and officers, and are exposed to the top leaders of our industry-leading company. As a member of the Emerging Leaders Program, you'll learn the business, inside and out, and when you are finished, you'll be ready for a future with enormous potential. Applicants must have at least a 3.5 overall GPA, with well-rounded education and demonstrated leadership experience. The program is designed as a comprehensive educational experience, including classroom sessions, leadership conferences, mentorship, hands-on training and one-on-one development.

GEICO's college recruiting team actively recruits for a variety of entry-level positions, including:

• Actuarial associates
• Senior business analysts
• Product management analysts
• Accounting associates
• Sales, customer service and claim counselors
• Auto damage adjusters

Strategic Plan and Diversity Leadership

Who has primary responsibility for leading diversity initiatives at your firm?

Thea Jenkins, director of management development and minority recruiting.

Does your firm currently have a diversity committee?

Yes.

If yes, does the committee's representation include one or more members of the firm's management/executive committee (or the equivalent)?

Yes.

If yes, how many executives are on the committee, and in 2005, what was the total number of hours collectively spent by the committee in furtherance of the firm's diversity initiatives?

Total Executives on Committee: Three, plus two attorneys and two managers. The committee meets at least once a month.

How many employees are on the committee, and how often does the committee convene in furtherance of the firm's diversity initiatives?

See above.

Does the committee and/or diversity leader establish and set goals or objectives consistent with management's priorities?

Yes.

Has the firm undertaken a formal or informal diversity program or set of initiatives aimed at increasing the diversity of the firm?

Yes, formal.

The Stats

Employees

2005: 20,000
2004: Over 20,000

Retention and Professional Development

Please identify the specific steps you are taking to reduce the attrition rate of minority and women employees.

• Increase/review compensation relative to competition
• Increase/improve current work/life programs
• Succession plan includes emphasis on diversity
• Work with minority and women employees to develop career advancement plans
• Strengthen mentoring program for all employees, including minorities and women

Diversity Mission Statement

GEICO is dedicated to assuring that all associates have an equal opportunity to achieve their full potential. The development and training of associates is vital to the success of the company. It is crucial that GEICO associates partner with the company in taking the initiative to look for opportunities to grow in their jobs, and to learn the skills that will help prepare them for greater growth and advancement. We are committed to providing an environment in which associates are recognized and rewarded based on results and their contributions to the organization's success.

unleash your
potential

... we have. GE's Evolution Series locomotive generates 16 cylinders' worth of power with only 12 cylinders, cutting emissions up to 40 percent as compared to our prior models. In addition, it was the first locomotive that met the new U.S. Environmental Protection Agency emissions standards. We call this ecomagination. At GE we invite you to unleash your ecomagination through a career in engineering, finance, manufacturing, sales and marketing, human resources, or information technology.

ecomagination℠

to learn more visit us at gecareers.com

an equal opportunity employer

GE

3135 Easton Tpke. Fairfield, CT 06828-0001 Phone: (203) 373-2211 Fax: (203) 373-3131 www.gecareers.com **Locations** 100 countries	**Employment Contacts** **Steve Canale** Manager Recruiting & Staffing E-mail: steve.canale@ge.com **Shari Hubert** Manager, Campus Recruiting Services 3135 Easton Turnpike Fairfield, CT 06828 Phone: (203) 373-2246 Fax: (203) 373-3292 E-mail: shari.hubert@ge.com

Recruiting

Please list the schools/types of schools at which you recruit.

• Ivy League schools
• Other private schools
• Public state schools
• Historically Black Colleges and Universities (HBCUs)
• Hispanic Serving Institutions (HSIs)
• *Other*: Predominantly minority and/or women's colleges

GE actively recruits at 41 focused schools in the U.S. and hires approximately 1,000 undergrad, master's and Ph.D. students each year in the U.S., and nearly an equal number outside the U.S.

Do you have any special outreach efforts that are directed to encourage minority students to consider your firm?

• Hold a reception for minority students
• *Conferences:* Consortium, DISCO, INROADS, NSBE, SHPE, NBMBA, NSHMBA, SWE
• Advertise in minority student association publication(s)
• Participate in/host minority student job fair(s)
• Sponsor minority student association events
• Firm's employees participate on career panels at schools
• Outreach to leadership of minority student organizations
• Scholarships or intern/fellowships for minority students
• *Other:* Jackie Robinson Foundation, National Action Council for Minorities in Engineering

What activities does the firm undertake to attract minority and women employees?

• Partner programs with women and minority associations
• *Conferences:* Consortium, DISCO, INROADS, NSBE, SHPE, NBMBA, NSHMBA, and SWE
• Participate at minority job fairs
• Seek referrals from other employees
• Utilize online job services

• *Other:* GE is a founding member of many of the organizations listed above. GE actively strives to recruit the best and brightest college students from all ethnic backgrounds.

Do you use executive recruiting/search firms to seek to identify new diversity hires?

No, not for entry-level college and MBA recruiting.

Internships and Co-ops

GE Early Identification (EID)

Deadline for application: Continuous
Number of interns in the program in summer 2005 (internship) or 2005 (co-op): 2,400
Pay: varies by degree and college year
Length of the program: Typically 10-12 weeks
Percentage of interns/co-ops in the program who receive offers of full-time employment: 50 percent of those eligible (graduating seniors)
Web site for internship/co-op information: gecareers.com

Other qualifications for the GE Early Identification program:

• GPA minimum of 3.0 (cumulative)
• Looking for bright students with demonstrated academic success, leadership skills and a willingness to learn and grow professionally.

Scholarships

All scholarship inquiries should be directed to the GE Foundation. The foundation provides scholarships to NSBE, Jackie Robinson, SWE, NBMBA and Consortium scholars, to name a few.

Affinity Groups

• African-American Forum
• Asian Pacific American Forum
• Hispanic Forum
• Women's Network

The purpose of all affinity groups is to provide an organization that can provide coaching, networking and career advancement opportunities to its members.

Entry-Level Programs/Full-Time Opportunities/Training Programs

Commercial Leadership Program (CLP)

As part of our strategy to achieve commercial excellence and drive organic growth, we are developing a pipeline of strong marketing and sales leaders at GE through the commercial leadership program (CLP). CLP offers a core curriculum that fosters the development of commercial skills and techniques that are critical to success in all GE businesses. The structure, duration and additional training are determined at the business level to meet their specific development and industry needs. Although the approach may vary by business, the end result is the same—CLP prepares candidates for a successful career in sales or marketing by providing the opportunity to learn about our products, industry and customers, while making valuable contributions to the organization.

Edison Engineering Development Program (EEDP)

A total development program—you bring the passion for technology and we'll supply technical training and projects for you to excel on a world-class team. EEDP will advance your technical problem-solving skills through advanced courses in engineering and real-life business experience.

EEDP is a two-year entry-level program providing three or more rotational assignments. All assignments are engineering projects driven by real GE business priorities.

Diverse experiences may include systems, analysis, design, quality, reliability, integration and test technical problem-solving skills developed via advanced engineering coursework, formal reports and presentations to senior leadership.

Participants in the program will gain business skills developed in corporate leadership courses. They will also have the opportunity to earn credit towards a MS degree in engineering and in real-world application technology.

Candidate Criteria:

• Passion for technology
• Demonstrated academic excellence
• Commitment to technology and quality
• Strong analytical, problem-solving and communication skills
• Engineering degree and relevant internship/co-op experience preferred
• Minimum GPA 3.0/4.0

Experienced Commercial Leadership Program (ECLP)

The experienced commercial leadership program (ECLP) accelerates the development of commercial-savvy talent through a structured program combining coursework, job assignments and interactive seminars. Candidates are hired into one of six businesses:

• Commercial finance
• Money
• Health care
• Infrastructure
• Industrial
• NBC Universal

ECLP is a two-year program consisting of four six-month, cross-segment rotational assignments within the commercial function of a GE business. Two rotations are marketing focused and two are sales focused. Program participants strengthen their commercial, business and leadership skills by completing an intensive curriculum consisting of eight weeks of classroom training, online training and in-residence global symposiums. International rotations are available based on performance and availability.

U.S. minimum candidate qualifications:

• MBA with two to four years marketing or sales experience
• Bachelor's degree with four to six years marketing or sales experience
• Demonstrated leadership, communication and analytical skills
• Geographic mobility
• Second language preferred (English required)
• Unrestricted work authorization in the United States, EMEA, China or Japan

Financial Management Program (FMP)

FMP is widely considered to be the premier program of its kind. It is the first step in many successful GE management careers. This intensive two-year entry-level program spans four rotational assignments.

Hands-on experience may include:

• Financial planning
• Accounting
• Operations analysis
• Auditing
• Forecasting
• Treasury/cash management
• Commercial finance
• Six Sigma quality

The program combines coursework, job assignments and interactive seminars to equip you with exceptional technical, financial and business skills. It is led by senior GE professionals and mentors, and develops world-class financial leaders for exciting positions.

Minimum criteria:

• Minimum cumulative GPA of 3.0 (no rounding)
• Undergraduate degree only, no MBA or master's degree
• Less than one year full-time external work experience
• Demonstrated interest or competency in finance
• Mobility
• Preferred criteria
• Leadership experience
• Communication skills
• Finance or business related internship
• Finance or business related major

Human Resources Leadership Program (HRLP)

HRLP will prepare you for a dynamic role in the human dimension of GE. As a true business partner, your work will influence the direction of our company. HRLP accelerates your development through two HR assignments and one cross-functional role.

The two-year program consists of three challenging eight-month assignments. Each participant will develop broad business skills via hands-on experience in two HR assignments, plus a third assignment in an area such as finance, quality or business development.

Other skills that participants will acquire include:

• Formal classroom training in HR leadership and business skills and concepts
• Extensive contact with peers and senior business leaders from around the world
• Expansion of your knowledge base, critical problem-solving skills and professional network

Candidate Criteria:

• Demonstrated academic excellence, business acumen and leadership ability
• Self-confidence, strong analytic problem-solving skills and exceptional communication skills
• MBA/MA in business or an HR-related discipline plus several years work experience preferred
• Geographic flexibility and global mindset; able to operate across cultures

Information Management Leadership Program (IMLP)

IMLP puts information management careers on the fast track. Program graduates are in tremendous demand throughout GE. IMLP develops strong technical and project management skills through coursework and meaningful assignments. The two-year program consisting of four six-month rotational assignments through different areas of a GE business.

• On-the-job training in business dynamics, career strategies, communication skills, problem solving, decision making and project leadership
• Formal coursework in advanced information technology and systems, and their strategic application within GE
• Develop strong technical foundation, project management skills and process knowledge that cuts across functions to support GE's boundless culture

Candidate Criteria:

• Strong interest in information technology applications
• Solid analytical abilities and sharp business acumen
• Bachelor's degree in computer science, information systems or computer engineering preferred; business degree or other related experience may be applicable

Operations Management Leadership Program (OMLP)

OMLP is an ideal entry point for engineers with the energy and drive to define and deliver world-class manufacturing processes, products and services. It is an intensive two-year entry-level program with at least three rotational assignments.

Possible assignments include:

• Manufacturing shop operations
• Process engineering, Six Sigma quality
• Materials management
• Supply chain management
• Environmental health and safety
• Mentoring, teamwork, ongoing reviews and defined deliverables
• Technical training in contemporary manufacturing, global supply chain management, APICS certification, Six Sigma quality training, environmental health and safety
• Business training and challenging experience in project management, team leading, negotiation, manufacturing finance

Candidate Criteria:

• Academic excellence, business acumen and leadership ability
• Strong communication and analytical problem-solving skills
• Geographic flexibility and global mindset; able to operate across cultures
• Degree in engineering or a technical discipline and relevant internship/co-op experience preferred
• Minimum GPA 3.0/4.0

Strategic Plan and Diversity Leadership

How does the firm's leadership communicate the importance of diversity to everyone at the firm?

The firm's leadership communicates diversity initiatives through e-mails, the web site, newsletters, meetings, etc.

Who has primary responsibility for leading diversity initiatives at your firm?

Deb Elam, manager, global employer of choice.

Does your firm currently have a diversity committee?

Diversity is reviewed annually at all levels during GE's formal HR refer process referred to as "Session C."

The Stats

2005 Employees

161,000 (U.S.)
155,000 (outside the U.S.)
316,000 (Total)

2005 Revenue

$72 billion (U.S.)
$78 billion (outside the U.S.)
$150 billion (Total)

Retention and Professional Development

How do 2005 minority and female attrition rates generally compare to those experienced in the prior year period?

About the same as in prior years.

Please identify the specific steps you are taking to reduce the attrition rate of minority and women employees.

The most important thing that GE does to retain all top talent is to provide them challenging and rewarding work. In addition, GE provides the tools and networks that give all employees an equal opportunity to grow and advance in their careers.

Diversity Mission Statement

Diversity and Inclusiveness

As a global company with operations in more than 100 countries, diversity isn't merely a noble idea—it's the reflection of our business. Every day GE works to ensure that all employees, no matter where they are located in the world and no matter where they come from, have an opportunity to contribute and succeed. Encompassed in that goal are promoting traditional ideas of diversity including ethnicity, race and gender, while at the same time exploring more contemporary concepts like inclusiveness.

We track diverse representation at all levels of the organization—by business, by geography and by function. We have robust reviews with the leadership of the company to show us where progress is being made, to glean best practices and where we have work to do, so that we can intensify efforts. Metrics are critical in setting goals and achieving results. While GE has made progress, significant efforts continue to improve the representation of women, U.S. minorities and non-U.S. citizens in leadership roles in the company.

In 2005, 34 percent of company officers and 40 percent of senior executives were diverse (women, U.S. minorities, and non-U.S. citizens) versus 22 percent of company officers and 29 percent of senior executives in 2000. Nearly one-quarter of GE's leadership is outside the U.S.

One of the key mechanisms for facilitating dialogue and progress in our diversity efforts is GE's affinity networks: The African-American Forum, The Asian Pacific American Forum, The Hispanic Forum and The Women's Network. These affinity networks play a critical role in attracting, developing, engaging and retaining employees at all levels across the company. These networks work in close partnership with Chairman and CEO Jeff Immelt, business leaders and the human resources team to continually uncover ways to improve in this area and opportunities for growth. These range from mentoring employees for professional growth to engaging customers for business growth. One powerful example of the impact the affinity networks have is in GE's philanthropic work in Africa. This initiative was a direct result of the chairman's involvement with The African-American Forum and a collective desire to make a difference in Africa.

Building off of the success of GE's Affinity Networks, employees in Japan were inspired to launch the "barrier-free network" in October 2004. This group aims to improve the mutual understanding between employees with disabilities and their colleagues by increasing awareness of key issues and their impact. This is one of the first employee groups for the disabled ever formed in a major company in Japan. This group will work to ensure that disabled employees have the same access to opportunity and the ability to reach their highest potential within the company. The group has launched a web site that details different types of disabilities and awareness activities developed by the network. The group has also started a sign language session with 20 participants who are learning the language for the first time.

Another facet of the GE diversity strategy is a commitment to diversity of its supply base. The company's supplier diversity program started more than 25 years ago and focuses on the development and inclusion of all capable suppliers.

Additional Information

Awards

• In *Fortune* magazine's 2006 Global Most Admired Companies list, GE ranked first overall (February 2006).
• In *Fortune* magazine's 2006 America's Most Admired Companies list, GE ranked second overall (February 2006).
• In *Fortune* magazine's 2005 50 Most Powerful Women, three GE female business leaders and two members of GE's board of directors were listed.
• In 2006, GE was ranked Number 1 for the Best Rotational Leadership Programs by Universum Communication Student Survey.
• In 2006, GE was named to *Black Enterprise*'s list of 40 Best Companies for Diversity.
• In 2005, GE was listed as World's Most Respected Global Companies by *Barrons*.
• GE was ranked first in *The Financial Times*' 2004 World's Most Respected Companies Survey for the seventh consecutive year since the survey's inception in 1998.
• GE was named to the Dow Jones Sustainability World Index as one of the world's leaders in environmental, social and economic programs.
• In March 2005, GE received the highest corporate governance rating of 10.0 from Governance Metrics International.
• In 2004, *BusinessWeek* ranked GE the fourth most valuable brand worldwide, after Coca-Cola, Microsoft and IBM (August 2004).
• In 2004, GE ranked second on the Forbes 2000 list, a comprehensive ranking of the world's biggest companies, measured by a composite of sales, profits, assets and market value (April 2004).
• GE ranked ninth on *Fortune* magazine's 50 Most Desirable MBA Employers list (April 2005).
• The Great Place to Work Institute Europe named two GE business units (Capital Aviation Services, Ireland, and Plastics, Spain) to the 100 Best Workplaces in the EU List (April 2004).
• GE received the 2004 Catalyst Award for comprehensive initiatives to advance women through its corporate ranks (March 2004).
• Executive Leadership Council Corporate Award for leadership in advancing diversity in corporate America.
• *Working Mother* magazine 100 Best Companies for Working Mothers in 2003, 2004 and 2005.
• *Diversity Inc*—Top 10 Best Companies for Asian-Americans
• *Woman Engineer*—No. 1 Company
• Top 50 Technology Companies—*Scientific American*

Goldman, Sachs & Co.

Locations

US:

Atlanta, GA • Boston, MA • Chicago, IL • Dallas, TX • Houston, TX • Jersey City, NJ • New York, NY • Philadelphia, PA • Princeton, NJ • Salt Lake City, UT • San Francisco, CA • Seattle, WA • Tampa, FL • Washington D.C.

International:

Auckland • Bangalore • Bangkok • Beijing • Buenos Aires • Calgary • Dublin • Frankfurt • Geneva • Hong Kong • Johannesburg • London • Los Angeles • Madrid • Melbourne • Mexico City • Miami • Milan • Moscow • Paris • Sao Paulo • Seoul • Shanghai • Singapore • Stockholm • Sydney • Taipei • Tokyo • Toronto • Zurich

Diversity Leadership

Edith Hunt
Managing Director

Lance LaVergne
Vice President, Global Head of Diversity Campus Recruiting

Employment Contact

Gina Moore
Analyst
85 Broad Street
New York, NY 10004
Phone: (212) 902-1000
Fax: (212) 902-3000
www.gs.com/careers

Recruiting

Please list the schools/types of schools at which you recruit.

• *Ivy League schools:* Harvard University, Princeton University, University of Pennsylvania, Columbia University, Brown University, Dartmouth College, Yale University, Cornell University
• *Other private schools:* Stanford University, New York University, University of Chicago, Northwestern University, Duke University, Georgetown University, Massachusetts Institute of Technology, Boston College, Villanova University, St. John's University, University of Southern California, University of Notre Dame, Amherst College, Emory University, Middlebury College, Vanderbilt University
• *Public state schools:* University of Illinois, University of California - Los Angeles, University of California - Berkeley, University of Michigan, University of Virginia, University of Texas, Rutgers University, City University of New York - Baruch College, University of North Carolina - Chapel Hill, University of Indiana
• *Historically Black Colleges and Universities (HBCUs):* Howard University, Morehouse College, Spelman College, Hampton University
• *Other predominantly minority and/or women's colleges:* Barnard College, Wellesley College, Smith College, Mt. Holyoke College

Do you have any special outreach efforts directed to encourage minority students to consider your firm?

• Hold a reception for minority students
• *Conferences:* National Association of Black Accountants, National Society of Black Engineers, Society of Women Engineers, Society of Hispanic Professional Engineers, National Black MBA Association, National Society of Hispanic MBAs, National Association of Women MBAs, Association of Latino Professionals in Finance and Accounting, Hispanic Alliance for Career Enhancement
• Advertise in minority student association publication(s)

• Participate in/host minority student job fair(s)
• Sponsor minority student association events
• Firm's employees participate on career panels at schools
• Outreach to leadership of minority student organizations
• Scholarships or intern/fellowships for minority students
• *Other:* Host workshops for graduate and undergraduate students through programs such as undergraduate and MBA camps

What activities does the firm undertake to attract minority and women employees?

• Partner programs with women and minority associations
• *Conferences:* National Black MBA Association, National Society of Hispanic MBAs, National Society of Black Engineers, Society of Hispanic Professional Engineers, National Association of Black Accountants, Association of Latino Professionals in Finance and Accounting, Hispanic Alliance for Career Enhancements, Consortium for Graduate Studies in Management, Society of Women Engineers
• Participate at minority job fairs
• Seek referrals from other employees

Internships and Co-ops

Summer Analyst Program

> ***Deadline for application:*** Winter 2006 (varies from school to school)
> ***Number of interns in the program in summer 2005 (internship) or 2005 (co-op):*** 1,498 interns
> ***Length of the program:*** 10 weeks
> ***Web site for internship/co-op information:*** www.gs.com/careers

Summer analysts join a 10-week comprehensive program, where they are given the opportunity to learn critical business skills, while gaining fundamental experience in their respective divisions. Goldman Sachs seeks highly motivated candidates who have demonstrated outstanding achievements in academic and extracurricular activities. We are looking for self-motivated, team players, who have excellent organizational and communication skills. While a background in finance or accounting is not required, candidates should have an interest in business and financial markets.

The following divisions hire summer analysts:

• Equities
• Fixed income, currency and commodities
• Finance (includes controllers, credit and corporate treasury and firmwide risk)
• Global investment research
• Human capital management
• Investment banking/corporate finance
• Investment management—asset management
• Investment management—private wealth management
• Global compliance
• Legal and management controls
• Merchant banking/private equity
• Operations (includes global operations)
• Services
• Technology

Scholarships

Scholarship for Excellence

Deadline for application for the scholarship program: December 2006

Scholarship award amount: $5,000 for sophomores, with an opportunity to be considered for an additional $7,500 in their junior year and $7,500 for juniors

Web site or other contact information for scholarship:

www.gs.com/careers/about_goldman_sachs/diversity/internships_scholarships/index.html

The Goldman Sachs Scholarship for Excellence Program was established in 1994 and is an integral part of our diversity recruiting effort, helping to attract undergraduate students of black, Hispanic and Native American heritage to careers at Goldman Sachs. Students of all majors and disciplines are encouraged to apply.

Recipients of the scholarship will receive:

• Sophomores—$5,000 scholarship to cover tuition and fees, and upon successful completion of summer internship, as well as the opportunity to receive an additional award and an offer to return for a second summer internship.

• Juniors—$7,500 scholarship to cover tuition and fees

An internship as a summer analyst in which the scholarship recipient will gain insight into the financial services industry, the firm and our unique culture; a coach/mentor that will help ensure a successful summer experience; and exposure to senior level managers and participation in firmwide networking opportunities.

The following are criteria we will consider when selecting our scholarship recipients:

• Black, Hispanic or Native American heritage
• Minimum cumulative grade point average of 3.4 or above on a 4.0 scale
• Interest in the financial services industry
• Community involvement—service to campus and community
• Demonstrated leadership and teamwork capabilities

Affinity Groups

At Goldman Sachs, we recognize that our ability to maintain and strengthen our edge requires a diverse workforce that can offer the widest possible range of perspectives. Through our diversity efforts, we work to provide a supportive and inclusive environment where all individuals, regardless of age, gender, race, religion, national origin, sexual orientation, gender identity, disability or other classification or characteristic, can maximize their full potential. Our affinity networks are an important part of the firm's diversity strategy because they serve as a forum to share ideas, concerns and successes, and provide opportunities for professional development. The primary focus of the networks is to:

• Promote the firm's business principles
• Foster leadership development and offer guidance on career management
• Increase the engagement and retention of historically underrepresented groups and women
• Facilitate relationship building between network members
• Create business development opportunities
• Enhance recruitment efforts for historically underrepresented groups and women
• Raise awareness, share ideas and create a sense of collaboration and community among everyone at Goldman Sachs
• Raise the visibility of our leadership and diversity commitment to external communities

The firm currently sponsors the following networks in the Americas:

- Asian Professionals Network
- Firmwide Black Network
- Firmwide Hispanic/Latin Network
- Gay and Lesbian Network
- Goldman Sachs Women's Network

Each network operates on a firmwide level and has chapters in divisions where greater interest and participation exists. Members of the firm's management committee and partnership committee sponsor each firmwide network. Network members meet on an ongoing basis and participate in network events throughout the year. Each network also organizes and participates in history and heritage months throughout the year. Every network has an internal web site which serves as a source of information for all Goldman Sachs employees on the network's mission, leaders, key initiatives and events.

Entry-Level Programs/Full-Time Opportunities/Training Programs

Full-Time Analyst Program

Geographic location(s) of program: Opportunities are available in the majority of our global offices

The main purpose of the analyst program is to provide analysts with critical business skills while gaining fundamental skills in their respective divisions. Goldman Sachs seeks highly motivated candidates who have demonstrated outstanding achievements in academic and extracurricular activities.

We are looking for self-motivated team players who have excellent organizational and communication skills. While a background in finance or accounting is not required, candidates should have an interest in business and financial markets.

Goldman Sachs hires full-time analysts for the following divisions:

- Equities
- Fixed income, currency and commodities
- Financing group
- Finance (includes controllers, credit and corporate treasury and firmwide risk)
- Global investment research
- Human capital management
- Investment banking/corporate finance
- Investment management—asset management
- Investment management—private wealth management
- Global compliance
- Legal and management controls
- Merchant banking/private equity
- Operations (includes global operations)
- Services
- Technology

Please visit our web site for specific divisional overviews at: www.gs.com

Strategic Plan and Diversity Leadership

The internal communications group focuses on reinforcing the culture of Goldman Sachs, keeping our people informed about news of the firm, our viewpoints on the global markets, our diverse businesses and management announcements. We use a variety of channels to communicate information throughout the firm—including GS Web (the firm's official Intranet site), "To All" memorandums, firmwide voice mails, global town halls and briefing toolkits.

The office of global leadership and diversity partners with the internal communications group to ensure that diversity messages are communicated effectively firmwide. As such, critical diversity messages are woven into senior leadership's announcements as well as in town halls. Key communications vehicles managed by:

GLD include:

• *Global leadership and diversity web site:* Goldman Sachs' global leadership and diversity internal web site provides a visible, informative and globally inclusive forum to share diversity-focused messages. The site, global in scope, is comprised of a home page that highlights articles from each region as well as separate sections dedicated to the Americas, Europe and Asia. The web site also houses all affinity network homepages globally. It is accessible via a direct link off the firm's GS Web.

• *GLD newsletters:* Goldman Sachs distributes formal global leadership and diversity newsletters to employees across the globe. These newsletters inform people about current initiatives and events such as history and heritage months, encourage them to become involved in affinity networks and highlight best practices and accomplishments across the firm.

In addition to the GLD web site, we also highlight diversity-related initiatives and events on GS Web, the firm's global internal web site.

Who has primary responsibility for leading diversity initiatives at your firm?

Edith Hunt, managing director.

Does your firm currently have a diversity committee?

Yes, in 1990, Goldman Sachs formed the Firmwide Diversity Committee (FDC) to support and promote an inclusive work environment that recruits, retains, develops, and rewards the best and brightest individuals and successfully supports a diverse workforce. Today, the FDC is led by Chairman and CEO Lloyd Blankfein. It consists of members of the firm's management committee and other senior leaders. The FDC meets on a quarterly basis.

If yes, does the committee's representation include one or more members of the firm's management/executive committee?

Yes.

If yes, how many executives are on the committee, and in 2005, what was the total number of hours collectively spent by the committee in furtherance of the firm's diversity initiatives?

Total Executives on Committee: 21

Does the committee and/or diversity leader establish and set goals or objectives consistent with management's priorities?

Yes.

One of the Firmwide Diversity Committee's (FDC) goals is to continue to promote an environment of mutual respect, cooperation and professionalism, and foster the teamwork essential to the firm's commitment to excellence. One of our most successful tools in driving our diversity initiatives throughout the firm has been the commitment and involvement of senior management. The FDC is not only accountable for diversity activities throughout the firm, but it is also a body that encourages serious debate and discussion on important diversity-related issues. To date, the FDC has helped develop numerous programs including one that enables employees to manage personal commitments, enhance career development and heighten sensitivity to diversity issues in the workplace. These programs range in scope from flexible work arrangements to generous family leave policies, and from mentoring programs to training programs.

Each year, the office of global leadership and diversity works with the FDC to create specific, measurable and actionable initiatives for the firm to focus on. These priorities align with the firm's overall business principles and vision for diversity. In 2006, our diversity priorities include:

• Increase the level of diversity dialogue among business leaders and managers
• Leverage our successes as a platform to increase diversity awareness
• Broaden our initiatives for black professionals and expand our retention strategies to focus on the Hispanic population
• Continue to maintain focus on women at all levels, with particular emphasis on the retention of midlevel women

Has the firm undertaken a formal or informal diversity program or set of initiatives aimed at increasing the diversity of the firm?

Yes, formal.

Goldman Sachs' office of global leadership and diversity directs the firm's diversity strategy and translates the firm's diversity commitments into specific actions. Aligned with both the executive office and human capital management, the office of global leadership and diversity is led by Edith Hunt, a managing director, and is driven by a central team that works collaboratively with divisional and regional leadership and diversity managers who ensure our diversity efforts are supported, coordinated and effective across the globe.

The office of global leadership and diversity seeks to drive leadership, commitment, and accountability from top to bottom. In order to fulfill this commitment, a structured set of annual priorities are set and division and region heads are held responsible for achieving them, as well as communicating them in key forums. Ultimately, the firmwide diversity committee is responsible for the state of diversity at Goldman Sachs and answers to our board of directors.

The office of global leadership and diversity employs a focused strategy that seeks to create real change and traction by (1) affecting cultural transformation, (2) advancing leadership and management skills across the firm, and (3) integrating diversity considerations into our key business and people processes such as: recruiting, training, career development, compensation, promotions, succession planning and other key retention strategies as a means to achieve our objectives. To accomplish this, we leverage four key catalysts: (i) leadership commitment; (ii) education and training; (iii) communication and involvement; and (iv) accountability.

To drive our diversity efforts deeper into our organization, Goldman Sachs has developed and implemented various formal systems, which focus on short and long-term priorities as well as measuring progress. These leading initiatives have played a significant role in advancing our diversity efforts.

Each year, division and region heads are responsible for presenting a diversity plan for their population to the firmwide Diversity Committee. The plan must align with the firm's annual diversity priorities and include a summary of successes, a review of their impact on the targeted population and new priorities for the coming year. This exercise requires division heads and managers to evaluate their own performance and formally commit to next steps for their respective populations. At year-end, each of our division heads are explicitly evaluated on their diversity efforts (looking at a range of indicators), so that in their performance review and compensation process they are held accountable by the firm's CEO.

Through our senior leaders' analysis, each division and region head meets with our chairman and CEO, to discuss the status of our high-potential women and minorities and to develop specific action steps to ensure we are broadening the pipeline and each professional's potential is maximized. These meetings are followed up on periodically, prior to key people processes such as promotion and compensation, to ensure that our decisions are consistent with the performance of the talent we identify. The executive office and division heads invest significant time to ensure that the right people are discussed and follow up responsibilities are completed.

Career development committees in each division and region ensure that managers are held accountable for diversity results. Led by each division's senior leadership, CDCs meet to review and provide clear development opportunities for our people across all professional levels. Through CDCs, divisional management proactively works to identify successors, mentor relationships, stretch assignments, mobility opportunities and potential for individuals' career advancement.

How often does the firm's management review the firm's diversity progress/results?

Quarterly.

How is the firm's diversity committee and/or firm management held accountable for achieving results?

Senior management reports to the board of directors annually on the state of the firm's diversity initiatives.

The Stats

	TOTAL IN THE U.S.		TOTAL OUTSIDE THE U.S		TOTAL WORLDWIDE	
	2005	2004	2005	2004	2005	2004
Number of employees (full-time employees)	12,141.27	11,701.27	7,489.47	6,683.7	19,630.74	18,384.97

Please note that these numbers are for 2004 and 2005. These numbers are listed as FTE (full-time employee) only.

Retention and Professional Development

Please identify the specific steps you are taking to reduce the attrition rate of minority and women employees.

• Develop and/or support internal employee affinity groups (e.g., minority or women networks within the firm)
• Increase/review compensation relative to competition
• Increase/improve current work/life programs
• Adopt dispute resolution process
• Succession plan includes emphasis on diversity
• Work with minority and women employees to develop career advancement plans
• Review work assignments and hours billed to key client matters to make sure minority and women employees are not being . excluded
• Strengthen mentoring program for all employees, including minorities and women
• Professional skills development program, including minority and women employees

Diversity Mission Statement

Goldman Sachs aims to be the employer, advisor and investment of choice by attracting and retaining the best and most diverse talent. Through our leadership and diversity efforts, including the affinity network program, we work to provide a supportive and inclusive environment where all individuals, regardless of gender, race, ethnicity, national origin, sexual orientation, gender identity, disability or other classification can maximize their full potential, which in turn leads to strengthening the firm's position as a leader in the industry.

The firm's commitment to diversity is evident at the most senior levels and is driven down through the firm by way of our seventh business principle:

We offer our people the opportunity to move ahead more rapidly than is possible at most other places. Advancement depends on merit and we have yet to find the limits to the responsibility our best people are able to assume. For us to be successful, our men and women must reflect the diversity of the communities and cultures in which we operate. That means we must attract, retain and motivate people, from many backgrounds and perspectives. Being diverse is not optional; it is what we must be.

We know that to manage diversity well, we have to manage people well. We realize that successful formal processes have a particularly positive influence on women, historically underrepresented groups and non-U.S. nationals. The office of global leadership and diversity reinforces our culture of meritocracy by advancing leadership and management skills, and integrating diversity considerations into our key business and people processes, such as recruiting, training, career development and other retention strategies.

Additional Information

At Goldman Sachs we recognize that having a diverse workforce encourages increased creativity and innovation. This is crucial to improved performance and continued business success. To that end, we are committed to creating an environment that values diversity and promotes inclusion. Goldman Sachs recruits individuals from diverse cultures and backgrounds. The result is a wealth of talent and creativity where exceptional individuals work together to provide a world-class service to a broad spectrum of corporate, government, institutional and private clients.

In our search for outstanding individuals we partner with organizations promoting diversity. Through our work with INROADS, Sponsors for Educational Opportunity, The Jackie Robinson Foundation, The Forte Foundation, The Employers Forum on Disability and others, we increase our commitment to recruiting women, students from ethnic minorities and those with disabilities.

Further, we have initiated and manage a number of programs designed to increase awareness of the firm and our industry. These programs allow us to offer academic scholarships, educational opportunities, summer internships and full-time positions to many outstanding students. Not all of these students have a finance or business background; we actively seek candidates from a broad array of academic disciplines and concentrations such as liberal arts, applied math, sciences and engineering, in order to reach a wide spectrum of strong candidates.

We invite to take a closer look at our firm and learn more about the different programs and opportunities available to you by visiting out web site at www.gs.com/careers.

Hallmark

Relationships are woven like fine fabric,

in colors of beauty and patterns of truth,

strengthened by *many distinct threads*.

AT HALLMARK, OUR COMMUNITY IS A WORK OF ART.

Hallmark Cards, Inc.

2501 McGee St.
Kansas City, MO 64108
Phone: (816) 274-5111
Fax: (816) 274-5061

Diversity Leadership

Valerie Steele
Corporate Diversity Manager

Vickie Harris
Corporate Diversity Director

Employment Contact

Dawn Harp
Corporate Staffing Manager
E-mail: hcorp01@hallmark.com
www.hallmark.com/careers

Recruitment

Please list the schools/types of schools at which you recruit.

• *Public state schools:* Central Missouri State Univ., Iowa State Univ., Kansas State Univ., Univ. of Kansas, Univ. of Missouri-Columbia, Univ. of Oklahoma

Do you have any special outreach efforts directed to encourage minority students to consider your firm?

• Participate in/host minority student job fair(s)
• Sponsor minority student association events
• Firm's employees participate on career panels at schools
• Outreach to leadership of minority student organizations
• Scholarships or intern/fellowships for minority students

What activities does the firm undertake to attract minority and women employees?

• Partner programs with women and minority associations
• *Conferences:* NSBE, FraserNet, National Urban League, SWE
• Participate at minority job fairs
• Seek referrals from other employees
• Utilize online job services

Do you use executive recruiting/search firms to seek to identify new diversity hires?

No.

Internships and Co-ops

Summer Internship

Deadline for application: October for all but creative, which does not have a deadline
Number of interns in the program in summer 2005 (internship) or 2005 (co-op): 29
Pay: $13.50-$18.50 per hour

Length of the program: 12 weeks

Percentage of interns/co-ops in the program who receive offers of full-time employment: Approximately 80 percent.

Web site for internship/co-op information: www.hallmark.com/careers

Our program includes rich assignments, many networking opportunities and social events for the interns. We search for interns for our marketing, finance, operations, retail, IT and creative divisions. The qualifications are that the student be obtaining a degree within the area of discipline appropriate to the division. Typically we look for students entering their senior year.

Affinity Groups

HAAL: Hallmark African-American Leadership

Mission is to ensure there is value for cultural differences and that those differences add value to the company by identifying solutions concerning education and awareness; recruitment, development and retention of African-Americans; product development and retail for African-Americans; and maintaining community alliances with organizations who have similar business interests to Hallmark.

HEART: Hispanic Education Awareness Resource Team

Mission is to enable our company to reach Hispanic consumers and to educate employees on Hispanic culture. Additionally, HEART focuses on the retention, recruitment and development of Hispanic employees, and leveraging the Hispanic culture, traditions and opportunities through local community involvement.

HERE: Hallmark Employees Reaching Equality

Mission is to provides Hallmark's gay, lesbian, bisexual and transgender (GLBT) employees with a support network, as well as a forum to work with management and peers on education and awareness of issues that affect them.

All affinity groups are open to all employees of Hallmark Cards, Inc. and meet monthly and host additional activities outside of monthly meetings.

Strategic Plan and Diversity Leadership

How does the firm's leadership communicate the importance of diversity to everyone at the firm?

By hosting events at Hallmark (e.g., CEO Walking the Talk Diversity Awards and Supplier Diversity Awards) and through articles in the daily company newsletter.

Who has primary responsibility for leading diversity initiatives at your firm?

Vickie Harris, corporate diversity director.

Does your firm currently have a diversity committee?

Yes.

If yes, please describe how the committee is structured, how often it meets, etc.

The Corporate Diversity Council (CDC) is made up of senior leaders from across Hallmark. They have bimonthly meetings to set the diversity strategy for the company and ensure that this strategy is executed both at corporate and division levels.

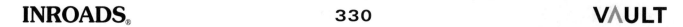

If yes, does the committee's representation include one or more members of the firm's management/executive committee (or the equivalent)?

Yes.

If yes, how many executives are on the committee, and in 2005, what was the total number of hours collectively spent by the committee in furtherance of the firm's diversity initiatives? How many employees are on the committee, and how often does the committee convene in furtherance of the firm's diversity initiatives?

There are 12 executives and two employees on the committee and they spent an estimated 1,300 hours collectively on council related initiatives in 2005.

Total Executives on Committee: 12

Does the committee and/or diversity leader establish and set goals or objectives consistent with management's priorities?

Yes, the strategy uses marketplace, workplace and workforce as the framework for setting goals and objectives that naturally fit with the priorities of the business and with HR. Also, since the CDC is comprised of business leaders, they are instrumental in ensuring that the objectives are aligned with the business goals.

Has the firm undertaken a formal or informal diversity program or set of initiatives aimed at increasing the diversity of the firm?

Yes, formal.

We: a) attend at least four diversity recruiting conferences every year, b) have division diversity councils, who often make increasing the diversity of their division a key goal, c) do targeted development, such as using INROADS interns, and d) have awareness raising programs for all employees.

How often does the firm's management review the firm's diversity progress/results?

Quarterly.

How are the firm's diversity committee and/or firm management held accountable for achieving results?

They are held accountable via their annual performance reviews.

Retention and Professional Development

How do 2005 minority and female attrition rates generally compare to those experienced in the prior year period?

About the same as in prior years.

Please identify the specific steps you are taking to reduce the attrition rate of minority and women employees.

• Develop and/or support internal employee affinity groups (e.g., minority or women networks within the firm)
• Increase/improve current work/life programs
• Adopt dispute resolution process
• Succession plan includes emphasis on diversity

Diversity Mission Statement

The Corporate Diversity Department exists to support Hallmark's goal of creating an environment that fully taps the potential of all individuals in pursuit of corporate objectives. We strive to accomplish this by:

- Developing a critical mass of change agents throughout the company who value diversity and will assist in driving a change process
- Offering programs that build awareness regarding diversity and the business success that results from effectively managing diversity
- Developing and supporting systems, processes and programs that serve to eliminate artificial barriers, which prevent individuals from achieving full potential
- Sustaining a positive image as a company that values diversity

Additional Information

Hallmark's Diversity Vision

Our corporate diversity vision is centered on providing shareholder value through:

- Our people create an environment that taps the full potential of every employee. We attract, develop and retain the best and brightest of a diverse talent pool.
- Our consumers, present and future, look to Hallmark to provide superior products and services that help them express their thoughts, feelings and emotions.
- Our products and services help all people express their heritage, and enrich their own lives and the lives of others.

Hallmark's Business Case for Diversity

Hallmark Cards, Inc. recognizes diversity as central to its success in the marketplace and as a key component of creating a competent workforce and an inclusive workplace.

Marketplace

Business success in the 21st century means responding to increasingly diverse consumer markets, which demand that companies understand them and be willing and able to address their specific needs through their products and services. As the industry leader in the personal expressions business, Hallmark has a distinct relationship with its consumers, who trust Hallmark to enrich their lives and enhance their relationships. Hallmark's brand and core competencies uniquely position it to meet the needs of all of its consumers in ways that are meaningful and memorable. Similarly, success as a retailer depends on Hallmark's ability to meet the needs of diverse consumers, and to provide products and services that link positive emotion to the retail experience for them.

Workplace

An environment in which diversity is embraced and diverse traits leveraged as strengths is one where every employee can perform to his or her potential and in which his or her contributions are respected and appreciated. Hallmark leaders demonstrating inclusiveness in all they do and challenging others to do the same will help employees contribute to a positive workplace for everyone.

Workforce

More than affirmative action, Hallmark focuses on attracting, developing, and retaining a competent and diverse workforce to improve productivity and ensure innovative problem solving and the development of relevant product solutions, all of which are good for business and help Hallmark meet consumer needs. This strength is drawn from differences in ethnic origin, religion, gender, age, sexual orientation, ability, lifestyle, economic background, regional geography, employment status, thinking style and more.

Additionally, Hallmark has an award-winning work/life balance program that includes the following:

- Flex-time

- Part-time schedules
- Job sharing
- Telecommuting
- Adjusted workday/workweek
- Compressed workweek
- Voluntary time off
- Leaves of absence
- Dependent care discounts and referral services
- Back-up child care
- Elder care consultation and referral
- Educational programs

HCA, Hospital Corporation of America

One Park Plaza
Nashville, TN 37203
Phone: (615) 344-2697
Fax: (615) 344-2555
www.hcahealthcare.com

Locations

US (in 23 states), England and
Switzerland

Diversity Leadership

Kim Sharp
V.P. Diversity

Employment Contact

Phone: (615) 344-9551
Fax: (615)344-1551
E-mail:
executive.recruitment@hcahealthcare.com

Recruiting

Please list the schools/types of schools at which you recruit.

• Private schools
• Public state schools
• *Historically Black Colleges and Universities (HBCUs):* Howard, TSU, Mehassy Medical College
• Other predominantly minority and women's colleges

Do you have any special outreach efforts that are directed to encourage minority students to consider your firm?

• *Participate in and host minority student job fairs:* Participate in local job fairs
• *Sponsor minority student association events:* NAHSE
• Firm's employees participate on early career panels at schools
• *Outreach to leadership of minority student organizations:* INROADS and at HBCUs
• *Other:* HCA Community Outreach Foundation has a scholarship program for the children of employees; HCA provides specific scholarship assistance for students pursuing areas where workforce shortage is critical to health care.

What activities does the firm undertake to attract minority and women employees?

• *Participate at minority job fairs:* Nashville Urban League Fair, NBMBAA, NASSE, NAHSE, NSHMBA, NABA, MED Week
• Seek referral from other employees
• Utilize online job services
• *Partner programs with women and minority associations:* INROADS and NAHSE
• *Other:* Has developed sourcing strategies for diverse talent

Do you use an executive recruiting/ search firm to seek to identify new diverse hires?

Yes.

If yes, list all women and or minority owned executive search recruiting firms to which the firm paid a fee for placement services in the past 12 months:

We use Computer Professional Inc., on a contract-to-hire basis.

Internship and Co-ops

Internship opportunities are available on a limited basis for students pursuing various majors including: accounting, supply chain (procurement), economics, human resources and areas of health care, such as nursing, medical technology, medical records. The number of internship positions vary on an annual basis and are usually available during the summer periods.

Scholarships

Scholarships are provided to specific schools to provide qualified students in specific disciplines an opportunity to complete their education and obtain work experience and potential employment. Students are identified through the school and interviewed by the firm. The scholarship program has been expanded and is in its first year of implementation.

Strategic Plan and Diversity Leadership

How does the firm's leadership communicate the importance of diversity to everyone at the firm?

For the leadership levels, multicultural symposia have been conducted covering 75 percent of the firm's leadership. A diversity task force made up of leaders from across the country is available to further the communication throughout the facilities. Annual report, monthly executive newsletter, quarterly updates, board presentations, senior leadership meetings, speakers and programs, and the ongoing message from the CEO of the firm have heightened the importance of diversity in the organization.

Who has primary responsibility for leading diversity initiatives at your firm?

Kim Sharp, vice president of diversity.

Does your firm currently have a diversity committee?

Yes, HCA has a diversity task force. The committee has senior leadership and leaders from various geographical areas of the country representing their divisions and facilities. They formulated the vision and provide guidance for the diversity strategic and implementation plan. The committee meets in person semiannually and is organized in teams to assist in reviewing specific policy guidelines.

If yes, how many executives are on the committee, and in 2005, what was the total number of hours collectively spent by the committee in furtherance of the firm's diversity initiatives? How many employees are on the committee, and how often does the committee convene in furtherance of the firm's diversity initiatives?

Yes.

Total Executives on Committee: 11

Total time collectively spent by the committee members was greater than 60 hours. There are 28 people on the committee. With the team structure, some teams have met three to four times by conference call (i.e. metrics, communications and patient care teams).

Does the committee and/or diversity leadership establish and set goals or objectives consistent with management's priorities?

The Diversity Committee recommended goals and the diversity leader has established goals and objectives consistent with management's priorities.

Has the firm undertaken a formal or informal diversity program or set of initiatives aimed at increasing the diversity of the firm?

The firm has a formal diversity program and initiatives aimed at increasing the diversity of the company. There are management development programs aimed at attracting diverse talent to enter the system and begin a formal leadership development training process that extends from two to four years.

How often does the firm's management review the firm's diversity progress/results?

Monthly reporting to the senior executive level and quarterly to the CEO level.

How is the firm's diversity committee and/or firm management held accountable for achieving results?

All executive leaders and senior officers have goals that include diversity initiatives which are tied to compensation.

The Stats

Employees

2005: 187,750
2004: 197,196
Women comprise 80.2 percent of the employee population.
Minorities comprise 22.7 percent of the employee population.

Diversity Mission Statement

At HCA, we will provide cross-cultural competent care to all patients we serve. We will foster a culture of inclusion and diversity across all areas of our company that embraces and enriches our workforce, physicians, patients, partners and communities.

HDR, Inc.

8404 Indian Hills Drive
Omaha, NE 68114
Phone: (402)399-4872
Fax: (402) 548-5002
www.hdrinc.com/careers

Locations

More than 5,200 employee-owners in over 130 locations worldwide in 36 states including Ontario, Canada and the United Kingdom.
HDR has worked in all 50 states and more than 60 countries.

Diversity Leadership

Judy Webster
Vice President, Employee Relations Director
Phone: (402) 399-4993
Fax: (402) 548-5002
E-mail: judy.webster@hdrinc.com

Employment Contact

Geralyn Bryant
Human Resources Representative
Phone: (402) 926-7052
Fax: (402) 548-5015
E-mail: geralyn.bryant@hdrinc.com

Recruiting

Please list the schools/types of schools at which you recruit.

• Ivy League schools
• Other private schools
• Public state schools
• Historically Black Colleges and Universities (HBCUs)
• *Other predominantly minority and/or women's colleges:* Hampton University, Howard University, Morgan State University, Southern University, Grambling State University, Tennessee State University, Tuskegee University

Do you have any special outreach efforts directed to encourage minority students to consider your firm?

• *Conferences:* NSBE (National Society of Black Engineers)
• Advertise in minority student association publication(s)
• Participate in/host minority student job fair(s)
• Firm's employees participate on career panels at schools
• Outreach to leadership of minority student organizations
• Scholarships or intern/fellowships for minority students

Yes, HDR, Inc. has partnered with INROADS for seven years, sponsoring one to three interns annually. The company made a decision to expand its corporate diversity initiative and in 2006 placed 24 INROADS interns in 13 locations. HDR received the Corporate Plus Award at the Ninth Annual Awards Banquet held in Omaha July 2005. HDR also has four MESA student interns in its California regional offices.

The first HDR/AMIE (Advancing Minorities' Interest in Engineering) scholarships were awarded to students at Morgan State University in Baltimore, Md. and Hampton University in Hampton, Va. The scholarships are a direct benefit of HDR's Platinum membership in AMIE which is a coalition of industry, government agencies and the ABET certified historically black colleges and universities (HBCUs) schools of engineering that seek to forge corporate/academic partnerships that serve to promote and support quality engineering programs.

HDR Howard University Fellowship Program: This program was created to support graduate students through their two-year education in the Howard Department of Civil Engineering and to give them opportunities for real-world experience in the field of water and wastewater treatment engineering. The $20,000 fellowship is awarded to a graduate student with exceptional technical talent in the field of water and wastewater. As part of the fellowship program, the recipient serves as a research assistant on HDR projects involving such innovations as membrane technology, and may intern at an HDR office over the summer.

HDR, Engineering, Inc. Diversity Scholarship Fund is for students attending the Peter Kiewit School of Engineering or the University of Nebraska.

What activities does the firm undertake to attract minority and women employees?

• Partner programs with women and minority associations
• Conferences
• Participate at minority job fairs
• *Seek referrals from other employees:* HDR has an employee referral program for employees to submit candidates for open positions and receive a referral bonus
• *Utilize online job services:* Utilize BlackCollegian.com and NSBE (National Society of Black Engineers) to list job postings

Do you use executive recruiting/search firms to seek to identify new diversity hires?

No.

Internships and Co-ops

HDR Internship and Cooperative Education Programs

Deadline for application: Recruiting for internships and co-ops runs year round. Typically recruiting begins in the fall and most students are hired and start their internship in May. HDR posts current open internship opportunities year round on its web site.

Number of interns in the program in summer 2005 (internship) Over 190 students interned

Pay: Salary ranges vary by location from $11 - $16 per hour, based on academic placement, experience and discipline

Length of the program: Summer internships typically run a 12 week period

Percentage of interns/co-ops in the program who receive offers of full-time employment: Offers are made to qualified students at a rate of 85 percent or more

Web site for internship/co-op information: www.hdrinc.com/careers

Majors: At HDR, we offer professional opportunities in many career fields. Engineering, architecture, planning, design, environmental or consulting jobs do make up the majority of our available positions, but we are also looking for talented individuals with accounting, human resources, legal, marketing, information technology and safety backgrounds. Through the internship program, HDR will typically employ students for two consecutive summers as interns.

Interns will be selected from a variety of schools and programs throughout the country. HDR accepts interns who apply on their own for an internship. Other interns are referred to HDR from programs with universities and other organizations, such as INROADS and MESA.

Internships

• Open to currently enrolled, full-time students
• Students work full-time during the summer or part-time during the semester
• Students are provided with career-related experience
• Students are compensated for work

Co-ops

• Open to currently enrolled, full-time students
• Students alternate university enrollment with terms of full-time employment
• Students are provided with career-related experience
• Students are compensated for work
• Students receive college credit

Strategic Plan and Diversity Leadership

How does the firm's leadership communicate the importance of diversity to everyone at the firm?

Through the companies' 2008 business plan and business meetings.

Does your firm currently have a diversity committee?

No.

Does the committee and/or diversity leader establish and set goals or objectives consistent with management's priorities?

Yes.

Has the firm undertaken a formal or informal diversity program or set of initiatives aimed at increasing the diversity of the firm?

Yes, informal.

How often does the firm's management review the firm's diversity progress/results?

Monthly, through the management dashboard.

Annually, through performance reviews.

How is the firm's diversity committee and/or firm management held accountable for achieving results?

Through goals and objectives and management dashboard.

Retention and Professional Development

Please identify the specific steps you are taking to reduce the attrition rate of minority and women employees.

• Work with minority and women employees to develop career advancement plans
• Strengthen mentoring program for all employees, including minorities and women
• Professional skills development program, including minority and women employees

Additional Information

HDR (hdrinc.com) is an architectural, engineering and consulting (A/E/C) firm that excels at managing complex projects and solving challenges for clients. More than 5,200 employee-owners, including architects, engineers, consultants, scientists, planners and construction managers, in 130 locations worldwide, pool their strengths to provide solutions beyond the scope of traditional A/E/C firms. Headquartered in Omaha, Nebraska, HDR serves the communities throughout all of it's locations through volunteer service, outreach, education and leadership.

A few of these include:

In one city, busloads of HDR employees travel to locations throughout the community to prepare meals for the homeless, renovate homes for the poor, rebuild community parks and escort underprivileged children to a science center.

In another, a team of employees crosses the border into an impoverished area of Mexico, where they build a day care center for children who are often victimized by crime.

And in still another, employees spend their free time cleaning up a community park.

Support for the following programs MESA—Math, Engineering & Science Achievement; and INROADS, an international career development organization. HDR is a long-time supporter of grade school and high school MESA programs, even bringing it to the college level in one city, and is one of the founding partners of INROADS in Omaha, Nebraska.

Also participates in local Habitat for Humanity and Paint-a-thon efforts.

HDR locally supported Creighton University's 2006 All-Nations Pow Wow.

Below are a few of the diversity efforts that HDR has been recognized for:

• April 5, 2006 — Ranked Fourth in Top Supporters of Black Engineering Schools

• January 18, 2006 — HDR's Chicago Office Receives Employer Of The Year Honors From Women's Transportation Group

• October 26, 2005 — First HDR/AMIE Scholarships Awarded To Students At Morgan State, Hampton Universities

• March 11, 2005 — HDR Ranks Among Top Corporate Supporters of Black Engineering Schools

• July 26, 2005 — HDR Employees to Participate in Brush Up Nebraska

• July 18, 2005 — HDR Donates Aluminum Cans to Habitat for Humanity

• *The Black Collegian,* 2006 — Top 100 Employers for the Class of 2006, No. 39 - Top Employer

• *US Black Engineer & Information Technology,* 2005 & 2006 — Among top 51 corporate supporters of black engineering schools

• Howard University Dean Attends Alexandria Office Event—Dr. James H. Johnson, Jr., dean of Howard University's College of Engineering, Architecture and Computer Sciences, and HDR Architecture President Merle Bachman joined the Alexandria office staff on Wednesday, November 9th for a surprise reception to celebrate Kathryn Prigmore's National Women of Color Lifetime Achievement Award. The award was presented during the 10th Annual National Women of Color in Technology Awards Conference, sponsored by the career communications group, held on October 20 to 22, 2005 in Atlanta, Georgia. The conference supports and recognizes minority women in technology careers and connects them with mentors and employers to help launch or re-energize their careers.

• Abad-Fitts honored as Technology All Star — San Antonio Assistant Department Manager Carmen Abad-Fitts selected to receive a national Women of Color Technology Award for her accomplishments in advancing technology and science. She received the Technology All-Star Award during the Atlanta conference October 28-30, 2004. The awards are sponsored by the career communications group.

Hershey Company, The

100 Crystal A Drive
Hershey, PA 17033
www.hersheys.com

Diversity Leadership
Andre Goodlett
Senior Director of Diversity & Inclusion

Employment Contact
Tonia Anderson
Manager of Diversity & Inclusion
100 Crystal A Drive
Harrisburg, PA 17110
Phone: (717) 508-3886
Fax: (717) 534-8053
E-mail: tanderson@hersheys.com

Recruiting

Please list the schools/types of schools at which you recruit.

• Ivy League schools
• Public state schools
• Historically Black Colleges and Universities (HBCUs)
• Hispanic Serving Institutions (HSIs)

Do you have any special outreach efforts directed to encourage minority students to consider your firm?

• Firm's employees participate on career panels at schools
• Scholarships or intern/fellowships for minority students

What activities does the firm undertake to attract minority and women employees?

• Partner programs with women and minority associations
• Participate at minority job fairs
• Seek referrals from other employees
• Utilize online job services

Do you use executive recruiting/search firms to seek to identify new diversity hires?

Yes.

Internships and Co-ops

Hershey's Intern Professional Program (HIPP)

Deadline for application: Ongoing all year
Number of interns in the program in summer 2005 (internship) or 2005 (co-op): 140 interns
Pay: Ranges from $11.75 - $21.60 per hour, depending on major and year in school

Length of the program: Typically interns 12 weeks, co-ops 12 months, though possibly longer, depending on a student's availability and department needs.

Percentage of interns/co-ops in the program who receive offers of full-time employment: Company-wide the figure is less than 10 percent. In the sales department it's 20 percent or more.

Web site for internship/co-op information: www.hersheys.com

Typically engineering, sales, human resources and finance have the majority of undergrad interns/co-ops.

Hershey's Inter Professional Programs (HIPP) formally began in 1978. Over the years, HIPP has grown to become a critical element in Hershey's strategic recruiting and hiring plans. The program provides students with opportunities to develop and apply their skills in a challenging, exciting and industry-leading corporate environment. Many interns have moved right into great jobs with Hershey's upon graduation. Future job offers have also been extended to some interns before returning to school to finish their senior year!

Scholarships

Hershey Scholar Program

Deadline for application for the scholarship program: February 15th

Scholarship award amount: $500-$3,000 paid in two equal installments on August 15 and December 30

Scholarships are available only for children of employees.

UNCF/Hershey Scholar Program

Deadline for application for the scholarship program: April 30

Scholarship award amount: $5,000

Scholarships are only available to minority Pennsylvania residents attending one of UNCF's 38 member colleges, or one of 14 institutions under the Pennsylvania state system of higher education.

Affinity Groups

Women's Council

The Women's Council has now been established. We have conducted focus group sessions with female employees at all levels of the organization to identify the issues relative to the female workforce. The council has broken off into subgroups to address several areas of opportunity. The group will also focus on networking, mentoring, education and developmental opportunities.

Entry-Level Programs/Full-Time Opportunities/Training Programs

New Employee On-Boarding

Length of program: Two days

Geographic location(s) of program: Hershey, Penn.

The program gives an overview of company heritage, organizational departments/functions, diversity, human relations, as well as a performance overview.

The role of the Hershey Leader

Length of program: Two days
Geographic location(s) of program: Hershey, Penn.

Leadership training, diversity overview, HR overview.

Strategic Plan and Diversity Leadership

How does the firm's leadership communicate the importance of diversity to everyone at the firm?

The Hershey Company has a dedicated diversity web site with a cultural calendar to help educate and share diversity-related information. In addition, the public relations department sends out monthly e-mails to employees highlighting diversity events and activities that are both internal and external.

Who has primary responsibility for leading diversity initiatives at your firm?

Andre Goodlett, senior director of diversity and inclusion.

Does your firm currently have a diversity committee?

Yes. The committee consists of several small councils e.g., manufacturing plants, field sales diversity councils in addition to multiple affinity groups. The leads of each group meet to form the corporate council.

If yes, does the committee's representation include one or more members of the firm's management/executive committee (or the equivalent)?

Yes.

If yes, how many executives are on the committee, and in 2005, what was the total number of hours collectively spent by the committee in furtherance of the firm's diversity initiatives?

Total Executives on Committee: Two

There are approximately 80 hours devoted to diversity initiatives. The full council consists of 31 members and they convene as a full council four times a year.

Does the committee and/or diversity leader establish and set goals or objectives consistent with management's priorities?

Yes.

Has the firm undertaken a formal or informal diversity program or set of initiatives aimed at increasing the diversity of the firm?

Yes, formal.

How often does the firm's management review the firm's diversity progress/results?

Quarterly.

The Stats

Employees

2005: 13,750
2004: 13,741

Revenue

2005: $4.429 billion
2004: $4.173 billion

Retention and Professional Development

How do 2005 minority and female attrition rates generally compare to those experienced in the prior year period?

Lower than in prior years.

Please identify the specific steps you are taking to reduce the attrition rate of minority and women employees.

• Develop and/or support internal employee affinity groups (e.g., minority or women networks within the firm)
• Increase/review compensation relative to competition
• Increase/improve current work/life programs
• Succession plan includes emphasis on diversity
• Work with minority and women employees to develop career advancement plans

Diversity Mission Statement

At The Hershey Company, diversity is a key ingredient in making us one of the finest companies in the world. We value the differences that make each individual, supplier, community, customer and consumer unique. Our success is a product of our ability to recognize, understand and incorporate those differences into everything we do. Hershey's strength and future success lie in its diversity—the diversity of thought, management styles, experience and abilities that only can come from bringing together people with different backgrounds and different ways of seeing the world. Hershey's approach to diversity emphasizes four areas: customer and consumer alignment, employee involvement and support, supplier diversity and community involvement.

Additional Information

Hershey's Initiatives:

Customer and consumer alignment: Hershey has significant opportunity in a diverse U.S. marketplace with an estimated ethnic buying power of one trillion dollars. Hershey's multifaceted partnership with Latina superstar Thalia and acquisition of Mexican candy company Grupo Lorena and its top brand, Pelon Pelo Rico, are significant steps in reaching these consumers. Hershey has introduced a new line of co-branded, Latin-inspired candies to build an awareness of a preference for its brands with this fast growing, dynamic population.

Employee involvement and support: Reaching out to employees through various diversity councils, affinity groups, continuous diversity education and internal cultural awareness campaigns are all vehicles through which The Hershey Company demonstrates its commitment to diversity.

Supplier diversity: One of the most important aspects of our business is our interaction with our suppliers. Like our employees, our suppliers make our success possible. Maintaining a diverse network of suppliers makes us a more efficient company while

contributing to the economic development of the communities in which we live and work. Our approach is to partner nationally and locally with organizations to identify diverse suppliers. We also aim to open up opportunities at all levels and in all categories of spending to certified diversity suppliers and, in areas where the diversity supplier is limited, to mentor promising minority and women businesses.

Community involvement: The Hershey Company has a long history of community leadership. Central to who we are as a company is our belief in making a difference in the lives of youth. We demonstrate our commitment through our participation with The Milton Hershey School, UNCF scholarships and the Hershey Youth Track and Field program. We also believe in the value of maintaining strong relationships with diversity focused organizations nationally and locally. We partner nationally with organizations like NAACP, La Raza and the United Way, and in the Hershey, Penn., area with organizations like the Urban League, Y Black Achievers and Junior Achievement.

Humana Health Plans

500 West Main Street
Louisville, KY 40202
Phone: (502) 580-1000
www.humana.com

Diversity Mission Statement

At Humana, we aspire to create a diverse and inclusive workforce that connects us with the consumer, drives innovation and engagement in the workplace, supports a multicultural community and promotes opportunity for our enterprise in the marketplace.

Our goal is for Humana to become the employer, health solution and community partner of choice.

Building talent at Humana is essential to achieving this goal. Therefore, we are using INROADS and other internship/professional development programs to infuse diverse talent into our workforce. Our hope is that many of these interns will go on to be full-time associates. We believe that having the right talent in place at all levels of our organization will drive Humana's business success.

International Business Machines Corporation

New Orchard Rd.
Armonk, NY 10504
Phone: (914) 499-1900
Toll Free: (800) 426-4968
Fax: (914) 765-7382
www.ibm.com/careers

Locations

170 locations in North America, South
America, Asia Pacific, Europe, Middle
East and Africa.

Diversity Leadership

Bill Lawrence
Senior Diversity Program Manager

Employment Contact

Margaret Ashida
Director, University Talent Programs

Recruiting

Please list the schools/types of schools at which you recruit.

• Ivy League schools
• Other private schools
• Public state schools
• Historically Black Colleges and Universities (HBCUs)
• Hispanic Serving Institutions (HSIs)
• Native American Tribal Universities

Do you have any special outreach efforts directed to encourage minority students to consider your firm?

• Hold a reception for minority students
• *Conferences:* American Indian Science and Engineering Society (AISES), Grace Hopper Conference for Women in Computing. HENAAC, National Association of Asian American Professionals (NAAAP), National Association of Women MBA (NAWM-BA), National Black MBA Association (NBMBAA), National Society of Black Engineers (NSBE), National Society of Hispanic MBAs (NSHMBA), Reaching Out, Society of Hispanic Professional Engineers (SHPE), Society of Mexican American Engineers and Scientists (MAES), Society of Women Engineers (SWE), Women In Technology International (WITI)
• Advertise in minority student association publication(s)
• Participate in/host minority student job fair(s)
• Sponsor minority student association events
• Firm's employees participate on career panels at schools
• Outreach to leadership of minority student organizations
• *Scholarships or intern/fellowships for minority students:* INROADS, National GEM Consortium, National Action Council for Minorities in Engineering (NACME), Sponsors for Educational Opportunity (SEO), Project View, Project Able and Entry Point (focused on People with Disabilities)

Web site: www.ibm.com/employment/us, click on "University," then "Diversity Recruitment Programs"

What activities does the firm undertake to attract minority and women employees?

• Partner programs with women and minority associations
• *Conferences:* American Indian Science and Engineering Society (AISES), Grace Hopper Conference for Women in Computing. HENAAC, National Association of Asian American Professionals (NAAAP), National Association of Women MBA (NAWM-

BA), National Black MBA Association (NBMBAA), National Society of Black Engineers (NSBE), National, Society of Hispanic MBAs (NSHMBA), Reaching Out, Society of Hispanic Professional Engineers (SHPE), Society of Mexican, American Engineers and Scientists (MAES), Society of Women Engineers (SWE), Women In Technology International (WITI)

• Participate at minority job fairs
• Seek referrals from other employees
• Utilize online job services

Do you use executive recruiting/search firms to seek to identify new diversity hires?

Yes.

Internships and Co-ops

Employment Pathways for Interns and Co-ops (EPIC)

Deadline for application: Applications accepted year round
Pay: Competitive with industry (pay varies by hire type, e.g. undergrad, grad student)
Length of the program: Internships are typically 10-14 weeks, co-ops are typically six or seven months
Web site for internship/co-op information: www.ibm.com/careers

A student employment assignment at IBM gives you real-world experience that offers you a competitive edge when you enter the workforce. Student employment assignments provide you the opportunity to become familiar with IBM's organization, work style and corporate culture. Co-op and internship programs are an important recruiting channel for IBM because they help management identify high-potential prospective employees. Participating students are often considered for a long-term commitment of regular employment. Our philosophy is recruit once, hire twice. As an IBM intern or co-op, you will be assigned to a paid technical or nontechnical position related to your major or career goals.

Extreme Blue

Deadline for application: Applications accepted year round
Pay: Competitive with industry
Length of the program: Typically 10-14 weeks
Web site for internship/co-op information: www.ibm.com/extremeblue

The Extreme Blue™ internship program—IBM's incubator for talent, technology and business innovation—challenges project teams of technical and MBA interns (along with their technical and business mentors) to start something big by developing new high growth businesses.

Scholarships

IBM-INROADS Scholarship

Scholarship award amount: $1,500 tuition scholarship (one-time scholarship)—several scholarships awarded

Web site or other contact information for scholarship available to INROADS interns at IBM only. The IBM-INROADS Scholarship provides $1,500 tuition scholarships to IBM INROADS interns who have demonstrated both academic and professional excellence.

Affinity Groups

Over 172 affinity networking groups globally.

Global Affinity Groups at IBM:

• Asian
• Black
• Gay, Lesbian, Bisexual, Transgender (GLBT)
• Hispanic/Latino
• Men
• Native American
• People with disabilities
• Women

Diversity Network Groups consist of employees who voluntarily come together with the ultimate goal of enhancing the success of IBM's business objectives by helping their members become more effective in the workplace through:

• Meeting and teaming
• Networking
• Mentoring and coaching
• Community outreach
• Social, cultural and educational events
• Developing professional skills
• Enhancing recruitment and welcoming

Entry-Level Programs/Full-Time Opportunities/Training Programs

International Business Machines Corporation, headquartered in Armonk, N.Y., is the world's largest information technology (IT) company. While we are the IT leader, the solutions and services we deliver to our clients span all major industries, including financial services, health care, government, automotive, telecommunications and education, among others. It is the breadth of our portfolio—across hardware, software, services, consulting, research, financing and technology—that uniquely separates IBM from other companies. We have a rich history of driving innovations that help our clients transform themselves into on demand businesses through our professional solutions, services and consulting businesses. IBM has a diverse and talented workforce that conducts business in 170 countries. For more information about IBM career opportunities, including our business areas and geographic locations, please visit www.ibm.com/careers.

Strategic Plan and Diversity Leadership

How does the firm's leadership communicate the importance of diversity to everyone at the firm?

The importance of diversity is communicated at all levels in IBM via electronic communication.

Who has primary responsibility for leading diversity initiatives at your firm?

Ted Childs, vice president, global workforce diversity.

Does your firm currently have a diversity committee?

Yes, a global diversity council governs over 70 local diversity councils around the world. Additionally, there are executive task forces for eight constituencies: Asian, black, gay, lesbian, bisexual, transgender, Hispanic/Latino, men, women, Native American and people with disabilities.

If yes, please describe how the committee is structured, how often it meets, etc.

Diversity councils are located at multiple IBM based locations worldwide.

If yes, does the committee's representation include one or more members of the firm's management/executive committee (or the equivalent)?

Yes.

Does the committee and/or diversity leader establish and set goals or objectives consistent with management's priorities?

Yes.

Has the firm undertaken a formal or informal diversity program or set of initiatives aimed at increasing the diversity of the firm?

Yes, formal.

How often does the firm's management review the firm's diversity progress/results?

Annually.

How is the firm's diversity committee and/or firm management held accountable for achieving results?

Through the annual chairman's review, senior level executives report on year to year progress.

The Stats

Employees

2005: 329,300
2004: 329,000

Revenue

2005: 91.1 billion
2004: 96.3 billion

EMPLOYEE DEMOGRAPHICS, 2005								
AREA	TOTAL	MEN	WOMEN	ALL MINORITIES	BLACK	ASIAN	HISPANIC	NATIVE AMERICAN
Officials/Mgrs	17,385	12,406	4,979	2,885	994	1,210	572	109
Professionals	55,827	37,269	18,558	13,873	3,995	7,170	2,400	308
Technicians	11,549	10,177	1,372	2,448	990	658	719	81
Marketing	40,052	28,832	11,220	10,106	2,815	5,561	1,505	225
Office/Clerical	5,951	1,764	4,187	1,945	1,289	217	375	64
Craft Workers	1,232	774	458	192	88	60	40	4
Operatives	1,971	1,266	705	391	155	153	75	8
Totals	133,967	92,488	41,479	31,840	10,326	15,029	5,686	799

Source: www-306.ibm.com/employment/us/diverse/employment_data.shtml

Retention and Professional Development

Please identify the specific steps you are taking to reduce the attrition rate of minority and women employees.

• Develop and/or support internal employee affinity groups (e.g., minority or women networks within the firm)
• Increase/review compensation relative to competition
• Increase/improve current work/life programs
• Adopt dispute resolution process
• Succession plan includes emphasis on diversity
• Work with minority and women employees to develop career advancement plans
• Review work assignments and hours billed to key client matters to make sure minority and women employees are not being excluded
• Strengthen mentoring program for all employees, including minorities and women
• Professional skills development program, including minority and women employees

Diversity Mission Statement

IBM leaders, in every generation, have believed that an inclusive workplace is right for the company, no matter what the prevailing views of the day represented. That kind of leadership didn't just happen—it is a natural companion to our shared beliefs and values. Diversity and the concept of workforce inclusion are key factors in helping define how we do business. "Diversity policies lie as close to IBM's core as they have throughout our heritage," says Sam Palmisano, IBM chairman and CEO. "Today we're building a workforce in keeping with the global, diverse marketplace to better serve our customers and capture a greater share of the on demand opportunity."

Additional Information

Project View is IBM's award-winning diversity recruitment program that offers black, Hispanic/Latino, Native American, Asian, women and people with disabilities, the chance to be considered for IBM career opportunities nationally. Travel, meals and lodging are included in this unique one-and-a-half-day visit. Only IBM makes a job search this much fun! Selection is based on work experience, skills, and overall academic achievement. This program is open to students receiving a BA, BS, MS or PhD. Project View is open to U.S. citizens or nationals, permanent residents, refugees, asylum seekers or those authorized to work under the amnesty provisions of the U.S. immigration law.

Multicultural People in Technology (MPIT) is a multicultural IBM employee initiative the focuses on:

• Support the growth, development, advancement and recognition of IBM's current multicultural technical talent
• Attract and recruit technical multicultural talent to IBM
• Encourage more multicultural youths (K-12) to pursue education and careers in science and technology

Currently, MPIT manages internal and external programs that address these needs in six multicultural constituencies: Asian, black, gay/lesbian/bisexual/transgender, Hispanic/Latino, Native American and people with disabilities.

EXploring Interests in Technology and Engineering (EXCITE) Camps are an extension of IBM's commitment to reach groups that are underrepresented in the technical workforce and to train and recruit individuals from those constituencies for technical careers. Through its EXITE Camps, IBM identifies 12- and 13-year-old girls with an interest or proficiency in math and science, and prepares them to fill the technical pipeline by introducing them to the potential of technology as well as the fun and exciting things they can do with it right now, and exposing them to women who have successful technology careers. Nearly 2,000 IBM volunteers, female and male, will participate in the EXITE Camps, developing, coordinating and overseeing such activities as web page design, computer chip design, laser optics, animation, robotics, and working with computer hardware and software. The volunteers will also introduce the girls to a variety of IBM technologies:

TryScience.org, an award-winning web site designed to make learning science more fun for kids. In addition, they will serve as e-mentors, corresponding with participants during the school year via e-mail, providing tutoring and encouraging the students to further pursue their interests in math, science and technology.

MentorNet is a not-for-profit educational organization focused on furthering women's progress in engineering and science fields through the use of an e-mentoring network. MentorNet matches protégés from various colleges and universities with mentors from industry and academia. IBM is a strategic partner of MentorNet, and IBMers comprise the program's largest source of professional mentors.

J.C. Penney Company, Inc.

6501 Legacy Dr.
Plano, TX 75024
Phone: (972) 431-1000
Fax: (972) 431-2320
www.jcpenneycareers.com

Locations

Plano, TX (HQ)
Store locations nationwide

Diversity Leadership

Fernando Serpa
VP of Diversity

Employment Contact

Juna Jones-Moore
College Relations
6501 Legacy Dr.
Plano, TX 75024
Phone: (972) 431-1000
Fax: (972) 431-2320
E-mail: jjone31@jcpenney.com

Recruiting

Please list the schools/types of schools at which you recruit.

• Ivy League schools
• Public state schools
• Historically Black Colleges and Universities (HBCUs)
• Hispanic Serving Institutions (HSIs)
• Native American Tribal Universities

Do you have any special outreach efforts directed to encourage minority students to consider your firm?

• *Conferences:* BEEP—Black Executive Exchange Program through National Urban League
• Advertise in minority student association publication(s)
• Participate in/host minority student job fair(s)
• Sponsor minority student association events
• Firm's employees participate on career panels at schools

What activities does the firm undertake to attract minority and women employees?

• Partner programs with women and minority associations
• *Conferences:* NUL, NAACP, LULAC, plus others
• Participate at minority job fairs
• Seek referrals from other employees

Do you use executive recruiting/search firms to seek to identify new diversity hires?

Yes.

If yes, list all women- and/or minority-owned executive search/recruiting firms to which the firm paid a fee for placement services in the past 12 months:

Pending.

Internships and Co-ops

Various ranging from sales manager interns, marketing interns, logistics interns, IT interns

Deadline for application: May 1st

Number of interns in the program in summer 2005 (internship) or 2005 (co-op): 50 in the internship program; four in the co-op program

Pay: Varies $12-$17 depending on the majors and positions)

Length of the program: Summer program—10 weeks; co-op—six months

Percentage of interns/co-ops in the program who receive offers of full-time employment: 75 percent

Web site for internship/co-op information: www.jcpenneycareers.com

Description: The 10-week summer intern program provides a realistic overview of the activities related to the specific departments: IT, marketing, sales, logistics, HR, procurement, legal. The main emphasis of this program is spent in the home office gaining a basic understanding of the process and a working knowledge of the departments that support the process.

Structure: The JCPenney Internship Program will provide a training schedule consisting of activities, training and projects designed to improve your knowledge of the specific department. A final written report or oral presentation will be made to marketing senior management.

Qualifications: Students between junior and senior years with a 3.0 minimum GPA are preferred. Most interns are marketing, HR, CIS, finance, supply change, management and business majors, but any student with a sincere interest in pursuing a career with JCPenney, who has strong leadership and analytical skills, can be successful.

Entry-Level Programs/Full-Time Opportunities/Training Programs

• Merchandising Training Program
• Direct Merchandising Training Program
• Assistant Designer Training Program
• Logistic Training Program
• Sales Manager Training Program

Length of programs: Six months

Geographic location(s) of programs: Varies—regional stores—all 50 states and corporate office in Plano, Texas.

Employee benefits and employee discounts are also provided.

Description

The six-month training program provides a realistic overview of the JCPenney process and operations. The main portion of the program is spent in the home office gaining a basic understanding of the process and a working knowledge of the departments that support the process. Upon successful completion of the training program and promotion into a full-time position, the annual salary will be increased.

Structure

The program will provide a training schedule, manual and web-based materials to facilitate the program. The schedule consists of activities, training and projects designed to improve your knowledge of JCPenney specific operations. Assignments, written reports and oral presentations will be made to senior executives.

Qualifications

College graduates with a 3.0 minimum GPA are preferred. Most graduates are business, finance, HR, management, marketing, finance and/or fashion merchandising majors, but any student with a sincere interest in pursuing a career in retail who has strong

leadership and analytical skills, and a flair for retail concepts, can be successful. Retail experience is strongly preferred plus a willingness to relocate.

Strategic Plan and Diversity Leadership

How does the firm's leadership communicate the importance of diversity to everyone at the firm?

The firm communicates diversity initiatives through mailings, the company web site, newsletters, meetings and pep rallies.

Who has primary responsibility for leading diversity initiatives at your firm?

Fernando Serpa, VP of diversity.

Does your firm currently have a diversity committee?

Yes.

If yes, does the committee's representation include one or more members of the firm's management/executive committee (or the equivalent)?

Yes.

How many employees are on the committee, and how often does the committee convene in furtherance of the firm's diversity initiatives?

Quarterly.

> *Total Executives on Committee:* Four

Does the committee and/or diversity leader establish and set goals or objectives consistent with management's priorities?

Yes.

Has the firm undertaken a formal or informal diversity program or set of initiatives aimed at increasing the diversity of the firm?

Yes, formal.

How often does the firm's management review the firm's diversity progress/results?

Twice a year.

The Stats

Employees
2005: 149,245 (U.S.)

Revenue
2005: $18,781,000 (U.S.)
2004: $18,096,000 (U.S.)

Diversity Mission Statement

OUR COMMITMENT

JCPenney is committed to valuing the diversity of our associates and the customers we serve. The goal of this positioning statement is to reinforce our commitment to valuing diversity and incorporating it into the Penney culture and the way we do business.

Additional Information

What is diversity?

Diversity refers to the uniqueness of each human being. Each person is an "original," a one-of-a-kind combination of characteristics—physical, personality, gender, ethnicity, race, religion, skills, cultural background and sexual orientation—that makes each person special and different.

Valuing diversity means appreciating the many advantages of diversity and behaving in a way that reflects respect for individual differences, while treating each person based on his or her own merit. For the company, valuing diversity means the inclusion of all our associates' and customers' differences as part of our overall business strategy.

Valuing diversity is in keeping wiht the Penney idea and philosophy

The Golden Rule was the company's original name and the principle by which James Cash Penney intended the business to be guided. The Penney Idea, adopted in 1913, set as its fifth principle, "To improve constantly the human factor in our business." We continue to broaden this vision by building more cultural diversity into our population. Our goal is to ensure that no gaps exist between our principles and our achievements.

Diversity is part of our business strategy

As our company has grown and prospered, it has become a citizen of the communities in which it operates worldwide. This has made it even more important for us to value and appreciate our diversity—because the successful retailer of the future will recognize diversity as a competitive strategy.

Valuing diversity is part of our strategic business plan and an important part of strengthening our competitive position. As we plan and run our business with customer diversity in mind, we will enhance our ability to gain and keep market share and increase sales and profits. Being customer driven requires that we have a mix of merchandise and workforce that are responsive to the customers we serve.

Our associate base represents a tremendous resource that we must continue to tap. We are committed to supporting diversity in our workforce through all of our personnel actions.

We believe a diverse workforce will enhance the quality of the decision-making process. This is, in fact, the essence of our team process.

Our vision

We see a JCPenney that is:

• Known by our associates as the place to work because we have an environment that makes it possible for all associates to contribute, be productive, receive recognition, grow and succeed.
• Known by our customers as the place to shop, since we can meet their needs through our stores, catalog and other businesses.
• Known by our suppliers as a company that provides and demands fair and equitable practices in all our business dealings.
• Known by our shareholders as a company that maximizes its diverse resources to provide a fair return.

Diversity is a shared responsibility

All associates share responsibility for respecting and utilizing the strengths of diversity in their actions with customers, suppliers and other associates.

Management must create an environment that encourages diverse viewpoints. This is accomplished through positive actions, such as attracting, hiring, training, developing, promoting and retaining a diverse workforce. Every level of management is accountable and responsible for accomplishing this.

JEA

JEA
21 West Church Street T6
Jacksonville, FL 32202
www.JEA.com

Locations

Jacksonville, FL

Diversity Leadership

Carol A. Higley, PHR
Manager, Corporate Workforce Planning
Phone: (904) 665-6045
Fax: (904) 665-5310
E-mail: higlca@jea.com

Employment Contact

Maria Salgueiro
Manager, Talent Acquisition and Retention
Phone: (904) 665-4699
Fax: (904) 665-5310
E-mail: salgme@jea.com

Recruiting

Please list the schools/types of schools at which you recruit.

Private schools: Jacksonville University, Jones College

Public state schools: Edward Waters College, Florida Agricultural & Mechanical University, Florida State University, University of Florida, University of North Florida

Do you have any special outreach efforts directed to encourage minority students to consider your firm?

• Advertise in minority student association publication(s)
• Participate in/host minority student job fair(s)
• Outreach to leadership of minority student organizations

What activities does the firm undertake to attract minority and women employees?

• Participate at minority job fairs
• Utilize online job services

Do you use executive recruiting/search firms to seek to identify new diversity hires?

Yes.

Internships and Co-ops

JEA CO-OP

Deadline for application: No deadline, depends on business needs
Number of co-op students in the program in summer 2005: 10
Pay: $10.50-12.50 hourly
Length of the program (in weeks): Varies
Percentage of interns/co-ops in the program who receive offers of full-time employment: 10 percent
Web site for internship/co-op information: www.JEA.com

Schedule: Part-time or full-time; flexible

Work groups include: Engineering, environmental services, finance, human resources, technology services

Strategic Plan and Diversity Leadership

How does the firm's leadership communicate the importance of diversity to everyone at the firm?

The firm's leadership communicates diversity information via the company's web site; corporate meetings and senior leadership meetings.

Who has primary responsibility for leading diversity initiatives at your firm?

Bill Hegeman, director, employee services.

Does your firm currently have a diversity committee?

Yes.

Has the firm undertaken a formal or informal diversity program or set of initiatives aimed at increasing the diversity of the firm?

Yes, informal.

How often does the firm's management review the firm's diversity progress/results?

Quarterly.

The Stats

Note: MSA Metropolitan Statistical Area (includes Clay, Duval, Nassau and St. Johns counties)
• Percentage of minorities: 25.8 percent
• Number of minorities: 485
• Percentage of female employees: 24 percent
• Number of female employees: 452
• Percentage of minorities on the executive team (Official/administrative job category): 14.4 percent
• Percentage of women on the executive team (Official/administrative job category): 24.7 percent

Retention and Professional Development

How do 2005 minority and female attrition rates generally compare to those experienced in the prior year period?

About the same as in prior years.

Please identify the specific steps you are taking to reduce the attrition rate of minority and women employees.

• Increase/review compensation relative to competition
• Increase/improve current work/life programs
• Adopt dispute resolution process
• Succession plan includes emphasis on diversity
• Work with minority and women employees to develop career advancement plans
• Strengthen mentoring program for all employees, including minorities and women
• Professional skills development program, including minority and women employees

Diversity Mission Statement

The Equal Opportunity/Equal Access Program applies without regard to race, creed, color, religion, political affiliation, sex, national origin, disability, age, veteran status, marital status or related personal characteristics. It pertains to every level of city government and all city implemented and/or sponsored programs and services related to employment. This includes, but is not limited to recruitment, hiring, compensation, training, placement, promotion, discipline, demotion, lay off, recall, termination, working conditions, and related terms and conditions of employment.

The Equal Opportunity/Equal Access Program is designed to challenge all city employees to achieve equality, accessibility and equal opportunity throughout all levels of city government. Consistent with this commitment, every manager, supervisor, elected and appointed official, staff member and employee is encouraged to join together in an effort to achieve the full realization of a better, more open equitable society.

Johnson & Johnson

501 George St.
New Brunswick, NJ 08901
Phone: (732) 524-1958
Fax: (732) 524-2587
www.jnj.com/careers

Locations
Worldwide

Employment Contact
Caridad Arroyo
Manager, Diversity Outreach
E-mail: carroy1@corus.jnj.com

Recruiting

Please list the schools/types of schools at which you recruit.

• Ivy League schools
• Other private schools
• Public state schools
• Historically Black Colleges and Universities (HBCUs)
• Hispanic Serving Institutions (HSIs)

Do you have any special outreach efforts directed to encourage minority students to consider your firm?

• Hold a reception for minority students
• *Conferences*: National Society of Black Engineers, Society of Hispanic Professional engineers, CGSM, GEM, National Society of Hispanic MBA, NBMBAA, Reaching Out, Disco, MBA Diversity Forum
• Advertise in minority student association publication(s)
• Participate in/host minority student job fair(s)
• Sponsor minority student association events
• Firm's employees participate on career panels at schools
• Outreach to leadership of minority student organizations
• Scholarships or intern/fellowships for minority students

What activities does the firm undertake to attract minority and women employees?

• Partner programs with women and minority associations
• *Conferences:* SWE chapter level, see list above
• Participate at minority job fairs
• Seek referrals from other employees
• Utilize online job services
• *Other*: Advertising

Do you use executive recruiting/search firms to seek to identify new diversity hires?

No.

Internships and Co-ops

Over 1,000 interns yearly and 90+ INROADers

Length of the program: Varies based on the student schedule, program
Percentage of interns/co-ops in the program who receive offers of full-time employment: 60 percent INROADS; the other programs are run by the operating companies—decentralized recruitment

Johnson & Johnson offers numerous internships. Please contact us for more information.

Scholarships

- Historically Black Colleges and Universities
- Hispanic Serving Institutions
- National Society of Black Engineers
- Society of Hispanic Professional Engineers
- Penn State
- GEM
- Consortium for Graduate Studies in Management

Scholarship award amount: Varies

Affinity Groups

- AALC: African-American Leadership Council
- AMENAH: Association of Middle Eastern & North African Heritage
- CAAJJ: Community of Asian Associates at Johnson & Johnson
- GLOBAL: Gay & Lesbian Organization for Business and Leadership
- HOLA: Hispanic Organization for Leadership and Achievement
- HONOR: Help our Neighbors with our Resources
- SAPNA: South Asian Professional Network & Association
- WLI: Women's Leadership Initiative

Entry-Level Programs/Full-time Opportunities/Training Programs

- Finance Leadership Dev. Program
- IM Leadership Dev. Program
- Engineering/Operations/Quality Leadership Dev. Program
- HR Leadership Dev. Program

Length of programs: Two years
Geographic location(s) of programs: Across the U.S. and Puerto Rico

Strategic Plan and Diversity Leadership

How does the firm's leadership communicate the importance of diversity to everyone at the firm?

Office of diversity, diversity minute "webinar," in-house conferences, e-mails, newsletters, web sites, meetings.

Who has primary responsibility for leading diversity initiatives at your firm?

Joann Heisen, vice president, office of diversity.

Does your firm currently have a diversity committee?

Yes.

If yes, does the committee's representation include one or more members of the firm's management/executive committee (or the equivalent)?

Yes.

Does the committee and/or diversity leader establish and set goals or objectives consistent with management's priorities?

Yes.

Has the firm undertaken a formal or informal diversity program or set of initiatives aimed at increasing the diversity of the firm?

Yes, formal.

The Stats

Employees
2005: 115,600 worldwide
Revenue
2005: $50.5 billion worldwide

Retention and Professional Development

How do 2005 minority and female attrition rates generally compare to those experienced in the prior year period?

About the same as in prior years.

Please identify the specific steps you are taking to reduce the attrition rate of minority and women employees.

- Develop and/or support internal employee affinity groups (e.g., minority or women networks within the firm)
- Increase/review compensation relative to competition
- Increase/improve current work/life programs
- Adopt dispute resolution process
- *Work with minority and women employees to develop career advancement plans*: done across the board for all employees
- Strengthen mentoring program for all employees, including minorities and women
- Professional skills development program, including minority and women employees

Diversity Mission Statement

Johnson & Johnson's credo sets forth our responsibilities to our employees. It recognizes their dignity and merit, their individuality and the requirement for equal opportunity in employment, development and advancement for those qualified. From these principles, modified over the years, Johnson & Johnson has fostered and encouraged the development of a diverse workforce—a workforce for the future. While we can point with pride to a commitment to diversity deeply rooted in our value system, we rec-

ognize that our former employees, customers and communities are far different from those of today. However, our commitment to these core stakeholders as they have evolved, and as Johnson & Johnson has evolved, is as strong as ever. Today's customers and employees come from all over the world and represent different ages, cultures, genders, races and physical capabilities. Through their life experiences, they provide a diversity of thought and perspective that must be reflected in our corporate culture.

To achieve this vision, we must build a workforce that is increasingly skilled, diverse, motivated and committed to dynamic leadership. This workforce should reflect our diverse customer base and be knowledgeable of the markets we serve. Being the employer of choice in a dynamic global environment means embracing the differences and similarities of all our employees and prospective employees. It also means the execution of innovative diversity and marketing initiatives to ensure our ability to recruit, develop, retain and promote exceptional talent from an array of backgrounds and geographies, while continuing our pursuit of excellence. Our goal is to ensure our ability to meet the demands of a changing world with a vision worthy of our values and our commitment to be the leader in health care across the globe. When we achieve our vision, diversity becomes one of our most important competitive advantages.

Additional Information

Because of J&J's decentralized structure, there are many other diversity initiatives that take place at the respective operating company levels.

JPMorgan Chase

277 Park Avenue
New York, NY 10172
www.jpmorganchase.com

Locations
4,252

Employment Contact
Sandra C. Dorsey
Vice President
Internship Program Manager
Phone: (212) 622-9458
Fax: (646) 534-3021
E-mail: sandra.dorsey@chase.com

Polina Kimlat
Officer
Phone: (212) 622-4330
Fax: (646) 534-3021
E-mail: polina.kimlat@jpmchase.com

Recruiting

Please list the schools/types of schools at which you recruit.

We recruit across a range of programs and campuses. Please check jpmorganchase.com/careers for events at your campus this fall and throughout the year.

Do you have any special outreach efforts to encourage minority students to consider your firm?

• *Conferences:* We participate in various industry-wide organizations and conferences. These include: Out for Undergraduates (BA), INROADS (BA), the United Negro College Fund (BA), Disability Mentoring Day (BA), JPMorgan Chase Smart Start Program (BA), The Consortium for Graduate Study in Management (MBA), The Forte Foundation (MBA), National Black MBA Association Conference, National Society of Hispanic MBAs Conference, National Association of Black Accountants (NABA) Convention and Reaching Out MBA Conference, which attracts gay, lesbian, bisexual and transgender (GLBT) students.

• *Other:* We visit a range of college campuses, including historically black colleges and universities, and conduct various outreach efforts to ensure that we meet and engage a diverse student population.

What activities does the firm undertake to attract minority and women employees?

In addition to the BA and MBA recruiting activities we described in the previous questions, the firm is committed to placing diverse, experienced professionals in open positions. We strive to place candidates internally and also work closely with our partner search firms to identify external candidates.

Internships and Co-ops

JPMorgan Chase has over 15 different summer internship programs, all of which hire a significant number of diverse candidates. Those divisions hiring interns include everything from technology and credit card services to investment banking and human resources. Summer interns are given a large amount of responsiblity and are expected to become integral membrs of their teams over the 10-week summer program.

In order to supplement our on-campus recruiting efforts, we work closely with INROADS, HACE, HBCUs and SEO to source diverse talent for our many summer programs. Deadlines vary for the internships, but most are in January and February, with interviews taking place in February and March. The pay also varies across the different lines of business within the bank and is competitive with the salaries paid by other financial service firms. The percentage of interns receiving offers of full-time employment varies from year to year, but is generally a very high percentage.

Scholarships

The JPMorgan Chase UNCF Scholars Program

A firmwide program dedicated to finding undergraduate students who have a commitment to diversity, the program is open to all students who can demonstrate this commitment, have a high academic achievement and strong leadership qualities. Each year, we select up to 20 students to join the program. Each receives up to $10,000 in scholarship money as well as a guaranteed summer internship. You can apply through the UNCF web site: www.uncf.org/internships.

Affinity Groups

JPMorgan Chase Employee Networks

The firm has more than 70 employee networks, initiated by and for employees, in locations across the globe. There are also several employee networks within the investment bank. These are groups of employees of a common cultural heritage, gender, age or interest. They are valued organizations within the firm and are actively supported by management.

Employee networks provide their members with a forum to communicate and exchange ideas, build a network of relationships across the firm, get access to volunteer opportunities in the community and support for career development and mentoring. More than 20,000 of the company's worldwide employees participate in one or more employee network. Employee networks strengthen our culture by:

- Supporting employees
- Promoting professional development
- Offering mentoring opportunities
- Helping employees understand the firm's culture
- Reinforcing JPMorgan Chase's commitment to inclusiveness and diversity
- Functioning as a resource to the Corporate Diversity Council
- Acting as a forum to accelerate the pace of change and cultivate an inclusive atmosphere

In the recent past, employee networks have hosted notable speakers and events. For example, AsPIRE, the employee network for Asian/Pacific Islanders, hosted Indra Nooyi, president and CFO of PepsiCo Inc. Additionally, PRIDE, the employee network for lesbian, gay, bisexual and transgender employees, hosted an appearance by acclaimed playwright Tony Kushner.

JPMorgan Chase Employee Networks (partial list)

- Access Ability: A resource on disability issues and a voice for employees with disabilities.

- Adelante: Promoting the development of Latino/Hispanic employees at JPMorgan Chase.

- AsPIRE (Asians and Pacific Islanders Reaching for Excellence): To enhance professional development and leadership opportunities for those of Asian/Pacific Island heritage.

- Investment Bank Finance and Business Management Women's Network: Formed to meet the needs of women at all levels in the investment bank finance and business management function globally, including networking, mobility, professional development and social responsibility.

- Investment Bank Junior Women in Banking: Formed to promote the retention and advancement of analyst and associate women in the investment bank area. To strengthen the pipeline of female employees, Junior Women in Banking focuses on leveraging senior leader engagement, networking, career development and mentoring.

- Investment Bank Women's Committee: A grassroots organization formed to address the needs and issues of women in the front office areas of the investment bank in North America. The committee's goal is to work together, and with management, to help attract, retain, develop and promote women across the businesses.

- Investment Bank Women Who Trade: Formed to foster communication among female traders in the investment bank and support recruiting efforts, this group is comprised completely of female traders across all of the investment bank's businesses and product groups.

- Native American Tribes Instilling Opportunities and Network Support: Native American employees and others supporting a diverse and inclusive workplace at JPMorgan Chase.

- Parents Networking Group: A network to help working parents in Europe, the Middle East and Africa successfully balance family and career.

- PRIDE: Supporting workplace fairness for lesbian, gay, bisexual and transgender employees.

- Professional Networking Association: Enthusiastic, outgoing young and young-minded professionals who want to grow personally and professionally.

- South Asian Society: A London-based network to maximize the impact of South Asians in making JPMorgan Chase successful.

- ujima: A forum for JPMorgan Chase employees of African descent, ujima is Swahili for "collective work and responsibility."

- Women of Color Connections: Designed to promote awareness of the unique challenges experienced by women of color.

- Women's Network: A forum for women at JPMorgan Chase to collaborate and grow as professionals.

- Working Families Network: A network to help JPMorgan Chase employees succeed in balancing family and career needs.

- Women in Risk Exchange: Formed to help retain talented women at all levels and give women at all stages of their careers concrete opportunities, both to develop professionally and to lead.

Entry-Level Programs/Full-Time Opportunities/Training Programs

We have 11 entry-level, full-time programs for undergrads:

- Asset & Wealth Management
- Audit
- Card Services
- Commercial Banking
- Corporate Finance
- Finance
- In Store Sales Management
- Operations, Management Services & Technology
- Research
- Sales & Trading
- Treasury & Securities Services

For detailed, up-to-date information, please visit us at jpmorganchase.com/careers.

Two aspects of our entry-level programs, in particular, differentiate JPMorgan Chase from other potential employers.

First, we take a holistic approach to managing our new BA (analyst) and MBA (associate) hires. The first few years are crucial in defining and establishing a strong career platform and mark the beginning of a road defined by targeted skills training and support. During that time, we want to ensure that training and development experiences are carefully structured so that our analysts and associates can build a strong foundation with the firm. We make significant investments in training and development, and our programs are considered to be among the best in the industry.

Second, we are serious about giving and getting clear direction and honest performance feedback. As Jamie Dimon, CEO, said in his 2005 annual shareholders letter, "We want our people to communicate openly, easily and constructively." One resource available is our rites of passage roadmap, which illustrates how to get ahead, the skills that are needed for each role and function, and the training programs that are available to close any gaps. Evaluation committees review performance and promotions across peer groups.

Strategic Plan and Diversity Leadership

How does the firm's leadership communicate the importance of diversity to everyone at the firm?

At JPMorgan Chase, we have been helping our clients do business for more than 200 years. To describe our firm and our people, there is no better phrase than that of one of our founders: "to at all times conduct first-class business in a first-class way." For us, this philosophy has everything to do with our people. Along with our reputation, our people are our most valuable asset. In an industry as dynamic, innovative and complex as financial services, we need to find and retain the very best employees.

To conduct first-class business in a first-class way, we understand the importance of fostering an environment of respect and inclusiveness. Our business principles serve as a roadmap for how and why we make decisions. As CEO Jamie Dimon said in his 2005 annual shareholder letter, "We are morally, programmatically and institutionally committed to inclusiveness and diversity."

At JPMorgan Chase, we constantly remind ourselves that the most important thing we can do for employees is to build a healthy, vibrant company that treats people with respect, and create an environment where everyone has the opportunity to succeed and performance is recognized and rewarded based on merit.

Managers are also encouraged to participate in a range of diversity activities, including:

- Mentoring
- Leadership and/or sponsorship roles in employee networks
- Participating in college recruiting
- Sponsorship of "fireside chats" with key employee groups

Who has primary responsibility for leading diversity initiatives at your firm?

Responsibility for creating a diverse and inclusive organization begins at the top. Our CEO, Jamie Dimon, leads the Corporate Diversity Council—a group of senior leaders from across the company, including the investment bank, who set the vision and strategy for diversity at the firm. Progress on diversity objectives is reviewed monthly by the executive management of the firm and regularly with the board of directors. In addition, managers understand that they are accountable for making measurable, sustainable progress in this regard.

The Stats

Revenue

2005: $59,149 billion

Diversity Mission Statement

At JPMorgan Chase, we constantly remind ourselves that the most important thing we can do for employees is to build a healthy, vibrant company that treats people with respect and creates opportunity. Everyone counts, and we have to remember that we all support one another. We strive to create a more inclusive work environment that draws on and develops the best talent. We want individuals of any race, nationality, gender, sexual orientation or physical ability to have the opportunity to excel based on their performance and contribution to the firm. Building a diverse and inclusive work environment requires effort and perseverance, which is why we make inclusiveness and diversity an integral part of how we manage the company.

Additional Information

What makes JPMorgan Chase a "best practice" firm?

We asked a range of JPMorgan Chase employeese why they joined and why they stay. From analysts to senior managers, there was a clear consensus on the six major attractions:

• The scale, scope and prestige of the bank
• Our reputation as a business innovator
• The chance to make a personal impact
• High-quality training and development
• Exceptional quality of work and deal flow
• A spirit of cooperation and teamwork

We understand that the best and brightest come from many backgrounds, many cultures and many outlooks. What the best and brightest share is a will and desire to achieve. By seeking out these candidates, by honoring and celebrating their diversity, by nurturing their strengths, we will stand apart from our competitors and be recognized by our clients as the best in the business.

Awards and Honors

We feel good about our efforts with regard to diversity and inclusiveness, and are especially gratified when external partners recognize them through awards and honors. For example:

• Top 50 Companies for Diversity by *DiversityInc* magazine, 2006 and five previous years running
• Top Companies for Women of Color by *Working Mother* magazine, 2006 and previous two years
• Top 10 Companies for Executive Women by *DiversityInc* magazine, 2006
• Top 10 Companies for Supplier Diversity by *DiversityInc* magazine, 2006
• Top 10 Companies for People with Disabilities by *DiversityInc* magazine, 2005
• Top 10 Companies for Latinos by *DiversityInc* magazine, 2005
• *Fortune* magazine's Top 50 Companies for Minorities for 2005 and previous six years
• 100 percent rating on the Human Capital Index, an evaluation conducted by the Human Rights Campaign to measure how well major corporations treat their gay, lesbian, bisexual and transgender employees and customers. Perfect score for five years running.
• Corporate Responsibility Award for outstanding leadership in corporate diversity efforts in the workplace from SAGE (Services and Advocacy for Gay, Lesbian, Bisexual & Transgender Elders), 2005
• Top 100 Companies by *Working Mother* magazine, 2005 and previous 10 years
• Top 50 companies by *LATINA Style* magazine, 2005 and previous four years
• No. 10 on *The Black Collegian*'s list of Top 100 Diversity Employers, 2005
• Top Six Companies for African American Women by *Essence* magazine, 2004
• The Ron Brown Award for Corporate Leadership—a Presidential Award recognizing JPMorgan Chase for outstanding achievement in employee and community relations, 2004
• Corporate Leadership for Children award from Child Care Inc. for our "extraordinary commitment to quality child care for children," 2003

- Top company for women by the New York City Mayor's Office/Women's Commission, 2003
- Top 50 best places to work by *Savoy* magazine, 2003
- Top 10 Companies for Recruitment and Retention by *DiversityInc* magazine, 2003
- Opportunity Now Award (U.K.)—for programs benefiting the careers of women, 2002
- Diversity Award for Excellence (U.K.), 2002
- CEO Diversity Leadership Award—from Diversity Best Practices, 2002
- *Careers & the disAbled* magazine—Top 50 Companies, 2000
- American Psychological Association: Psychologically Healthy Workplace Award, 2003
- New York State Psychological Association: Psychologically Healthy Workplace Award, 2002
- *Enable* magazine—Top Companies for people with disabilities, 2002
- *Hispanic* magazine—Corporate 100, 2003
- New York State Rehabilitation Association—Top Company for supporting individuals with disabilities, 2002
- Conference Board Work-Life Innovators Award, 2002
- Top Company for gay, lesbian, bisexual, transgender employees by *DiversityInc* magazine, 2003
- Catalyst Award for innovative programs that advance the careers of women, 2001
- Outie Award from the Out & Equal organization for most significant progress toward gay, lesbian, bisexual and transgender employees
- Gay-Friendly Public Companies in Corporate America Award, the Gay Financial Network (gfn.com)

As proud as we are of our achievements and recognitions, we know that there is always more that can be done. We'll encourage you to share your interests in ways that help raise standards on all sides, giving you the challenges, experiences, development and support you need to fulfill your potential, because that's how we will achieve ours.

Kellogg Company

One Kellogg Square
Battle Creek, MI 49016-3599
Phone: (269) 961-2000
www.kellogg.com/careers

Locations

North America, Latin America, Europe,
Asia Pacific

Diversity Leadership
Velois Bowers
VP Diversity & Inclusion

Employment Contact
Byron R. Foster

Recruiting

Please list the schools/types of schools at which you recruit.

- *Public state schools:* Western Michigan University, DePaul University, Michigan State University,UTEP, UCLA, Indiana University
- *Historically Black Colleges and Universities (HBCUs):* Lincoln University (MO.), Central State University, Clark Atlanta University, Howard University, Morgan State University, Chicago State University, Alabama A&M, University of Arkansas-Pine Bluff, Hampton University, Wilberforce University
- *Hispanic Serving Institutions (HSIs):* Texas A&M

Do you have any special outreach efforts directed to encourage minority students to consider your firm?

- Host a reception for minority students
- Conferences
- Participate in/host minority student job fair(s)
- Sponsor minority student association events
- Outreach to leadership of minority student organizations
- Scholarships or intern/fellowships for minority students

What activities does the firm undertake to attract minority and women employees?

- Partner programs with women and minority associations
- *Conferences:* NSBE, Consortium, NBMBAA, NABA, NSHMBA, ALPHA, SHPE, SWE, NSN, NAWMBA
- Participate at minority job fairs
- Seek referrals from other employees
- Utilize online job services
- Network with diversity organizations

Do you use executive recruiting/search firms to seek to identify new diversity hires?

Yes.

Internships and Co-ops

The internship programs are in several Kellogg business groups and are typically recruited for during the academic year. Most of the internships are during the summer, following the close of the academic year. The internships consist of undergraduate and graduate students.

> *Length of the programs:* 12 weeks
> *Percentage of interns/co-ops in the programs who receive offers of full-time employment:* 75 percent
> *Web site for internship/co-op information:* www.kellogg.com/careers

The internships are designed as developmental tools which are meaningful projects providing a bridge to full-time positions following graduation. The quality of work and successful project completion are among the key factors to determine if an intern will receive an offer of employment.

Scholarships

Kellogg's Corporate Citizen Fund (KCCF)

KCCF has provided funding for scholarship programs that are weighted to selection of diverse students, including the following:

- Carson's Scholars Fund—$25,000 to support the Carson's Scholars Fund offered to Battle Creek Public School students
- Consortium for Graduate Study in Management—$15,000 to support Millenium Campaign for Educational Excellence
- Hispanic College Fund—$10,000
- Hispanic Scholarship Fund—$6,000
- MESAB—$10,000 scholarship support for Medical Education for South African blacks
- National Association for Black Accountants (NABA)—$6,000
- Women's Grocer Association—$1,000

Affinity Groups

Kellogg employee resource groups offer opportunities for employees who are connected by some common dimension of diversity to come together to build relationships, identify and generate potential solutions to real or perceived barriers that interfere with their ability to realize their full potential, and to create opportunities to aid Kellogg Company in driving positive business results.

Women of Kellogg (WOK)

This community is dedicated to the personal and professional growth and development of the women within Kellogg Company. They join together to project a common voice for the shared experiences, perceptions and needs of women in the Kellogg workplace and to help members reach their full potential.

> *Meet:* Monthly
> *Web site:* www.kellogs.com

Kellogg African American Resource Group (KAARG)

This group contributes to company objectives by ensuring the professional development of its members, and serving as a resource to positively influence the Kellogg environment. They provide career development strategies and activities, advise company leadership as appropriate and actively drive retention.

> *Meet:* Monthly

Web site: www.kelloggs.com

Kellogg Young Professionals

This group provides professional and social networking opportunities for young employees (30 years and under) to assist in their acclimation & development within the company. Professional development opportunities are focused on enhancing the understanding of Kellogg Operations while providing both macro- and micro-level learning.

> *Meet:* Monthly
> *Web site:* www.kelloggs.com

Other employee resource groups currently in development:

• Hispanic Employee Resource Group
• Multicultural Employee Resource Group (KMERG)

Entry-Level Programs/Full-Time Opportunities/Training Programs

Global learning and development opportunities (25 workshops offered in 2005).

Strategic Plan and Diversity Leadership

Who has primary responsibility for leading diversity initiatives at your firm?

VeLois Bowers, vice president diversity and inclusion.

Does your firm currently have a diversity committee?

No.

Does the committee and/or diversity leader establish and set goals or objectives consistent with management's priorities?

Yes.

Has the firm undertaken a formal or informal diversity program or set of initiatives aimed at increasing the diversity of the firm?

Yes, formal.

How often does the firm's management review the firm's diversity progress/results?

Quarterly.

How is the firm's diversity committee and/or firm management held accountable for achieving results?

At the core of Kellogg's diversity and inclusion initiative is accountability. That is the essence and strongest component of the initiative. Performance measures were added to the evaluations of all people managers around the initiative. The success of the initiative became one of several factors that played a part in performance evaluations, promotions and bonuses.

Human resources and people managers knew that the Executive Management Council (EMC) was reviewing the overall diversity and inclusion plan quarterly. A standing agenda item for the EMC was the number of women and minorities who are being prepared for positions of increasing responsibility in the company.

A diversity scorecard was designed to allow the company to see its progress on the initiative. It had measurable objectives for hiring, retention and promotion of women and minorities. The scorecard kept track of company sponsored training of women and minorities, demographics, affirmative action deficiencies, and women and minority underutilization. On a quarterly basis, managers were given their scorecard to determine their progress.

Retention and Professional Development

Please identify the specific steps you are taking to reduce the attrition rate of minority and women employees.

• Develop and/or support internal employee affinity groups (e.g., minority or women networks within the firm)
• Increase/review compensation relative to competition
• Increase/improve current work/life programs
• Succession plan includes emphasis on diversity
• Work with minority and women employees to develop career advancement plans
• Strengthen mentoring program for all employees, including minorities and women
• Professional skills development program, including minority and women employees

Diversity Mission Statement

Valuing Diversity

At Kellogg Company, we're dedicated to the things that set us apart and make us better. With different backgrounds, cultures and experiences, everyone brings something valuable to our team. We thrive on the diverse talents of our employees, and we expect all of our team members to show dignity and respect to those talents. There's always a better idea just around the corner and, with support, creative thoughts become brilliant working solutions. At Kellogg Company, it's all about being yourself, being accepted, and being successful.

Additonal Information

People are our most important asset.

Kellogg Diversity and Inclusion Strategy focuses on four key strategic areas:

• Build accountability for diversity and inclusion throughout the organization
• Recruit, retain and develop talented people
• Drive, understanding, education and awareness
• Create the environment

Companies are constantly in flux as to who is responsible for making sure that the people of the organization are developed, trained and motivated to give their best for the success of the company. The question is continually being asked as to who is accountable for providing skill-building experiences so that employees are always learning and continually creating innovative products. At Kellogg, the world's leading producer of cereal and a leading producer of convenience foods, the answer is its strategy. Accountability: everyone, every level. Every management level and every people manager within the organization must have measurable accountabilities which help to ensure that Kellogg attracts, retains and promotes people from the broad range of backgrounds that comprise the diverse global marketplace it serves.

Such accountability is broad in its scope. But the creation of the K Values made it reasonable to believe that the company could embrace and support such an initiative. The K Values, six guiding Kellogg values, encompass the way the company runs its business and builds relationships with its employees.

The K Values are:

- We act with integrity and show respect
- We are all accountable
- We are passionate about our business, our brands, and our food
- We have the humility and hunger to learn
- We strive for simplicity
- We love success

The key value underpinning the diversity and inclusion initiative is "We act with integrity and show respect." This K Value calls for everyone in the company to show respect and value all individuals for their diverse backgrounds, experience, styles, approaches and ideas. Also, it requires every member of the organization to listen to others.

Everyone who manages people at Kellogg has measurable performance requirements around the initiative. But, three groups in particular are accountable for ensuring the integration of the initiative within the company. They are:

- The Executive Management Committee (EMC)
- Human resource professionals
- The company's people managers

The specific tasks and deliverables for each group differ, but each has accountabilities in the four key strategic focuses of the Diversity and Inclusion Strategy:

- Build accountability for diversity and inclusion throughout the organization
- Recruit, retain and develop talented people
- Drive understanding, education and awareness
- Create the environment

Three programs help to ensure that the key accountabilities are driven throughout the organization:

- Kellogg's performance management review
- The diversity and inclusion scorecard
- Managing inclusion training

Kelly Services

999 West Big Beaver Rd.
Troy, MI 48084
E-mail: talentmanagement@kellyser-
vices.com
www.kellyservices.com (choose United
States to go to our US homepage)

Recruiting

Please list the schools/types of schools at which you recruit.

• *Other private schools:* Duke University, Raleigh, NC
• *Public state schools:* University of Illinois, Chicago, IL
• *Historically Black Colleges and Universities (HBCUs):* Central State University, Wilberforce, OH; Prairie View A&M, Prairie
  View, TX

Do you have any special outreach efforts directed to encourage minority students to consider your firm?

Kelly services is affliated with the following organizations:

• American Association of Retired Persons (AARP)
• Black Data Processing Association (BDPA)
• Hispanic Alliance for Career Enhancement (HACE)
• National Association of Black Accountants (NABA)
• National Association of Colleges and Employers (NACE)
• Navy League
• National Urban League
• Operation Able

Internships and Co-ops

Kelly is dedicated to supporting INROADS, Inc. Working in one of our many Kelly offices as a member of the INROADS internship program is an exciting and rewarding opportunity for any student. In fact, it's the perfect opportunity to prepare for our
Manager-in-Training program. Our internships are an educational strategy designed to help students merge their career goals and
classroom studies with real-world experience. This is accomplished though mentorships, professional support, guidance, training
and development.

The partnership between Kelly and INROADS began in 1994 and is a cornerstone of Kelly's diversity initiative. Since starting
the relationship, we have hired students to work in field and corporate capacities.

Entry-Level Programs/Full-Time Opportunities/Training Programs

Our 18-month College Graduate Manager-in-Training (CGIT) Program is designed to provide career opportunities to talented individuals with the desire to grow with Kelly. Our program will train you in all aspects of our branch office operations and sales process, ultimately promoting you into a management and leadership role for your own market.

What does a Kelly Manager do?

As the manager of your own branch operation, you will have complete responsibility for the business development of your market as well as the development and coaching of the inside service team. You'll consult with our clients to develop human resource business solutions, while managing a multi-million dollar portfolio of business. Our managers:

• Manage branch operations to meet and exceed financial targets
• Select, train, and develop staff
• Identify potential new clients through outside business development activities
• Lead team efforts in service delivery, customer and employee retention, recruiting and expense management (e.g., workers' compensation, unemployment compensation, general operating expenses)
• Build and maintain relationships with key customers and business leaders in the community, as well as local, regional and corporate Kelly management
• Design and conduct presentations and proposals to potential customers

We'd like to meet you if you have…
• A bachelor's degree in marketing, management, liberal arts or other business majors
• GPA 3.0 +
• Ability to relocate
• The ability to build relationships and communicate effectively
• The ability to collaborate effectively with others to ensure both Kelly's and the customers' business goals are met and/or exceeded
• The ability and desire to lead and contribute to the personal and professional development of others
 • Knowledge of financial concepts and a keen level of awareness on current labor, business, and community issues

Diversity Mission Statement

Kelly Services is committed to and has a long history of supporting a diverse workplace.

With a workforce of more than 700,000 employees globally, we place a premium on creating a culture of inclusion in order to attract, retain and develop a diverse talent pool. At Kelly Services, an inclusive culture encompasses diversity acceptance and respect for each of our employees and their contributions. We strive to maintain a diverse workforce that reflects the population of each community in which we do business.

Kelly Services has a long history of supporting a diverse workplace and maintaining a commitment to an inclusive environment.

Our shared values of diversity, individual dignity and mutual respect reflect our clear commitment to diversity throughout our organization. To strengthen our commitment, diversity is one of our core strategies in the corporate business plan, which is used as a guide for all of our employees. We are also in the process of implementing a five-part diversity strategic plan that includes the following components: recruitment, talent management, outreach, education and communication.

Our main goal is to create an environment of inclusion where diverse ideas and perspectives flourish to create the best business solutions for our customers. Our success is directly tied to the success of our employees.

Additional Information

Kelly Services, Inc. is a Fortune 500 company headquartered in Troy, Mich. that provides staffing services to customers in various industries worldwide. Kelly offers staffing solutions that include temporary staffing services, staff leasing, outsourcing, vendor on-site and full-time placement. Kelly owns and operates nearly 2,600 offices in 30 countries and territories. Kelly provides employment to more than 700,000 employees annually, with skills including office services, accounting, engineering, information technology, law, science, marketing, light industrial, education, health care and home care.

Key Bank

127 Public Square
Cleveland, OH 44114
Phone: (216) 689-6300
Fax: (216) 689-7009
www.key.com

Locations
950 locations in 13 states

Internships and Co-ops

Key internship programs offer college students an opportunity to experience working at Key on a short-term basis. Internships prepare students for full-time opportunities in the undergraduate programs and other opportunities upon graduation. Key recruits for its internship program at college campuses across the country and target undergraduate students who major in finance, business, accounting and information technology.

Internships also help to build a foundation of diversity at Key, as Key partners with organizations such as INROADS and the United Negro College Fund (UNCF).

Web site address for employment: www.key.com/jobs

Entry-Level Programs/Full-Time Opportunities/Training Programs

Undergraduate Programs

Key undergraduate programs help connect recent college graduates with exciting opportunities at Key. By combining on-the-job training, hands-on experience and department rotations, Key analyst program graduates are well prepared for a career with the firm.

We presently offer five rotational programs in:

- Key technology services
- Key corporate and investment banking
- Finance
- National consumer finance
- McDonald financial group

The Stats

Employees

2005: 19,694

Revenue

2006: $93.4 billion

Retention and Professional Development

Diversity Awareness

Key offers training, mentoring programs and partnerships to our employees and to our communities.

Training

• Diversity Training: Valuing Differences reinforces basic diversity concepts and provides skill-building exercises; training focuses on understanding oneself and others, cultural conflicts, resolving diversity conflicts, workplace behavior, managing diverse relationships and dealing with inappropriate humor in the workplace.

• Weatherhead Executive Experience (1Key Diversity Leadership Challenge): Provides diversity training for senior-level executives as part of the Weatherhead Executive Experience.

Mentoring

• Mentoring helps employees confront barriers, providing exposure to critical decision-making and helps build relationships in informal and formal organizational networks. Through mentoring, minority and female employees receive professional development coaching from executives

Employee Leadership

• Diversity Councils: Comprised of employees who represent a cross-section of the organization, help drive our diversity efforts with the full support of senior management.

• Board of Inclusion: Comprised of senior level managers who represent various lines of businesses and strengthen our efforts to attract and retain a diverse workforce. We recognize the need for a diverse set of talents to be a leader in today's marketplace.

Partnerships

Key partnerships include:

• *National Black MBA Association*—The National Black MBA Association, Inc. (NBMBAA) is a nonprofit organization of minority MBAs, business professionals, entrepreneurs and MBA students.

• *National Society for Hispanic MBAs*—National Society of Hispanic MBAs (NSHMBA) is a nonprofit organization whose mission is fostering Hispanic leadership through graduate management, education and professional development to improve society.

• *INROADS Program*—An international, world-class nonprofit organization that helps to recruit, source and develop talented young people of color.

• *Esperanza*—Serves the educational needs of Cleveland's Hispanic community since 1983 and offers programs for elementary, middle school and high school students.

• *United Negro College Fund (UNCF)*—Oldest and most distinguished higher education assistance organization in the United States.

• *Historically Black Colleges and Universities (HBCU)*—We have partnerships with the following nationally ranked HBCU colleges and universities: Hampton University, Morehouse College and Spelman College.

• *Diversity Hiring Coalition*—active member of the Diversity Hiring Coalition in Maine where resources are shared to help Maine employers to increase, support and retain racial and ethnic diversity in the workplace.

Web site address for diversity: http://www.key.com/html/A-3.6.1.html

KPMG LLP

345 Park Ave.
New York, NY 10154-0102
Phone: (212) 758-9700
Fax: (212) 758-9819
www.kpmgcareers.com

Locations
93 US offices

Diversity Leadership
Jennifer Neal
Diversity Recruiting Manager
1660 International Drive
Tysons Corner
McLean, VA 22102
Phone: (703) 286-8218

Employment Contact
Clyde Jones
Three Chestnut Ridge Road
Montvale, NJ 07645

Recruiting

Please list the schools at which you recruit.

KPMG maintains recruiting relationships with well over 100 colleges and universities across the United States at both private and public institutions.

- *Historically Black Colleges and Universities (HBCUs):* Howard University, Hampton University, Florida A&M, University, North Carolina A&T State University, Clark Atlanta University.

Do you have any special outreach efforts that are directed to encourage minority students to consider your firm?

- *Conferences:* National Association of Black Accountants (NABA), Association of Latino Professionals in Finance and Accounting (ALPFA), Hispanic Student Business Association (HSBA)
- Advertise in minority student association publication(s)
- Sponsor minority student association events
- Firm's employees participate on career panels at school
- Outreach to leadership of minority student organizations
- Scholarships or intern/fellowships for minority students
- *Other:* Host Case Study Competitions for NABA and ALPFA

Do you use executive recruiting/search firms to seek to identify new diversity hires?

Yes. KPMG does use executive search firms that focus on minority and women professionals.

KPMG's Recruiting Strategy

Recruiting is another important way the firm demonstrates that diversity is profoundly important to its success. KPMG's campus recruiting team is actively involved in recruiting at historically black colleges and universities (HBCUs) and participates at the NABA and ALPFA student chapter level on a regional basis. Campus and experienced hire recruiters participate in numerous career fairs held by diverse organizations. Recruiting literature includes messaging on the firm's commitment to being a great place to work and inclusive environment.

Our interest in increasing our presence on HBCU campuses is exemplified by our participation in the Howard 21st Century Advantage Program for the past three years. Through the program, we've worked closely with groups of 20 students each year and have provided mentoring on a one-to-one basis by minority employees from KPMG.

Internships and Co-ops

INROADS

Deadline for application: May
Number of interns in the program in summer 2005 (internship) or 2005 (co-op): 52
Pay: Varies
Length of the program: Eight weeks
Percentage of interns/co-ops in the program who receive offers of full-time employment: 100 percent of those eligible to receive offers of full-time employment did receive a full-time offer.
Web site for internship/co-op information: www.inroads.org

KPMG is a member of INROADS, a program that places minority students in intern positions in our offices throughout the country.

Through this program we are able to offer internships at an early stage, (i.e., prior to entering college) and for as many as four years, compared to our traditional one-year internship beginning the summer before graduation.

Scholarships

KPMG Foundation/Frank Ross Professorship

Deadline for application for the scholarship program: April
Scholarship award amount: $2,500
Web site or other contact information for scholarship: Awarded through NABA

Frank Ross, a retired partner with KPMG, continues his active commitment to diversity education and recruitment in the accounting field beyond his retirement from the firm. Mr. Ross, a founder of NABA, has created, in collaboration with the foundation and the firm's Washington, D.C. office, a $650,000 endowment fund. KPMG's partners and employees can contribute to this endowment fund and KPMG's foundation will match their contribution.

We provide four $2,500 scholarships during the national NABA convention. The students are chosen by NABA based on the criteria and weightings below.

• GPA: 40 percent
• Financial need: 20 percent
• Essay: 15 percent
• Leadership: 15 percent
• Working for education funds: 10 percent

Minority Doctoral Scholarship Program

The KPMG Foundation invested seven million dollars to establish a Minority Doctoral Scholarship Program, open to African-American, Hispanic-American and Native-American accounting doctoral students (scholarships were also awarded to information systems doctoral students from 1997-2002). This program annually awards nearly $600,000 in scholarships. This is in addition to the teaching and research assistantship and waiver of tuition and fees normally provided by doctoral-granting institutions. To date, 50 percent of the minority doctoral scholarships have been awarded to women.

Howard University Student Business Executive Leadership Honors Program

KPMG is a part of the Howard University student business executive leadership honors program. In this venture, KPMG works with a team of students and provides mentoring, in addition to career advice and professional development opportunities for future accounting, finance and computer professionals.

Affinity Groups

Over the past several years, KPMG has developed a number of internal networks to engage our diverse groups in career development. These networks help increase visibility of diverse people among the general workforce, and enhance a feeling of inclusiveness between leadership and employees.

KPMG's diversity networks include:

• APIN (Asian Pacific Islander Network)
• African-American Network
• AALA (African-American Latino Americans)
• KNOW (KPMG's Network of Women)
• Hispanic-Latino Network
• International Circle (for those engaged on an international assignment or considering one)
• Pride@KPMG (gay, lesbian, bisexual, and transgender professionals)

Women's Initiatives

Constituting nearly half of all new hires, women represent an enormous part of KPMG's talent pool. To help women realize their full potential, KPMG formed a women's advisory board in 2003, charged with developing programs and initiatives designed to help support, advance and reward women.

One such program, KPMG's network of women (KNOW), has been helping to foster women's networking, mentoring and leadership opportunities in nearly half of KPMG's U.S. offices. Further expansion is planned in the years ahead. So far, KNOW has positively affected more than 8,500 women.

In addition, the Women's Advisory Board and KNOW leaders have collaborated to develop external events that bring together senior-level executive women and showcase the firm's commitment to women.

Entry-Level Programs/Full-Time Opportunities/Training Programs

Diversity Training

KPMG has always believed strongly in setting and maintaining high standards of integrity. To promote integrity and inclusiveness, KPMG requires all employees and partners to undergo "respect and dignity and diversity in the workplace" training.

Professional Training and Development

Training is available to entry-level employees and availability continues throughout each individual's career through learning opportunities to audit, tax and advisory professionals to keep all individuals technically current in their accounting discipline and fully prepared to apply their auditing and accounting knowledge to the particular industry context relevant to the clients they serve.

Complementary learning opportunities are available to increase skill in client relationship management, collaboration, leadership and other personal effectiveness skills. All told, partner and employee training averages 72 hours per person annually, which significantly exceeds the National State Boards of Accountancy (NASBA) annual and triennial requirements.

KPMG has also enhanced the curriculum available to our client service support (CSS) staff to better enable their individual skills development and career success within KPMG and beyond. Areas of training include business writing and making effective presentations, building effective relationships with colleagues and clients, problem solving and decision making, leading and mobilizing teams, performance management, project management, and self-management of one's career. The overall management of learning and development is carried out by the firm's center for learning and development (CLD). The CLD is staffed with a team of experienced, dedicated professionals who are the backbone of KPMG's education and training environment. Their efforts are complemented by the contributions of hundreds of audit, tax and advisory professionals, who are drawn in to develop and deliver the comprehensive curriculum that is available to employees of the firm.

KLEARN LIVE! is key to the firm's blended learning approach. Its Centra software-based, virtual classroom delivers training in an efficient, nonintrusive way. Individuals simply log in for the training they need. Instructors and subject matter experts lead training sessions from anywhere, using slides, multimedia, whiteboards, questions, chats and other training tools.

Strategic Plan and Diversity Leadership

How does the firm's leadership communicate the importance of diversity to everyone at the firm?

KPMG uses a variety of communication methods to help foster a supportive and inclusive work environment such as *KPMG Today,* the firm's Outlook-delivered daily update on news and events both internal and external to the firm, and, *KPMGLife* magazine which profiles our people and their accomplishments.

Who has primary responsibility for leading diversity initiatives at your firm?

Clyde Jones, national director, diversity and EEO/AAP.

Does your firm currently have a diversity committee?

Yes.

If yes, please describe how the committee is structured, how often it meets.

KPMG's national diversity team, led by Clyde Jones, drives and supports the firm's national and grassroots efforts in support of KPMG's commitment to being an all-inclusive workplace. Such programs and initiatives include events like national diversity celebrations in local offices, KPMG diversity networks and external minority professional organization sponsorships.

Has the firm undertaken a formal or informal diversity program or set of initiatives aimed at increasing the diversity of the firm?

KPMG's Commitment to Diversity:

KPMG embraces diversity and encourages our employees to share their views and lifestyles, thereby broadening everyone's awareness of differences. We believe in fostering an environment of inclusion that encourages partners and employees to be successful. By valuing our differences we build upon our individual, team and firm strengths. It's an approach that we believe benefits our people and our clients.

Our Team
Joseph Maiorano, Executive Director, Workplace Solutions
Phone: (201) 307-7269
E-mail: jmaiorano@kpmg.com

Clyde Jones, National Director, Diversity and EEO/AAP
Phone: (201) 307-8368
E-mail: clydejones@kpmg.com

Kathy Rohan, Manager, EEO
Phone: (201) 307-7780
E-mail: krohan@kpmg.com

Mentoring

KPMG prides itself on its mentoring culture, with thousands of partners and employees benefiting from the mentoring experience every day. The firm has several resources to help individuals establish and maintain a mentoring relationship, and leverage it for personal growth, career development and potential advancement. People can also visit the KPMG mentoring web site, and the firm helps partners and employees initiate and develop a mentoring relationship, as a mentor or mentee.

Equal Employment Opportunity

KPMG LLP reaffirms its longstanding policy of providing equal opportunity for all applicants and employees, regardless of their race, color, creed, religion, age, gender, national origin, citizenship status, marital status, sexual orientation, gender identity, disability, veteran status or other legally protected status.

This policy applies to recruiting, recruitment advertising and/or other communications media, hiring, rates of pay and other compensation, benefits, overtime, promotions, transfers, demotions, terminations, reductions in force, discipline and all other terms, conditions or privileges of employment.

How often does the firm's management review the firm's diversity progress/results?

Annually.

The Stats

Employees

19,600 (U.S.)

Revenue

2005: $4.7 billion (fiscal year ending Sept. 30, 2005)

Retention and Professional Development

How do 2005 minority and female attrition rates generally compare to those experienced in the prior year period?

Lower than in prior years.

Please identify the specific steps you are taking to reduce the attrition rate of minority and women employees.

- Develop and/or support diversity networks
- Increase/review compensation relative to marketplace
- Increase/improve current work/life programs
- Professional skills development programs

Diversity Mission Statement

Our Mission

Foster a work environment that is inclusive and embraces diversity of our people, their ideas and lifestyles, professional insights and personal perspectives. This is vital for KPMG to stand apart from other audit, tax and advisory services firms, and as an employer of choice.

Our Vision

Our aim is to make enhancements to the firm's work environment by valuing our differences and including them in what we do. Our values support it. Our clients value it. And our success depends on it.

Our Strategy

Leveraging, valuing and encouraging diversity of thought, perspective and approach to create an open and inclusive work environment where both business and personal objectives and growth can be met through:

Awareness: Promote KPMG's strategy and commitment to diversity and inclusion internally and externally.
Recruitment: Recruit, retain and promote the best and the brightest.
Education: Provide orientation into KPMG through consistent and ongoing messaging around our culture of values, our competencies and our diversity strategy.

Career Development: Provide information regarding career planning internally, including networking and mentoring and external exposure through workshops, seminars and community involvement.

Additional Information

KPMG is committed to diversity. We embrace diversity and encourage our partners and employees to share their views and lifestyles, thereby broadening everyone's awareness of differences and hopefully creating an inclusive environment free of discrimination. The varied backgrounds and experiences of our professionals are crucial to understanding and meeting our clients' needs in an increasingly diverse marketplace. Diversity is a critical component to being an employer of choice, and one of KPMG's genuine strengths. People are KPMG's most important asset and the driving force behind its success. The firm is committed to creating an inclusive work environment that is built on the firm's standards and values. These help build the trust, support and openness necessary for successful people and, in turn, a successful firm.

KPMG's Values

KPMG's values define our culture and our commitment to the highest principles of personal and professional conduct. They represent how we relate to each other, what we expect from our clients, and what our clients and the marketplace should expect from us. As such, they will continue to be at the heart of how we operate as a firm.

The following is a list of KPMG's seven values:

• We lead by example—we, as a firm and as individuals, act in a manner that exemplifies what we expect of each other and our clients, and what our clients should expect of us.
• We work together—forging relationships across diverse teams, cultures, functions and practices to enhance team and business results.
• We respect the individual—we respect all individuals for their diversity, who they are and what they bring as individuals and as team members for the benefit of our clients and the firm.
• We seek the facts and provide insight—we listen to and proactively challenge different points of view in order to arrive at the right judgments.
• We are open and honest in our communication—we encourage timely, clear and constructive two-way communication.
• We are committed to our communities—we, as individuals and teams, use our time and resources to support our local communities.
• Above all, we act with integrity—we are professional first and foremost, take pride in being part of KPMG and are committed to objectivity, quality and service of the highest standards.

External Diversity Outreach

NABA and ALPFA

KPMG is a corporate sponsor of the National Association of Black Accountants (NABA) and the Association of Latino Professionals in Finance and Accounting (ALPFA) annual conventions. We provide financial support for, and sponsor KPMG

professionals to attend, these conventions. Many KPMG partners and employees currently hold national and local leadership positions in these organizations.

KPMG sponsors NABA and ALPFA student case study competitions that provide finance and accounting students with the opportunity to showcase their business, accounting, research and presentation skills.

KPMG maintains memberships and plays a leading role in various organizations focused on promoting diversity in accounting, including:

- ALPFA/National Society of Hispanic MBAs
- American Indian Business Leaders
- Diversity Career Group
- Executive Diversity
- Hispanic Association for Career Enhancement
- National Association for Asian American Professionals
- National Council of Philippine American & Canadian Accountants
- National Urban League
- Out and Equal
- Professional Strategies LLC
- Urban Financial Services Coalition
- Women for Hire
- WorkplaceDiversity.com

Memberships

KPMG is a member of the American Institute of Certified Public Accountants (AICPA), where Clyde Jones, national director, diversity and EEO/AAP, sits on the minorities initiative committee, a group that is focused on increasing the number of minority CPAs in the accounting profession. This is an appointed position and Mr. Jones is in the second year of a three-year term. The committee meets quarterly and subgroups operate throughout the year. Mr. Jones chairs the academic support task force which seeks to increase the minority CPA population through innovative academic scholarship programs. Mr. Jones is also a member of the Association of Latino professionals business advisory council (ALPFA). ALPFA is the premier Latino organization dedicated to enhancing opportunities for its members in the accounting, finance and related professions.

Diversity Begins on Day One

Communicating KPMG's culture starts early and goes beyond the first day of hire. Each new employee attends a new hire orientation session, which includes information about the firm's values, culture and structure. During this orientation, new hires hear from leadership about why KPMG is a great place to work and what it takes to be successful. The orientation provides all the necessary information to help ensure the new hire has a solid understanding of KPMG's strategy, policies, benefits and programs.

Supplier Diversity Program

The firm actively seeks to promote participation of minority-owned, women-owned, veteran-owned and special disabled veteran-owned businesses in our purchasing supplier process. Equal opportunity is given to minority-owned, women-owned, veteran-owned and special disabled veteran-owned businesses to join our supplier base by competing and participating in the purchasing process, subject to established purchasing policies and procedures.

In this regard, KPMG is the only Big Four firm that supports Women Business Enterprise National Council (WBENC), a national organization dedicated to the advancement of women-owned businesses (WBEs). KPMG contributes an annual funding of nearly $40,000 to support the group's mission through sponsorships and events. Additionally, KPMG has participated in several networking events with WBEs, where our purchasing team members network with WBEs as potential vendors. KPMG is also a member of the National Minority Supplier Development Council, Inc.

KPMG Foundation

KPMG Foundation is the creator, cofounder and administrator of The PhD Project, one of the most far-reaching and ambitious diversity programs ever conceived to address the underrepresentation of minority Americans in business, higher education and the corporate workforce. A landmark effort, The PhD Project aims to put more minorities on business school faculties, with the goal of attracting more minority students and creating greater diversity among future business students.

In December 1994, The PhD Project, with additional funding from academia and leading corporations, held a conference to bring together 266 potential minority doctoral candidates with current doctoral students, business school faculty, deans and heads of doctoral programs for a two-day conference. Less than one year after the first PhD Project conference, the nation's business schools reported a 42 percent one-year increase in the number of African-Americans, Hispanic-Americans and Native Americans entering doctoral programs in business. Half of those newly created PhD students were individuals who had been reached by The PhD Project. Now in its 11th year, The PhD Project has increased the number of minority business professors from 294 in 1994 to 746 in 2005.

The PhD Project Statistics

Forty-five of the 266 individuals who attended The PhD Project conference in 1994 began a doctoral program the following year; 62 percent of them were women. Of the 45, 19 have finished the doctoral program and are currently teaching at a university; 13 are women.

Since 1994, 10,027 individuals have submitted applications for the annual November conference, of which 4,584 were selected and 4,233 have attended.

Of the 4,233 past conference attendees, 374 started a business doctoral program, of which 109 have finished the doctoral program and are currently teaching at a university, 58 of those new faculty are women.

PhD Project Doctoral Students Associations

In August 1994, KPMG Foundation formed the first African-American Accounting Doctoral Students Association (AADSA), now known as The PhD Project Accounting Doctoral Students Association. Since 1994, the foundation has expanded the associations to include finance, information systems, management and marketing students, and membership has been extended to Hispanic-Americans and Native Americans. The PhD Project Doctoral Students Associations (DSAs) help sustain a high level of commitment and sense of connection among minority students in business through networking, joint research opportunities, peer support and mentoring. As a result, 92 percent of DSA members have completed or are continuing in their doctoral programs, compared with 70 percent among doctoral candidates generally. AACSB International reports that 60.5 percent of those who earn business doctorates are in teaching positions. For The PhD Project, that number is an astounding 99 percent.

KPMG's Recognitions for Diversity

KPMG's local offices have won numerous awards for their efforts in diversity and community service including:

• The *Black Collegian Magazine*'s Top 100 Employers
• American Cancer Society's National Team Program Recognition award
• Award for Excellence in Workplace Volunteer programs/Points of Light
• Human Rights Campaign Foundation's Corporate Equality Index
• *Working Mother* magazine's 100 Best Companies
• *Hispanic* magazine's corporate 100 Best Places for Latinos to Work and Top 50 Recruitment Companies
• *Asian Enterprise* magazine's 10 Best Companies for Asian Americans
• American Society of Women Accountants' Balance Award: Celebrating the Dimensions of Success
• *DiversityInc* Top 10 Companies for Executive Women, Top 10 Companies for Asian Americans, 20 Noteworthy Companies
• Center for Companies that Care, 2005 Honor Roll Volunteerism award
• National Fatherhood Initiative (NFI) Fatherhood award
• Abilities, Inc./NBDC at the National Center for Disability Services, Making a Difference award on celebrating diversity year-round
• YAI/NIPD (National Institute of People with Disabilities)—Corporation of the Year
• The Human Rights Campaign (HRC) Best Places to Work

The materials contained within this document provide a general overview of some of KPMG's programs, practices and policies.

It is important to remember that individual situations do and will vary. Further, the programs, policies and practices described generally herein do change from time to time and we reserve the right to make such changes and/or discontinue any of them at any time and for any reason, subject to applicable federal, state and/or local laws.

Lehman Brothers

745 Seventh Avenue
New York, NY 10019
Phone: (212) 526-7000
www.lehman.com/careers

Locations

America
Asia
Europe

Diversity Leadership

Anne Erni
Managing Director, Chief Diversity Officer

Deirdre O'Donnell
Senior Vice President, Global Head of
Diversity Recruiting

Erica Irish Brown
Senior Vice President, Head of Diversity
Lateral Recruiting

745 Seventh Avenue
New York, NY 10019
Phone: (212) 526-7000
www.lehman.com/careers

Recruiting

Please list the schools/types of schools at which you recruit.

• *Ivy League schools:* Brown University, Columbia University, Cornell University, Dartmouth College, Harvard University, University of Pennsylvania, Princeton University and Yale University
• *Other private schools:* Amherst College, Carnegie Mellon University, Duke University, Georgetown University, George Washington University, Johns Hopkins University, Massachusetts Institute of Technology, Middlebury College, New York University, Northeastern University, Northwestern University, Rochester Polytechnic Institute, Rochester Institute of Technology, University of Chicago, University of Maryland, University of Miami, University of Notre Dame, Stanford University and Williams College
• *Public state schools:* University of California Berkeley, University of California Los Angeles, University of Florida, University of Michigan, University of North Carolina Chapel Hill, University of Texas at Austin and the University of Virginia
• *Historically Black Colleges and Universities (HBCUs):* Morehouse College and Spelman College
• *Other predominantly minority and/or women's colleges:* Barnard College, Mt. Holyoke College, Smith College and Wellesley College

Do you have any special outreach efforts directed to encourage minority students to consider your firm?

• Hold a reception for minority students
• *Conferences:* National Black MBA (NBMBAA), National Society of Hispanic MBAs (NSHMBA), Reaching Out Conference, Out for Business Conference, MBA Jumpstart, Society of Hispanic Engineers (SHPE), National Society of Black Engineers (NSBE), Society of Women Engineers (SWE), Hispanic Alliance for Career Enhancement (HACE)
• The Emerging Leaders internship program focusing on students with disabilities
• Advertise in minority student association publication(s)
• Participate in/host minority student job fair(s)
• Sponsor minority student association events
• Firm's professionals participate on career panels at school
• Outreach to leadership of minority student organizations

• Scholarships or intern/fellowships for minority students

•*Other:* Resume and interview skills workshops

What activities does the firm undertake to attract minority and women employees?

All of the firm's diversity initiatives are aimed at attracting, hiring and retaining qualified diverse candidates and employees. In 2005, the firm hired a full-time diversity lateral recruiting team that concentrates solely on identifying top female and minority candidates for new job openings. The group focuses on hiring qualified individuals into front, middle and back office positions at the analyst level and above.

All internal recruiters assist hiring managers in sourcing diverse candidates through various professional and charitable organizations, organization and job posting web sites, conferences and other contacts. These resources include the Financial Women's Association, 85 Broads, Toigo Foundation, LatPro.com, America's Job Bank, Hot Jobs and alumni networks such as Columbia Business School's African-American Alumni Association. Hiring managers are encouraged to post all new openings internally and externally for all employees and others to have the opportunity to apply and to ensure that there is a diverse slate of qualified candidates for open positions before extending the offer. In addition, the firm offers a training program entitled "Interviewing Through a Diversity Lens" which helps hiring managers identify candidate strengths beyond their first impression and enables the managers to be more objective during the recruiting and interview process.

In addition to campus recruiting, the lateral recruiting team attends annual conferences for the National Black MBA Association (NBMBAA), the National Society of Hispanic MBAs (NSHMBA), the National Association of Black Accountants (NABA) and the Association of Latino Professionals in Finance and Accounting (ALPFA) as well as the National Association of Securities Professionals (NASP). Lehman Brothers participates in various professional career fairs including the Annual Diversity Career Expo sponsored by the National Association of African Americans in Human Resources (NAAAHR) and WorkplaceDiversity.com, the Hispanic Alliance for Career Enhancement (HACE), Women for Hire, the Wall Street Business and Disability Council and the Toigo Foundation Annual Career Fair for Fellows and Alumni.

In addition to the external sources of candidates mentioned above, employee referrals for lateral professional hires are actively solicited from the firm's employee networks, Women's Initiatives Leading Lehman, Lehman Employees of African Decent, The Latin American Council, Lehman Brothers Asian Network, Lehman Brothers Disability Working Forum and Lehman Brothers Gay and Lesbian Network.

Another innovative program launched in 2005 to strengthen Lehman Brothers' recruiting efforts was Encore. Encore was our corporate response to the *Harvard Business Review* research "Off-Ramps and On-Ramps" published in 2005. This study, of which Lehman Brothers was one of the sponsors, focused on how difficult it is for women to re-enter the workforce after having taken time off to have children, care for elderly parents, or address other life responsibilities. Gathered for a unique half-day experience, 71 female participants visited Lehman Brothers looking for a possible "on ramp" in their professional careers. The attendee list included employees who formerly worked at Lehman Brothers and former employees of other financial entities. The Encore event included networking, self-reflection and informational sessions. Those interested in pursuing positions with the firm were asked to submit a resume. Introductory screening and counseling sessions were conducted with the majority of women who submitted their resumes, and subsequent follow-up interviews with the businesses have been granted when appropriate. Encore has since expanded globally and was launched in Europe on February 9, 2006 with 49 women attending. Future efforts in other geographies are being considered as are subsequent Encore reunion events in the New York metropolitan area.

Additional evidence of our commitment to diversity is the firm's requirement that search firms provide hiring managers with diverse slates for each and every job opening on which they are retained. This policy is reinforced by the firm's annual "search firm breakfast" where senior management reiterates the firm's commitment to diversity and the need for search firms who wish to do business with Lehman Brothers to be equally committed.

Do you use executive recruiting/search firms to seek to identify new diversity hires?

Yes.

Internships and Co-ops

Investment Banking, Investment Management, Equities & Fixed Income Summer Analyst Programs

Pay: Competitive

Length of the program: Eight weeks

Web site for internship information: www.lehman.com\careers

Lehman Brothers' eight-week summer analyst programs provides motivated college juniors with an internship position in one of three programs: investment banking, capital markets (fixed income and equities) or investment management. These summer analyst programs offer an exciting opportunity for talented individuals interested in exposure to the financial services industry. Lehman Brothers' summer internships in the U.S. are managed as two separate sequential summer programs (Term 1 and Term 2). Each program runs for eight weeks and the exact term maps to the summer vacation schedules of our participating schools.

In all programs, weekly workshops and seminars are provided to expose analysts to all areas of the firm. Summer analysts are assigned junior and senior mentors to provide guidance throughout the summer. They will also benefit from contact with Lehman Brothers' professionals of all levels through group events and informal functions. Summer analysts are provided with detailed feedback twice during the summer—first, midway through the eight-week program and then at the end. The divisions look upon the summer analyst programs as a primary source for hiring full-time analysts. Accordingly, those who are interested in full-time employment are strongly encouraged to apply to one of our three summer programs.

What we look for in a summer analyst:

• Students currently pursuing an undergraduate degree in their penultimate year of graduation
• Record of distinctive academic performance
• Distinctive problem-solving skills
• Strong professional presence to include self-confidence and maturity
• Marked leadership potential
• Strong initiative—the ability to make things happen
• Ability to contribute in a team-based environment
• Interest in a career in finance

Our Programs:

Investment Banking Summer Analyst Program

The investment banking division provides comprehensive financial advisory and capital raising services. This includes advice relating to mergers and acquisitions, privatizations, and debt and equity financings and restructuring. A summer analyst will be placed in an industry or product coverage group where he or she will assist bankers on financing and advisory projects as a member of the project team. Each summer analyst is given a hands-on opportunity to work as a full member of a client team on a variety of transactions.

Capital Markets START Summer Analyst Program (Fixed Income and Equities)

Both our fixed income and equities divisions have sales, trading and research functions. These functions provide advice, ideas and execution services to the institutional investing community. Additionally, an origination function exists in the fixed income division in the real estate, securitization banking and public finance groups. The divisions' main goals are to enhance relationships with key clients of the firm and to facilitate transactions. During the program, summer analysts will be placed directly in a product area within one of the fixed income or equities sales, trading, or research areas. Summer analysts will be exposed to the daily flow of business and often are asked to assist in a variety of special projects for their particular business group.

Investment Management Summer Analyst Program

The Lehman Brothers' investment management division provides investment planning, financial advisory and asset management services to institutions and high net worth individuals. We offer a broad range of investment vehicles such as separately managed accounts, mutual funds, hedge funds and private equity. The investment management division is the fastest growing business within the firm. Summer analysts typically rotate through one or two placements within different functional areas of our investment management business such as: investments and research, client advisory and solutions, strategy and business management and private investment management. Each analyst participates as a fully contributing member of selected project teams, working with individuals at all levels on diverse assignments. Analysts will be exposed to the daily flow of business and often are asked to assist in a variety of special projects for their particular business group.

Finance Summer Analyst Programs

>**Pay:** Competitive
>**Length of the program:** 10 weeks
>**Web site for internship information:** www.lehman.com\careers

The finance summer analyst program provides you with the opportunity to gain experience working in one of the major departments of our finance division in a concentrated 10-week period. You will get the chance to interact with senior managers on a daily basis. Your exact placement will depend on our business needs at the time we are hiring. Your training will include an introductory course in global capital markets, seminars taught by internal faculty, online PC training, professional skills development courses, and a weekly seminar familiarizing you with the different departments within the finance division. You will also be given the opportunity to present a summary of your experience within the finance division and an opportunity to collaborate on a group presentation at the end of the summer.

The division looks upon the summer analyst program as a primary source for hiring full-time analysts. So we strongly encourage all those interested in full-time employment to apply to the summer program.

Operations Summer Analyst Programs

>**Pay:** Competitive
>**Length of the program:** 10 weeks
>**Web site for internship information:** www.lehman.com\careers

This is your opportunity to gain 10 weeks of solid experience within an industry-leading operations division building your skills in a specific business area. As a summer analyst, you will get the chance to contribute as a full and valued member of the team to which you are assigned and have responsibilities similar to a first-year analyst. We want to ensure you receive the best possible exposure to the department in that time, so we provide you with a comprehensive curriculum to supplement your on-the-job experience. This includes management-led overviews, presentations by internal and external experts on relevant financial products and market topics, and a tour of the New York Stock Exchange. Our division utilizes the summer analyst program as a primary source for hiring full-time analysts, we strongly encourage all those interested in full-time roles to apply to the summer program.

Information Technology Summer Analyst Programs

>**Pay:** Competitive
>**Length of the program:** 10 weeks
>**Web site for internship information:** www.lehman.com\careers

The firm offers a 10-week summer program for computer science, computer/electrical engineering and information systems students entering in the summer of their junior year. Students in other majors with a strong technical background will also be considered. Information technology summer analysts will join either application development or infrastructure technology teams and take an active role in developing the technology that drives our businesses. While your actual role is determined by the group you join, it is similar to the role of a full-time analyst, providing you with the opportunity to obtain real responsibility while learning the team values of our "One Firm" approach. During your training you will receive exposure to senior management and the business of Wall Street, which will include a weekly speaker series featuring our chief information officer and senior IT professionals. The summer analyst program can provide an opening to a full-time position and a rewarding long-term career with the firm.

Affinity Groups

Lehman Brothers' diversity initiatives are aimed at attracting the best people. Our firm's culture and work environment proves that having a diverse workforce encourages increased creativity and innovation, which are crucial drivers for continued business success. To help achieve our diversity goals, the firm endorses employee networks. Networks are encouraged to meet as often as necessary; the frequency is determined by the networks. Network meetings take the form of steering committee meetings, sub-committee meetings, town halls, general events and monthly network leader meetings with the global diversity and inclusion office. In 2005 network leaders were invited to present to the firm's CEO on issues relevant to their constituencies and the firm. In the U.S., Europe and Asia there is active participation in one or more of the following networks listed below.

Lehman Brothers Asian Network (LBAN)

LBAN forms an integral part of the firm's diversity initiatives by enhancing professional development and maximizing the contributions of every Lehman Brothers' employee of Asian descent.

Lehman Brothers Disability Working Forum (LBDWF)

LBDWF works to develop a strategy to raise awareness about disability issues, to form relationships and represent the firm with external disability-related organizations, and to enhance the scope of the recruiting outreach efforts to attract candidates with disabilities.

Lehman Brothers Employee & Family Network (LEAF)

LEAF (Lehman Brothers Employees and Families Network) is a network aimed at providing education and support for employees who are caregivers of all ages and family situations.

Lehman Brothers Gay & Lesbian Network (LBGLN)

LBGLN helps to provide a supportive environment for the firm's lesbian, gay, bisexual and transgender (LGBT) employees to enhance career development and to ensure that Lehman Brothers is an "employer of choice" for members of the LGBT community.

Lehman Employees of African Descent (LEAD)

LEAD's mission is to enhance the careers and employment experiences of employees of African descent at Lehman Brothers by creating an empowering culture of inclusion that will enable the firm to achieve its overall mission. We LEAD to achieve, empower, and include through opportunity and unity.

The Latin American Council (TLAC)

The mission of The Latin American Council (TLAC) is to create career, educational and social opportunities for Latin American/Hispanic professionals within Lehman Brothers. The Latin American Council seeks to identify, retain and enhance Lehman Brothers' Latin American/Hispanic talent, fostering an environment for personal and professional advancement that contributes to the firm's growth and continued success.

Women's Initiatives Leading Lehman (WILL)

WILL's mission is to encourage, inspire and support women in their career development at Lehman Brothers, thereby attracting and retaining women who will contribute to the firm's long-term success.

For more information please visit our web site at: www.lehman.com/who/diversity/networks.htm

Entry-Level Programs/Full-Time Opportunities/Training Programs

Equities & Fixed Income Analyst Program

> ***Length of program:*** Two to three years
> ***Geographic location(s) of program:*** New York

The START analyst program is a two-year program with a third-year option in which analysts are trained, placed in businesses, coached and reviewed on an ongoing basis.

The initial training takes place in New Jersey for the Asian and U.S. analysts and in London for the European analysts. The initial training provides a comprehensive overview of capital markets instruments and businesses and includes an introduction to asset management. Investment management analysts as well as finance and risk analysts take part in this training along with the capital markets analysts.

Following training, the generalist analysts in capital markets begin rotations through businesses in equities and fixed income. Analysts have the opportunity to explore various areas and roles and to state their placement preferences following these intensive interactions. Placement decisions are made by the global heads of both the equities and fixed income divisions at the end of the rotation process and are based on the overall business needs, appropriate fit and analyst preferences.

After two years, all START analysts are eligible for promotion to associate. Senior analysts, those analysts that have a master's degree or related work experience, are eligible to be considered for promotion to associate after one year at Lehman Brothers. Promotion decisions are communicated to START analysts in the spring of their second year. If an analyst is not promoted after two years, she or he generally either exits the firm or will be offered the opportunity to remain in the program for a third year. If promoted, an analyst assumes the associate title and continues work in his or her current business. Those analysts who remain in the program for a third year are eligible to be considered for promotion to associate at the end of the third year. At that time, the third year analyst is either promoted to associate or exits the firm.

Role of a Full-Time Analyst

Each analyst works as part of a team on various assignments, with extensive learning on the job. The responsibilities each analyst undertakes are a function of individual performance, achievement and individual business needs.

Our two-year full-time program has been specifically developed to build your immediate skills as well as to enable your long-term career development. The program begins in New Jersey with several weeks of intensive classroom training in which all Sales, Trading and Research Training (START) analysts participate.

The training consists of an orientation to the firm and a comprehensive capital markets course. This covers a variety of topics including stock and bond analysis and an overview of all the major capital markets instruments and businesses, including an introduction to asset management. Analysts gain exposure to many aspects of the firm through a series of business presentations, lectures and interactive projects. You will also receive training for the Series 7 and Series 63 licensing exams.

Most analysts are hired into a generalist pool and are then placed in one of the sales, trading and research functions in the New York office. On occasion, there are also a few opportunities in our Boston, Chicago and San Francisco branch offices. If you have a particular relevant skill set and inclination, it may be possible to pre-place you into specific positions. Securitization banking, public finance, global commercial real estate, and fixed income and equity analytics all pre-place analysts into their respective businesses.

At the completion of the training program, generalist analysts will begin a rotation process through our fixed income and equities divisions. These intensive interactions will give you the ability to explore various areas and roles. Within individual rotations, analysts learn on the job as they are exposed to experienced professionals and contribute to a variety of assignments as part of a team. The responsibilities that analysts are given reflect their individual performance and achievements. Following your rotations, you will have the opportunity to state your placement preferences. Placement decisions are made by the global heads of

both the fixed income and equities divisions at the end of the rotation process and are based on a combination of business needs and analyst preferences.

Each analyst's progress is carefully managed by the capital markets program and development team. Shortly after placement, analysts complete a goal setting form with their manager to determine their development objectives for their first six months in the firm. After this, analysts complete a performance review every six months during the two-year program to review their progress and set their goals. Throughout, the capital markets program and development team may recommend a specific training course to support an analyst's development.

Investment Banking Analyst Program

> *Length of program:* Two to three years
> *Geographic location(s) of program:* New York, Los Angeles, Menlo Park, Chicago, Houston

Our analyst program represents your entry point into our investment banking and our private equity divisions. It has been specifically developed to build your immediate skills and to enable your long-term career development. The two- to three-year program begins with four to five weeks of training in New York. This training introduces you to the firm and its uniquely team-based approach, and reinforces skills that you will apply as an investment banker.

The new hire classroom curriculum includes technical skills training in accounting, computer modeling and financial valuation techniques. You will also participate in small teams on projects that provide you with a better understanding of the firm's capabilities and help you to develop a global network of peers. Following this, you will return to the region where you were hired and join one of the firm's industry, product or regionally-focused groups or the private equity division. Your placement will be based on both your preference as well as the firm's needs.

As an analyst you will participate as a fully contributing team member, working with bankers at all levels on diverse assignments. Projects you may be involved in include: company valuation, strategic advisory, execution of debt and equity offerings and new business origination. Your specific responsibilities may include financial analysis and modeling, industry research, coordination of internal and external processes related to a financing or sale and assistance in the preparation of offering memoranda, proposals and other written materials. In addition, you'll receive confidential 360-degree performance reviews to assist your future development. From the outset, you will have a clear path of opportunity for career growth, which will begin with the chance to be promoted to associate after three years of tenure in the program.

Investment Management Analyst Program

> *Length of program:* Two to three years
> *Geographic location(s) of program:* New York

This is your opportunity to become part of a two- to three-year analyst program with a global leader in the investment management arena. You will join a program that provides a full orientation to the firm, as well as comprehensive, classroom-based capital markets curricula covering a varied range of topics. These include stock and bond analysis and a broad overview of the major capital markets instruments and businesses.

You will gain further exposure to many aspects of the firm through a series of business presentations, lectures and interactive projects. Following the capital markets module, you will receive in-depth training on our investment management division's platform, products and capabilities, as well as being prepared for the Series 7 and Series 63 registration exams. You will also receive on-the-job training. As an analyst, you will gain a broad understanding of the investment management business through our generalist program. The program gives you the opportunity to work in different areas, such as: investments and research, client advisory and solutions, or strategy and business management.

Investments and Research

- Participating in the analysis of outside hedge fund and money manager selections
- Developing and maintaining asset allocation models
- Working with fixed income or equity analysts across industry groups

• Performing in-depth company and macro industry/sector analysis

Client Advisory and Solutions

• Developing marketing plans and strategies to increase new sales opportunities and client retention
• Working with our sales force on new business strategies; advising clients and our sales force on specialized product opportunities
• Collaborating with business groups to create and execute marketing communication programs and branding initiatives

Strategy and Business Management

• Supporting executive management and partnering with multiple internal groups—investment research, marketing, operations, legal and sales—to incubate and execute new products, strategic investments and processes for the division

• Undertaking a variety of tasks—from developing new investment vehicles and business lines to analyzing potential acquisitions for the division

Operations Analyst Program

> *Length of program:* Two years
> *Geographic location(s) of program:* New York, New Jersey

The two-year program begins with an orientation to the firm and a comprehensive overview to include our capital markets and professional development training curriculum. The program's curriculum is designed to provide you with the professional skills, industry knowledge and development opportunities that will enable you to achieve success within the operations division.

During orientation, analysts are also given the opportunity to hear about the various placements that are available within our division. Placement decisions are made based on business needs and analyst preferences. After one year of successful performance within their initial placement, analysts are eligible to explore other opportunities within operations such as:

• Equity operations: Provides the support and control infrastructure that enables the firm to develop and deliver financial products through the global capital markets. Working with sales, trading, information technology, finance and the firm's clients, operations' aims are to enhance the firm's overall performance by minimizing operational and consequent market risk and by adding value to our clients.

• Fixed income operations: The focus for the group is to support Lehman Brothers' activities with respect to interest rate and credit-based fixed income cash and derivative products, ensuring that profitability and risk are appropriately managed and reported on behalf of Lehman Brothers fixed income businesses.

• Investment management division operations: responsible for supporting the delivery of quality products, services, and account information and analytics to our clients. Through our organization, we assist in the processing of trades, reconciliation of daily client activity, managing client risk exposure, problem resolution, and the production of standard and customized client statements and portfolio analytics for the IMD business division.

• Information and exposure management: This group primarily focuses on monitoring and acting on margin exposures with clients, and ensuring that the firm has a central and consistent set of product and pricing data for use in all client reporting. The group also directly oversees the production of cost basis reporting and mailed statements for IMD/prime broker clients.

• Clearance and custody services: responsible for various functions, ranging from clearance and settlement with global clearing banks and depositories, to custodial control.

• Operations control America: Responsible for a wide range of reconciliation and reporting processes that support the firm's trading and operations activities. The main responsibilities of the department are to reconcile/balance all bank accounts and securities positions and ensure regulatory compliance for all reported customer and firm differences.

• Business analysis group: Functions as change agents for the division, facilitating value-added change in an effective and cost efficient manner.

Finance Analyst Program

Length of program: Two years

Geographic location(s) of program: New York

We offer you the chance to benefit from a two-year rotational program. During this time you will be eligible to undertake three successive eight-month rotations in various departments of the finance division, including: financial control and analysis, capital markets control, infrastructure reporting and treasury and tax. The rotational structure of the program is specifically designed to expose you to a broad range of functions and departments within the finance division, enabling you to build your financial skills and gain experience with capital markets products. You will develop your interests and prepare for a successful management career.

Here are some of the major responsibilities of the departments to which you will be assigned:

Financial control and analysis

- Financial reporting and analysis for all business units
- Management of the firm's annual budget process and business review process
- Assurance of a robust internal control environment

Global treasury

- Asset and liability management
- Cash management
- Credit and bank relations
- Insurance risk management
- Financial planning and analysis

Tax

- Analysis of specific trading strategies aimed at optimizing the firm's effective tax rate
- Evaluation of the firm's foreign source income across multiple legal entities
- Domestic and foreign tax law compliance

Capital Markets Control

- Daily revenue analyses explaining why a desk made or lost money
- Balance sheet reporting to ensure all balance sheet usage requirements are met
- Cash capital/regulatory capital reviews to ensure that as a firm we are optimizing usage of our capital

Infrastructure Control

- Expense management
- Information technology finance
- Operations finance
- Corporate support and control

Information Technology Analyst Program

Geographic location(s) of program: New York

The technology development program is an intensive three-month course that includes technical training, financial markets instruction, professional development and leadership skills guidance. It includes a speaker series led by senior management in the information technology division, as well as other networking opportunities.

The interview process and subsequent job placements are made based on your background, skills, experience and interest. Technical training is then customized to reflect the area in which you have been placed.

Application Development provides technical training in areas such as:

• Object oriented development tools, including: C++, Java, EJB and J2EE
• Database design and development using Sybase and Oracle
• Front-end technologies including HTML, XML, JavaScript and JSP
• Middleware object development using TIBCO and Orbix
• Multi-tier application development in Weblogic
• Project and presentation design replicating real-life systems

After completing the program, you will immediately apply your technical skills in business analysis, systems design and implementation roles. Our front office groups develop and maintain applications in pricing, sales and trading, collateral and margin processing, position tracking and e-commerce. The middle and back office groups comprise the firm's information management and control systems. The applications supported include risk management, collateral management, global funding, clearance and settlement, and payment processing as well as the firm's finance and legal functions.

Infrastructure Engineering provides technical training in areas such as:

• Windows NT/2000 support, including troubleshooting, installation and workstation configuration.
• UNIX systems administration in Solaris environments.
• Database administration for current database management products.
• Network support, design, configuration, installation and administration of IP based networks.
• Project and presentation design replicating real-life systems.

After completing the program, you are eligible to become part of an infrastructure group in an engineering, operations or support role. The data center group maintains the central processing facility, provides 24-hour support and administers our corporate data-bases. The distributed systems group installs and maintains the Firm's UNIX, NT and Windows servers. The market data and middleware group configures and supports our client workstations and supplies our users with the desktop tools and market data information they need to do their jobs. The network services group provides research, design, implementation and around-the-clock support services for on-network data, voice and video traffic, including e-mail and remote access.

Strategic Plan and Diversity Leadership

How does the firm's leadership communicate the importance of diversity to everyone at the firm?

Leadership communication related to diversity utilizes all avenues available within the firm, including:

Divisional town hall meetings, e-mails to all employees from senior leaders, awards and recognition e-mails, postings to the firm's Intranet (known as LehmanLive) and the global home page, the Lehman Daily News (a broadcast e-mail to highlight news impacting the entire firm), the quarterly corporate newsletter, event invitations, periodic diversity newsletters, recruiting updates, the *Global Diversity & Inclusion* brochure, brochures, posters in elevators and floor lobbies.

Who has primary responsibility for leading diversity initiatives at your firm?

Anne Erni, managing director, chief diversity officer.

Does your firm currently have a diversity committee?

Yes, the firm does have regional and divisional councils chaired by their representative business leaders but we do not have a corporate-wide diversity council.

If yes, does the committee's representation include one or more members of the firm's management/executive committee?

Yes.

If yes, how many executives are on the committee, and in 2005, what was the total number of hours collectively spent by the committee in furtherance of the firm's diversity initiatives? How many employees are on the committee, and how often does the committee convene in furtherance of the firm's diversity initiatives?

There are approximately 15 to 18 members of each of the regional and divisional diversity councils, all of whom are senior vice presidents or managing directors. The councils meet on average eight to 10 times during the year.

Does the committee and/or diversity leader establish and set goals or objectives consistent with management's priorities?

Yes.

Has the firm undertaken a formal or informal diversity program or set of initiatives aimed at increasing the diversity of the firm?

Yes.

How often does the firm's management review the firm's diversity progress/results?

Twice a year.

How is the firm's diversity committee and/or firm management held accountable for achieving results?

Lehman Brothers holds all managers, including those at the top of the organization accountable for diversity. Each business division is responsible for developing an annual diversity plan which addresses their particular opportunities and defines measurable action steps for achieving results. Regional CEOs and the firm's president review the diversity plans. To the extent a division is successful in achieving their diversity goals, they are rewarded with an additional pool of incentive compensation to allocate to employees who have made a significant contribution to the divisional diversity effort. Our performance management system incorporates criteria on diversity practices for all employees.

Diversity Mission Statement

Chairman and Chief Executive Officer, Richard S. Fuld, Jr. has made the following statement with regard to diversity and inclusion:

At Lehman Brothers, we have achieved momentum across our businesses and regions because we have built a culture where our people come together as a team to deliver all of the firm's resources to our clients. Our firm has come a long way by many measures. One of the greatest changes is in the wide variety of perspectives and backgrounds of our people today. We have made substantial progress in recruiting and developing the very best people, creating a diverse and inclusive culture and establishing ourselves as leaders in the community.

To reach our next level of success, we must continue to foster a culture that is full of opportunity, where exceptional people want to build their careers. Our commitment to being a world class organization goes hand in hand with our commitment to building a truly diverse and inclusive culture and to ensuring that all employees are valued for their unique abilities and contributions and their diversity of thought and perspective.

Our diversity efforts are integral to strengthening our 'One Firm' culture and to delivering on the firm's client-focused strategy. A truly diverse and inclusive culture enables us to deliver the best service and products and to generate the most innovative ideas for our clients. There are remarkable opportunities for us to take this firm to its next level of success. I am confident that the people here at this firm and those who will join us in the time ahead will help us build on that success.

Additional Information

At Lehman Brothers we are committed to attracting, retaining and developing the best people from the broadest backgrounds, and to nurturing our inclusive culture that fosters employee development and contributes to our commercial success. Each of our employees comes from a unique background, each brings a diverse perspective to the firm based on his or her variety of life experiences. This variety of thought and perspective is of intrinsic value to us in our talent evaluation process. To assist in the retention and development of our people, we emphasize tools such as networking opportunities, mentoring programs, employee and management education and training, and corporate citizenship.

Following are a sample of our employee programs:

• Employee networks in all geographic regions open to all employees
• Over 500 employees act as mentors in one of over 20 mentoring programs
• Over 13,000 employees have taken part in our awareness training program since 2004, with another 1,000 more slated for this year

The firm and its networks partnered with over 70 diversity related community organizations in 2005, either through financial or volunteer sponsorship. These include:

• Student organizations: SEO, Robert A. Toigo, Posse, Capital Chances, Opportunity Now
• Community organizations: Robin Hood, Harlem's Children Zone, Girl Scouts
• Professional organizations: New York Women's Foundation, National Association of Asian Professionals, The Hispanic Federation, The Twenty First Century Foundation

Life Balance

Investment banking is characterized by fast-paced, demanding work environments, however, Lehman is highly committed to fostering a culture that supports and respects our employees' need to balance the complex and sometimes competing demands of their careers and personal lives.

Our enhanced policies and benefits reflect our commitment to this culture; resources are dedicated specifically to ensuring we maintain our best practices.

Some key highlights of our life balance strategy enhancements since 2004 are:

• An extra week of paid vacation for nearly all employees
• Implementation of firm-sponsored flexible work arrangements including reduced or compressed work week, flex-time, telecommuting or flexspace for employees with conducive roles
• Introduction of a partially-paid sabbatical for tenured employees
• Increased subsidies for adoption, additional time off for elder care, bereavement, and secondary caregivers after childbirth or adoption.
• July 2004—Introduced online FWA application process, with online training
• July 2004—Created position of full-time retention manager as ombudsperson for the FWA program
• Monthly—Conduct training workshops for managers and employees on working and managing flexibly, facilitated by both internal staff and external consultants
• 2005—Expanding workplace flexibility included as goal for 2005 (and 2006) diversity business plans
• September 2005—Life balance featured in global diversity and inclusion brochure
• November 2005—Rolled out Encore, a new recruitment program aimed at bringing women back to the workplace who have off-ramped; the availability of flexibility is a key component in attracting women back
• January 2006—Conducting pilot program (unique on Wall Street) to install technology in key employees homes to facilitate working away from the office (in response to the threat of Avian flu)

All these policies reinforce the value we place on contributions and results versus face time.

Career mobility is also emphasized through the firm's support of internal transfers; managers are encouraged to fill staffing vacancies through the transfer or promotion of current employees of the firm, whenever possible.

Recognition of our Efforts

Selected achievements in 2005:

• Top 100 Companies for Working Mothers by *Working Mother* magazine

• Securities Industry Association (SIA) Innovative Leadership Award for Diversity

• Gold Standard for Commitment to Diversity by Race for Opportunity, a U.K.-based organization. The firm's score rose to 83 percent in 2005, from 56 percent in 2004

• 100 percent on the Human Rights Campaign's Corporate Equality Index for the past three years

• America's largest gay, lesbian, bisexual, and transgender organization

• One of *DiversityInc.'s* 25 Noteworthy Companies for Diversity

• Top 40 Ideal Diversity Employers in the *Black Collegian*/Universum campus survey (both MBA and undergraduate students) for 2004 and 2005

• Ranked among the 50 Best Workplaces in the U.K. by the Great Place to Work Institute (U.K.)

• Ranked number one for overall satisfaction in the *Vault Guide to the Top 50 Banking Employers*, including ranking among the top seven for diversity with respect to minorities, women and gays and lesbians

• Winner of the Respect Award presented by the Gay, Lesbian and Straight Education Network (GLSEN), for tireless efforts to promote GLBT leadership and equality

Thank you so much for your interest in Lehman Brothers, we are proud of our commitment to diversity and inclusion, and wish you good fortune in your career aspirations.

Liberty Mutual Insurance Company

175 Berkeley Street
Boston, MA 02116
Phone: (617) 357-9500

Locations

Boston, MA (HQ)
900 locations worldwide

Employment Contact

Ann Nowak
Manager of College Relations
175 Berkeley St
Boston, MA 02129
Phone: (617) 357-9500
Fax: (617) 574-5616
E-mail: campus.recruiting@libertymutual.com
www.libertymutual.com/careers

Recruiting

Please list the schools/types of schools at which you recruit.

Liberty Mutual visits campuses throughout the U.S. including HBCUs, and HSIs, as well as private and public institutions of higher education. If we are not on a particular campus and we welcome resumes through our web site.

Do you have any special outreach efforts that are directed to encourage minority students to consider your firm?

• Conferences
• Advertise in minority student association publication(s)
• Sponsor minority student association events
• Firm's employees participate on career panels at school
• Outreach to leadership of minority student organizations
• Scholarships or intern/fellowships for minority students

Liberty Mutual is eager to meet minority students on the campuses we visit and will participate in activities, association meetings and job fairs. Scholarship opportunities are also available through the Hispanic Scholarship Fund and the United Negro College Fund as well as to students at Morehouse College.

What activities does the firm undertake to attract minority and women employees?

• Partner programs with women and minority associations
• Participate at minority job fairs
• Utilize online job services

Internships and Co-ops

Liberty Mutual Internship Program

Deadline for application: Early spring semester
Number of interns in the program in summer 2006 (internship) or 2006 (co-op): 325
Pay: Competitive
Length of the program: 10-12 weeks
Percentage of interns/co-ops in the program who receive offers of full-time employment: 85 percent
Web site for internship/co-op information: www.libertymutual.com/campus

INROADS

Liberty Mutual will hire approximately 325 undergraduate interns each summer and approximately 25 MBA level interns. Approximately half of these undergraduate interns will come from the INROADS program. Pay is competitive and positions are throughout the U.S. Internships are based on business needs, so interns work in a variety of functional areas throughout the organization including traditional business jobs, accounting, finance, IT and HR. Positions also exist in the functional areas specific to the insurance industry including claims, underwriting, sales, loss prevention and actuarial. During the summer interns participate in training programs to learn about the business of insurance as well as the organization. Undergraduate rising seniors have the opportunity to visit the Boston headquarters and meet with senior executives and interview for positions. Development plans are developed for each student so that returning interns see a progression through a job family. MBA interns will meet with senior executives to gain a perspective on strategic initiatives.

Scholarships

Target School Scholarship Program

Liberty Mutual has a scholarship program at a number of our targeted campuses:

Deadline for application for the scholarship program: Spring of sophomore year
Scholarship award amount: Varies by school
Web site or other contact information for scholarship: www.libertymutual.com/campus

UNCF

Deadline for application for the scholarship program: See web site for details
Web site or other contact information for scholarship: www.uncf.org

HSF

Deadline for application for the scholarship program: See web site for details
Web site or other contact information for scholarship: www.hsf.net

Entry-Level Programs/Full-Time Opportunities/Training Programs

Liberty Mutual anticipates hiring 800+ college grads during the upcoming academic year. Opportunities exist in accounting, finance, IT, sales, claims, underwriting and HR. Some of the development programs include:

Fellowship in Finance and Accounting (FIFA)

Length of program: Two years (three eight-month assignments within the corporate finance and accounting and strategic business units).
Geographic location(s) of program: Boston

Training opportunities include a two-week employee orientation, professional development, on-the-job training and technical training programs.

Foundations for Sales Success

Length of program: Four to 12 months
Geographic location(s) of program: Field based

Includes technical classroom training and field experience.

Technical Development Program (TDP)

Length of program: Three to five years
Geographic location(s) of program: Portsmouth, Wausau (some opportunity for rotations in Indianapolis)

Three phases of your development include a classroom orientation, a business assignment, technical immersion as well as up to four Information Systems Rotations.

Corporate Real Estate Rotational Program

Length of program: 18-24 months
Geographic location(s) of program: Boston, MA

Within rotations, on-the-job training will develop participants skills. Rotations include: strategic planning, budget preparation and monitoring of office relocation projects within corporate real estate, tenant services and procurement

HRDP — Human Resource Development Program

Length of program: 18-24 months
Geographic location(s) of program: Boston, MA

Individual rotations included all areas of HR, benefits, HR systems, and compensation within the corporate and business groups strategic plan and diversity leadership.

Has the firm undertaken a formal or informal diversity program or set of initiatives aimed at increasing the diversity of the firm?

Liberty Mutual has a strategy in place to attract and retain minority representation and to build a more inclusive work environment as part of each individual business unit workforce plan. The strategy is multi-pronged and includes implementation of a mentoring program across business units, training for all new managers on inclusion, increased financial support to professional minority organizations, enhanced college relations and recruitment programs, and improved communications to external candidates as well as our internal employee population to better articulate our employment value propositions. Visit our web site at www.libertymutual.com/aboutus for more information.

How often does the firm's management review the firm's diversity progress/results?

Quarterly.

How is the firm's diversity committee and/or firm management held accountable for achieving results?

Business unit heads are held responsible for effective implementation of their inclusive workforce plans to meet the respective business needs.

The Stats

As of December 31, 2005, Liberty Mutual Group had $78.8 billion in consolidated assets and $21.2 billion in annual consolidated revenue. The company ranks 102nd on the Fortune 500 list of largest corporations in the United States based on 2005 revenue.

LMG offers a wide range of insurance products and services, including personal automobile, homeowners, workers compensation, commercial multiple peril, commercial automobile, general liability, global specialty, group disability, assumed reinsurance, fire and surety.

LMG (www.libertymutual.com) employs over 39,000 people in more than 900 offices throughout the world.

Retention and Professional Development

How do 2005 minority and female attrition rates generally compare to those experienced in the prior year period?

About the same as in prior years.

Additional Information

Liberty Mutual has a strong promote-from-within philosophy, therefore it is critical that we bring strong talent into the organization from college campuses. This initiative includes working with diversity associations on campus, INROADS, professional associations including NBMBAA, NSHMBA, ALPFA, NABA, the Consortium, NAACP and Urban League among others. Our recruiting on campus includes visits to HBCUs.

Inclusion is critical to our success. By tapping all available pools of talent, we will better serve the needs of our customers in the communities we serve and want to serve. An inclusive company also treats people with dignity and respect and provides the opportunity to grow and succeed based on ability, performance and aspirations.

Liz Claiborne, Inc.

1441 Broadway, 20th Floor
New York, NY 10018
Phone: (212) 354-4900

Locations

US:

Arleta, CA • Atlanta, GA • Commerce, CA • Dallas, TX • Los Angeles, CA • New York, NY • North Bergen, NJ • Vernon, CA • Wakefield, MA

International:

Amsterdam, The Netherlands • Hong Kong • Huxquilucan, Mexico • Jakarta, Indonesia • Madrid, Spain • Manila, Philippines • Montreal, Quebec, Canada • Ontario, Canada • Shanghai, China • Sri Lanka • Taiwan • Voorschoten, the Netherlands

Distribution Center Locations

Breinigsville, PA • Dayton, NJ • Lincoln, RI • North Bergen, NJ • Montreal, Canada • Mt. Pocono, PA • Ontario, Canada • Santa Fe Springs, CA • Vernon, CA • West Chester, OH

Employment Contact

Marla Schwartz
College Relations
1441 Broadway, 20th Floor
New York, NY 10018
Phone: (212) 626-5447
Fax: (212) 626-5527
E-mail: marla_schwartz@liz.com
www.lizclaiborneinc.com

Recruiting

Please list the schools/types of schools at which you recruit.

• Ivy League schools
• Other private schools
• Public state schools
• Historically Black Colleges and Universities (HBCUs)
• Other predominantly minority and/or women's colleges

Do you have any special outreach efforts directed to encourage minority students to consider your firm?

• Advertise in minority student association publication(s)
• Participate in/host minority student job fair(s)
• Firm's employees participate on career panels at school
• Scholarships or intern/fellowships for minority students

What activities does the firm undertake to attract minority and women employees?

• Partner programs with women and minority associations
• Participate at minority job fairs
• Seek referrals from other employees
• Utilize online job services
• Black Retail Association Group (BRAG) and INROADS

Do you use executive recruiting/search firms to seek to identify new diversity hires?

No.

Internships and Co-ops

Liz Claibourne Inc. Summer Internship Program

> *Deadline for application:* March 2005
> *Number of interns in the program in summer 2005 (internship) or 2005 (co-op):* 70 students (65 undergraduate, five MBAs)
> *Pay:* undergraduate: $10 per hour, IT/IS undergraduate: $12 per hour, MBA: $1,500 for 10 weeks
> *Percentage of interns/co-ops in the program who receive offers of full-time employment:* Of the ones we identify as stand-outs, we hire at least 50 percent depending on business needs (head count)
> *Web site for internship/co-op information:* www.lizclaiborneinc.com

The Summer Internship Program starts in mid-June and runs through mid-August for 10 weeks. We offer internships in the following areas: design, merchandising/planning, production/manufacturing, sales, finance, information systems, human resources and legal.

Each intern is also given a summer project that will take six to eight weeks to complete. The summer project will create a hands-on experience for each intern to gain better exposure to the area in which they have been placed.

The Summer Internship Program also provides exposure to different areas of the company as the interns complete their assignments. There are weekly activities that include brown bag lunches, field trips and other activities for the interns to interact with each other as well as gain more exposure to other areas of the organization.

Affinity Groups

We do not currently have any affinity groups, although every intern is paired with a mentor/buddy to help them with the transition into Liz Claiborne Inc. and our corporate environment.

Entry-Level Programs/Full-Time Opportunities/Training Programs

Our two programs, the Finance Management Training Program and the Accounting Management Program, are both four-month rotations through our finance and accounting divisions. Once the rotation is completed, a full-time opportunity is identified.

Through our organizational development department an extensive list of training programs and classes for Liz Claiborne associates are offered.

Classes included are: Civil Treatment® for Employees, Civil Treatment® for Managers, ValuEthics™, Basic Retail Math, Presentation Skills for Designers, Presentation Skills for Sales Associates, Business Simulation, Business Writing 1, Business Writing 2, Coaching & Counseling for the Experienced Manager, Dale Carnegie, Executive Presentation Skills, Focus - Time

Management, Frontline Leadership, Management Effectiveness, Positive Power & Influence Skills, The Accounting Game and The Finance Game. Also, see below for Attraction, Retention, Professional and Leadership Development.

Strategic Plan and Diversity Leadership

How does the firm's leadership communicate the importance of diversity to everyone at the firm?

Our diversity and inclusion efforts are our CEO's number one non-financial initiative. There is constant discussion and reminders of the importance of expanding our diversity and inclusion efforts at all levels. Our CEO's diversity and inclusion statement is featured on our Intranet.

Who has primary responsibility for leading diversity initiatives at your firm?

Dennis Butler, vice president of associate relations. Diversity is a company-wide effort and initiative, so every manager, executive, etc. is committed to its growth.

Does your firm currently have a diversity committee?

Yes. Currently, the diversity committee includes an executive VP, a group president, the senior VP of HR, the VP of associate relations and a director of HR. We are currently in the process of identifying 10-15 additional members at the VP level or higher from a cross section of our organization.

If yes, does the committee's representation include one or more members of the firm's management/executive committee? Yes.

If yes, how many executives are on the committee, and what was the total number of hours collectively spent by the committee in furtherance of the firm's diversity initiatives? How many employees are on the committee, and how often does the committee convene in furtherance of the firm's diversity initiatives?

Currently, the committee is meeting monthly.

Does the committee and/or diversity leader establish and set goals or objectives consistent with management's priorities?

The most senior members of the committee (EVP, GP, and SVP) have non-financial objectives relative to increasing and valuing the diversity of our workforce.

Has the firm undertaken a formal or informal diversity program or set of initiatives aimed at increasing the diversity of the firm?

Yes, informal. As a federal contractor, we are an affirmative action employer with written AAPs that are reviewed and updated annually. Where underutilization exists, specific formal goals are set.

Additionally, we recognize that having a diverse workforce that reflects the diversity of our marketplace makes good business sense. Accordingly, we are actively working to increase awareness and the valuing of diversity.

How often does the firm's management review the firm's diversity progress/results? Quarterly

How is the firm's diversity committee and/or firm management held accountable for achieving results?

Key executive non-financial objectives reflect inclusion goals.

The Stats

Employees

2005: 15,400
2004: 9,374 (U.S.)
2004: 14,000 (worldwide)

Revenue

2005: $4.85 billion

Overall Demographics

76 percent female
36 percent minority

Executives Demographics

60 percent female leadership council
9 percent min leadership council
40 percent female exec council

Retention and Professional Development

How do 2005 minority and female attrition rates generally compare to those experienced in the prior year period?

About the same as in prior years.

Please identify the specific steps you are taking to reduce the attrition rate of minority and women employees.

• Increase/review compensation relative to competition
• Increase/improve current work/life programs
• Succession plan includes emphasis on diversity
• Work with minority and women employees to develop career advancement plans
• Strengthen mentoring program for all employees, including minorities and women
• Professional skills development program, including minority and women employees
• Attraction, retention, professional and leadership development:

The survival of any organization depends on the attraction, retention and development of quality associates. The stewardship review and talent management process provide the opportunity to review the performance of key executives and other high-potential associates. HR generalists and executives meet on a regular basis (formally and informally) to discuss cross-functional, promotional and other developmental opportunities for high-potential employees. During this process, we make a conscious effort to identify minorities as candidates for these opportunities. By recognizing these outstanding performers, we are able to strategically develop and create a diverse pipeline for the future leadership of Liz Claiborne.

In addition to many internal and external training/leadership development courses offered, following are programs we have established to enhance the developmental opportunities, retention and promotability of all associates. In implementing these programs, specific attention is given to assuring that the current and future leadership of our organization appropriately reflects the diversity of the labor pool and marketplace.

This year, we introduced the "Leader Studio." This three-phase program includes an experiential learning opportunity and on-the-job practice using concepts of adult learning styles and generational influences which can be effectively applied to managing a diverse workforce. As part of the learning, participants visit the Civil Rights Museum in Memphis, Tenn. This event enhances

their appreciation of peoples' differences by encouraging them to better understand the experiences of those who were involved in the Civil Rights movement.

We have increased funding and support for associates' participation in networking conferences specific to women of color. This year, the Working Mother Women of Color Conference (NY, NY), the Hispanic Women's Conference (Phoenix, Ariz.) and the NAFE Conference (NY, NY) were attended by female associates of various ethnic backgrounds and at all levels.

Additionally, we have implemented the following:

• Senior Executive Stewardship Reviews: Annually, the chairman/CEO and human resources meet with each of the division presidents and corporate department senior vice presidents to discuss their direct reports and any high-potential associates that should be considered part of our strategic succession planning process. Developmental needs and opportunities are discussed as part of this process. The process also helps uncover and address skill gaps and to surface any other real or perceived barriers that may be blocking the advancement or development of associates. As part of this process, the chairman specifically charges his executive team with assessing their recruiting, retention and development strategies to be sure they adequately address the needs of our diverse workforce and marketplace.

• Organizational Reviews: Annually, each division and corporate department in partnership with human resources reviews their organization to identify high potentials/promotables, performers/technical experts and any non-performers. Managers discuss their subordinates with their supervisors to ensure that appropriate development plans exist and are being executed. This process follows the setting of individual performance and development plans by associates and their managers.

• Talent Management: As an expansion and enhancement of the existing organizational review process, the talent management process was developed. All human resources generalists, recruiters and organizational development leadership meet formally several times throughout the year to review the internal talent pool in great detail. The group discusses career paths, strengths, development needs and explores any existing and future, new and/or cross-functional opportunities for each high potential/potential high potential employees (approximately 500 of whom are women). The opportunity to share information regarding top and emerging talent—our future leaders—results in more efficient and timely promotion of internal movement and development. As part of this process we annually conduct all-day talent management summits.

Diversity Mission Statement

From our CEO:
February 7, 2005
To: All Liz Claiborne Associates
Subject: Diversity & Inclusion

The creation of a diverse portfolio has been a cornerstone of our strategy. Multiple brands that are sold in multiple channels and geographies and that touch multiple consumer demographics have generated an enviable record of consistent performance and growth. In order to be successful in this environment, we must be innovative, responsive, dynamic and adaptable to the demands of a global marketplace. While it is our consistency of execution that creates our competitive advantage, it is our ability to understand and translate the distinct differences of our consumers, brands and channels of distribution that distinguishes us.

We are a global corporation and take pride in a culture of achievement and excellence. Among our standards of excellence is the consistent goal to create a workplace in which our behaviors, practices and policies promote respect, opportunity and advancement for all our associates. A key to these standards in our culture is inclusion.

Inclusion reflects the diversity of backgrounds, experiences and outlooks our associates bring to the workplace. More importantly, inclusion focuses on behaviors and actions that reflect our value for diversity in our workplaces, communities and markets.

In our workplace, inclusion must be embodied in everything we do and be a vital part of our cultural fabric from ideas, concepts and processes to training, development, mentoring and our day-to-day relationships. Inclusion will allow us to attract and retain the best talent.

In our communities and the workforce from which we draw our associates, inclusion must be evident in our recruiting outreach and community involvement.

In our marketplace, inclusion is visible in our suppliers and in our sales and marketing initiatives.

Most of all, inclusion is a shared responsibility. My senior executives and I have a responsibility as leaders of our company to demonstrate a visible commitment to fostering an environment of inclusion. As associates of this company, we all have a responsibility to model behaviors that honor and celebrate the unique contributions and perspectives our associates bring to this work we share.

Great companies accelerate the pace of change and push beyond the status quo to uncover new ideas, concepts and opportunities. Great companies fuel that acceleration by increasing inclusion initiatives and renewing the values and beliefs that guide their actions.

We are a great company that I believe can be greater. Embracing differences, leading change through innovation, committing to common goals, valuing integrity in everything we do and engaging the minds and energies of each and every associate—these will enable us to realize that greatness.

Paul R. Charron

Additional Information

We are a visionary and progressive company that actively supports the advancement of qualified minorities and women. We have a workforce that mirrors the diversity of our marketplace. Women and minorities are well-represented throughout all levels of the company.

CEO commitment to inclusion has resulted in the establishment of a Diversity Steering Committee and the communication of the CEO's inclusion statement to all associates. We have increased representation of Latinas across the company. Additionally, key executive non-financial objectives reflect inclusion goals, our intern program has successfully targeted and recruited more minorities, and we have expanded funding to support associate attendance at conferences for Latinas and other women of color.

Our programs give associates the opportunity to focus on professional development while balancing their work and family needs. We offer a very generous paid time-off program, alternative work arrangements, summer hours, steep clothing discounts and more. Additionally, our "traditional" benefits are very competitive, including healthcare, employee assistance programs, 401(k) matching, tuition reimbursement, gym membership discounts (including an on-site facility).

The focus of the Liz Claiborne's Foundation is women's issues and we have implemented corporate initiatives relative to domestic violence and helping women, including minorities, achieve their life goals for safety, professional achievement and family.

We continue to develop strategic approaches for creating a more inclusive culture in which behaviors, values and practices promote respect, representation, career development and success across all forms of diversity. Our culture, which empowers associates to achieve their full potential, attracts and retains loyal, dedicated, promotable associates, including women and minorities.

413

We're privileged to help build the future.
One inspired mind at a time.

Children are eager to learn. And the men and women of Lockheed Martin are eager to help. That's why we support educational initiatives that help children reach their greatest potential – from one-on-one mentoring to broad-based programs designed to excite students about math and science. We also provide grants and local programs for students of all grades – from elementary school to universities. At Lockheed Martin, we're serious about education. Because we believe that giving back is the very best way forward.

Lockheed Martin Corporation

6801 Rockledge Drive
Bethesda, MD 20817

Locations
Major sites in:
Dallas/Fort Worth, TX area
Denver, CO area
Orlando, FL area
Palmdale, CA
Philadelphia, PA area
San Jose/Bay, CA area
Washington, D.C. area
Marietta, GA
As well as many other national and international sites.

Diversity Leadership
Shantella Carr-Cooper
Vice President for Diversity and Equal
Opportunity Programs

Employment Contact
Leslie L. Chappell
Director, University Relations
www.lockheedmartin.com/careers

Recruiting

Please list the schools/types of schools at which you recruit.

- Ivy League schools
- Other private schools
- Public state schools
- Historically Black Colleges and Universities (HBCUs)
- Hispanic Serving Institutions (HSIs)
- Other predominantly minority and/or women's colleges

Do you have any special outreach efforts directed to encourage minority students to consider your firm?

- Hold a reception for minority students
- *Conferences:* HACU, HENAAC, NSBE, SWE, SHPE, AISES, MAES, NAMEPA, BEY
- *Advertise in minority student association publication(s): Minority Engineer, Woman Engineer*
- Participate in/host minority student job fair(s)
- Sponsor minority student association events
- Firm's employees participate on career panels at school
- Outreach to leadership of minority student organizations
- Scholarships or intern/fellowships for minority students
- Internship/co-op opportunities, workshops, special speakers, mentors

What activities does the firm undertake to attract minority and women employees?

- Partner programs with women and minority associations
- *Conferences:* HACU, HENAAC, NSBE, SWE, SHPE, AISES, MAES, NAMEPA, AMIE
- Participate at minority job fairs
- Seek referrals from other employees
- Utilize online job services

Do you use executive recruiting/search firms to seek to identify new diversity hires?

Yes.

Internships and Co-ops

Deadline for application: Ongoing

Number of interns in the program in summer 2006 (internship) or 2006 (co-op): 1,701

Pay: Varies by academic level, major and geographic location

Length of the program: Typically, nine to 11 weeks

Percentage of interns/co-ops in the program who receive offers of full-time employment: 52 percent

Web site for internship/co-op information: www.lockheedmartin.com/careers

Lockheed Martin seeks students at all academic levels in the following majors:

• Aeronautical engineering
• Computer engineering
• Computer science
• Electrical engineering
• Mechanical engineering and systems engineering

We also have limited opportunities in

• Finance
• Human resources
• Accounting and business

Scholarships

Lockheed Martin participates in the following scholarship programs aimed at women and minority students, please see their web sites for details on deadlines, amounts and eligibility requirements:

• American Indian College Fund—Tribunal Scholarships:
   www.collegefund.org/

• American Indian Science and Engineering Society:
   http://aises.org/highered/scholarships/

• Hispanic Association of Colleges & Universities (HACU) Scholarships:
   https://scholarships.hacu.net/applications/applicants/

• Hispanic Scholarship Fund:
   www.hsf.net/scholarships.php

• League of Latin American Citizens Scholars (LULAC):
   www.chci.org/chciyouth/scholarship/listofscholarships.htm

•Mexican-American Engineering Society (MAES) Scholarship:
   www.maes-natl.org/index.php?module=ContentExpress&func=display&ceid=237&meid=241

• National Society of Black Engineers Corporate Scholarships:
   www.nsbe.org/programs/nsbescholarships.php

•Society of Women Engineers Scholarship:
   www.swe.org/stellent/idcplg?IdcService=SS_GET_PAGE&nodeId=9&ssSourceNodeId=5

• Society of Hispanic Professional Engineers Foundation (Scholarships):
www.shpe.org/index.php/docs/239

Lockheed Martin also offers many scholarships for diversity students that are administered directly by the schools with whom we partner, most are in engineering. These scholarships have a wide range of eligibility requirements, deadlines and award amounts.

Entry-Level Programs/Full-Time Opportunities/Training Programs

Leadership Development Program (LDP) (various specialties)

Length of program: Two to three years of rotational assignments
Geographic location(s) of program: Nationwide

Employees receive week-long training each summer and periodic communications throughout the year. Most large worksites have dedicated LDP managers who help guide the employees.

Tuition reimbursement is provided so that employees in this program can pursue a masters degree. In some cases, paid time off is provided in order to attend classes or to study for examinations. In some cases, flexible work schedules can be arranged so that the employee can attend day classes if necessary.

Strategic Plan and Diversity Leadership

Who has primary responsibility for leading diversity initiatives at your firm?

Shantella Carr-Cooper, vice president for diversity and equal opportunity programs.

Does your firm currently have a diversity committee?

Yes, our Executive Diversity Council (EDC) is chaired by our Chairman, President and CEO, Robert J Stevens, and vice-chaired by our CFO, Chris Kubasik. The members consist of 26 of the top leaders of the corporation, including executive vice presidents, operating business unit presidents, the chief information officer (CIO) and senior vice president of human resources. The EDC serves as an advisory function to our executive management council. It is their vision and strategy that is driven down through out the corporate via the diversity councils at our business units.

If yes, does the committee's representation include one or more members of the firm's management/executive committee (or the equivalent)?

Yes.

If yes, how many executives are on the committee, and in 2005, what was the total number of hours collectively spent by the committee in furtherance of the firm's diversity initiatives? How many employees are on the committee, and how often does the committee convene in furtherance of the firm's diversity initiatives?

Total Executives on Committee: 26

The EDC spends approximately 1,000 hours amongst the 26 members furthering Lockheed Martin's diversity initiatives. There are approximately 36 business unit diversity councils. It is difficult to calculate how many hours they spend furthering the diversity initiatives, due to the large number of members in this diversity community.

Does the committee and/or diversity leader establish and set goals or objectives consistent with management's priorities?

Yes. We have aligned our business processes with our people management process to ensure our goals & objectives are consistent with management's priorities.

Has the firm undertaken a formal or informal diversity program or set of initiatives aimed at increasing the diversity of the firm?

Yes, formally. Lockheed Martin views diversity in a broad sense of the term that goes beyond race and gender. While those are two aspects of our view on how we define diversity, we look at things like educational background, geographic location, personal style, etc. Our efforts at creating a more inclusive environment focuses on all aspects of diversity. When we talk about increasing the number of women and minorities, we use the term increasing representation. Our approach to increasing representation is maintaining a positive compliance posture, as defined by the affirmative action regulations to address underutilization.

How often does the firm's management review the firm's diversity progress/results?

Quarterly.

How is the firm's diversity committee and/or firm management held accountable for achieving results?

We have put an assessment process in place to measure the performance of a business unit in the area of diversity inclusion. The assessment process takes employee opinion, as well as the kinds of processes and practices in place to foster inclusion. The business unit receives a numeric score associated with the assessment and BU leaders are held accountable for results through their incentive compensation plan.

The Stats

Employees

2005: 135,000

Revenue

2005: $37.2 billion
Of our total workforce, 24 percent is female and 20 percent is minority.

Retention and Professional Development

How do 2005 minority and female attrition rates generally compare to those experienced in the prior year period?

Lower than in prior years.

Please identify the specific steps you are taking to reduce the attrition rate of minority and women employees.

• Develop and/or support internal employee affinity groups (e.g., minority or women networks within the firm) at some locations and with our company executive leadership
• Increase/review compensation relative to competition for all employees
• Increase/improve current work/life programs alternative work schedule, telecommuting, flexible work schedules, etc.
• Adopt dispute resolution process corporate policy statement to address dispute resolution
• Succession plan includes emphasis on diversity
• Work with minority and women employees to develop career advancement plans
• Review work assignments and hours billed to key client matters to make sure minority and women employees are not being excluded

Diversity Mission Statement

Lockheed Martin is committed to creating one company, one team, all inclusive, where diversity contributes to mission success. Diversity at Lockheed Martin is an inclusive team that values and leverages each person's individuality.

Additional Information

At Lockheed Martin, we recognize that diversity is not just a short-term trend. It is a business imperative. Our long-term success depends on a commitment to diversity. We have to leverage the individuality of each employee as a competitive advantage by eliminating barriers to inclusiveness. Diversity is about creating an environment that welcomes, respects and develops our individual differences as a competitive strength. It begins with our core values of ethics, excellence, "can-do" attitude, integrity, people and teamwork. It extends to every activity involved in attracting and retaining a talented workforce that reflects the diversity of our customers, suppliers and our world.

There's a difference between stating our commitment to diversity and living it. We are dedicated to a process that listens to the voices of our employees and partners to help shape our course. It is through this process that we set goals and develop a strategy that will hold us accountable for making Lockheed Martin a place of "institutionalized inclusion."

Our approach to diversity is analogous to our work as system integrators. Each element, each subsystem must do its job, but function as part of a larger, integrated whole, which together achieve astounding results. The whole is definitely stronger than its individual parts. In similar fashion, Lockheed Martin is made stronger by the combined efforts of each employee and each operating business unit working as one team.

The Lockheed Martin team is naturally diverse, encompassing 130,000 people with a wide variety of skills, backgrounds, perspectives and lifestyles. We draw from this tremendous source of talent to forge a great company—one team that is committed to the success of our customers on projects of profound significance to our world.

As a world-class advanced technology leader, we must continually reach out to new and different points of view to succeed in the global marketplace. This means we must have an environment that attracts the best people with the biggest dreams and the highest standards and give them the support and encouragement they need to reach their full potential. It also keeps us focused on assuring the widest possible circle of suppliers with whom we do business.

Diversity must be more than words. Having an inclusive environment really demands an engagement process that starts at the top —in my office—and extends throughout the corporation to each and every employee and stakeholder in this enterprise. We share in this commitment as a team because it is right for people and right for business.

That's what diversity is all about for Lockheed Martin and the people and institutions we serve. Diversity is a journey, and we are on this journey together.

JOHN P.
PACKAGING DEVELOPMENT ENGINEER

VINCENT T.
MARKETING MANAGER

ALICE F.
FORMULA DEVELOPMENT ENGINEER

L'ORÉAL
WORLD LEADER IN BEAUTY PRODUCTS

JOIN US. WITH $4 BILLION IN ANNUAL SALES AND ACCOLADES THAT INCLUDE THE FIRST EVER DIVERSITY BEST PRACTICES GLOBAL LEADERSHIP AWARD, L'ORÉAL USA IS A PLACE WHERE YOUR UNIQUE TALENTS CAN LEAD THE WAY TO A GREAT CAREER.

L'ORÉAL USA MANAGEMENT DEVELOPMENT PROGRAM
MARKETING ▪ SALES ▪ FINANCE ▪ INFORMATION SYSTEMS ▪ LOGISTICS ▪ MANUFACTURING ▪ RESEARCH & DEVELOPMENT

IF YOU ARE AN IMAGINATIVE AND RESULTS-FOCUSED GRADUATING SENIOR WITH AN ENTREPRENEURIAL SPIRIT AND COMMITMENT TO EXCELLENCE, THEN L'ORÉAL USA MAY HAVE THE OPPORTUNITY FOR YOU. UPON ENTERING OUR ROTATIONAL TRAINING PROGRAM, YOU WILL BECOME AN INTEGRAL PART OF OUR TEAM, WITH CONCRETE RESPONSIBILITY FROM DAY ONE. YOU WILL WORK ALONGSIDE TOP PROFESSIONALS WHO SHAPE THE INDUSTRY, CONTRIBUTING TO THE CREATION OF IDEAS AND THE PROCESSES THAT TURN THOSE IDEAS INTO REALITIES. IN ADDITION TO PROFESSIONAL DEVELOPMENT TRAINING HELD AT OUR MANAGEMENT DEVELOPMENT CENTER, WE OFFER COMPETITIVE COMPENSATION AND BENEFITS. LEARN MORE ABOUT THIS EXCITING FULL-TIME OPPORTUNITY, AS WELL AS INTERNSHIP OPPORTUNITIES, AND APPLY AT **WWW.LOREALUSA.COM**. EQUAL OPPORTUNITY EMPLOYER.

         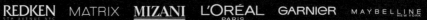 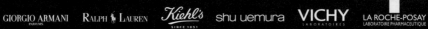

L'Oréal USA

575 Fifth Avenue
New York, NY 10017
Phone: (212) 984-4000
www.lorealusa.com

Diversity Leadership
Ed Bullock
Chief Diversity Officer

Employment Contact
Jennifer Peters
Manager, Corporate Strategic Recruitment

Recruiting

Please list the schools/types of schools at which you recruit.

• Ivy League schools
• Other private schools
• Historically Black Colleges and Universities (HBCUs)
• Other predominantly minority and/or women's colleges

Do you have any special outreach efforts directed to encourage minority students to consider your firm?

• Hold a reception for minority students
• *Conferences:* NBMBAA, NSHMBA
• Advertise in minority student association publication(s)
• Participate in/host minority student job fair(s)
• Sponsor minority student association events
• Firm's employees participate on career panels at schools
• Outreach to leadership of minority student organizations
• Scholarships or intern/fellowships for minority students

What activities does the firm undertake to attract minority and women employees?

• Partner programs with women and minority associations
• Conferences
• Participate at minority job fairs
• Seek referrals from other employees
• Utilize online job services

Internships and Co-ops

L'Oréal Summer Internship Program

Deadline for application: Rolling application, but most offers are finalized by April 1st
Number of interns in the program in summer 2006 (internship) or 2006 (co-op): 90 undergraduate interns
Pay: Competitive
Length of the program: 10-12 weeks
Web site for internship/co-op information: www.lorealusa.com

L'Oréal USA offers a formal internship program consisting of three main elements: (1) the day to day functional job assignment, (2) a business related project to be completed and presented to management and (3) educational and professional development sessions. The individual job assignments will vary with department needs, but you will get a chance to release your creativity and gain a new view to the world's leading beauty company.

Interns may be placed in the following areas: marketing, sales, finance, accounting, information systems, logistics, manufacturing, research & development, or human resources.

Entry-Level Programs/Full-Time Opportunities/Training Programs

Management Development Program for Marketing, Sales, Finance, Information Systems, Manufacturing or Research & Development

> *Length of program:* Two years for undergraduates; one year for MBAs
> *Geographic location(s) of program:* Specific to the division and function

The management development program is designed for students graduating with a bachelor's degree who want to pursue a career in marketing, sales, finance, information systems, logistics, manufacturing or research & development. L'Oréal USA's management development program has been designed to develop our future leaders.

As part of the L'Oréal USA management development program, students are placed into one of the channels of trade at L'Oréal USA—consumer products, luxury products, professional products, active cosmetics or one of our corporate functions i.e. finance, accounting, manufacturing or research & development. The program is designed to give you the opportunity to gain exposure and hone your skills through hands-on assignments and puts a strong emphasis on professional development through formal training held at our management development center and individual check-points with members of the HR community. L'Oréal USA takes a three-pronged approach to the program whereby successful candidates will experience a period of integration, participate in training rotationals, and ultimately be placed in an entry-level management position.

Strategic Plan and Diversity Leadership

How does the firm's leadership communicate the importance of diversity to everyone at the firm?

The president of the company presents diversity communication annually in the corporate newsletter and through executive leadership meetings with divisions for L'Oréal.

A diversity video featuring Lindsay Owen-Jones, chairman of L'Oréal, has been created to convey the L'Oréal diversity philosophy. This video is featured at all orientations and leadership programs.

Who has primary responsibility for leading diversity initiatives at your firm?

CEO Jean Paul Agon supported by the Office of Diversity.

Does your firm currently have a diversity committee?

Yes.

Does the committee and/or diversity leader establish and set goals or objectives consistent with management's priorities?

Yes.

Has the firm undertaken a formal or informal diversity program or set of initiatives aimed at increasing the diversity of the firm?

Yes, formal. Four programs that provide employee orientation, management to leadership, global executive leadership as well as mandatory diversity training for all employees.

How often does the firm's management review the firm's diversity progress/results?

Quarterly.

The Stats

	TOTAL IN THE U.S.		TOTAL OUTSIDE THE U.S		TOTAL WORLDWIDE	
	2005	2004	2005	2004	2005	2004
Number of employees	7,900	7,629	44,503	43,274	52,403	50,903
Revenue	€4.186 billion	€3.280 billion	€10.35 billion	€10.94 billion	€14.53 billion	€14.22 billion

Retention and Professional Development

Please identify the specific steps you are taking to reduce the attrition rate of minority and women employees.

• Increase/improve current work/life programs
• Succession plan includes emphasis on diversity

Additional Information

L'Oréal is dedicated to serving all expressions of beauty and well being, which it seeks to make accessible to women and men all over the world. We believe our approach to diversity and inclusion must stand on a firm foundation of respect for the individual as stated in our L'Oréal code of business ethics. We embrace the philosophy of first being diverse from within and in order to become more diverse from within, we have established the office of diversity reporting to the president of L'Oréal USA and supporting global initiatives. This position will insure our steady progress toward a more inclusive and innovative organization.

Our Definition of Diversity

Diversity is the mosaic of people who bring a variety of backgrounds, styles, perspectives, values, beliefs and differences as assets to the groups and organizations with which they interact.

Our Thoughts on Diversity

"Today we live and work in an increasingly diverse world, a world of individuals with different cultural and ethnic backgrounds, unique styles, perspectives, values and beliefs. A diverse workforce in all functions and levels enhances our creativity and our understanding of consumers and allows us to develop and market products that are relevant."

Jean-Paul Agon, president and CEO, L'Oréal USA   June 2002

"At L'Oréal we manage diversity by giving value and respect to our employees, our consumers and our business partners as core ingredients in the formula for our success. We respect the talents, creativity and diversity they bring to our entire brand portfolio. We are committed to the recruitment, retention and development of a diverse workforce without regard to gender, ethnicity, religion, disabilities or sexual orientation."

Edward W.Bullock, VP diversity, L'Oréal USA

Lucent Technologies

600 Mountain Ave.
Murray Hill, NJ 07974
Phone: (908) 582-8500
www.lucent.com/careers

Diversity Leadership

Ethel Batten
HR Vice President and Chief Diversity Officer
600 Mountain Ave.
Murray Hill, NJ 07974
Phone: (908) 582-8500
www.lucent.com/careers

Recruiting

Please list the schools/types of schools at which you recruit.

• *Ivy League schools:* Harvard University, University of Pennsylvania, Columbia University and Cornell University
• *Other private schools:* Purdue, Stanford University, Massachusetts Institute of Technology, Seton Hall University, Stevens Institute of Technology, Babson College, St. Peters College, Boston College, Emory University, Northwestern University, University of Chicago and Duke University
• *Public state schools:* Rutgers University, University of Illinois, Penn State University, Boston University, University of Georgia, New Jersey Institute of Technology, Ohio State University and University of Illinois-Chicago
• *Historically Black Colleges and Universities (HBCUs):* Howard University and Tennessee State University

Do you have any special outreach efforts directed to encourage minority students to consider your firm?

• Conferences
• Participate in/host minority student job fair(s)
• Outreach to leadership of minority student organizations
• Scholarships or intern/fellowships for minority students

What activities does the firm undertake to attract minority and women employees?

• Conferences
• Participate at minority job fairs
• Seek referrals from other employees
• Utilize online job services

Do you use executive recruiting/search firms to seek to identify new diversity hires?

Yes.

Internships and Co-ops

Lucent Summer Internship Program

Deadline for application: January 31st
Number of interns in the program in summer 2005 (internship) or 2005 (co-op): 160
Pay: Depends on year, degree and experience
Length of the program: 10 weeks

Web site for internship/co-op information: www.lucent.com/work/collegerecruitment.html

Lucent's Summer Internship Program provides valuable work experience within a corporate environment to outstanding college students ranging from first year through the masters level, PhD levels and college faculty members. The objective of the program is to provide summer employment with positive work/training experience, identify and track potential regular full-time employees and establish "goodwill ambassadors" for Lucent on campuses. Interns receive project-focused assignments and challenging objectives consistent with their career goals. Interns also are assigned a mentor in addition to their supervisor/coach.

Interns receive a broad orientation to Lucent, the specific business unit and the individual work group to which they will be contributing. Developmental opportunities may include meetings with corporate executives, various educational workshops, business unit information exchanges, networking events and facility tours.

All offers for our summer internship program will be extended by April 15th. Submit your resume by January 31st, however we will accept resumes after this date. Please see the instructions below for submitting your resume.

To participate in Lucent's Early Career Identification Programs, you must meet the following criteria:

• GPA: Overall GPA of 3.0/4.0 or above.
• Citizenship: U.S. citizen, permanent or conditional permanent resident, temporary resident, asylum seeker or refugee. We will accept students on F-1 or J-1 Visas.
• Student status: Full-time students will be considered from any four or five year accredited U.S. college or university. Students must be enrolled to return as a full-time student following the internship.

Majors: Accounting, behavioral science, business administration, chemical engineering, chemistry, computer engineering, computer science, economics, electrical engineering, engineering mechanics, finance, industrial engineering, journalism, management, manufacturing engineering, mathematics, mechanical engineering, operations research, physics, public relations, sales/marketing, statistics, systems engineering and telecommunications.

> *Principal U.S. locations:* North & Central New Jersey, Naperville Ill.
> *Network Solutions:* AMPS/PCS co-op program
> *Length of the program:* 26 weeks

Bell Labs Graduate Research Fellowship Program

> *Deadline for application:* mid-January for the fall program
> *Web site for internship/co-op information:* http://www.lucent.com/social/blgrfp/

The Bell Labs Graduate Research Fellowship Program is designed to increase the number of minorities and women in the fields of science, math, engineering and technology. A Bell Labs Graduate Research Fellowship is a wonderful opportunity to help outstanding minorities and women enhance their knowledge and to pursue a PhD in science and engineering.

Fellowships are awarded to women and members of a minority group currently underrepresented in the sciences who are U.S. citizens, permanent residents or non-residents here on an F1 student visa. The program is primarily directed to graduating college seniors, but applications from first-year graduate students will be considered. Ten fellowships are awarded each year.

Candidates are selected on the basis of scholastic attainment in their fields of specialization, and other evidence of their ability and potential as research scientists. A distinctive feature of the program is the opportunity for fellowship participants to gain first-hand research and development experience, through on-site activities at Lucent Technologies Bell Labs, under the guidance of research scientists and engineers. Each participant is expected to spend the first summer working with their mentor at Bell Labs on a research project in their area of interest. Fellowship participants are encouraged to continue their association with their mentors during the following academic year and throughout their graduate studies.

Scholarships

Project GRAD Scholarships

Through the Lucent Foundation, Lucent funds four-year college scholarships for Project GRAD (Graduation Really Achieves Dreams), a major educational reform initiative at Malcolm X Shabazz High School and Central High School in Newark, NJ Project GRAD works to raise student achievement in reading, writing and math at the two high schools. The goal of the program is to significantly increase the number of students from these high schools who graduate and go on to college. Lucent has supported this program since its inception in 1999.

To qualify, students must have come from one of the feeder elementary schools in Newark to either Shabazz or Central High School. High school students also must participate in enrichment programs during their high school years and graduate with a GPA of 2.5 or higher.

For more information on Project GRAD, contact the Lucent Foundation at foundation@lucent.com

Affinity Groups

Lucent actively supports and encourages its Employee Business Partner (EBP) Groups; individual organizations that offer programs to address the needs of different ethnic and social groups. Lucent's EBP groups are an important part of our culture, and help advance the professional and personal growth of all employees through networking forums, career development programs and community service.

Lucent's Employee Business Partner Groups are:

• 4A—Asian-Pacific American Association for Advancement at Lucent Technologies
• ABLE—Alliance of Black Lucent Technologies Employees
• EQUAL—Lesbian, Bisexual, Gay and Transgendered Employees of Lucent Technologies
• HISPA—Hispanic Association of Lucent Technologies Employees
• IDEAL—Individuals Dedicated to Enabling Accessiblity in Life
• LUNA—United Native Americans of Lucent Technologies
• WILL—Women in Leadership at Lucent Technologies

To provide guidance and support to these groups while they continue this work, several Lucent leaders have been named EBP advisors, and work closely with each EBP group on a rotating basis.

Entry-Level Programs/Full-Time Opportunities/Training Programs

Lucent's Tuition Assistance Program

Lucent employees are eligible for $7,000 per year for undergraduate and other education and $9,000 per year for graduate education. The purpose of this program is to broaden employees' knowledge, keep them current with business and technology changes, enhance their abilities and help them meet the competitive challenges of a global business.

Supply Chain Network MBA Leadership Development Program

Length of program: 36 months
Geographic locations(s) of program: United States

SCN LDP candidates are recruited and interviewed each year between September 1st and March 15th. Resumes for both full-time and summer intern positions are gathered during this time frame. From March 15th through September 1st resumes are collected but not reviewed until after September 1st.

The Leadership Development Program sponsored by Supply Chain Networks (SCN) originates, and is supported, by the entire SCN senior leadership team. The program is focused on developing future global leaders while engaging them in challenging projects critical to Lucent's future. The LDP is a rigorous 36-month program consisting of three to four rotations, approximately 12 months in duration. The summer intern component consists of a 10-week work assignment, which may lead to future full-time opportunities.

Each position offers a wide range of responsibilities and business opportunities for the new hire and the LDP executive mentoring program enhances this growth.

Supply Chain Networks provides Lucent with all supplier and supply chain engineering and management, manufacturing, logistics, and distribution functions for global provisioning from end to end. SCN LDP is seeking advanced level degree graduates to work on projects that focus on several areas including:

- General management
- Business development/strategy
- Supply chain management
- Demand management
- Product design chain
- Operations
- Customer facing
- Order fulfillment
- Supplier management
- Provisioning/manufacturing

Qualifications/experience criteria:

- Minimum of five years post-bachelor's degree full-time work experience, with previous overseas work assignment(s) desirable.
- Must have the right to work in the U.S. on a permanent/full-time basis.
- Undergraduate degree in engineering or business/finance desirable.
- Proficiency in two or more languages preferred and/or willingness to acquire a second language skill.
- Demonstration of leadership characteristics and/or experience, change agent, thinks strategically, results oriented, proven high level of performance.
- Demonstrated ability to work in a global environment as well as experience doing business in a different culture.

If you meet Lucent's criteria and are interested in applying for an SCN Leadership Development Program position, please submit your resume online: www.lucent.com/hireme.

Lucent's leaders have placed a top priority on the continued development of our talent. To address this, a comprehensive program talent management program, "Developing Great Talent" (DGT), is being launched to ensure all managers at Lucent understand the critical role they play in identifying, acquiring, developing and retaining great talent. Lucent's mentoring program, Leading Lucent's Future, is being revamped. This program works to accelerate Lucent's performance through increased contributions of rising leaders and build a diverse group of future leaders.

Strategic Plan and Diversity Leadership

How does the firm's leadership communicate the importance of diversity to everyone at the firm?

Lucent's chairman & CEO was keynote speaker during Black History Month activities sponsored by one of Lucent's employee business partners.

- Lucent senior leaders, including the chairman and CEO have released diversity statements to employees stressing the importance of diversity.

• Articles in LT Today (Lucent's daily electronic newsletter) and business unit publications on the importance of diversity.
• Employee Business Partner Groups.
• Each of Lucent's employee business partner groups has an executive advisor.
• Agenda item on the leaders' team meetings.

Who has primary responsibility for leading diversity initiatives at your firm?

Ethel Batten, human resources vice president and global diversity officer.

Does your firm currently have a diversity committee?

Yes.

The committee is comprised of representation both nationally and internationally. There is representation from all business segments and corporate centers as well as levels. The committee meets on a bi-monthly basis.

The primary responsibility of the committee is to align business objectives with diversity priorities, translating the priorities of the senior management committee into realities for the business segments. The committee also tracks the progress of Lucent's five-year diversity strategy and serves as a voice of the people on an ongoing basis.

If yes, does the committee's representation include one or more members of the firm's management/executive committee (or the equivalent)?

Yes.

If yes, how many executives are on the committee, and in 2005, what was the total number of hours collectively spent by the committee in furtherance of the firm's diversity initiatives? How many employees are on the committee, and how often does the committee convene in furtherance of the firm's diversity initiatives?

Total Executives on Committee: Three

There are a total of 34 employees on the committee.

The committee convenes on a bi-monthly basis (six times per year).

Does the committee and/or diversity leader establish and set goals or objectives consistent with management's priorities?

Yes.

Has the firm undertaken a formal or informal diversity program or set of initiatives aimed at increasing the diversity of the firm?

Yes, formal.

How often does the firm's management review the firm's diversity progress/results?

Quarterly.

How is the firm's diversity committee and/or firm management held accountable for achieving results?

Diversity measurements/objectives are included in the committee's scorecard. They are annually assessed during performance management.

Retention and Professional Development

Please identify the specific steps you are taking to reduce the attrition rate of minority and women employees.

• Develop and/or support internal employee affinity groups
• Increase/review compensation relative to competition
• Increase/improve current work/life programs
• Adopt dispute resolution process
• Succession plan includes emphasis on diversity
• Work with minority and women employees to develop career advancement plans
• Review work assignments and hours billed to key client matters to make sure minority and women employees are not being excluded
• Strengthen mentoring program for all employees, including minorities and women
• Professional skills development program, including minority and women employees

Diversity Mission Statement

We achieve our shared purpose by embracing the full richness of our people's differences. We believe the diversity of our people enriches our work experience and is the source of our innovation and our competitive advantage. We adhere to Lucent's core values and treat everyone with dignity and deepest respect.

Additional Information

Diversity is an important part of Lucent's heritage. We have always valued and remain strongly committed to diversity through our corporate culture, recruiting and development programs. Diverse people and ideas are vital to our corporate culture, to our success as a global business and to our ability to attract and retain talented employees. Over the last few years, Lucent has faced a changing telecom industry and a challenging market. Our company has had to adjust to this new reality. Our workforce has been affected, but our commitment to diversity as a business imperative has not.

At Lucent, we work to respect each other, acknowledge others' ideas and appreciate what makes us distinct as individuals. Respecting our differences is an integral part of our culture and values, and it shows.

Lucent has a strong set of core values, which is clearly evident in our internal and external web sites, as well as in "Business Guideposts." "Business Guideposts" is Lucent's code of conduct, which all employees are required to read and certify online. "Business Guideposts" describes Lucent's standards for ethical business behavior and addresses a wide range of business and personnel issues. People with different backgrounds, experiences and cultures bring very different perspectives to Lucent and enrich the quality of our performance for our customers. The debate and discussion, the creativity, innovations and the diversity of ideas that diverse perspectives generate are essential for any successful global company.

Lucent formed a Global Diversity Council to build on diversity efforts already in place, as well as expand our focus on diversity. This council, which has the commitment and participation of our top business leaders, will work to evaluate current programs and suggest ways to further endorse diversity efforts. In addition to the Global Diversity Council, there are a number of diversity councils on the business unit level.

Lucent has always been and continues to be a strong advocate for supplier diversity. This is a critical requirement for Lucent and our key customers. To be a leading player in the global market, the whole team needs to be diverse, and our suppliers and business partners are a critical part of the team working to meet our customers' expectations. We also work hard to incorporate diversity suppliers into the business and work to strengthen our relationships with them. AT&T was the first Fortune 500 to add sexual preference to its EO/AA policy in 1974 and the first company to have a gay and lesbian affinity group. In 1999, Lucent continued its trend setting legacy by adding "gender identity, characteristics and expressions" to the EO/AA policy. Lucent was the first company to include that language in their policy.

Marriott International, Inc.

Marriott Drive
Washington, D.C. 20058
Phone: (301) 380-3000

Diversity Leadership

Maruiel Perkins Chavis
Vice President, Workforce Effectiveness and Diversity
Marriott Drive
Washington, D.C. 20058
Phone: (301) 380-8391
Fax: (301) 380-4202
http://marriott.com/careers/default.mi

Employment Contact

Steve Bauman
Vice President, Talent Acquisition & HR Research

Recruiting

What activities does the firm undertake to attract minority and women employees?

Marriott maintains a strong commitment to national recruitment advertising, with placements in such publications as *Black Collegian*, *Black Enterprise*, *Black MBA*, *CAREERS and the disABLED*, *DiversityInc*, *Hispanic Business* and *Working Mother*.

Our strategic relationships with dozens of affinity organizations and media outlets help us get the word out that minorities and women have a great future at Marriott as associates, vendors, franchisees and guests. Examples include: The National Association of Black Accountants, the National Black MBA Association, the National Society of Minority Hoteliers, the Organization of Chinese-Americans, National Council of La Raza, the Women Business Enterprise Council, National Hispanic Corporate Council, the U.S. Hispanic Chamber of Commerce, the NAACP and the National Urban League.

Scholarships

Marriott is actively involved in the Emerging Markets Program of the International Franchise Association. The company contributes monetary, in-kind and management executive talent resources to IFA and has partnered with the association to launch a Minority Entrepreneurs Scholarship program.

Contact information for scholars:

Mr. John Reynolds, president
IFA Educational Foundation
1350 New York Ave. NW
Suite 900
Washington, D.C. NW 20005
Phone: (202) 662-0764
E-mail: johnr@franchise.org

Strategic Plan and Diversity Leadership

Does your firm currently have a diversity committee?

The Marriott board of directors has established a subcommittee on diversity which meets regularly to set significant goals and monitor progress at every level of the corporation.

Has the firm undertaken a formal or informal diversity program or set of initiatives aimed at increasing the diversity of the firm?

Six regional diversity councils drive our corporate diversity message home in the field with implementation of diversity-related initiatives to include strategic partnerships, targeted recruitment campaigns, leadership development programs, internships, conferences and other outreach to women and minorities.

The Stats

Our commitment to diversity begins at home. Marriott's 143,000 associates hail from dozens of nations, speak more than 50 languages and work under the Marriott banner in 66 countries and territories around the world. 60 percent of our associates are minorities and 54 percent are women, many of whom take advantage of the company's professional development programs to move up and map out long-term careers with the company.

Nearly 3,000 of Marriott's current managers began their careers with Marriott in hourly positions. Currently, 55.7 percent of the company's supervisors—the first step toward achieving a management post—are minorities.

Of the new managers hired during 2005, 26 percent were minorities and 48 percent were women.

Diversity Mission Statement

At Marriott International, diversity is more than a goal...it's our business. From our global workforce and vendors, to our franchisees, our customers and communities, we thrive on the differences that give our company its strength and competitive edge. In the process, we've set the standard for the entire hospitality industry. And it shows:

• *DiversityInc* ranked Marriott #22 on its list of the "Top 50 Companies for Diversity." Marriott was the highest-ranking lodging company on the list. (June 2006)

• Marriott was recognized as one of the Top 50 Companies for Supplier Diversity by *Hispanic Trends Magazine* (Jan./Feb. 2005 issue)

• National Society of Minorities in Hospitality presented Marriott International with its first ever "Lifetime Commitment Award" as a result of our work and support of the association.

• In October 2004, John W. Marriott, III co-chaired the 2004 National Minority Supplier Development Council Conference. The conference, which drew more than 6,400 attendees, represents the nation's largest convergence of minority suppliers and corporate purchasing organizations.

• The National Urban League awarded David M. Sampson, senior vice president, diversity initiatives, and Priscilla J. Hollman, vice president, diversity relations, the prestigious Donald H. McGannon Award for their commitment to ideals and beliefs in equal opportunity.

• Black Data Processing Associates (BDPA) and WorkplaceDiversity.com have awarded Marriott International, Inc. their "Best Companies for Blacks in Technology Award."

• *Essence* magazine named Marriott as one of the publication's "Best Companies for Black Women."

• *Hispanic* magazine's "Corporate 100" recognizes Marriott International as one of the 100 "Best Places to Work for Latinos."

• Marriott was ranked in the top ten U.S. companies for diversity in the "Best of the Best" Corporate Awards for Diversity & Women by Diversity Best Practices and Business Women's Network.

• The NAACP has ranked Marriott #1 in its *Lodging Industry Report* seven out of the past eight years.

• *Latina Style* magazine has named Marriott to its list of "The 50 Best Companies for Latinas to Work for in the U.S." the sixth year in a row.

• J.W. Marriott, Jr. received the Jackie Robinson Foundation's 2004 ROBIE Award for Achievement in Industry for the company's commitment to diversity. The foundation recognized Marriott for the company's success in employment and supplier diversity.

• *Working Mother* magazine has listed Marriott among its "100 Best Companies for Working Mothers" for 14 years.

• *Fortune* magazine recognized Marriott as one of the "100 Best Companies to Work For" for the last nine consecutive years.

Additional Information

Our stakeholders know we're serious about diversity.

Marriott International's stakeholders know that our commitment to diversity can be summed up in one word: absolute.

• Marriott Chairman and CEO J.W. Marriott, Jr., sits on the board of trustees of the National Urban League.

• In February 2003, J.W. Marriott, Jr. was awarded the Lifetime Achievement Award by the Hospitality Industry Diversity Institute for his commitment to recognizing and including women, minorities and people with disabilities in the hospitality industry.

Suppliers and vendors: A world of opportunity at Marriott

Every big company begins as a small business. Marriott did…back in 1927. We've never forgotten the opportunities that others gave us to succeed. Today, we proudly continue the tradition by reaching out to a whole new generation of entrepreneurs.

• Marriott is on track to exceed the minority ownership and supplier diversity goals it set itself in 2005. The 2010 goal to have 500 minority-and women-owned Marriott hotels is well on its way to being met with over 400 minority-and women-owned hotels in the Marriott system.

• In 2005, through our company-wide supplier diversity program, Marriott purchased and facilitated spending of more than $347 million in goods and services from more than 11,000 minority- and women-owned businesses.

• Marriott retains the mutual fund management services of Ariel Capital Management LLC—a premier African-American owned investment management company—to administer the company's profit-sharing retirement savings plan.

• In 2004, Marriott spent more than one million dollars with Land-Ron, a Hispanic-owned architecture and construction contractor. Asian-American owned company Tronex recently signed a $1.4 million annual contract to supply latex gloves to Marriott. Our company expects to save more than $200,000 annually with our new supplier.

Minority franchisees and owners grow with us.

As Marriott pursues its growth plan and continues to expand, we want diverse partners and stakeholders to grow and prosper alongside us.

Our minority ownership initiative helps us attract and develop relationships with quality-minded minority and female owners and franchisees, and support them through every step of the development process. Today, 15 percent of franchise units are owned by minorities. As of July 2006, more than 400 Marriott hotels are owned, operated or under development by women or ethnic minorities.

Four Fires LLC, a financial consortium composed of four Native American tribes, has teamed up with Marriott in a first-of-its-kind partnership to build a 13-story Residence Inn in downtown Washington, D.C., near the Smithsonian's new National Museum of the American Indian, which is slated to open in late 2004.

Marriott International, Inc. received the 2006 Ronald E. Harrison Award, by the International Franchise Association (IFA), for its significant contributions to minorities in franchising.

In 2006, Marriott announced RLJ Development, owned by Black Entertainment Television (BET) founder Robert L. Johnson, expects to purchase 90 Marriott International hotels from White Lodging Services Corporation by year end 2006. RLJ Development will become one of Marriott's largest hotel owners upon completion of the transaction.

Mirroring our stakeholders and our communities

We won't be satisfied until every aspect of our business reflects the rich diversity of the people and communities that touch Marriott's world.

For more information:

• External diversity initiatives: Dave Sampson, senior vice president, diversity initiatives, at (301) 380-3046 or Priscilla Hollman at (301) 380-1223.
• Supplier Diversity: Louise Rosamont at (301) 380-5889.
• University Relations & Recruiting: Steve Bauman at steve.bauman@marriott.com
• Media inquiries: corporate communications at (301) 380-7770.

Marsh Inc.

Marsh
1166 Avenue of the Americas
New York, NY 10036
Phone: (212) 345-6000

Locations
Worldwide

Employment Contact
College Recruiting
1166 Avenue of the Americas
New York, NY 10036
Phone: (212) 345-6000
Fax: (212) 345-2088
www.marsh.com

Recruiting

Please list the schools/types of schools at which you recruit.

• Ivy League schools
• Other private schools
• Public state schools
• Historically Black Colleges and Universities (HBCUs)

Do you have any special outreach efforts directed to encourage minority students to consider your firm?

• Hold a reception for minority students
• Conferences
• Advertise in minority student association publication(s)
• Participate in/host minority student job fair(s)
• Sponsor minority student association events
• Firm's employees participate on career panels at schools
• Outreach to leadership of minority student organizations
• Scholarships or intern/fellowships for minority students

What activities does the firm undertake to attract minority and women employees?

• Partner programs with women and minority associations
• Conferences
• Participate at minority job fairs
• Seek referrals from other employees
• Utilize online job services

Do you use executive recruiting/search firms to seek to identify new diversity hires?

No.

Internships and Co-ops

Summer Risk Analyst Program

Deadline for application: February 1, 2007
Number of interns in the program in summer 2005 (internship) or 2005 (co-op): 50

Length of the program: 10 weeks

Percentage of interns/co-ops in the program who receive offers of full-time employment: 85 percent

Web site for internship/co-op information: www.marsh.com (careers/college recruiting)

All majors are considered.

Required Qualifications:

• Must be a U.S. citizen or have unrestricted authorization to work for an employer in the U.S.

• Progress towards a BA/BS degree with a 3.0 GPA.

• Proficient in Microsoft Office.

• Ability to work in a fast paced team environment with rapidly changing priorities and demands.

• Candidates must be prepared to discuss work location preferences during the on-campus/first interview.

• Qualified candidates must be highly motivated and demonstrate a strong interest in business.

• Candidates must possess superior detail orientation and excellent communication and interpersonal skills. Candidates should also be service-oriented individuals with strong analytical, research, and problem-solving skills.

• Some previous business experience is preferred.

Scholarships

Marsh Diversity Scholarship Program (Tuskegee University)

Deadline for application for the scholarship program: February 28, 2007

Scholarship award amount: $2,000 for the entire scholarship

Web site or other contact information for scholarship: Available in the career office

Required Qualifications:

• Must be a U.S. citizen or have unrestricted authorization to work for an employer in the U.S.

• Progress towards a BA/BS degree with a 3.0 GPA.

• Proficient in Microsoft Office.

• Ability to work in a fast-paced team environment with rapidly changing priorities and demands.

• Candidates must be prepared to discuss work location preferences during the on-campus/first interview.

• Candidates must be highly motivated and demonstrate a strong interest in business.

• Candidates must possess superior detail orientation and excellent communication and interpersonal skills. Candidates should also be service-oriented individuals with strong analytical, research, and problem-solving skills.

• Some previous business experience is preferred.

All majors are considered.

Marsh Diversity Scholarship Program (Howard University)

Deadline for application for the scholarship program: February 28, 2007

Scholarship award amount: $8,000 for the entire scholarship

Web site or other contact information for scholarship: Available in the career office

Required Qualifications:

• Must be a U.S. citizen or have unrestricted authorization to work for an employer in the U.S.

• Progress towards a BA/BS degree with a 3.0 GPA.

• Proficient in Microsoft Office.

• Ability to work in a fast-paced team environment with rapidly changing priorities and demands.

• Candidates must be prepared to discuss work location preferences during the on-campus/first interview.

• Qualified candidates must be highly motivated and demonstrate a strong interest in business.

• Candidates must possess superior detail orientation and excellent communication and interpersonal skills.

• Candidates should also be service-oriented individuals with strong analytical, research, and problem-solving skills.

• Some previous business experience is preferred.

All majors are considered.

Marsh Diversity Scholarship Program (Temple University)

> *Deadline for application for the scholarship program:* February 28, 2007
> *Scholarship award amount:* $3,000 for the entire scholarship
> *Web site or other contact information for scholarship:* Available in the career office

Required Qualifications:

• Must be a U.S. citizen or have unrestricted authorization to work for an employer in the U.S.

• Progress towards a BA/BS degree with a 3.0 GPA.

• Proficient in Microsoft Office.

• Ability to work in a fast paced team environment with rapidly changing priorities and demands.

• Candidates must be prepared to discuss work location preferences during the on-campus/first interview.

• Qualified candidates must be highly motivated and demonstrate a strong interest in business.

• Candidates must possess superior detail orientation and excellent communication and interpersonal skills.

• Candidates should also be service-oriented individuals with strong analytical, research, and problem-solving skills.

• Some previous business experience is preferred.

All majors are considered.

Entry-Level Programs/Full-Time Opportunities/Training Programs

Risk Analyst Program

> *Length of program:* Two years
> *Geographic location(s) of program:* Atlanta, Boston, Chicago, Detroit, Houston, Los Angeles, New York and San Francisco.

The Risk Analyst Orientation Curriculum is a development program that integrates formal learning, on-the-job experiences, networking, recommended books and performance support. The orientation program takes place during the first year of the risk analysts employment with Marsh. After two years in a role, colleagues will be eligible for a future development program based on a nomination process.

Strategic Plan and Diversity Leadership

How does the firm's leadership communicate the importance of diversity to everyone at the firm?

Marsh uses ongoing communication through broadcast e-mail communications and the firm's Intranet web site.

Who has primary responsibility for leading diversity initiatives at your firm?

Susan Reid, managing director

Does your firm currently have a diversity committee?

Yes.

If yes, does the committee's representation include one or more members of the firm's management/executive committee (or the equivalent)?

Yes.

Does the committee and/or diversity leader establish and set goals or objectives consistent with management's priorities?

Yes.

Has the firm undertaken a formal or informal diversity program or set of initiatives aimed at increasing the diversity of the firm?

Yes, formal.

How often does the firm's management review the firm's diversity progress/results?

Quarterly.

The Stats

Employees

2005: 30,000

Revenue

2005: $5 billion

Retention and Professional Development

How do 2005 minority and female attrition rates generally compare to those experienced in the prior year period?

About the same as in prior years.

Please identify the specific steps you are taking to reduce the attrition rate of minority and women employees.

- Develop and/or support internal employee affinity groups
- Increase/improve current work/life programs
- Succession plan includes emphasis on diversity
- Work with minority and women employees to develop career advancement plans
- Review work assignments and hours billed to key client matters to make sure minority and women employees are not being excluded
- Strengthen mentoring program for all employees, including minorities and women
- Professional skills development program, including minority and women employees

Diversity Mission Statement

Marsh fosters an environment in which each colleague values what every other colleague has to offer. We expect all of our people to view differences—whether they are differences of race, ethnicity, gender, age, sexual orientation, function, geography or other facets of experience—as a powerful source of organizational strength. We will creatively leverage these different experiences and perspectives into a rich collection of skills and knowledge to provide innovative approaches to our business and unparalleled service to our clients. We will continue to ensure that all Marsh colleagues are valued and respected so that they are able to apply their unique capabilities in the pursuit of personal and organizational effectiveness.

Marshall and Ilsley Corporation

770 N. Water St.
Milwaukee, WI 53202
Phone: (414) 765-7700
www.micorp.com

Diversity Leadership

Walt A. Buckhanan
Vice President, Corporate Diversity/Inclusion
Manager
770 N Water St
Milwaukee, WI 53202
Phone: (414) 765-7771
Fax: (414) 765-7514
E-mail: walt.buckhanan@micorp.com

Recruiting

Please list the schools/types of schools at which you recruit.

• Private schools
• Public state schools

Do you have any special outreach efforts directed to encourage minority students to consider your firm?

• *Conferences:* Black MBA and NEON
• Participate in/host minority student job fair(s)
• Sponsor minority student association events
• Firm's employees participate on career panels at school

What activities does the firm undertake to attract minority and women employees?

• Partner programs with women and minority associations
• *Conferences:* Black MBA, NEON, M&I Milwaukee and You
• Participate at minority job fairs
• Seek referrals from other employees
• Utilize online job services

Do you use executive recruiting/search firms to seek to identify new diversity hires?

Yes.

Internships and Co-ops

INROADS

Deadline for application: February 28th
Pay: TBD (Based on experience and grade level)
Length of the program: 12 weeks
Web site for internship/co-op information: www.micorp.com

Jr. Associate Program

Deadline for application: February 28th
Pay: TBD (Based on experience and grade level)
Length of the program: 12 weeks
Web site for internship/co-op information: www.micorp.com

Each manager develops a job description on an annual basis.

Affinity Groups

We are in the process of developing criteria for employee resource groups.

Entry-Level Programs/Full-Time Opportunities/Training Programs

Financial Sales Program

Length of program: Seven to 12 months
Geographic location(s) of program: Arizona, Minnesota, Missouri and Wisconsin

Treasury Management Sales Program

Length of program: Seven to 12 months
Geographic location(s) of program: Arizona, Minnesota, Missouri and Wisconsin

Corporate Banking Program

Length of program: Seven to 12 months
Geographic location(s) of program: Arizona, Minnesota, Missouri and Wisconsin

Trust Operations Program

Length of program: Seven to 12 months
Geographic location(s) of program: Arizona, Minnesota, Missouri and Wisconsin

Audit Analysis Program

Length of program: Seven to 12 months
Geographic location(s) of program: Arizona, Minnesota, Missouri and Wisconsin

Strategic Plan and Diversity Leadership

How does the firm's leadership communicate the importance of diversity to everyone at the firm?
Corporate newsletter, e-mails, meetings and training.

Who has primary responsibility for leading diversity initiatives at your firm?
Walt A. Buckhanan, VP corporate diversity/inclusion manager.

Does your firm currently have a diversity committee?

Yes.

If yes, please describe how the committee is structured, how often it meets, etc.

It is made up of business line managers representing key areas of responsibilities.

If yes, does the committee's representation include one or more members of the firm's management/executive committee?

Yes.

If yes, how many executives are on the committee, and in 2005 what was the total number of hours collectively spent by the committee in furtherance of the firm's diversity initiatives? How many employees are on the committee, and how often does the committee convene in furtherance of the firm's diversity initiatives?

Our diversity council make up is apprised of: one executive sponsor, the CEO, and nine business line managers. The council meets quarterly.

Does the committee and/or diversity leader establish and set goals or objectives consistent with management's priorities?

Yes.

Has the firm undertaken a formal or informal diversity program or set of initiatives aimed at increasing the diversity of the firm?

Yes, formal.

How often does the firm's management review the firm's diversity progress/results?

Quarterly.

Retention and Professional Development

How do 2005 minority and female attrition rates generally compare to those experienced in the prior year period?

About the same as in prior years.

Please identify the specific steps you are taking to reduce the attrition rate of minority and women employees.
• Increase/review compensation relative to competition
• Succession plan includes emphasis on diversity
• Work with minority and women employees to develop career advancement plans
• Strengthen mentoring program for all employees, including minorities and women

Diversity Mission Statement

Marshall & Ilsley corporation is committed to a diverse workforce that reflects the communities we serve. We value our employees' talents and support a work environment that is inclusive and respectful.

Mattel, Inc.

333 Continental Boulevard
El Segundo, CA 90245-5012
Phone: (310) 252-2000

Locations

With worldwide headquarters in El Segundo, California, Mattel employs more than 25,000 people in 42 countries and sells products in more than 150 nations throughout the world.

Diversity Leadership

Graciela Meibar
VP Global Diversity

Employment Contact

Teresa Newcomb
Corporate Staffing
333 Continental Blvd.
El Segundo, CA 90245
Phone: (310) 252-2000
E-mail: teresa.newcomb@mattel.com
www.mattel.com

Recruiting

Please list the schools/types of schools at which you recruit.

• Ivy League schools
• Other private schools
• Public State schools
• Historically Black Colleges and Universities (HBCUs)
• Hispanic Serving Institutions (HSIs)
• Other predominantly minority and/or women's colleges

Do you have any special outreach efforts that are directed to encourage minority students to consider your firm?

• *Conferences:* NSHMBA and NBMBAA
• Firm's employees participate on career panels at schools

What activities does the firm undertake to attract minority and women employees?

• Partner programs with women and minority associations
• *Conferences:* NSHMBA and NBMBAA
• Seek referrals from other employees

Do you use executive recruiting/search firms to seek to identify new diversity hires?

No.

Scholarships

Mattel offers scholarships to the children of employees.

Affinity Groups

None at this time, although the company is starting a women's network.

Strategic Plan and Diversity Leadership

How does the firm's leadership communicate the importance of diversity to everyone at the firm?

The firm communicates diversity information via e-mails and newsletters.

Who has primary responsibility for leading diversity initiatives at your firm?

Graciela Meibar, vice president of global diversity.

Does your firm currently have a diversity committee?

No.

Does the committee and/or diversity leader establish and set goals or objectives consistent with management's priorities?

Yes.

Has the firm undertaken a formal or informal diversity program or set of initiatives aimed at increasing the diversity of the firm?

Yes, informal.

How often does the firm's management review the firm's diversity progress/results?

Quarterly.

The Stats

2005 Emloyees

U.S. Employees: 5,000
Employees outside the U.S.: 20,000
Employees Worldwide: 25,000

2004 Employees

U.S. Employees: 5,000
Employees outside the U.S.: 20,000
Employees Worldwide: 25,000

Revenue

2005: $5.2 Billion (Worldwide)
2004: $5.1 Billion (Worldwide)

Retention and Professional Development

How do 2005 minority and female attrition rates generally compare to those experienced in the prior year period?

About the same as in prior years.

Please identify the specific steps you are taking to reduce the attrition rate of minority and women employees.

• Develop and/or support internal employee affinity groups
• Strengthen mentoring program for all employees, including minorities and women
• Professional skills development program, including minority and women employees

Diversity Mission Statement

Diversity is a strategic business plan imperative to Mattel, Inc. As we get closer to our consumers, we will become more successful. The best way to do so is by having a work force that reflects our worldwide consumers.

McDonald's Corporation

Oak Brook, IL 60523
Phone: (630) 623-4833
Fax: (630) 623-7232
www.mcdonalds.com

Locations

Oak Brook, IL (HQ)

Diversity Leadership

Pat Harris
Chief Diversity Officer
2111 McDonald's Drive, Dept. 147
Oak Brook, IL 60523

Employment Contact

Lynda DuBovi
Admin., Diversity & Inclusion
2111 McDonald's Drive
Oak Brook, IL 60523
Phone: (630) 623-4833

Recruiting

What activities does the firm undertake to attract minority and women employees?

• Partner programs with women and minority associations
• *Conferences:* NAACP, NUL, NCLR, NAAAP, WFF, HACU, LULAC, JASC, NBMBA, ALPFA, Bennet College for Women
• Seek referrals from other employees

Do you use executive recruiting/search firms to seek to identify new diversity hires?

No.

Scholarships

RMHC/African-American Future Achievers Scholarship Program

Commitment to Education

The RMHC/African-American Future Achievers Scholarship program is a program of the Ronald McDonald House Charities global office and its U.S. chapters. It is one of several RMHC scholarships designed to assist specific students who face a widening education gap. The goal of this RMHC program is to provide scholarships to graduating high school seniors who may need an extra hand getting in and staying in college. Studies show that the more difficult it is for a student to get into college, the less likely they are to graduate. Funding from RMHC can sometimes make the difference between attending and not attending the college of someone's choice. During the 2003-2004 RMHC/African-American Future Achievers program, over $1.3 million was awarded in scholarships.

The RMHC/Future Achievers Scholarship program provides financial support to students who are committed to pursuing post-secondary education in their chosen field at an accredited institution. The RMHC/Future Achievers program recognizes young peoples' educational accomplishments, their potential and their commitment to serve the community. Local chapters of RMHC operate the program in their respective geographic areas with support from the global office of RMHC, local McDonald's restaurants and other businesses and organizations in the community.

To apply for a RMHC/Future Achievers scholarship, students must:

• Have at least one parent of African-American origin
• Be eligible to enroll in and attend a two-year or four-year accredited college with a full course of study
• Attend college in the U.S.
• Reside in a participating local chapter's geographic area

Scholarships are generally a minimum of $1,000 and are designated for graduating high school seniors, although some local programs may award different scholarship amounts.

Scholarship recipients are selected based on:

• Academic achievement
• Financial need
• Community involvement
• Personal qualities and strengths as portrayed in a required essay

Recipients must enroll in and attend an accredited institution in the academic year after their selection and provide verification of enrollment. Scholarship funds are paid directly to the schools and no funds will be dispersed to students directly.

Additional eligibility information and instructions are provided on the scholarship application.

Participating Areas

The deadline for the 2004-2005 academic year was February 15, 2005. Please check back in the fall for a list of areas participating in the program in the next academic year.

Scholarship Applications

The deadline for the 2004-2005 academic year was February 15, 2005. Please check back in the fall for an application for the program.

RMHC/ASIA (Asian Students Increasing Achievement) Scholarship Program

Commitment to Education

The RMHC/ASIA Scholarship program is a program of the Ronald McDonald House Charities global office and its U.S. chapters. It is one of several RMHC scholarships designed to assist specific students who face a widening education gap. The goal of the RMHC/ASIA program is to provide scholarships to graduating high school seniors who may need an extra hand getting in and staying in college. Studies show that the more difficult it is for a student to get into college, the less likely they are to graduate. Funding from RMHC can sometimes make the difference between attending and not attending the college of someone's choice. During the 2003-2004 RMHC/ASIA program, over $600,000 was awarded in scholarships.

The RMHC/ASIA Scholarship program provides financial support to students who are committed to pursuing post-secondary education in their chosen field at an accredited institution. The RMHC/ASIA program recognizes young peoples' educational accomplishments, their potential and their commitment to serve the community. Local chapters of RMHC operate the program in their respective geographic areas with support from the global office of RMHC, local McDonald's restaurants and other businesses and organizations in the community.

To apply for a RMHC/ASIA scholarship, students must:

• Have at least one parent of Asian-Pacific origin (any major Asian-American, Southeast Asian, South Asian or Pacific Islander group)
• Be eligible to enroll in and attend a two-year or four-year accredited college with a full course of study
• Attend college in the U.S.
• Reside in a participating local chapter's geographic area

Scholarships are generally a minimum of $1,000 and are designated for graduating high school seniors, although some local programs may award different scholarship amounts.

Scholarship recipients are selected based on:

• Academic achievement
• Financial need
• Community involvement
• Personal qualities and strengths as portrayed in a required essay

Recipients must enroll in and attend an accredited institution in the academic year after their selection and provide verification of enrollment. Scholarship funds are paid directly to the schools and no funds will be dispersed to students directly.

Additional eligibility information and instructions are provided on the scholarship application.

Participating Areas

The deadline for the 2004-2005 academic year was February 15, 2005. Please check back in the fall for a list of areas participating in the program for the next academic year.

RMHC/HACER (Hispanic American Commitment to Educational Resources) Scholarship Program

Commitment to Education

The RMHC/HACER Scholarship program is a program of the Ronald McDonald House Charities global office and its U.S. chapters. It is one of several RMHC scholarships designed to assist specific students who face a widening education gap. The goal of this RMHC program is to provide scholarships to graduating high school seniors who may need an extra hand getting in and staying in college. Studies show that the more difficult it is for a student to get into college, the less likely they are to graduate. Funding from RMHC can sometimes make the difference between attending and not attending the college of someone's choice. During the 2003-2004 RMHC/HACER program, more than two million dollars was awarded in scholarships.

The RMHC/HACER Scholarship program provides financial support to students who are committed to pursuing post-secondary education in their chosen field at an accredited institution. The RMHC/HACER program recognizes young peoples' education accomplishments, their potential and their commitment to serve the community. Local chapters of RMHC operate the program in their respective geographic areas with support from the global office of RMHC, local McDonald's restaurants and other businesses and organizations in the community.

History of the Program

As a former educator, McDonald's franchisee Richard Castro from El Paso, TX, was keenly aware of the alarming number of Hispanic students who dropped out of high school in his hometown and across the country. Driven by his commitment to give back, Castro acted to change the situation by leading the effort to create a scholarship program that would serve as encouragement for young Hispanics to complete high school and continue their education.

Castro rallied his fellow McDonald's franchisees and the McDonald's corporation and secured the support of Ronald McDonald House Charities to establish the RMHC/HACER program in 1985. An initial fund of $97,000 served to launch the program, providing $1,000 awards to high school seniors in various communities. Today, the RMHC/HACER Scholarship Program has become the largest high school-to-college scholarship program for Hispanic students and a nationally-recognized program.

To apply for a RMHC/HACER scholarship, students must:

• Have at least one parent of Hispanic origin
• Be eligible to enroll in and attend a two-year or four-year accredited college with a full course of study
• Attend college in the U.S.
• Reside in a participating local chapter's geographic area

Scholarships are generally a minimum of $1,000 and are designated for graduating high school seniors, although some local programs may award different scholarship amounts.

Scholarship recipients are selected based on:

• Academic achievement
• Financial need
• Community involvement
• Personal qualities and strengths as portrayed in a required essay

Recipients must enroll in and attend an accredited institution in the academic year after their selection and provide verification of enrollment. Scholarship funds are paid directly to the schools and no funds will be dispersed to students directly.

Additional eligibility information and instructions are provided on the scholarship application.

Participating Areas

The deadline for the 2004-2005 academic year was February 15, 2005. Please check back in the fall for a list of areas participating in the program for the next academic year.

www.rmhc.org/mission/scholarships/index.html

Affinity Groups

Asian Employee Network, McDonald's African-American Employee Network, Hispanic Employee Network, Hispanic Leadership Council, Women's Leadership Network

Entry-Level Programs/Full-Time Opportunities/Training Programs

LAMP

> *Length of program:* 12 months
> *Geographic location(s) of program:* U.S.

The purpose of the Leadership at McDonald's Program (LAMP) is to accelerate the development of high potential leaders in a way that drives results, shapes organizational culture and builds leadership depth.

Development focuses on leveraging on-the-job experiences, while providing appropriate skills that can be applied and practiced in each participant's day-to-day job. It will also focus on developing the leadership abilities of each participant. The framework that will be used to guide leadership development is based upon three leadership challenges: leading oneself, leading high performance teams and leading the organization.

Strategic Plan and Diversity Leadership

How does the firm's leadership communicate the importance of diversity to everyone at the firm? Who has primary responsibility for leading diversity initiatives at your firm?

Pat Harris, chief diversity officer.

Does your firm currently have a diversity committee?

Yes, we have a diversity council.

If yes, please describe how the committee is structured, how often it meets, etc.

The council was started in 2004 under the direction of the CEO of McDonald's USA. With a focus on diversity and inclusion the council participants represent diversity thought leaders throughout our corporation.

If yes, does the committee's representation include one or more members of the firm's management/executive committee (or the equivalent)?

Yes.

If yes, how many executives are on the committee, and in 2005, what was the total number of hours collectively spent by the committee in furtherance of the firm's diversity initiatives? How many employees are on the committee, and how often does the committee convene in furtherance of the firm's diversity initiatives?

There are five executives on the council. There are an additional 28 employees on the council and they meet on a quarterly basis.

Does the committee and/or diversity leader establish and set goals or objectives consistent with management's priorities?

Yes.

Has the firm undertaken a formal or informal diversity program or set of initiatives aimed at increasing the diversity of the firm?

Yes, formal.

How often does the firm's management review the firm's diversity progress/results?

Twice a year.

Retention and Professional Development

How do 2005 minority and female attrition rates generally compare to those experienced in the prior year period?

About the same as in prior years.

Please identify the specific steps you are taking to reduce the attrition rate of minority and women employees.

• Develop and/or support internal employee affinity groups (e.g., minority or women networks within the firm)
• Succession plan includes emphasis on diversity
• Strengthen mentoring program for all employees, including minorities and women

Diversity Mission Statement

The McDonald's mission is to ensure our employees, owner/operators and suppliers reflect and represent the diverse population McDonald's serves around the world. We will harness the multi-faced qualities of our diversity—individual and group differences among our people—as a combined complimentary force to run great restaurants.

Additional Information

Diversity—It's Everybody's Business

It is our belief that diversity is a shared accountability across the U.S. business.

The Diversity Initiatives Department provides the strategic direction for diversity. This department is charged with developing the internal framework to integrate diversity into business strategies. This framework is delivered through consulting with the Divisions and Home Office Departments to ensure the alignment of diversity initiatives with the "Plan to Win" key business strategies. The Diversity Initiatives Department serves as brand ambassadors to external organizations to strengthen and optimize McDonald's national partnerships with diverse community, political and educational organizations.

In the spirit of "Diversity—It's Everybody's Business" partnerships across the U.S field and the U.S. corporate departments, diversity has become a part of the fabric of the organization. These partnerships have positioned core diversity strategies to leverage our current strengths and to develop actionable initiatives for areas of diversity development.

Monsanto Company

800 No. Lindbergh Blvd
St. Louis, MO 63167
www.monsanto.com

Employment Contact

Jack Nesbitt
University Relations Lead and
Employment Marketing Lead
800 No. Lindbergh Blvd
St. Louis, MO 63167

Recruiting

Please list the schools/types of schools at which you recruit.

• *Other:* Several Big 10 schools; private schools
• Public state schools
• Historically Black Colleges and Universities (HBCUs)
• Hispanic Serving Institutions (HSIs)

Do you have any special outreach efforts directed to encourage minority students to consider your firm?

• *Conferences:* FFA, AFA, HACE, MANRRS
• Advertise in minority student association publication(s)
• Firm's employees participate on career panels at schools

What activities does the firm undertake to attract minority and women employees?

• Partner programs with women and minority associations
• *Conferences:* HACE, MANRRS
• Participate at minority job fairs

Internships and Co-ops

IT Coop Program & Internships

> *Deadline for application:* April
> *Number of interns in the program in summer 2005 (internship) or 2005 (co-op):* 170 combined
> *Pay:* Based on completed year in school—pay is every two weeks
> *Length of the program:* IT co-op six months/ interns 10-12 weeks
> *Percentage of interns/co-ops in the program who receive offers of full-time employment:* Varies
> *Web site for internship/co-op information:* www.monsanto.com

College Recruiting: Interns and Co-ops

The Monsanto Intern Program (in St. Louis or other U.S. locations)

This program offers college students on-the-job experience through paid temporary, full-time positions. Participants gain valuable professional experience and develop an insider's understanding of how Monsanto operates. Students typically participate in the intern program during their summer semester break. Interns generally work 40 hours per week and assignments may vary in length from 10 to 12 weeks during the summer. Internships are for students who wish to explore a career at Monsanto. If you are interested, we encourage you to respond online.

Children of employees may be considered for internships, but must go through the same selection process as all other candidates. If selected, children may not work in any direct or indirect reporting relationship to their parent.

Program Requirements

You must be currently enrolled as a full-time student in a bachelor's, master's, or PhD degree program at an accredited university. In most cases, you must have completed at least the freshman year.

Preferred candidates should have:

• Demonstrated leadership, communication and business acumen.

• One of the following majors: accounting, finance, human resources, law, information systems, agronomy, animal science, agricultural business, plant breeding, plant physiology, genetic engineering, chemical engineering, biological sciences, botany, chemistry, or other agricultural-oriented major.

• Interns could be assigned to work in one of the following functional areas: engineering, operations, research & development, finance/accounting, sales, animal agriculture, manufacturing/seed operations, and technology.

Selection

Selection is based on student credentials, behavioral-based interview results and the matching of student's skills to available openings.

Program details

Dates: The intern program typically begins in May and continues through August. We usually fill positions by mid-February.

Locations: We have opportunities located throughout North America. Our headquarters are located in St. Louis, MO.

Logistics

Transportation: Students are primarily responsible for securing their own transportation to and from the worksite on a daily basis. Monsanto is able to provide information to students regarding carpools, rental cars and public transportation.

Travel Lump Sum: The travel lump sum provision of the program provides a relocating student with a predetermined dollar amount based upon the mileage traveled round trip between the city in which the school is located and the city in which the work site is located.

Why should you consider a Monsanto Internship for the summer?

• Networking: You'll interact with senior executives at a variety of meetings and receptions, and interact with each other at First Day Welcome, volunteer activities and social events.

• Professional Development: Your work will be measurable and realistic and allow you to stretch your ability. To give you practice interacting with managers and demonstrating your business acumen, you may be chosen to present a summary of your project work to managers and peers at the end of your internship.

• Guidance: At the start of the summer, we'll help you develop a career development plan, and you'll receive a mid-point and end-of-summer performance evaluation. We'll also pair you with a mentor on an individual basis.

• Compensation: Internship compensation is very competitive.

• Lunch and learn: Senior executive presentations

Affinity Groups

- African-Americans in Monsanto
- Hispanic Network and Asian Network

The Stats

Employees

2006: 16,694 (worldwide)

Revenue

2005: $6.2 million

Retention and Professional Development

Please identify the specific steps you are taking to reduce the attrition rate of minority and women employees.

- Develop and/or support internal employee affinity groups
- Increase/review compensation relative to competition
- Increase/improve current work/life programs
- Adopt dispute resolution process
- Succession plan includes emphasis on diversity
- Work with minority and women employees to develop career advancement plans
- Review work assignments and hours billed to key client matters to make sure minority and women employees are not being excluded
- Strengthen mentoring program for all employees, including minorities and women
- Professional skills development program, including minority and women employees

Diversity Mission Statement

Monsanto's goal is to build an inclusive and diverse organization, which values and engages all of our people's talents and perspectives. We also strive to leverage our diversity to achieve outstanding business success overall, and to ensure the growth and acceptance of biotechnology. This commitment has launched a number of actions. In addition, the importance of diversity is also reflected in our external pledge under the heading of respect.

Specifically, we will respect the religious, cultural and ethical concerns of people throughout the world. We will act with integrity, courage, respect, candor, honesty, humility and consistency. We will place our highest priority on the safety of our employees, the communities where we operate, our customers, consumers and the environment.

Additional Information

At Monsanto, we believe diversity is a business imperative. We have created a culture that reinforces diversity. As part of Monsanto's ongoing Create a Winning Environment initiative, all employees are encouraged to recognize, appreciate and leverage diversity. People managers and employees alike are trained to look for and appreciate the unique value that each individual brings to work and strive to create a more inclusive environment where everyone can contribute what they can to the collective goals of the organization.

To foster a highly inclusive environment for all, the company offers several different training experiences that range from basic diversity awareness to advanced relationship skills for people managers. In addition, each employee is expected to set at least one DPR goal related to how they will create a more inclusive work environment. Our innovative staffing process seeks to provide a slate of diverse candidates for available positions.

We fundamentally believe that diversity leads to outstanding business success. Our commitment is driven by an urgency to create a Monsanto that better reflects the skills and perspectives required for continued global success.

Some creative examples of our diversity efforts are listed below.

• The global diversity web site
• Quarterly featured employee called "Who Am I"
• Town halls
• Demonstration by African dancers to increase cultural awareness
• Visibility for Network Leads to update organization on activities
• Viewing of CBT's created by employees on local diversity issues
• Pledge report
• Examples of fostering participation and collaboration
• Diversity fairs
• Networking and sharing
• Poster sessions on what's happening around the world
• Speaker series
• Leadership skills for Asian Pacific professionals
• Dale Carnegie training
• Language lessons
• French and Spanish classes offered by employees

Nationwide

One Nationwide Plaza 1-01-20
Columbus, OH 43215
Toll Free: (800) 882-2822

Locations

All 50 U.S. states, District of Columbia,
Virgin Islands, Asia, Europe and Latin
America

Diversity Leadership

Candice Barnhardt
VP Organizational Effectiveness Practice

Employment Contact

One Nationwide Plaza 1-01-13
Columbus, OH 43215
Toll Free: (800) 882-2822
www.nationwide.com/nw/careers/university-relations/index.htm

Recruiting

Please list the schools/types of schools at which you recruit.

• Ivy League schools
• Other private schools
• Public state schools
• Historically Black Colleges and Universities (HBCUs)

Do you have any special outreach efforts that are directed to encourage minority students to consider your firm?

• Hold a reception for minority students
• Advertise in minority student association publication(s)
• Participate in/host minority student job fair(s)
• Sponsor minority student association events
• Firm's employees participate on career panels at schools
• Outreach to leadership of minority student organizations
• Scholarships or intern/fellowships for minority students

What activities does the firm undertake to attract minority and women employees?

• *Conferences:* National Urban League Conference (NUL)
• Participate at minority job fairs
• Utilize online job services
• The firm participates in the following organizations: National Association for the Advancement of Colored People (NAACP). The firm participates in the following organizations: National Black MBA Association (NBMBAA), National Society of Hispanic MBAs (NSHMBA), National Association of Asian American Professionals (NAAAP)

Do you use executive recruiting/search firms to seek to identify new diversity hires?
Yes.

Internships and Co-ops

Tom Joyner/Nationwide, "On Your Side" internship program

Deadline for application: March 31st

Number of interns in the program in summer 2006 (internship) or 2006 (co-op): 10 undergraduate and graduate interns

Pay: Range $13-$27 per hour

Length of the program: 10 weeks

Web site for internship/co-op information: www.nationwide.com/nw/careers/university-relations/index.htm

INROADS

Number of interns in the program in summer 2006 (internship) or 2006 (co-op): Five interns

Pay: $13-$16 per hour

Length of the program: 12 weeks

Web site for internship/co-op information: www.nationwide.com/nw/careers/university-relations/index.htm

Leader Development Institute (LDI) graduate level internship program

Deadline for application: Driven by manager's request (no later than March 31st). Students can post their resume for internship opportunities year round.

Number of interns in the program in summer 2006 (internship) or 2006 (co-op): 20 interns

Pay: $22-$27 per hour

Length of the program: 12 weeks

Percentage of interns/co-ops in the program who receive offers of full-time employment: 70 percent in 2005

Web site for internship/co-op information: www.nationwide.com/nw/careers/university-relations/index.htm

Qualification for our graduate level internship program—LDI consist of: completion of first year at an accredited MBA program, minimum 3.2 GPA, at least three years work experience, competitive academic performance, coursework concentration in finance, marketing, actuarial science, risk management business or information technology. Features of the LDI program include a variety of activities to enhance learning.

Interns Today...Leaders Tomorrow (Corporate Internship Program)

Deadline for application: Driven by manager's request March 31st. Students can post their resume for internship opportunities year round.

Number of interns in the program in summer 2006 (internship) or 2006 (co-op): 100 (includes Tom Joyner, INROADS and LDI programs)

Pay: $13-$16 per hour

Length of the program: 10-12 weeks

Percentage of interns/co-ops in the program who receive offers of full-time employment: 40 percent

Web site for internship/co-op information: www.nationwide.com/nw/careers/university-relations/index.htm

Interns are placed in various business units across Nationwide. Placement stems from our managers' request. Once they've identified a hiring strategy, University Relations works to identify and recruit the best and brightest for that area. Qualified candidates should have at least a 3.0 GPA, status as a rising junior or senior, solid academic achievement, strong oral and written communication skills, involvement in various student organizations, and prior internship experience (preferred but not required). Each business unit identifies projects and assignments for their intern.

Our Tom Joyner program requires the same qualifications with one addition, student must be enrolled at a historically black college or university.

Scholarships

Tom Joyner/Nationwide, "On Your Side" Scholarship

Deadline for application for the scholarship program: March 31
Scholarship award amount: Entire scholarship up to $2,500, based on unmet financial need
Web site or other contact information for scholarship:
www.nationwide.com/nw/careers/university-relations/index.htm

Only interns selected to participate in the Tom Joyner/Nationwide, "On Your Side" internship program are eligible. The scholarship amount is up to $2,500 and is based on the student's unmet financial need. The scholarship is dDirectly related to the internship program mentioned above.

Affinity Groups

Asian Awareness Network

This group works to network and create awareness and understanding of the Asian cultures within Nationwide through business, social and multicultural activities.

Pride Gay & Lesbian Club

This club meets to network on social, service and cultural activities. In addition, the group provides support and other resources for members who seek to improve their relationships with friends or family members who are gay or lesbian.

Raising Interest in Spanish Awareness (RISA)

This group is for those interested in building a more inclusive environment through education, social and business networking. The members participate in a variety of activities including: mentoring Hispanic students, child car seat inspections, job fairs, the Latino Festival, and educational and cultural events.

Umoja Network

The mission of the Umoja Network is to recognize, celebrate, educate and raise awareness of the African-American contribution. The group promotes a message of inclusion and shares knowledge about topics that are important to success in the workplace and as members of the larger community.

Entry-Level Programs/Full-Time Opportunities/Training Programs

Financial Leadership Rotation Program (FLRP)

Length of program: Two years
Geographic location(s) of program: Columbus, OH

The program includes a tailored orientation lasting two weeks, mentoring partnerships, project assignments, coaching and feedback, professional networking, and recognition through placement.

Nationwide Financial Leader Development Program (NFLDP)

Length of program: 12 months
Geographic location(s) of program: Columbus, OH

Components include but are not limited to:

• Coaching sessions
• Team building
• Presentation skills
• Surveys/assessments
• 360 feedback
• Mentoring

Strategic Plan and Diversity Leadership

Who has primary responsibility for leading diversity initiatives at your firm?

Candance Barnhardt, vice president, organizational effectiveness practice.

Does your firm currently have a diversity committee?

Yes.

Nokia

North American Headquarters:
6000 Connection Dr.
Irving, TX 75039
Phone: (972) 894-5186
Fax: (972) 894-5814

Locations

Argentina • Austria • Brazil • Canada • Chile • Columbia • Czech Republic • Denmark • Ecuador • Egypt • Ethiopia • Finland • France • Germany • Greece • Hungary • India • Indonesia • Iran • Japan • Kazakhstan • Kenya • Kuwait • Lebanon • Mexico • Morocco • Netherlands • Nigeria • Pakistan • Philippines • Poland • Portugal • Russia • Saudi Arabia • Singapore • South Africa • Spain • Switzerland • Taiwan • Thailand • Tunisia • Turkey • UK • Ukraine • US • Venezuela

Diversity Leadership

Catherine Simin Rousteau
HR Manager/University Relations
6000 Connection Dr.
Irving, TX 75039
Phone: (972) 894-5186
Fax: (972) 894-5814
E-mail: simin.rousteau@nokia.com
www.nokia.com/careers

Recruiting

Please list the schools/types of schools at which you recruit.

• *Ivy League schools:* Columbia, Cornell, Harvard, Penn/Wharton, Yale
• *Other private schools:* MIT SMU, TCU, USC, Carnegie Mellon University, Duke, University of Chicago, Stanford
• *Public state schools:* UT, UTD, UTA, UCLA, University of California Berkeley, University of San Diego, University of Maryland

Do you have any special outreach efforts directed to encourage minority students to consider your firm?

• *Conferences:* National Society of Black Engineers, Society of Hispanic Professional Engineers
• Advertise in minority student association publication(s)
• *Participate in/host minority student job fair(s):* National Society of Black Engineers, Society of Hispanic Professional Engineers, National Society of Black MBAs, Society of Women Engineers, National Society of Hispanic MBAs
• Sponsor minority student association events
• Firm's employees participate on career panels at schools
• Outreach to leadership of minority student organizations
• *Other:* We advertise in the minority issue of NACE's campus publication. We also advertise extensively in several minority pub-
 lications, in addition to posting our open jobs on DiversityInc, LatPro and other diversity job boards.

What activities does the firm undertake to attract minority and women employees?

• Partner programs with women and minority associations
• *Conferences:* Society of Women Engineers, National Society of Black Engineers, Society of Hispanic Professional Engineers

- *Participate at minority job fairs:* Society of Women Engineers, National Society of Black Engineers, Society of Hispanic Professional Engineers
- Seek referrals from other employees
- *Utilize online job services:* LatPro, SWE, NSBE online

Do you use executive recruiting/search firms to seek to identify new diversity hires?

Yes.

Internships and Co-ops

Nokia hires interns to fill specific positions, based on need. Most interns are hired at the beginning of the fall, spring, and summer semester, corresponding with most university calendars. Assignments/projects generally last three months, or 1,000 hours.

Qualifications to be an intern:

- Currently be enrolled in a degree program (bachelors, masters, PhD) at an accredited university
- Preferably at least junior level
- Preferably at least a 3.0 GPA

Intern benefits:

- Competitive hourly wages
- Holiday pay
- Additional perk benefits, based on position
- If an intern is hired as a regular employee, he /she will be given credit for their time as an intern
- Access to other Nokia perks

Entry-Level Programs/Full-Time Opportunities/Training Programs

As with the intern positions, specific entry-level positions are based on business group need.

Our networks group does have a rotational program for entry-level technical service managers.

Strategic Plan and Diversity Leadership

Who has primary responsibility for leading diversity initiatives at your firm?

Simin Rousteau, manager, diversity - North America.

Does your firm currently have a diversity committee?

Yes.

If yes, does the committee's representation include one or more members of the firm's management/executive committee (or the equivalent)?

Yes.

> *Total Executives on Committee:* Five

Does the committee and/or diversity leader establish and set goals or objectives consistent with management's priorities?

Yes.

Has the firm undertaken a formal or informal diversity program or set of initiatives aimed at increasing the diversity of the firm?

Yes, formal.

How often does the firm's management review the firm's diversity progress/results?

Annually.

How is the firm's diversity committee and/or firm management held accountable for achieving results?

Diversity results and next year plans have to be presented to Nokia's CEO on an annual basis by the head of each Nokia business group.

The Stats

	TOTAL IN THE U.S.		TOTAL OUTSIDE THE U.S		TOTAL WORLDWIDE	
	2005	2004	2005	2004	2005	2004
Number of employees	5,863	6,677	51,033	46,834	56,896	53,511
Revenue	$5,863 billion	$677 million	$34.2 billion	N/A	$29.3 billion	N/A

Retention and Professional Development

How do 2005 minority and female attrition rates generally compare to those experienced in the prior year period?

Higher than in prior years.

We had changes in our business model in United States that led to some reorganization in our R&D groups. These groups have a larger minority population.

Please identify the specific steps you are taking to reduce the attrition rate of minority and women employees.

• Succession plan includes emphasis on diversity
• Work with minority and women employees to develop career advancement plans
• Strengthen mentoring program for all employees, including minorities and women
• Professional skills development program, including minority and women employees

Diversity Mission Statement

Our main goal is to evolve the company culture toward a more inclusive work environment. This means, among other things, that we're committed to seeking, respecting and harnessing the broad range of diversity at Nokia, including gender, race, age, cultural background, physical ability, religion, sexual orientation, and/or any other attribute that shapes an individual's perspective.

461

NORTH CAROLINA
Office of State Personnel

Thomas H. Wright, Director

The Office of State Personnel – Paving the way for change!

Join an organization whose name is synonymous with innovation and creativity in the field of human resource systems.

The Office of State Personnel is a leader in the public sector in its application of best practices and innovations. It is recognized and valued as a strategic business partner by agencies, universities and the General Assembly.

The Office of State Personnel provides leadership and supports agencies and universities in creating and sustaining dynamic human resource systems to attract, retain, develop, and motivate a diverse and competent workforce.

The Office of State Personnel is charged with the responsibility of maintaining the human resource systems for the North Carolina State Government. Come and join an organization where your unique talents can flourish. North Carolina State Government offers competitive salaries and excellent benefits.

North Carolina Office of State Personnel

1331 Mail Service Center
Raleigh, NC 27699-1331
Phone: (919) 807-4800
Fax: (919) 733-065

Diversity Leadership
Nellie Riley
Human Resources Managing Partner

Employment Contact
Charlene Shabazz
HR Partner
116 West Jones Street
Raleigh, NC 27603
E-mail: Charlene.shabazz@ncmail.net
OSP.state.nc.us

Recruiting

Please list the schools/types of schools at which you recruit.

• Public state schools
• Historically Black Colleges and Universities (HBCUs)
• Other predominantly minority and/or women's colleges

Do you have any special outreach efforts directed to encourage minority students to consider your firm?

• Participate in/host minority student job fair(s)
• Firm's employees participate on career panels at schools
• Outreach to leadership of minority student organizations
• Scholarships or intern/fellowships for minority students

What activities does the firm undertake to attract minority and women employees?

• Partner programs with women and minority associations
• Participate at minority job fairs
• Seek referrals from other employees

Do you use executive recruiting/search firms to seek to identify new diversity hires?
No.

Internships and Co-ops

INROADS

Deadline for application: December
Number of interns in the program in summer 2005 internship: 11
Budget for the entire program: $89,975
Length of the program: 12 weeks
Percentage of interns/co-ops in the program who receive offers of full-time employment: Two percent

Web site for internship/co-op information: www.inroads.org

Qualifications for the INROADS Program is at least a 2.5 grade point average and selection is competitive based on interviews by INROADS staff. Participants must major in courses specified by the position description. Supervisors in departments and agencies select students.

NC state government participating departments include:

- Commerce
- Insurance
- Juvenile Justice and Delinquency Prevention
- Revenue
- Administration
- State Treasurer and the Office of State Personnel

Model Cooperative Education

Deadline for applications: Varies by semester
Number of interns in the program in summer 2005 (internship) or 2005 (co-op): 11 interns
Budget for the entire program: $21,000
Length of the program: 12 weeks
Percentage of interns/co-ops in the program who receive offers of full-time employment: Three percent

Qualifications:

- At least a 2.0 grade point average.
- Majoring in the area specified on the position announcement.
- Resident of North Carolina.

Students are referred from college placement offices/co-op coordinators. Supervisors in departments and agencies select co-op students.

Summer Assistance Department of Transportation

Deadline for application: April 1st each year
Number of interns in the program in summer 2005 (internship) or 2005 (co-op): 90 interns
Budget for the entire program: $75,000
Length of the program: 12 weeks
Percentage of interns/co-ops in the program who receive offers of full-time employment: 60 percent
Web site for internship/co-op information: www.NCDOT.org

Qualifications:

This program is for students majoring in civil engineering. Must have at least a 2.5 grade point average and 21 semester hours and a legal resistant of North Carolina.

Summer Internships: NC Youth Advocacy and Involvement Office-Department of Administration.

Deadline for application: January each year
Number of interns in the program in summer 2005 (internship) or 2005 (co-op): 100
Budget for the entire program: $82,500
Length of the program: 10 weeks
Web site for internship/co-op information: www.ncyaio.com

Summer internships are offered in virtually all areas of state government.

Qualifications:

• Students must have completed their first year of college.

• Be enrolled in a community college, law or graduate school in or out-of-state for the semester following the internship.

• Be a legal resident of NC and have at least an overall 2.5 GPA on a 4.0 scale

Department of the Controller- Beacon Project College Internship Program

Deadline for application: Accept applications throughout the year

Number of interns in the program in summer 2005 (internship) or 2005 (co-op): Six students—salaries are $12.89 per hour.

Budget for the entire program: $110,592. This amount will expire July 2007. Anticipate a new budget after that date.

Length of the program: 12 weeks in summer and during the spring and fall semesters- length varies

Web site for internship/co-op information: www.beacon.nc.gov

Qualifications:

Applicants should be juniors, seniors or graduate students majoring in business management, public administration or management information systems.

Affinity Groups

No specific names, but affinity groups/networks have been established for females and African-American males. Opportunities to network and career development are the reasons the groups have been established. The groups meet at least every other month.

Entry-Level Programs/Full-Time Opportunities/Training Programs

DOT Transportation Engineering Associate Program

Deadline for application: November 30th and March 30th each year

Number of associates slots: 100 slots continuously. Hire at least 20 December grads and 20 May grads

Length of the program: 18 months

Geographic location of program: Statewide

Web site for internship/co-op information: www.NCDOT.org (employment opportunities—recruitment programs)

Training/training component of this program: This program is for new engineers. These engineers rotate assignments throughout the department during the 18 month training cycle.

Educational components of this program: This program provides tuition reimbursement and career development assistance with the professional engineering license.

Strategic Plan and Diversity Leadership

How does the firm's leadership communicate the importance of diversity to everyone at the firm? E-mails, web site, newsletters, and meetings are used to promote and communicate the importance of diversity. Diversity is part of the mission statement for the Office of State Personnel—the headquarters for the state personnel system that has approximately 88,000 employees subject to the State Personnel Act.

Who has primary responsibility for leading diversity initiatives at your firm?

Nellie Riley, HR managing partner—EEO and diversity expert for the state.

Does your firm currently have a diversity committee?

Yes.

The council includes representatives from most demographic groups (women, veterans, American Indians, Hispanics/Latinos, African-Americans, the disabled and older workers), the director of Civil Rights, Department of Transportation, and the director of the Human Relations Commission and the state's historically underutilized business director.

If yes, does the committee's representation include one or more members of the firm's management/executive committee (or the equivalent)?

> *Total Executives on Committee:* Three.

In 2005 the executives spent 24 hours in furtherance of the State's diversity initiatives. The council meets at least quarterly for at least two hours. There are 14 committee members. Collectively the committee spent 104 hours in 2005 on the furtherance of the State's diversity issues.

Does the committee and/or diversity leader establish and set goals or objectives consistent with management's priorities?

Yes, the council established a purpose and mission statement and objectives. Its mission is to develop and support diversity initiatives to ensure that North Carolina State Government delivers effective services to citizens by recognizing, optimizing, and championing a diverse work force. Further, the mission statement of the Office of State Personnel includes attracting and retaining a diverse workforce.

Has the firm undertaken a formal or informal diversity program or set of initiatives aimed at increasing the diversity of the firm?

Yes, formal. The Special Emphasis Project for African-American males, females, older workers, the disabled and people of color includes initiatives to increase the representation, career development and retention of different demographic groups.

How often does the firm's management review the firm's diversity progress/results?

Annually.

How is the firm's diversity committee and/or firm management held accountable for achieving results?

Through work plans.

The Stats

Employees

2005: 88,000

Retention and Professional Development

How do 2005 minority and female attrition rates generally compare to those experienced in the prior year period?

About the same as in prior years.

Please identify the specific steps you are taking to reduce the attrition rate of minority and women employees.

• Develop and/or support internal employee affinity groups (e.g., minority or women networks within the firm)
• Increase/review compensation relative to competition
• Increase/improve current work/life programs
• Adopt dispute resolution process
• Work with minority and women employees to develop career advancement plans
• Strengthen mentoring program for all employees, including minorities and women
• Professional skills development program, including minority and women employees

Note—all if these initiatives are being undertaken in the Special Emphasis Project.

Additional Information

The State of North Carolina is committed to diversity through several means which include: A requirement that all new managers and supervisors attend the Equal Employment Opportunity Institute within the first year of appointment; Executive Order Number Five that requires that all occupational categories reflect diversity of the State' working population; Statewide Diversity Council (Diversity Advocacy Partnership) that was organized by the Office of State Personnel; a specific project entitled Special Emphasis that focuses on the needs of all demographic groups (women, African-American males, older workers, the disabled, people of color and white male inclusion).

ACHIEVEMENT STARTS WHEN
YOU HARNESS THE POWER
OF MANY PERSPECTIVES.

WE KNOW GREATNESS IS OFTEN THE PRODUCT OF PEOPLE BRINGING FRESH PERSPECTIVES TO THE TABLE.

That's why Northrop Grumman is committed to the internships and educational programs that support fresh thinking and diversity in our organization. By partnering with organizations like the Society of Hispanic Professional Engineers and offering company-wide mentoring, we're fostering a breadth of perspectives to power our world-class aerospace and defense projects. Perspectives like yours.

Achievement never ends.

NORTHROP GRUMMAN

DEFINING THE FUTURE™

www.careers.northropgrumman.com

Northrop Grumman Corporation

1840 Century Park East
Los Angeles, CA 90067-2199
Phone: (310) 553-6262
Fax: (310) 553-2076
www.careers.northropgrumman.com

Recruiting

Please list the schools/types of schools at which you recruit.

• Ivy League schools
• Other private schools
• Public state schools
• Historically Black Colleges and Universities (HBCUs)
• Hispanic Serving Institutions (HSIs)
• Native American Tribal Universities
• Other predominantly minority and/or women's colleges

Do you have any special outreach efforts that are directed to encourage minority students to consider your firm?

• Hold a reception for minority students
• *Conferences:* SHPE, NSBE, HENAAC, SWE
• Advertise in minority student association publication(s)
• Participate in/host minority student job fair(s)
• Sponsor minority student association events
• Firm's employees participate on career panels at schools
• Outreach to leadership of minority student organizations
• Scholarships or intern/fellowships for minority students
• *Other:* UNCF, INROADS, United Negro College Fund; provide speakers for minority targeted luncheons & banquets, workshops

What activities does the firm undertake to attract minority and women employees?

• Partner programs with women and minority associations
• *Conferences:* SHPE, AISE, NSBE HENAAC, SWE
• Participate at minority job fairs
• Seek referrals from other employees
• Utilize online job services
• *Other:* Host/sponsor regional diversity organization monthly meetings

Do you use executive recruiting/search firms to seek to identify new diversity hires?

Yes.

Internships and Co-ops

NASA-Sharp & Cams CA. Academy Math & Science, Monster Diversity Leadership Program

> *Deadline for application:* Varies
> *Pay:* Varies by location
> *Length of the program:* Flexible to meet student's needs
> *Percentage of interns/co-ops in the program who receive offers of full-time employment:* Varies by business area
> *Web site for internship/co-op information:* www.definingthefuture.com

Typically a 3.0 GPA and sophomore status from an accredited college or university is required. Requirements may vary by business unit.

Scholarships

- UNCF/NG Diversity Scholarship
- HIP Scholarship
- Diversity ENS Scholarship Program

Affinity Groups

- WINGS
- Women's Networking Group, Community Practice

Entry-Level Programs/Full-Time Opportunities/Training Programs

Engineering & Business Prof. Dev. Programs (ES); Leadership Training Program

> *Length of program:* 15 months
> *Geographic location(s) of program:* Baltimore, MD
> *Please describe the training/training component of this program:* Rotational assignments supported by internal & external coursework
> *Please describe any other educational components of this program:* Tuition reimbursement; mentoring programs

Strategic Plan and Diversity Leadership

Does your firm currently have a diversity committee?

Yes.

Does the committee and/or diversity leader establish and set goals or objectives consistent with management's priorities?

Yes.

Has the firm undertaken a formal or informal diversity program or set of initiatives aimed at increasing the diversity of the firm?

Yes, formal.

The Stats

Employees

2005: 125,000 (U.S.)

Revenue

2005: $30.721 billion
2004: $29.853 billion

Retention and Professional Development

Please identify the specific steps you are taking to reduce the attrition rate of minority and women employees.

Support to local chapters of minority organizations such as SHPE, WSBE, etc.

Looking for an internship
that offers more?

INTERNSHIPS   CAREERS   PERSONAL PLANNING   BUSINESS PLANNING

Learn more. Grow more. Explore more. An internship with
the Northwestern Mutual Financial Network allows you to
learn about our financial products and share what you know
with our clients. Find out more. www.internship.nmfn.com

Northwestern Mutual
FINANCIAL NETWORK®
The Quiet Company.®

Northwestern Mutual Financial Network

720 East Wisconsin Avenue
Milwaukee, WI 53202
Phone: (414) 271-1444
www.careers.nmfn.com

Locations
350 locations nationwide

Employment Contact
www.internship.nmfn.com

Recruiting

Please list the schools/types of schools at which you recruit.

• Other Private schools
• Public state schools
• Historically Black Colleges and Universities (HBCUs)
• Hispanic Serving Institutions (HSIs)
• Other predominantly minority and/or women's colleges

Do you have any special outreach efforts directed to encourage minority students to consider your firm?

• *Conferences*: U.S. Hispanic Chamber of Commerce, Women in Insurance and Financial Services, Graduate Career Enrichment Diversity Conferences, National Black MBA, National Hispanic MBA
• Advertise in minority student association publication(s)
• Participate in/host minority student job fair(s)
• Sponsor minority student association events
• Firm's employees participate on career panels at schools
• Scholarships or intern/fellowships for minority students

What activities does the firm undertake to attract minority and women employees?

• Partner programs with women and minority associations
• *Conferences:* Host national Graduate Career Enrichment Conferences in 22 markets
• Participate at minority job fairs
• Seek referrals from other employees
• *Utilize online job services:* Advertise on diverse internet sites of Yahoo, Careerbuilder and Monster.com
• *Other:*
   Sponsorships: Women in Insurance and Financial Services, NAACP, Hispanic Chamber of Commerce, black and Hispanic MBA associations; offer local office diversity scholarships; media outreach

Do you use executive recruiting/search firms to seek to identify new diversity hires?

No.

Internships and Co-ops

Financial Representative Internship Program

Deadline for application: Ongoing

Pay: Performance-based plus stipends

Length of the program: Both summer and year long—can lead to full-time opportunity

Percentage of interns/co-ops in the program who receive offers of full-time employment: 35 percent

Web site for internship/co-op information: www.internhsip.nmfn.com

Financial representative interns with the Northwestern Mutual Financial Network have the opportunity to experience the career by addressing the needs of individuals and businesses in the areas of retirement, insurance and investment services, estate analysis, education funding and employee benefits. Interns can develop their own practice, but they are not alone. They are supported by our network of specialists, a variety of training programs and mentors. Financial representatives and financial representative interns are independent contractors, and not employees of Northwestern Mutual.

Has the firm undertaken a formal or informal diversity program or set of initiatives aimed at increasing the diversity of the firm?

Yes, formal.

Northwestern Mutual strives to build a field force that represents the diversity within the communities where we do business. Company-driven initiatives focus on increasing the diversity of the Northwestern Mutual Financial Network. Our field diversity area in the recruitment division seeks to recruit and retain more women and minorities as financial representative interns, full-time financial representatives and in field leadership roles. Programs include national sponsorships and a variety of campus recruitment programs designed to reach women and minority candidates.

How often does the firm's management review the firm's diversity progress/results?

Quarterly.

How is the firm's diversity committee and/or firm management held accountable for achieving results?

Results are tracked as part of our recruitment and marketing balanced scorecard. This includes the number of diverse employees in financial representation, internships and in leadership.

Additional Information

Northwestern Mutual is the largest direct provider of individual life insurance in the U.S. Although the company has offered insurance since 1857, today, through its subsidiaries, it also provides financial guidance, estate planning, trust services and a variety of investment products. With $133 billion in assets, the company was ranked 116 by revenue in the 2006 Fortune 500. In February 2006, *Fortune* named Northwestern Mutual the "most admired life insurance company" for the 23rd straight year.

The Northwestern Mutual Financial Network is the marketing name for the sales and distribution arm of Northwestern Mutual.

The company, its subsidiaries and affiliates provide life insurance, annuities, mutual funds, long-term care insurance and disability income insurance. Among its affiliated companies are those that comprise the Russell Investment Group, which provide investment management and advisory services; Northwestern Mutual Investment Services, LLC (NMIS), a wholly-owned company of Northwestern Mutual, broker-dealer and member NASD and SIPC; and Northwestern Mutual Wealth Management Company, a wholly-owned company of Northwestern Mutual, limited purpose federal savings bank and a registered investment adviser which provides financial planning, investment management and trust services. A subsidiary, Northwestern Long Term Care Insurance Company, offers long-term care insurance.

Office Depot, Inc.

2200 Old Germantown Road
Delray Beach, FL 33445
Phone: (561) 438-4800
Fax: (561) 438-8246
www.officedepot.com/links/jobs

Locations
Delray Beach, FL(HQ)
Worldwide locations

Diversity Leadership
Daniela Saladrigas
Recruiter

Jewell Crute
College Recruiter
E-mail: collegerelations@officedepot.com

Employment Contact
Daniela Saladrigas
Recruiter

Recruiting

Please list the schools/types of schools at which you recruit.

- Ivy League schools
- Other private schools
- Public state schools
- Historically Black Colleges and Universities (HBCUs)

Do you have any special outreach efforts directed to encourage minority students to consider your firm?

- Sponsor minority student association events
- Firm's employees participate on career panels at school
- Outreach to leadership of minority student organizations
- *Other:* work with INROADS

What activities does the firm undertake to attract minority and women employees?

- Partner programs with women and minority associations
- *Conferences:* Office Depot Success Strategies for Business Women Conference
- Participate at minority job fairs
- Seek referrals from other employees
- Utilize online job services

Do you use executive recruiting/search firms to seek to identify new diversity hires?

No.

Internships and Co-ops

Retail Management Internship Program

Deadline for application: March 15
Pay: $10-12 per hour

Length of the program: 10 weeks

Web site for internship/co-op information: www.officedepot.com/links/jobs

Corporate Internship Program*

*Openings vary from year to year and often exist in IT, Marketing/Merchandising, HR, Finance/Accounting/Tax and others

Deadline for application: March 15

Number of interns in the program in summer 2005 (internship) or 2005 (co-op): 39

Pay: $11-18 per hour

Length of the program: 12 weeks

Web site for internship/co-op information: www.officedepot.com/links/jobs

Office Depot offers several types of paid undergrad internship programs. The programs are highly structured and individualized. Our interns work on meaningful projects, contribute to business units and achieve amazing results. All interns are responsible for an individual project which they ultimately present to senior management. We strive to place successful interns as full-time Office Depot employees after graduation.

Our Retail Management Internship Program is offered at store locations throughout the country. It is designed to expose the intern to the day-to-day life of retail management. The program offers hands-on experience in a fun, fast-paced environment and helps build skills in management, customer service, time management, problem solving and relationship building that the intern can utilize in all future endeavors.

The Corporate Internship Program is based at our corporate headquarters in Delray Beach, Florida. Each intern is assigned to a specific division within the company and follows a curriculum created by the specific intern's manager. Opportunities vary from year to year and often exist in the following areas: information technology, e-commerce, merchandising/replenishment, marketing, finance/accounting/tax, internal audit, customer relations and human resources.

Entry-Level Programs/Full-Time Opportunities/Training Program

Onboarding Program

Length of program: One week

Geographic location(s) of program: Delray Beach, Florida

The one-week program to orient and acclimate new college hires into Office Depot consists of:

• Buddy programs
• Exposure to executives
• Company history, values and culture
• Benefits
• Diversity and ethics workshops
• Systems training
• Team building activities
• Transition to work discussion
• Store and warehouse visits
• Touch base meetings/feedback surveys quarterly for up to 12 months after date of hire

Strategic Plan and Diversity Leadership

How does the firm's leadership communicate the importance of diversity to everyone at the firm?

Web sites, monthly calendars, corporate cultural celebrations, newsletters and e-mails.

Who has primary responsibility for leading diversity initiatives at your firm?

Virginia Rebata, vice president of organizational development and diversity for Office Depot.

Does your firm currently have a diversity committee?

Yes. The EVPs, VPs and directors meet quarterly.

If yes, does the committee's representation include one or more members of the firm's management/executive committee?

Yes.

If yes, how many executives are on the committee?

Total Executives on Committee: Seven

Does the committee and/or diversity leader establish and set goals or objectives consistent with management's priorities?

Yes.

Has the firm undertaken a formal or informal diversity program or set of initiatives aimed at increasing the diversity of the firm?

Yes, formal.

How often does the firm's management review the firm's diversity progress/results?

Quarterly.

How is the firm's diversity committee and/or firm management held accountable for achieving results?

We utilize a balance score card to measure all of our executives. The Diversity Committee is an integral part of that score card.

The Stats

Employees

2005: 47,000 (U.S.)

Revenue

2005: $14 billion (U.S.)

Diversity Mission Statement

At Office Depot, we are committed to creating an inclusive environment where all people are valued and respected. Diversity is an important dimension of respect for the individual—one of our core values—and a key to our success in a global marketplace.

Olin Corporation, Brass & Winchester Divisions

Corporate Headquarters
190 Carondelet Plaza
Suite 1530
Clayton, MO 63105-3443

Brass & Winchester Divisions
427 N. Shamrock
East Alton, IL 62024

Locations

Brass Division: East Alton, IL (HQ)
Waterbury, CT; Seymour, CT; Cuba, MO;
Bryan, OH and Multiple production and
distribution sites throughout the U.S.,
Puerto Rico, Queretaro, Mexico and
Guangzhou, China. Sales offices through-
out the U.S. and internationally in
Singapore, Japan, China and Europe
Winchester Locations: East Alton, IL;
Oxford, MS

Diversity Leadership

Valerie Peters
Director, Human Resources

Angie Standefer
Manager, Employment and Records

Employment Contact

Angie Standefer
Manager, Employment & Records
427 N. Shamrock
East Alton, IL 62024
Phone: (618) 258-2976
E-mail: akstandefer@olin.com
www.olin.com

Additional Information

Olin Corporation's Brass & Winchester Divisions are leaders in their respective industries. Brass products include copper and copper alloy sheet, strip, foil, rod, welded tube, fabricated parts, and stainless steel and aluminum strip. Winchester products include sporting ammunition, canister powder, reloading components, small caliber military ammunition and components, and industrial cartridges.

We are an equal opportunity employer and proud of our diverse workforce. Since our birth in 1892, Olin has demonstrated a commitment to excellence. Our values are simple, but powerful: integrity, innovation, continuous improvement, our employees, our customers, and our shareholders. Diversity of ideas and diversity within our workforce helps us achieve excellence.

Our efforts to encourage minority students to consider Olin as an employer include advertising in minority student association publications, participating in minority student job fairs, participating in career panels at colleges, universities and high schools; and sponsoring scholarships and internships for minority students. For more information, go to our web site at www.olin.com.

Remember dreaming about the perfect job?

At OSRAM SYLVANIA, our business is the creation of light. As a global lighting leader, our name has defined innovation in the industry. The power behind our vision is our people – a wealth of talented professionals. At the root of our global team is our Associate Development Program – an innovative two-year immersion program that places new associates in the center of our core business functions. Candidates are considered for one of five program tracks: engineering and manufacturing, finance, human resources, information technology, or marketing and sales. Upon completion of the program, successful associates qualify for positions throughout the company. We offer generous compensation and incomparable growth opportunities for luminous minds to excel. Visit www.sylvania.com or your career placement office for more information. We are an EOE.

OSRAM SYLVANIA

100 Endicott Street
Danvers, MA 01923
Phone: (978) 777-1900
Fax: (978) 750-2152
www.sylvania.com

Locations

Asia
Canada
Europe
Mexico
United States

Diversity Leadership

Leah Weinberg
Manager of Diversity, Inclusion and the
Associate Development Program
E-mail: leah.weinberg@sylvania.com

Employment Contact

Maureen Crawford Hentz
Corporate Recruiter
100 Endicott Street
Danvers, MA 01923
Phone: (800)-SYLVANIA
E-mail: maureen.crawford@sylvania.com or
diversity.recruiter@sylvania.com

Recruiting

Please list the schools/types of schools at which you recruit.

• Ivy League schools
• Other private schools
• Public state schools
• Historically Black Colleges and Universities (HBCUs)
• Hispanic Serving Institutions (HSIs)
• Native American Tribal Universities

* Specific schools listed for recruiting on www.sylvania.com

Do you have any special outreach efforts directed to encourage minority students to consider your firm?

• Hold a reception for minority students
• *Conferences:* NSBE, SHPE, SWE, WITI, CAREERS and the disABLED, and Jobapalooza
• Advertise in minority student association publication(s)
• Participate in/host minority student job fair(s)
• Sponsor minority student association events
• Firm's employees participate on career panels at schools
• Outreach to leadership of minority student organizations
• Scholarships or intern/fellowships for minority students
• *Other*: Advertise in the Minority College Edition of *Diversity/Careers in Engineering and Information Technology*

What activities does the firm undertake to attract minority and women employees?

• Partner programs with women and minority associations
• *Conferences:* NSBE, SHPE, SWE
• Participate at minority job fairs
• Seek referrals from other employees
• Utilize online job services

Internships and Co-ops

OSRAM SYLVANIA Intern and Co-op Program

Deadline for application: Our program is year-round. We have intern and co-op positions available throughout the year; resumes are accepted on a continuous basis.

Pay: Pay schedule is according to function and year in school.

Length of the program: 12-52 weeks. This depends upon the intern or co-op's availability and the needs of the hiring manager.

Web site for internship/co-op information: http://www.sylvania.com/aboutus/careers/jobs/

Anyone interested in an intern or co-op position should send his/her resume to the intern coordinator at intern.coordinator@sylvania.com.

Opportunities within our Intern and Co-op Program are available in, but are not limited to, the following areas:

• Engineering
• Finance and accounting
• Human resources
• Information technology
• Marketing and national customer service

Availability is based upon the company's needs at any given time.

Affinity Groups

We presently have eight affinity groups in our organization:

• African-American Network
• OSAN—Osram Sylvania Asian Network
• SPECTRUM—Sylvania's GLBT network
• Latino Alliance for Motivation & Production (LAMP)
• Advocates for people with disabilities
• Women's Affinity Group

The Women's Network currently has two subgroups—the Sales & Marketing Women's Network and the Women In Science and Engineering (WISE) Network. The purpose of each of these groups is to embrace the unique characteristics of, empower and support the employees who compose our increasingly diverse workforce.

Examples of affinity group mission statements:

African-American Network (AAN)

The African-American Network is committed to promoting the value and benefits of diversity within OSRAM SYLVANIA, while encouraging people of African descent to achieve their full potential, professionally and personally, as they pursue careers and leadership positions within the company.

Advocates for People with Disabilities (APWD)

Advocates for People with Disabilities will create an inclusive work environment and through support, advocacy and assistance, strive to level differences towards the goal of promoting individual growth and adding value to OSRAM SYLVANIA.

Sales & Marketing Women's Network

The Sales & Marketing Women's Network will provide support and assistance to women who sell OSRAM SYLVANIA products and have either direct or indirect contact with our customers. This network will address the unique challenges that women face in the business world and give us a forum for ideas and learning. In addition, this network will provide opportunities for women across all sales channels to form alliances from the field to headquarters to make us all more effective and increase sales of OSRAM SYLVANIA products.

Women in Science & Engineering (WISE)

The Women in Science and Engineering Network encourages women to achieve their full potential in careers as scientists, engineers, technologists and leaders within OSRAM SYLVANIA.

Entry-Level Programs/Full-Time Opportunities/Training Programs

Associate Development Program

Length of program: 24 months
Geographic location(s) of program: United States, Mexico, Canada and Germany

During the course of the program, associates are given three different assignments throughout the company. This rotational component of the program provides training in and exposure to various areas of our business.

The mission of the Associate Development Program is to develop both the leadership skills and professional work ethics of the highest quality college graduates, while also providing access to positions of increasing responsibility within OSRAM SYLVANIA. All of this, in turn, works with the company-wide goal of leading OSRAM SYLVANIA to become the number one global lighting manufacturer in the world. The program consists of three eight-month assignments rotated over a two-year period to encourage exploration and advance leadership, problem-solving, decision-making and other skills. The program is comprised of six disciplines:

1) Engineering

Engineering at OSRAM SYLVANIA is directly responsible for technological breakthroughs that have revolutionized the world of lighting and precision materials. The scope and diversity of engineering at OSRAM SYLVANIA are as far-reaching as our achievements. As an engineering associate, you will be given assignments in the areas of research and development, product development, process engineering, equipment development, materials development, or testing and analysis.

Assignments may include opportunities to:

• Assist in the transfer of technology from pilot stage to full-scale production
• Design and develop innovative processes that result in increased efficiency, quality and cost reduction
• Develop high speed automated assembly equipment
• Introduce new materials for use in lighting and other products

Academic Requirements:

• BS or MS in material science engineering, electrical engineering, mechanical engineering, optical engineering, chemical engineering or ceramic engineering

2) Finance

OSRAM SYLVANIA's position of leadership in the lighting industry and its vision for the future requires the financial organization to play a key role through continuous improvement in measurement, analysis, and resource allocation. Total quality and internal and external customer satisfaction are constant goals. As a finance associate, you will be given assignments with immediate exposure to our business.

Assignments are at the corporate, division, and plant level and will include diverse responsibilities in financial analysis, accounting and internal auditing such as:

• Coordinating and consolidating the development of an annual budget and analyzing results and variances
• Working closely with factory personnel to develop standards, identify cost reduction opportunities and prepare capital expenditure requests
• Developing an integrated reporting system which measures the profitability and key indicators of product lines within a division
• Analyzing historical and forecasted market price trends and recommending short and long term actions to enhance product profitability

Academic Requirements:

• BS in accounting, business, finance or economics
• Minimum of 12 credit hours of accounting

3) Human Resources

With a workforce of approximately 10,590 employees, OSRAM SYLVANIA believes its greatest strength is its employees. As a human resources associate, you will apply your skills and academic training toward maximizing employee commitment, satisfaction and productivity—the stated goals of the OSRAM SYLVANIA's human resources charter. Your responsibilities will include:

• Recruiting and selecting new employees whose education, skills and work philosophies match the organization's needs
• Implementing performance management programs that effectively motivate and provide rewards for results
• Developing labor strategies and participating in the resolution of labor negotiations, grievances and arbitration
• Managing programs that facilitate employee involvement and team problem-solving processes

Academic Requirements:

• BS, MS or MBA in human resources management or industrial relations

4) Information Technology

Information technology that provides accurate and timely data for all levels of a corporation is essential to compete in today's business environment. OSRAM SYLVANIA's Corporate Information Technology group is considered leading edge in its use of client server technology to ensure that marketing, sales, manufacturing and financial personnel always have the right information at the right time. The Associate Development Program in Information Technology offers an unequaled opportunity to gain professional competency through real-world business exposure. As an information technology associate, you will be given assignments that focus on different facets of the information technology function such as:

• Being part of the group which is the single point of contact for all OSRAM SYLVANIA's business users for the resolution of information technology problems
• Participating as a member of a key information technology project or process team and having the opportunity to do programming, systems design, testing and implementation
• Implementing new technologies associated with network, server or desktop design and analysis, including working with computer platforms, operating systems and various network technologies

Academic Requirements:

• BS in computer information systems or related field

5) Manufacturing

The production of quality products using state of the art equipment, in an efficient, cost effective way is the cornerstone of success for a world class manufacturing organization. The OSRAM SYLVANIA Associate Development Program in manufacturing offers an unequaled opportunity to experience this highly technical field, as well as to give you professional competency through real-world business exposure. As a manufacturing associate, you will be given challenging opportunities to participate in, or lead, continuous improvement programs such as:

• Analyzing manufacturing processes, recommending and implementing changes to improve material and/or labor efficiencies

• Applying new systems and measurements such as Total Cycle TimeSM, First Pass Yield and ISO 9000 to existing processes to create a streamlined, consistent means of operating departments and businesses
• Participating in team activities to promote involvement, share ideas and gain the commitment of employees at all levels of the organization
• Supervising a department or work area with responsibility for meeting safety, quality, production and cost targets

Academic Requirements:

• BS or MS in mechanical engineering, industrial engineering, electrical engineering, material science, ceramic engineering or chemical engineering

6) Marketing and Sales

At OSRAM SYLVANIA, we value innovation not only in product development but also in how we approach the various markets that we serve. From large city skyscrapers to the living room, from rock concerts to the operating table, lighting is an essential part of daily life. As a marketing/sales associate, you will be exposed to the realities of a competitive and rewarding marketplace. Assignments may include the following responsibilities:

• Market planning and research
• Product management
• Sales
• Advertising and promotion
• Training and education
• Competitive analysis
• Logistics and customer service

Academic Requirements:

• BS in business or marketing or BA in liberal arts

While in the program, associates receive the same benefits as all other OSRAM SYLVANIA employees. We offer multiple medical and dental plans, along with a competitive, non-contributory pension program. Here are some highlights:

• Indemnity, medical plans, dental plans, and vision plan
• A company match to individual 401(k) investments
• Generous company-paid life insurance benefits with options to buy additional life insurance for oneself, a spouse and dependents at group rates
• Convenience, care and income protection benefits including:
  • Discounted auto and homeowner's insurance
  • Short-term and long-term disability insurance
  • Optional long-term care insurance for self or a family member
  • Physical fitness programs on site or through a reimbursement program

Many OSRAM SYLVANIA employees use our educational assistance/tuition reimbursement plan for themselves and our scholarship program for their children. We match employee gifts to schools at all grade levels, and distribute cash grants to organizations with whom our employees volunteer. Relocation assistance is also available for associates who move more than 50 miles while in the program.

Strategic Plan and Diversity Leadership

How does the firm's leadership communicate the importance of diversity to everyone at the firm?

Communications include letters from executives, e-mails, an internal diversity web site and diversity topics being addressed at quarterly meetings held by executives. There is an executive advocate for each affinity group, providing support, barrier removal and a direct conduit to the executive committee of OSRAM SYLVANIA.

Who has primary responsibility for leading diversity initiatives at your firm?

Leah Weinberg, manager of diversity inclusion and the Associate Development Program, in cooperation with the diversity council.

Does your firm currently have a diversity committee?

Yes.

Geoff Hunt, senior vice president of human resources & communication, champions the diversity council. The diversity council was established by our company president in 2001 "to analyze the diversity situation at OSRAM SYLVANIA and to keep (management) attuned to changes that need to be made if the diversity initiative is to be successful, especially over the long term."

How many employees are on the committee, and how often does the committee convene in furtherance of the firm's diversity initiatives?

The council is comprised of 28 employees from various business units, one advisor and one champion. The council meets four times per year. The council has a chairperson, facilitator and an administrator elected by the council at large on an annual basis. It is organized into five committees focusing on communications, training, recruitment and retention, employee involvement and metrics.

The goals established by the council are:

• To develop measurements of success for diversity at OSRAM SYLVANIA and monitor progress
• Provide management with suggestions for improving diversity at OSRAM SYLVANIA
• Communicate the benefits of diversity within the company and provide employees with an avenue to voice their concerns or issues regarding diversity in our facilities without fear of repercussion

Has the firm undertaken a formal or informal diversity program or set of initiatives aimed at increasing the diversity of the firm?

Yes, formal.

The council has been tasked with identifying systems required to support diversity, identifying enablers and barriers to success, and making recommendations to management on direction and more specifically on programs and policies. The council has successfully recommended and implemented a mentoring program, a communications plan, an affinity group initiative and other programs. These programs are designed to support diversity in both employee representation and customer support. Goals for 2006 include building a supplier diversity program.

How is the firm's diversity committee and/or firm management held accountable for achieving results?

The diversity council is required to present progress to the executive committee each quarter. This includes a review of progress on programs and initiatives as well as making recommendations for future activities. The manager of diversity integration is responsible for achieving the desired results.

The Stats

	2005 STATS	
	U.S.	**WORLDWIDE**
Number of employees	11,000	38,000
Revenue	€1.5 billion	€4.3 billion

DEMOGRAPHIC PROFILE				
	MALE	FEMALE	NON-CAUCASIAN	CAUCASIAN
Employees	69.1%	30.9%	9.9%	90.1%
Interns	62.5%	37.5%	25.5%	74.5%

Retention and Professional Development

Please identify the specific steps you are taking to reduce the attrition rate of minority and women employees.

• Develop and/or support internal employee affinity groups
• Maintain competitive compensation rates
• Maintain strong work/life programming
• Succession plan includes emphasis on diversity
• Work with minority and women employees on career development plans
• Continue to build mentoring program for all employees, including minorities and women
• Professional skills development program, including minority and women employees

Diversity Mission Statement

OSRAM SYLVANIA is committed to developing an increasingly diverse workforce with fair and open access to career opportunities. We cultivate an inclusive, supportive climate, thereby enabling us to better meet the needs of our employees and customers. We believe that variety of opinion, approach, perspective and talent are the cornerstones of a strong, flexible and competitive company.

Additional Information

OSRAM SYLVANIA is committed to developing and retaining an increasingly diverse workforce. In the area of recruitment, we have established a corporate commitment to programs that serve minority student populations, such as INROADS. We are solidifying strategic relationships and partnerships with colleges, universities and professional organizations that have significant female and minority populations. With regard to retention, our programs and strategies will result in a more diverse and inclusive work environment. These programs include affinity groups and a mentoring program. Increased emphasis is being placed upon diversity in our succession planning. With the powerful commitment of our executives and management team, OSRAM SYLVANIA is an environment where every talented individual can be proud to work.

Owens & Minor

9120 Lockwood Blvd.
Mechanicsville, VA 23116-2029
Phone: (804) 723-7000

Additional Information

At Owens & Minor our vision is to be a world class organization that builds its strength through the successful integration of the diverse cultures, backgrounds and experience of our teammates and business partners. Our inclusive environment enhances our efforts as we work to find solutions for our customers and supply chain partners. All of our teammates, customers, suppliers, as well as the communities we serve have differing views. They trust that we take these views into account as we plan our business. In order for us to be the best we can be, we must clearly understand these diverse needs and perspectives. Strategically, this can be best accomplished by capitalizing on the value of a diverse workforce and supplier base.

We believe that the diversity of our teammates will help our company "deliver" the difference in this increasingly diverse market. At Owens & Minor we look toward our leadership team to:

• Establish diversity as a key component of how we conduct business

• Encourage all teammates to support Owens & Minor's diversity plan and diversity efforts

• Measure the success of the team at achieving specific goals for hiring, developing, promoting and retaining teammates in under-represented or underutilized job groups and businesses

It is our belief that diversity and business success go hand in hand.

Pearson Education

One Lake Street
Upper Saddle River, NJ 07458
Phone: (201) 236-3419
Fax: (201) 236-3381
E-mail: anne.adamo@pearsoned.com
www.pearsoned.com/careers

Locations

US:
Arlington, VA • Boston, MA • Columbus, OH • Eagan, MN • Bloomington, MN • Glenview , IL • Champaign, IL • Indianapolis, IN • Mesa, AZ • Iowa City, IA • Lawrence, KS • New York, NY • Old Tappan, NJ • Parsippany, NJ • San Francisco, CA • UpperSaddle River, NJ • White Plains, NY
International:
Africa • Asia • Australia • Canada • Europe • India • the Middle East • New Zealand • South America

Diversity Leadership

Christine Pfeiffer
Diversity Team Leader

Ryan Darlington
College Recruiting

Employment Contact

Anne Adamo
Manager, Employee Relations

Recruiting

Please list the schools/types of schools at which you recruit.

• *Ivy League schools:* Harvard
• *Other private schools:* Marist, William Patterson, Syracuse, Seton Hall, Muhlengerg, Mt. St. Mary, Quinnipiac
• *Public state schools:* Rutgers

Do you have any special outreach efforts directed to encourage minority students to consider your firm?

• *Conferences:* Monster Diversity Leadership Program, Black Wharton Undergraduate Association, Southern Christian Leadership Conference
• Participate in/host minority student job fair(s)
• Sponsor minority student association events
• Firm's employees participate on career panels at schools

What activities does the firm undertake to attract minority and women employees?

• Participate at minority job fairs
• Seek referrals from other employees
• *Utilize online job services:* Monster.com, DiversityHire.com, AmericasJobBank.com
• *Other:* Advertise in minority publications such as *Hispanic Network Magazine, Professional Women's Magazine, Black Enterprise* magazine, and *Black EOE Journal*

Do you use executive recruiting/search firms to seek to identify new diversity hires?

No.

Internships and Co-ops

Pearson Intern Program

Deadline for application: April 15
Number of interns in the program in summer 2005 (internship) or 2005 (co-op): 100 at multiple locations throughout the U.S.
Pay: Varies
Length of the program: Minimum eight weeks during June/July/August
Percentage of interns/co-ops in the program who receive offers of full-time employment: Varies by position/location
Web site for internship/co-op information: www.pearsoned.com/careers

Pearson maintains a Summer College Intern Program that enables the company to recruit and train a diverse group of people for careers in publishing by providing students an opportunity to expand their theoretical knowledge, clarify their career goals and enhance opportunities for full-time employment. Students will be placed in departments that suit their interests, as well as their major course of study. The departmental structure includes corporate functions, editorial, marketing, sales, production, design and human resources.

Entry-Level Programs/Full-Time Opportunities/Training Programs

General Accounting Program

Length of program: Two years
Geographic location(s) of program: Upper Saddle River Facility

Hands-on experience in four major accounting areas.

Tuition Reimbursement is offered, but as company policy, not just for this program.

Strategic Plan and Diversity Leadership

Who has primary responsibility for leading diversity initiatives at your firm?

Christine Trum, senior VP human resources.

Does your firm currently have a diversity committee?

Yes.

If yes, please describe how the committee is structured, how often it meets, etc.

Diversity council meets quarterly and includes executive management.

If yes, does the committee's representation include one or more members of the firm's management/executive committee (or the equivalent)?

Yes.

Total Executives on Committee: Nine

Does the committee and/or diversity leader establish and set goals or objectives consistent with management's priorities?

Yes.

Has the firm undertaken a formal or informal diversity program or set of initiatives aimed at increasing the diversity of the firm?

Yes, formal, including:

• HR Diversity Team
• Metrics
• Internship program
• Training initiatives

How often does the firm's management review the firm's diversity progress/results?

Quarterly.

How is the firm's diversity committee and/or firm management held accountable for achieving results?

Diversity metrics and practices are reviewed by the Pearson PLC Board each year. Goals are set and scrutinized annually.

The Stats

2005 Employees

Total number of employees: 16,500
Pearson Education: 7,489

2005 Revenue

Pearson Education: $600 million

Retention and Professional Development

Please identify the specific steps you are taking to reduce the attrition rate of minority and women employees.

• Develop and/or support internal employee affinity groups (e.g., minority or women networks within the firm)
• Increase/improve current work/life programs
• Succession plan includes emphasis on diversity
• Strengthen mentoring program for all employees, including minorities and women
• Professional skills development program, including minority and women employees

Diversity Mission Statement

We want to be: (1) A diverse company—to attract the very best candidates, at all levels, regardless of race, gender, age, physical ability, religion or sexual orientation; we always try to hire the best person for the job, and to ensure that our candidate pool is diverse and our hiring is non-discriminatory; (2) a fair company—to ensure that pay, retention, promotions and terminations are determined without regard to race, gender, age, physical ability, religion or sexual orientation; and (3) a company which uses diversity to help achieve its commercial goals and targets new opportunities in growing markets.

Additional Information

Pearson was awarded both a Bronze Corporate Spirit Award for leadership in fully making the INROADS mission a part of our daily work and a Growth Award for significantly increasing the number of INROADS internships. Additionally, Pearson's Corporate INROADS liaison was named Business Advisor of the Year.

Pitney Bowes

1 Elmcroft Road
Stamford, CT 06926
Phone: (203) 356-5000
www.pitneybowes.com

Locations

Locations in 130 countries.

Diversity Leadership

Denise Rawles-Smith
Manager, Diversity External Relationships
1 Elmcroft Road
Stamford, CT 06854
Phone: (203) 351-7910
Fax: (203) 348-1289
E-mail: denise.rawles@pb.com

Employment Contact

Michael T. Holmes
Director, Strategic Talent Management Global

Recruiting

Please list the schools/types of schools at which you recruit.

• *Ivy League schools*: Cornell, Columbia
• *Other private schools:* Rensselaer Polytechnic Institute (RPI), Rochester Institute of Technology (RIT) and Fairfield University
• *Public state schools:* University of Connecticut and the University of Waterloo
• Historically Black Colleges and Universities (HBCUs)
• Hispanic Serving Institutions (HSIs)
• Native American Tribal Universities

Do you have any special outreach efforts directed to encourage minority students to consider your firm?

• Hold a reception for minority students
• Advertise in minority student association publication(s)
• Sponsor minority student association events
• Firm's employees participate on career panels at schools
• Outreach to leadership of minority student organizations
• Scholarships or intern/fellowships for minority students
• *Other*: Participate in college and university job fairs

What activities does the firm undertake to attract minority and women employees?

• Partner programs with women and minority associations
• *Conferences:* INROADS, National Society of Black Engineers, National Urban League, Association of Latino Professionals, National Society of Hispanic MBAs, National Black MBA Association, National Sales Network and the Society of Women Engineers
• *Participate at minority job fairs:* See conference list
• Seek referrals from other employees
• Utilize online job services
• *Other:* We advertise our career opportunities in publications such as *Hispanic Business, Black MBA, Asian Enterprise, Black Enterprise, Diversity/Careers, DiversityInc, Fortune, Hispanic Professional, National Society of Black Engineers, New York Times Magazine, CAREERS & the disABLED, Society of Women Engineers* and *Diversity & The Bar*

Do you use executive recruiting/search firms to seek to identify new diversity hires?

Yes.

Internships and Co-ops

INROADS

> *Deadline for application:* January; candidates are interviewed in March; offers made in April
> *Number of interns in the program in summer 2005 (internship) or 2005 (co-op):* 13 interns
> *Pay:* $12.50-$16.00 per hour
> *Percentage of interns/co-ops in the program who receive offers of full-time employment:* 66 percent
> *Web site for internship/co-op information:* www.pb.com/careers

Between August and September, we inform INROADS of our intern commitments for the upcoming year (that number includes students eligible to return for another internship and new students). Between October and December, we maintain communication with students we are expecting to return. We discuss their academic performance, career interests and opportunities for their next internship. Several students intern over the mid-semester break with their previous managers or potential new managers for their next internship.

Between January and February, Pitney Bowes employees participate in INROADS Talent Pool training sessions, helping conduct mock interviews and facilitate workshops. Between March and April, Pitney Bowes' HR team interviews candidates at the annual INROADS Corporate Interview Day (CID).

After the CID, we determine which candidates best fit the internship opportunities and fast-paced work environment of Pitney Bowes. Within three business days following CID we communicate to INROADS a list of candidates to whom we will extend verbal offers.

Once our offers are accepted, we review the internships in greater detail and agree upon starting and ending dates. Interns are matched with Pitney Bowes managers who demonstrate a strong track record of performance in coaching and employee development. As required by INROADS, all interns receive mid- and end-of-internship performance evaluations, as well as appropriate supervision and timely feedback.

All internships are designed to challenge our interns with work that allows them to make immediate contributions and demonstrate their potential for full-time professional level employment.

Internships and Co-ops

Engineering CO-OP/Interns

> *Deadline for application:* Varies throughout the year
> *Number of interns in the program in summer 2005 (internship) or 2005 (co-op):* 43 interns
> *Pay:* $17-26 per hour
> *Length of the program:* Three to six months
> *Percentage of interns/co-ops in the program who receive offers of full-time employment:* 5 percent
> *Web site for internship/co-op information:* www.pb.com/careers

Most Pitney Bowes co-ops work in our Technology Center in Shelton, Connecticut. Our Technology Center project leaders hire co-ops to be on engineering teams drawing from four functional groups:

• Mechanical/electrical/systems
• Software
• Product usability and design
• Technical support/operations

Co-ops find support for their career development on the functional side while working toward specific deadlines and output goals on their various product assignments.

Pitney Bowes' Advanced Concepts in Technology, a unit dedicated to capturing the advantages of technologies likely to emerge in the next 10 years, also employs engineers on its research and development projects.

Our co-op positions are designed to challenge students with work that allows them to make immediate contributions and demonstrate their potential for full-time professional level employment.

Scholarships

Pitney Bowes INROADS/FWC Hispanic Scholarship

Scholarship award amount: Award depends on the year the participant is in school and his or her GPA. The scholarship ranges from $500-$2,000. Award is announced at the Annual Awards reception.

Affinity Groups

DMT Women's Forum

This forum is composed of women helping women succeed and grow. The objective is to engage women in the Document Messaging Technologies business unit in leveraging each other to develop each woman's career by exposing them to internal and external leaders, ideas and best practices. They also learn to share best practices around managing work and personal lives. The DMT Women's Forum creates a renewed sense of employee engagement and exposure for members of the steering committee to interface with key business leaders as they organize events. This can help further the company's long-term strategic objectives and immediate business goals. They meet monthly and hold two to three evening events a year.

Entry-Level Programs/Full-Time Opportunities/Training Programs

Pitney Bowes TechCentral Professional Development Program (PDP)

Length of program: Three year rotational program for students who have just completed a bachelor's or master's degree
Geographic location(s) of program: Connecticut

The Pitney Bowes TechCentral Professional Development Program (PDP) is a rotational program to develop technical and managerial leaders within our IT organization. The program offers challenging "real job" assignments based on an individual's specific education, experience, development needs and interests. It consists of two or three assignments over a three-year period, followed by a final placement. Throughout the three years, participants can expect to be provided with:

• Exposure to business leaders across Pitney Bowes
• Work assignments with challenges and learning opportunities
• Personal development coaching & feedback
• Opportunities to network with peers

The program approach is to hire extremely talented people, nurture their growth and give them opportunities to make an impact. We are working to identify great technical talent and to assist recent graduates in acquiring the unique skills and experiences they need to excel in their careers.

Strategic Plan and Diversity Leadership

How does the firm's leadership communicate the importance of diversity to everyone at the firm?

Our most senior level leaders (CEO, COO, CFO, chief HR officer, general counsel and business unit presidents) regularly communicate the business value of diversity via weekly voice mail power talks, town hall meetings, Intranet announcements, internal publications, diversity forums and quarterly operational reviews. These leaders also agree on collaborations with our customers and suppliers on mutually beneficial diversity initiatives.

Who has primary responsibility for leading diversity initiatives at your firm?

Susan Johnson, vice president, strategic talent management, and Michael T. Holmes, director, strategic talent management & global diversity leadership.

Does your firm currently have a diversity committee?

No.

Does the committee and/or diversity leader establish and set goals or objectives consistent with management's priorities?

Yes. Diversity governance is an enterprise-wide initiative, which includes accountability to the CEO and board level. The CEO receives detailed reports regarding diversity, succession planning, as well as performance assessments. In addition, business unit presidents and their direct reports, including senior corporate staff, are held accountable for the success of diversity initiatives within their individual business units. The number of employees and hours spent on these initiatives vary from business unit to business unit. Diversity is an objective of senior management and the board of directors and is enforced by tying compensation to successful completion of the diversity objective. The diversity strategic planning process outlines goals for the company and places responsibility for meeting those goals in the hands of employees organized into what is known as our Diversity Leadership Councils. Through these councils, we have diversity champions throughout all of Pitney Bowes who are actively engaged to help foster employee involvement.

Has the firm undertaken a formal or informal diversity program or set of initiatives aimed at increasing the diversity of the firm?

Yes, formal. Pitney Bowes has established a strategic architecture to define enterprise goals and objectives within the organization. Each business unit and staff function defines their goals in alignment with the company's including:

• Strategic architecture
• Engaged workforce
• Leadership talent
• Diversity
• Business unit strategic planning process
• Staffing and recruitment
• Leadership development

How often does the firm's management review the firm's diversity progress/results?

Twice a year.

How is the firm's diversity committee and/or firm management held accountable for achieving results?

We have built diversity metrics into our corporation's objectives through specific metrics. The CEO, SVP of HR and executive director of global diversity leadership have accountability to the Corporate Responsibility Committee (a subset of the board of directors). Each business leader is held accountable for furthering our diversity efforts. We have a leadership model that describes and holds leaders accountable for their behaviors (explicit and implicit). Managers are accountable for the development of their people and diversity is an objective of senior management and the board of directors and is enforced by tying compensation to successful completion of the diversity objective.

The Stats

	TOTAL IN THE U.S.		TOTAL OUTSIDE THE U.S		TOTAL WORLDWIDE	
	2005	2004	2005	2004	2005	2004
Number of employees	25,319	27,152	8,846	8,031	34,165	35,183
Revenue	$4.09 billion	$3.70 billion	$1.40 billion	$1.25 billion	$5.49 billion	$4.96 billion

Retention and Professional Development

Please identify the specific steps you are taking to reduce the attrition rate of minority and women employees.

• Develop and/or support internal employee affinity groups (e.g., minority or women networks within the firm)
• Increase/review compensation relative to competition
• Increase/improve current work/life programs
• Adopt dispute resolution process
• Succession plan includes emphasis on diversity
• Work with all employees including minority and women employees to develop career advancement plans
• Strengthen mentoring program for all employees, including minorities and women
• Professional skills development program, including minority and women employees

To help advance women and minorities, Pitney Bowes has an initiative to augment its leadership and professional development programs into upper management. LEAD! is Pitney Bowes' multi-faceted, comprehensive initiative that provides managers with the training, tools and processes to enhance their leadership skills and to help them become successful.

Pitney Bowes also believes in providing its employees opportunities to advance in the company with the flexibility to manage their time between their careers and their life commitments. We offer programs such as flexible work arrangements, transportation programs, employee resources fairs, on-site amenities that include fitness centers and medical clinics, an employee assistance program (EAP) and on-site financial education programs.

Diversity Mission Statement

Pitney Bowes does business in workplaces characterized by significant diversity. We value, actively pursue and leverage diversity in our employees, and through our relationships with customers, business partners and communities. Diversity is essential to innovation and growth. Pitney Bowes' commitment to diversity is also consistent with and further supports the company's values and practices.

Additional Information

Pitney Bowes has a long and admirable history of corporate-wide commitment to diversity dating back to the 1960s. Diversity is the foundation of our company's success. The company is consistently recognized for its ongoing commitment to building a truly diverse organization (See awards list below). The continued focus on transformation and on talent and leadership lays the foundation for future growth.

Pitney Bowes has a diverse network of strategic partnerships and alliances with over 40 key organizations. Among our partners are the National Urban League, Women's Business Enterprise National Council, National Society of Hispanic MBAs, National

Black MBA Association, the Connecticut Asian Pacific American Bar Association, Society of Women Engineers, National Society of Black Engineers, Congressional Hispanic Caucus Institute, Congressional Black Caucus and National Minority Supplier Development Council.

We also have impactful strategic relationships with our internal partners and provide programs for our employees and stakeholders. Examples of some of the internal diversity-related programs are:

MBA Leadership Summit

We host the MBA Leadership Summit at our world headquarters facility, in partnership with our local chapters of the National Society of Hispanic MBAs (NSHMBA) and the National Black MBA Association (NBMBAA).

Speed Networking

Speed Networking is a process Pitney Bowes uses to facilitate networking and learning. Started in 2004, Speed Networking was piloted as an initiative to help with the retention and engagement of women at middle and senior levels, and to promote the professional advancement of women in our workplace.

Prism Award

The Prism Award was created to recognize Pitney Bowes' teams for strategies and initiatives that were implemented at the business or corporate level to sustain our commitment to diversity and inclusion.

Diversity Festival

The Diversity Festival is a celebration of diversity in race, religion, customs, cultures, origins and beliefs. We celebrate Pitney Bowes' employees, customers, communities and business partners worldwide, and foster greater understanding of all that we have in common.

2005 Recognition & Awards

Pitney Bowes has earned many awards during its long history of investing in the community and partnering with nonprofits nationally and internationally. Here are some of the awards we have won that highlight our commitment to diversity:

• Awarded the Corporate Award by the Executive Leadership Council, 2005.
• Ranked among the 50 Top Employers for Minorities by *Fortune* magazine, 2005.
• Awarded the Brillante Award in the Corporate Award Category by the National Society of Hispanic MBAs, 2005.
• Ranked among Best Employers for Workers 50 and Over by AARP, 2005, 2004.
• Ranked one of the 30 Best Companies for Diversity by *Black Enterprise* magazine.
• Recognized on *Latin Business'* 2005 Corporate Diversity Honor Roll, 2005.
• Ranked among DiversityInc.com's Top 50 Companies for Diversity, 2005, 2004, 2003, 2002 and 2001; ranked the No. 1 Company for Diversity in 2004.
• Rated in the 100 Best Corporate Citizens by *Business Ethics* magazine, 2005, 2004, 2003, 2002, 2001 and 2000.
• Awarded Corporate Partner of the Year by the Connecticut Chapter of the National Society of Hispanic MBAs, 2005, 2001.
• Ranked among DiversityBusiness.com's (formerly known as Div2000.com)America's Top Organizations for Multicultural Business—Opportunities, 2005, 2004, 2003, 2002, 2001.
• Ranked among Top 100 Companies for Hispanics by *Hispanic Magazine*, 2005, 2004, 2003, 2002, 2001, 2000 and 1999.
• Ranked among *Hispanic Magazine*'s Top 50 Recruitment Programs, 2005, 2004, 2003, 2002, 2001, 2000, 1999 and 1998.
• Awarded the Outstanding Corporate Supplier Diversity Award by the National Minority Business Council, 2005.
• Named to *Asian Enterprise Magazine*'s 10 Best Companies for Asian/Pacific Americans, 2005, 2004, 2003, 2001 and 2000.

PNC Financial Services Group, Inc.

249 Fifth Avenue
Pittsburgh, PA 15222
Phone: (412) 762-2000

Locations

Pittsburgh, PA (HQ)
Philadelphia, PA
Cincinnati, OH
Washington, DC
Delaware
New Jersey

Diversity Leadership

Davie S. Huddleston
VP, Manager, Strategic Talent Acquisition

Employment Contact

Brian A. Rider, PHR, AVP
Manager, University Relations
249 Fifth Avenue
Pittsburgh, PA 15222
Phone: (412) 762-0288
Fax: (412) 768-2819
E-mail: brian.rider@pnc.com
www.pnc.com/careers

Recruiting

Please list the schools/types of schools at which you recruit.

• Public state schools
• Historically Black Colleges and Universities (HBCUs)

Do you have any special outreach efforts directed to encourage minority students to consider your firm?

• *Conferences:* Lead sponsor of the Minorities in Pittsburgh conference
• Participate in/host minority student job fair(s)
• Sponsor minority student association events
• Firm's employees participate on career panels at schools
• Outreach to leadership of minority student organizations
• Scholarships or intern/fellowships for minority students

What activities does the firm undertake to attract minority and women employees?

• Partner programs with women and minority associations
• Conferences
• Participate at minority job fairs
• Seek referrals from other employees
• Utilize online job services

Do you use executive recruiting/search firms to seek to identify new diversity hires?

Yes.

PNC uses a broad range of executive recruiting/search firms to identify talent in the marketplace. We generally request diverse slates of candidates from both majority and minority/women-owned firms, and have worked specifically with diversity practice groups at some of the larger firms over time.

Internships and Co-ops

PNC Internship Program

Deadline for application: No formal deadline although the majority of our recruiting is conducted in the fall semester

Number of interns in the program in summer 2005 (internship) or 2005 (co-op): 56

Pay: 2005 ranges from $11.50-$16.50 per hour

Length of the program: 10-12 weeks

Percentage of interns/co-ops in the program who receive offers of full-time employment: Percent is based on those eligible for hire

Web site for internship/co-op information: www.pnc.com/careers/collegerecruiting.html

The PNC Internship Program is a 10- to 12-week internship experience that provides meaningful work assignments and professional development exposure to senior and executive level management and exposure to the host city. Candidates should have a finance and/or accounting background, 3.2 GPA minimum, relevant work and/or past internship experience, preferably in a banking or financial services environment, and be involved on their campus in student-focused organizations/activities, preferably in a leadership role.

Scholarships

PNC Fellows

Deadline for application for the scholarship program: Typically mid-summer (late July)

Scholarship award amount: Ranges from $1,000-$5,000 for undergraduates

The PNC Fellowship was initiated to help diversify our workforce by identifying and recruiting top students of color. Eligible students must maintain a high academic standing, be involved within their community and campus environment and be in good standing with INROADS (if the candidate is an INROADS intern).

Affinity Groups

PNC convened four Employee Resource Groups (ERGs) aimed at giving a voice to specific segments of our employee population. Initial target audiences were managerial and professional-level African-Americans and senior-level women in Philadelphia and Pittsburgh. These groups were charged with recommending specific business objectives, including identifying ways to increase employee and community engagement and business development in their target demographic group.

PNC's Employee Resource Groups are, by design, not networks or affinity groups. Typically, networks or affinity groups are broad cross-sections of particular demographic groups that convene primarily to address employee satisfaction issues. Many diversity efforts have seen these groups devolve into social clubs that sponsor member-focused social events and relevant cultural days. They often do not reach their full potential to be catalysts for change within an organization due to a lack of strategic focus.

The ERGs at PNC, however, are positioned as strategic bodies with clear business objectives. They meet on company time to discuss the issues, often engaging in very candid dialogue. Members are provided with access to a broad range of information to help them formulate their recommendations.

The Employee Resource Groups are small, each consisting of about 15 high-performing employees, and are sponsored by members of the executive team. PNC's chairman and CEO, Jim Rohr, and his executive team are committed to championing their recommendations. Five senior-level employees serve as sponsors for the four ERGs (one of the four groups is co-sponsored). Their active involvement with the groups not only demonstrates support, but also ensures that the ERG maintains a strategic focus.

Vision statements for the groups follow:

African-American Employee Resource Group

The African-American ERG is a catalyst that causes PNC to become an inclusive organization known for its diverse workforce and as a preferred place to work and bank for the African-American community.

Senior-Level Women Employee Resource Group

The Senior Women ERG impacts PNC's culture in a way that results in a significant number of diverse senior women holding and being actively considered for line and staff executive roles.

Strategic Plan and Diversity Leadership

Diversity is one of PNC's corporate values, and thus is an integral part of communications within the organization. Specific messages about diversity and its importance in the organization are communicated via "push" e-mail messages to the employee base (ex. Black History Month kick-off message), via our Intranet and Internet sites, in corporate publications (including electronic and print), and as a part of other verbal communications.

Who has primary responsibility for leading diversity initiatives at your firm?

Kathleen C. D'Appolonia, senior vice president, manager, corporate recruitment and employee inclusion, and Kenneth E. Spruill, Jr., vice president, manager, diversity strategies

Does your firm currently have a diversity committee?

No.

Though PNC does not currently have a "diversity committee" in its traditional format (i.e., a diversity council), PNC's Employee Resource Groups (mentioned above) provide a great deal of insight into diversity-related matters for the organization. Some of PNC's business units have started more traditional diversity councils at the business level.

Does the committee and/or diversity leader establish and set goals or objectives consistent with management's priorities?

Yes.

Has the firm undertaken a formal or informal diversity program or set of initiatives aimed at increasing the diversity of the firm?

Yes, formal.

How often does the firm's management review the firm's diversity progress/results?

Quarterly.

How is the firm's diversity committee and/or firm management held accountable for achieving results?

Diversity results are built into PNC's performance management process, and are a component of all employees' performance.

The Stats

Employees

2005: 21,437
2004: 21,335

Revenue

2005: $1.3 billion
2004: $1.2 billion

Retention and Professional Development

How do 2005 minority and female attrition rates generally compare to those experienced in the prior year period?

About the same as in prior years.

Please identify the specific steps you are taking to reduce the attrition rate of minority and women employees.

• Develop and/or support internal employee affinity groups (e.g., minority or women networks within the firm)
• Increase/review compensation relative to competition
• Increase/improve current work/life programs
• Succession plan includes emphasis on diversity
• Work with minority and women employees to develop career advancement plans
• Strengthen mentoring program for all employees, including minorities and women
• Professional skills development program, including minority and women employees

Diversity Mission Statement

PNC's corporate value of diversity is defined as follows:

We recognize the critical value of our differences and of our individual and collective strengths and skills.

Additional Information

PNC has been a proud supporter of INROADS and the local INROADS/Pittsburgh-Erie chapter. Through corporate representation in the INROADS Leadership Development Institute (LDI) regional conferences as well as significant financial support of LDI regional conferences held in Pittsburgh in 2001, 2004, 2005 and upcoming in 2006, PNC has been recognized by INROADS as a "Corporate Plus" recipient for "true commitment to the INROADS mission." By supporting the social and developmental events during LDI, the 2005 LDI was among the highest rated LDI experiences in the country. Each year, PNC has been recognized by INROADS nationally for its support both financially and in people-hours for planning, organizing and facilitating throughout the year.

PPG Industries

One PPG Place
Pittsburgh, PA 15272
Phone: (412) 434-3131

Locations
Pittsburgh, PA (HQ)

Diversity Leadership
Laura Randall
Manager, Diversity

Employment Contact
John Coyne
Manager, Corporate Recruiting
Phone: (412) 434-2015
Fax: (412) 434-2011
E-mail: jpcoyne@ppg.com
www.ppg.com

Recruiting

Please list the schools/types of schools at which you recruit.

• Ivy League schools
• Other private schools
• Public state schools
• *Historically Black Colleges and Universities (HBCUs):* Hampton, NC A&T, Florida A&M
• *Hispanic Serving Institutions (HSIs):* University of Houston, Texas A&M

Do you have any special outreach efforts directed to encourage minority students to consider your firm?

• Hold a reception for minority students
• Conferences
• Advertise in minority student association publication(s)
• Participate in/host minority student job fair(s)
• Sponsor minority student association events
• Firm's employees participate on career panels at schools
• Outreach to leadership of minority student organizations
• Scholarships or intern/fellowships for minority students

What activities does the firm undertake to attract minority and women employees?

• Partner programs with women and minority associations
• Conferences
• Participate at minority job fairs
• Seek referrals from other employees
• Utilize online job services

Do you use executive recruiting/search firms to seek to identify new diversity hires?

Yes.

Internships and Co-ops

We have internship programs in the engineering, chemistry, finance, IT and marketing departments each summer. Pay varies by position and we attempt to offer full-time employment if there is a fit and we have jobs.

Scholarships

We have a scholarship program available for each school at which we recruit.

Entry-Level Programs/Full-Time Opportunities/Training Programs

We hire full-time graduates in various disciplines, technical and business. They are placed across the U.S. and have a variety of training programs.

Strategic Plan and Diversity Leadership

Who has primary responsibility for leading diversity initiatives at your firm?

Laura Randall.

Does your firm currently have a diversity committee?

Yes.

If yes, please describe how the committee is structured, how often it meets, etc.

The committee meets four times a year and has all levels of employees on the committee.

If yes, does the committee's representation include one or more members of the firm's management/executive committee (or the equivalent)?

Yes.

Total Executives on Committee: Eight

Does the committee and/or diversity leader establish and set goals or objectives consistent with management's priorities?

Yes.

Has the firm undertaken a formal or informal diversity program or set of initiatives aimed at increasing the diversity of the firm?

Yes, formal.

How often does the firm's management review the firm's diversity progress/results?

Quarterly.

How is the firm's diversity committee and/or firm management held accountable for achieving results?

Reports to CEO and board of directors.

The Stats

Total Employees

2005: $10.20 billion
2004: 32,000

Total Revenue

2005: 30,800
2004: $8.5 billion

Retention and Professional Development

How do 2005 minority and female attrition rates generally compare to those experienced in the prior year period?

Lower than in prior years.

Please identify the specific steps you are taking to reduce the attrition rate of minority and women employees.

• Develop and/or support internal employee affinity groups (e.g., minority or women networks within the firm)
• Increase/improve current work/life programs
• Adopt dispute resolution process
• Succession plan includes emphasis on diversity
• Work with minority and women employees to develop career advancement plans
• Strengthen mentoring program for all employees, including minorities and women
• Professional skills development program, including minority and women employees

Like you, we have some distinctive characteristics of our own.*

For the fifth year in a row, PricewaterhouseCoopers was voted the #1 ideal employer in our profession in the Universum Undergraduate Survey of business students.

visit pwc.com/lookhere

*connectedthinking

PRICEWATERHOUSE COOPERS

PricewaterhouseCoopers LLP

300 Madison Avenue
New York, NY 10017
Phone: (646) 471-4000
Fax: (646) 471-3188

Locations

PricewaterhouseCoopers LLP is a network
of professional service firms located in
144 countries.

Diversity Leadership

Rod Adams
Director of Diversity Recruiting
www.pwc.com/bringit

Recruiting

Please list the schools/types of schools at which you recruit.

- *Private and Public schools:* PwC actively recruits at over 200 private and public colleges and universities.
- *Historically Black Colleges and Universities (HBCUs):* Howard University, Florida A&University, Hampton University, North Carolina A&T University, Atlanta University Center
- *Hispanic Serving Institutions (HSIs):* Florida International University

Do you have any special outreach efforts directed to encourage minority students to consider your firm?

- Hold a reception for minority students
- Advertise in minority student association publication(s)
- Participate in/host minority student job fair(s) and conferences
- Sponsor minority student association events
- Firm's employees participate on career panels at schoools
- Scholarships or intern/fellowships for minority students
- Partner with universities to offer H.S. programs to promote accounting awareness

What activities does the firm undertake to attract minority and women employees?

- Partner programs with women and minority associations
- *Conferences:* Association of Latino Professionals in Finance and Accounting Annual Conference, National Association of Black Accountants Annual Convention, National Black MBA Association Annual Convention, National Society of Hispanic MBAs Annual Conference, *Working Mother* magazine, WorkLife Congress, National Association of Black Accountants Regional Student Conferences, National Hispanic Business Association, National Asian American Society of Accountants
- Offer minority scholarship/leadership/internship program - eXceed
- Platinum Sponsor of the Monster Diversity Leadership Program
- Seek referrals from other employees
- Utilize online job services
- Advertise in National Publications (*DiversityInc.*, *Black Collegian*, etc.)

Internships

INROADS

Deadline for application: Need to apply during fall semester or early spring semester (winter quarter)
Number of interns in the program in summer 2005 (internship): 219
Pay: Varies
Length of the program: Eight to10 weeks
Percentage of interns in the program who receive offers of full-time employment: 85 percent
Web site for internship/co-op information: www.pwc.com/bringit

In our eight to 10 week (may extend longer) summer program PricewaterhouseCoopers LLP interns get a taste of what it's like to work here full-time. It is an internship involving multi-dimensional, integrated learning coupled with a practical paid work experience. Interns attend orientation, offsite training and receive a laptop computer for the duration of their internship. All internships include social events and community service activities.

Rising freshman, sophomores and juniors are assigned to work in an internal firm services (IFS) group - human resources/recruiting, marketing, learning and education (may require travel), finance, diversity and work life, meeting and event services, information technology and/or sales and business development. They will receive exposure to client service through shadow days, mentor assignments, training and workshops.

Rising seniors will function in a client service role in assurance, tax or advisory. They will have responsibilities similar to a first year associate on client engagement. They will be a part of a team of business advisors, serving diverse clients and developing optimal strategies for those clients. Interns will help advise our clients on solutions to the issues facing them and as a member of a client service team, they'll help offer clients a thorough understanding of current and emerging issues and the underlying business concerns. Interns will be challenged to think, stimulated to grow and encouraged to contribute. If successful, interns will receive a full time offer.

Leadership Programs

Deadline for application: Need to apply during fall semester or early spring semester (winter quarter)
Pay: None
Length of the program: Three to five days
Web site for internship/co-op information: www.pwc.com/bringit

Multi-event innovative programs inspiring teamwork and leadership development, geared to bridge the gap between academic education and initial intern assignments

Events may include:

• Client shadowing
• Etiquette dinners
• Social activities

Scholarships

eXceed

Deadline for application for the scholarship program: Application process runs from September through December
Scholarship award amount: $ 3,000
Web site or other contact information for scholarship: www.pwc.com/exceed

For PwC, diversity is a business imperative that will help it sustain its position as the U.S. professional services firm. Since 1990, PwC has awarded scholarships to some of the best and brightest African-American, Hispanic/Latino and Native American students in the U.S. Our scholarship program includes:

• A $3,000 scholarship
• An invitation to our annual Diversity in Business Leadership Conference
• A winter or summer internship with PricewaterhouseCoopers

Qualifications:

• Freshman or sophomore
• Overall GPA of 3.2 or higher
• An academic and career interest in accounting, management information systems and/or computer science

Affinity Groups

Networking Circles

At PricewaterhouseCoopers LLP, we are committed to creating an inclusive culture where everyone can succeed in achieving their professional and personal goals. We recognize that networks are critical to career success. Networks provide access to information and new business leads, as well as support and guidance in achieving career goals. Research shows that exclusion from informal networks and limited access to mentors can be barriers to advancement. A key goal of our affinity group circles is to provide that connection.

Circle members receive valuable career advice, expand skills, increase their knowledge of the firm's businesses and share best practices—all within a community of talented women and our diverse staff. Circle members meet regularly to exchange ideas, analyze developmental issues and receive feedback and guidance as a group. They also advise and mentor each other as relationships develop.

Circle Goals:

• To ignite and empower women and our diverse staff to achieve their personal and professional ambitions
• To provide a sense of community and connectivity
• To create opportunities for networking and visibility
• To present opportunities for professional and personal development, and
• To provide role models and a mentoring environment

The following Circles in PwC offices around the country:

• Women's Networking Circles
• Parenting Circles
• Diversity Circles
• GLBT Circles

Entry-Level Programs/Full-Time Opportunities/Training Programs

At PricewaterhouseCoopers LLP, you'll learn on the job, with your clients and in formal training programs. No matter where you are in your career, you will find the accelerated learning and coaching experiences you need to be successful. PwC invests over $130 million in training, offers over 750 courses for ongoing learning, and provides over 800,000 hours in training per year. We offer distinctive training programs as well as a number of self-study programs to further develop your skills and expand your knowledge base through a wide range of programs and resources that can be tailored to your needs.

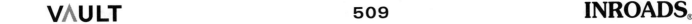

Signature Training Programs for Assurance, Advisory, and Tax

Signature programs are comprehensive, engaging, residential programs that are offered during advancement milestones or at annual or biannual industry or line of service conferences. These programs are opportunities for you to learn valuable skills, network with colleagues and interact with leadership directly. Below are some examples of signature programs.

Go Audit: A program for first-year associates in PwC's assurance line of service around a group learning experience, Go Audit is a dynamic, two-week introduction to the way we work on audit engagements at PwC. Your team will face a variety of tasks that challenge you to demonstrate an understanding of audit and business processes, incorporating technology and critical thinking skills as a team. The program is delivered nationally at central training locations, allowing you to begin to build the professional peer network that will serve you well throughout your career.

Advisory University: This annual premier learning event for the advisory line of service brings together all advisory client service professionals across the country and several international attendees, from members of the global leadership and senior U.S. partners to associates and analysts. In addition to a full curriculum that includes both technical and professional development courses instructed by internal and external experts, this week-long event provides everyone, from entry-level staff through partner, the opportunity to listen to leadership and obtain an understanding of the firm's strategy and goals, to acquire new relevant skills and knowledge, and to build and develop relationships across the practice.

Tax Associate Series and Tax Select: Instructor-led courses, ranging from three to ten days in length, form the cornerstone of development for tax associates in a wide variety of tax technical, professional and business skills areas. Tax associates receive in-depth technical training from both internal and external experts in the taxation of corporations, pass-through entities, individuals, international transactions and multi-state transactions, supplemented with project management and relationship management skills training designed to accelerate their development into world-class business and tax advisors. Senior associates attend the annual tax select program, featuring the latest strategies, available products and services and technical developments in taxation, along with a wide array of professional skills development opportunities. Over 100 courses are offered, empowering them to take control of their professional development with a plan tailored specifically to their individual needs and interests.

Educational Support Plan

The PwC Educational Support Plan provides staff with educational support of up to $5,250 per calendar year. The program is designed to provide staff the opportunity to further their education through pursuit of a degree and/or to improve their skills by pursuing educational courses that are directly related to their current position.

Strategic Plan and Diversity Leadership

How does the firm's leadership communicate the importance of diversity to everyone at the firm?

The U.S. firm's senior partner communicates the importance of diversity in his "Weekly Wrap" e-mail communication to our partners and his bi-monthly "Staff Update" e-mail to all employees. In addition our chief diversity officer hosts web casts, goes office-to-office for town hall meetings and communicates through e-mails.

Who has primary responsibility for leading diversity initiatives at your firm?

Chris Simmons, chief diversity officer and member of the U.S. Leadership Team.

Does your firm currently have a diversity committee?

Yes.

If yes, please describe how the committee is structured, how often it meets, etc.

Our office of diversity is comprised of the following:

• Chief diversity officer
• Director of minority retention and advancement
• Director of women's retention and advancement
• Director of gender initiatives and dependent care

- Director of diversity for firmwide people initiatives
- Director of Diversity Sourcing
- Director of diversity metrics/EEO/AA
- Diversity communications leader
- Gender initiatives/dependent care manager
- Four partner diversity champions in each of our lines of service
- 14 local diversity leaders in our larger markets

The national team of the office of diversity has weekly calls, and the entire team has bi-weekly calls to share updates, best practices and discuss strategic issues.

Has the firm undertaken a formal or informal diversity program or set of initiatives aimed at increasing the diversity of the firm?

Yes, formal. PricewaterhouseCoopers LLP is committed to creating an inclusive workplace where everyone can succeed in achieving his or her professional and personal goals. An inclusive workplace enables us to embrace the diversity and richness of backgrounds and perspectives of our people and to leverage their diverse talents to arrive at winning business solutions.

At PricewaterhouseCoopers, we believe the term "diversity" incorporates all the characteristics that make us both alike and unique: our backgrounds, cultures, nationalities, lifestyles, identities, points of view, approaches to solving problems, ways of working, and views of personal and career success. Our commitment to creating an inclusive work environment that leverages this diversity is a business imperative tied directly to our bottom line and the sustainability of our organization's success. We view inclusion as encompassing work/life flexibility and diversity. An inclusive workplace is fundamental to our business—it enhances overall business performance through global market understanding, attracting and retaining the best talent and serving clients through the most effective solutions.

PricewaterhouseCoopers continues to demonstrate its commitment to making its workplace inclusive through:

- Its chief diversity officer reporting directly to the chairman of the firm and being part of the firm's core executive leadership team
- Its office of diversity under the leadership of the chief diversity officer includes local diversity managers in 14 of the firm's major markets
- Diversity partner champions appointed in each of the firm's four lines of businesses
- National and local initiatives to recruit retain and advance our best diverse talent
- A flexible work environment to respond in the most agile way to the demands of a client service business while providing our partners and staff with the control and influence over their own quality of life
- Incorporating inclusion, diversity and work/life values and practices as priorities in our people strategy
- Mentoring and networking initiatives to increase leadership opportunities for women and minorities
- Learning and education opportunities for leaders, managers and staff to better manage diversity and inclusion

PricewaterhouseCoopers' diversity programs are an integral component of its strategy to identify and remove barriers to our people achieving high performance. It enhances fairness and equal employment opportunity for minorities, women, individuals with disabilities, and covered veterans by ensuring that these groups have equal access to PricewaterhouseCoopers' employment opportunities.

We also believe that our people are more productive at work when they have the flexibility to successfully manage their lives outside of work. Flexibility is an individual's ability, over time, to meet the demands of his or her role and accomplish the things he or she identifies as priorities outside the office. Our senior leadership's goal is to create a flexible work environment where we can respond in the most agile way to the demands of a client service business while providing our partners and staff with control over their own quality of life.

We have created or expanded many of our work/life programs and initiatives to specifically address work/life flexibility for our people. Examples of these efforts include:

- Generous vacation and time off benefits-ranking first in our industry and third among large Fortune 100 "Best Companies"
- Extended holiday time off, when business needs allow. In FY '06 this included five and a half days off over the 2005 July 4th holiday and 10 consecutive days off between December 24th and January 2nd.

• A wide range of flexible work arrangements
• An employee assistance program
• Child care and elder care resource and referral services
• National child care center discounts
• Backup child care centers in many of our major markets
• Generous emergency dependent care reimbursement program
• Adoption leave and generous adoption financial assistance
• Generous parental leave for men and women
• A dependent care expense account
• Mom's lactation program (also for partners/wives of PwC partners and staff)

The Stats

Employees

2005 Number of partners and staff: More than 130,000

Revenue

2005: $20.3 billion

Retention and Professional Development

Please identify the specific steps you are taking to reduce the attrition rate of minority and women employees.

• Develop and/or support internal employee affinity groups (e.g., minority or women networks within the firm)
• Increase/improve current work/life programs
• Succession plan includes emphasis on diversity
• Work with minority and women employees to develop career advancement plans
• Review work assignments and hours billed to key client matters to ensure proportional representation on top client engagements
• Strengthen mentoring program for all employees, including minorities and women
• Professional skills development program for all employees, including minority and women employees

Additional Information

We believe an inclusive workplace enables us to take advantage of the talent of our diverse workforce to improve the quality of our services and grow our business.

—Dennis Nally, U.S. chairman

Diversity is about attracting and retaining top talent. It's about building a great place to work for all our people.

—Chris Simmons, chief diversity officer

In a period of time when many organizations may have reduced their budgets, our leadership has made significant investments in our diversity effort by providing diversity leadership in each of our lines of service and supporting our diversity strategy locally with diversity leaders in 14 of our major markets. Our diversity leaders serve as change agents on the ground that collaborate with office managing partners and HR leaders to develop locally customized strategies to promote inclusion and dedicate all of their time and attention to developing diverse leaders, improving minority retention and increasing work/life quality for all our staff.

Our story is one of commitment—from the chairman's office that sets national policy to the local offices where our client teams are on the ground working with our diversity leaders. We are committed to building a culture of equity and fairness, of integrity and excellence in everything we do. We demand the best of our people and they, in turn, demand the best from us. They demand that we demonstrate a visible commitment to diversity not just policy statements and programs, but tangibly though the actions of their leadership and peers—and visibly by the results.

We are very proud of our diverse workforce, our leadership position in the profession and the quality service we deliver to clients. Half of our new hires—and of our total PwC population—are women. And this year, 28 percent of our new partners were women, an increase of seven percent over the prior year. People of color represent one quarter of our new hires and our client service staff. We have been recognized externally for our commitment and actions, including:

• Named one of *Fortune* magazine's "100 Best Companies to Work For" two consecutive years in 2005 and 2006.
• Named one of the "Top 10 Companies for Working Mothers" by *Working Mother* magazine in 2005 the 10th consecutive year we were on the Top 100 list and the third time we've been recognized as a Top 10 company.
• Ranked #6 in *DiversityInc.'s* list of Top 50 Best Companies for Diversity in 2006.
• Named one of the "Best Companies for Women of Color" by *Working Mother* magazine in 2005.
• Ranked #1 in the 2005 Universum Business Student Survey. And our recruiting web site ranked #1 ahead of Microsoft, Google, Disney and others.
• Ranked #2 on *The Black Collegian Magazine*'s list of The Top 100 Employers of the Class of 2004.
• Ranked #13 in *Training* magazine's list of Top 100 Companies in 2005.
• The #1 employer of INROADS interns in 2005.

We acknowledge that it is a journey, yet we are strengthened knowing that diversity is now imbedded in everything we do as a firm—from recruiting to coaching and developing, from succession planning to winning clients. We know that the success of our firm depends entirely upon our people—and we can't afford not to invest in each and every one.

Procter & Gamble

One Procter & Gamble Plaza
Cincinnati, OH 45202
Phone: (513) 983-1100

Locations

Cincinatti, OH (HQ)
180 countries
Main offices (international):
Brussels, Belgium
Caracas, Venezuela
Geneva, Switzerland
Guangzhou, China
Kobe, Japan
Mexico City, Mexico
San Juan, Puerto Rico

Diversity Leadership

Jorge Rivera
Manager, Diversity Recruiting

Employment Contact

Shaun Howard
Recruiting Specialist
2 P&G Plaza
Cincinnati, OH 45202
Phone: (513) 983-1100
E-mail: howard.sd.1@pg.com
pgjobs.pg.com

Recruiting

Please list the schools/types of schools at which you recruit.

• Ivy League schools
• Other private schools
• Public state schools
• Historically Black Colleges and Universities (HBCUs)
• Hispanic Serving Institutions (HSIs)
• Native American Tribal Universities
• Other predominantly minority and/or women's colleges

Do you have any special outreach efforts directed to encourage minority students to consider your firm?

• Hold a reception for minority students
• Conferences
• Advertise in minority student association publication(s)
• Participate in/host minority student job fair(s)
• Sponsor minority student association events
• Firm's employees participate on career panels at schools
• Outreach to leadership of minority student organizations
• Scholarships or intern/fellowships for minority students

What activities does the firm undertake to attract minority and women employees?

• Partner programs with women and minority associations
• *Conferences:* NSHBMA, SHPE, NSBE, NBMBAA, SWE, AISES, NAAAP, ADI, CGSM, COSD, NHBA
• Participate at minority job fairs
• Seek referrals from other employees
• Utilize online job services

Do you use executive recruiting/search firms to seek to identify new diversity hires?

Yes.

If yes, list all women- and/or minority-owned executive search/recruiting firms to which the firm paid a fee for placement services in the past 12 months:

HACU.

Internships and Co-ops

Corporate Internship Program/Includes INROADS

Deadline for application: Varies by discipline

Length of the program: 12 weeks

Percentage of interns/co-ops in the program who receive offers of full-time employment: 80 percent

Web site for internship/co-op information: pgjobs.pg.com

Qualifications for this program differ by function and department.

Careers in Business Initiatives

Deadline for application: May 1

Number of interns in the program in summer 2005 (internship) or 2005 (co-op): 25

Length of the program: Eight weeks

Qualifications for this program differ by function and department.

Scholarships

The P&G Fund

Deadline for application for the scholarship program: Varies

Web site or other contact information for scholarship: pg.com

Affinity Groups

• Hispanic (H) Leadership Team
• African-American (AA) Leadership Team
• Asian or Pacific American (APA) Leadership Team
• Native American (NAI) Leadership Team

Each leadership team within P&G focuses on mentorship, recruiting, retention and development and meets once a month.

Other affinity groups within Procter & Gamble:

• H Advertising Team
• AA Advertising Team
• APA Marketing Market Knowledge Team
• AA IT Team
• Multicultural Multinational Team
• APA IT team

• AA F&A Team
• APA F&A Team
• H F&A Team

Strategic Plan and Diversity Leadership

How does the firm's leadership communicate the importance of diversity to everyone at the firm?

The firm's leadership committee communicates diversity initiatives via e-mails, the P&G web site, newsletters, meetings and presentations.

Who has primary responsibility for leading diversity initiatives at your firm?

Every employee at P&G owns diversity.

Does your firm currently have a diversity committee?

Yes.

If yes, does the committee's representation include one or more members of the firm's management/executive committee (or the equivalent)?

Yes.

Does the committee and/or diversity leader establish and set goals or objectives consistent with management's priorities?

Yes.

How often does the firm's management review the firm's diversity progress/results?

Quarterly.

The Stats

Employees
2005: 110,000
2004: 100,000

Revenue
2005: $56.7 billion
2004: $58 billion

Retention and Professional Development

How do 2005 minority and female attrition rates generally compare to those experienced in the prior year period?

Lower than in prior years.

Please identify the specific steps you are taking to reduce the attrition rate of minority and women employees.

• Develop and/or support internal employee affinity groups (e.g., minority or women networks within the firm)
• Increase/review compensation relative to competition

- Increase/improve current work/life programs
- Adopt dispute resolution process
- Work with minority and women employees to develop career advancement plans
- Strengthen mentoring program for all employees, including minorities and women
- Professional skills development program, including minority and women employees

Progress Energy

410 S. Wilmington St.
Raleigh, NC 27601-1748
www.progress-energy.com

Locations

Florida
North Carolina
South Carolina

Employment Contact

Christie Hill
College Recruiter
410 S. Wilmington Street; PEB 20 REC
Raleigh, NC 27601
Phone: (919) 546-6490
Fax: (919) 546-7784
E-mail: Christie.hill@pgnmail.com

Recruiting

Please list the schools/types of schools at which you recruit.

• Public state schools
• Historically Black Colleges and Universities (HBCUs)
• Native American Tribal Universities
• Other predominantly minority and/or women's colleges

Do you have any special outreach efforts directed to encourage minority students to consider your firm?

• Advertise in minority student association publication(s)
• Participate in/host minority student job fair(s)
• Sponsor minority student association events
• Firm's employees participate on career panels at schools
• Outreach to leadership of minority student organizations
• Scholarships or intern/fellowships for minority students

What activities does the firm undertake to attract minority and women employees?

• Partner programs with women and minority associations
• Participate at minority job fairs
• Seek referrals from other employees
• Utilize online job services
• *Other*: Advertise in minority publications

Strategic Plan and Diversity Leadership

How does the firm's leadership communicate the importance of diversity to everyone at the firm?

Via diversity councils, the diversity web site and internal communications.

Who has primary responsibility for leading diversity initiatives at your firm?

We have a centralized Corporate Diversity and Inclusion Office. Other key organizations include: a supplier diversity organization, a recruiting organization that is responsible for diversity recruiting and corporate communications.

Does your firm currently have a diversity committee?

Yes—both corporate and business unit level committees.

If yes, does the committee's representation include one or more members of the firm's management/executive committee (or the equivalent)?

Yes, the CEO leads the Corporate Diversity Council and the business unit executives lead their respective business unit diversity councils.

Does the committee and/or diversity leader establish and set goals or objectives consistent with management's priorities?

Yes, diversity initiatives are aligned with corporate diversity and inclusion strategies and initiatives and they are also customized for specific business needs.

How often does the firm's management review the firm's diversity progress/results?

Monthly and quarterly.

How is the firm's diversity committee and/or firm management held accountable for achieving results?

Monthly discussions at our senior leaders meeting and a quarterly diversity scorecard.

Retention and Professional Development

Please identify the specific steps you are taking to reduce the attrition rate of minority and women employees.

• Develop and/or support internal employee affinity groups
• Increase/review compensation relative to competition
• Increase/improve current work/life programs
• Succession plan includes emphasis on diversity
• Work with minority and women employees to develop career advancement plans
• Professional skills development program, including minority and women employees

Diversity Mission Statement

Diversity at Progress Energy is more than a way to profitability. It's a way of life. Beyond simply hiring the best people into the right jobs—regardless of race, sex or creed—we have taken the goals of diversity many steps farther. In fact, few companies can match our ability to blend unique knowledge, individual interpretations, singular experiences and personal points of view across a broad workforce. Our diversity energizes our thinking, making us more flexible. It is the fuel that sparks true innovation and opens the door to new ideas. We believe in developing in our people the power to embrace and ultimately leverage their differences to attain heights impossible to reach individually.

Treat Others the way you would like to be treated.

A corporate strategy anyone can understand.

It's worked for Protective for almost one hundred years. Offer great products at highly competitive prices and provide the kind of attentive, personal service we'd hope to get from others. Sound too simple? Maybe, but it's helped us become one of the fastest growing companies in the life insurance industry. Isn't it reassuring to know that, "Doing the right thing is smart business"?

Doing the right thing is smart business.^{SM}

www.Protective.com

Life Insurance • Annuities • Retirement Savings • Asset Protection Products

Protective Life Corporation, P.O. Box 2606, Birmingham, AL, 35202
PLC-1002 (8-02)

Protective Life Corporation

2801 Highway 280 South
Birmingham, AL 35223
Phone: (205) 268-1000
Toll Free: (800) 866-3555

Locations

Alabama • Arizona • California •
Connecticut • Florida • Georgia • Indiana
• Illinois • Kansas • Louisiana •
Massachusetts • Maryland • Michigan •
Minnesota • Missouri • Mississippi •
North Carolina • Nebraska • Nevada •
Ohio • Oregon • Pennsylvania • Rhode
Island • South Carolina • Tennessee •
Texas • Virginia • Washington •
Wisconsin

Employment Contact

Darcell Streeter
Manager of Opportunity
2801 Hwy 280 South
Birmingham, AL 35223
Phone: (205) 268-3801
Fax: (205) 268-7202
E-mail: darcell.streeter@protective.com
www.protective.com

Recruiting

Please list the schools/types of schools at which you recruit.

• Private schools
• Public state schools
• Historically Black Colleges and Universities (HBCUs)

Do you have any special outreach efforts directed to encourage minority students to consider your firm?

• Advertise in minority student association publication(s)
• Participate in/host minority student job fair(s)
• Scholarships or intern/fellowships for minority students

Internships and Co-ops

Bridges—building the future of Protective

Length of the program: summer program: 10-12 weeks

Entry-Level Programs/Full-time Opportunities/Training Programs

Managing Inclusion (managers), Exploring Inclusion (individual contributors/non-managers), on-line learning and knowledge builders

Length of programs: Four hours, three hours, two hours, and one and a half hours
Geographic location(s) of program: All offices

This program will provide managers and others with the right tools to put the full range of people in demanding positions where they acquire skills and knowledge that will make them indispensable assets to the high-value economy.

Strategic Plan and Diversity Leadership

How does the firm's leadership communicate the importance of diversity to everyone at the firm?

The firm communicates diversity initiatives via training, focus groups, workshop, employee communication, e-mails, roundtables, etc.

Who has primary responsibility for leading diversity initiatives at your firm?

Opportunity council, managed by Darcell Streeter.

Does your firm currently have a diversity committee?

Yes.

If yes, please describe how the committee is structured, how often it meets, etc.

The opportunity council meets monthly. The purpose of the council is to facilitate and complement Protective Life's commitment to inclusion and opportunity, provide recommendations for achieving wholesale inclusion at Protective Life and identify barriers to Protective Life's quest to become a complete meritocracy.

If yes, does the committee's representation include one or more members of the firm's management/executive committee (or the equivalent)?

Yes. The council spent a total of about 300 hours in the furtherance of our initiative in 2004. There are seven members at the VP level or above, two directors, two individual contributors, and the program manager. Each member represents a business unit or a major division within a business unit.

Does the committee and/or diversity leader establish and set goals or objectives consistent with management's priorities?

Yes.

Has the firm undertaken a formal or informal diversity program or set of initiatives aimed at increasing the diversity of the firm?

Yes, formal.

How often does the firm's management review the firm's diversity progress/results?

Quarterly.

How is the firm's diversity committee and/or firm management held accountable for achieving results?

Evaluations, an employee feedback survey, exit interviews, training, personal development plans and inclusion goals.

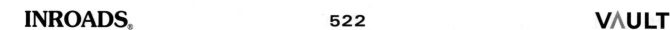

Diversity Mission Statement

Our mission is to promote an environment in which all employees are recognized and appreciated for their unique talents and contributions, encouraged and motivated to perform at their full potential and rewarded for outstanding performance. We are committed to Protective people having an equal opportunity for growth and development by ensuring that no barriers, real or perceived, exist. By upholding these principles we drive our company's ultimate business objective—to serve others by providing quality products, superior financial results and a merit-based work setting.

Additional Information

Guidance on Opportunity at Protective

At Protective, we are firmly committed to providing equal opportunity to all individuals, regardless of a person's gender, race, age, national origin, religion, sexual orientation or other matters not relevant to job performance or career advancement. We want our company to be a meritocracy, a place where talent, hard work, good results and commitment to our values are appreciated and rewarded. This commitment to a merit-based workplace is consistent with our values and critically important to our future success.

If our company is to be a place where all employees have an equal opportunity to reach their potential as employees and human beings, Protective people must believe that they have an equal opportunity to advance. If they do not, a barrier to this goal will exist, even if equal opportunity does in fact exist. We want to make sure that no such barrier, real or perceived, exists at Protective.

One of our company's core values is growth. By growth, we mean not only growth of our company, but also the personal growth and development of Protective people within the company. As our company grows, we must also make sure that we give all Protective people the opportunity for career and personal growth.

Another of our values is serving people. To fulfill this value, we must recognize that people see the world in many different ways and that our success as a company depends upon our ability to respond to the needs of the many different types of people we serve as customers. Thus, the fact that we have a varied and diverse employee group supports our commitment to serving people and can be a competitive advantage to the extent we derive from our people the capacity to better understand the diverse needs and points of view of our customers.

This is not to say that we favor advancing a less qualified individual over a more qualified individual. Rather, it is to say that we must create an environment in which all employees will be appreciated for their unique talents and contributions, encouraged to perform at their full potential and rewarded for doing the best job possible of satisfying the needs of the diverse customer base that we serve.

To reach our full potential as a company, we must have a highly motivated, loyal and talented workforce. We simply cannot afford to lose any talented employee because of any factor not related to job performance. We want to be the employer of choice for the best and the brightest of the people available for employment wherever we do business.

For these reasons, we encourage and embrace variety and diversity in the workplace at all levels of this company. Adherence to these principles is the right thing to do, and it is clearly smart business.

PSEG

80 Park Plaza, T21D Newark, NJ 07102 Phone: (609) 278-4248 Fax: (973) 623-5389 www.pseg.com **Locations** **New Jersey (HQ)** New York Connecticut	**Employment Contact** Chandra Ledford Recruiter & Outreach Specialist E-mail: chandra.ledford@pseg.com

Recruiting

Please list the schools/types of schools at which you recruit.

• Ivy League schools
• Other private schools
• Public state schools
• Historically Black Colleges and Universities (HBCUs)

Do you have any special outreach efforts directed to encourage minority students to consider your firm?

• *Conferences:* Society of Hispanic Professional Engineers Region IV Conference (s); Thurgood Marshall Scholarship Fund Leadership Conference
• Advertise in minority student association publication(s)

What activities does the firm undertake to attract minority and women employees?

• Conferences. See above
• Participate at minority job fairs
• Utilize online job services

Internships and Co-ops

Generation Engineer Program (three year program)

Deadline for application: Summer/fall of each year

This program is for college graduates, not students, but the company interviews students during their senior year of school.

The successful candidate will be hired into an entry-level engineering position as a generation engineer. The new generation engineer will be involved in a three-year training and development program within the PSEG Fossil, LLC organization. During this period, the generation engineer will be assigned to various power plant locations, with subsequent other rotational assignments, along with a variety of leadership development sessions and technical training. This broad experience will aid in developing the generation engineer's skills and knowledge of PSEG Fossil, LLC and PSEG Power, LLC.

The station assignments will allow the generation engineer to understand the operation and maintenance activities associated with a power generating station through participation in selected operating and maintenance type activities. During this period, shift-work is required and overtime compensation is offered. Other assignments will enable the engineer to understand the various roles and responsibilities of the support organizations and the services they provide to the generating stations. Throughout the three-year development period, there will be opportunities to participate in specific leadership development programs, as well as other special training.

We are looking for college graduates with:

BS degrees primarily in: Electrical engineering (EE), mechanical engineering (ME), civil engineering (CE), and chemical/environmental engineering with a GPA of 3.0 or higher. We are looking for individuals who are interested in a career at a major energy company in power generation, which includes engineering, operations and maintenance applications. A valid driver's license is also required.

PSEG Management Associate Program-MAP

This program is a three-year Rotational Development Program.

As part of the Management Associate Program (MAP), successful candidates will participate in a three-year management development program, designed to prepare recent college graduates for future decision-making roles within the enterprise. MAP associates rotate typically every nine to 12 months through various organizations to gain high-level exposure in strategic financial and operational areas of the company.

Rotational assignments have included the following areas:

- Corporate finance
- Financial risk management
- Energy trading
- Mergers and acquisitions
- Internal audit
- Accounting
- Human resources
- Marketing
- Customer services (supervisory role)
- Treasury services

New areas for rotational assignments are continuously being explored.

Program participants are required to begin to pursue an MBA on a part time basis before the last year in the program. PSEG offers generous tuition reimbursement.

Qualified candidates must be pursuing a bachelor's degree with a business major or have relevant intern/work experience. A minimum GPA of 3.25 is required. A GPA of 3.5 or higher is desired. Candidates must be authorized to work in the United States for the full length of the three-year program.

Successful applicants must be knowledgeable in core business disciplines such as accounting, economics, finance, marketing and management.

Candidates must have proven leadership potential, strong interpersonal skills and balanced quantitative and qualitative skills.

Affinity Groups

Adelante

Vision

To cultivate an environment where Hispanics/Latinos are recognized and represented at all levels throughout PSEG.

Mission

• To be a resource for PSEG employees at all levels who want to gain a greater understanding of, or contribute to, the Hispanic/Latino experience and perspective
• To communicate the collective needs of PSEG Hispanic/Latino employees and the Hispanic/Latino community
• To help PSEG leadership increase its awareness of the intellectual and technological capital provided by Hispanics/Latinos that support the successful performance and achievement of Adelante and PSEG goals

Black Data Processing Associates

The New Jersey chapter of Black Data Processing Associates (NJ BDPA) was originally established in 1981 and was known as Northern New Jersey, one of the premier chapters of the National BDPA. Chapter membership rose to over 125 members and eventually experienced a decline that resulted in the chapter becoming inactive in 1998.

NJ BDPA proudly stands with over 40 active chapters of the National BDPA, which was founded in 1975, in Philadelphia and is currently headquartered in Washington D.C. In the tradition of the national organization, NJ BDPA is a nonprofit, member-focused organization that exists to provide professional development programs and services to position its members at the forefront of the information technology industry.

NJ BDPA offers monthly program meetings featuring special guest speakers who share their knowledge and professional experiences.

American Association of Blacks in Energy (AABE)

Established over 20 years ago, AABE is a nonprofit national organization comprised of energy professionals dedicated to ensuring the input of minorities in the discussion and development of energy policies, regulations, R&D technologies, entrepreneurship opportunities and environmental issues in the United States. Today, there are 32 chapters in six geographic regions in the United States.

For more information on AABE, visit the AABE web site.

Minority Interchange (MI)

Minority Interchange (MI) is a not-for-profit corporation that provides a forum for the development and nurturing of leadership ability and the promotion of career-enhancing skills and techniques. This goal is accomplished through education, employment and networking opportunities. MI is run entirely by volunteers and membership is open to everyone. MI's tone is upbeat, motivational and inspirational. To learn more about the Minority Interchange, please visit their national web site: www.mi-hq.org.

Women's Network

The PSEG Women's Network is an informal group that meets at lunchtime about eight times a year, with speakers from inside and outside of the company. Their mission is to be a forum to provide professional women at PSEG with career development insight and skills to aid in their success in both job satisfaction and advancement, as well as providing an environment that will foster collaborative mentoring and support.

Strategic Plan and Diversity Leadership

Does your firm currently have a diversity committee?

Yes.

If yes, please describe how the committee is structured, how often it meets, etc.

Structured as follows: EOG diversity steering committee; PSEG enterprise diversity council; business area councils

If yes, does the committee's representation include one or more members of the firm's management/executive committee (or the equivalent)?

Yes.

Retention and Professional Development

Please identify the specific steps you are taking to reduce the attrition rate of minority and women employees

• Develop and/or support internal employee affinity groups (e.g., minority or women networks within the firm)
• Increase/improve current work/life programs
• Strengthen mentoring program for all employees, including minorities and women
• Professional skills development program, including minority and women employees

Diversity Mission Statement

PSEG Diversity Vision

PSEG strives to be a company that truly values diversity and where all associates support each other, customers and vendors in ways that allow their unique characteristics to become enablers of, rather than barriers to, corporate success and shareholder value.

Diversity is a value that is demonstrated through mutual respect and appreciation of the similarities and differences (such as age, culture, education, ethnicity, experience, gender, race, religion, sexual orientation, etc.) that make people unique. An environment where diversity is respected is one where—as individuals and united as members of teams—we can effectively apply all of our talents, skills and experiences in pursuit of achieving business objectives.

PSEG Diversity Commitment

• Foster strong leadership, dedication and support
• Attract and recruit from a diverse pool of candidates; focus on identifying and leveraging the most effective sources for qualified talent
• Create and sustain a respectful and inclusive environment and culture, to support retention of a diverse workforce
• Align diversity with human resources practices, including leadership development and training; integrate with business planning and operations
• Assure representation of the diversity of the company in internal and external communications

Pulte Homes Inc.

100 Bloomfield Hills Parkway
Bloomfield Hills, MI 48304
Phone: (248) 644-7300
www.Pulte.com

Additional Information

In the summer of 1950, 18-year-old Bill Pulte built and sold his first home in Detroit, Michigan. It was the inception of today's Pulte Homes Inc., the largest, most diversified homebuilder in the United States, with revenues exceeding $14.7 billion in 2005. Today, Pulte Homes has expanded across 27 states and constructed more than 450,000 homes, with experience that ranges from luxury homes to urban in-fill projects to active adult communities and virtually everything in between. The Pulte Homes family of brands includes:

• Pulte Homes—traditional homebuilding operations from entry-level homes to million dollar homes to urban communities
• Del Webb—the nation's leading brand of active adult communities
• DiVosta Homes—one of Florida's leading and most recognized home brands

At Pulte, we view diversity as a business priority, it is critical to our success. Innovation is one of our core business strategies, so leveraging diversity just makes sense! We believe in the value of each other's differences and in treating one another fairly and with respect and dignity. We are working hard to ensure that our future workforce reflects the diversity of our customers, partners, trade contractors, stockholders and the communities around the nation that have embraced our beautiful homes and neighborhoods. We need the insight, creativity and perspectives that a range of diverse employees can bring to the table in order to become a stronger, smarter and more innovative company.

As our workforce continues to evolve to reflect the growing diversity of our communities, our ability to understand, value and incorporate differences becomes increasingly important. Diversity, like any other part of our long-term business plan, requires focus and resolve. Our commitment starts at the top and filters through every geographic area. A few of the things that we're doing to maintain diversity in our culture: diversity training, outreach and scholarship programs and web-based communications.

Pulte is proud to sponsor our employee-run Diversity Council and Women's Leadership Council to ensure that everyone in our organization visibly encourages and values the contributions and differences of employees from various backgrounds. Key objectives of both councils include:

• Creating a more inclusive environment for all employees

• Heightening and increasing employee and management awareness

• Increasing representation of women and diverse employees at all levels of the organization through focused training, development, mentoring and retention plans

• Increasing our capabilities and results in recruiting diverse employees into our workforce

At Pulte, our employees may all look different, but they share one thing in common: an unbridled passion for what we do…we deliver the homes that people dream of!

If you are excited about opportunities at Pulte Homes, we want to talk to you! Please visit us at www.pulte.com.

QUALCOMM Incorporated

5775 Morehouse Drive
San Diego, CA 92121
Phone: (858) 587-1121
Fax: (858) 658-2100

Locations

San Diego, CA (HQ)
20 locations in the US and 40 offices
internationally.

Employment Contact
Lee Wills-Irvine
Diversity Staffing Manager
5775 Morehouse Drive
San Diego, CA 92121
Phone: (858) 658-3641
Fax: (858) 658-2102
E-mail: lwi@qualcomm.com
https://jobs.qualcomm.com

Recruiting

Please list the schools/types of schools at which you recruit.

- *Other private schools:* Stanford, MIT, University of Southern California
- *Public state schools:* UC Berkeley, Georgia Tech, UC San Diego, UCLA, San Diego State University, University of Illinois, University of Texas, University of Waterloo, North Carolina State, University of Michigan, University of Colorado, Virginia Tech
- *Historically Black Colleges and Universities (HBCUs):* Atlanta University Center Schools
- *Hispanic Serving Institutions (HSIs):* University of Texas and San Diego State University

Do you have any special outreach efforts directed to encourage minority students to consider your firm?

- Hold a reception for minority students
- *Conferences:* National Black MBA Association National Conference, National Society of Black Engineer National Conference, National Society of Hispanic MBAs, Society of Hispanic Professional Engineers National Conference, Society of Women Engineers National Conference, MESA- Math Engineering and Science Achievement Annual Conference hosted on-site with three different Universities- SDSU, UCSD and one Junior College;
- Advertise in minority student association publication(s)
- Participate in/host minority student job fair(s)
- Sponsor minority student association events
- Firm's employees participate on career panels at schools
- Outreach to leadership of minority student organizations
- Scholarships or intern/fellowships for minority students
- We offer financial support through scholarships
- We are a GEMS organization
- We host on-site recruiting events for minority students

What activities does the firm undertake to attract minority and women employees?

- Partner programs with women and minority associations
- *Conferences:* National Black MBA Association National Conference, National Society of Black Engineer National Conference, National Society of Hispanic MBAs, Society of Hispanic Professional Engineers National Conference, Society of Women Engineers National Conference, WITI Conference, Black Engineer of the Year Conference, Association of Latino Professionals in Finance and Accounting Conference, National Urban League Conference
- *Participate at minority job fairs:* NSBE Career Fair, SHPE Career Fair, SWE Career Fair, WITI Career Fair, NBMBA career fair and Urban League Career Fair.

• Seek referrals from other employees
• Utilize online job services

Do you use executive recruiting/search firms to seek to identify new diversity hires?

Yes.

If yes, list all women- and/or minority-owned executive search/recruiting firms to which the firm paid a fee for placement services in the past 12 months:

We do not provide firm information which may be construed as an endorsement.

Internships and Co-ops

QUALCOMM Internship Program

> *Deadline for application:* No deadline—internships are ongoing
> *Number of interns in the program in summer 2005 (internship) or 2005 (co-op):* Approximately 300
> *Pay:* Our interns are paid competitively based on their year in school
> *Length of the program:* Internships typically last three to six months
> *Percentage of interns/co-ops in the program who receive offers of full-time employment:* 70 percent
> *Web site for internship/co-op information:* https://jobs.qualcomm.com/college/

QUALCOMM accepts resumes from students at the bachelor's, master's and PhD levels for internships. Preference is given to junior class standing or higher with a minimum GPA of 3.0.

Most of our openings are in the areas of hardware, software, systems and test engineering for technical majors in:

• Computer engineering
• Computer science
• Electrical engineering

We have a limited number of business openings for majors in:

• Accounting
• Finance
• Information technology

Scholarships

"Q" Award of Excellence

> *Deadline for application for the scholarship program:* Awards are usually granted each school year in the second semester or term
> *Scholarship award amount:* Generally three awards are made per school with a scholarship amount of $3,000
> https://jobs.qualcomm.com/diversity/scholarships

The QUALCOMM "Q" Awards of Excellence are scholarships given to student members of professional engineering organizations, such as:

• American Indian Science and Engineering Society (AISES)
• National Society of Black Engineers (NSBE)
• San Diego MESA Alliance (SDMA)
• Society of Latino Engineers and Scientists (SOLES)
• Society of Hispanic Professional Engineers (SHPE)

• Society of Women Engineers (SWE)

Qualifications:

• Applicants must be full-time students with a declared major in computer science, computer engineering or electrical engineering.
• Students must be currently enrolled, in good standing, and have a minimum cumulative GPA of 3.25/4.0.
• The current year's fall term grades are factored into the award decision.
• Generally three awards are made per school with a scholarship amount of $5,000

Eligible schools include:

• Atlanta University Center
• Georgia Tech
• Massachusetts Institute of Technology
• North Carolina State University
• San Diego State University
• Stanford University
• University of California, Berkeley
• University of California, San Diego
• University of California, Los Angeles
• University of Cincinnati
• University of Michigan
• University of Southern California

If you meet the above criteria, you may apply directly to QUALCOMM or through your school's Minority Engineering Program or similar type of office.

Affinity Groups

QUALCOMM strongly believes in fostering its diverse environment through its involvement with internal and external organizations. We regularly offer our facilities and resources to host organization meetings and events such as:

• Society of Hispanic Professional Engineers (SHPE)
• San Diego Industry Liaison Group (SDILG)
• Association of Iranian American Professionals in San Diego (AIAP)
• AFROAM—QUALCOMM African-American employee group
• Society of Women Engineers (SWE)
• National Black Society of Engineers
• Asian Business Association
• San Diego Black MBA Association
• LAMBDA Pride—Gay/Lesbian/Bisexual employee group
• Indian Cultural Club

SHPE—Society of Hispanic Engineers

SHPE was created in 1994 to provide Qualcomm management and Hispanic employees with a link to the community. SHPE was selected as a parent organization because it has a national agenda that bridges corporations, universities, colleges, K-12 schools, and the local communities.

AFROAM—QUALCOMM

AFROAM-QUALCOMM started as an internal mailing list created for the dissemination of information by and for African-American employees at QUALCOMM, Incorporated. The mailing list has grown from an information outlet to an organization that has sponsored several special events here at QUALCOMM celebrating diversity and ethnicity.

Mission Statement: AFROAM's mission is to contribute to the success of QUALCOMM by recruiting qualified candidates, encouraging employees to further develop professional skills and cultural awareness, and promoting education and communication technologies in our communities.

LAMBDA—Gay, Lesbian, Bisexual Group

The group meets to socialize, celebrate and support each other through social gatherings, participation in community events, and daily conversation on our own internal mailing lists.

QSWE, QUALCOMM Society of Women Engineers

QSWE is a network of women engineers who collaborate with the San Diego chapter of the Society of Women Engineers to facilitate professional development programs and community outreach to encourage young women to enter the field of engineering.

Entry-Level Programs/Full-Time Opportunities/Training Programs

Management Skills Training Program

Length of program: Four days
Geographic location(s) of program: San Diego

Designed to develop and enhance competencies as a manager, this program offers a valuable opportunity to add to management skills. Attendees will study key management topics. Through interactive discussions with other QUALCOMM managers, attendees will acquire new ideas, thoughts and suggestions which will improve your ability to handle your daily management challenges.

QUALCOMM also offers tuition reimbursement for those who are pursuing job-related courses, or a course of study leading to a job-related degree, and attending an approved university.

Strategic Plan and Diversity Leadership

Who has primary responsibility for leading diversity initiatives at your firm?

We take a cross-functional approach to diversity and inclusion at QUALCOMM and diversity is an important component of our company culture. Lee Wills-Irvine, diversity staffing manager, is the primary contact.

Does your firm currently have a diversity committee?

Yes. The committee meets on a bi-weekly basis to discuss diversity issues related to recruiting, retention and development.

If yes, how many executives are on the committee, and in 2005, what was the total number of hours collectively spent by the committee in furtherance of the firm's diversity initiatives? How many employees are on the committee, and how often does the committee convene in furtherance of the firm's diversity initiatives?

This committee spent approximately 35 hours working collectively on the furtherance of the firm's diversity initiatives in 2005. There are seven people on this committee.

Total Executives on Committee: Two

Does the committee and/or diversity leader establish and set goals or objectives consistent with management's priorities?

Yes.

Has the firm undertaken a formal or informal diversity program or set of initiatives aimed at increasing the diversity of the firm?

QUALCOMM's diversity program is based on business logic—global diversity and inclusion positively impacts our bottom line by increasing revenues, increasing productivity and decreasing costs. We have undertaken many initiatives to increase diversity at QUALCOMM including: community involvement, engaging minority and diversity organizations, as well as QUALCOMM's dedication to furthering math and science in schools and universities through its support of programs such as High Tech High. We also participate in many diversity focused career fairs and attend universities with significant minority populations in our recruitment process.

How often does the firm's management review the firm's diversity progress/results?

Monthly.

The Stats

	TOTAL IN THE U.S.		TOTAL OUTSIDE THE U.S		TOTAL WORLDWIDE	
	2005	2004	2005	2004	2005	2004
Number of employees	7,975	7,000	1,222	1,000	9,197	8,000
Revenue	N/A	N/A	N/A	N/A	$5.67 billion	$4.88 billion

Global diversity and inclusion is evident at QUALCOMM with over 10,000 employees representing more than 100 different countries, speaking more than 60 languages, and ranging in age from 18 to 77 years.

Diversity Mission Statement

Global diversity & inclusion is the catalyst for raising the consciousness about how diversity positively impacts all aspects of our business—employees, customers and communities. At QUALCOMM we foster a global environment with business locations in over 30 countries where our employees from diverse backgrounds are encouraged to build on their individual strengths and contribute to the overall success of the company.

At QUALCOMM, we recognize that business success is driven by creativity and diversity. By valuing our differences and appreciating our similarities, we encourage the exchange of unique ideas and perspectives and build upon our individual, team and business strengths. Our diversity creates an energy that carries our global teams forward in developing new and superior products worldwide. At the heart of global diversity & inclusion is QUALCOMM's commitment to provide all employees, regardless of their backgrounds and perspectives on the world, the opportunity to achieve their personal and professional goals.

Additional Information

We are a communications company that thrives on the ideas and perspective that are evident in a diverse and multinational workforce. Our teams are charged with energy that comes from different backgrounds coming together in a working environment that embraces creativity and open minds. Diversity plays an integral role in our global viewpoint and provides an atmosphere that fosters the kind of free flow of ideas that has made us a technology leader. By communicating with people from diverse backgrounds and groups all over the world, we engage in a dialogue that drives the wireless communication's industry.

Our value of global diversity and inclusion is reflected in our employees, corporate culture, programs and activities throughout the world. We take this philosophy into our communities where we live and work by supporting initiatives that further opportunities for education, cultural enrichment and community needs. An active employee volunteer program fosters understanding by partnering with local community activities in a wide variety of opportunities. We also recognize the importance of future generations and launched what we call the NEXT Generation Workforce Initiative to increase minority and women representation in the engineering, computer science, information technology and related fields.

Qwest Communications International Inc.

1801 California Street
Denver, CO 80202
Phone: (800) 899-7780
www.qwest.com/careers

Internships and Co-ops

Qwest partners with the INROADS organization to provide internships for minority youth across the nation for 20 years. The locations vary each year, as do the number and type of opportunities. For more information regarding INROADS please visit their web site at www.inroads.org.

Affinity Groups

Qwest has a number of employee diversity groups. These groups are comprised of current Qwest employees with a common interest in promoting the Qwest diversity philosophy. Qwest recognizes the following self-governing groups:

• ABTP (Alliance of Black Telecommunications Professionals)
• Qwest Women
• Voice of Many Feathers (Native American)
• SOMOS (Qwest Hispanic Resource Network)
• Qwest Friends (Persons With Disabilities))
• EAGLE (Employee Association for Gays and Lesbians)
• Qwest Veterans
• PAAN (Pacific Asian-American Network)

The focus of these groups includes:

• Act as a resource and/or mentor to their membership
• Provide a unique cultural perspective to Qwest on how to increase market share and improve performance
• Provide a link between Qwest and the diverse communities it serves

Qwest provides each resource group an operating budget, meeting space and an Intranet site for member communications. In addition, each resource group has an annual Qwest Foundation budget of $5,000 to be used for grants to community organizations recommended by the resource groups that meet foundation guidelines. Activities of the resource groups are open to all Qwest employees and are publicized through the company's employee communications channels.

Additional Information

Qwest Communications International Inc. (NYSE: Q) is a leading provider of voice, video and data services. The company's employees are committed to the "Spirit of Service" and providing world-class services that exceed customers' expectations for quality, value and reliability. Whether you're a single household, a small business or a global corporation, from voice to data to video, Qwest has a solution just for you.

Diversity awareness is an important part of Qwest's values and has been incorporated into each management employee's annual objectives. Our business culture promotes mutual respect, acceptance, cooperation and productivity among employees who are diverse in age, color, race, national origin, veteran status, religion, sexual orientation, ethnicity, marital or family status, disability and any other legally protected category.

Our diversity philosophy extends to our customers and states, "At Qwest, we embrace diversity in all aspects of the business. We meet competitive challenges by understanding and valuing all our existing and potential customers and the dedicated employees who meet their needs each day."

At Qwest, we meet competitive challenges by understanding and valuing all our customers and the dedicated employees who meet their needs each day. What makes Qwest's approach to the advancement of diversity in the workplace unique is that it is accomplished within the context of—not at the expense of—the company's overall corporate strategy.

For more information about Qwest please visit our web site qwest.com. If you are interested in career opportunities available at Qwest, please visit our career web site at qwest.com/careers.

RR Donnelley

111 South Wacker Drive
Chicago, IL 60606-4301
Phone: (312) 326-8000
www.rrdonnelley.com

Locations

US:
Bolingbrook, IL • Chicago, IL • New York, NY • Reno, NV
International:
Mississauga, ON, Canada • Santiago, Chile • Shanghai, China • The Netherlands

Employment Contact

Dr. Damayanti Vasudevan
Vice President, Diversity & Inclusion
E-mail: Damayanti.Vasudevan@rrd.com
or e-mail your resume to
rrdonnelley@trm.brassring.com

Recruiting

Please list the schools/types of schools at which you recruit.

- Private schools
- Public state schools
- Historically Black Colleges and Universities (HBCUs)
- Other predominantly minority and/or women's colleges

Do you have any special outreach efforts directed to encourage minority students to consider your firm?

- Advertise in minority student association publication(s)
- Participate in/host minority student job fair(s)
- Firm's employees participate on career panels at schools
- Outreach to leadership of minority student organizations
- Scholarships or intern/fellowships for minority students
- *Other*: Sponsor professional development associations that would target graduate students, such as National Black MBA Association, Executive Leadership Conference

What activities does the firm undertake to attract minority and women employees?

- Partner programs with women and minority associations
- *Conferences:* INROADS, UNCF, Rainbow/PUSH; Executive Leadership Council (mid-level managers) Symposium, Catalyst, Global Summit for Women, Empowering Women Network, National Black MBA Association Conference
- Participate at minority job fairs
- Seek referrals from other employees
- Utilize online job services

Internships and Co-ops

INROADS and UNCF

Deadline for application: Spring
Pay: $1,800-$2,700 per month
Length of program: Eight to 10 weeks

Diversity is a critical factor in RR Donnelley's business success. Through effective recruiting, we have the opportunity to make a significant difference and improve diversity in the organization.

These are the internship programs we partner with in our diversity recruiting efforts:

INROADS (Intern Program)

25 East Washington Avenue, Suite 801
Chicago, IL 60602
Phone: (312) 553-5000
www.inroads.org

The United Negro College Fund (UNCF) Universities
8260 Willow Oaks, Corporate Drive
Fairfax, VA 22031
Phone: (703) 205-3400
www.uncf.org

Scholarships

RR Donnelley contributes scholarship support by sponsoring external organizations like N'DIGO Foundation, UNCF, ELC Foundation and PUSH Excel.

Affinity Groups

RR Donnelley has site and regional active inclusion councils throughout the United States.

Inclusion councils at RR Donnelley strive to be a diverse representation of the employee population. They advocate for and promote an inclusive workforce by implementing programs, activities and education resources that address workplace culture, community partnerships and marketplace relationships.

Entry-Level Programs/Full-Time Opportunities/Training Programs

Corporate Mentoring Program

Length of Program: One to three years
Geographic location(s) of program: Primarily domestic United States

Protégés of the program participate in various development opportunities, including training, personal career management, goal-setting, special projects and mentor assignment.

Strategic Plan and Diversity Leadership

How does the firm's leadership communicate the importance of diversity to everyone at the firm?

RR Donnelley promotes the importance of diversity through efforts of the inclusion councils, external/internal web site, online resource library, e-learning courses, management and sales training, CEO and executive commitment, community relations and supplier diversity program.

Who has primary responsibility for leading diversity initiatives at your firm?

Dr. Damayanti Vasudevan, Vice President, Diversity and Inclusion.

Does your firm currently have a diversity committee?

Yes.

If yes, please describe how the committee is structured, how often it meets, etc.

Conducts a quarterly review of progress, and an annual review of strategy and progress.

If yes, does the committee's representation include one or more members of the firm's management/executive committee (or the equivalent)?

Yes, the CEO, COO, and SVP of HR.

If yes, how many executives are on the committee, and in 2005, what was the total number of hours collectively spent by the committee in furtherance of the firm's diversity initiatives? How many employees are on the committee, and how often does the committee convene in furtherance of the firm's diversity initiatives?

Strategy committee does not have employees. Inclusion councils are sponsored by executives and have employee participation.

Does the committee and/or diversity leader establish and set goals or objectives consistent with management's priorities?

Yes.

Has the firm undertaken a formal or informal diversity program or set of initiatives aimed at increasing the diversity of the firm?

Yes, formal.

How often does the firm's management review the firm's diversity progress/results?

Quarterly.

How is the firm's diversity committee and/or firm management held accountable for achieving results?

RR Donnelley leaders are held accountable through Management By Objective Goals. All employees are held accountable via the performance management competency of "*Promoting Inclusion*."

The Stats

Employees

2005: 35,510 (U.S.)
2004: 32,330 (U.S.)
2005/2004: 50,000+ (worldwide)

Retention and Professional Development

Please identify the specific steps you are taking to reduce the attrition rate of minority and women employees.

- Develop and/or support internal employee affinity groups (e.g., minority or women networks within the firm)
- Increase/review compensation relative to competition
- Increase/improve current work/life programs
- Adopt dispute resolution process
- Succession plan includes emphasis on diversity
- Work with minority and women employees to develop career advancement plans
- Strengthen mentoring program for all employees, including minorities and women
- Professional skills development program, including minority and women employees

Diversity Mission Statement

RR Donnelley will build strong and lasting relationships with diverse partners in the workplace, marketplace and community. We will create a workplace in which behaviors, practices and policies promote respect, inclusion, utilization, career development and success across all forms of diversity.

Additional Information

Diversity and Inclusion at RR Donnelley

To be a successful leader in the 21st century, our business practices must align with the changes in our world. The demographics of our business and workforce partners are changing rapidly, and we must stay ahead of the changes. This means we need to be diligent in ensuring that our workforce and business practices reflect the diversity and needs of the customers we serve around the world today and in the future.

Employment

RR Donnelley is building an inclusive workforce, through our employment practices, such as internal and external recruiting, hiring, employee development, evaluation, promotion and retention. This includes opportunities for training, development, recognition and advancement for all employees.

Workplace Quality

RR Donnelley is committed to providing an environment in which everyone can contribute fully, feel valued and respected, and be rewarded for their contributions to the company's goals. RR Donnelley's policy on discrimination is simple: we do not tolerate it. Each of us is responsible for pointing out actions that are inconsistent with our company's values. Through our open door policy, employees are encouraged to bring concerns, issues or complaints to any member of management, with the assurance that they will receive prompt, thorough attention without fear of retaliation. Our managers and supervisors are responsible for investigating complaints and taking prompt and appropriate disciplinary action if these standards are violated.

Every action we take—in everything we do every day—supports our goal of building a better workplace. Our inclusion councils engage employees at all levels to address diversity and inclusion issues and concerns. Our focus on shared responsibility and accountability is essential to our progress in diversity.

Through education and training on diversity and inclusion, we enable cultural change and integration of diverse talent.

Supplier Relationships

RR Donnelley is committed to building relationships with a variety of business partners. Our supplier diversity program has been in place for more than 20 years. We seek out opportunities to conduct business with underutilized organizations, such as minority-owned and female-owned businesses. We strive to identify and develop qualified underutilized suppliers, cultivating relationships with these businesses and monitoring our progress in these areas. In establishing these relationships, RR Donnelley contributes to the economic growth and development of diverse businesses.

Customers

In the dynamic world of business, we know our customers are changing. Our increasingly diverse customers rely on us and our insight and knowledge, to deliver the right solutions at the right time and at the right price. Meeting these expectations is a priority for RR Donnelley. We continually assess our strategies, capabilities, practices and policies to ensure that we can serve all of our customers.

Community Involvement

RR Donnelley strives to be the neighbor of choice. We believe in being a good corporate citizen of society and the communities in which we operate. With programs focused on literacy, youth and families, our company has a long-standing tradition of supporting a wide range or organizations, many of which serve underrepresented and nontraditional groups.

Robert Half International Inc.

2884 Sand Hill Road, Suite 200
Menlo Park, CA 94025

Locations

330 offices throughout the United States, Canada, Europe and Asia/Pacific.

Diversity Leadership

Ranelle Newson
Manager, Diversity Program
2884 Sand Hill Road, Suite 200
Menlo Park, CA 94025
Phone: (925) 598-8475
Fax: (925) 598-8943
E-mail: ranelle.newson@rhi.com
www.rhi.com

Recruiting

Please list the schools/types of schools at which you recruit.

• Ivy League schools
• Other private schools
• Public state schools
• Historically Black Colleges and Universities (HBCUs)
• Hispanic Serving Institutions (HSIs)

Do you have any special outreach efforts directed to encourage minority students to consider your firm?

• *Conferences:* National Association of Black Accountants, Association of Latino Professionals in Finance and Accounting (ALPFA)
• Advertise in minority student association publication(s)
• Participate in/host minority student job fair(s)
• Sponsor minority student association events
• Firm's employees participate on career panels at schools
• Outreach to leadership of minority student organizations
• Scholarships or intern/fellowships for minority students

What activities does the firm undertake to attract minority and women employees?

• Partner programs with women and minority associations
• *Conferences:* National Association of Black Accountants, Association of Latino Professionals in Finance and Accounting (ALPFA), Working Mother Media (Women of Color Conference)
• Participate at minority job fairs
• Seek referrals from other employees
• Utilize online job services
• *Other:* Advertise in key niche publications

Scholarships

RHI provides scholarships through the following organizations: National Association of Black Accountants, American Institute of Certified Public Accountants—Minority Initiatives Program, Association of Latino Professionals in Finance and Accounting (ALPFA), NAACP, National Hispanic University, Hispanic Scholarship Fund and United Negro College Fund.

Entry-Level Programs/Full-Time Opportunities/Training Programs

Robert Half International Inc. makes it a priority to provide its employees with the tools, resources, training and learning opportunities to be successful. New employees participate in a structured series of training programs that combine online learning with hands-on coaching. Training is continued to a wide range of facilitated programs that foster professional growth. To accommodate schedules of employees, RHI's training resources include an extensive library of online, video and audio courses, and a comprehensive electronic university called RHI University. Educational programs are provided for employees at all stages of their careers and the investment in training and development programs continues throughout employees' careers.

Strategic Plan and Diversity Leadership

How does the firm's leadership communicate the importance of diversity to everyone at the firm?

The firm provides diversity training and information is communicated via e-mail messages and meetings.

Who has primary responsibility for leading diversity initiatives at your firm?

Ranelle Newson, manager, diversity program.

Does the committee and/or diversity leader establish and set goals or objectives consistent with management's priorities?

Yes.

Has the firm undertaken a formal or informal diversity program or set of initiatives aimed at increasing the diversity of the firm?

Yes, formal.

How often does the firm's management review the firm's diversity progress/results?

Quarterly.

The Stats

Employees

2005: Approximately 11,000 (worldwide)

Revenue

2005: $3 billion (U.S.)

Diversity Mission Statement

To be the premier provider of specialized staffing services in all markets we serve while adhering to the highest professional standards. This includes identifying, recruiting, retaining and promoting a diverse workforce. We value an environment that respects differences and leveraging these differences allows us to be competitive in an increasingly changing global market. We believe these differences along with an inclusive environment will continue to make Robert Half International Inc. an employer of choice.

Additional Information

RHI is recognized as a leader in the global business community for our commitment to the highest professional standards. As a leader, RHI's diversity strategy goes far beyond simply valuing individual differences or developing human resources policies. Our diversity strategy builds on our strong commitment to ethics first, takes into account the globalization of the world economy and leverages dynamic changes in the demographic characteristics of the population (diversity) in our talent and business markets. We actively recognize these changes as a business and social opportunity to increase productivity and growth and have developed a diversity strategy that will have a positive effect on our business, employees, suppliers, customers, products, and services and thereby position us to gain a competitive advantage. Our strategy incorporates the following major fundamentals for building our business, growing our talent and expanding our markets:

• Maximize our ability to identify, hire, and deploy professional talent
• Support commitment to our company's guiding principles which include "ethics first"
• Contribute to our continued success as a global employer of choice
• Develop new client markets and win market share in new, emerging client communities and markets

Different thinking
makes us great.

Great thinking
makes us different.

For more than 70 years,
Rockwell Collins has been dedicated to
providing innovative and dependable
aviation electronics and comunications
solutions worldwide.

Rockwell
Collins

www.rockwellcollins.com/careers

Rockwell Collins

400 Collins Road NE
Cedar Rapids, IA 52498
Phone: (319) 295-7415
Fax: (319) 295-9347
www.rockwellcollins.com

Locations

105 US locations

Employment Contact

Patty Stephens
Manager, University Relations
E-mail: pjstephe@rockwellcollins.com

Recruiting

Please list the schools/types of schools at which you recruit.

• *Private schools:* Rose Hulman Institute of Technology, LeTourneau University, Embry-Riddle Aeronautical University—Prescott/Daytona campus
• *Public state schools:* Milwaukee School of Engineering, University of Wisconsin—Madison, Iowa State University, University of Iowa, Northern Iowa University, South Dakota School of Mines and Technology, North Dakota State University, University of North Dakota, University of Michigan—Ann Arbor, Michigan Tech University, Texas A&M, University of Illinois—Urbana/Champaign, University of Texas—Austin, University of Texas—Dallas, University of Texas—El Paso, Virginia Tech University, Purdue, Florida Institute of Technology, University of Florida—Gainsville, University of California—Irvine, California Polytechnic University—Pomona, Rensselaer PolyTech
• *Historically Black Colleges and Universities (HBCUs):* North Carolina Agriculture and Technology

Do you have any special outreach efforts directed to encourage minority students to consider your firm?

• Hold a reception for minority students
• *Conferences:* Purdue Diversity weekend/career fair
• Advertise in minority student association publication(s)
• Participate in/host minority student job fair(s)
• Sponsor minority student association events
• Firm's employees participate on career panels at school
• Outreach to leadership of minority student organizations
• Scholarships or intern/fellowships for minority students
• *Other*: K-12 program

What activities does the firm undertake to attract minority and women employees?

• Partner programs with women and minority associations
• *Conferences:* SWE, NSBE, SHPE
• Participate at minority job fairs
• Seek referrals from other employees
• Other: Employee networking groups, minority supplier program, external web presence

Do you use executive recruiting/search firms to seek to identify new diversity hires?

Yes.

Internships and Co-ops

Rockwell Collins Internship and Co-op Program

Deadline for application: Ongoing, request that students apply online at www.rockwellcollins.com/careers

Number of interns in the program in summer 2006 (internship) or 2006 (co-op): 280

Pay: Depends on number of credit hours completed for interns and number of sessions for the co-op program

Length of the program: Intern program: 12 weeks, Co-op Program: three work sessions that rotate with school session and total 12 months of work experience when complete.

Web site for internship/co-op information: www.rockwellcollins.com

Strategic Plan and Diversity Leadership

How does the firm's leadership communicate the importance of diversity to everyone at the firm?

• E-mail communication and leader/employee meetings
• Newsletters
• Videos
• Posters/signage
• Internal web site and external billboards

Who has primary responsibility for leading diversity initiatives at your firm?

Susan Nelson, director, corporate diversity.

Does your firm currently have a diversity committee?

Yes, executive diversity council and diversity advisory council.

If yes, please describe how the committee is structured, how often it meets, etc.

The Executive Diversity Council meets quarterly.

If yes, does the committee's representation include one or more members of the firm's management/executive committee (or the equivalent)?

Yes.

If yes, how many executives are on the committee, and in 2005, what was the total number of hours collectively spent by the committee in furtherance of the firm's diversity initiatives? How many employees are on the committee, and how often does the committee convene in furtherance of the firm's diversity initiatives?

Total hours: 20 meetings

Total Executives on Committee: 11

Does the committee and/or diversity leader establish and set goals or objectives consistent with management's priorities?

Yes.

Has the firm undertaken a formal or informal diversity program or set of initiatives aimed at increasing the diversity of the firm?

Yes, formal.

How often does the firm's management review the firm's diversity progress/results?

Monthly.

How is the firm's diversity committee and/or firm management held accountable for achieving results?

Each business area has a diversity scorecard, including diversity program metrics, that is cadenced on a monthly basis.

The Stats

Employees

17,000 (worldwide)

Retention and Professional Development

Please identify the specific steps you are taking to reduce the attrition rate of minority and women employees.

• Develop and/or support internal employee networking groups
• Increase/review compensation relative to competition
• Increase/improve current work/life programs
• Succession plan includes emphasis on diversity
• Work with minority and women employees to develop career advancement plans
• Strengthen mentoring program for all employees, including minorities and women
• Professional skills development program, including minority and women employees

Diversity Mission Statement

Valuing and leveraging differences to fuel innovations and build a stronger company.

Russell Corporation

3330 Cumberland Suite 800
Atlanta, GA 30339
Phone: (678) 742-8810
Fax: (256) 500-9064
employment@russellcorp.com

Locations

US, Honduras, Mexico, Asia, Japan,
Continental Europe, United Kingdom,
Canada and Australia.

Diversity Leadership

Nina Choudhuri

Employment Contact

Jackie Parker
Director, Diversity
3330 Cumberland Suite 800
Atlanta, GA 30339
Phone: (678) 742-8810
Fax: (256) 500-9064
E-mail: parkerjackie@russellcorp.com

Recruiting

Please list the schools/types of schools at which you recruit.

• Ivy League schools
• Historically Black Colleges and Universities (HBCUs)
• Hispanic Serving Institutions (HSI)

Do you have any special outreach efforts directed to encourage minority students to consider your firm?

• Hold a reception for minority students
• Firm's employees participate on career panels at school
• Scholarships or intern/fellowships for minority students

What activities does the firm undertake to attract minority and women employees?

• Partner programs with women and minority associations
• Participate at minority job fairs
• Seek referrals from other employees

Do you use executive recruiting/search firms to seek to identify new diversity hires?

Yes.

If yes, list all women- and/or minority-owned executive search/recruiting firms to which the firm paid a fee for placement services in the past 12 months:

• Pathfinders, Inc.
• Diversity Search Inc.
• Staff Source
• First Pro
• Ingenium Partners, Inc.

Internships and Co-ops

Although Russell Corporation does not have a formal undergraduate internship program, we have been pleased to provide internship opportunities to both minority and non-minority undergraduate students from a variety of southeastern regional colleges and universities.

> *Number of interns in the program in summer 2005 (internship) or 2005 (co-op):* Four
> *Pay:* Hourly rate paid bi-monthly
> *Length of the program:* Typically 12 weeks
> *Percentage of interns/co-ops in the program who receive offers of full-time employment:* None, as these are full-time students returning to college.

Russell has had the pleasure of hosting summer undergraduate interns in our finance, IT and marketing departments. Students are channeled into appropriate departments based on their vocational interests/majors. They work closely with managers on a day-to-day basis to gain critical hands-on experience in a fast-paced corporate environment.

Affinity Groups

- AHLC (African Heritage Leadership Council)—Atlanta
- AHLC (African Heritage Leadership Council)—Alexander City
- RLAHN (Russell Latin American Heritage Network)—Atlanta
- RWLN (Russell Women's Leadership Network)—Atlanta
- RWLN (Russell Women's Leadership Network)—Alexander City

The objective of the employee networks is to assist the company in identifying opportunities and issues that uniquely exist within these segments of the Russell employee population. They meet monthly on company time to address and manage these issues. Their main goals are focused against four pillars: workplace, workforce, community and marketplace strategies.

Strategic Plan and Diversity Leadership

How does the firm's leadership communicate the importance of diversity to everyone at the firm?

Communication is done through monthly operating meetings, newsletters, e-mails and the company web site.

Who has primary responsibility for leading diversity initiatives at your firm?

Kevin Clayton, VP of diversity and Jackie Parker, director of diversity.

Does your firm currently have a diversity committee?

Yes.

If yes, please describe how the committee is structured, how often it meets, etc.

The team is comprised of Russell's most senior managers who meet on a quarterly basis. The purpose of the team is to remove barriers that may get in the way of the organization's diversity vision/goals.

If yes, does the committee's representation include one or more members of the firm's management/executive committee (or the equivalent)?

Yes.

Does the committee and/or diversity leader establish and set goals or objectives consistent with management's priorities?

Yes.

Has the firm undertaken a formal or informal diversity program or set of initiatives aimed at increasing the diversity of the firm?

Yes, formal.

• To create awareness and confirm diversity as a business imperative.
• To increase the representation of women and minorities in mid to senior level professional and management positions.
• To integrate diversity into the talent management initiative and processes.
• To increase the use of women and minority owned enterprises as suppliers of products and services to SunTrust.
• To create management accountability for diversity.

How often does the firm's management review the firm's diversity progress/results?

Monthly.

How is the firm's diversity committee and/or firm management held accountable for achieving results?

All bonus eligible employees' compensation is tied to a diversity scorecard.

The Stats

Employees

2005/2004 Number of employees worldwide: Approximately. 14,000

Revenue

2005/2004: Approximately $1.3 billion

2005/2004 STATS				
ASIAN AMERICAN	ASIAN INDIAN	BLACK	HISPANIC	WHITE
.06%	.01%	36.5%	7.8%	55%
MALE			FEMALE	
49.4%			50.6%	

Retention and Professional Development

How do 2005 minority and female attrition rates generally compare to those experienced in the prior year period?

About the same as in prior years.

Please identify the specific steps you are taking to reduce the attrition rate of minority and women employees.

• Develop and/or support internal employee affinity groups (e.g., minority or women networks within the firm)
• Increase/review compensation relative to competition
• Succession plan includes emphasis on diversity
• Work with minority and women employees to develop career advancement plans

Diversity Mission Statement

To create a fair and equitable culture in which every member of the Global Russell Team reinforces our values and contributes to achieving our business goals.

Additional Information

Russell also has a strong workplace diversity initiative with a goal of creating an environment where each employee is respected and valued, a place where people can celebrate his or her similarities and his or her differences. In today's competitive global marketplace, Russell feels its greatest strength is its people and that it needs all employees willing and able to contribute to move the company forward. Our focus areas are:

- **Workforce:** To attract and retain superior talent
- **Workplace:** To foster an empowering culture that respects both differences and similarities
- **Marketplace:** To leverage our diversity and to capitalize on unique revenue opportunities
- **Communities:** To support the communities where we live and operate

Ryder System, Inc.

11690 NW 105th Street
Miami, FL 33178
Phone: (305) 500-4049
Fax: (305) 500-5758

Locations

Argentina • Australia• Brazil• Canada•
Chile • China• Germany• Ireland• Mexico•
Poland• Singapore• The Netherlands• UK

Diversity Leadership

Gerri Rocker
Group Director, Corporate Diversity and
Work/Life Planning

Employment Contact

Gerri Rocker
Group Director, Corporate Diversity and
Work/Life Planning
E-mail: grocker@ryder.com
www.ryder.com/jobbank/employment.jsp

Recruiting

Please list the schools/types of schools at which you recruit.

• *Other private schools:* Duke University, Georgia Institute of Technology, Rochester Institute of Technology, University of Miami, University of North Carolina, University of Virginia, University of Chicago
• *Public state schools:* Texas A & M University, Purdue, University of Florida, Florida Atlantic University, Florida International University, Florida A&M, University of Michigan, Florida State University

Do you have any special outreach efforts directed to encourage minority students to consider your firm?

• *Conferences:* National Society of Hispanic MBAs (NSHMBA), Black MBAs (NBMBA), LaRaza, National Urban League, National Association of Black Accountants
• *Participate in/host minority student job fair(s):* University of Miami Martin Luther King Jr. Job Fair and Florida A&M University Job Fair

What activities does the firm undertake to attract minority and women employees?

• Partner programs with women and minority associations
• *Conferences:* NSHMBA, NBMA, LaRaza, National Urban League
• Participate at minority job fairs University of Miami MLK Job Fair and Florida A&M University
• Seek referrals from other employees
• Utilize online job services
• Other: Affinity group referrals

Do you use executive recruiting/search firms to seek to identify new diversity hires?

No, we encourage the search firms to provide diverse slates of candidates.

Internships and Co-ops

INROADS

Deadline for application: February 2006
Number of interns in the program in summer 2005 (internship) or 2005 (co-op): Two co-op participants
Pay: $1,500 per student, entire program
Length of the program (in weeks): Eight

Scholarships

Ryder Rental Master Scholarship

Deadline for application for the scholarship program: December 31, 2006
Scholarship award amount: 1st place, $6,000; 2nd place, $4,000; 3rd place, $3,000; entire scholarship
Web site or other contact information for scholarship:
Ryder System, Inc.
c/o Marketing Department
11690 NW 105th Street
Miami, FL 33178-1103

Qualifications:

• Applicants must be a full-time or part-time Ryder employee
• Applicants must be enrolled or have been accepted as a student in an accredited post-high school institution of higher learning (junior college, university, technical and/or trade school)
• Full-time employees must be enrolled in no fewer than two classes, or the equivalent of six credit hours
• Part-time employees must be enrolled in no fewer than three classes, or the equivalent of nine credit hours
• A minimum GPA of 3.0 on a 4.0 scale, 4.0 on a 5.0 scales, or the cumulative equivalent of a "B" is required for consideration

Ryder Roundtable Scholarship

Deadline for application for the scholarship program: December 31, 2006
Scholarship award amount: 1st place, $10,000; 2nd place, $7,500; 3rd and 4th place, $5,000; 5th place, $2,500; entire scholarship
Web site or other contact information for scholarship:
Ryder System, Inc.
c/o Marketing Department
11690 NW 105th Street
Miami, FL 33178-1103

Qualifications:

• All applicants must be a member of the immediate family of a full-time Ryder employee who has been employed by Ryder for at least one year, a retired Ryder employee or of a deceased Ryder employee
• Applicants must be enrolled or have been accepted as a student in an accredited post-high school institution of higher learning (junior college, university, technical and/or trade school)

Ryder Team Excellence Scholarship

Deadline for application for the scholarship program: December 31, 2006
Scholarship award amount: 1st place, $6,000; 2nd place, $4,000; 3rd place, $2,000; entire scholarship

Web site or other contact information for scholarship:
Ryder System, Inc.
c/o Marketing Department
11690 NW 105th Street
Miami, FL 33178-1103

Qualifications:

• All applicants must be a vehicle sales employee or immediate family member/relative of a vehicle sales employee
• Applicants must be enrolled or have been accepted as a student in an accredited post-high school institution of higher learning (junior college, university, technical and/or trade school)

Affinity Groups

• Ryder Black Employee Network
• Ryder Hispanic Network
• Ryder Administrative Professional Association
• Ryder Women's Management Association

The groups are chartered by the company to assist with meeting company goals and objectives and to provide employees with developmental opportunities, networking venues and enhance morale.

Strategic Plan and Diversity Leadership

How does the firm's leadership communicate the importance of diversity to everyone at the firm?

• Mandatory diversity training for all employees
• Business Unit Diversity Scorecard which measures hiring, promotion and retention rates for women and people of color
• Supplier diversity program for WMBE's
• Diversity brochure, "Driven by Differences, Driven by Diversity, Driven by You," spotlighting diversity initiatives and awards used by sales team for RFPs and by staffing group for recruiting events/diversity conferences and external distribution
• Diversity and work/life planning web site: ryder.com/about_us_dwl.shtml
• "Diversity Spotlight," an electronic communication mechanism which provides employees company-wide with informative articles on diversity-related issues in the workplace such as religion, sexual orientation, differing perspectives, etc.
• Multicultural heritage calendar: An annual calendar highlights major holidays/traditions celebrated around the world

Who has primary responsibility for leading diversity initiatives at your firm?

Gerri Rocker, group director, corporate diversity and work/life planning.

Does your firm currently have a diversity committee?

No.

Does the committee and/or diversity leader establish and set goals or objectives consistent with management's priorities?

Yes.

Has the firm undertaken a formal or informal diversity program or set of initiatives aimed at increasing the diversity of the firm?

Yes, formal.

• Identifying target positions for enhanced recruitment of women and people of color
• Requiring a signed Diversity Commitment Letter from all external search firms
• Identifying diverse candidates for upward mobility through succession planning process

• The Inclusion Journey (phase I)—company-wide mandatory training of all Ryder employees, implemented in 1998
• Continuing the Journey—Building an Inclusion Toolkit (phase II)—developed for supervisors/managers to enhance understanding of diversity as a business imperative and the role of leadership in creating an environment that respects and values different perspectives, ideas and experiences. Training will be offered on an "as needed" basis upon requests of function heads and/or human resources managers.

How often does the firm's management review the firm's diversity progress/results?

Quarterly and annually.

How is the firm's diversity committee and/or firm management held accountable for achieving results?

During year-end reviews, managers are held accountable through their performance review. Ratings are specific to business unit.

The Stats

	STATS WORLDWIDE	
	2005	2004
Number of employees	27,800	26,300
Revenue	$5.7 billion	$5.2 billion

	MALE (All Employees)	WOMEN (All Employees)	MINORITIES (All Employees)	WOMEN (Upper Mgmt)	WOMEN (Middle Mgmt)	MINORITIES (Upper Mgmt)	MINORITIES (Middle Mgmt)
2005	84.5%	15.5%	26.4%	13.9%	20.0%	13.4%	19.1%
2004	84.9%	15.1	25.8%	13.1%	20.1%	12.4%	18.5%

Retention and Professional Development

How do 2005 minority and female attrition rates generally compare to those experienced in the prior year period?

About the same as in prior years. See chart for turnover rates.

ATTRITION RATES	WOMEN (PERCENT)	MINORITY (PERCENT)
2005	20.2%	27.8%
2004	20.2%	27.6%

Please identify the specific steps you are taking to reduce the attrition rate of minority and women employees.

• Development of career advancement plans for women and people of color
• Provide opportunity for professional skills development
• Increase/improve current work/life offerings to ensure balance between personal/professional life
• Enhance and/or support internal employee affinity groups

Diversity Mission Statement

Mission

Create a supportive environment which values individual differences and enables all employees to contribute their full potential in pursuit of business objectives.

Corporate philosophy

Ryder's corporate philosophy is based on respect for one another and recognition that each person brings his or her own unique attributes to the corporation. We are committed to providing equal opportunity for all employees to reach their full potential; it is a fundamental value and it makes good business sense.

Additional Information

One of Ryder's goals is to have an environment where all employees can contribute their full potential to helping the company meet its business objectives. Ryder realizes that many of the traditional jobs in the transportation and logistics industry are not ones that readily attract women and people of color. We know that our success is based on the commitment and contribution of all our employees. We are striving to ensure that every employee has the opportunity to fully participate, to grow professionally and to develop to his or her potential. Our diversity initiatives help ensure that we utilize our available pool of talent, develop all employees to their fullest potential and provide the company with a competitive advantage.

Ryder firmly believes it is important for the company to be involved in, and a contributor to, the communities in which it lives and works, and employees are encouraged to be involved in community activities. The company's support—both directly and through the Ryder Charitable Foundation, which is funded by company earnings—is focused in the areas of human needs, culture and education with increasing attention being given in recent years to education.

Our Chairman and Chief Executive Officer Gregory Swienton has made a deep personal diversity commitment, not only to Ryder, but also to our community in general. He says, "The world—and Ryder—is changing so rapidly, that we need to draw on all available resources and talent to remain competitive and ensure success."

Company Policies

• Diversity awareness training: Required company-wide training to heighten awareness of diversity issues and provide employees with the skill set to deal effectively with workplace diversity.
• Flex-time policy: Provide employees with an opportunity to better balance work and family/personal responsibilities.
• Domestic Partner Benefits: Provided to employees whose partners are of the same or opposite sex.

Recognition and Awards

• *Latina Style* Top 50—Recognized Ryder as being among the 50 Best Companies for Hispanic Women to Work
• Hispanic "Corporate 100"—*Hispanic* magazine recognized Ryder for providing the most opportunities for Hispanics in the areas of recruitment, scholarships, minority supplier programs and support for Hispanic organizations
• *Network Magazine*—Recognized Ryder as being among the Top 5 Companies for Black Professionals in south Florida
• Human Rights Campaign—Recognized as equitable of gay, lesbian and transgendered employees
• Red Cross Award—Recognition of charitable and in-kind services in the aftermath of September 11, 2001
• 2001 United Way Campaign—Corporate Globe Setter recognition
• Family Christian Association of America—Black Achievers Youth Sponsor
• 500 Role Models of Excellence Sponsor—Annual Martin Luther King, Jr. Awards Breakfast

Corporate Sponsorships

• National Black and Hispanic MBA Conferences
• National Association of Black Accountants
• Urban Leagues of Greater Miami and Broward County
• National Council of LaRaza Conference
• Florida Regional Minority Purchasing Council

Philanthropic programs:

• The Jackie Robinson Foundation
• The Nat Moore Foundation
• INROADS
• Florida Memorial College
• United Way
• Batten Fellows Program—Black Professional Leadership Program
• Miami-Dade League of Women Voters
• Boy Scouts of America

Ryland Group Inc., The

24025 Park Sorrento Suite 400
Calabasas, CA 91302
Phone: (818) 223-7500
www.ryland.com

Locations

Calabasas, CA (HQ)
Ryland Mortgage:
Scottsdale, AZ
Woodland Hills, CA
Ryland builds in 28 of the nation's top housing markets, including:
North Central:
Austin, TX • Baltimore, MD • Delaware •
Chicago, IL • Cincinnati, OH • Dallas, TX •
Houston, TX • Indianapolis, IN • Minneapolis,
MN • San Antonio, TX • Washington, DC
Southeast:
Atlanta, GA • Charleston, SC • Charlotte, NC
• Myrtle Beach, SC • Fort Myers, FL •
Greensboro, NC • Greenville, SC •
Jacksonville, FL • Orlando, FL • Tampa, FL
West:
Central Valley • Denver, CO • Inland Empire •
Las Vegas, NV • Phoenix, AZ • Sacramento,
CA • San Diego, CA

Employment Contact

Karen Ball
Recruiter
E-mail: campushires@ryland.com

Recruiting

Please list the schools/types of schools at which you recruit.

• Private schools
• Public state schools
• Historically Black Colleges and Universities (HBCUs)
• Hispanic Serving Institutions (HSIs)

Do you have any special outreach efforts directed to encourage minority students to consider your firm?

• Participate in/host minority student job fair(s)
• Firm's employees participate on career panels at schools
• Outreach to leadership of minority student organizations
• Scholarships or intern/fellowships for minority students

What activities does the firm undertake to attract minority and women employees?

• Partner programs with women and minority associations

- Participate at minority job fairs
- Seek referrals from other employees
- Utilize online job services

Entry-Level Programs/Full-Time Opportunities/Training Programs

Ryland Homes Management Training Program and Ryland Mortgage Management Training Program

Length of program: Three years

Ryland's Management Training Programs are company diversity initiatives created to increase the number of women and ethnically diverse employees within our management team. By providing participants with a 360-degree view of the residential construction or mortgage industry, Ryland will create a strong pool of employees from which future leaders can emerge.

Ryland's three years of on-the-job training expose management trainees to all aspects of the residential construction or mortgage industry. Through each rotation, a mentor and performance evaluations will provide on-going guidance and feedback to address a management trainee's needs and interests.

Please visit www.ryland.com/careers for current opportunities and locations.

Strategic Plan and Diversity Leadership

How does the firm's leadership communicate the importance of diversity to everyone at the firm?

The firm communicates diversity initiatives through the Intranet, Internet and company newsletter.

Has the firm undertaken a formal or informal diversity program or set of initiatives aimed at increasing the diversity of the firm?

Yes, formal—for example, through Ryland's two Management Training Programs.

The Stats

	TOTAL (U.S.)	
	2005	2004
Number of employees	3,200	2,829
Revenue	$4.8 billion	$3.9 billion

Safeway, Inc.

5918 Stoneridge Mall Road
Pleasanton, CA 94588
Phone: (925) 467-3536
Fax: (925) 467-3736
www.safeway.com

Diversity Leadership
Kim Farnham
Director, Human Resouces Planning

Employment Contact
Hieu Sweeney
Human Resources Rep.
E-mail: hieu.sweeney@safeway.com

Recruiting

Please list the schools/types of schools at which you recruit.

• Ivy League schools
• Other private schools
• Public state schools
• Historically Black Colleges and Universities (HBCUs)
• Hispanic Serving Institutions (HSIs)

Do you have any special outreach efforts directed to encourage minority students to consider your firm?

• Hold a reception for minority students
• Participate in/host minority student job fair(s)
• Sponsor minority student association events
• Firm's employees participate on career panels at schools
• Outreach to leadership of minority student organizations
• Scholarships or intern/fellowships for minority students

What activities does the firm undertake to attract minority and women employees?

• Partner programs with women and minority associations
• Conferences
• Participate at minority job fairs
• Seek referrals from other employees
• Utilize online job services

Do you use executive recruiting/search firms to seek to identify new diversity hires?

Yes.

Internships and Co-ops

Safeway, Inc. Summer Internship Program

Deadline for application: Open

Number of interns in the program in summer 2005 (internship) or 2005 (co-op): 2005 first year of program

Length of the program: 12 weeks

Percentage of interns/co-ops in the program who receive offers of full-time employment: Not yet tracked

Scholarships

Safeway offers undergraduate scholarships through DECA and graduates scholarships from NSHMBA.

Entry-Level Programs/Full-Time Opportunities/Training Programs

Marketing Trainee Program

Length of program: Three to nine months

Geographic location(s) of program: Pleasanton, Calif.

Three to nine month training program in which trainees will be introduced to marketing functions including pricing, procurement and category management. After the successful completion of the trainee program, you will be placed in one of three areas of marketing.

Strategic Plan and Diversity Leadership

How does the firm's leadership communicate the importance of diversity to everyone at the firm?

Statement from CEO, training, diversity web site on Intranet, diversity library and cultural heritage videos.

Who has primary responsibility for leading diversity initiatives at your firm?

Kim Farnham, director, HR planning.

Does your firm currently have a diversity committee?

Yes. Thirteen diversity advisory boards with over 150 members. One senior level board for all of Safeway, and 12 division boards. Individual advisory boards determine frequency of meetings, ranging from every month to once a quarter.

If yes, does the committee's representation include one or more members of the firm's management/executive committee (or the equivalent)?

Yes.

Does the committee and/or diversity leader establish and set goals or objectives consistent with management's priorities?

Yes.

Has the firm undertaken a formal or informal diversity program or set of initiatives aimed at increasing the diversity of the firm?

Yes, formal.

How often does the firm's management review the firm's diversity progress/results?

Quarterly.

The Stats

	TOTAL IN THE U.S.		TOTAL OUTSIDE THE U.S		TOTAL WORLDWIDE	
	2005	2004	2005	2004	2005	2004
Number of employees	172,905	151,043	32,115	23,453	205,020	174,496
Revenue	$34 million	N/A	$38 million	N/A	$72 million	N/A

MINORITIES	FEMALES	MALES
64,678	80,637	92,016

Retention and Professional Development

Please identify the specific steps you are taking to reduce the attrition rate of minority and women employees.

• Develop and/or support internal employee affinity groups (e.g., minority or women networks within the firm)
• Increase/review compensation relative to competition
• Increase/improve current work/life programs
• Succession plan includes emphasis on diversity
• Work with minority and women employees to develop career advancement plans
• Strengthen mentoring program for all employees, including minorities and women
• Professional skills development program, including minority and women employees

Diversity Mission Statement

Scope

This policy applies to all Safeway employees and applicants.

Policy

At Safeway, the diversity of our employees, customers, and the communities in which we operate is a key ingredient in our success.

• We value and celebrate the diversity of the men and women who make up our workforce
• We respect the personal worth and unique contributions of each individual
• We expect that each of us grant others the same respect, cooperation and fair treatment that we seek for ourselves

Safeway supports equal employment opportunity in hiring, development and advancement for all qualified persons without regard to race, color, religion, age, gender, national origin, ancestry, physical or mental disability, veteran status, sexual orientation, or marital status. Safeway provides reasonable accommodations for applicants and employees with disabilities. We will not tolerate unlawful discrimination in any aspect of employment, nor will we tolerate harassment of any individual or group.

Every officer, manager, supervisor, and employee is expected to support and contribute to an environment that respects and values the diversity of our workforce and ensures the success of Safeway's equal employment opportunity commitment. Employees are encouraged to bring complaints and issues of concern to the company through their management or directly to the human resources department. We take all complaints and concerns seriously, and will handle them promptly.

The principles described in this statement, while founded in state and federal laws, also reflect Safeway traditions and our beliefs that lie at the heart of everything we do.

Schering-Plough Corporation

2000 Galloping Hill Road
Kenilworth, NJ 07033
Phone: (908) 298-4144
Fax: (908) 298-3505

Locations

We have a presence in more than 100 countries in North America, Europe, Asia, Africa, Australia and Latin America.

Diversity Leadership

Sylvester Mendoza
Senior Director Diversity Strategies
2000 Galloping Hill Road
Kenilworth, NJ 07033
Phone: (908) 298-7496
Fax: (908) 298-3505
E-mail: sylvester.mendoza@spcorp.com
www.schering-plough.com/careers

Recruiting

Please list the schools/types of schools at which you recruit.

• Ivy League schools
• Public state schools
• Historically Black Colleges and Universities (HBCUs)
• Hispanic Serving Institutions (HSIs)

Do you have any special outreach efforts directed to encourage minority students to consider your firm?

• Hold receptions for minority students
• Advertise in minority student association publications
• Participate in/host minority student job fairs
• Sponsor minority student association events
• Firm's employees participate on career panels at schools
• Outreach to leadership of minority student organizations
• Provide scholarships or intern/fellowships for minority students

What activities does the firm undertake to attract minority and women employees?

• Partner programs with women and minority associations
• Participate at minority job fairs

Do you use executive recruiting/search firms to seek to identify new diversity hires?

Yes.

Internships and Co-ops

INROADS, Research, Manufacturing and Finance

Deadline for application: February of each year

Pay: Depends on the education major of the intern; weekly pay.

Length of the program: 11 weeks

Percentage of interns/co-ops in the program who receive offers of full-time employment: Five percent

Web site for internship/co-op information: Same as above

Strategic Plan and Diversity Leadership

How does the firm's leadership communicate the importance of diversity to everyone at the firm?

The firm communicates diversity information via the company web site, newsletter and meetings.

Who has primary responsibility for leading diversity initiatives at your firm?

Paul Graves, vice president, global staffing, diversity and public affairs.

Does your firm currently have a diversity committee?

Yes.

Does the committee and/or diversity leader establish and set goals or objectives consistent with management's priorities?

Yes.

Has the firm undertaken a formal or informal diversity program or set of initiatives aimed at increasing the diversity of the firm?

Yes, formal.

How often does the firm's management review the firm's diversity progress/results?

Quarterly.

How is the firm's diversity committee and/or firm management held accountable for achieving results?

Performance evaluation.

The Stats

2005 Employees

13, 086 (U.S.)

18,914 (outside the U.S.)

32,000 (worldwide)

Revenue

2005: $9.5 billion

Women represent 47.5 percent and men represent 52.5 percent of the U.S. population. There are a total of 12 board members. Women represent 16.67 percent and minorities represent 16.67 percent. The management team consists of 35 members. 14.3 percent are women and 8.57 percent are minorities.

Retention and Professional Development

Please identify the specific steps you are taking to reduce the attrition rate of minority and women employees.

- Develop and/or support internal employee network groups (e.g., minority or women networks within the firm)
- Increase/review compensation relative to competition
- Increase/improve current work/life programs
- Work with minority and women employees to develop career advancement plans
- Strengthen coaching program for all employees, including minorities and women
- *Other:* Talent planning includes emphasis on diversity

Shell Oil Company

910 Louisiana
Houston, TX 77002
www.shell.com/careers

Diversity Leadership

Jeff Wallace
Diversity Outreach Administrator

Carmen Wright
Manager, Graduate Recruitment & University Relations

Employment Contact

Julie A. Sacco
Attraction & Branding Consultant

Recruiting

Please list the schools/types of schools at which you recruit.

• Private schools
• Public state schools
• Historically Black Colleges and Universities (HBCUs)
• Hispanic Serving Institutions (HSIs)

Do you have any special outreach efforts directed to encourage minority students to consider your firm?

• Hold a reception for minority students
• Conferences
• Advertise in minority student association publication(s)
• Participate in/host minority student job fair(s)
• Sponsor minority student association events
• Firm's employees participate on career panels at schools
• Outreach to leadership of minority student organizations
• Scholarships or intern/fellowships for minority students

What activities does the firm undertake to attract minority and women employees?

• Partner programs with women and minority associations
• Conferences
• Participate at minority job fairs
• Seek referrals from other employees
• Utilize online job services

Do you use executive recruiting/search firms to seek to identify new diversity hires?

Yes.

Internships and Co-ops

Shell Internship Program

Deadline for application: Year round, best availability October to March
Length of the program: 10 to 12 weeks
Web site for internship/co-op information: www.shell.com/careers

Come and experience working with us

What's working life like at a world-class company? Could Shell be the place to start your career? If you're a talented and promising individual, you could get a taste of working with us during the summer.

A paid internship with Shell gives you real work responsibility and the chance to test your abilities on genuine business challenges.

To ensure that you get the maximum benefit from your experience with us, your internship will be tailored to your specific abilities and interests, and will be certain to provide you with an opportunity to prove yourself in a true business environment. The work experience also gives you the opportunity to find out whether you and Shell are right for each other.

A Great Opportunity

• See inside the energy industry
• Take part in real projects
• Try out business challenges
• Work with Shell employees or other students
• Get feedback from senior Shell managers
• Track the long-term results of your work

Throughout your time with us your performance will be assessed and you will receive structured feedback in order to further develop your skills, knowledge and business acumen.

We have a number of summer internship opportunities available for both technical and commercial students. Most take place during the summer in the U.S. However, as a global organization, there will be always be a number of international opportunities for exceptional candidates.

Scholarships

Shell Oil Company Technical Scholarship

Deadline for application for the scholarship program: December 31st
Scholarship award amount: Undergraduate—$5,000 per year (four year renewable scholarship or until bachelor's degree requirements are completed, whichever occurs first). Technical—$2,500 total—(Payable over a two-year period).

Shell Oil Company offers scholarships to selected students pursuing two-year technical training in process technology or industrial instrumentation or a four-year college degree in engineering or geosciences at certain colleges as described herein. Scholarship recipients will be selected on a competitive basis by a selection committee and will be notified of their award in the early summer after the submission of their application.

To qualify you must:

• Be enrolled in an undergraduate program
• Be a U.S. citizen or a permanent resident of the United States
• Be enrolled full-time and a sophomore, junior or senior in one of the institutions listed here

• Have a minimum 3.2 GPA, which must be maintained throughout your participation in the program
• Major in one of the following disciplines: geology, geophysics or physics, chemical, civil, electrical, mechanical, petroleum, geological or geophysical engineering

Technical Training Program

• Be a U.S. citizen or a permanent resident of the United States
• Be enrolled full-time and have completed at least 12 semester hours in one of the community college technical schools listed here
• Have a minimum 3.0 GPA, which must be maintained throughout your participation in the program
• Major in Process Technology, Industrial Instrumentation or a related field to oil industry

Affinity Groups

• Network Next (Generation X Network)
• SAIL (Society Absent of Individual Limitations)
• SAPENG (Shell Asian Pacific Employee Network Group)
• SBNG (Shell Black Network Group)
• SEA Shell (Support, Equality, & Awareness at Shell)
• SHEN (Shell Hispanic Employee Network)
• Support Equality Awareness
• WAVE (Women Adding Value Everywhere)
• WIN (Women's Information Network)
• SPAAN (Shell Progressive African-American Network)

Strategic Plan and Diversity Leadership

Who has primary responsibility for leading diversity initiatives at your firm?

Director of diversity.

Does your firm currently have a diversity committee?

Yes.

Has the firm undertaken a formal or informal diversity program or set of initiatives aimed at increasing the diversity of the firm?

Yes, formal.

Smurfit-Stone Container

150 N. Michigan Avenue
Chicago, IL 60601
Phone: (312) 580-4800
Fax: (312) 649-4332
www.smurfit-stone.com

Diversity Leadership

Jackie Thomas
Manager of Recruitment and Diversity
8182 Maryland Avenue
Saint Louis, MO 63105
Phone: (314) 746-1155
Fax: (314) 746-1331
E-mail: jsthomas@smurfit.com

Recruiting

Please list the schools/types of schools at which you recruit.

• Public state schools
• Historically Black Colleges and Universities (HBCUs)

Do you have any special outreach efforts directed to encourage minority students to consider your firm?

• Hold a reception for minority students
• Advertise in minority student association publication(s)
• Outreach to leadership of minority student organizations
• Scholarships or intern/fellowships for minority students

What activities does the firm undertake to attract minority and women employees?

• Partner programs with women and minority associations
• Participate at minority job fairs
• Seek referrals from other employees
• Utilize online job services

Do you use executive recruiting/search firms to seek to identify new diversity hires?

Yes.

If yes, list all women- and/or minority-owned executive search/recruiting firms to which the firm paid a fee for placement services in the past 12 months.

Just began using in 2005.

Internships and Co-ops

• City of Chicago
• Kidstart

Scholarships

Washington University Scholarship

Scholarship award amount: 10,000 per year

Scholarship given to a minority student at Washington University based upon grades, other activities and need. We are in the process of putting together a recommendation and a budget for scholarships to be distributed on campus in 2006.

Affinity Groups

Women in Leadership

The team focuses on the recruitment, development and advancement of females within the organization. The team meets every other month and is working on modifications to make more policies more family-friendly. They are also organizing networking/professional development events for professional females across the company. Two events are scheduled in Q3, 2005. We are scheduled to form an African-American team in Q4.

Entry-Level Programs/Full-Time Opportunities/Training Programs

Management Development Program

Length of program: Two years (four six-month rotations)
Geographic location(s) of program: Chicago and St. Louis

Aimed at increasing the internal pool of qualified, diverse future leaders, the management development program was created as a part of Smurfit-Stone's diversity initiative. The program will recruit recent college graduates to participate in an organization-wide rotation program, and equip them with industry knowledge and professional development opportunities to grow within the organization.

Training Component:

Specific training programs are designed for each rotation, during the program. Program participants will receive training focused on the following key areas:

• Accounting/finance/management budgeting
• Leadership development
• Packaging industry marketplace/Smurfit-Stone operating philosophy
• Presentation skills
• Managing conflict
• Effective communication

Strategic Plan and Diversity Leadership

How does the firm's leadership communicate the importance of diversity to everyone at the firm?

Our strategy is to infuse diversity as a piece in everything that we do. Diversity components are included in e-mails, speeches from CEO and key leadership, incorporation into meeting topics and company newsletters.

Who has primary responsibility for leading diversity initiatives at your firm?

Jackie Thomas, manager of recruitment and diversity.

Does your firm currently have a diversity committee?

Yes.

If yes, please describe how the committee is structured, how often it meets, etc.

The Diversity Steering Committee is made up of key participants from the operating groups leadership (VP level and HR director) and others in corporate (i.e. communications, legal, supplier diversity, recruiting). The team is sponsored by the CEO and VP of HR who attend meetings regularly. The team meets every quarter. Each of the operating units have also formed teams to drive the corporate strategy into the facilities.

If yes, does the committee's representation include one or more members of the firm's management/executive committee (or the equivalent)?

Yes.

If yes, how many executives are on the committee, and in 2005, what was the total number of hours collectively spent by the committee in furtherance of the firm's diversity initiatives? How many employees are on the committee, and how often does the committee convene in furtherance of the firm's diversity initiatives?

The committee has a total of 15 people and was reorganized in 2006 to include key executive leadership. In addition, several members of the steering team moved to the diversity tactical team, to better focus on driving the implementation of the diversity initiatives. In 2005 the team met every other month and the members are also working to drive diversity into their operating units.

Total Executives on Committee: Five VP level executives, four director level executives

Does the committee and/or diversity leader establish and set goals or objectives consistent with management's priorities?

Yes.

Has the firm undertaken a formal or informal diversity program or set of initiatives aimed at increasing the diversity of the firm?

Yes, formal. We have formed the diversity committee that is setting strategy for the operating units. We also have formed partnerships with professional organizations (i.e. NSHMBA) and are working with colleges with the intent of increasing the diversity representation in our hires. We are also working through succession planning and performance management to retain and promote diverse individuals particularly into the manager ranks.

How often does the firm's management review the firm's diversity progress/results?

Quarterly.

How is the firm's diversity committee and/or firm management held accountable for achieving results?

The metrics are presented to the Executive Committee and board of directors each quarter. Diversity progress is incorporated into the HR Leadership and CEO's incentives and we are working on getting incorporated into all leadership's incentives in 2007.

The Stats

Employees

2005: 33,500 (U.S.)

Revenue

2005: $8.4 billion (U.S.)

	INDUSTRY	SSCC
Overall population		
White	69 percent	69 percent
Minority	31 percent	31 percent
Male	79 percent	83 percent
Female	21 percent	17 percent

Compared to industry we are competitive as it relates to minorities. We are currently working to increase our percentage of females.

Retention and Professional Development

Please identify the specific steps you are taking to reduce the attrition rate of minority and women employees.

• Develop and/or support internal employee affinity groups (e.g., minority or women networks within the firm)
• Increase/review compensation relative to competition
• Increase/improve current work/life programs
• Succession plan includes emphasis on diversity
• Work with minority and women employees to develop career advancement plans
• Strengthen mentoring program for all employees, including minorities and women
• Professional skills development program, including minority and women employees

Diversity Mission Statement

To establish a company-wide culture that supports our CustomerONE philosophy and capitalizes on the differences and uniqueness of our employees.

Additional Information

Activities in 2005:

• Formation of diversity-related affinity groups (e.g. Women in Leadership and Multicultural Team)
• Creation of division diversity teams to drive change into the divisions and facilities
• Lunches/dinners with CEO and high performing diverse groups of employees at facilities and at corporate
• Pilot of new hire coaching program
• Refinement of career path model and continued emphasis on succession planning with tracking of diverse employees
• Incorporate diversity training into relevant existing training courses
• Creation of campus recruitment strategy
• Corporate management development program
• Strong focus on supplier diversity—to achieve our goal of five percent of total applicable spending, we developed a progressive step-up plan that would increase our targeted growth goal over a five year period
• Measures provided quarterly to board of directors
• Reengineering exit interview process to collect more accurate data on employees reasons for leaving—by Q3

Sodexho

9801 Washingtonian Boulevard
Gaithersburg, MD 20878
Phone: (800) 763-3946

Locations

6,000

Diversity Leadership

Nereida (Neddy) Perez
Senior Director Diversity & External Relations
9801 Washingtonian Blvd.
Gaithersburg, MD 20878
Phone: (301) 987-4063
Fax: (301) 987-4186
E-mail: neddy.perez@sodexhousa.com

Employment Contact

John Lee
Director of College
200 Continental Drive, Suite 400
Newark, DE 19713
Phone: (302)738-9500 Ext. 5206
E-mail: john.lee@sodexhousa.com
www.sodexhousa.com

Recruiting

Please list the schools/types of schools at which you recruit.

• Private schools
• Public state schools
• Historically Black Colleges and Universities (HBCUs)
• Hispanic Serving Institutions (HSIs)
• Native American Tribal Universities
• Other predominantly minority and/or women's colleges

Do you have any special outreach efforts directed to encourage minority students to consider your firm?

• Hold a reception for minority students
• *Conferences:* National Society of Minority Hospitality Students (National and Regional), Multi Cultural Food and Hospitality Association
• Advertise in minority student association publication(s)
• Participate in/host minority student job fair(s)
• Sponsor minority student association events
• Firm's employees participate on career panels at schools
• Outreach to leadership of minority student organizations
• Scholarships or intern/fellowships for minority students

What activities does the firm undertake to attract minority and women employees?

• Partner programs with women and minority associations
• *Conferences:* Women's Food Service Forum
• Participate at minority job fairs
• Seek referrals from other employees

• Utilize online job services

Do you use executive recruiting/search firms to seek to identify new diversity hires?

Yes.

Internships and Co-ops

Sodexho Future Leaders Program

Number of interns in the program in summer 2005 (internship): 17

Pay: $420 per week

Length of the program: 10 weeks

Percentage of interns/co-ops in the program who receive offers of full-time employment: 50 percent (anticipated)

Scholarships

National Society of Minority Hospitality Students

Deadline for application for the scholarship program: January 15, 2006

Scholarship award amount: $1,500

Affinity Groups

• AALF—(African-American Leadership Forum)
• SOL—(Sodexho Organization of Latinos)
• PANG—(Pan Asian Network Group)
• WING—(Women's Network Information Group)
• PRIDE—(People Respecting Individuality, Diversity and Equality)

Entry-Level Programs/Full-Time Opportunities/Training Programs

Beginning Your Career—The First 90 Days

Length of program: Approximately 90 days

Geographic location(s) of program: Field operations throughout the United States

The program is a combination of three-day classroom orientations coupled with self-guided workbooks and two videos that provide managers with activities and on-the-job experiences that focus on the critical knowledge and skills needed by managers within their first year.

We have a tuition reimbursement program. We also offer an extensive list of training programs through Sodexho University and its resource library.

Strategic Plan and Diversity Leadership

How does the firm's leadership communicate the importance of diversity to everyone at the firm?

Sodexho's commitment to diversity and inclusion is communicated at Sodexho on a daily basis as it is a part of how we do business. These messages are communicated from our president and CEO, our SVP and chief diversity officer, Sodexho's office of diversity, network group and diversity council members and managers and employees across the company. Sodexho utilizes e-mails, our internal and external web sites, internal presentations at staff and regional/district meetings, diversity newsletters, employee network group newsletters, and other means to continually reinforce and update employees on our diversity and inclusion activities. Additionally, each year Sodexho publishes and distributes a diversity annual report to all managers and clients which highlights our accomplishments and successes for the fiscal year.

Who has primary responsibility for leading diversity initiatives at your firm?

Dr. Rohini Anand, chief diversity officer.

Does your firm currently have a diversity committee?

Yes.

If yes, please describe how the committee is structured, how often it meets, etc.

Sodexho currently has a diversity leadership council that is lead by our president and CEO, our SVP and chief diversity officer, and other executive team members.

In addition, each of our market segments have diversity councils that help to drive diversity and inclusion within their respective market segments.

If yes, does the committee's representation include one or more members of the firm's management/executive committee (or the equivalent)?

Yes.

If yes, how many executives are on the committee, and in 2005, what was the total number of hours collectively spent by the committee in furtherance of the firm's diversity initiatives? How many employees are on the committee, and how often does the committee convene in furtherance of the firm's diversity initiatives?

The diversity leadership council is staffed exclusively by executive team members and meets quarterly. In addition, our diversity councils meet on a quarterly basis, with monthly subcommittee meetings.

Does the committee and/or diversity leader establish and set goals or objectives consistent with management's priorities?

Yes.

Has the firm undertaken a formal or informal diversity program or set of initiatives aimed at increasing the diversity of the firm?

Yes, formal. Sodexho has a comprehensive and measurable diversity strategy designed to create and maintain a diverse and inclusive workplace. The strategy is focused on building a diverse and inclusive workplace and activities are targeted around our employees, our culture/climate, our customers and clients and the communities in which we serve.

How often does the firm's management review the firm's diversity progress/results?

Monthly.

How is the firm's diversity committee and/or firm management held accountable for achieving results?

Sodexho utilizes an annual diversity scorecard which is linked to incentive compensation, and impacts 10-15 percent of manager bonuses and 25 percent of executive team bonuses. Additionally, Sodexho's CEO has committed to the diversity scorecard incentive link regardless of the financial performance of the company, emphasizing the importance of diversity and inclusion to the organization. Lastly, our company's core competencies include competencies in diversity management, and employees performance objectives are inclusive of actions that help to drive key initiatives (e.g., mentoring) which further support our diversity and inclusion strategy.

Retention and Professional Development

Please identify the specific steps you are taking to reduce the attrition rate of minority and women employees.

• Develop and/or support internal employee affinity groups
• Increase/review compensation relative to competition
• Increase/improve current work/life programs
• Adopt dispute resolution process
• Succession plan includes emphasis on diversity
• Work with minority and women employees to develop career advancement plans
• Review work assignments and hours billed to key client matters to make sure minority and women employees are not being excluded
• Strengthen mentoring program for all employees, including minorities and women
• Professional skills development program, including minority and women employees

Diversity Mission Statement

Diversity and inclusion is an inherent part of our culture and business growth. The energy and talent at all levels of the organization is unleashed, resulting in innovative solutions that contribute to a spirit of team, service and progress. With diversity and inclusion as a competitive advantage, Sodexho is an employer of choice and the benchmark for customers, clients and communities domestically and globally.

Additional Information

Sodexho has implemented many initiatives to support our diversity and inclusion strategy. These include Sodexho's comprehensive diversity learning strategy, Champions of Diversity employee recognition program, Spirit of Mentoring programs, and redesigned diversity scorecard—all of which demonstrate Sodexho's strong commitment to developing our people. In program profiles such as the one for our action learning degree program, we believe that you will see strong evidence of the results we have achieved by fully engaging and empowering diverse employees at every level of our company.

Our success, in part, has been significantly driven by the following five strategic accomplishments:

• Diversity and inclusion is one of Sodexho's six strategic imperatives that drives our business strategy and smart growth operations, and consequently is reported/reviewed monthly at executive team meetings along with financials.

• Sodexho utilizes an annual diversity scorecard which is linked to incentive compensation, and impacts 10-15 percent of manager bonuses and 25 percent of executive team bonuses.

• Sodexho's CEO has committed to the diversity scorecard incentive link regardless of the financial performance of the company, emphasizing the importance of diversity and inclusion to the organization.

• Sodexho's senior vice president and chief diversity officer reports directly to the CEO.

• Sodexho has recently created three senior director of diversity positions within each of our market segments (education, corporate, and health care) that report directly into the market president, with dotted line to the chief diversity officer, which drives accountability through direct connection to business operations.

Beyond what we believe to be the best practices referenced above, over the past year, Sodexho's executive team, office of diversity, division diversity councils and diverse employee network groups have worked to fully empower our managers and executives to implement our corporate diversity and inclusion strategy. Among our more recent accomplishments:

We introduced a redesigned Sodexho diversity scorecard, containing revised quantitative as well as new qualitative components and related tools, to help our managers and executives to recognize and reward exemplary efforts in hiring, promoting and retaining minority and women managers (2004). These tools include our new diversity resource guide which assists managers with creating a diverse and inclusive workplace.

We have launched four mentoring programs: a formal program connected to succession planning called "IMPACT," a midlevel manager mentoring program through our employee network group called "Peer 2 Peer," a divisional mentoring program called "Bridge" for frontline managers and a frontline employee program called "CHAMP."

As part of our comprehensive diversity learning strategy, launching our new diversity learning labs which build upon the foundation established by our mandatory spirit of diversity course. For all managers these learning labs provide in-depth diversity training and skills in areas such as cross-cultural communications, culturally-competent recruiting, communication across gender and generational lines of difference and other topics.

Also as part of our comprehensive diversity learning strategy, launching the EEO/AA "TOPS" training modules for our frontline, hourly employees and new diversity "TOPS" awareness and skills training modules.

Sodexho launched an impressive work/life effectiveness initiative with a cross divisional task force that includes executive team sponsorship and involvement. The task force includes a "matures" subcommittee that is focused on issues pertaining to our older workforce. There is on-going diversity management training for our executive committee (provided by Catalyst, Inc. and other top consultants). In addition, we support our employee network groups to promote awareness and celebration of the contributions of diverse employees within the firm.

Sodexho has been recognized with the following awards:

• Top 10 Best Company for Hispanics by *Hispanic Business Magazine*
• Top 10 Company for Asian-American Employees by *Asian Enterprise Magazine*
• Top 100 Employers for 2005 (No. 6) by *The Black Collegian*
• Hispanic Corporate 100 by *Hispanic Magazine/Hispanic Trends*
• 25 Notable Companies for Diversity by *DiversityInc.*
• Top 10 Company for People with Disabilities by *DiversityInc.*
• Top 10 Company for Supplier Diversity by *DiversityInc.*
• Top 25 Company for African-Americans by *Black Professionals Magazine*
• Top 50 Corporations for Supplier Diversity by *Hispanic Magazine/Hispanic Trends*
• Latina Style Top 50 Company by *Latina Style Magazine*
• International Innovation in Diversity Award by *Profiles in Diversity Journal*
• Diversity Innovator Award by The Women's Business Center
• Joseph Papp Corporate Diversity Award Foundation for Ethnic Understanding
• 2005 Career FOCUS Eagle Award—James Taylor National Eagle Leadership Institute

Sprint Nextel Corporation

2001 Edmund Halley Drive
Reston, VA 20191
Phone: (703) 433-4000

Employment Contact
Tammy Edwards
Director, Inclusion and Diversity
2001 Edmund Halley Dr.
Reston, VA 20191
Phone: (703) 433-4000
www.sprint.com/careers

Recruiting

Please list the schools/types of schools at which you recruit.

• *Public state schools:* Iowa State University, Kansas State University, Truman State University, University of Nebraska -Lincoln, University of Kansas, University of Maryland, University of Missouri - Columbia, University of Missouri - Kansas City, University of Missouri - Rolla, University of Virginia, Central Missouri State University, Florida A&M University, Florida State University, Northwest Missouri State University, Pittsburg State University, Purdue University, Southwest Missouri State University, University of Florida, Virginia Tech, Kansas City, MO Community Colleges
• Historically Black Colleges and Universities (HBCUs)

Do you have any special outreach efforts directed to encourage minority students to consider your firm?

• Hold a reception for minority students
• Advertise in minority student association publication(s)
• Participate in/host minority student job fair(s)
• Sponsor minority student association events
• Firm's employees participate on career panels at schools
• Outreach to leadership of minority student organizations
• Scholarships or intern/fellowships for minority students

What activities does the firm undertake to attract minority and women employees?

• Partner programs with women and minority associations
• *Conferences:* NABA, NSBE, SHPE, SWE, NSHMBA, NBMBAA
• Participate at minority job fairs
• Seek referrals from other employees
• Utilize online job services

Do you use executive recruiting/search firms to seek to identify new diversity hires?

No.

Internships and Co-ops

Deadline for application: Varies depending on campus interviews for fall and spring
Pay: $10-$22 hourly wage depending on school classification and prior intern experience
Length of the program: 10 to 12 weeks
Percentage of interns/co-ops in the program who receive offers of full-time employment: 60 percent

Web site for internship/co-op information: www.sprint.com/hr/college_intern.html

The Internship Program is designed to enhance Sprint's recruitment efforts and reinforce the relationships developed through these efforts. The program objectives are to:

• Promote meaningful assignments to enhance the student's learning
• Provide intern program orientation materials to students and their supervisors
• Coordinate opportunities for interaction with Sprint managers, executives and other interns
• Enhance recruiting efforts with conversion to hire

Internships are 10-12 weeks in duration. During the internship, the intern learns about the company, the department functions and gains valuable work experience enhancing his or her educational goals. Sprint hires interns based on education and experience and business needs. They are placed in business sales, consumer sales, finance, information or permanent residents, through scholarships of up to $5,000 and paid summer internships at Sprint locations. The program accepts juniors majoring in accounting, business administration, economics, finance, (computer, electrical, industrial, management) engineering, mathematics, statistics and management information systems.

Scholarships

Sprint Minority Engineering Scholarship Program

Deadline for application for the scholarship program: April 1st
Scholarship award amount: Full scholarship
Web site or other contact information for scholarship: www.kcmetro.edu/pubs/campusScholarshipLists.pdf

The Sprint Minority Engineering Scholarship Program is co-sponsored by the Kansas City Metropolitan Community Colleges, the University of Missouri-Rolla and Sprint to attract, encourage and support promising minority students wishing to enter the field of engineering or computer science.

UNCF/Sprint Scholars Program

Deadline for application for the scholarship program: January 1st
Scholarship award amount: $5,000 annual award
Web site or other contact information for scholarship: http://www.uncf.org

The UNCF/Sprint Scholars Program provides educational opportunities for African-Americans, American Indians/Alaskan Natives, Asian Pacific Islander Americans and Hispanic American students who are U.S. citizens.

Affinity Groups

Diamond Network

The Diamond Network is an African-American-focused employee resource group whose mission is to aid Sprint in recruiting, retaining, developing and promoting African-American employees. The vision of the Diamond Network is to be recognized as an organization that promotes inclusion and diversity as a competitive advantage for Sprint. The goals of the Diamond Network are:

• Represent Sprint in recruitment activities
• Foster professional development
• Provide networking opportunities
• Promote diversity and inclusion

Enlace

Vision: To be a Sprint resource for communicating, supporting and engaging the Hispanic community, employees and the Hispanic culture.

Mission: Enlace is committed to supporting the partnership with Sprint and the Hispanic community. From community involvement and Hispanic cultural enrichment to employee development and market initiatives, Enlace is dedicated to promoting diversity.

Our Commitments:

• Community involvement: To strengthen relationships and opportunities between Enlace and the Hispanic community
• Cultural enrichment: To encourage the learning of and appreciation for Hispanic heritage and culture
• Employee development: To encourage and promote self-development and career employment
• Market initiative: To support Sprint initiatives that provide a competitive advantage for Hispanic marketing initiatives

Entry-Level Programs/Full-Time Opportunities/Training Programs

The programs are currently being redesigned.

Strategic Plan and Diversity Leadership

How does the firm's leadership communicate the importance of diversity to everyone at the firm?

Sprint communicates its commitment to inclusion via e-mail, newsletters, training, web casts, and executive presentations.

Who has primary responsibility for leading diversity initiatives at your firm?

Tammy Edwards, director inclusion and diversity.

Does your firm currently have a diversity committee?

Yes.

If yes, please describe how the committee is structured, how often it meets, etc.

The Sprint Executive Inclusion Council is composed of executives from various business units. The council is chaired by Gary Forsee, CEO.

If yes, does the committee's representation include one or more members of the firm's management/executive committee (or the equivalent)?

Yes.

Does the committee and/or diversity leader establish and set goals or objectives consistent with management's priorities?

Yes.

Has the firm undertaken a formal or informal diversity program or set of initiatives aimed at increasing the diversity of the firm?

Yes, formal.

How often does the firm's management review the firm's diversity progress/results?

Quarterly.

How is the firm's diversity committee and/or firm management held accountable for achieving results?

The success of the company's inclusion initiatives is part of the executive's performance review evaluations.

Retention and Professional Development

How do 2005 minority and female attrition rates generally compare to those experienced in the prior year period?

Lower than in prior years.

Please identify the specific steps you are taking to reduce the attrition rate of minority and women employees.

• Develop and/or support internal employee affinity groups (e.g., minority or women networks within the firm)
• Increase/improve current work/life programs
• Succession plan includes emphasis on diversity
• Work with minority and women employees to develop career advancement plans
• Strengthen mentoring program for all employees, including minorities and women
• Professional skills development program, including minority and women employees

Additional Information

To learn more about Sprint's inclusion initiatives, please visit www.sprint.com/diversity.

St. Paul Travelers Companies, Inc., The

One Tower Square
Hartford, CT 06183
Phone: (860) 954-2781
Fax: (860) 277-1970
www.stpaultravelers.com

Locations

National

Diversity Leadership

Allison Keeton
Director College Relations

Employment Contact

Laurie Buyniski
College Relations Consultant
E-mail: lebuynis@spt.com

Recruiting

Please list the schools/types of schools at which you recruit

• Private schools
• Public state schools
• Historically Black Colleges and Universities (HBCUs)

Do you have any special outreach efforts directed to encourage minority students to consider your firm?

• Advertise in minority student association publication(s)
• Participate in/host minority student job fair(s)
• Sponsor minority student association events
• Firm's employees participate on career panels at schools
• Outreach to leadership of minority student organizations
• Scholarships or intern/fellowships for minority students

What activities does the firm undertake to attract minority and women employees?

• Partner programs with women and minority associations
• Participate at minority job fairs
• Seek referrals from other employees
• Utilize online job services

Internships and Co-ops

Information Technology Leadership Development Internship

Deadline for application: January
Number of interns in the program in summer 2005 (internship) or 2005 (co-op): 40 interns
Length of the program: 10 weeks
Percentage of interns/co-ops in the program who receive offers of full-time employment: 50 percent
Web site for internship/co-op information: www.stpaultravelers.com/careers/new_grads/interns/index.html

Actuarial Leadership Development Program Internship

Deadline for application: January
Number of interns in the program in summer 2005 (internship) or 2005 (co-op): 15 interns
Length of the program: 10 weeks
Percentage of interns/co-ops in the program who receive offers of full-time employment: 90 percent
Web site for internship/co-op information: www.stpaultravelers.com/careers/new_grads/interns/index.html

Financial Management Leadership Development Program Internship

Deadline for application: January
Number of interns in the program in summer 2005 (internship) or 2005 (co-op): Eight interns
Length of the program: 10 weeks
Percentage of interns/co-ops in the program who receive offers of full-time employment: 60 percent
Web site for internship/co-op information: www.stpaultravelers.com/careers/new_grads/interns/index.html

Personal Lines Product Management Internship Program

Deadline for application: January
Number of interns in the program in summer 2005 (internship) or 2005 (co-op): 15 interns
Length of the program: 10 weeks
Web site for internship/co-op information: www.stpaultravelers.com/careers/new_grads/interns/index.html

Investments Internship

Deadline for application: January
Number of interns in the program in summer 2005 (internship) or 2005 (co-op): Two interns
Length of the program: 10 weeks
Web site for internship/co-op information: www.stpaultravelers.com/careers/new_grads/interns/index.html

INROADS Internship

Deadline for application: January
Number of interns in the program in summer 2005 (internship) or 2005 (co-op): 12 interns
Percentage of interns/co-ops in the program who receive offers of full-time employment: 40 percent (two of five seniors)
Web site for internship/co-op information: http://www.stpaultravelers.com/careers/new_grads/interns/index.html

Underwriting Internship

Deadline for application: January
Number of interns in the program in summer 2005 (internship) or 2005 (co-op): Five interns
Length of program: 10 weeks

The St. Paul Travelers summer internship programs provide college students with an excellent opportunity to gain firsthand experience. Our internship programs are designed to attract talented and motivated students who desire a career in actuarial, finance, information technology, or underwriting. Our opportunities extend beyond the work station. Beside our challenging assignments, St. Paul Travelers interns are busy with many activities within St. Paul Travelers as well as within the Saint Paul, Minn. and Hartford, Conn. communities.

Scholarships

Basic requirements include overall GPA of 3.0 or above, majors in actuarial science, finance, MIS, CS, risk management & insurance, economics (GPA and majors depend on the school), and ability to work in the U.S. The scholarship is a one-time award. For deadline and award amount, see school for details.

- Babson College
- Bentley College
- Bryant College
- Cal State-Fullerton
- Central Connecticut State University
- Georgia State
- Hamilton College
- Howard University
- Illinois State
- Lafayette
- Olivet College
- Rensselear Polytechnic Institute
- SUNY - Geneseo
- SUNY - Stonybrook
- Temple
- University of CT
- University of GA
- University of Hartford
- UMASS
- University of MN
- University of Notre Dame
- University WI - Eau Claire
- University WI - Madison
- Williams College
- WPI

Entry-Level Programs/Full-Time Opportunities/Training Programs

Information Technology Leadership Development Program

Length of program: Three to five years
Geographic location(s) of program: St. Paul, MN and Hartford, CT

ITLDP is a challenging, multi-faceted program designed to develop well-rounded information systems leaders capable of mastering a dynamic business and technical environment. Each rotation increases in level of responsibility and complexity. Through the series of rotational assignments, participants receive in-depth exposure to information systems at St. Paul Travelers, while becoming familiar with the insurance and financial services industry. The program curriculum includes a study of insurance, various technical skills, and project management. In addition, seminars are held covering information resource management, strategic planning and effective leadership. The program curriculum is supplemented with specific training required by each rotation.

Actuarial Leadership Development Program

Length of program: Three years
Geographic location(s) of program: St. Paul, MN and Hartford, CT

The St. Paul Travelers Actuarial Leadership Development Program (ALDP) focuses on building actuarial and business expertise and stimulating leadership development for individuals interested in pursuing an actuarial career in the insurance industry. Rotational work assignments give the ALDP participant an opportunity to experience the core actuarial functions across the various St. Paul Travelers business lines. Examples of rotational assignments include: pricing/product development, reserving, business planning and research. In addition to the actuarial exam support and rotational work assignments, the ALDP offers a core leadership training curriculum designed to give ALDP participants the tools necessary to achieve a leadership position in the organization. This curriculum includes seminars covering topics like management communications, information resource management, strategic planning, and effective leadership. The program curriculum is also supplemented with specific training required for each rotation.

Financial Management Leadership Development Program

Length of program: Three years
Geographic location(s) of program: St. Paul, MN and Hartford, CT

The St. Paul Travelers Financial Management Leadership Development Program focuses on leadership development for individuals interested in pursuing a career in financial management within the property & casualty insurance industry. The FMLDP exposes you to senior management, whether it's during your rotation, at a business meeting, or during networking opportunities. As you work through your various rotations you will be in roles key to business function and will be leaned on by management to push yourself, for your continued learning, as well as to help the business succeed. Throughout all phases of the Financial Management Leadership Development Program you will receive both technical and leadership training. The leadership training consists of one to three day seminars/workshops on various topics, such as management communications, strategic planning and effective leadership. The program curriculum is also supplemented with specific technical training required for each rotation.

Personal Lines Product Management

Length of program: One year
Geographic location(s) of program: Hartford, CT

Based in personal lines headquarters in Hartford, CT, our product management organization operates in 11 regions across the country. Each team provides market, product and pricing analysis to rapidly deliver our products via increasingly sophisticated segmentation strategies. As a part of this program you will learn how to determine adequate pricing of products, analyze the marketplace first hand, as well as through competitor and industry data, quantify the impact of pricing and underwriting decisions, negotiate pricing decisions with various distribution channels, respond to state insurance department inquiries, build and monitor local agency strategy and performance, and facilitate peer development. The educational programs provided for participants of this program include technical training, interpersonal and management skills, business skills, project management and other skills training.

Environmental Claim Assistance Account Executive Program

Length of program: 12-14 weeks
Geographic location(s) of program: Baltimore, MD; Dallas, TX; Denver, CO; Fairfax, VA; Hartford, CT; Houston, TX; Indianapolis, IN

In this position, candidates work closely with our clients, brokers, and legal professionals to resolve coverage issues and settle high-risk environmental claims. Types of claims include asbestos, toxic chemicals, pharmaceutical products, hazardous waste and pollution. Formal paid training program which combines classroom and independent study. Practical training is designed to give trainees hands-on experience and confidence and is an integral part of our program. One-on-one mentoring provides for career guidance and sharp insights into current business and case law.

Underwriting Program

Length of program: One year

Geographic location(s) of program: National opportunities

The Underwriting Development Program's main goal is to attract students from a diverse background and prepare them for the role of a commercial lines account executive/underwriter. The program is designed to develop a group of business leaders skilled in insurance underwriting, sales, marketing and product knowledge through a structured rotational program, coupled with training and mentoring. After being hired into a business unit, participants receive nine weeks of classroom training in our insurance operations office in Hartford, CT. They will then receive an additional three months of on-the-job training at their assigned locations followed by six months of a small assignment. To facilitate the learning process, participants in the program will develop a mentoring relationship with individuals in senior management positions.

Bond Account Manager Trainee

Length of program: Six months to one year

Geographic location(s) of program: National Opportunities

Our account managers have a diverse role. Responsibilities include: sales and underwriting, including evaluating exposures and negotiating terms and conditions, interaction with our independent agents and customers, and acting as a marketing representative to promote and expand travelers' bond business. Formal classroom training in our offices in Hartford, CT and practical training at one of our field offices will prepare you for this position. The training period is typically six months to one year. The combination of classroom and on-the-job training is designed to provide employees with the tools to develop leadership, sales, underwriting and management skills. Additionally, we encourage all of our employees to direct their own careers by taking the initiative to identify opportunities that will help them succeed, including tuition reimbursement.

Diversity Mission Statement

A diverse workforce builds positive relationships with our communities, customers, and investors. By incorporating diversity into the fabric of our business, we expand our business opportunities and contribute to the company's success.

St. Paul Travelers provides equal employment opportunities to all employees and applicants for employment free from unlawful discrimination based on race, color, religion, gender, age, national origin, disability, veteran status, marital status, sexual orientation or any other status or condition protected by local, state or federal law.

Staples, Inc.

500 Staples Drive
Framingham, MA 01702
Phone: (508) 253-5000
Fax: (508) 253-4227

Employment Contact
Catharine Jennings
College Relations Specialist
E-mail: Catharine.Jennings@staples.com
www.staples.com/jobs

Recruiting

Please list the schools/types of schools at which you recruit.

- *Ivy League schools:* Harvard, Dartmouth, MIT
- *Other private schools:* Northeastern University, Babson, Bentley, Boston College, Boston University, Worcester Polytechnic Institute, Providence, Suffolk, Wentworth, Syracuse, Stonehill
- *Public state schools:* UMASS Amherst, UMASS Lowell, UMASS Dartmouth, Arizona State University, Ohio State University, Michigan State University, Pennsylvania State University, Farmingham State, Bridgewater, Fitchburg
- *Historically Black Colleges and Universities (HBCUs):* Morehouse, Spelman, Clark Atlanta, Morris Brown, Howard, Wilberforce, Xavier

Do you have any special outreach efforts directed to encourage minority students to consider your firm?

- *Conferences:* National Society of Hispanic MBAs (NSHMBA), National Black MBA Association (NBMBAA), Association of Latino Professionals in Finance and Accounting (ALPFA), National Association of Black Accountants (NABA)
- Participate in/host minority student job fair(s)
- Outreach to leadership of minority student organizations
- Scholarships or intern/fellowships for minority students

What activities does the firm undertake to attract minority and women employees?

- Partner programs with women and minority associations
- *Conferences:* National Society of Hispanic MBAs (NSHMBA), National Black MBA Association (NBMBAA), Association of Latino Professionals in Finance and Accounting (ALPFA), National Association of Black Accountants (NABA), National Association of Asian American Professionals (NAAAP)
- Participate at minority job fairs
- Seek referrals from other employees
- Utilize online job services

We also have our diversity team go on campus and speak to classes at local schools about diversity in the workplace. We take at least two INROADS interns each summer.

Do you use executive recruiting/search firms to seek to identify new diversity hires?

Yes.

Internships and Co-ops

Deadline for application: April 30th for internships, March 1st or October 1st for co-ops

Number of interns in the program in summer 2006 (internship) or 2006 (co-op): 42 interns, 24 co-ops

Pay: $10-12 hourly for interns, $12-24 for grad interns, $16 for co-ops

Length of the program: We have spring, summer, fall internships and some are full-time for summer and continue part-time into fall and spring. We also have six month co-ops.

Percentage of interns/co-ops in the program who receive offers of full-time employment: 25 percent

Web site for internship/co-op information: www.staplescampuscareers.com

We have interns in our home office in many different functional groups including merchandising, information systems, finance/accounting, marketing, strategy, public relations and media. Students must have a GPA of 3.0 and typically our opportunities are best suited for rising sophomores or above. In addition to the day-to-day responsibilities of the internship, Staples interns are given the opportunity to participate in the "Lunch and Learn" speaker series which gives the intern the opportunity to hear from and learn from senior level executives in the company. Past luncheons have focused on learning about Staples web site usability, Staples sports marketing, and Staples brands. We take the interns on a tour of our planogram and they get to collectively have lunch and Q&A with the COO. It is a great summer experience that is capped off with Intern Presentation Day—an opportunity for the interns to strut their stuff and give a presentation on what they did during their internship.

Scholarships

Staples participates with many national diversity organizations to give scholarships to minority students affiliated with those organizations. Students should contact Catharine Jennings to learn more about how to qualify.

Entry-Level Programs/Full-Time Opportunities/Training Programs

Logistics Rotational Program

Length of program: Two years

Geographic location(s) of program: Multiple U.S. locations

General Format:

Each participant will be placed in one of the following positions for the described period of time:

• Supervisor-in-training—fulfillment center (12 months)
• Supervisor-in-training—service delivery operation (six months)
• Project Manager-in-training—corporate office (six months)

During each of the rotations, the associate will report to an operations manager who will be responsible for exposing the associate to all departments and functions of the location. Specified training plans for each piece of the rotation ensures both classroom and on the job learning. Also, each associate will be partnered with a mentor to provide guidance and direction throughout the entire two-year program.

Preferred Customer Account Manager

With just the right combination and innovation, Staples has grown into a $16.1 billion world-class powerhouse of the office supply industry. As part of our dedicated and talented sales force, you will be part of an industry leader.

This is an inside sales role.

The Account Management Preferred Customer Program focuses on retaining and developing above average Staples Business Delivery Customers. Monthly contacts range from sales calls focusing on differing products and categories to service escalation calls. The account manager is wholly responsible for the satisfaction, growth and development of his/her account base of approximately 650 accounts. Utilize internal resources to overcome obstacles. Discover and analyze prospects needs, determine which features/benefits of Staples will appeal the most to the customer and present those features/benefits to the customer. Create a sense of satisfaction as related to purchasing with Staples based on offers presented. Meet or exceed productivity requirements. Collect marketing intelligence and customer data as required. Leverage marketing dollars used throughout Staples, Inc. to proactively sell Staples products. Generate sales dollars for Staple Business Delivery. Appropriately channel leads for Staples Contract Division. Solve all service escalation for every account managed, proactively contact the party responsible for solving the customer's dilemma and follow through to ensure customer satisfaction. Act as the customer's primary liaison to Staples in regards to product, pricing, billing,etc. Exceptional decision making skills are necessary.

Qualifications

• Strong oral and written communication skills.
• Proven ability to set and adjust priorities based on activity.
• Works well in a fast-paced environment with little supervision.
• Strong sales skills.
• Strong customer service skills.
• Proficient PC skills, including Microsoft Office.

We need driven, smart sales executives who can THINK BIG to develop new and existing business, open new doors and establish and build accounts. You must be a self-starter with proven energy and motivation, willing to develop and close sales leads. You must be results oriented, self-motivated and driven by both financial and career opportunities. Excellent verbal and written communication skills are essential objectives. Time management skills are a must! Industry knowledge is a plus. As a Staples associate, you can expect a competitive base salary, monthly commission plan, comprehensive health care benefits, 401(K), employee stock purchase plan, union reimbursement and ongoing training and development.

Customer Service Rotation

Length of program: Two years
Geographic location(s) of program: Kentucky; Hackensack, NJ; Framingham, MA; Rochester, NY

General Format:

• Each participant will be placed in one of the following positions for the described period of time:
• Manager-in-training—Kentucky call center (12 months)
• Manager-in-training—Rochester or Hackensack call center (six months)
• Manager-in-training—Corporate office / service improvement office (six months)

During each of the rotations, the associate will report to a manager who will be responsible for exposing the associate to all departments and functions of the location. Specified training plans for each piece of the rotation ensures both classroom and on the job learning. Also, each associate will be partnered with a mentor to provide guidance and direction throughout the entire two-year program.

Position Locations:

• Kentucky call center—Florence, Kentucky
• Rochester call center—Rochester, New York
• Hackensack call center—Hackensack, New Jersey
• Corporate office—Framingham, Massachusetts

Strategic Plan and Diversity Leadership

How does the firm's leadership communicate the importance of diversity to everyone at the firm?

Diversity messages are interwoven within general corporate updates either via satellite broadcast, Staples News, or internal communications.

Who has primary responsibility for leading diversity initiatives at your firm?

Doreen Nichols, director of associate relations and diversity.

Does your firm currently have a diversity committee?

No.

Has the firm undertaken a formal or informal diversity program or set of initiatives aimed at increasing the diversity of the firm?

Yes, informal.

How often does the firm's management review the firm's diversity progress/results?

Annually.

How is the firm's diversity committee and/or firm management held accountable for achieving results?

Goals are set for the recruiting department and this is a component of each recruiter's performance appraisal.

The Stats

Employees

2005: 69,000
2004: 65,000

Revenue

2005: $16.1 billion
2004: $14.4 billion

Retention and Professional Development

How do 2005 minority and female attrition rates generally compare to those experienced in the prior year period?

About the same as in prior years.

Please identify the specific steps you are taking to reduce the attrition rate of minority and women employees.

Succession plan includes emphasis on diversity.

Diversity Mission Statement

Reflecting the face of our customer through diversity is a commitment deeply embedded in Staples' corporate culture. We are dedicated to providing a work environment of inclusion and acceptance, and look for associates who will also embrace these values.

Additional Information

To understand why diversity is so important to us, you don't have to look farther than your nearest Staples store. Our customers—whether they're shopping in our stores, online, or through Staples contract or business delivery—are a mosaic of different cultures, ethnicities, genders, and ages. So it's not surprising that we strive for a workforce and a supplier network that reflect the diverse multicultural "face" of our customers.

Staples has been quietly building a workforce of diverse and talented associates, developing a network of diverse suppliers, and supporting diversity in our communities through the Staples Foundation for Learning. In recognition of our achievement in this area, *DiversityInc.* magazine named Staples one of the top ten companies for recruitment and retention of a diverse workforce in 2004.

We know there's much to do, but the results are starting to show. Our recent focus on diverse college recruitment initiatives and partnerships with professional organizations has been highly successful. Our supplier diversity program was the first in the industry to build a network of established regional Minority Women Business Enterprise (MWBE) partners, which allows customers to purchase directly from and be billed by diversity suppliers. In our local communities, we support diversity through the Staples Foundation for Learning, which provides job skills and educational opportunities for people of all backgrounds, with a special emphasis on disadvantaged youth.

At Staples, we are proud of our commitment to diversity and the great strides we've made toward achieving it. Our success is as multi-faceted as our associates and customers.

Starwood Hotels & Resorts Worldwide, Inc.

1111 Westchester Avenue
White Plains, NY 10604
Phone: (914) 640-8487

Locations
Located in over 85 countries globally

Employment Contact
Mary Anne McNulty
Manager, Staffing & College Relations
E-mail:
maryanne.mcnulty@starwoodhotels.com
www.starwood.jobs

Recruiting

Please list the schools/types of schools at which you recruit.

- Ivy League schools
- *Other private schools:* Cornell University, Boston University, University of Delaware, University of Houston, University of Massachusetts, Purdue University, University of Nevada - Las Vegas, University of Hawaii
- *Public state schools:* Washington State University, Michigan State University, Penn State University
- *Historically Black Colleges and Universities (HBCUs):* Bethune-Cookman College, Morgan State University

Do you have any special outreach efforts directed to encourage minority students to consider your firm?

- *Conferences:* NBMBAA, NSHMBA, NSMH
- Advertise in minority student association publication(s)
- *Participate in/host minority student job fairs:* NSMH, Thurgood Marshall
- Sponsor minority student association events
- Outreach to leadership of minority student organizations
- *Scholarships or intern/fellowships for minority students:* Hispanic College Fund, NSMH scholarship support

What activities does the firm undertake to attract minority and women employees?

- Partner programs with women and minority associations
- *Conferences:* OCA, NSMH, NSHMBA, NBMBAA, NAACP
- Participate at minority job fairs

Internships and Co-ops

INROADS

Number of interns in the program in summer 2004 (internship) or 2004 (co-op): Four INROADS interns
Pay: Varies by geographic placement
Length of the program: 10-12 weeks
Web site for internship/co-op information: www.starwood.jobs

Entry-Level Programs/Full-Time Opportunities/Training Programs

Management Training Program

Length of program: Six months
Geographic location(s) of program: Across U.S.

Starwood's Management Training Program combines professional development, mentorships and immersion into the service-oriented realm of hotel operations. Associates in this program will be poised for entry into management positions including rooms, food and beverage, sales, revenue management, human resources, catering/convention services, accounting and more. At the completion of a 12-week rotational program, each associate is placed in a position of responsibility at the same hotel where the training was completed.

Strategic Plan and Diversity Leadership

Who has primary responsibility for leading diversity initiatives at your firm?

Shelley Freeman, director of diversity.

Does your firm currently have a diversity committee?

Yes.

If yes, does the committee's representation include one or more members of the firm's management/executive committee (or the equivalent)?

Yes.

Additional Information

What We Believe: Diversity & Inclusion

Culture of Inclusion

At Starwood, we recognize and appreciate the diversity of people, ideas and cultures, and believe that diverse experiences and people are required for our business to succeed. We strive to create an environment that embraces the diversity of all of our constituencies: associates, customers, guests, owners, suppliers and shareholders. We support a culture of inclusion where associates at every level, including the full range of backgrounds, cultures and orientations can reach their maximum potential. We are passionate about attracting and retaining the best and the brightest talent, unleashing their potential and stretching them beyond their comfort zone. Through this diversity of viewpoints, we deliver unprecedented business results by satisfying all of our guests and customers with superior innovation and service.

Built on Diversity

Starwood Hotels & Resorts is a global organization that is built on diversity. With seven distinct brands—Sheraton® Hotels & Resorts, Four Points® by Sheraton Hotels, St. Regis® Hotels & Resorts, The Luxury Collection®, Le Méridien®, W Hotels® and Westin® Hotels & Resorts—operating in over 95 countries, we maintain an associate and customer base as diverse as the world's population. Each brand's distinctive appeal affords us a unique position in the global marketplace that caters to travelers of all backgrounds and from almost every culture. Therefore, creating an environment of inclusion for our associates, guests and suppliers is not just the right thing to do, it is the very core of our business.

National Partnerships

Focusing on blending and mining the talents of our more than 145,000 associates from around the world and taking care of guests who frequent our approximately 850 Starwood properties is a commitment that begins at the top of our organization, but is the shared responsibility of each associate. By creating national partnerships with associations focused on serving the needs and concerns of many types of visible and invisible differences—race, gender and sexual orientation, to name a few—we hope to have a far-reaching impact by making a difference in the markets in which we operate and the guests we serve.

Diversity Council

Our Diversity Council is made up of senior leaders at Starwood. Its role is to partner with other company leaders to drive the strategy forward with the support of a dedicated staff of change agents in our Office of Diversity and Inclusion.

Just as we approach other vital business imperatives, our Corporate Diversity Council has developed a strategy and multiyear plan for accelerating change, particularly in the area of representation. As an organization, we are committed to setting the pace for the industry, raising the bar on how we deploy and develop associates and, in the process, understanding how diversity yields business success.

Positive Messages

It takes time. We are committed to the task. Our associates must know that embracing diversity and learning how to mine different talents and opinions in a business like ours improves our company, our product and all of us as individuals. Valuing individual differences is not new here; for years, we have offered domestic partner benefits for all of our associates without hesitation. Through inclusion training, we reinforce positive messages. By continuing to introduce metrics, like linking compensation to achieving diversity goals, and clarifying the diversity goals of each department, there is a shared understanding of how serious we are about making this an unconscious part of how we do business everyday, everywhere, for everyone.

This is the Starwood way.

State Street Corporation

State Street Financial Center
One Lincoln Street
Boston, MA 02111

Locations

US:

Massachusetts (HQ)

California • Georgia • Illinois • Missouri •
New Jersey • New Hampshire • New York
• North Carolina

International:

Austria • Australia • Belgium • Canada •
Cayman Islands • Channel Islands • Chile
• China • France • Germany • Ireland •
Italy • Japan • Luxembourg • The
Netherlands • Singapore • South Africa •
South Korea • Switzerland • Taiwan •
Thailand • United Arab Emirates • United
Kingdom.

Employment Contact

Maia Germain
College Relations and Diversity Initiatives
Manager
State Street Financial Center
One Lincoln Street
Boston, MA 02111
Phone: (617) 786-3000
E-mail: mgermain@statestreet.com
www.statestreet.com (Click on Careers, then
Job Opportunities)

Recruiting

Please list the schools/types of schools at which you recruit.

• Ivy League schools
• Other private schools
• Public state schools
• Historically Black Colleges and Universities (HBCUs)
• Hispanic Serving Institutions (HSIs)
• Other predominantly minority and/or women's colleges

Do you have any special outreach efforts directed to encourage minority students to consider your firm?

• Participate in/host minority student job fair(s)
• Sponsor minority student association events
• Firm's employees participate on career panels at schools
• Outreach to leadership of minority student organizations

What activities does the firm undertake to attract minority and women employees?

• Partner programs with women and minority associations
• Conferences
• Participate at minority job fairs
• Seek referrals from other employees
• Utilize online job services

Do you use executive recruiting/search firms to seek to identify new diversity hires?

Yes.

Internships and Co-ops

INROADS, PIC (Private Industry Council), Year Up, internal program

Deadline for application: Open, depending on program

Number of interns in the program in summer 2006 (internship) or 2006 (co-op): 300+ interns

Length of the program: Summer—two weeks, other depending on need

Web site for internship/co-op information: Currently under construction

Affinity Groups

In the United States, State Street's eight employee affinity groups will play an active role in this process. These groups include an Asian Professionals Group, Bible Study Group, Black Professionals Group, Chinese Affinity Group, Disability Awareness Alliance, Gay, Lesbian, Bisexual and Transgender Group, Latin American Professional Network and Professional Women's Network. Group members meet throughout the year to share ideas and experiences, mentor and network, and sponsor internal programs around national and international events like Black History Month, International Women's Day, Asian and Latin American Heritage Months and PRIDE. All of the affinity groups have the support of the corporation and are provided a discretionary budget to use in outreach, community service, membership promotion, etc. State Street affinity groups are publicized in employee communications, new employee orientation, meeting announcements and through the company's Intranet.

Entry-Level Programs/Full-Time Opportunities/Training Programs

Fund Accountant, Portfolio Accountant, Portfolio Administrator

Length of program: Two weeks (each)

Geographic location(s) of program: Boston/Quincy, MA

Strategic Plan and Diversity Leadership

State Street's global inclusion initiative brings together a team of employee opinion leaders from across the corporation representing myriad levels, cultural, professional and lifestyle backgrounds, geographic locations and walks of life. The goal of the initiative is to provide all employees and managers with the tools, guidance and opportunities to perform to their potential and be valued, engaged and productive.

A global inclusion steering committee, comprised of representatives from State Street's senior leadership globally, leads the effort and is responsible for setting strategy and ultimately driving change centered on the work environment, gender/ethnicity and culture issues, internal mobility, management development and turnover management.

The steering committee is supported by three global inclusion regional groups, representing North America, Europe and the Asia/Pacific area. These groups are actively working to complete recommendations on improving the quality of working life at the regional and corporate levels, currently focusing on management practices, recruitment and retention of a diverse work force, and improved communication effectiveness.

The Stats

	TOTAL IN THE U.S.		TOTAL OUTSIDE THE U.S		TOTAL WORLDWIDE	
	2005	2004	2005	2004	2005	2004
Number of employees	13,143	13,174	7,822	6,751	20,965	19,925
Revenue	$3.39 billion	$3.18 billion	$2.13 billion	$1.82 billion	$5.52 billion	$4.95 billion

Retention and Professional Development

Please identify the specific steps you are taking to reduce the attrition rate of minority and women employees.

• Develop and/or support internal employee affinity groups (e.g., minority or women networks within the firm)
• Increase/review compensation relative to competition
• Increase/improve current work/life programs
• Work with minority and women employees to develop career advancement plans
• Professional skills development program, including minority and women employees

Diversity Mission Statement

To be a place where all employees are engaged and valued.

In addition to being a great place to bank.... we're also a great place to work.

Headquartered in Atlanta, Georgia, SunTrust operates an extensive distribution network primarily in Florida, Georgia, North Carolina, South Carolina, Tennessee, Maryland, Virginia and the District of Columbia - and also serves customers in selected markets nationally. Our primary businesses include deposit, credit, trust and investment services, and through various subsidiaries, we provide credit cards, mortgage banking, insurance, brokerage, and capital markets services.

SunTrust was recently ranked as one of DiversityInc's "Top 50 Companies for Diversity" for 2006. Among the programs which contributed to SunTrust's inclusion on this list were:

- *Mentoring and leadership development programs for minorities*
- *Work-life benefits*
- *An aggressive Diversity recruiting strategy - resulting in a diverse workforce*
- *An active Corporate Diversity Council*
- *Diversity training programs*

SunTrust makes a significant investment in both the training and development of its employees. Our comprehensive, professional internship and full-time Training Programs provide a solid platform on which to build your career.

SunTrust is proud of its established partnership with INROADS, and provides internship opportunities throughout our footprint for talented minority students.

Visit us online to learn more about our outstanding careers at:

suntrust.com/campus

SunTrust supports a diverse workforce and is a Drug Testing and Equal Opportunity Employer. M/F/V/D.

SunTrust Banks, Inc.

303 Peachtree Street
Atlanta, GA 30308
Phone: (404)588-7711
Fax: (404)588-8047
www.suntrust.com

Locations

1,700 branches across the southeast and mid-Atlantic regions

Diversity Leadership

Carolyn Cartwright
Director of Diversity
303 Peachtree Street
Atlanta, GA 30308
Phone: (404)588-7711
Fax: (404)588-8047
www.suntrust.com/campus

Recruiting

Please list the schools/types of schools at which you recruit.

- *Private schools:* Duke, Emory, Rollins College, University of Richmond, Vanderbilt, Wake Forest, Washington and Lee
- *Public state schools:* Florida State, Clemson, Georgia Tech, James Madison University, University of Central Florida, University of Florida, University of Georgia, University of Maryland, University of North Carolina - Chapel Hill, University of South Florida, University of Tennessee - Knoxville, University of Virginia, Virginia Commonwealth University, and Virginia Tech
- *Historically Black Colleges and Universities (HBCUs):* Florida A&M, Howard University, Spelman, and Tennessee State
- *Hispanic Serving Institutions (HSIs):* Florida International University and University of Miami

Do you have any special outreach efforts directed to encourage minority students to consider your firm?

- Hold a reception for minority students
- *Conferences:* Howard Financial Services Institute and Monster Diversity Leadership Program
- Advertise in minority student association publication(s)
- Participate in/host minority student job fair(s)
- Sponsor minority student association events
- Firm's employees participate on career panels at school
- Outreach to leadership of minority student organizations
- Scholarships or intern/fellowships for minority students
- *Other:* Participate in the Florida A&M Industry Cluster; participate in the SWEPT Program at Spelman; established an Executive Liaison Program where we have assigned SunTrust executives to each of our core HBCUs and HSIs; participate in the 21st Century Advantage Program at Howard University

What activities does the firm undertake to attract minority and women employees?

- Partner programs with women and minority associations
- *Conferences:* Black Data Processing Associates, Career Opportunities for Students with Disabilities (COSD), Emerging Leaders Program, Monster Diversity Leadership Program, National Black MBA, National Society of Hispanic MBAs, National Urban League, Urban Financial Services Coalition, Women for Hire, and Women of Color Technology Awards Conference
- Participate at minority job fairs
- Seek referrals from other employees
- Utilize online job services
- Partnership with INROADS
- Send SunTrust representatives to facilitate sessions at the INROADS Leadership Development Institute events

Do you use executive recruiting/search firms to seek to identify new diversity hires?

No.

Internships and Co-ops

In addition to the internship programs listed below, SunTrust also typically has intern opportunities in the following areas: credit, marketing, strategic sourcing, and wealth and investment management. These internship opportunities vary each year, so be sure to check the careers section of suntrust.com for a complete listing of our openings.

INROADS

Number of interns in the program in summer 2005 (internship) or 2005 (co-op): 25
Pay: Intern pay varies based on geographic location, department placement, and year in school.
Length of the program: 10-12 weeks
Percentage of interns/co-ops in the program who receive offers of full-time employment: Approximately 70 percent
Web site for internship/co-op information: www.suntrust.com/campus

SunTrust typically places INROADS interns throughout the company's footprint, in the following lines of business: business banking, commercial banking, commercial real estate, mortgage banking, retail banking, and wealth and investment management. Interns generally spend from two to four summers with the organization learning analytical and/or sales skills through direct, hands-on participation. The summer experience includes some combination of client exposure, job-shadowing, and classroom training. In addition, all interns complete a summer project and presentation that reflects appropriate research and analysis for their particular function.

All INROADS interns are paired with a mentor and Human Resources local coordinator. They also participate in special programming activities throughout the summer, including a variety of professional development seminars. Rising seniors are invited to participate in SunTrust's annual INROADS Senior Summit. This two day event, which is held at our corporate headquarters in Atlanta, gives interns the opportunity to interact with senior management, gain exposure to our business strategies, and network with other interns and recent college hires.

Qualifications:

Varies by line of business and functional area.

Corporate and Investment Banking Internship Program

Number of interns in the program in summer 2005 (internship) or 2005 (co-op): Seven
Pay: Intern pay varies based on geographic location, department placement, and year in school.
Length of the program: 10-12 weeks
Percentage of interns/co-ops in the program who receive offers of full-time employment: Approximately 60 percent
Web site for internship/co-op information: www.suntrust.com/campus

The Summer Internship Program provides the opportunity to gain exposure to a number of disciplines within Corporate and Investment Banking. The intern will be assigned to a specific group to work on various analyses, modeling and underwriting assignments for the bank's corporate clients. Interns will sharpen financial analysis skills, develop an understanding of corporate markets and clients, and build expertise in corporate finance and investment banking products through on-the-job training. Potential assignments include: advisory services, asset securitization, diversified industries, energy finance, financial risk management, fixed income sales, trading and research, food and beverage finance, foreign exchange, health care finance, syndicated finance, private debt placements, public debt issuance or structured real estate leasing. The overall goal of the program is for the intern to develop a solid understanding of our industry, our organization and our strategy. At the end of the summer, interns will be considered for a full-time analyst position in client management corporate finance, Debt Capital Markets or Investment

Banking upon graduation. Most of our opportunities will be in Atlanta, however there is a potential for positions in Nashville, Orlando or Richmond.

Qualifications:

- Completed junior year of BA/BS degree required; any major
- Finance coursework preferred
- Overall GPA of 3.0 or above required
- Solid leadership and interpersonal skills
- High degree of academic and extracurricular achievement
- Proven analytical ability and attention to detail
- Proven ability to work well in a team environment
- Excellent written and oral communication skills

Mortgage Internship Program

Number of interns in the program in summer 2005 (internship) or 2005 (co-op): Six
Pay: Intern pay varies based on geographic location, department placement, and year in school.
Length of the program (in weeks): 10 weeks
Web site for internship/co-op information: www.suntrust.com/campus

Mortgage interns will provide project management support to various divisions within the SunTrust mortgage line of business. Summer placements within SunTrust mortgage may include: marketing, finance, customer care, or production operations. Interns will participate in project team meetings and perform related assignments. They will participate in the development and tracking of formal project plans and key milestones. Interns will have the opportunity to develop valuable relationships while working with project managers and other interns in the program. They will also gain exposure to the various divisions within SunTrust mortgage through scheduled seminars and training sessions. In addition, all interns are assigned an experienced mentor as a part of the internship program. Mortgage internship opportunities are available in Richmond, Virginia.

Qualifications:

- Any major: Business majors strongly preferred
- Overall GPA of 2.8 or above required
- Solid interpersonal skills and customer service orientation
- Leadership experience and analytical aptitude
- High motivation and ability to meet deadlines
- Strong computer skills to include: Microsoft Word, Excel, Internet Explorer, and PowerPoint

Affinity Groups

We do not have formal affinity groups at SunTrust. However, we do have diversity site councils located across the enterprise in 20 geographic regions. These diversity site councils have sub-committees that focus on certain dimensions of diversity (i.e., women, GLBT, African-Americans, Hispanics, Asians and people with disabilities). These sub-committees focus on some of the same issues as affinity groups. Their purpose is to represent diversity in action at the local market level. Their activities include cultural celebrations, networking, recruiting new employees, mentoring, business development and community outreach. For example, our councils across the enterprise participated in Disability Employment Awareness Month by creating sub-committees to develop programs to support Disability Mentoring Day. The site councils also established African-American sub-committees to observe Black History Month. The groups sponsored events like "Juneteenth" and internal and external events around the documentary "Summer Hill." "Summer Hill" was a first person narrative describing Jim Crow. The councils meet at least once per quarter. They have market or regional web sites where they can report their local information. Additionally, each site council has a page on the corporate web site.

We also have two informal/unofficial affinity groups in place—a group that supports GLBT issues called Diversity Works, and an African-American group called SunTrust League of Employees (SALE). Meeting frequency varies from monthly to quarterly. The groups focus on employee support, mentoring, community outreach, business development and recruiting.

Entry-Level Programs/Full-Time Opportunities/Training Programs

Business Banking Associate Program

Length of program: Approximately six months

Geographic location(s) of program: SunTrust Business Banking has offices throughout the company's footprint in Georgia, Florida, Maryland, North Carolina, South Carolina, Tennessee, Virginia and the District of Columbia.

SunTrust Business Banking focuses on providing a full range of financial products and services to small businesses throughout the southeast and mid-Atlantic regions. Business bankers are sales specialists who focus on new business development of clients and prospects with annual revenues of one to five million dollars. Associates participate in a six month training program that begins their progression towards a business banker position within the retail line of business. The program focuses on four key areas: business development skills, sales abilities, analytical skills and product knowledge. Associates participate in classroom training in Atlanta, Georgia and complete on-the-job rotations in the bank location where they were hired. Associates support business bankers and managers by analyzing a wide variety of companies, industries, and markets, performing financial statement analysis, and assisting with call preparation. Associates are equipped with the tools needed to be successful contributors by participating in on-the-job rotations reinforced by classroom training.

Qualifications:

• BA/BS required
• Any major. e.g. accounting, finance, or equivalent analytical coursework strongly preferred
• Overall GPA of 2.8 or above required
• Strong sales orientation
• Solid interpersonal skills and communication skills
• Motivation to succeed
• Analytical aptitude

Commercial Banking Associate Program

Length of program: Approximately 11 months

Geographic location(s) of program: SunTrust Commercial Banking has offices throughout the company's footprint in Georgia, Florida, Maryland, North Carolina, South Carolina, Tennessee, Virginia, and the District of Columbia.

The SunTrust Commercial Banking line of business focuses on providing comprehensive financial solutions, superior value and outstanding services to targeted companies throughout the SunTrust footprint. The majority of commercial banking clients are privately held companies with annual revenues between five and 250 million dollars. Commercial banking associates participate in an 11-month training program that begins their progression towards a relationship manager position. The program focuses on three key areas—sales skills, analytical ability and product knowledge. Associates have the opportunity to build a professional network with their peers and commercial banking managers throughout the SunTrust system by participating in centralized classroom training in Atlanta, Georgia. Associates also complete on-the-job training in their local banking units where they support relationship managers and portfolio specialists in financial statement analysis, industry research, and client call preparation.

Qualifications:

• BA/BS required
• Any major, e.g. accounting, finance or equivalent analytical coursework strongly preferred
• Overall GPA of 2.8 or above required
• Interest in business and finance

• Strong sales orientation
• Solid interpersonal and communication skills
• Analytical aptitude
• Strong work ethic
• Desire to learn and grow professionally

Commercial Real Estate Associate Program

Length of program: Approximately 11 months
Geographic location(s) of program: SunTrust Commercial Real Estate has offices throughout the company's footprint in Georgia, Florida, Maryland, North Carolina, South Carolina, Tennessee, Virginia, and the District of Columbia.

SunTrust commercial real estate is a specialized, full-service banking group dedicated to providing financial solutions to commercial developers, real estate investors, national and local residential homebuilders, affordable housing groups, and real estate investment trusts. Commercial real estate clients are a combination of privately-held and publicly traded companies ranging in size and complexity and a number of them have market capitalization over one billion dollars. Commercial real estate associates participate in an 11-month program that begins their progression towards a relationship manager position. The program focuses on three key areas: sales skills, analytical ability, and product knowledge. Associates participate in centralized classroom training in Atlanta, Georgia and complete on-the-job assignments in the bank location where they were hired. Associates support relationship managers and portfolio specialists by analyzing companies, industries, markets and real estate projects, performing financial statement analysis and reviewing the clients' current credit relationship with SunTrust.

Qualifications:

• BA/BS required
• Any major, e.g. accounting, finance or equivalent analytical coursework strongly preferred
• Overall GPA of 2.8 or above required
• Interest in business and finance
• Strong sales orientation
• Solid interpersonal and communication skills
• Analytical aptitude
• Strong work ethic
• Desire to learn and grow professionally

Client Management Corporate Finance Analyst Program

Length of program: Two to three year analyst position
Geographic location(s) of program: Program is based in Atlanta; however potential rotation and placement opportunities exist in Atlanta, Nashville, Orlando and Richmond.

Client managers in corporate and investment banking are organized along both industry and geographic lines. Their mission is to utilize their expertise, along with that of the various product specialists and risk managers, to deliver creative ideas and solutions to their clients. This track of the Corporate and Investment Banking Analyst Training Program prepares analysts to become associates in many areas of corporate and investment banking and SunTrust. The program combines relevant classroom training in Atlanta with two, one-year practical on-the-job assignments. Assignments may be in any of our specialty groups—energy, health care, financial institutions, food and beverage, media, asset-based lending—or in one of our diversified industry groups located in Atlanta, Nashville, Orlando and Richmond. Analysts will sharpen financial analysis skills, develop an understanding of corporate markets and clients, and build expertise in corporate finance and investment banking products.

Qualifications:

• BA/BS required
• Any major; business major preferred
• Accounting or finance courses preferred
• Overall GPA of 3.0 or above required

• Proved analytical ability and attention to detail
• Solid leadership and interpersonal skills
• Effective oral and written communication skills

Debt Capital Markets Analyst Program

Length of program: Two to three year analyst position
Geographic location(s) of program: Program is based in Atlanta

The Debt Capital Markets track of the Corporate and Investment Banking Analyst Training Program combines a brief classroom schedule on the front end followed by six to 12-month group assignments with product specialists, during the initial two to three year analyst appointment. Analysts will support both external and internal clients in various industries with an assortment of capital markets products. Analysts will sharpen their corporate finance and modeling skills, as well as develop a broad understanding of capital markets and investment banking products and learn how they are leveraged in a vast number of industries. The majority of analysts will complete their assignments in Atlanta. Other assignments may include Nashville, Orlando or Richmond.

Qualifications:

• BA/BS required
• Any major
• Overall minimum GPA of 3.0 required
• Finance courses preferred
• High degree of academic and extracurricular achievement
• Interest in finance and investment banking
• Willingness to commit substantial time and energy to the program
• Proven analytical ability and attention to detail
• Proven ability to work well in a team environment
• Excellent written and oral communication skills

Investment Banking Analyst Program

Length of program: Two years
Geographic location(s) of program: Atlanta, Georgia

SunTrust Robinson Humphrey's Investment Banking Analyst Program is a two-year program designed to provide recent college graduates with an introduction to investment banking through an intensive learning experience. Analysts play integral roles on project teams by working closely with senior bankers on all aspects of investment banking transactions. After a three-week classroom training period, analysts work as generalists for the first six months, serving clients in various industries with an assortment of investment banking products. This generalist orientation offers analysts the opportunity to develop a broad base of skills while also gaining exposure to a wide variety of industries. After six months, analysts join industry-specific teams, providing them the opportunity to develop industry and product knowledge and make significant contributions to transaction teams. The majority of analysts will be placed at our headquarters in Atlanta. SunTrust Robinson Humphrey also has satellite investment banking offices in Boston, Nashville and Orlando.

Qualifications:

• BA/BS required
• Any major
• Overall minimum GPA of 3.0 required
• Finance courses preferred
• High degree of academic and extracurricular achievement
• Interest in finance and investment banking
• Willingness to commit substantial time and energy to the program
• Proven analytical ability and attention to detail
• Proven ability to work well in a team environment
• Excellent written and oral communication skills

Strategic Plan and Diversity Leadership

How does the firm's leadership communicate the importance of diversity to everyone at the firm?

- New employee orientation program
- Company web site: www.suntrust.com
- Employee web site
- Employee newsletter
- Annual report on diversity
- Diversity brochures
- Diversity commitment statements in the *Employee Handbook*
- Collateral materials for marketing, benefits, and new hire orientation
- Diversity training

Who has primary responsibility for leading diversity initiatives at your firm?

Our diversity initiatives are led by Carolyn Cartwright, senior vice president.

Does your firm currently have a diversity committee?

Yes.

If yes, please describe how the committee is structured, how often it meets, etc.

We have a Corporate Diversity Council made up of 20 senior executives across the enterprise that are responsible for setting the strategic direction as thought leaders, monitoring activities and evaluating the overall effectiveness of the initiative. The chairman/CEO and the president/COO co-chair the Corporate Diversity Council. The corporate council has sub-committees that serve as the working arms for moving ideas into action. The corporate council meets at least quarterly. The 20 Diversity Site Councils report to the Corporate Diversity Council.

If yes, does the committee's representation include one or more members of the firm's management/executive committee (or the equivalent)?

Yes.

> *Total Executives on Committee:* 20

Does the committee and/or diversity leader establish and set goals or objectives consistent with management's priorities?

Yes. Diversity is a business imperative at SunTrust. It aligns and supports SunTrust's strategic intent.

Specifically:

We intend to be recognized as the leading provider of high value financial services to consumers, businesses and institutions within our designated geographies.

Our success and financial market recognition will flow from our ability to enhance the economic well being of our customers, our shareholders, our people and our communities.

Our diversity mission and goals are tied to the mission, goals and values of the organization. The Corporate Diversity Council objectives are to:

- Confirm diversity as a business imperative in our workforce, marketplace and community.
- Convey management accountability for a diversity inclusive business environment.
- Maintain management accountability for increasing diversity representation.
- Create and sustain diversity awareness among all employees.
- Deliver diversity education and training

SunTrust recognizes that we are in the midst of a changing landscape. We identified four areas for marketplace changes that we will address in our diversity strategy. They include Hispanic, female, African-American entrepreneurs, and the 50+ age group.

Has the firm undertaken a formal or informal diversity program or set of initiatives aimed at increasing the diversity of the firm?

Yes, formal. Our diversity initiatives focus on the five previously stated diversity objectives. Some of the programs related to these objectives include an emerging and ethnic markets strategy, a development program for high potential people of color (POC) that is designed to accelerate the promotion rate of POC, the maintenance of a diversity representation scorecard, education and training for managers, a web-based training program for employees and a diversity recruiting strategy.

How often does the firm's management review the firm's diversity progress/results?

Programmatic review of diversity events and strategies occurs at least quarterly and an annual evaluation is made on progress-to-date against goals. Goals are maintained or new ones established during annual planning meetings.

How is the firm's diversity committee and/or firm management held accountable for achieving results?

Managers are held accountable for their diversity efforts and representation scorecard results. The bank's performance appraisal system has a diversity performance factor. Additionally, diversity is one of the leadership elements of the Management Incentive Program.

The Stats

	TOTAL (U.S. AND WORLDWIDE)	
	2005	2004
Number of employees	35,170	33,156
Revenue	$7.802 million	$6.348 million

There are two women and two people of color, or 17 percent, on the SunTrust board of directors (note: one woman is also a person of color.) Our workforce is made up of 70 percent females and 33 percent minorities. Women account for 62 percent of all promotions to executive, senior and middle management positions. Women make up 36 percent of senior vice presidents and 75 percent of entry-level managers. People of color account for 13 percent of middle managers and senior professionals.

Retention and Professional Development

How do 2005 minority and female attrition rates generally compare to those experienced in the prior year period?

About the same as in prior years. Our turnover for women and people of color is about the same as it is for white males.

Please identify the specific steps you are taking to reduce the attrition rate of minority and women employees.

• Increase/review compensation relative to competition
• Increase/improve current work/life programs
• Adopt dispute resolution process
• Succession plan includes emphasis on diversity

- Work with minority and women employees to develop career advancement plans
- Strengthen mentoring program for all employees, including minorities and women
- Professional skills development program, including minority and women employees
- Diversity Training for managers and associates
- Employee assistance programs
- Tuition reimbursement program
- SunTrust University—SunTrust's training and development division

Diversity Mission Statement

Vision

To create an inclusive environment and culture at SunTrust that emphasizes respect and leverages diversity in our marketplace, workforce, workplace and communities so that we can beat our competition in making SunTrust a superior employer and financial services provider, thus enhancing shareholder value.

Mission Statement

To be recognized as being among the best financial service providers in developing a diverse employee base that successfully meets the needs of our clients within our designated geographies.

Additional Information

SunTrust has development programs in place that focus on providing exceptional work experiences and mentoring opportunities. We have both formal and informal mentoring throughout the organization. We have also established a focused Leadership Development Program for minorities. The goal of the program is to accelerate the representation of ethnic minorities in key leadership and management positions. 15 participants were selected for a two year program which includes structured development activities, a business project, mentoring, coaching, 360 degree feedback and networking opportunities. It is a high level program to support SunTrust's talent management and diversity goals related to attracting, developing, promoting and retaining a diverse workforce.

We have targeted recruiting efforts which allow us to maintain strong relationships with minority colleges and organizations. Some of our college connections include Florida A&M, Howard, Spelman and Tennessee State University. For example, SunTrust is a participant in the 21st Century Advantage Program (CAP) at Howard University. A key element is the Corporate Team Adoption Program. Adoption means regular contact between STI executives and the students. The students learn about culture, history and business dynamics through case studies and site visits at SunTrust. A SunTrust executive, who acts as a corporate liaison, has been assigned to each of our core HBCUs and HSIs. Our hope is that their relationships with key faculty and staff will allow us to identify top talent from these institutions. We have also established a national partnership with INROADS and currently have 25 interns working with us.

To attract the best and brightest employees who reflect the diversity of our communities, we have established networks with key professional organizations, to include:

- Black Data Processing Associates
- Hispanic Chamber of Commerce
- National Black MBA Association
- National Society of Hispanic MBAs
- National Urban League
- Urban Financial Services Coalition
- Women for Hire
- Women of Color in Technology

SunTrust has achieved many successes through our Diversity Initiatives Program. Some of our accomplishments include:

- Ranked number 38 out of 50 by *DiversityInc* magazine as one of the Best Places to Work for Minorities
- Presented the Corporate Award of the Year for support of diversity in the financial services industry
- 2004 Recipient of the New Freedom Initiative Award presented by the Department of Labor, as an initiative of President Bush for employers with practices that address the needs of people with disabilities
- We placed in the top 100 of *Fortune* magazine's Best Places to Work for Minorities
- Awarded the best diversity web site by *DiversityInc Magazine*
- Given a grade of 100 (out of 100) by the Human Rights Campaign for our programs for the GLBT community
- Ranked as one of the best places to work by *The Atlanta Tribune* and *The Atlanta Business Chronicle*

SunTrust is known as a good corporate citizen in the communities where we operate. We give time and financial support to organizations like:

- 100 Black Men
- Jack and Jill Organization
- Latin American Association
- Hispanic Chamber of Commerce
- Urban League
- Rainbow PUSH Coalition
- Asian-American Chamber of Commerce
- Women in Finance
- M.L. King Centers
- Minority/Women Business Owners' Councils
- SCLC
- Asian-American Heritage Foundation
- Human Rights Campaign
- YWCA
- Career Opportunities for Students with Disabilities
- Women's Resource Center to End Domestic Violence

Symbol Technologies, Inc.

One Symbol Plaza, MS A-2
Holtsville, NY 11742
Phone: (631) 738-2400

Locations

Holtsville, NY (HQ)
Locations in over 50 countries.

Employment Contact

Margaret-Ann Douglas
Manager, Human Resources
One Symbol Plaza, MS A-2
Holtsville, NY 11742
Phone: (631) 738-4086
Fax: (631) 738-4763
E-mail: Margaret-ann.douglas@symbol.com
www.symbol.com/about/careers/careers.html

Recruiting

Please list the schools/types of schools at which you recruit.

• Ivy League schools
• Other private schools
• Public state schools
• Historically Black Colleges and Universities (HBCUs)
• Hispanic Serving Institutions (HSIs)

Do you have any special outreach efforts directed to encourage minority students to consider your firm?

• Participate in/host minority student job fair(s)
• Sponsor minority student association events

What activities does the firm undertake to attract minority and women employees?

• Participate at minority job fairs
• Seek referrals from other employees
• Utilize online job services

Do you use executive recruiting/search firms to seek to identify new diversity hires?

No.

Affinity Groups

SWAT—Symbol Women's Action Team

SWAT is a channel through which women can achieve their full potential professionally and personally. By serving as a network of professionals, SWAT engenders an environment in which its members communicate successes and share solutions available to women in the workplace.

SWAT meets monthly. The group's main goals are as follows:

• Recruitment and retention of women at Symbol Technologies, Inc.
• Promote and enhance relationship building among females in the Symbol workforce
• Provide an environment for women professionals to network and form support structures among female colleagues

Strategic Plan and Diversity Leadership

How does the firm's leadership communicate the importance of diversity to everyone at the firm?

• The Intranet—diversity web site
• Diversity training for managers
• Staff meetings
• Memos

Does your firm currently have a diversity committee?

No.

Has the firm undertaken a formal or informal diversity program or set of initiatives aimed at increasing the diversity of the firm?

Yes, informal.

How often does the firm's management review the firm's diversity progress/results?

Annually.

The Stats

	TOTAL IN THE U.S.		TOTAL OUTSIDE THE U.S		TOTAL WORLDWIDE	
	2005	2004	2005	2004	2005	2004
Number of employees	2,391	2,679	2,842	2,638	5,233	5,317
Revenue	$1.1 billion	$1.1 billion	$0.6 billion	$0.6 billion	$1.7 billion	$1.8 billion

The figure in the US column represents revenue for TASS (the Americas international - Mexico, Latin America and Canada).

Retention and Professional Development

How do 2005 minority and female attrition rates generally compare to those experienced in the prior year period?

Higher than in prior years. The company underwent significant changes and had a number of reorganizations in which a number of positions were eliminated. We are now in the turnaround mode, recruitment is picking up and we will be engaging in some targeted minority and female recruiting activities this year.

Please identify the specific steps you are taking to reduce the attrition rate of minority and women employees.

• Develop and/or support internal employee affinity groups
• Increase/review compensation relative to male non-minorities
• Increase/improve current work/life programs
• Adopt dispute resolution process
• Succession plan includes emphasis on diversity and identifies diverse candidates

Diversity Mission Statement

At Symbol, we know it is our associates that make us a great company. We respect and value diversity and are committed to creating a culture of inclusion where all of our associates can thrive—a culture that unlocks our enormous reservoirs of talent, innovation, and commitment and tears down barriers to collaboration.

We are actively working toward creating a workforce that mirrors and responds to the communities in which we operate and reflects the growing diversity of the marketplace—increasing our competitiveness, living our values and assuring our position as the enterprise mobility company.

Additional Information

Symbol's diversity program is currently under review. We have quite a few activities planned for this year, including the provision of five scholarships to Stony Brook University, two of which must go to women; targeted outreach to women and minority colleges and we are working closely with the Hispanic Association on Corporate Responsibility to promote Hispanics in the workforce. The following are just a couple of the activities in which we have been involved in the community:

In 2005 we provided a grant of $50,000 to the Urban League of Long Island to support the development of a computer resource room to provide educational services to youth vocational exploration programs, college prep programs and youth development and leadership programs.

A grant of $10,000 was provided to Pronto to support Hispanics. The program includes ESL classes and job placement for youth and adults.

A grant of $15,000 was provided to the Long Island Fund for Women and Girls to support "Smart Careers for Girls," a program designed to expand the interest of girls and young women in science, technology and engineering and math careers through increasing their exposure to specific information directly from women in these fields.

Synovus Financial Corp.

1000 5th Avenue Columbus, GA 31901 Phone: (706) 644-0679 Fax: (706) 649-5793 www. synovus.com **Locations** Worldwide	**Diversity Leadership** Audrey D. Hollingsworth Senior Vice President, Director, HR Services **Employment Contact** Jeff Hart Manager, Employment Services

Recruiting

Please list the schools/types of schools at which you recruit.

• Public state schools
• Historically Black Colleges and Universities (HBCUs)
• Other predominantly minority and/or women's colleges

Do you have any special outreach efforts directed to encourage minority students to consider your firm?

• Advertise in minority student association publication(s)
• Participate in/host minority student job fair(s)
• Sponsor minority student association events
• Firm's employees participate on career panels at schools

What activities does the firm undertake to attract minority and women employees?

• Participate at minority job fairs
• Seek referrals from other employees
• Utilize online job services

Do you use executive recruiting/search firms to seek to identify new diversity hires?

No.

Internships and Co-ops

Synovus Inter/CO-OP PROGRAM

Deadline for application: Varies depending on the position
Pay: $8.00 - $12.00 per hour
Length of the program: 10 - 12 weeks
Percentage of interns/co-ops in the program who receive offers of full-time employment: 40 percent
Web site for internship/co-op information: www.synovus.com

The internship program encompasses several departments within our family of companies. It varies from year to year.

Scholarships

Jack Parker Scholarship Fund (internal scholarship program)

> *Deadline for application for the scholarship program:* Applications for the scholarship will be accepted each spring, with the award winners announced in the summer. Applications are reviewed and ranked by an independent, external scholarship selection committee.

Number and size of the awards to be granted will be determined each year by the board of directors of the Jack B. Parker Foundation Inc., based on available funds. The most outstanding applicant is chosen to be the Jack Parker Scholar.

Our company strives to assist the families of our team members through the Jack Parker Centennial Scholarship Program. The Jack Parker Scholarship Program was established in 1988, as a part of the commemoration of the 100th Anniversary of Columbus Bank and Trust Company. The scholarship program is managed by the Jack B. Parker Foundation, Inc., to award college or vocational institution scholarships to the children of Synovus family team members. The scholarship program and the foundation were named in memory of Jack B. Parker, whose career with our family of companies spanned 44 years. Jack's enthusiastic attitude, keen sense of duty and good heart were evident throughout his career. He served as resident historian, confidant and trainer for countless team members. Less well-known was the role Jack played as an anonymous benefactor. Children of current, retired or deceased employees are eligible to submit an application for the scholarship program.

Entry-Level Programs/Full-Time Opportunities/Training Programs

Management Associate Program

> *Length of program:* Six to nine months
> *Geographic location(s) of program:* Columbus, GA and several banks in the southeastern U.S.

On-the-job training and classroom training encompassing several areas of retail and commercial banking.

Strategic Plan and Diversity Leadership

Our diversity council and the president of our company provides planned communication throughout the year. We use a variety of communication vehicles and messages. The value of diversity to our organization is displayed on our company web site to communicate our commitment to external sources. We use a formal print piece that is available for our CEO population to use during community or business meetings involving external audiences. Through our Intranet (INSITE) we deliver bi-monthly articles to team members regarding various topics of interest on the subject of diversity. We also conduct an annual leadership presentation that includes progress results, goals and new year targets on diversity. Our council meets semi-monthly to address issues of diversity, develop programmatic initiatives and prepare for focus groups session with team members.

Who has primary responsibility for leading diversity initiatives at your firm?

Audrey D. Hollingsworth, senior vice president, director, financial services HR.

Does your firm currently have a diversity committee?

Yes, the Synovus Diversity Council is comprised of various senior/executive level corporate leaders from throughout the enterprise. The council convenes every other month to discuss goals, progress and additional efforts that can be made to further our commitment to diversity.

If yes, does the committee's representation include one or more members of the firm's management/executive committee (or the equivalent)?

Yes.

If yes, how many executives are on the committee, and in 2005, what was the total number of hours collectively spent by the committee in furtherance of the firm's diversity initiatives? How many employees are on the committee, and how often does the committee convene in furtherance of the firm's diversity initiatives?

In 2005 there were 20 senior/executive leaders on the Synovus Advisory Council. The council meets at least six times per year for approximately 20 hours per year.

Does the committee and/or diversity leader establish and set goals or objectives consistent with management's priorities?

Yes, we continue to set three major goals that align with our leadership priorities: diversity training for all of our leaders, targeted development plans for minorities and females and representation progress in the leadership tier.

Has the firm undertaken a formal or informal diversity program or set of initiatives aimed at increasing the diversity of the firm?

Yes, formal. There are five areas that we use to measure and assess progress toward improving representation in our organization. Those areas are: workforce, leadership, top salaried, new hires and board of directors (we are substituting board of directors for termination results). We measure our progress against our community statistics, establish targets and measure progress. This year we will introduce a report card to assess individual company results.

How often does the firm's management review the firm's diversity progress/results?

Quarterly.

How is the firm's diversity committee and/or firm management held accountable for achieving results?

There is no formal accountability that is specifically directed at the council. However, the council holds itself accountable by publishing our goals to our team members and providing the team members with updates on progress toward our diversity goals. Essentially, our total workforce holds the council accountable for delivering on the expectations that are established. It is about our credibility for doing what we say we will do.

The Stats

Employees
2005: 12,351
2004: 11,904

Revenue
2005: $2.6 billion
2004: $2.1 billion

Retention and Professional Development

How do 2005 minority and female attrition rates generally compare to those experienced in the prior year period?

About the same as in prior years.

Diversity Mission Statement

We are committed to creating an environment that appreciates individuality. And now, more than ever, we're renewing our commitment to diversity. We continue to recognize diversity as a broad collection of differences that encompasses many elements: beliefs, race, work styles, age, education, ethnic origin, gender, ideas, physical ability, perspectives and more.

We believe that a wide "band of inclusion" helps to increase team member performance, empowerment, satisfaction, productivity, equity, creativity, respect and fairness. Our focus on diversity will also position us to better promote diverse business partnerships, expand our customer base, attract and retain the top talent in the market, make the company a better place to work, better understand our diverse customers' unique needs, give customers and communities outstanding service and deliver greater value to our stakeholders. At Synovus, valuing and leveraging our differences is an essential part of our organization's success.

Our diversity strategy includes:

• Education—discussing the benefits value and management of diversity
• Representation—visible diversity at all levels of the organization
• Business Partnerships—developing relationships with diverse business partners
• Development—establishing mentoring and networking models that facilitate the continued growth and development of our team members
• Work Place Practices—modifying our recruiting and hiring strategy to position us to compete for a diverse talent pool

Diversity creates an environment where team members can contribute innovative ideas, seek challenge, assume leadership and continue to focus on and exceed business, professional and personal objectives. One approach toward individual success is to give people meaningful, challenging work and mentors to help them along the way.

T. Rowe Price

100 E. Pratt Street
Baltimore, MD 21202
Phone: (410) 345-2000
www.troweprice.com

Locations

Amsterdam • Argentina • Australia •
Denmark • Hong Kong • Japan • London
• Singapore • Stockholm

Diversity Leadership

Jeff Sube
Manager, Organizational Development and
Diversity

Employment Contact

Sholeh Dadressan
Corporate Recruiter
100 E. Pratt Street
Baltimore, MD 21202
Phone: (410) 345-2715
Fax: (410) 345-2394
E-mail: sholeh_dadressan@troweprice.com
www.troweprice.com/careers

Recruiting

Please list the schools/types of schools at which you recruit.

• Ivy League schools
• Other private schools
• Public state schools
• Historically Black Colleges and Universities (HBCUs)
• Other predominantly minority and/or women's colleges

Do you have any special outreach efforts directed to encourage minority students to consider your firm?

• Hold a reception for minority students
• Conferences
• Advertise in minority student association publication(s)
• Participate in/host minority student job fair(s)
• Sponsor minority student association events
• Firm's employees participate on career panels at schools
• Outreach to leadership of minority student organizations
• Scholarships or intern/fellowships for minority students
• *Other:* Longstanding partnership with INROADS for recruiting T. Rowe Price interns and full-time hires

What activities does the firm undertake to attract minority and women employees?

• Partner programs with women and minority associations
• *Conferences:* Robert Toigo Foundation, The Consortium for Mgmt. Studies, National Assoc. of Women MBAs, National Association of Black MBAs
• Participate at minority job fairs
• Seek referrals from other employees
• Utilize online job services

Do you use executive recruiting/search firms to seek to identify new diversity hires?

We use executive recruiting/search firms to identify qualified candidates.

Internships and Co-ops

T. Rowe Price Summer Internship Program

Number of interns in the program in summer 2005 (internship) or 2005 (co-op): 81 interns two co-op students

Pay: Depends on year of study, previous internships with T. Rowe, skill set, etc.

Length of the program: 10-12 weeks

Percentage of interns/co-ops in the program who receive offers of full-time employment: 64 percent of eligible interns in 2005 were extended full-time offers

Web site for internship/co-op information: www.troweprice.com/careers

As a summer intern at T. Rowe Price, students will gain meaningful experience that will help position their future careers for success. Our structured, firmwide program provides a thriving business environment where interns can apply their academic knowledge and grow both personally and professionally. With ongoing guidance and coaching from the manager, our interns will work on real world projects that contribute to the daily operation of our business.

We offer exciting opportunities across many of today's in-demand career areas such as: accounting, communications and design, economics, finance, human resources, information technology, investments, investment operations and marketing and sales.

Scholarships

T. Rowe Price offers numerous scholarship opportunities.

Entry-Level Programs/Full-time Opportunities/Training Programs

T. Rowe Price provides rotational programs such as the two-year Investment Fellowship program as well as full-time opportunities for many of our entry-level positions.

Strategic Plan and Diversity Leadership

How does the firm's leadership communicate the importance of diversity to everyone at the firm?

The T. Rowe Price board of directors participates in an annual review of the firm's diversity strategy with the director of global human resources (e.g. recruiting, retention, development, succession planning, mentoring, community outreach). At T. Rowe Price, workplace diversity is primarily accomplished via inclusive business practices at the corporate level and also within individual business units.

The Stats

2005 Employees

4,212 (U.S.)

142 (outside of U.S.)

4,354 (worldwide)

Retention and Professional Development

T. Rowe Price invests in initiatives designed to promote inclusion in all aspects of retention and professional development of its associates. In part, the firm addresses retention and professional development of its associates through targeted training and development programs, innovative internships, a corporate mentoring program, a robust succession planning process, a comprehensive achievement-based recognition program, and a wide spectrum of community outreach initiatives.

Diversity Mission Statement

At T. Rowe Price, diversity is a leadership standard and a core business strategy built upon a foundation of integrity, initiative, service, teamwork and learning. We recruit, develop, and retain highly motivated and skilled individuals with varied backgrounds and experience who share our vision of a diverse workforce. The result is a creative and productive environment that promotes inclusion and demonstrates exceptional ability to attain shareholder, client and organizational objectives. Workplace diversity contributes to our firm's reputation as a global employer of choice, is key to our competitive advantage, and guides our decisions to invest and become involved in the communities where we live and work.

Target Corporation

1000 Nicollet Mall, TPS-0955
Minneapolis, MN 55403
Phone: (612) 696-6705
Fax: (612) 696-5400
www.target.com

Locations

Target store headquarters is located in Minneapolis, Minnesota. Target has over 1,400 store locations in 47 states, 23 distribution centers and three import warehouses and has offices in over 40 countries throughout the world to support our global sourcing initiatives.

Diversity Leadership

Tamika Curry
Director of Diversity

Employment Contact

www.target.com/careers

Recruiting

Please list the schools/types of schools at which you recruit.

- Ivy League schools
- Other private schools
- Public state schools
- Historically Black Colleges and Universities (HBCUs)
- Hispanic Serving Institutions (HSIs)
- Other predominantly minority and/or women's colleges

Do you have any special outreach efforts directed to encourage minority students to consider your firm?

- Hold a reception for minority students
- *Conferences:* National Black MBA, National Society of Hispanic MBAs, Hispanic Alliance for Career Enhancement, National Hispanic Business Association, Monster Diversity Leadership Program, National Association of Asian American Professionals, National INROADS Alumni Association, Consortium for Graduate Study in Management, Society of Hispanic Professional Engineers, National Society of Black Engineers
- Advertise in minority student association publication(s)
- Participate in/host minority student job fair(s)
- Sponsor minority student association events
- Firm's employees participate on career panels at schools
- Outreach to leadership of minority student organizations
- Scholarships or intern/fellowships for minority students

What activities does the firm undertake to attract minority and women employees?

- Partner programs with women and minority associations
- Conferences
- Participate at minority job fairs
- Seek referrals from other employees
- Utilize online job services

Do you use executive recruiting/search firms to seek to identify new diversity hires?

No.

Internships and Co-ops

Target Headquarters, Stores or Distribution Internship

Deadline for application: On campus interviews fall and spring

Number of interns in the program in summer 2005 (internship) or 2005 (co-op): Approximately 1,000

Pay: Depends on position

Length of the program: 10-12 weeks

Percentage of interns/co-ops in the program who receive offers of full-time employment: 50 percent general/75 percent INROADS

Web site for internship/co-op information: Target.com/campus

Stores Overview

10 week program with rotations in the following areas:

• Logistics
• Sales floor
• Human resources
• Assets protection
• Guest services
• Perishables
• Pharmacy
• Opportunity to complete a hands-on project within your focus area
• Executive partnership and shadow rotation
• Interact with executives & top leaders in a Fortune 100 company
• Opportunity to strengthen your leadership skills
• Learn about merchandising, guest service and inventory management to maximize sales
• Availability to attend executive level leadership training classes

Qualifications:

• *Undergrad:* Currently enrolled or accepted in a four-year degree program with strong academic performance
• Leadership and strong decision making skills
• Ability to communicate clearly and effectively in all situations
• Team-oriented thinking
• Committed to self development and developing others
• Strong cognitive skills, including problem analysis, decision making, financial and quantitative analysis
• Desire to pursue a career in retail management

Distribution Overview

• 10-week program designed to provide a realistic sense of distribution operations, an executive's role and our culture
• Achieved through technical and leadership training, project work, committee participation

Key training objectives:

• Gain an understanding of distribution operations and supply chain management
• Gain an understanding of Target culture

• Learn what it means to be an effective Target leader
• Gain a picture of how a world-class supply chain organization operates
• Work in a fast-paced, technologically advanced, clean, bright operation
• Become part of a leadership organization that moves boxes
• Leave an imprint on the organization

Qualifications:

• Thrives in a fast-paced, results-focused, collaborative environment
• Strong ability to develop relationships with others
• Strong communication skills
• Interested in leading others
• Approaches the opportunity with initiative
• Commitment to learning
• Ready to have fun!

Headquarters Overview

The 10-week HQ internship is designed to give hands-on real world experience in the following areas:

• Target technology services
• Property development (real estate, construction, architecture, engineering, store planning & design, building services)
• Target sourcing services
• Finance/accounting
• Merchandising/merchandising presentation
• Target.com
• Graphic design marketing
• Store support/assets protection
• Target financial services
• Housing and airfare available for out of state interns

Interns will:

• Work with a team, manager and mentor
• Play a significant role in analyzing/developing company strategies
• Responsible for completing a project and presenting results at the conclusion of the internship
• Receive developmental feedback through classroom training, on the job application and the formal review process
• Participate in social networking events, executive lunches, Metro Intern Exchange, volunteer opportunities and involvement with Target's diversity business councils

Qualifications:

• Excellent analytical skills
• Outstanding verbal and written communication skills
• Demonstrated leadership skills
• Superior planning and organizational skills
• Strong computer skills

Scholarships

We fund undergraduate scholarships through general scholarship funds of the schools where we recruit as well as provide graduate scholarships through our partnerships with NBMBAA, NSHMBA and CGSM. We also provide funding to the United Negro College Fund and the Hispanic Scholarship Fund.

Affinity Groups

- African-American Business Council
- Asian-American Business Council
- GLBT Business Council
- Hispanic Business Council

Target's diversity business councils aim to create an inclusive environment and provide a forum to exchange information, share common interests and establish mentoring relationships. Each business council is focused on helping team members grow professionally and has specific programs and objectives centered on retention and development.

Entry-Level Programs/Full-Time Opportunities/Training Programs

Team Leader In-Training (Distribution Centers, Business Analyst (HQ/Merchandising), Human Resouces In-Training (Distribution, HQ, and Stores), Executive Team Leader-In-Training (Stores), Target Technology Leadership Program (HQ)

Length of program: 12 week training program
Geographic location(s) of program: Nationally

Our extensive training program involves classroom and on-the-job experience and a mentor who works with the team member throughout the training.

Tuition reimbursement is available.

Strategic Plan and Diversity Leadership

How does the firm's leadership communicate the importance of diversity to everyone at the firm?

Target uses all of the corporation's communication channels to share diversity information including e-mails, web site, newsletters, posters, brochures, etc. Furthermore, Target annually administers an internal communication campaign centered on diversity awareness.

Who has primary responsibility for leading diversity initiatives at your firm?

Tamika Curry, director of diversity.

Does your firm currently have a diversity committee?

Yes. Target has a cross-functional diversity steering committee chaired by a member of senior management. The committee meets bi-monthly and is comprised of leaders from throughout the corporation. The objective of the committee is to provide direction, feedback, and guidance on Target's corporate diversity efforts.

If yes, does the committee's representation include one or more members of the firm's management/executive committee (or the equivalent)?

Yes.

If yes, how many executives are on the committee, and in 2005, what was the total number of hours collectively spent by the committee in furtherance of the firm's diversity initiatives? How many employees are on the committee, and how often does the committee convene in furtherance of the firm's diversity initiatives?

A total of 22 employees are on the committee, which meets bi-monthly.

Total Executives on Committee: 19

Does the committee and/or diversity leader establish and set goals or objectives consistent with management's priorities?

Yes.

Has the firm undertaken a formal or informal diversity program or set of initiatives aimed at increasing the diversity of the firm?

Yes, formal.

How often does the firm's management review the firm's diversity progress/results?

Bi-monthly.

How are the firm's diversity committee and/or firm management held accountable for achieving results?

Management is required to report annually to the Target board of directors on its progress in achieving greater diversity of our workforce.

The Stats

	TOTAL IN THE U.S.		TOTAL WORLDWIDE	
	2005	2004	2005	2004
Number of employees	Tot: 336,000 Min: 138,000 Fem: 198,000	Tot: 292,000 Min: 115,000 Fem: 172,000	Tot: 336,000 Min: 138,000 Fem: 198,000	Tot: 292,000 Min: 115,000 Fem: 72,000
Revenue	N/A	N/A	$52,620 mil	46,839 mil

Our long-standing commitment to equal opportunity has increased the diversity of our work force as reflected in our Equal Employment Opportunity (EEO) report for 2005 (the most relevant portions of which follow).

Target percentage of all employees in the following job categories:

	FEMALE	MINORITY
Officials & Managers	44%	23%
Professionals	20.2%	14%
Sales Workers	63%	43%
Professionals	59%	40%

Gender and ethnic diversity is reflected at the highest levels of the corporation, including Target's board of directors.

Diversity Mission Statement

Target is a performance-based company with equal opportunities for all who perform.

Our commitment

We respect and value the individuality of all team members and guests. We know that valuing diversity makes good business sense and helps to ensure our future success.

Our definition of diversity

We define diversity as individuality. This individuality may include a wide spectrum of attributes like personal style, age, race, gender, ethnicity, sexual orientation, language, physical ability, religion, family, citizenship status, socio-economic circumstances, education and life experiences. To us, diversity is any attribute that makes an individual unique that does not interfere with effective job performance.

Additional Information

Discrimination based upon race, color, religion, sex, age, national origin, disability, sexual orientation or other characteristics protected by law is not tolerated in our work place. In addition to prohibiting such discrimination, we attempt to create an environment that recognizes the value of diversity and enhances the opportunity for success of all team members regardless of their differences.

The following are examples of initiatives within Target that are intended to promote diversity throughout our organization:

Minority recruitment-employees of diverse backgrounds are sought by attending minority job fairs (National Black MBA Association, National Society of Hispanic MBAs and Consortium for Graduate Study in Management), placing ads in minority media, posting jobs and looking for candidates on minority-focused web sites (such as DiversityInc and HireDiversity), posting positions at schools and other public places with high minority populations, attending national meetings of minority organizations, and publishing and distributing recruitment literature emphasizing our commitment to diversity.

Target also hires interns from INROADS at the corporate, store and distribution center levels. Target is a charter sponsor for the INROADS Retail Management Institute, aimed at attracting more students of color to retail careers. In addition, Target has the Executive In-Training Program, where a priority is placed on sourcing and staffing positions with diversity candidates.

Target is a national leader in providing job opportunities for people with disabilities. Target participates in community-based training by seeking out agencies, school programs and government incentive programs in an effort to hire people with disabilities.

Diversity Training: Target provides training programs to all its employees and leadership development to all supervisory level team members—and diversity training is an integral part of that development. We provide training that is intended to enhance awareness of diversity in the work place and to build skills necessary to promote that diversity and the benefits it offers.

Diversity Team: Target has formed an internal diversity team that is solely dedicated to leveraging diversity throughout the organization. The team focuses on recruitment and retention, awareness and communication, and measurement, and works with business partners throughout the company to provide diversity guidance and drive change.

Diversity Steering Committee: Target has a cross-functional committee, comprised of leaders representing all areas of the company, that help provide direction, feedback and guidance on the corporation's diversity efforts.

Diversity Business Councils: Target sponsors a variety of diversity business councils that provide a forum for individuals to grow and develop and all have specific goals around recruitment and retention, mentoring, training and coaching.

Involvement and Partnerships: Target has partnerships with many diversity-focused organizations, including:

• INROADS
• The Consortium For Graduate Study in Management (CGSM)
• Monster Diversity Leadership Program (Monster DLP)
• National Association of Asian American Professionals (NAAAP)
• The National Black MBA Association Conference (NBMBAA)
• The National Society of Hispanic MBAs (NSHMBA)
• Hispanic Alliance for Career Enhancement (HACE)
• National Hispanic Business Association (NHBA)
• Black Data Processing Association (BDPA)
• The National Minority Supplier Development Council (NMSDC)
• The Women's Business Enterprise National Council (WBENC)
• Society for Women in Engineering (SWE)
• The Urban League
• The United Negro College Fund (UNCF)
• The Hispanic College Fund (HCF)

Diversity has been one of the strengths of our company and will continue to be an important part of our business strategy as we expand into new and different markets. We are committed to promoting and reinforcing diversity throughout our company as we position our business for continued success in the 21st century.

Tech Data Corporation

5301 Tech Data Drive
Clearwater, FL 33760
Phone: (727) 539-7429
Fax: (727) 539-7429

Locations

Clearwater, FL (HQ)

Diversity Leadership

Ed Krauss
www.techdata.com/careers

Employment Contact

Amy Blake
Manager, Employment
5301 Tech Data Drive
Clearwater, FL 33760
Phone: (727) 539-7429
Fax: (727) 539-7429

Recruiting

Please list the schools/types of schools at which you recruit.

- *Public state schools:* University of South Florida, University of Florida, Florida State, University of Tampa, Eckerd College, University of Central Florida
- *Historically Black Colleges and Universities (HBCUs):* Florida A&M University

Do you have any special outreach efforts directed to encourage minority students to consider your firm?

- Advertise in minority student association publication(s)
- Participate in/host minority student job fair(s)
- Scholarships or intern/fellowships for minority students
- INROADS internship program

What activities does the firm undertake to attract minority and women employees?

- Partner programs with women and minority associations
- Participate at minority job fairs
- Seek referrals from other employees
- Utilize online job services

Do you use executive recruiting/search firms to seek to identify new diversity hires?

Yes.

Internships and Co-ops

INROADS

Deadline for application: Fall
Pay: $10-12 per hour (full-time), paid bi-weekly
Length of the program: 12 weeks
Percentage of interns/co-ops in the program who receive offers of full-time employment: 100 percent

Strategic Plan and Diversity Leadership

How does the firm's leadership communicate the importance of diversity to everyone at the firm?

E-mail, quarterly employee meetings, web site, town hall meetings.

Who has primary responsibility for leading diversity initiatives at your firm?

Ed Krauss, senior manager, employment operations.

Does your firm currently have a diversity committee?

Yes.

If yes, please describe how the committee is structured, how often it meets, etc.

14 members who meet once a month.

If yes, does the committee's representation include one or more members of the firm's management/executive committee (or the equivalent)?

Yes.

Does the committee and/or diversity leader establish and set goals or objectives consistent with management's priorities?

Yes.

Has the firm undertaken a formal or informal diversity program or set of initiatives aimed at increasing the diversity of the firm?

Yes, formal.

How often does the firm's management review the firm's diversity progress/results?

Twice a year.

Retention and Professional Development

Please identify the specific steps you are taking to reduce the attrition rate of minority and women employees.

• Increase/improve current work/life programs
• Succession plan includes emphasis on diversity
• Work with minority and women employees to develop career advancement plans
• Professional skills development program, including minority and women employees
• *Other:* We also analyze exit interview data to identify opportunities for improvements and trends

Diversity Mission Statement

Tech Data's philosophy has always striven to place the greatest emphasis on the role of the individual within the company. That emphasis on the individual, at the same time, requires Tech Data to pay attention to the fact that each employee brings a wealth of different perspectives to the work environment. Tech Data and its employees need to be respectful not only of those differences, but learn how to make difference, in itself, an additional value which can be incorporate into how others are treated and customers are approached.

The concept of meaningful sameness and meaningful difference is not a new one. Meaningful sameness is needed in order for people to operate within the context of a common set of standards and values for everyday operation. Employees also need to

contribute meaningfully to the company in the performance of their jobs. Concurrently, Tech Data and its employees must respect and encourage meaningful difference, with the assumption that people from different perspectives provide vitality, creativity, new ideas and growth.

Multiculturalism seeks to look at difference in the broadest parameters. Culture is often defined to include terms of race, gender, and national origin, and these specific indices are, of course, vital in shaping values. Additionally, culture also involves values derived from considerations relating to one's age, marital status, religion, sexual orientation, gender identity and/or expression and disability. All of these factors, and more, shape an individual's value system, and all of these have actual potential value to Tech Data as a company.

Tech Data provides equal opportunity for all employees and applicants for employment regardless of race, color, creed, religion, national origin, sexual orientation, age, or sex. Similarly, Tech Data has stated that individuals with physical and mental limitations are evaluated on their ability to perform a specific job rather than on stereotypical assumptions about their disability, and that reasonable accommodations are made when appropriate. Tech Data continues to hold steadfast to this philosophy.

A policy limited to equal opportunity, however, is not sufficient to attract and retain members of historically underrepresented groups. While Tech Data has attracted an immensely talented workforce, the nets must be cast much more widely to attract available talent. The process Tech Data uses for that purpose is affirmative action; it is a means for Tech Data to achieve multiculturalism, i.e., the existence and valuing of difference. Tech Data's operating assumption is that talent is randomly distributed in all populations and that Tech Data benefits from the participation of different groups in its workforce.

Affirmative action is a concept misunderstood by many. In many people's minds, it has meant lowered standards or preferential treatment. Tech Data's position is that we can behave affirmatively while retaining the highest standards, but that more energy, planning, and commitment must be committed to the inclusion of competitive talent from all segments of the population. That effort requires dedication, personal responsibility and investment of resources. Tech Data needs to continue to find ways to encourage and support hiring managers to make the extra efforts needed to attract the best people.

Multiculturalism is crucial to Tech Data domestically within the United States and as a global corporation. Tech Data's future success in the United States depends heavily upon the ability to harness and include the vitality of the burgeoning minority populations, both as employees and customers. No one group will have majority status within 10 years and demographic factors will have major implications for the workforce composition, as well as customers.

Globally, the world is getting smaller and Tech Data's presence internationally becomes more prominent every day. Tech Data has always sought local talent in order to compete effectively, and Tech Data needs to be open to and inclusive of ideas and values that originate outside the United States. Tech Data will continue to seek ways to incorporate different perspectives in global operations.

Managing multiculturalism is a critical part of success for any twenty-first century company and it is a challenge Tech Data is ready to pursue.

Tenet Healthcare Corporation

13737 Noel Road, Suite 100
Dallas, TX 75240
Phone: (469) 893-6026
Fax: (469) 893-7026
www.tenethealth.com

Locations

Dallas, TX (HQ)

More than 60 hospitals owned and operated by Tenet subsidiaries offer a wide array of medical services in the following 12 states:
Alabama • California • Florida • Georgia • Louisiana • Missouri • Nebraska • North Carolina • Pennsylvania • South Carolina • Tennessee • Texas.
We have corporate and regional offices locations in:
California • Florida • Texas • Georgia • Missouri

Diversity Leadership

Rhonda Price
Senior Director, Human Resources

Employment Contact

Beth Crooms
Manager, National Recruitment Strategies
E-mail: beth.crooms@tenethealth.com
Career web site address:
www.teamtenet.com/vault

Recruiting

Please list the schools/types of schools at which you recruit.

• Ivy League schools
• Other private schools
• Public state schools
• Historically Black Colleges and Universities (HBCUs)
• Hispanic Serving Institutions (HSIs)
• Other predominantly minority and/or women's colleges

Do you have any special outreach efforts directed to encourage minority students to consider your firm?

• Hold a reception for minority students
• Advertise in minority student association publication(s)
• Participate in/host minority student job fair(s)
• Sponsor minority student association events
• Firm's employees participate on career panels at schools
• Outreach to leadership of minority student organizations
• Scholarships or intern/fellowships for minority students

What activities does the firm undertake to attract minority and women employees?

• Partner programs with women and minority associations
• *Conferences:* National Association of Hispanic Nurses, Black Nurses Association
• Participate at minority job fairs

• Seek referrals from other employees
• Utilize online job services
• Conduct workshops for the Women's Job Corp.

Do you use executive recruiting/search firms to seek to identify new diversity hires?

Yes.

Affinity Groups

Tenet hospitals direct and manage initiatives and programs of all types at a local level, including diversity, to best meet each community and workforce's unique circumstances. As a result, the existence and type of affinity groups vary by hospital. Affinity groups have been established at some hospitals in response to local interest and need.

Entry-Level Programs/Full-Time Opportunities/Training Programs

Hospitals offer a host of training programs including Leadership Essentials and Nurse Leader Academy.

There is a student loan repayment program to assist employees in repaying school loans, and tuition reimbursement to continue education.

Strategic Plan and Diversity Leadership

How does the firm's leadership communicate the importance of diversity to everyone at the firm?

With strategy and leadership of diversity managed at a local hospital level, the communication approach varies by hospital. Generally, communication regarding the importance of diversity is incorporated into new employee orientation, department head communications, diversity class, ethics training, and incorporated into various annual training programs.

Who has primary responsibility for leading diversity initiatives at your firm?

Leadership of diversity initiatives is managed at the local hospital level. Generally it is the responsibility of either the chief human resource officer or the CEO.

Does your firm currently have a diversity committee?

Yes, in some hospitals.

If yes, please describe how the committee is structured, how often it meets, etc.

It varies by hospital.

Has the firm undertaken a formal or informal diversity program or set of initiatives aimed at increasing the diversity of the firm?

It's informal at a corporate level, allowing each hospital to tailor an approach that best suits their situation.

The Stats

Employees

2005: 77,800

Revenues

2005: $9.6 billion

At Tenet, our total workforce is 79 percent female and 21 percent male. Our senior leadership team, composed of senior directors, hospital administrative teams and vice presidents, is currently 65 percent female and 35 percent male.

At the core of our workforce is our talented nurse community. The most recent survey conducted by the Department of Health & Human Services, the 2004 National Sample Survey of Registered Nurses, indicates that of the total RN community available nationwide, only 4.6 percent are black, 3.3 percent are Asian or Pacific Islander and 1.8 percent are Hispanic. We recently compared ourselves to these national statistics and are proud to report that at Tenet, our diverse workforce of nurses is 15 percent black, 14 percent Asian or Pacific Islander and 8 percent Hispanic. We feel this is a reflection of our approach to serve and respond to the needs of our hospital's local communities.

Retention and Professional Development

How do 2005 minority and female attrition rates generally compare to those experienced in the prior year period?

About the same as in prior years.

Please identify the specific steps you are taking to reduce the attrition rate of minority and women employees.

- Increase/review compensation relative to competition
- Increase/improve current work/life programs
- Adopt dispute resolution process
- Succession plan includes emphasis on diversity
- Strengthen mentoring program for all employees, including minorities and women
- Professional skills development program, including minority and women employees
- *Other*: This varies according to each hospital's approach and strategy but many hospitals have a Retention Committee that focuses on ways to retain employees throughout the hospital.

Diversity Mission Statement

Our overall vision is that Tenet will distinguish itself as a leader in redefining health care delivery and will be recognized for the passion of all its people and partners in providing quality and innovative care to the patients it serves in each community.

"Toyota taught me how to take **the road less traveled.**"

The Toyota Way of doing business centers on respect for others and the continued growth of everyone. In order to maintain this high-performing environment, we need the best people. People from all walks of life. People just like you.

At Toyota Motor Sales, USA, Inc., we take pride in what the Toyota name represents – innovation, quality, and reliability. TMS is the U.S. sales, marketing, and distribution arm that oversees operations in 49 states for Toyota, Scion and Lexus products.

We would like to invite you to explore career opportunities at Toyota Motor Sales U.S.A., Inc. and discover how you can achieve great success as part of a team of which you too can be proud of. Toyota offers excellent salaries and a benefit package that includes medical, dental and vision plans. Not to mention, a great vehicle leasing program. So come join our team and take your career in a whole new direction.

For more information on employment opportunities, please visit us at: **www.toyota.com/talentlink**

⊙ TOYOTA | toyota.com/talentlink

Toyota is an equal opportunity employer. M/F/D/V.

Toyota Motor Company

19001 S. Western Ave, A134
Torrance, CA 90501
Phone: (310) 468-2083
Fax: (310) 381-6842
www.toyota.com/talentlink

Locations

Torrance, CA

Diversity Leadership

Fabiola Gonzalez
College Recruiter

Employment Contact

Jennifer Gonzalez
HR Representative
E-mail: jennifer_gonzalez@toyota.com

Recruiting

Please list the schools/types of schools at which you recruit.

• Private schools
• Public state schools
• Historically Black Colleges and Universities (HBCUs)
• Other predominantly minority and/or women's colleges

Do you have any special outreach efforts directed to encourage minority students to consider your firm?

• *Conferences:* Atlanta University Center (AUC) and National Hispanic Business Association
• Advertise in minority student association publication(s)
• Participate in/host minority student job fair(s)
• Sponsor minority student association events
• Outreach to leadership of minority student organizations
• Scholarships or intern/fellowships for minority students

What activities does the firm undertake to attract minority and women employees?

• Partner programs with women and minority associations
• *Conferences:* see above
• Participate at minority job fairs
• Seek referrals from other employees
• Utilize online job services

Do you use executive recruiting/search firms to seek to identify new diversity hires?

No.

Internships and Co-ops

Corporate Summer Intern Program

Deadline for application: September 1-February 28
Number of interns in the program in summer 2005 (internship) or 2005 (co-op): 60

Pay: $14 per hour

Length of the program: 10 weeks

Percentage of interns/co-ops in the program who receive offers of full-time employment: 67 percent

Web site for internship/co-op information: www.toyota.com/talentlink

The program is designed to provide the intern with exposure to the automotive industry while working in a corporate environment. While internship assignments vary based on company business need, specific functions will revolve around project-based work aimed at supporting the work group. Examples of past internships include:

• Advertising
• Financial planning
• Toyota certified used vehicles
• Vehicle marketing
• Scion
• Market representation
• Supplier diversity
• Toyota dealer consulting
• Distribution operations
• Toyota Rent-A-Car (TRAC)
• Interactive marketing
• Business

Location:

TMS national headquarters, located in Torrance, California.

Qualifications:

• Must have only one semester/year left of school
• Candidates should be pursuing a BA/BS in business, communications, marketing, liberal arts or other related degrees

Customer Relations Internship

Deadline for application: September 1-March 15

Number of interns in the program in summer 2005 (internship) or 2005 (co-op): 20

Pay: $17 per hour

Length of the program: 10 weeks full-time in the summer; part-time during final school year

Percentage of interns/co-ops in the program who receive offers of full-time employment: 50 percent

Web site for internship/co-op information: www.toyota.com/talentlink

The customer relations intern program provides college students with exposure to the automotive industry while working in a corporate environment. As a customer relations intern, you will receive an initial three-and-a-half weeks of classroom training that includes: comprehensive training on all Toyota vehicles, products, services and policies. Training in the areas of communication, problem-solving, negotiation and customer satisfaction is also provided.

After training, your primary responsibility will be communicating with customers who contact the customer experience center's toll-free number. You will work within a team environment where you will act as a liaison between Toyota owners, prospective consumers, dealerships, Toyota region offices and Toyota headquarters. You will be required to analyze customer concerns (i.e. requests for financial assistance, dealer sales or service-related complaints, or product-related concerns), and determine the appropriate action to positively impact owner satisfaction and retention.

Customer relations is one of the key entry-level positions for Toyota and offers a tremendous opportunity to learn about Toyota products, the inner workings of the company and how to work effectively with a diverse customer base. As a CR intern, your overall mission is to document the voice of the customer and build lifetime advocates for Toyota. The skills you acquire will be invaluable for your career in business.

Location:

TMS national headquarters, located in Torrance, California.

Qualifications:

• You should have achieved junior status and be within two semesters or three quarters of graduation

• You must exhibit sound customer service orientation and the ability to work within a professional corporate setting, along with the following skills: written and oral communication, time management, negotiation and problem solving, initiative, teamwork, planning and organization

• You should have direct experience in dealing with customers in challenging situations and the ability to make appropriate decisions when considering the interests of both the customer and Toyota

• A desire to work in the automotive industry long-term

• Previous automotive experience is a plus

Additional Information:

This internship is designed as a 12-month program. During the summer months, you will work full-time (40 hours per week).

During the school year, you will work part-time (approx. 15 hours per week) on a flexible schedule, but with a commitment to work a minimum of four hours every Monday.

Upon completion of the internship, consideration for full-time Toyota openings will be available to you.

Automotive Technology Internship

Deadline for application: September 1-February 28
Number of interns in the program in summer 2005 (internship) or 2005 (co-op): 12
Pay: $16 per hour
Length of the program: 10 weeks
Percentage of interns in the program who receive offers of full-time employment: 70 percent
Web site for internship/co-op information: www.toyota.com/talentlink

The program is designed to provide the intern with exposure to the automotive industry while working in a corporate environment.

The intern will be assigned various duties to support the activities of the department. The focus is primarily on projects scheduled for completion over the summer. Internship assignments vary based on the business need of the company. Examples of past internships and possible projects include:

• Lexus technical support—Provide support to product engineers for model launch activities including preparing support materials for region or area offices and dealership technical associates
• North American production support—Assist with new vehicle launch activities
• Product quality assurance, body—Support TAS operations with call volume analysis, conduct hands-on body department problem investigations and conduct field report analysis to determine extent of problems
• Product quality assurance, chassis—Gather and report technical information on customer concerns reported by Toyota-Lexus field offices, investigate recovered parts to determine root cause of customer complaint, update and maintain technical databases
• Product quality assurance, electrical—Gather and report technical information on customer concerns reported by Toyota-Lexus field offices, coordinate part recovery and parts test requests assigned to the department
• Product quality assurance, powertrain—Warranty analysis, warranty part recovery, assist in the development of powertrain TSBs and assist with the installation and evaluation of test parts on fleet vehicles
• Service technology—Support of scan tool software development activities and perform tool and equipment group support activities

• Technical training—Assist in the development of training curriculum for dealership service technicians which includes: researching, drafting and proof-reading of technical material and photo and video shoots for new model training
• Vehicle service center—Greet customers and dispatch repair orders to available technicians, process Toyota and Lexus warranty claims, inventory Toyota special tools and perform parts inventory

Location:

TMS National headquarters, located in Torrance, California

Qualifications:

• Must have only one semester/year left in school
• Major in automotive technology or related degree
• Proficiency in MS Word, Excel and Powerpoint

Summer Relocation Assistance:

For candidates more than 50 miles away, Toyota will cover the following expenses:

• Round-trip airfare or driving reimbursement
• Subsidized housing
• Subsidized lease car for out-of-state
• Shipping of 50 lbs. to and from Torrance, CA

INROADS Summer Internship

Deadline for application: INROADS deadline
Number of interns in the program in summer 2005 (internship) or 2005 (co-op): Nine
Pay: $13-14 per hour, depending on year in school
Length of the program (in weeks): 10 weeks
Percentage of interns/co-ops in the program who receive offers of full-time employment: 100 percent
Web site for internship/co-op information: www.toyota.com/talentlink

The program is designed to provide the intern with exposure to the automotive industry while working in a corporate environment. While internship assignments vary based on company business need, specific functions will revolve around project-based work aimed at supporting the work group. Examples of past internships include:

• Advertising
• Financial planning
• Toyota certified used vehicles
• Vehicle marketing
• Scion
• Market representation
• Supplier diversity
• Toyota dealer consulting
• Distribution operations
• Toyota Rent-A-Car (TRAC)
• Interactive marketing
• eBusiness

Location:

TMS national headquarters, located in Torrance, California.

Qualifications:

• Must have only one semester/year left in school.
• Candidates should be pursuing a BA/BS in business, communications, marketing, liberal arts or other related degrees.

Affinity Groups

TODOS: Toyota Organization for the Development of Latinos

TODOS is dedicated to the enhancement of the personal and professional development of its members. Our goal is to provide opportunities for mentoring, networking and community involvement. Furthermore, we represent a community that values diversity and inclusion. This community will foster creativity and thoughtful risk-taking to assist Toyota in becoming the most successful and respected car company in America.

AAC: African-American Collaborative

We, as a group of dedicated associates of Toyota North America, have elected to form an organization to support Toyota's success by encouraging, through information and education, an environment that recognizes and respects diversity in the workplace, thereby creating a positive environment for all associates.

AAC is currently active in the Greater Kentucky/Cincinnati area.

GALA: Gay and Lesbian (Bisexual Transgender and Friends) Alliance at Toyota

As a group of dedicated associates of Toyota Motor Sales, we have chosen to form an organization to support the success of TMS by developing and supporting an environment that recognizes and respects diversity in the workplace, thereby creating a positive environment for all associates.

TAASiA: Toyota Asian American Society in Alliance

Our goal is to represent the diverse Asian American cultures and heritages within Toyota and in the broader community. We will leverage the strength and growing population of Asian Americans to foster an environment and corporate culture of diversity and inclusion in order to become the most respected automotive company in the world.

Torque: Women's Business Partnering Group

Torque is a catalyst to advance the personal and professional development of women at Toyota, enabling our full contribution by influencing systemic change, while increasing inclusion opportunities and human capital.

Entry-Level Programs/Full-Time Opportunities/Training Programs

Sales, Marketing and Service Trainee (MT) Program

The sales, marketing and service trainee program is designed to provide you with broad exposure to automotive wholesale and retail operations prior to becoming a field traveler in a Toyota, Scion or Lexus field office. Through this rotational training program, you will gain hands-on experience in several departments within Toyota's national headquarters. The program incorporates on-the-job training as well as classroom training in time management, computer skills and retail operations.

Field analyst: Following successful completion of training, you will interview for an open position as a field analyst and be relocated to one of the Toyota or Lexus field sales offices throughout the United States. As an analyst, your function may vary as a merchandising or customer satisfaction analyst, among others.

Field traveler: After one to two years as a field analyst, you will be assigned to a position as a field traveler. As a field traveler, you will be the primary contact for a district of eight to 12 dealerships, representing TMS to assist dealers in achieving business objectives. The field traveler position typically requires heavy travel (80-90 percent travelling) during the week, as well as possible weekend assignments.

In preparation for the field analyst and field traveler positions, you will spend six to 12 months in a rotational training program involving two to three job rotations within corporate headquarter departments, such as the Toyota or Lexus customer assistance center, warranty, marketing, advertising, product education, sales administration or service and parts operations.

Location:

Training takes place at Toyota's national headquarters, located in Torrance, California. Upon completion of corporate rotational assignments, trainees transition to one of our nationwide field offices (Portland, San Francisco, Los Angeles, Denver, Cincinnati, Chicago, Boston, New York or Atlanta). Candidates must be willing to relocate within the U.S. Placement is determined by business need.

Qualifications:

Candidates should possess a BA or BS in business administration, marketing, management, automotive technology or related degree. Desired skills include strong interpersonal skills, the ability to think on one's feet, effective customer relationship management skills and proficiency in Word, Excel and PowerPoint. Dealership experience and/or automotive industry internship is helpful, but not required.

Technical Service Corporate Trainee

12- to 24-month training program in the product technical services department, which consists of six-month rotations. This allows trainees to immerse themselves in projects resulting in a stronger understanding of the technical aspects of Toyota and Lexus products, as well as current dealer vehicle repair practices.

Rotations (Possible assignments include):

Product quality assurance (four groups: body, chassis, electrical and powertrain): This department reports and tracks vehicle technical issues from the first reports of a potential concern until the issue has been researched and if necessary resolved with a field fix or production change.

Technical and body training: This department is responsible for the development of technical and body-training courses offered to Toyota and Lexus dealership associates.

Accessory product quality assurance: This department is responsible for all aspects of accessory quality. Accessory product quality works to establish and maintain stringent accessory quality standards for companies producing accessories for Toyota and Lexus vehicles.

Service technology: This department is responsible for developing and researching special tools which dealerships will be required to purchase. Duties include project-oriented assignments within one of three program tracks: product quality assurance, technical training or technical operations. At the beginning of the program you will also be matched with a mentor.

Location:

TMS national headquarters, located in Torrance, California.

Qualifications:

• BA or BS in automotive technology, industrial management, automotive service management or related degree
• Proficiency in MS Word, Excel and PowerPoint

Information Technology Corporate Trainee

Toyota offers a 24-month training program in the information systems division, which consists of four six-month rotation assignments. The program allows corporate trainees to immerse themselves in IT projects, resulting in a technical understanding of IT systems for Toyota, Lexus and Scion divisions.

Rotation assignments:

A variety of rotation assignments for corporate trainees are available, including technical, business and field rotations. Examples of possible rotation assignments include:

Technical rotations

Enterprise data management (EDM): EDM's long-term strategy is to create single databases that encompass a particular subject area, enabling all users of data to use data from a single source—eliminating redundancy and maximizing efficiency.

Automotive or Toyota customer services: These groups provide support for large-scale, multi-platform applications—defining, developing and delivering enhancements projects for the vehicles business units. Rotations through various phases of IT system enhancements or implementations provide corporate trainees the ability to learn about the various lifecycles of a system. Project management skills are developed during this rotation.

Business rotations

IS strategy and governance: This department is responsible for the IS strategic planning and governance processes, providing strategic research, process improvements, project recommendations and executive presentations.

Field rotation for technical and business programs

Toyota technology field operations: The IT field rotation offers exposure to the sales organization from an IT perspective. Field rotations may include Georgia, Illinois, Iowa, Maryland, New Jersey or Oregon.

Location:

Rotation assignments located in Torrance, CA and U.S. field locations.

Qualifications:

- BA or BS in computer engineering or technology, information systems, business administration, or related degree.
- Proficiency in MS Word, Excel and PowerPoint.
- Strong written and verbal communication skills.

Logistics training and development program

An 18-month on-the-job training program which develops high performing logistics professionals into leaders who model Toyota values and continually challenge existing systems to improve quality, costs and lead times within Toyota's North American parts logistics division operations.

Tracks:

Candidates hired for the program will be matched with one of the following tracks and locations:

- Procurement and inventory control: Headquarters located in Torrance, CA; North American parts center in Ontario, CA; North American parts center in Hebron, KY
- Physical distribution management: A parts distribution center in a metropolitan location: Los Angeles, Chicago, Boston, Cincinnati, Kansas City, New York, Portland, Baltimore or San Francisco
- Planning and strategy: Headquarters located in Torrance, CA

Duties may include an on-the-job training plan to be completed at the rotational training site. This training is designed to provide the trainee with hands on learning, leadership opportunities and business insight within one of the three tracks listed above. Included in overall training program will be a short departure from the individual's assigned track to gain insight into the other two tracks, which are also key operating areas of the division. In addition, each individual will receive core standardized training courses, which include, but are not limited to, Toyota production system, total quality management, total parts logistics, kaizen and leadership development.

Typical Career Path:

• Operations: logistics trainee > group leader > warehouse supervisor > operations supervisor > manager
• Procurement: logistics trainee > procurement analyst > procurement administrator > manager

Locations:

Toyota has warehouse operations in: Chicago, Cincinnati, Baltimore, Kansas City, Boston, Portland, San Francisco, Los Angeles and New York. Procurement positions are at the Hebron, KY and Ontario, CA locations. Planning and strategy positions are located at Toyota's headquarters located in Torrance, CA.

Qualifications:

• Bachelor's degrees in supply chain management, operations management or general business degrees are preferred for all tracks. Individuals with other degrees (psychology, education, etc.), but possessing supervisory experience are considered for the physical distribution track. Operations research and purchasing or procurement-related degrees are considered for the procurement track.
• Proficiency in MS Word, Excel and PowerPoint.

Strategic Plan and Diversity Leadership

How does the firm's leadership communicate the importance of diversity to everyone at the firm?

• Internal diversity web site
• Speaking engagements at business partner group meetings
• E-mails
• Availability of diversity and inclusion training for everyone
• Champions for diversity and inclusion effort

Who has primary responsibility for leading diversity initiatives at your firm?

Jerome Miller, VP, diversity and inclusion.

Does your firm currently have a diversity committee?

Yes. The diversity steering committee comprises five senior executives who meet on a periodic basis to provide oversight and guidance on diversity opportunities and initiatives.

Has the firm undertaken a formal or informal diversity program or set of initiatives aimed at increasing the diversity of the firm?

Yes, formal.

Champions for Diversity and Inclusion:

• Partner with officers and department heads to enhance inclusion and leverage diversity within their division/department
• Move the organization forward to diversity and inclusion awareness through formal and informal education
• Apply diversity and inclusion subject matter expertise to business priorities, objectives and opportunities

How often does the firm's management review the firm's diversity progress/results?

Monthly.

The Stats

Employees

2005: 260,000

Revenue

2005: $7.4 million

Retention and Professional Development

Please identify the specific steps you are taking to reduce the attrition rate of minority and women employees.

• Develop and/or support internal employee affinity groups
• Strengthen mentoring program for all employees, including minorities and women

Diversity Mission Statement

Mission

To guide TMS in making diversity and inclusion an integral part of every aspect of our business to support Toyota in becoming the most respected and successful car company in America.

Vision

In an inclusive environment, all associates are respectfully and fully engaged in the work and life of the organization.

At TMS, diversity is our competitive advantage; understanding, embracing and leveraging our differences enables us to achieve our business goals.

Additional Information

Company Overview

Toyota Motor Sales, U.S.A., Inc. (TMS) is a wholly owned subsidiary of Toyota Motor Corporation, one of the largest automotive manufacturers in the world. TMS is the marketing, sales, distribution and customer service arm of Toyota, Lexus and Scion in the United States, marketing products and services through a network of 1,415 Toyota, Lexus and Scion dealers in 49 states. Established in 1957, TMS and its subsidiaries also are involved in distribution logistics, motor sports, R & D and general aviation.

U.S. Steel Corporation

600 Grant Street
Pittsburgh, PA 15219
Phone: (412) 433-6919
Fax: (412) 433-6917

Locations

US:
Chicago, IL • Detroit, MI • Fairfield, AL •
Gary, IN • Granite City, IL • Lorain, OH •
Michigan • Minnesota • Pittsburgh
International:
Mexico • Kosice, Slovak Republic • Serbia

Employment Contact

F. David Coleman
General Manager of Corporate Diversity
E-mail: fdcoleman@uss.com
www.ussteel.com

Recruiting

Please list the schools/types of schools at which you recruit.

- *Other private schools:* Case Western Reserve University, Gannon University, LaRoche College, Rose Hulman Institute of Technology, University of Notre Dame, Valparaiso University, Duquesne University, Dayton University, Lehigh University, St. Vincent College, Vanderbilt University, Northwestern University, Marquette University, Thiel College, Waynesburg College, Westminster College

- *Public state schools:* Auburn University, California University of Pennsylvania, Cleveland State, Colorado School of Mines, Georgia Institute of Technology, Michigan State University, Michigan Tech Houghton, Mississippi State, North Dakota State University, Oakland University (Michigan), Penn State University, Purdue University Calumet (Indiana), Robert Morris University, Southern Illinois University - Edwardsville, Southern Illinois University - Carbondale, University of Alabama - Birmingham, University of Alabama - Tuscaloosa, University of Illinois - Champaign, University of Michigan - Dearborn, University of Minnesota - Twin Cities, University of Minnesota - Duluth, University of Missouri - Rolla, University of Missouri - Columbia, University of North Dakota - Grand Forks, University of Pittsburgh, University of Toledo, West Virginia University, Youngstown State University (Ohio), Wayne State University (Michigan), Bradley University, Carnegie Mellon University, Grove City College, Indiana University - Bloomington, Indiana University of Pennsylvania, Ohio State University, Ohio University, Slippery Rock University, South Dakota School of Mines, St. Louis University, Tennessee Tech University, University of Alabama - Huntsville, University of Cincinnati, University of Michigan - Ann Arbor, University of Missouri - St. Louis, University of South Alabama, University of St. Francis - Joliet, Virginia Tech, Western Michigan, Bowling Green University, Eastern Michigan, Ferris State University, Indiana State University, Iowa State, Milwaukee School of Engineering, New Mexico State, Ohio Northern University, Rensselaer Poly Institute, Tri-State University - Angola, University of Akron, Washington University - St. Louis

- *Historically Black Colleges and Universities (HBCUs):* Alabama A&M, Howard University, Southern University, Tennessee State, Tuskegee University, Hampton University, Morgan State, University of Illinois - Chicago

- *Hispanic Serving Institutions (HSIs):* University of Texas - El Paso

- *Other predominantly minority and/or women's colleges:* Carlow University

Do you have any special outreach efforts directed to encourage minority students to consider your firm?

- Hold a reception for minority students
- Participate in/host minority student job fair(s)
- Outreach to leadership of minority student organizations

What activities does the firm undertake to attract minority and women employees?

U.S. Steel offers a program for women who are or once were in the steel business. The program is called Ciloets. U.S. Steel participates in job fairs for both woman and minority employees.

Do you use executive recruiting/search firms to seek to identify new diversity hires?

Yes.

Internships and Co-ops

INROADS

Number of interns in the program in summer 2005 (internship) or 2005 (co-op): Three to five
Pay: $15.00 per hour. Interns are paid every two weeks.
Length of the program: Summer

U.S. Steel is proud to have been affiliated with INROADS since its inception in the late 1970s. In support of their efforts, we have hired three to five interns from INROADS to work for us each summer. Each year, interns from INROADS have proven themselves as positive assets not only for our company, but also for our community. Several interns are now successful full-time employees. In response to the positive contributions of the INROADS program, U.S. Steel is proud to sponsor the greater Pittsburgh 2006 INROADS banquet, which will be held on August 10th at the Heinz museum.

Scholarships

Employee Sons & Daughters Scholarship

Deadline for application for the scholarship program: November 30th
Scholarship award amount: The amount is up to 15 individual $10,000 scholarships, payable in four annual installments of $2,500. Payments are made direct to colleges and universities by Scholarship America and designated for tuition, room and/or board. The college or university is instructed to return unused funds to the United States Steel Foundation at the end of each academic year.

The scholarship program is limited to sons and daughters of active, full-time employees of U.S. Steel. Applicants must be high school seniors who have applied for full-time admissions to an accredited, four-year college or university. Foreign colleges and universities are excluded.

Entry-Level Programs/Full-Time Opportunities/Training Programs

New Managers Program

Length of program: The program is a five-day seminar to provide a broad picture of United States Steel Corporation.
Geographic location of program: Pittsburgh, Penn.

Included are presentations on United States Steel Corporation history and organization, steel business simulation, communications, personnel planning, as well as an orientation to what is required of managers. This workshop shows participants how a new manager's life changes, both personally and professionally, on becoming a manager. The program also includes presentations by executives and general managers who provide updated information on subjects like general business conditions, key customers, United States Steel Corporation Strategies, business ethics and human resources policies.

Strategic Plan and Diversity Leadership

How does the firm's leadership communicate the importance of diversity to everyone at the firm?

The leadership at U.S. Steel communicates diversity by making diversity a business imperative and core value.

Who has primary responsibility for leading diversity initiatives at your firm?

F. David Coleman, general manager of corporate diversity.

Does your firm currently have a diversity committee?

Yes, the committee meets every other month.

If yes, does the committee's representation include one or more members of the firm's management/executive committee (or the equivalent)?

Yes.

If yes, how many executives are on the committee, and in 2005, what was the total number of hours collectively spent by the committee in furtherance of the firm's diversity initiatives?

U.S. Steels Diversity Committee consists of 16 members. The committee convenes every other month.

Does the committee and/or diversity leader establish and set goals or objectives consistent with management's priorities?

Yes. U.S. Steel as a company has made diversity its primary focus. When it comes to making the workforce a more diverse environment, both the Diversity Committee and management see diversity as an important issue for the future of the company.

Has the firm undertaken a formal or informal diversity program or set of initiatives aimed at increasing the diversity of the firm?

Yes, formal.

How often does the firm's management review the firm's diversity progress/results?

Quarterly.

How is the firm's diversity committee and/or firm management held accountable for achieving results?

U.S. Steel holds itself accountable for achieving results by building diversity into the metrics of the corporation. U.S. Steel employees are trained in diversity.

The Stats

	TOTAL IN THE U.S.		TOTAL OUTSIDE THE U.S		TOTAL WORLDWIDE	
	2005	2004	2005	2004	2005	2004
Number of employees	20,000	20,000	26,000	26,000	46,000	46,000
Revenue	$10.69 billion	$11.13 billion	$3.34 billion	$2.84 billion	$14.03 billion	$13.97 billion

Retention and Professional Development

How do 2005 minority and female attrition rates generally compare to those experienced in the prior year period?

About the same as in prior years.

Please identify the specific steps you are taking to reduce the attrition rate of minority and women employees.

• Increase/review compensation relative to competition
• Succession plan includes emphasis on diversity
• Work with minority and women employees to develop career advancement plans
• Strengthen mentoring program for all employees, including minorities and women
• Professional skills development program, including minority and women employees

Diversity Mission Statement

At United States Steel our goal is to be the best: making steel, driving financial performance, building business partnerships, increasing stakeholder value and supporting our communities. This starts with our inclusive culture that values the diversity of our people and their talents. As a result, our employees contribute in creative ways to secure our future as a world competitive company.

Unilever USA

800 Sylvan Avenue
Englewood Cliffs, NJ 07632
Phone: (800) 272-6296
Fax: (201) 541-5230
www.unilever.com

Locations

Global

Diversity Leadership

Lois Rubin
Diversity Manager
800 Sylvan Avenue
Englewood Cliffs, NJ 07632
Phone: (800) 786-6988
Fax: (201) 541-5230
www.unileverusa.com

Employment Contact

Jennifer Feuer
University Relations Manager
700 Sylvan Avenue
Englewood Cliffs, NJ 07632
Phone: (800) 786-6988
Fax: (201) 541-5230
www.unileverusa.com

Recruiting

Please list the schools/types of schools at which you recruit.

• Ivy League schools
• Other private schools
• Public state schools
• Historically Black Colleges and Universities (HBCUs)
• Hispanic Serving Institutions (HSIs)

Do you have any special outreach efforts directed to encourage minority students to consider your firm?

• Hold a reception for minority students
• Advertise in minority student association publication(s)
• Sponsor minority student association events
• Firm's employees participate on career panels at schools
• Outreach to leadership of minority student organizations
• Scholarships or intern/fellowships for minority students

What activities does the firm undertake to attract minority and women employees?

• Partner programs with women and minority associations
• Conferences
• Seek referrals from other employees
• Utilize online job services
• Various minority scholarship programs

Internships and Co-ops

Summer Internship Program, Supply Chain Co-op Program

Number of interns in the program in summer 2005 (co-op): 70
Length of the program (in weeks): 10 weeks
Percentage of interns/co-ops in the program who receive offers of full-time employment: 55 percent
Web site for internship/co-op information: www.unileverusa.com

We hire interns from various campuses throughout New Jersey in the following fields: marketing, finance, IT, sales, supply chain and R&D for a 10-12 week summer internship program. Additionally, we hire INROADS and Jackie Robinson Foundation Scholars. We also have a supply chain co-op program.

Scholarships

• Jackie Robinson Foundation Legacy Award
• National Merit Scholarship Program

Affinity Groups

• African-American Business Network
• Asian Business Council
• Gay and Lesbian Business Network
• Hispanic Business Network
• Women's Interactive Network

Entry-Level Programs/Full-Time Opportunities/Training Programs

• Marketing
• Finance
• IT
• R&D
• Supply Chain Management Leadership Program

(all full-time opportunites)

Strategic Plan and Diversity Leadership

How does the firm's leadership communicate the importance of diversity to everyone at the firm?

The firm's leadership communicates diversity initiatives through e-mails, the company Intranet, newsletters and meetings, training, diversity speakers/events, posters, banners and inter-office communications.

Who has primary responsibility for leading diversity initiatives at your firm?

Lois Rubin, diversity manager.

Does your firm currently have a diversity committee?

Yes.

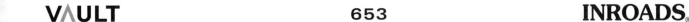

If yes, please describe how the committee is structured, how often it meets, etc.:

The committee is multi-leveled, multi-ethnic and composed of both men and women. The committee meets in person three times a year, in addition to holding three conference calls per year.

If yes, does the committee's representation include one or more members of the firm's management/executive committee (or the equivalent)?

Yes.

Does the committee and/or diversity leader establish and set goals or objectives consistent with management's priorities?

Yes.

Has the firm undertaken a formal or informal diversity program or set of initiatives aimed at increasing the diversity of the firm?

Yes, formal.

How often does the firm's management review the firm's diversity progress/results?

Quarterly.

The Stats

Employees

2005: Approximately 15,000 (U.S.)
2005: 223,000 (worldwide)

Revenue

2005: $9 billion (U.S.)

Retention and Professional Development

How do 2005 minority and female attrition rates generally compare to those experienced in the prior year period?

About the same as in prior years.

Please identify the specific steps you are taking to reduce the attrition rate of minority and women employees.

- Develop and/or support internal employee affinity groups
- Increase/improve current work/life programs
- Succession plan includes emphasis on diversity
- Strengthen mentoring program for all employees, including minorities and women
- Professional skills development program, including minority and women employees
- *Other*: Organization assessments, functional diversity plans, strategy-into-action plan that includes accountability for diversity inclusion success

SMART. DRIVEN. BOLD.

It's nice to work for a company that's just like me.

UnitedHealthcare®, a UnitedHealth Group® company, provides network-based health and well-being benefits and services for employers and consumers nationwide. We use our strength, diversity and innovation to improve the lives of the more than 18 million people who receive our unique products and services. And our endless pursuit for excellence in everything we do extends to your career as well. Join us today for an inspired and purposeful mix of professional growth opportunities and personal rewards.

For details on opportunities with UnitedHealthcare, visit our CAREERS page at **www.unitedhealthgroup.com** and search in your area of interest.

Diversity creates a healthier atmosphere: An equal opportunity employer. M/F/D/V.

United Healthcare, formerly PacifiCare, a UnitedHealth Group Company

9900 Bren Rd. East
Minnetonka, MN 55343
www.unitedhealthgroup.com

Locations

Minnetonka, MN (HQ)
Regional offices throughout the nation

Employment Contact

Heather Cooper
Account Executive, Recruitment Services
E-mail: heather_cooper@uhc.com

Recruiting

Please list the schools/types of schools at which you recruit.

• Ivy League schools
• Other private schools
• Public state schools
• Historically Black Colleges and Universities (HBCUs)

Do you have any special outreach efforts directed to encourage minority students to consider your firm?

• Participate in/host minority student job fair(s)
• Sponsor minority student association events
• Firm's employees participate on career panels at schools
• Scholarships or intern/fellowships for minority students

What activities does the firm undertake to attract minority and women employees?

• Partner programs with women and minority associations
• Conferences
• Participate at minority job fairs
• Seek referrals from other employees
• Utilize online job services

Do you use executive recruiting/search firms to seek to identify new diversity hires?

No.

Internships and Co-ops

INROADS Internship Program

Deadline for application: March 31
Number of interns in the program in summer 2006 (internship) or 2006 (co-op): 24

Visit Vault at www.vault.com for insider company profiles, expert advice, career message boards, expert resume reviews, the Vault Job Board and more.

VAULT CAREER LIBRARY

657

UnitedHealthcare (formerly Pacificare) has been a national partner of INROADS since 2004, offering internship programs throughout the nation in the primary functions of underwriting, sales and finance.

Corporate MBA Internship Programs

Our corporate MBA internship program offers general management internships nationwide.

Actuarial Summer Internship Program

> *Deadline for application:* March 31
> *Number of interns in the program in summer 2005 (internship) or 2005 (co-op):* Five
> *Pay:* $13-15 per hour
> *Length of the program:* 10 weeks
> *Percentage of interns/co-ops in the program who receive offers of full-time employment:* Since inception in 1999, approximately 50 percent of the interns have been offered full-time positions.
> *Web site for internship/co-op information:* www.pacificare.com (employment, college recruitment)

The Actuarial Summer Internship Program (ASIP) at PacifiCare, a UnitedHealthcare Company, is a 10-week program from June to September, with flexible start and end dates depending on each intern's summer schedule. Interns will work 40 hours per week at either the Cypress or Santa Ana office in Orange County, California. Salary is competitive and will take into account any actuarial exams passed.

Interns will work on projects ranging from product pricing and provider contract analysis to reserves calculation and financial reporting. During the process, interns will go through various training programs to learn more about the managed care industry, PacifiCare's business models, and how to use database query language and Microsoft applications to perform actuarial calculations. Interns will also be guided through the examiniation preparation process in a full-time work setting, and study materials will be provided for the November exam sitting.

Qualifications:

- Working toward a bachelor's or master's degree in mathematics, statistics, actuarial science or other major with relevant experience.
- At least junior standing with minimum 3.2 GPA
- Strong computer, analytical and communication skills.
- Completion of one actuarial exam preferred; however, candidates with high GPA and analytical skill will be considered.

Scholarships

Latino Health Scholars Program

* The Scholarship program outlined below is for high school seniors who are entering college.

> *Deadline for application for the scholarship program:* May 29th annually (scholarship opportunity at least through 2006)
> *Scholarship award amount:* 70 $2,000 total scholarships and two $25,000 total scholarships available
> *Web site or other contact information for scholarship:* www.pacificare.com; www.pacificarelatino.com

PacifiCare, a UnitedHealthcare Company, introduced the PacifiCare Latino Health Scholars Program in 2003 to address the critical shortage of Spanish speakers in the educational pipeline for health professions. Under the program, PacifiCare offers annual scholarships of $2,000 each for bilingual, bicultural high school students interested in pursuing careers in the health care industry. In 2004, PacifiCare increased the number of scholarships available from 33 to 50, for a two-year total scholarship opportunity of $166,000. Through this program, PacifiCare hopes to reverse what is currently a widening gap between the Latino population and the number of bilingual and bicultural professionals in the health care field.

For 2005 and 2006, PacifiCare further expanded its Latino Health Scholars program to include—in addition to the 70 $2,000 scholarships the company will award this fall—two $25,000 scholarships for the most deserving bilingual and bicultural students dedicated to pursuing careers in health care. These two scholarships, entitled PacifiCare Freedom Awards, recognize outstanding individuals and organizations that have demonstrated tremendous sacrifice and commitment to make a positive difference in our communities. The award was inspired by the heroic actions of U.S. Marine Sgt. Rafael Peralta who was killed last November by enemy action in Iraq. Fighting alongside his fellow marines in Falluja, Peralta, wounded by gunshots, reached out for a grenade that was hurled by an insurgent and cradled it to his body to protect others from the blast. His heroism saved the lives of five of his fellow Marines.

Strategic Plan and Diversity Leadership

Does your firm currently have a diversity committee?

No.

Does the committee and/or diversity leader establish and set goals or objectives consistent with management's priorities?

Yes.

Has the firm undertaken a formal or informal diversity program or set of initiatives aimed at increasing the diversity of the firm?

Yes, informal.

How often does the firm's management review the firm's diversity progress/results?

Monthly.

The Stats

Employees

2005: 18,717

Revenue

2005: $27 billion

Retention and Professional Development

How do minority and female attrition rates generally compare to those experienced in the prior year period?

About the same as in prior years.

Please identify the specific steps you are taking to reduce the attrition rate of minority and women employees.

- Increase/review compensation relative to competition
- Succession plan includes emphasis on diversity
- Work with minority and women employees to develop career advancement plans
- Strengthen mentoring program for all employees, including minorities and women
- Professional skills development program, including minority and women employees

Diversity Mission Statement

Diversity creates a healthier atmosphere. UnitedHealthcare is an equal opportunity employer.

Additional Information

UnitedHealth Group is a Fortune 50 company listed as one of the top two most admired health care companies in *Fortune* magazine since 1995. We have the privilege each day—directly or indirectly—to make a significant difference in someone's life.

Although our employees have diverse cultural backgrounds, beliefs and lifestyles, they have one thing in common: their ability to excel.

At United, we not only respect diversity—we believe diverse viewpoints are assets. We depend on our employees' broad range of talents, personalities and ideas to help us design services specifically tailored to meet the needs of the diverse communities we serve and generate the innovations of tomorrow.

United Parcel Service (UPS)

World headquarters 55 Glenlake Parkway, N.E. Atlanta, GA 30328 Phone: (404) 828-6000 Fax: (404) 828-6562 www.ups.com	**Employment Contact** For information concerning employment opportunities at UPS, please go to www.upsjobs.com. UPS is an equal opportunity employer.

The Stats

Employees

2005: 348,400 (U.S.)
2005: 58,800 (outside the U.S.)
2005: 407, 200 (worldwide)

Revenue

2005: $36.6 billion (worldwide)

Diversity Mission Statement

Founded: August 28, 1907 in Seattle, WA
Chairman & CEO: Michael L. Eskew

Diversity and UPS People

UPS's workforce is multicultural, multidimensional and reflective of the broad attributes of our global communities. In fact, each year since 1999, UPS has been consecutively ranked by *Fortune* magazine as one of the "50 Best Companies for Minorities."

UPS understands that diversity encompasses more than ethnicity, gender and age. It's how employees think, the ideas they contribute and their general attitude toward work and life.

Diversity is encouraged by recognizing the value of people's different experiences, backgrounds and perspectives. Diversity is a valuable, core component of UPS because it brings a wider range of resources, skills and ideas to the business.

Long-standing company policies—such as employee ownership, equal opportunity, promotion from within and teamwork—have helped make UPS a preferred employer. Diversity impacts UPS's business from many perspectives, whether it's in meeting the needs of a diverse customer base, working with a diverse supplier network or gaining momentum from the varied contributions of our diverse workforce.

- African-Americans, Hispanics, Asian-Pacific Americans and other minorities make up 35 percent of the company's 348,400 employees in the United States.
- Minorities accounted for half of UPS's new employees in 2003.
- Women represent 27 percent of the U.S. management team and 21 percent of the overall workforce, holding jobs from package handlers, to drivers, to senior management and to the UPS board of directors.
- Among the company's 58,000 U.S. managers, minorities hold nearly 30 percent of those executive positions. Positions held include district managers, the UPS management committee and UPS's board of directors.

UPS Diversity Steering Council

UPS expects diversity to be fostered and encouraged by every UPSer in their daily commitment to the company. UPS also has a Diversity Steering Council whose vision is to "ensure that workforce, customer and supplier diversity remain a visible core value that is integral to our business, our community relationships and the UPS charter."

The UPS Diversity Steering Council is co-chaired by Chairman and CEO Mike Eskew and Senior Vice President, Human Resources Allen Hill. This cross-functional council consists of internal and external representatives.

Employer of Choice

UPS is frequently recognized for its commitment to diversity. Since 1999, UPS has been consecutively ranked by *Fortune* magazine as one of the 50 Best Companies for Minorities.

UPS was profiled as a leader in *Hispanic* magazine's 13th annual Corporate 100 list, "a list of the top U.S. companies that excel in creating business and job opportunities for Hispanic Americans, as well as donating to philanthropies that target Latino communities."

Since 2000, UPS has been consecutively named a top corporation for Women's Business Enterprises (WBEs) by the Women's Business Enterprise National Council (WBENC).

UPS was honored with the coveted NAACP (National Association for the Advancement of Colored People) Corporate Citizen of the Year Award.

UPS placed third in *DiversityInc*'s Diversity Top 30 poll. The poll rates corporations on a range of criteria from employment and advancement of people of color to advertising in ethnic media.

Community

Throughout our history at UPS, we've found that we grow by not only investing in our business but also in the communities where we live and work.

UPS does extensive work and partners with various organizations to improve social conditions that exist within the communities we serve. Below is a sample of the organizations UPS and UPS people partner with:

- 100 Black Men of America (100 BMOA)
- Family and Workplace Literacy Programs
- Hispanic Chamber of Commerce (HCC)
- INROADS
- National Association for the Advancement of Colored People (NAACP)
- NASCAR
- National Urban League (NUL)
- National Council of La Raza (NCLR)
- Native American Business Alliance (NABA)
- Organization of Chinese Americans (OCA)
- The National Newspapers Publishers Association (NNPA)
- Special Olympics
- UNCF Corporate Scholars
- Women's Business Enterprise National Council (WBENC)

Customers

UPS understands that customer diversity requires understanding the differences in cultural backgrounds and the unique needs of each customer.

Every day, more than 370,000 UPSers serve nearly 8 million customers in over 200 countries and territories worldwide. Because of its global impact, UPS has many unique opportunities to reach a broad range of diverse customers. UPS understands that diversity is essential as the company expands and finds ways to solve the individual needs of all customers.

Supplier Diversity

Formally launched in 1992, the UPS Supplier Diversity Program is committed to providing business opportunities to minority- and women-owned businesses.

UPS strives to have diversity among its business partners. In addition to developing strategic relationships with minority- and women-owned businesses, UPS encourages majority suppliers to support women- and minority-owned firms. We are committed to ensuring that our supplier diversity process strengthens the minority- and women-owned businesses that drive economic development in our communities.

More than 25,000 businesses across America are partners in the UPS supplier network.

United Technologies Corporation

United Technologies Building
Hartford, CT 06101
Phone: (860) 728-7000

Locations
Hartford, CT (HQ)

UTC is the parent company for the following companies:
Carrier Corporation (HQ—Farmington, CT)
Pratt and Whitney (HQ—East Hartford, CT)
Hamilton Sundstrand (HQ—Windsor Locks, CT)
Otis Elevator (HQ—Farmington, CT)
Sikorsky Aircraft (HQ—Stratford, CT)
UTC Fire and Security (HQ—Farmington, CT)
UTC Power (HQ—South Windsor, CT)
UTC Research Center (R&D) (HQ—East Hartford)

All companies have multiple international and domestic operation locations.

Our U.S. presence beyond the Hartford, CT metropolitan area is in:
Carrier: Syracuse, NY, Athens, GA, Collierville, TN, Charlotte, NC
Hamilton Sundstrand: Rockford, IL, San Diego, CA, Miramar, FL
Sikorsky and Pratt & Whitney: West Palm Beach, FL
Otis: Every major city
Otis and Carrier: Many satellite sales and distributions offices

Diversity Leadership
Grace Figueredo
Director, Workforce Diversity

The diversity campus recruiting aspect for the corporation falls under Joelle Hayes.

Employment Contact
Joelle Hayes
Manager
Corporate Recruiting and Diversity Partnerships
One Financial Plaza, MS 504
Hartford, CT 06101
Phone: (860) 728-6516
Fax: (860) 660-9260
E-mail: joelle.hayes@utc.com
www.utc.com/careers

Recruiting

Please list the schools/types of schools at which you recruit.

We recruit at the following schools: Cornell University, Purdue University, Renssalaer Polytechnic Institute, MIT, UCONN, GA Tech, University of Michigan, Penn State, University of Illinois—Champaign-Urbana, Howard, North Carolina A&T State, University of Puerto Rico—Mayaguez

Do you have any special outreach efforts directed to encourage minority students to consider your firm?

• Hold a reception for minority students
• *Conferences:* NSBE, SHPE, SWE, BEYA
• Advertise in minority student association publication(s)
• Participate in/host minority student job fair(s)
• Sponsor minority student association events
• Firm's employees participate on career panels at schools
• Outreach to leadership of minority student organizations
• Scholarships or intern/fellowships for minority students

What activities does the firm undertake to attract minority and women employees?

• Partner programs with women and minority associations
• *Conferences:* NSBE (National and Regional), SWE, SHPE, BEYA (entry-level), NSHMBA, NBMBAA, NAWMBA (MBA hires); an additional 11 focus schools for MBA hires.
• Participate at minority job fairs
• Seek referrals from other employees
• Utilize online job services
• Career services, job boards

Do you use executive recruiting/search firms to seek to identify new diversity hires?

Yes, mostly executive hires, some manager and professional level hires.

If yes, list all women- and/or minority-owned executive search/recruiting firms to which the firm paid a fee for placement services in the past 12 months.

Granville and Webb, Millette Granville and Principal. At one particular business unit, 30 percent of all search firms retained are women and minority owned.

Internships and Co-ops

INROADS is UTC's only internship program outside of its internal internship programs. Hamilton Sundstrand has an extremely robust co-op/experiential education program.

INROADS

Number of interns in the program in summer 2005 (internship) or 2005 (co-op): 170
Pay: Varies by major (technical/nontechnical) and classification
Length of the program (in weeks): 10-12
Percentage of interns/co-ops in the program who receive offers of full-time employment: 75 percent
Web site for internship/co-op information: www.inroads.org

Scholarships

UTC INROADS Scholarship

Deadline for application for the scholarship program: July (varies each year)

Scholarship award amount: $20,000 total annually—award amount varies—two awards at $3,500, two at $2,500, two at $1,000, five at $500

Web site or other contact information for scholarship: Only for eligible returning INROADS interns employed by UTC.

Affinity Groups

- African-American Forum
- Hispanic Leadership Forum
- Women's Leadership Forum
- Asian Pacific Forum
- Women's Finance Forum
- Veteran's Forum
- New Hire Forum

UTC has established operating guidelines for affinity groups within its business units. Most of them meet on a monthly/quarterly basis. They have executive champions who support/sponsor their activities and related events. The groups have charters, which support the overall diversity mission/vision of UTC. Most of the groups are focused on supporting the recruitment, development, advancement and retention of UTC's minority employees. In addition, these groups mentor and participate in various community outreach activities. They have web sites that inform membership of their mission, upcoming events, resources, etc.

Entry-Level Programs/Full-Time Opportunities/Training Programs

- UTC Financial Leadership Program: 24 months; Connecticut
- UTC Information Technology Leadership Program: Three nine-month rotations (27 months); Connecticut
- Hamilton Sundstrand HR Rotational Program: 24 months; various locations
- Pratt and Whitney Manufacturing Engineering Development Program: 24 months; Connecticut
- Carrier Technical Sales Management Trainee Program: Various locations
- Career Engineering Leadership Program: Various locations

All full-time and part-time UTC employees are eligible for the Employee Scholar Program, which pays full tuition, fees and books towards degree study in any area.

Strategic Plan and Diversity Leadership

How does the firm's leadership communicate the importance of diversity to everyone at the firm?

UTC has a decentralized cascade-down approach to diversity. At the start of the year, each respective business unit sets key objectives and diversity is embedded into these. The senior leadership of each business unit utilizes various communication vehicles to share, monitor and report on the progression of these objectives throughout the course of the year, e.g. "roadmaps," scorecards, etc. These are posted on web sites and discussed through meetings, e-mail communiqués, and town hall meetings etc. are conducted to discuss the performance and results in these areas. The CEO reviews diversity metrics at quarterly senior level operating management meetings.

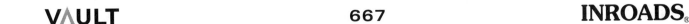

Who has primary responsibility for leading diversity initiatives at your firm?

Grace Figueredo, director, work force diversity.

In addition, each business unit has a diversity manager, who makes up the UTC Diversity Council.

Does your firm currently have a diversity committee?

No. However, some of the business units do have diversity committees that were formed at the grass root level.

Has the firm undertaken a formal or informal diversity program or set of initiatives aimed at increasing the diversity of the firm?

Yes, formal. UTC has a decentralized cascade-down approach to diversity. At the start of the year, each respective business unit sets goals regarding representation. In addition, we track, monitor and report on the associated activity, such as hiring, promotions, and attrition. Each business unit sets a strategic approach to addressing their opportunities. HR has the responsibility of partnering with line leaders to develop action and implementation plans. Every quarter at operating management meetings, each of the business unit presidents presents a status update to the CEO, and diversity performance/results are reported, reviewed and discussed.

How often does the firm's management review the firm's diversity progress/results?

Quarterly.

How is the firm's diversity committee and/or firm management held accountable for achieving results?

As stated above, the UTC diversity progression metrics are reviewed at operating management meetings quarterly by the CEO with the divisional presidents. At the conclusion of each year, executive incentive compensation is linked to their respective performance/results in all business deliverables, with diversity being one of the elements.

The Stats

2005 STATS			
	IN U.S.	OUTSIDE U.S.	WORLDWIDE
Number of employees	72,600	147,400	220,000
Revenues	$16.6 billion	$26.1 billion	$42.7 billion

	EXECUTIVE	MANAGERIAL	PROFESSIONAL
Female	9.2%	17.1%	16.6%
Minority	7.9%	12.8%	13.6%
OVER 55% OF EMPLOYEES ARE OUTSIDE OF THE U.S.			

Retention and Professional Development

How do 2005 minority and female attrition rates generally compare to those experienced in the prior year period?

Higher than in prior years.

Please identify the specific steps you are taking to reduce the attrition rate of minority and women employees.

Currently standardizing and taking a more proactive and strategic approach to retention and other related drivers that affect turnover.

Diversity Mission Statement

UTC Diversity Vision

Our diversity vision is to create an environment where people want to work and contribute their fullest potential. It defines the value that is placed on the differences in the workforce and recognizes that diversity is key in broadening our experience and technical competency base to compete effectively in the global marketplace.

UTC Diversity Mission

To create an environment where all associates are encouraged to reach their fullest potential and where everyone values, accepts and respects the differences in our workforce.

Additional Information

Since 1995, United Technologies Corporation has made significant progression in its diversity representation goals and has been recognized for numerous awards and honors regarding the area of diversity—most recently, the Brillante Award from NSHMBA (National Society of Hispanic MBAs), the Golden Torch Award for Corporate Diversity Leadership from NSBE (National Society of Black Engineers) and an Innovator Award from INROADS, to name a few.

UTC believes that innovation springs from knowledge and is committed to supporting a highly educated work force. Currently, more than 13,000 employees participate in the UTC Employee Scholar Program, which provides pre-paid tuition and fees, time off to attend classes and study and the award of UTC common stock upon graduation. The company encourages all employees to enroll in college classes to broaden their horizons, expand their thinking and sharpen their skills. Employees are free to explore their own interests, which need not be directly related to their work. The program is open to all UTC employees and the response is enthusiastic. Since the program's inception in 1996, UTC has invested more than $450 million in the Employee Scholar Program. Approximately 16,000 employees have received their degrees through the program. Retention among employees in the Employee Scholar program is greater than for those that are not.

In 2005, UTC granted $20,000 to fund scholarships for INROADS students to prepare them for positions of leadership in corporate America. Further, through the efforts of the UTC African-American Forum, $40,000 was provided in scholarship support to INROADS interns who were impacted by the effects of Hurricane Katrina. UTC also supports several historically black colleges and universities, such as North Carolina A&T, Howard University and Tuskegee.

In order to address employees' needs for resource and referral services, the Lifechoices program was established through the support of a consulting firm to provide employees with a variety of services including child and elder care referral services, emergency dependent care referral services, fertility and adoption consulting services and a homework hotline. Last year, more than 22 percent of UTC's U.S. employees used the resources of Lifechoices.

UTC employees value the corporation's role in strengthening our communities through innovative and significant monetary contributions. Each year, UTC donates more than $16 million to organizations around the world that support community programs,

the arts, education and the environment. This money is supplemented by the priceless contributions of time and effort made by thousands of employee volunteers. Each year, our employees spend more than 50,000 hours volunteering their time and expertise to their communities and nonprofit organizations. Like many companies, UTC matches the donations of their employees to nonprofit organizations. The company also recognizes and encourages volunteer activities by contributing to specific organizations to which employees donate a significant amount of their personal time. UTC is a leader in its support for Special Olympics. In 2005, UTC celebrated its 28th year of partnership with Special Olympics Connecticut. As a title sponsor of the state Summer Games, UTC supports Special Olympics Connecticut with more than 2,000 volunteers and $100,000 annually.

2005 UTC Facts

• We employ 220,000 employees in 180 countries in over 4,000 locations
• 42nd largest U.S. corporation (2006 list, *Fortune*)
• 120th largest in the world (2005 list, *Fortune*, Global 500)
• Named "Most Admired" aerospace and defense company (six years in a row, *Fortune*)

US Airways

Corporate Headquarters 4000 East Sky Harbor Blvd. Phoenix, AZ 85034 Phone: (480) 693-0800 Fax: (480) 693-8664 www.usairways.com	**Diversity Leadership** Linda Garza Kalaf, MA, SPHR, GPHR 111 Rio Salado Parkway Tempe, AZ 85281 Phone: (480) 693-8631 Fax: (480) 693-8664 www.linda.kalaf@usairways.com

Recruiting

Please list the schools/types of schools at which you recruit.

• Ivy League schools
• Private schools
• Public state schools
• Technical schools

Do you have any special outreach efforts that are directed to encourage minority students to consider your firm?

• *Conferences:* Hispanic Women's Conference, National Black MBA Association, National Society of Hispanic MBAs, Organization of Black Airline Pilots, Women in Aviation
• Participate in minority student job fairs
• *Other:* Advertise on minority web sites, for example,. www.latinosforhire.com

What activities does the firm undertake to attract minority and women employees?

• Partner programs with women and minority associations
• Participate at minority job fairs
• Utilize online job services

Do you use executive recruiting/search firms to seek to identify new diversity hires?

No.

Internships and Co-ops

INROADS: A number of interns participated in 2005 and returned in 2006, and participated in human resources, engineering and accounting.

US Airways' Summer Internship Program, "Intern With US" commenced in 1998, and is designed to provide students with airline experience that aligns with their educational and career interests.

> *Deadline:* April 14
> *Number of interns:* 15
> *Length of Program:* 10-12 weeks
> *Pay:* $10-$12 per hour (depending on school level)

Affinity Groups

Management Club

The US Airways Management Club is an organization that fosters cooperation, communication and understanding between all members of the corporate management team by providing opportunities for education, information and interaction in an environment which stimulates personal and corporate growth.

Minority Professional Association

MPA was organized in 1993 to provide an opportunity for management level African-American professionals to network and further their career development via a variety of seminars and workshops. Through the years, the scope of the organization has expanded to include all minority professionals at US Airways. The MPA has hosted several annual conferences.

Professional Women's Group

PWG was organized in 2000 as a networking organization for professional women. The PWG works to recognize, develop and promote women in the company. One of the biggest successes of the organization is the creation of the speaker series, which provides an opportunity for our members to hear from and interact with successful women within and outside of US Airways.

Spectrum

Spectrum is a networking organization that is open to all gay, lesbian, bisexual, transgender and straight employees. Spectrum was organized in 2003, and is committed to promoting equality and recognition of sexual identity as it relates to the workplace through awareness, education and communication. Spectrum has conducted focus group meetings and membership drives in the corporate office and Philadelphia.

Strategic Plan and Diversity Leadership

Who has primary responsibility for leading diversity initiatives at your firm?

Linda Garza Kalaf, manager, diversity programs.

Does your firm currently have a diversity committee?

Yes. Since the US Airways and America West Airlines merger in 2005, US Airways has recently re-established the Diversity Council to further expand the newly merged company's commitment to diversity. The Diversity Council meets on a quarterly basis.

If yes, does the committee's representation include one or more members of the firm's management/executive committee (or the equivalent)?

No. The diversity council consists of a cross section of front-line management, front line employees and a designee from each Affinity Group/Employee Network.

If yes, how many employees are on the committee?

The Diversity Council consists of 15 employees.

Does the committee and/or diversity leader establish and set goals or objectives consistent with management's priorities?

Yes.

Has the firm undertaken a formal or informal diversity program or set of initiatives aimed at increasing the diversity of the firm?

Yes, formal.

How often does the firm's management review the firm's diversity progress/results?

Monthly.

How is the firm's diversity committee and/or firm management held accountable for achieving results?

• Department profile (affirmative action goals)
• Inclusion of a diverse slate of qualified candidates in selection processes
• Diversity initiatives (training and outreach) completed annually
• Completion of diversity education to leadership team and front line employees
• Summer internship program conversation to hires

Diversity Mission Statement

Creating a culture that values diversity by maximizing and embracing the talents, skills, backgrounds, experiences and perspectives of all employees, thereby reflecting the diversity of customers served by US Airways.

Valero Energy Corporation

One Valero Way
San Antonio, TX 78249
Phone: (210) 345-2000
www.valero.com

Diversity Leadership

Kim Griffin
Employment Services Manager
One Valero Way
San Antonio, TX 78249-1112
Phone: (210) 345-2028
Fax: (210) 345-2778
E-mail: kim.griffin@valero.com

Employment Contact

Ruth Pina
Staffing & Employee Services
One Valero Way
San Antonio, TX 78249-1112
Phone: (210) 345-2000
Fax: (210) 345-2646
Toll Free: (800) 531-7911
www.valero.com

Recruiting

Please list the schools/types of schools at which you recruit.

• Private schools
• Public state schools
• Hispanic Serving Institutions (HSIs)

Do you have any special outreach efforts that are directed to encourage minority students to consider your firm?

• Advertise in minority student association publication(s)
• Firm's employees participate on career panels at schools

What activities does the firm undertake to attract minority and women employees?

• Partner programs with women and minority associations
• Seek referrals from other employees
• Utilize online job services

Do you use executive recruiting/search firms to seek to identify new diversity hires?
Yes.

If yes, list all women- and/or minority-owned executive search/recruiting firms to which the firm paid a fee for placement services in the past 12 months:

Alpha Quality Services, Badon's Employment, Inc.; Bullock Personnel, CAS Consulting Group, LLC; Channel Personnel Services, Energy Search Enterprises, Energy and Technical Associates, Inc.; FSC Technologies, LLC; Graves Recruiters for

Professionals, Deacon Recruiting, SMR Consulting Services, L.V. Havlik and Associates, Inc.; L.K. Jordan and Associates, Lang Technology Services, J. Rawley Personnel Solutions, Inc.

Internships and Co-ops

Valero Internship Program

Deadline for application: Rolling

Number of interns in the program in summer 2005 (internship) or 2005 (co-op): 49 interns; 21 co-ops

Pay: $14.00 per hour for interns; $24.00 per hour for co-ops.

Length of the program: Approximately 12 weeks

Percentage of interns/co-ops in the program who receive offers of full-time employment: 86 percent

Web site for internship/co-op information: www.valero.hrdpt.com/intern/

Scholarships

Since Valero began the scholarship program in 1981, the company has recognized outstanding children of all demographics including minority groups in support of their efforts to obtain a college education. Valero has awarded 265 scholarships totaling nearly two million dollars.

In addition, for the past two years Valero has awarded scholarships to children of Aruban employees. Fourteen Aruba scholarships have been granted totaling $140,000.

Strategic Plan and Diversity Leadership

Who has primary responsibility for leading diversity initiatives at your firm?

Collective responsibility of HR group.

Does your firm currently have a diversity committee?

No.

Has the firm undertaken a formal or informal diversity program or set of initiatives aimed at increasing the diversity of the firm?

Yes, informal.

How often does the firm's management review the firm's diversity progress/results?

Annually.

The Stats

The corporate office in San Antonio, Texas and operational sites throughout the United States are located in geographically diverse areas that enable the company to hire personnel of all demographics including minorities and females. As of December 2005, Valero employed a total of 18,067 individuals which included 38 percent minorities and 36 percent females. In addition, the CEO's leadership team consists of six executives including two females. Valero generated $55 billion in revenues in 2004 and a record $82 billion in 2005.

Retention and Professional Development

Please identify the specific steps you are taking to reduce the attrition rate of minority and women employees.

• Adopt dispute resolution process
• Succession plan includes emphasis on diversity
• Strengthen mentoring program for all employees, including minorities and women
• Professional skills development program, including minority and women employees

Valero is participating in Linkage conferences which target high potential employees as well as women and minorities. These conferences are pre-paid by the company and are made available to female managers and above. The sessions focus on diversity, women's issues in the workplace, and effective leadership strategies.

Valero has an executive development program which was implemented in August of 2004. This program is comprised of a three-day live simulation and feedback experience for current and emerging senior leaders throughout the organization. Graduate school incentives are also available to all employees. Costs for graduate school are reimbursed at a rate of 80 percent contingent upon sustaining a B average or above.

Valero strives to maximize retention of all managers within the organization, including minority and female managers. This is accomplished through one-on-one coaching, training, online educational tools, HR generalist services, employee performance reviews, 360 degree performance reviews and on-going performance feedback. Valero believes that retention really begins during the selection and hiring process and puts a great deal of time and effort into maximizing the effectiveness of this process and thus minimizing efforts on the retention side. Through commitment to our affirmative action plans, minority-targeted succession planning efforts and behavior-based interviews and personality assessments, Valero's selection process very effectively supports the hiring of minority managers as well as on-going promotion of managers from within the minority talent pools.

Diversity Mission Statement

Valero has a comprehensive competency model that specifies the competencies required for success in positions throughout the organization. The model provides valuable information to employees regarding the areas most relevant to success in their current job and for jobs where they might want to consider in the future. The model includes core competencies, such as diversity, required for all Valero employees, core supervisor competencies for all Valero supervisors and organization and contributor level competencies.

These competencies are incorporated into many of the Valero human resources functions including behavioral interviewing, employee performance review, 360 degree assessment, training and development, career planning and the development library. Within this model, "value diversity" is defined as someone who shows and fosters respect and appreciation for each person whatever their background, race, age, gender disability, values, lifestyle, perspectives, or interests; seeks to understand the worldview of others; see differences in people as opportunities for learning about and approaching things differently. Valuing diversity is being receptive to a wide range of people unlike oneself, according to any number of distinctions: national origin, physical ability, age, race, color, gender, class, native language, religion, sexual orientation, veteran status, professional experience, personal preferences, and work style.

These initiatives are a commitment to all employees and promote practices that demonstrate respect, trust and the value of each individual to ensure a pleasant work environment for all personnel. Valero demonstrates its fair treatment to all employees by providing everyone the opportunity to be considered for promotions through company-wide job postings. Diversity training is incorporated in "What Do Great Managers Do?," "Promises, Promises," "Sexual Harassment," retail new employee orientation, retail assistant and store manager training and the AIM training for retail area managers. These programs are provided for the purpose of maintaining a workplace that respects and dignifies each and every employee.

Additional Information

Affirmative Action Program

Valero's affirmative action program supports the company's diversity initiatives through the consistent and accurate administration of activities throughout the company's locations. The corporate human resources department works with a human resources representative from each location during the planning and preparation of their respective affirmative action plan.

Activities include:

• Communication of goals to hiring supervisor when a job is posted.

• Dissemination of quarterly reports to human resources representatives at each location, which include a summary of personnel activities and updates on progress toward meeting their site's goals.

• Annual presentations are conducted for corporate human resources managers to the management teams at each of the 19 refinery locations highlighting the company's yearly affirmative action activities and goals.

• Completion of internal audits of affirmative action procedures at randomly selected Valero locations.

• Past recipient of the Department of Labor's prestigious Exemplary Voluntary Efforts (EVE) Award based on Valero's successful recruitment of minority and female college interns, high retention rate post-graduation in professional positions at Valero and notable progression into supervisory roles.

Names of Minority Associations which Valero Supports:

• San Antonio Hispanic Chamber of Commerce
• Corpus Christi Hispanic Chamber
• National Hispanic Institute
• La Prensa
• Avance Corpus Christi
• Avance San Antonio
• Guadalupe Cultural Arts Center
• Avendia Guadalupe Association
• Texas Diversity Council

Awards and Recognition

• Ranked No. 3 among the nation's best employers on *Fortune's* listing of the "100 Best Companies to Work For"—up from its No. 23 ranking in 2005. Received the Great Place to Work Institute's "Pride Award" in 2004

• Ranked among *Hispanic* magazine's "Corporate 100" in 2002, 2003, 2004 and 2006 for providing business and job opportunities for Hispanic Americans

• One of just five companies honored, Valero received the U.S. Department of Labor's prestigious "Exemplary Voluntary Efforts" (EVE) Award for exemplary and innovative equal employment opportunity programs in 2002

Verizon Communications

1095 Avenue of the Americas
New York, NY 10036
Phone: (212) 395-2121
Fax: (212) 869-3265
Toll Free: (800) 621-9900
www22.verizon.com/about/careers

Diversity Leadership

Monice Sanders
Director, Staffing and Diversity,Telecom
Human Resources
13100 Columbia Pike
Silver Spring, MD 20904
Phone: (301) 236-1281
E-mail: monice.h.sanders@verizon.com

Employment Contact

Mesha Mendenhall Mott
Manager, College Relations and Recruitment
Telecom Human Resources

Diversity Contact

Dianne Campbell
Senior Staff Consultant, Workforce Diversity
Telecom Human Resources

Recruiting

Please list the schools/types of schools at which you recruit.

- *Ivy League schools:* Cornell
- *Private schools:* Carnegie Mellon, Devry University, Georgia Tech, ITT Technical Institute, Purdue University, Rensselaer Polytechnic Institute, Stevens Institute of Technology
- *Public state schools:* City University of New York, Rutgers University, University of Illinois—Urbana Champaign, University of Maryland—Baltimore & College Park, University of Massachusetts—Amherst, University of North Texas, University of Oklahoma, Texas A&M—College Station, University of California—Los Angeles, University of California—Riverside, University of South Florida, University of Southern California, University of Texas-Austin, University of Texas-Arlington
- *Historically Black Colleges and Universities (HBCUs):* Clark University, Florida A&M, Hampton University, Howard University, Morehouse, Morgan State University, Norfolk State University, North Carolina A&T, Spelman
- *Hispanic Serving Institutions (HSIs):* City University of New York colleges, University of Texas—San Antonio

Do you have any special outreach efforts directed to encourage minority students to consider your firm?

- Participate in/host minority student job fair(s)
- Sponsor minority student association events
- Firm's employees participate on career panels at school
- Outreach to leadership of minority student organizations

What activities does the firm undertake to attract minority and women employees?

- Partner programs with women and minority associations
- *Conferences:* National Black MBA Association, Hispanic Business Student Association, Hispanic Engineer National Achievement Awards Conference, Society for Women Engineers, Society for Hispanic Professional Engineers, National Society

of Black Engineers, American Indian Science & Engineering Society, National Society of Hispanic MBAs, Organization of Chinese Americans

• Participate at minority job fairs
• Seek referrals from other employees

Do you use executive recruiting/search firms to seek to identify new diversity hires?

No.

Internships and Co-ops

Verizon Young Leaders Program

Deadline for application: Candidates are sent directly from the Hispanic Association of Colleges and Universities and the Hispanic College Fund
Pay: Varies depending on location and class level
Length of the program (in weeks): 12 weeks

The Verizon Young Leaders program is a partnership with the Hispanic Association of Colleges and Universities and the Hispanic Scholarship Fund to increase the number of Hispanic summer interns at Verizon. In addition to the summer internship, each student is awarded a need-based scholarship. The departments that hire will vary each summer and the responsibilities will be based on the needs of the business.

INROADS

Deadline for application: Candidates are sent directly from INROADS.
Number of interns in the program in summer 2004 (internship) or 2004 (co-op): Nine internships
Pay: Varies depending on location and class level.
Length of the program : Approximately 12 weeks; however, there may be an opportunity for interns to continue working throughout the year in a part-time capacity.
Percentage of interns/co-ops in the program who receive offers of full-time employment: 4.5 percent

Verizon has been a major participant and supporter of the INROADS Internship Program. Recruiting interns is integral to identifying talented, diverse candidates. A key to our company's long-term success is to identify challenging and mutually beneficial internship positions within Verizon each year. We are working to enhance the INROADS relationship and the number of interns we will employ going forward.

Scholarships

Verizon College Scholarships

Deadline for application for the scholarship program: Varies. Scholarships are awarded in the fall. Candidates are then selected during the spring or summer for the following school year by the colleges.
Scholarship award amount: Scholarship amounts per school vary from $1,000-14,000.
Web site or other contact information for scholarship: Candidates apply directly to the department at the school awarded the scholarship.

Scholarships are awarded to all of Verizon's targeted colleges and universities. They are awarded to students majoring in engineering (electrical, mechanical, industrial, computer), computer science, math or business. The criteria for scholarships: students must possess, at a minimum, a 3.0 GPA and must have a specific major. Scholarships will be awarded to students that are underrepresented in the field that Verizon is targeting.

Affinity Groups

Our Employee Resource Groups (ERGs) are Verizon-supported and employee-run. They are organized affinity groups that promote personal and professional growth for employees with common interests. Through networking, mentoring, special initiatives, seminars and conferences, ERGs promote personal and professional employee growth, enhance career advancement and provide a stronger sense of community within the company and broader community. More than 10,000 employees are affiliated with our 10 Employee Resource Groups.

Asian Pacific Employees for eXcellence (APEX)

APEX aims to provide personal and professional development programs for its members. In addition, APEX strives to fulfill its social responsibilities by reaching out and supporting the communities in which they serve, and by increasing cultural awareness and championing the corporation's response to issues facing the Asian/Pacific Islander community.

Consortium of Information and Telecommunications Executives (CITE®)

CITE provides employee advocacy, issue awareness and professional development within Verizon. CITE serves as a resource for the African-American community at large. CITE makes a positive impact by hosting annual conferences, providing scholarships, implementing training and development programs and being actively involved in communities. Visit CITE's web site at www.forcite.com to learn more about their history, initiatives, state chapters and upcoming events.

Disabilities Issues Awareness Leaders (DIAL)

DIAL's mission is to recognize the talents and develop the maximum potential of Verizon employees with disabilities. DIAL provides insight, recommendations and support to individuals with disabilities and to Verizon. This effort is in keeping with the stated corporate commitment to universal design principles, the spirit of the Americans with Disability Act (ADA) and to managing diversity.

Gay, Lesbian, Bisexual and Transgender Employees of Verizon and Their Allies (GLOBE)

GLOBE's purpose is to address the needs and concerns of employees of Verizon who are Gay, Lesbian, Bisexual or Transgender or who have family, friends or colleagues who are, thereby creating a working environment in which each individual is treated with respect and dignity. For more information, visit GLOBE's web site at http://globe-of-verizon.org.

The Hispanic Support Organization (HSO)

HSO is the voice of the Hispanic employee who is committed to increasing opportunities for professional and personal development. HSO counsels and educates leaders to raise the awareness and increase responsiveness to issues affecting the Hispanic community within and outside Verizon Communications. To learn more about HSO, visit their web site at http://www.hispanicsupportorganization.org.

The National Jewish Cultural Resource Group (NJCRG)

NJCRG strives to create and maintain an environment in which members are encouraged to grow, participate and contribute to the company's overall success. NJCRG provides a unique cultural perspective to Verizon on various issues, which will increase our competitive advantage with our changing customer base.

Native American People of Verizon (NAPV)

NAPV has a mission to support, educate and acknowledge, through cultural exchange, the historical and contemporary contributions of American Indians/Alaskan Natives. Additionally, NAPV aims to enhance development, advancement and recruitment of American Indians at Verizon, and to support Verizon corporate values in our diverse workplace and community.

South Asian Professionals Inspiring Cultural Enrichment (SPICE)

SPICE is committed to sharing the rich heritage of South Asian cultures, providing a forum for communication of common interests and goals, and strengthening the fabric of diversity throughout the corporation. Verizon serves a diverse customer base externally and hence a multicultural perspective internally can prove invaluable. SPICE seeks to provide and refine that perspective throughout Verizon with respect to the South Asian community it serves.

Veterans Advisory Board of Verizon (VABVZ)

VABVZ has a mission to provide to senior management assistance, guidance and representation, regarding Veterans issues such as employment, health care, changes in health care as directed by the U.S. Veterans Administration, and legislation passed by U.S. Congress.

Women's Association of Verizon Employees (WAVE)

WAVE encourages an environment for learning new skills, addressing real women-in-the-workplace issues, networking and mentoring. Reaching out to women from associates through senior level executives at Verizon, WAVE works within the Consortium of Resource Groups to address issues such as child care, harassment in the workplace and opportunities for advancement.

Entry-Level Programs/Full-Time Opportunities/Training Programs

The Company: Verizon is one of the world's leading providers of high-growth communications services. Verizon is a major wireline carrier, wireless service provider, directory supplier and leader in data networking. To win in the marketplace, Verizon needs top talent. We seek the best people (those with diverse experience, perspectives, knowledge and backgrounds) and continue to provide the training they need to develop new or stronger skills, advance in the company, and achieve their goals, while contributing to Verizon's success.

The Benefits: Verizon provides an outstanding employee benefits package, including medical and dental plans, company-match 401(k) savings plan, life insurance, short- and long-term disability coverage, pension plan, personal lines of insurance, employee assistance program, domestic partner benefits, employee resource groups, flexible spending accounts and generous educational assistance programs.

Contact Information: If you are interested in the following programs and meet the designated qualifications, contact your college placement office. For more information and to submit your resume online, please visit www.verizon.com/college. Verizon is an equal opportunity employer and supports workforce diversity.

The Verizon Development Program

Length of program: This two-year rotational program consists of two hands-on staff marketing assignments, each lasting about six months, plus a one-year assignment in a supervisory or customer contact role. The initial six-month assignments may involve any aspect of business-to-business or consumer marketing, including product management, product development, product launch, market analysis, promotional campaigns, distribution and pricing.

Geographic location(s) of program: These assignments are typically based in a headquarters environment. Locations include but are not limited to: MA, NY, PA, MD, DC, VA, NC, FL, OH, IN, TX, CA and WA

Marketing provides a solid early career foundation to outstanding individuals who can address Verizon's marketing challenges, manage others and ultimately assume leadership roles in one of Verizon's largest business units, Retail Markets. The focus of this program is Verizon consumer and business customer segments. The program is designed to provide broad exposure to Verizon's consumer and business-to-business marketing initiatives, complemented by customer contact experiences and the opportunity to supervise a team—an unbeatable formula for launching a successful career.

Participants then transition from this headquarters exposure to the front line, where they may experience the dynamics of customer interaction and the challenges of supervising others. They gain both line and staff, headquarters and field perspectives, which will serve them well throughout their careers. Along the way, they are exposed to a broad array of telecommunications products and services—voice and data, network and hardware. At program completion, the career path typically leads to front-line management, with career progression to general marketing management in Verizon Retail Markets.

The program provides abundant training, with coursework in telecom technology, project management, presentation skills, leadership, supervision, customer relations, financial skills and time management. Participants also attend Verizon Development Program Orientation. Orientation includes presentations by business leaders, team-building exercises, workshops and social activities that provide opportunities to meet and network with peers.

Qualifications:

• BS in marketing.
• Excellent academic preparation and achievement with a minimum of 3.0 out of 4.0 overall GPA
• Superior oral and written communications, leadership, analytical and interpersonal skills
• Evidence of mature, flexible and innovative approaches to work experiences
• Potential to assume supervisory responsibilities
• Willingness to relocate during the program experience
• Must have authorization to work permanently in the United States

Software/Systems Architect Development Program Verizon Information Technology (VZIT)

> *Length of program:* The program format typically entails two rotational assignments, each lasting about six to nine months.
> *Geographic location(s) of program:* Including, but not limited to, Dallas, Tampa, Boston and the DC metro area.

The Verizon Software/Systems Architect Development Program (SSADP) provides innovative, technically sophisticated MS and PhD graduates the opportunity to immerse themselves in the dynamic environment of Verizon Information Technology (VZ-IT). Verizon IT represents the best of both worlds for technical professionals. We are a company that successfully takes advantage of the resources and security of a big corporation while maintaining a spirited and highly educated workforce. What this program offers you is the opportunity to make an impact on the future—to work within a financially stable but technologically creative environment.

You will be part of a brave new world, as the overarching Verizon IT goal is to become a technical innovator in developing and marketing information technology and eBusiness solutions. You can be part of this growth: contribute to it, develop and learn from it, establish your place in the industry and refine your career as an IT professional.

The Software/Systems Architect program is designed to perpetuate your academic success by developing well-rounded software engineers with a broad technology foundation, strong Verizon systems knowledge and the potential to ultimately assume technical leadership and/or general management roles at Verizon. These assignments provide exposure to different phases of the software development life cycle (i.e. requirements, design, development and testing), different technologies and different sides of the Verizon business. SSADP Participants are also exposed to various facets of software design including, but not limited to: data (logical modeling, physical database, DBMS), applications (object modeling, systems development/ integration, high level object-oriented design) and infrastructure computing (networking platforms, operating systems and software). Technologies include Java, .Net, XML, J2EE, C# and web services, among others. These hands-on assignments enable you to gain valuable experience in the design and development of large-scale systems applications with mentorship from Verizon project leads.

Qualifications:

- MS/PhD in computer science, electrical/computer engineering or related fields
- Excellent academic preparation and achievement with a minimum of 3.0 out of 4.0 overall GPA
- Software design or development experience; experience with various platforms
- Exceptional analytical, interpersonal, teamwork, leadership and communications skills
- Willingness to relocate during the program experience

Verizon Finance Professional Development

Geographic location(s) of program: NY/NJ, Philadelphia, Boston, DC/MD/VA, Tampa, FL, Irving TX

This comprehensive development program, which encompasses special orientation to Verizon and the finance function, is a personal development and training plan, with a targeted competency-based curriculum. Participants have access to extensive Verizon training opportunities via Verizon's NetLearn programs and access to the Verizon educational assistance program as well as ongoing performance feedback and coaching.

Mentoring circle participation is used to encourage creating opportunities for collaborative learning experiences, exchanging ideas as a group, analyzing developmental issues, receiving feedback and guidance, providing ongoing support and a sense of community and developing a strong peer network.

Developmental forums will include exposure to senior leadership, business issues and technology, skill assessment and creation of formal development/career plans and coming face-to-face with mentoring circles.

In addition, possible rotational assignment opportunities will help participants gain knowledge and experience of other finance disciplines, understand the inter-relationship between the finance organizations and develop and sharpen additional finance skills and interests. These jobs will also give them the chance to demonstrate strengths and skill sets to other managers and supervisors.

Qualifications:

- Most roles: BS/MBA in finance/accounting
- Technical Financial Analysis roles should have a BS in MIS/IT/computer engineering
- Verizon Capital Corp. role: math, operations research and engineering majors will be considered
- For all roles: minimum 3.3 out of 4.0 GPA preferred
- In-depth knowledge of MS Office products (and knowledge of Hyperion for some positions)
- Superior organizational, analytical, critical thinking, communication and interpersonal skills.
- Excellent quantitative skills
- For some roles, outstanding modeling and operations research skills
- Able to work effectively under pressure to meet critical deadlines
- Must have authorization to work permanently in the United States

Verizon Finance & Accounting Full-Time/Internship Positions

Geographic location(s) of program: NY/NJ, PA, MA, DC, MD, VA, TX, FL

Verizon financial and accounting roles provide excellent opportunities to apply your finance/accounting/technical background in a corporate finance setting.

Sample internships and full-time positions are in the areas of:

- *Consolidations*—Analyze subsidiary financial reports; prepare consolidated subsidiary financial statements
- *External Reporting*—Prepare and file periodic financial reports (Forms 10Q, 10-K); track, analyze impacts of SEC, GAAP developments
- *Staff Accounting*—Assist with monthly closing procedures, financial analyses, journal entries, account reconciliation, report results

- *Financial Performance and Assurance, Specialist-Business Development*—Evaluate business operations, financial projections, strategies, budgets and opportunities by developing financial models and conducting market/industry research
- *Line of Business Expenses*—Handle expense budgeting, planning and reporting for a Verizon line of business
- *Billing and Collections*—Handle billing for telecom industry customers, including adjustments, negotiations, settlements, documentation, tracking and accruals
- *Financial Planning & Analysis*—Develop and execute financial presentations, analysis and supporting documentation; support assigned business units
- *Financial Policies*—Assist with the operational implementation of new FASB and SEC accounting standards, support assigned business units, encompassing mergers and acquisitions, financial instruments, business combinations, etc.
- *Financial Reporting*—Prepare comparative financial data for quarterly earnings release, review trends, unusual items and variances to present a complete, accurate and balanced view of Verizon's financial performance to Wall Street analysts.
- *Corporate Consolidations*—Review business unit data submissions for data integrity, including consistency, comparability and GAAP compliance; prepare, process inter-segment elimination activity and topside adjustments; perform inter-segment out-of-balance reviews and reconciliation; generate consolidated financial statement.
- *Financial Planning & Analysis (Verizon Capital Corp)*—Provide pricing, valuation and transaction support of existing VCC portfolio, using sophisticated financial modeling and forecasting tools.
- *Technical Financial Analysis*—Implement, maintain sophisticated support systems; conduct economic cost studies; make entry and exit decisions for product lines; perform ad hoc analyses and studies; develop models for policy makers and executives.

Qualifications:

Same as those for the Verizon Finance Professional Development Program above

Full-Time Regular Positions Only:

The Professional Development: Members of the Verizon Finance team participate in special developmental and mentoring activities, including an orientation to Verizon and the finance function.

Contact Information: If you are interested and meet specified qualifications, please submit your resume to sandra.magwood@verizon.com; please reference "FT" or "Intern" in the subject field of your e-mail. For more information, please visit www.verizon.com/college. Verizon is an equal opportunity employer and supports workforce diversity.

Strategic Plan and Diversity Leadership

How does the firm's leadership communicate the importance of diversity to everyone at the firm?

Advocacy for Verizon's diversity strategy incorporates various communications vehicles including corporate/line of business-specific Intranet web sites and diversity-specific forums/meetings Examples include, but are not limited to:

- Verizon executives feature or incorporate diversity into their speeches and presentations to an internal employee audience and external groups
- Verizon's Development and Leadership Initiative (DLI) Symposium provides the opportunity for Verizon's executives to articulate Verizon's diversity strategy and engage DLI participants in discussion
- Employee Resource Group (ERG) events and activities (seminars, conferences, cultural celebrations, mentoring, etc.) provide the opportunity to communicate Verizon's diversity strategy and its commitment to having an aligned and integrated workplace where diversity is transparent, and where Verizon is an inclusive organization that leverages the diversity of employees, customers and suppliers for increased productivity, profitability and an enhanced reputation. Each of the 10 ERGs receive assistance in promoting their events and activities through the corporate e-mail systems
- HR Weekly is an online publication available through the Human Resources Communications web page. In addition to an ongoing calendar of events, stories highlighting the ERG program are also featured. Weekly distribution to all employees is utilized through the corporate e-mail systems
- The individual lines of business and ERGs design and deploy intranet web sites/web pages showcasing their support and commitment to Verizon's diversity strategy

Who has primary responsibility for leading diversity initiatives at your firm?

Tracey Edwards, Vice President—Staffing and Diversity, Domestic Telecom—Human Resources, has the primary responsibility for the overall design, implementation and program management of various diversity initiatives within the Domestic Telecom Lines of Business in support of Verizon's diversity strategy.

Does your firm currently have a diversity committee?

Yes.

If yes, please describe how the committee is structured, how often it meets, etc.

Verizon strives for diversity at every level within the company from the top down. To make progress through diversity and to ensure that it remains an integral part of our business, each business unit across the company relies on its diversity councils to help them develop and implement customized diversity plans. Those plans are designed to meet the specific requirements of that business unit and help them execute the Verizon diversity strategy.

Each council chooses a chair. The chair can be anyone from a senior leader within a line of business, to a human resources business partner, to a member of the diversity council. Councils meet at least once a month via conference call and at least once a year in person to set goals and objectives, to strategize and to implement the various diversity initiatives.

Each council is required to create and implement a diversity plan that includes diversity goals for their specific lines of business. Verizon's diversity goals include, but are not limited to:

(1) Employee Development—Encourage employees to take advantage of the specific leadership/management training classes available including the affinity workshops. Advocate continuous learning including enrollment in diversity training offered by Verizon through various mediums such as free online or classroom-based diversity classes. Ensure all director-level and above managers mentor lower-level employees

(2) Communication—Ensure all employees have a clear understanding of Verizon's diversity strategy. Encourage employees to get involved with all diversity efforts and to let them know that the senior leaders stand behind diversity. Host diversity weeks, panel discussions, etc.

(3) External Outreach and Partnerships—Work within the communities Verizon serves to educate people on diversity, technology, humanitarian projects.

If yes, does the committee's representation include one or more members of the firm's management/executive committee (or the equivalent)?

Yes.

If yes, how many executives are on the committee, and in 2005, what was the total number of hours collectively spent by the committee in furtherance of the firm's diversity initiatives? How many employees are on the committee, and how often does the committee convene in furtherance of the firm's diversity initiatives?

Executive representation and the number of employees on each committee vary by each line of business diversity council. Councils meet at least once a month via conference call and at least once a year in person to set goals and objectives, to strategize, and to implement the various diversity initiatives.

> *Total Executives on Committee:* Varies by line of business.

Does the committee and/or diversity leader establish and set goals or objectives consistent with management's priorities?

Yes. Corporate Diversity sets the overall Verizon diversity strategy, and Workforce Diversity provides the councils with the human resources focus for the year (e.g. employee development for 2005). However, each line of business council creates action plans and initiatives in support of those plans depending on the needs of their particular line of business. These plans are created with input for the line of business senior management team.

Has the firm undertaken a formal or informal diversity program or set of initiatives aimed at increasing the diversity of the firm?

Yes, formal. To ensure that diverse members of our multicultural work force are prepared for career advancement, we have established mentoring and leadership development programs, such as the Verizon Development and Leadership Initiative (DLI). The DLI provides tools that help participants identify professional goals and network with Verizon executives, while helping Verizon identify and develop a diverse pool of high-potential candidates.

The DLI and Verizon's employee development resources have strengthened Verizon's leadership team by developing high quality managers from diverse backgrounds who are prepared to assume new job assignments and additional responsibilities.

Verizon's mentoring initiative is critical to our strategy to win in the global marketplace and be the premier telecommunications company in the world. Mentoring helps drive this strategy because it fosters the development, growth and contributions of our most important asset—our people. Mentoring achieves this objective by leveraging informal work relationships, and enhancing the skills and capacity of our people to achieve their professional and personal objectives, while adding value to the business.

How often does the firm's management review the firm's diversity progress/results?

Quarterly.

How is the firm's diversity committee and/or firm management held accountable for achieving results?

We have a commitment to diversity that stems from the top of the business. In addition to a leadership team that is becoming more and more diverse, we are also governed by a diverse board of directors representing a variety of industries and experiences.

Our management executives are held accountable for promoting diversity in their organizations and our Diversity Performance Incentive links our employment efforts to recruit, retain and develop a diverse population of employees to meet the needs of the diverse marketplace that we serve.

Retention and Professional Development

Please identify the specific steps you are taking to reduce the attrition rate of minority and women employees.

• Develop and/or support internal employee affinity groups (e.g., minority or women networks within the firm)
• Increase/review compensation relative to competition
• Succession plan includes emphasis on diversity
• Work with minority and women employees to develop career advancement plans
• Strengthen mentoring program for all employees, including minorities and women
• Professional skills development program, including minority and women employees

Diversity Mission Statement

Verizon is committed to maintaining an inclusive corporate culture that embraces and leverages the diversity of employees, customers and suppliers for increased productivity, profitability and an enhanced reputation. The culture of inclusion that defines our company will earn the trust of our employees and the diverse customers and communities we serve.

Additional Information

Verizon is at the forefront of the transformation of the telecommunications industry and we remain committed to creating and fostering an inclusive culture that values the diversity of our employees. Competition in our industry is pervasive, and we recognize that in order to meet the ever changing and growing demands of our customers we must rely on the innovation and creativity that a diverse employee base provides. Verizon is proud of the broad range of products and services we offer and prouder still of our ability to foster, promote and preserve the diversity and human rights of our employees, customers and communities.

Awards and Recognition

Verizon has been recognized nationally for its commitment to diversity:

2006 Diversity Awards/Honors

• *Black MBA* magazine ranked Verizon 1st on the publication's Top 50 Companies for African-American MBAs to Work (2006).

• *Black Engineer and Information Technology (USBE&IT) Magazine* selected Verizon as a Top Supporter of Historically Black Colleges (2006).

• *DiversityInc* magazine ranked Verizon No. 1 on the 2006 list of Top 50 U.S. Companies for Diversity.

• Moms in Business Network/The International Association of Working Mothers named Verizon National Company of the Year.

• *Training* Magazine named Verizon Communications and Verizon Wireless to their annual "Training Top 100" list of organizations that excel at employee development.

• WBENC (Women's Business Enterprise National Council) selected Verizon to its annual listing of America's Top Corporations for Women, in March 2006. The award recognizes a select group of companies for their "world class" supplier diversity programs.

• *Working Mother* named Verizon one of 2006 Best Companies for Women of Color.

2005 Diversity Awards/Honors:

• *BLACK ENTERPRISE* magazine named Verizon one of the "30 Best Companies for Diversity." The publication noted Verizon's commitment to diversity among senior management, board of directors and suppliers.

• *CAREERS & the disABLED* magazine named Verizon the Private-Sector Employer of the Year for its commitment to recruiting, hiring and advancing people with disabilities.

• DiversityBusiness.com honored Verizon with its "America's Top Organizations for Multicultural Opportunities" award.

• Employee Assistance Society of North America presented Verizon with its Corporate Award of Excellence for its innovative employee assistance program, VZ-LIFE. Verizon received the award for offering comprehensive work/life solutions to its diverse work force.

• EPA (Environmental Protection Agency) Verizon was named U.S. EPA WasteWise Partner of the Year.

• EPA and DOT (Department of Transportation) recognized Verizon as one of the Best Workplaces for Commuters.

• Montgomery County MD recognized Verizon at its 6th annual Recycling Awards Week Ceremony for our comprehensive waste reduction and recycling program—Verizon surpassed the objective of 50 percent (exceeded to 70 percent).

• *Essence* magazine placed Verizon 2nd for African-American women on its list of 35 Great Places to Work.

• HESTEC (Hispanic Engineering Science and Technology) presented Magda Yrizarry, vice president, with the UTPA Foundation Latina Pioneer Award.

• *Hispanic* magazine named Verizon to its Corporate 100 list for providing opportunities for Hispanics. It also named Verizon as having one of the Top 25 Diversity Recruitment Programs and one of the Top 25 Supplier Diversity Programs.

• Hispanic Association on Corporate Responsibility (HACR) ranked Verizon second on the HACR Corporate Index, in 2005. The index grades the Fortune 100 companies on their commitment to the Hispanic community.

• *Hispanic Business* magazine named Verizon to its list of 25 Best Companies to Work For. Verizon was ranked one of the magazine's top five companies for Hispanics.

• *Latin Business* magazine named Verizon to its Corporate Diversity Honor Roll (2004, 2005).

• *Latina Style* magazine named Verizon to its special Top 13 list of the 50 Top Companies for Hispanic Women.

• *Diversity Journal* profiled Maura Breen, Keiko Harvey, Jerri DeVard, senior vice presidents at Verizon; Katherine Linder, Kathy Harless and Sheila Lau, presidents, were also profiled as "Women of Initiative."

• *Scientific American* magazine named Verizon to its first list of the 55 top companies making a difference in the way people with disabilities live and work.

• *Training Magazine* named Verizon and Verizon Wireless to its list of the Top 100 companies that excel at human capital development.

• United States Pan Asian American Chamber of Commerce (USPAACC) named Verizon "Corporation of the Year."

• Women's Venture Fund presented Magda Yrizarry, vice president, with the "Highest Leaf Award." The award honors women whose business or professional action positively impacts their fields and exemplifies an understanding of the balance between outcome and responsibility in their workplace.

Wachovia Corporation

One Wachovia Center
Charlotte, NC 28288-0013
www.wachovia.com

Wachovia Securities
Riverfront Plaza
901 East Byrd Street
Richmond, VA 23219
www.wachoviasec.com

Evergreen Investments
200 Berkeley Street
Boston, MA 02116
Phone: (617) 210-3200
www.evergreeninvestments.com

Employment Contact
E-mail: jobs@wachovia.com
Jobs@evergreeninvestments.com
www.wachovia.com/careers

Recruiting

Please list the schools/types of schools at which you recruit.

• *Ivy League schools:* Harvard University, Princeton University, and University of Pennsylvania
• *Other private schools:* Duke University, Wake Forest University, Vanderbilt University and others
• *Public state schools:* University of North Carolina, University of Virginia, University of Texas, University of Florida, and others
• *Historically Black Colleges and Universities (HBCUs):* Morehouse College, Spelman College, Hampton University, Howard University, Florida A&M University and others
• *Hispanic Serving Institutions (HSIs):* Florida International University and University of Houston

Do you have any special outreach efforts directed to encourage minority students to consider your firm?

• Hold a reception for minority students
• *Conferences:* National Society of Hispanic MBAs, National Black MBA Association, NABA, NAACP, ALPFA, Thurgood Marshall Career Fair Toigo
• Advertise in minority student association publication(s)
• Participate in/host minority student job fair(s)
• Sponsor minority student association events
• Firm's employees participate on career panels at schools
• Outreach to leadership of minority student organizations
• Scholarships or intern/fellowships for minority students

What activities does the firm undertake to attract minority and women employees?

• Partner programs with women and minority associations
• *Conferences:* National Association of Black Accountants, Black Data Processing Association, Association of Latino Professionals in Finance & Accounting, National Black MBA Association, National Society of Hispanic MBAs
• Participate at minority job fairs
• Seek referrals from other employees
• Utilize online job services

Do you use executive recruiting/search firms to seek to identify new diversity hires?

Yes.

Internships and Co-ops

There are a variety of internship programs in eight different lines of business. The specific programs vary each year and are updated on our web site in December. Please see www.wachovia.com/college for details.

Deadline for application: February 1st

Number of interns in the program in summer 2005 (internship) or 2005 (co-op): 141 undergraduate interns and 41 graduate interns in 2005.

Pay: $12 to $18 per hour for undergraduate programs, based on class year and varies slightly by line of business

Length of the program: Eight to 10 weeks

Percentage of interns/co-ops in the program who receive offers of full-time employment: Varies by line of business

Web site for internship/co-op information: www.wachovia.com/college

Scholarships

A variety of scholarships are available.

Scholarship award amount: $500 to $2,000

Entry-Level Programs/Full-Time Opportunities/Training Programs

There are a variety of entry-level associate and analyst programs in eight different lines of business. The specific programs vary each year and are updated on our web site in August and January. Please see www.wachovia.com/college for details.

Length of program: Three to six month rotations in various areas, two to three year placements, or permanent placement depending on the program

Geographic location(s) of program: In every location within the Wachovia footprint

Varies from six weeks initial training to ongoing training depending on the program.

Strategic Plan and Diversity Leadership

How does the firm's leadership communicate the importance of diversity to everyone at the firm?

Wachovia's corporate Intranet has a section called Wachovia Diversity, accessible from the homepage, where CEO Ken Thompson talks about the importance of creating a diverse and inclusive workplace. Employees can also find Wachovia's Values Statement, Diversity Strategies for the current year, and diversity resources on this site. In addition, twice a year, Ken provides an update on diversity to all employees through e-mail, Intranet and over Wachovia's internal television network.

Who has primary responsibility for leading diversity initiatives at your firm?

Rosie Saez, director of diversity integration practices.

Does your firm currently have a diversity committee?

Yes.

If yes, please describe how the committee is structured, how often it meets, etc.

The Corporate Diversity Council, headed by CEO Ken Thompson, meets approximately six times per year to determine and direct the strategic diversity effort for the entire Wachovia footprint. The council is made up of a diverse representation of leaders from across Wachovia. The purpose of the council is to convert the ideal of what we think our company stands for into processes and procedures that ensure that the ideal becomes real. The council determines the current state of diversity in the corporation, defines corporate objectives relative to diversity and works to continuously reinforce the practice of diversity at Wachovia.

If yes, does the committee's representation include one or more members of the firm's management/executive committee (or the equivalent)?

Yes.

If yes, how many executives are on the committee, and in 2005, what was the total number of hours collectively spent by the committee in furtherance of the firm's diversity initiatives? How many employees are on the committee, and how often does the committee convene in furtherance of the firm's diversity initiatives?

Total Executives on Committee: Six

Does the committee and/or diversity leader establish and set goals or objectives consistent with management's priorities?

Yes.

Has the firm undertaken a formal or informal diversity program or set of initiatives aimed at increasing the diversity of the firm?

Yes, formal.

How often does the firm's management review the firm's diversity progress/results?

Annually.

How is the firm's diversity committee and/or firm management held accountable for achieving results?

The CEO is a member of the committee. Also, the committee is advised by the director of diversity integration practices.

Diversity Mission Statement

Teamwork. Synergy. The collective ideas and insights of our employees forge our solid and unified vision for success.

At Wachovia, we treat people with respect, recognize them for their individuality, and provide opportunities for advancement based on performance. Race, gender, gender identity, sexual orientation, work/life status, ethnic origin, culture, spiritual beliefs and practices, age, education level, physical ability, veteran status, and other differences make us unique as individuals and enhance our company as a whole.

A Corporate Diversity Council, lead by CEO Ken Thompson, guides the Wachovia diversity commitment. The council meets regularly to:

• Define corporate diversity objectives
• Raise awareness and sensitivity to diversity within our company
• Determine the state of affairs within our company and prescribe strategies and action plans when needed
• Implement programs and policies effectively
• Update and improve diversity commitments on an as-needed basis

Our commitment to diversity is also felt outside of our company. Today, we have outreach programs in place that have a significant affect on the communities we serve. These include community development products and services, purchasing programs with minority-owned firms, women's financial advisory initiatives, and products and services for underserved diverse customer groups.

Wachovia is an active participant in the INROADS internship program. If interested, please contact your local INROADS office for more information.

Additional Information

National Diversity Recruiting Partner Alliances
National Association of Black Accountants
Web site: http://www.nabainc.org
2006 National Association of Black Accountants Conference & Career Expo—Hollywood, Fl; June 13-17 Wachovia is Corporate Sponsor

Association of Latino Professionals in Finance and Accounting
Web site: http://www.alpfa.org
August 5th-September 2006, Annual Convention, Ft Worth, TX; Wachovia is Corporate Sponsor

National Society of Hispanic MBA
Web site: http://www.nshmba.org
October 26-28, 2006; 17th Annual National Conference, Cincinnati, OH; Wachovia is Corporate Sponsor

Urban Financial Services Coalition
Web site: http://www.ufsc.org/
May 29-June 4, 2006; National Conference, Dallas, TX; Wachovia is Corporate Sponsor

Black Data Processors Association
Web site: http://www.bdpa.org/portal/
August 2-6, 2006; National Conference, Los Angeles, CA; Wachovia is Corporate Sponsor

Gay & Lesbian Professional Career Network (National Online Job Board & Professional Alliance)
Careers Web site: http://www.GLPCareers.com

National Association of Asian American Professionals
Web site: http://www.naaap.org
August 17-20, 2006; National Conference, Seattle, WA; Wachovia is Corporate Sponsor

National Black MBA Association
Web site: http://www.nbmbaa.org
October 26-28, 2006; National Conference & Career Expo, Atlanta, GA; Wachovia is Corporate Sponsor

Special Diversity Outreach Partnership Programs for 2006:
National Black MBA Local Empowerment Initiative—Dallas/Ft Worth
National Society of Hispanic MBA—Hispanic Executive Summit—New York
Association of Latino Professionals in Finance & Accounting—Women of ALPFA Leadership—National/Regional focus

Wal-Mart Stores, Inc.

702 Southwest 8th Street
Bentonville, AR 72716
Phone: (479) 273-4000

Additional Information

"Diversity doesn't just happen. Just saying we are committed to diversity is not enough—we must put in the right processes and leadership to make it happen."

Lee Scott
President and CEO
Wal-Mart Stores, Inc.

At Wal-Mart, we embrace diversity at all levels in our organization. We believe that success requires both an environment where people are respected and valued, along with a talented workforce that represents our diverse customer base. This ensures that we create an environment that is as distinct as the suppliers that we buy from, the shareholders we serve and the global communities in which we operate.

Today, we are indeed a diverse workforce with more than 1.8 million associates worldwide. With stores and operations in China, Mexico, Germany, the United Kingdom, Brazil, Japan, and other countries, our associates bring a host of talents, perspectives and experience that have helped to make us one of the nation's most admired companies. Yet, we are more than just a great place to shop. We are also a great place to work. Currently, we are proud to be a leading employer of African-Americans and Hispanics in the United States. This is the one reason Wal-Mart was named on the *DiversityInc* Top 50 Companies for Diversity list in 2005!

This is also why Wal-Mart is committed to key diversity initiatives including leadership development programs specifically designed to support women and minorities in the advancement of their careers. Wal-Mart also demonstrates the importance of diversity through its Good Faith Efforts Program. This program builds and enhances relationships with organizations that support the advancement of women, minorities, seniors, individuals with disabilities, and gay, lesbian, bisexual, and transgender individuals. The Good Faith Efforts Program enhances the company's reputation with these groups and also ensures that we continue to recruit and retain qualified, interested and diverse associates.

Wal-Mart is also committed to diversifying its workforce by actively recruiting top talent from colleges and universities with significant populations of diverse students, including many women's colleges, historically black colleges and universities, and colleges with a high Hispanic representation. We also recruit at military locations and at diversity career fairs throughout the nation.

Ensuring our commitment to diversity requires our management team to meet their diversity goal requirements. In 2005, the number of associates accountable for meeting their diversity goals was expanded from 3,500 officers and senior managers to include more than 51,000 facility-level managers. By including our field operations team in our diversity efforts, we are ensuring that our corporate diversity initiatives are met nationally. Additionally, we are pleased to note that 100 percent of our officers achieved both their diversity placement and Good Faith Effort goals in 2005!

Supplier diversity is also an important initiative for Wal-Mart as we strive to be a preferred business partner and drive the diversity of our suppliers. We spent more than $4.2 billion in 2005 with women and minority-owned businesses. To foster their growth, Wal-Mart established a $25 million private equity fund to provide capital to women and minority-owned businesses. Additionally, we provided a $1 million grant to the Business Consortium Fund, an initiative of the National Minority Supplier Development Council. Driving our supplier diversity is a continual focus for Wal-Mart and one that helps us better serve the communities in which we operate.

We continue to earn recognition for our diversity programs and our progress to date. To name a few, we are honored to have been included among *Black Enterprise* magazine's Top 35 Companies for Diversity, Hispanic Association on Corporate Responsibility Corporate Index's Top 10 Companies for Inclusion of the Hispanic Community, and *Asian Enterprise* magazine's Top 10 Companies for Asian-Americans.

For more information regarding diversity at Wal-Mart, including other diversity-based awards or recognition, our Voices of Color film series, our support of the Martin Luther King, Jr. National Memorial, our *Profiles in Pride* booklet and other related programs, please visit our web site at www.walmartstores.com/diversity and www.walmartfacts.com.

"Our people make the difference, and it is our collective difference—in perspective, experience and understanding—that allows us to better serve our customer."

Susan Chambers
Executive Vice President People Division
Wal-Mart Stores, Inc.

Wells Fargo & Company

420 Montgomery Street
San Francisco, CA 94104

Locations

San Francisco (HQ)
Offices in all 50 states

Diversity Leadership

Linda McConley
Diversity Manager
420 Montgomery St.
San Francisco, CA 94104
Phone: (612) 667-0643
Fax: (612) 667-5353
E-mail: Linda.k.mcconley@wellsfargo.com

Employment Contact

Lane Ceric
Corporate Recruitment Manager
333 Market Street
San Francisco, CA 94105
www.wellsfargo.com/employment

Recruiting

Please list the schools/types of schools at which you recruit.

• *Ivy League schools:* Examples include Harvard and University of Pennsylvania
• *Other private schools:* Examples include Knox College, Kenyon College, Pepperdine University, Claremont McKenna Schools, Emory University, Texas A&M
• *Public state schools:* Examples include UC Berkeley, UCLA, ASU, ISU, UTA, Iowa State, University of Minneapolis, UC Davis, USC
• *Historically Black Colleges and Universities (HBCU's):* Examples include Clark Atlanta Schools, Xaviers, Jackson State University
• *Hispanic Serving Institutions (HSIs):* Examples include St. Mary's College, Our Lady of The Lake
• *Native American Tribal Universities:* Examples include American Indian Business Leaders Conference

Do you have any special outreach efforts directed to encourage minority students to consider your firm?

• Hold a reception for minority students
• *Conferences:* Please see below.
• *Advertise in minority student association publication(s):* For every event we attend or host on campus, we actively advertise o events to those student groups that have listed themselves on the campus sites.
• *Participate in/host minority student job fair(s):* We participate in the Diversity Career Fair in the spring at UC Berkeley.
• *Sponsor minority student association events:* This year, we were Golden Bear Sponsors ($15,000 - the highest level) at the Conference for African-Americans at UC Berkeley.
• Firm's employees participate on career panels at school
• Outreach to leadership of minority student organizations
• Scholarships or intern/fellowships for minority students

What activities does the firm undertake to attract minority and women employees?

• Partner programs with women and minority associations

• *Conferences:* American Indian Business Leaders, Graduate Women in Business, National Association of Black Accountants, National Black MBA Association, National Hispanic Business Association, National Society of Hispanic MBAs, Students in Free Enterprise, and various regional and campus student organizations
• Participate at minority job fairs
• Seek referrals from other employees
• Utilize online job services

Do you use executive recruiting/search firms to seek to identify new diversity hires?
No.

Internships and Co-ops

Corporate/Wholesale Banking Undergraduate Summer Analyst and MBA Summer Associate Program

Deadline for application: February 2006
Number of interns in the program in summer 2005 (internship) or 2005 (co-op): 43 undergraduates and 10 MBAs
Length of the program: 10-12 weeks
Percentage of interns/co-ops in the program who receive offers of full-time employment: TBD.
Web site for internship information: http://www.wellsfargo.com/employment/undergraduates/summer/corporate

Internet Services Summer Intern Program

Deadline for application: March 2006
Number of interns in the program in summer 2005 (internship) or 2005 (co-op): 12 undergraduates/three MBAs
Length of the program: 10-12 weeks
Percentage of interns/co-ops in the program who receive offers of full-time employment: TBD.
Web site for internship information: http://www.wellsfargo.com/employment/undergraduates/summer/internet

Scholarships

Hispanic Scholarship Fund (HSF)

Deadline for application for the scholarship program: April 2006
Scholarship award amount: 25 scholarships, $2,500 per scholarship for each year up to four years.
Web site or other contact information for scholarship: http://www.hsf.net/scholarships.php

Wells Fargo offers scholarship awards (as well as internships and future employment opportunities) to Latino students in partnership with the Hispanic Scholarship Fund (HSF).

Asian and Pacific Islander American Scholarship Fund (APIASF)

Scholarship award amount: $2,000
Web site or other contact information for scholarship: www.apiasf.org

Wells Fargo is one of several founding sponsors of the Asian and Pacific Islander American Scholarship Fund (APIASF). The scholarship is designed for college-bound students from underrepresented Asian and Pacific Islander communities interested in pursuing careers in banking and financial services.

Summer Search Foundation

Deadline for application for the scholarship program: Please contact (415) 362-0500
Scholarship award amount: $5,000 donation and compensation associated with participation in the intern programs detailed above.
Web site or other contact information for scholarship: http://www.summersearch.org/about/s.php?P=home.html

The mission of Summer Search is to identify low-income high school youth who demonstrate resiliency in overcoming hardship and possess the desire to help others. Nurturing those qualities over time in students who have often been neglected allows them to become empowered future everyday leaders. Our ambitious mission is accomplished through a program that combines full scholarships to summer experiential education programs with intensive long-term mentoring. Summer Search currently works with 600 students a year in San Francisco, Boston, Napa-Sonoma, New York City and Seattle. Wells Fargo sponsors three to five interns per summer.

Students Rising Above (KRON Channel 4)

Deadline for application for the scholarship program: Mid-April 2006
Scholarship award amount: Compensation associated with participation in the intern programs detailed above.
Web site or other contact information for scholarship: http://www.studentsrisingabove.org/

This scholarship was created by KRON 4 News reporter and anchor Wendy Tokuda for students living in dangerous or low-income neighborhoods.

Qualifications include:

• Low-income or living on government assistance
• Highly recommended by teachers, counselors or mentors
• Cannot already be receiving a four-year scholarship
• Personal character
• Has overcome obstacles that are not of their own making
• Committed to earning a college degree
• Willing to talk about life experiences on camera
• Must live within nine-county Bay Area
• 3.0+ GPA.

Wells Fargo sponsors three to five interns per summer.

UC Berkeley SAGE Scholars Program

Deadline for application for the scholarship program: Varies annually
Scholarship award amount: $3,800 administrative fee per scholar/per summer and compensation associated with participation in the intern programs detailed above
Web site or other contact information for scholarship: http://students.berkeley.edu/sagescholars/

UC Berkeley's SAGE (Student Achievement Guided by Experience) Scholars Program is an academically rigorous program that combines workplace experience with the professional skills needed to succeed in a competitive economy. SAGE works with highly motivated UC Berkeley's students from low-income and diverse backgrounds. SAGE promotes quality professional leadership and career development training through internships, mentoring and education. Wells Fargo is on the Corporate Advisory Board for this organization, hired five interns in 2005 and potentially five interns for 2006.

University of Texas, Austin Jumpstart Program

> *Deadline for application for the scholarship program:* Varies annually
> *Scholarship award amount:* Compensation associated with three years of pre-program employment and all tuition and fees associated with enrollment in the UT-Austin MBA program.

A new program from The University of Texas at Austin's McCombs School of Business aims to expand the pool of top students who consider an MBA degree. The Jump Start program targets undergraduate seniors who are academically qualified for a top-ranked MBA program but lack the required work experience. Companies agree to provide the experience by hiring the students for three years. The McCombs School then offers candidates deferred admission to the MBA program based on the completion of their job commitment.

INROADS

> *Scholarship award amount:* Administrative fee per intern/per summer and compensation associated with participation in the intern programs detailed above.

Affinity Groups

Wells Fargo has 80 Team Member Resource Groups across the company. The networks offer employees with a common background with professional growth opportunities, personal enrichment, networking, mentoring and educational opportunities. They also help us attract, retain and advance diverse team members. Any Wells Fargo team member can join an existing group or propose to start a new group. Groups include:

• Arab
• African-American ("CheckPoint")
• Asian/Pacific Islander ("Asian Connection")
• Team Members Dealing with Disabilities ("disAbilities Awareness")
• Hispanic/Latino ("Amigos")
• Native American ("Native Peoples")
• Persian ("Persian American Connection")
• Gay, Lesbian, Bi-sexual and Transgender ("PRIDE")

Entry-Level Programs/Full-Time Opportunities/Training Programs

Wells Fargo has many programs in place designed to attract and retain diverse team members, to enhance our diversity objectives and provide management opportunities. These programs have been in place for several years. Past experience has shown that many of these individuals quickly move up within the organization to leadership roles. Participants in these programs, like all Wells Fargo team members, are eligible for tuition reimbursement.

Corporate Banking: Credit Management Training Program (MBA)

> *Length of program:* Six months
> *Geographic location of program:* San Francisco

This program familiarizes participants with how Wells Fargo analyzes and evaluates credit situations. Associates work directly with corporate clients in building and strengthening relationships and recommending the necessary credit or other financial products to meet their needs.

Corporate Banking: Financial Analyst Program (BA/BS)

Length of program: 18-24 months
Geographic location of program: Major cities in California, Texas, the Pacific Northwest, Chicago, Minneapolis, New York and other U.S. locations

The Financial Analyst Program provides analytical and operational support to senior bankers during the deal making process, corporate meetings and presentations to senior managers. Formal training in accounting, corporate finance, treasury management and commercial credit.

Corporate Banking: Marketing Operations and Project Manager/Leadership Development Program (BA/BS)

Length of program: 12-18 months
Geographic location of program: San Francisco, St. Paul

This program is designed to train qualified diversity candidates for management roles in corporate banking support services. Provides comprehensive exposure to the Wells Fargo corporate/wholesale businesses in preparation for an individual contributor or management position within the business group.

Business Banking Services: Business Banking Associate Program (UG)

Length of program: 12 months (two six-month rotations)
Geographic location of program: San Francisco, Sacramento, Concord, Boise, Minneapolis, San Antonio

Rotations include operations/customer service, finance/credit analysis, systems, mergers and acquisitions and human resources. Also includes formal training in technical, business and interpersonal skills.

Finance: Finance Associate Program (UG)

Length of program: 12 months
Geographic location of program: San Francisco

The Finance Associate Program prepares recent graduates for a career in finance through a combination of hands-on experience, classroom and web-based training and peer interaction. It moves trainees through project teams in various finance business lines, and one rotation in an unassociated Wells Fargo business line.

Internet Services: Internet Business Consultant Program (MBA)

Length of program: 12 months
Geographic location of program: San Francisco

The Internet Business Consultant Program provides participants the opportunity to develop skill sets in the world of e-commerce and address key challenges in our business. Participants learn what makes an Internet business successful and have the chance to contribute to that success.

Internet Services: Information Technology Associate (BS/BA)

Length of program: 12 months
Geographic location of program: San Francisco

Includes three project-based rotations over 12 months. The ITA program uses a combination of classroom training, computer-based training, project team participation, peer interaction and working one-on-one with e-commerce technology professionals to prepare participants for their first assignment as an Internet services IT professional.

Audit Services Group: Auditor Rotational Training Program (BA/BS)

Length of program: 36 months
Geographic location of program: Des Moines, Minneapolis, Phoenix, San Francisco

A rotational program wherein individuals complete a formal training curriculum related to technical, business and behavioral skills while rotating among different audit groups.

Wells Fargo Services: Leadership Development Program (BA/BS)

Length of program: 12 months
Geographic location of program: Minneapolis, Phoenix, San Francisco

A rotational program providing exposure to a variety of functional enterprises within the services company. Participants may work in a retail store, a phone bank center, and/or in entry-level operations and technology assignments. They will also receive a personal mentor, guidance from the program manager and various assignment managers.

Corporate Human Resources: HR Leadership Program (MBA)

Length of program: 10-12 months
Geographic location of program: San Francisco

A program developing HR core competencies in recent MBAs. Participants work as consultants on projects in various corporate HR business lines/lines of business.

"Class of" Program

Length of program: Six months
Geographic location of program: Major cities nationwide

Trainees in the programs detailed above participate in corporate human resource's "Class of" Program. The goal of this program is to offer participants exposure to the larger company, senior management and each other, creating a sense of community and strong working relationships across business lines. The six-month curriculum includes a two-day executive exposure forum, networking opportunities with management and peers throughout the company and webcasts on professional development and Wells Fargo's visions & values.

Strategic Plan and Diversity Leadership

How does the firm's leadership communicate the importance of diversity to everyone at the firm?

The company distributes diversity information through e-mail, internal and external web sites, newsletters, meetings, speeches, brochures, videos, training courses, phone announcements and letters from executives.

Who has primary responsibility for leading diversity initiatives at your firm?

Linda McConley, diversity manager.

Does your firm currently have a diversity committee?

Yes.

If yes, please describe how the committee is structured, how often it meets, etc.

Thirty-two members representing each Wells Fargo business line (one Diversity Council representative per 5,000 team members). The committee meets six times per year (three face-to-face meetings and three teleconferences).

If yes, does the committee's representation include one or more members of the firm's management/executive committee (or the equivalent)?

Yes.

Does the committee and/or diversity leader establish and set goals or objectives consistent with management's priorities?

Yes.

Has the firm undertaken a formal or informal diversity program or set of initiatives aimed at increasing the diversity of the firm?

Yes, formal. Wells Fargo has a company-wide diversity platform called "Six Steps to Got Diversity" to guide and measure the company's progress towards becoming a more inclusive environment for everyone. It includes six initiatives that the entire company is working on (executive involvement and accountability, recruiting and retention, diverse segment marketing, diverse community giving, supplier diversity, and communications).

How often does the firm's management review the firm's diversity progress/results?

Twice a year.

How is the firm's diversity committee and/or firm management held accountable for achieving results?

Our Corporate Diversity Council reports directly to our Executive Management Committee twice a year. We discuss progress and action items within our Six Steps platform.

The Stats

	TOTAL WORLDWIDE	
	2005	2004
Number of employees	156,320	149,593
Revenue	$33 billion	N/A

DEMOGRAPHIC PROFILE				
U.S. MINORITIES:	MALE EMPLOYEES:	FEMALE EMPLOYEES:	MINORITIES ON EXECUTIVE TEAM:	WOMEN ON EXECUTIVE TEAM:
30.8%	38.2%	61.8%	8.1%	19.5%

Retention and Professional Development

How do 2005 minority and female attrition rates generally compare to those experienced in the prior year period?

About the same as in prior years.

Please identify the specific steps you are taking to reduce the attrition rate of minority and women employees.

• Develop and/or support internal employee affinity groups (e.g., minority or women networks within the firm)
• Increase/review compensation relative to competition
• Increase/improve current work/life programs
• Adopt dispute resolution process
• Succession plan includes emphasis on diversity
• Work with minority and women employees to develop career advancement plans
• Review work assignments and hours billed to key client matters to make sure minority and women employees are not being excluded
• Strengthen mentoring program for all employees, including minorities and women
• Professional skills development program, including minority and women employees

Diversity Mission Statement

Wells Fargo team members should expect to work in an environment where each person feels valued for individual traits, skills and talents, and has the opportunity to fulfill ambitions and contribute to the success of the company.

Additional Information

Diversity is central to Wells Fargo's success on several levels. We have more than 80 businesses, which diversifies our risk so we do not over-rely on the revenue stream of any one business. We have a diversity of products that help us satisfy all our customers' financial needs and achieve steady growth. We do business in diverse geographies which helps insulate us from local economic downturns. We also have millions of diverse customers. We have greater creativity and multiple perspectives when our teams have different experiences and backgrounds. We believe that all these levels of diversity make Wells Fargo a stronger company and a great place to work.

We're the No. 17 Best Company for Diversity according to *DiversityInc* magazine's "Top 50 Companies for Diversity" and among the "Top 50 Employers for Minorities and Women" according to *Fortune* magazine. We scored a perfect 100 on the Human Rights Campaign "Corporate Equality Index." and were recognized by the National Federation of the Blind for being the first financial institution to make online banking services on www.wellsfargo.com accessible to the visually impaired.

Wells Fargo has a company-wide diversity platform called "Six Steps to Got Diversity." The six steps help guide and measure our success at hiring and retaining team members, serving customers and partnering with communities that are more diverse. Every Wells Fargo business line can set objectives and measure success against these six things:

• Our CEO and executive management team take responsibility for diversity and hold themselves and others accountable. Diversity is a part of Wells Fargo's vision and values. The corporate diversity council reports to the executive management team. Upper management references our diversity in internal and external, written and verbal communications.

• People from diverse backgrounds are in all levels of management. Managers are accountable for attracting diverse candidates and for developing and retaining a diverse leadership pipeline. Wells Fargo has a plan for increasing diversity among its upper management.

• We establish long-term relationships with diverse communities. Wells Fargo tailors products and services to diverse communities and communicates those products and services through targeted marketing and advertising.

• We contribute to the communities we work, live and do business in. Wells Fargo continues to foster a supplier-diversity program and diverse philanthropic and educational efforts.

• Diversity is present in all of our company communications. Diversity information and examples can be seen throughout corporate-wide, regional and business line communications and marketing materials (even if the word "diversity" isn't used). Diversity links are easily found on both our Intranet and on wellsfargo.com.

• We are known as a diverse company. Job candidates, customers, vendors and shareholders seek Wells Fargo out because of its diverse reputation. Existing team members have avenues to voice their opinions on how inclusive Wells Fargo is. Wells Fargo earns credibility through national and community-based groups.

We can't grow without you. And you. And you. And you.

Your ideas, your talent, your unique perspective. We've got a place for you at Weyerhaeuser, a forest products company with business strengths from forestry to manufacturing. We recognize that the fastest way to grow as a company is to seek out diverse, creative people and provide opportunities to lead. From engineering to sales, from I.T. to operations, you can have a voice in our growth. To learn more, visit us at www.weyerhaeuser.com/careers.

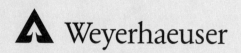

Weyerhaeuser

P.O. Box 9777
Federal Way, WA 98063-9777
Phone: (253) 924-2345
Fax: (253) 924-4151
www.weyerhaeuser.com/careers

Diversity Leadership
Effenus Henderson
Director, Workforce Representation &
Diversity

Darvi Mack
Diversity Manager

Employment Contact
Rhonda Stickley
Director Staffing

Recruiting

Please list the schools/types of schools at which you recruit.

• Ivy League schools
• Other private schools
• Public state schools
• Historically Black Colleges and Universities (HBCUs)
• Hispanic Serving Institutions (HSIs)
• Native American Tribal Universities
• Other predominantly minority and/or women's colleges

Do you have any special outreach efforts directed to encourage minority students to consider your firm?

• Hold a reception for minority students
• *Conferences:* National Black MBA, National Society Hispanic MBA, Society Women Engineers, INROADS, CATALYST, National Association Black Accountants, National Urban League Convention, Women in Construction
• Advertise in minority student association publication(s)
• Participate in/host minority student job fair(s)
• Sponsor minority student association events
• Firm's employees participate on career panels at schools
• Outreach to leadership of minority student organizations
• Scholarships or intern/fellowships for minority students

What activities does the firm undertake to attract minority and women employees?

• Partner programs with women and minority associations
• *Conferences:* National Black MBA, National Society Hispanic MBA, INROADS, Black Data Processing Association, Association Latino Professionals & Accountants; National Association Black Accountants, National Urban League Convention, Women in Construction, Society Women Engineers, CATALYST
• *Participate at minority job fairs all major national Diversity job fairs as indicated:* National Black MBA, National Society Hispanic MBA, Black Data Processing Association, Association Latino Professionals & Accountants; National Association Black Accountants, National Urban League Convention, Women in Construction, Society Women Engineers
• Seek referrals from other employees
• Utilize online job services

Do you use executive recruiting/search firms to seek to identify new diversity hires?

No.

Internships and Co-ops

Weyerhaeuser/UNCF Corporate Scholars Program

Deadline for application: End of February

Number of interns in the program in summer 2005 (internship) or 2005 (co-op): 18 interns (25 interns budgeted for 2006)

Pay: $15.00 per hour

Percentage of interns/co-ops in the program who receive offers of full-time employment: 95 percent

Web site for internship/co-op information: http://www.uncf.org/internships/internshipdetail.asp?Sch_ID=16607

Weyerhaeuser/UNCF Corporate Scholars Program was established to increase student interest in Weyerhaeuser and to expand the pool of prospective diverse employees. Sophomores and juniors enrolled in the areas of engineering (chemical, mechanical, electrical, industrial, pulp & paper technology, forest), industrial manufacturing/production technology, forestry, information technology or related are eligible to apply.

Scholarships

Weyerhaeuser/UNCF Corporate Scholars Program

Deadline for application for the scholarship program: February 12th

Scholarship award amount: Up to $10,000.00 for entire scholarship

Web site or other contact information for scholarship: www.uncf.org/internships/internshipdetail.asp?Sch_ID=16607

The Weyerhaeuser/UNCF Corporate Scholars Program was established to increase student interest in Weyerhaeuser and to expand the pool of prospective diverse employees. Sophomores and juniors enrolled in participating schools in the areas of forestry, forest product sales and marketing, industrial/manufacturing/electrical engineering and operation management and supervision are eligible to apply.

Affinity Groups

- Women in Action (WIA)
- Gay, Lesbian, Bisexual, Transgender Employees (GLBTE)
- Weyerhaeuser Black Employees Alliance (WEBA)
- Hispanics for Outstanding Leadership and Advancement (HOLA)

All business support groups serve as support for its membership and are committed to assisting the company in recruiting and retention of diverse employees, group professional development and fostering a respectful inclusive workplace.

Entry-Level Programs/Full-Time Opportunities/Training Programs

Managed Entry

Length of program : Varies by program; 18 months or longer

Geographic location(s) of program: National

Please describe the training/training component of this program: Accounting, engineering, sales, production, IT, HR

Please describe any other educational components of this program: All full-time employees are eligible for tuition reimbursement.

Strategic Plan and Diversity Leadership

How does the firm's leadership communicate the importance of diversity to everyone at the firm?

E-mails, company newsletters, business specific newsletters, web site, meetings, employee forums, training, brochures and via affinity groups/business networks.

Who has primary responsibility for leading diversity initiatives at your firm?

Steve R. Rogel, CEO and president, supported by Effenus Henderson, chief diversity officer.

Does your firm currently have a diversity committee?

Yes.

If yes, please describe how the committee is structured, how often it meets, etc.

The committee meets three times a year. Committee focuses on the firm's diversity high impact strategies areas which include leadership, governance, talent management, culture/climate and outreach.

If yes, does the committee's representation include one or more members of the firm's management/executive committee (or the equivalent)?

Yes.

If yes, how many executives are on the committee, and in 2005, what was the total number of hours collectively spent by the committee in furtherance of the firm's diversity initiatives?

Total Executives on Committee: Seven executives, one diversity director; meets quarterly; 50 hrs

Does the committee and/or diversity leader establish and set goals or objectives consistent with management's priorities?

Yes. The executive diversity team sets the diversity goals that align with business strategy.

Has the firm undertaken a formal or informal diversity program or set of initiatives aimed at increasing the diversity of the firm?

Yes, formal. The EDT has set five high impact action areas aimed to increase diversity and retention of talent.

How often does the firm's management review the firm's diversity progress/results?

Quarterly.

How is the firm's diversity committee and/or firm management held accountable for achieving results?

Accountability: 20 percent is linked to the Management Incentive Program Bonus Plan.

The Stats

Employees
2005: 41,217 (U.S.)
2004: 42,974 (U.S.)

Revenue
2005: 23.0 billion
2004: 19.7 billion

Retention and Professional Development

How do 2005 minority and female attrition rates generally compare to those experienced in the prior year period?

Lower than in prior years.

Please identify the specific steps you are taking to reduce the attrition rate of minority and women employees.

• Develop and/or support internal employee affinity groups (e.g., minority or women networks within the firm)
• Increase/review compensation relative to competition
• Increase/improve current work/life programs
• Adopt dispute resolution process
• Succession plan includes emphasis on diversity
• Work with minority and women employees to develop career advancement plans
• Strengthen mentoring program for all employees, including minorities and women
• Professional skills development program, including minority and women employees
• *Other:* Work with industry attrition group to monitor attrition and turnover trends

Diversity Mission Statement

We are an employer of choice with high-performing people who are treated with respect and work together in a safe and healthy workplace where diversity, development, teamwork and open communication are valued and recognized.

Additional Information

The Weyerhaeuser Way

The Weyerhaeuser Way consists of a set of statements and principles that represent our aspirations and desired culture. At the operational level, they are reflected in our Roadmap for Success. Our values statements are further amplified by Weyerhaeuser's business conduct guidelines outlined in our code of ethics, "Our Reputation: A Shared Responsibility."

Our Vision

The best forest products company in the world and a global leader among all industries.

Our Mission

Produce superior returns for shareholders by focusing on our customers and working safely to:

• Grow and harvest trees

- Manufacture and sell forest products
- Build and sell homes

Our Values

• *Customers and suppliers:* We listen to our customers and suppliers to improve our products and services to meet their present and future needs.

• *People:* We are an employer of choice with high-performing people who are treated with respect and work together in a safe and healthy workplace where diversity, development, teamwork and open communication are valued and recognized.

• *Accountability:* We expect superior performance and are accountable for our actions and results. Our leaders set clear goals and expectations, are supportive, and provide and seek frequent feedback.

• *Citizenship:* We support the communities where we do business, hold ourselves to the highest standards of ethical conduct and environmental responsibility and communicate openly with Weyerhaeuser people and the public.

• *Financial responsibility:* We are prudent and effective in the use of the resources entrusted to us to create shareholder value.

Whirlpool Corporation

2000 N. M-63
Benton Harbor, MI 49022
Phone: (269) 923-5000
Fax: (269) 923-2874
www.whirlpoolcorp.com

Locations

Corporate Headquarters: Benton Harbor, Michigan
European Operations Center: Comerio, Italy
Regional Headquarters: Shanghai, China and Sao Paulo, Brazil

Additionally, Whirlpool has 50 manufacturing and technology centers around the world.

Employment Contact

www.whirlpoolcareers.com
careers@whirlpool.com

Recruiting

Please list the schools/types of schools at which you recruit.

• *Private schools:* University of Notre Dame
• *Public state schools:* University of Michigan, Michigan State University, Purdue University, Indiana University, Ohio State University, University of Florida, University of North Carolina-Chapel Hill, University of Georgia, University of Tennessee, Northern Illinois University, Michigan Technology University, Arizona State University

Do you have any special outreach efforts directed to encourage minority students to consider your firm?

We partner with minority chapters in business and engineering at our core target programs, where we sponsor initiatives, hold learning sessions and training workshops to give minority individuals any assistance they need.

What activities does the firm undertake to attract minority and women employees?

• *Conferences:* National Society of Black Engineers, Society of Women Engineers, National Association of Black Accountants, Association of Latino Professionals in Finance & Accounting, National Hispanic Business Association, Society of Hispanic Professional Engineers
• *Other:* Referrals from campus diversity organizations and Leaders, online job boards, campus job boards

Do you use executive recruiting/search firms to seek to identify new diversity hires?

No, we feel that there is no better way to reach out to new talent than to utilize existing diverse talents to target those individuals.

Internships and Co-ops

Deadline for application: January 2, 2006
Length of the program: Nine to 12 weeks
Percentage of interns/co-ops in the program who receive offers of full-time employment : 75 percent
Web site for internship/co-op information: www.whirlpoolcareers.com/campus

Exciting internships are available in all of Whirlpool's functional departments. With an internship program of over 75 people you create your own little beach community at one of the top 10 beaches in the nation!

Whirlpool's internship program provides real, hands-on work experience to give each intern a better understanding of the type of work they may perform as full-time employees. Whirlpool's internship program educates participants about the different areas of the company, its strategic objectives and the plans in place to achieve those objectives. We take interns to our Greenville Manufacturing site, home of the KitchenAid stand mixer where interns tour the plant and are put on the line to test their capability and have a little fun!

The program also provides interns with an opportunity to experience the surrounding communities. Interns get involved in the two beach volleyball leagues, golf leagues, and softball leagues to develop lasting friendships with other interns, and get to know Whirlpool employees outside of the work environment. They also enjoy the wine tours at many of the surrounding 35 wineries within a 30 minute radius.

Finally, the program evaluates each intern's work performance, as well as allows him or her to evaluate whether Whirlpool Corp. would be a good fit for his or her full-time career aspirations.

Affinity Groups

Whirlpool African-American Network; Whirlpool Hispanic Network; Whirlpool Women's Network; Whirlpool Gay, Lesbian, Bisexual, and Transgender Network; Whirlpool Asian Network; and Whirlpool Native American Network, and The Young Professional Organization.

Entry-Level Programs/Full-Time Opportunities/Training Programs

Real Whirled

Length of program: Seven weeks of intensive training
Geographic location(s) of program: Training conducted in Benton Harbor, Mich. Training program graduates then relocate to various locations throughout the United States.

The Real Whirled program begins with a seven-week intensive training program, both classroom and experiential. Participants live together in a house outfitted with Whirlpool and KitchenAid appliances for the entire training program.

The purpose of the program is to provide the participants with all the necessary information and skill development required for their new positions as market brand representatives. The classroom component of the training is focused on learning about the products sold by Whirlpool Corporation throughout the United States, as well as developing leadership, communication and selling skills. The experiential component of the program is centered around activities like job shadowing, mystery shopping and using the products in the house on a daily basis. It is common for Whirlpool's senior executives to join the class discussion and to come by the Real Whirled house for dinner during the training program. Once the initial seven weeks are over, the training continues through monthly webcasts, teleconferences and occasionally regionally based face-to-face meetings.

Human Resource Leadership Development Program (HRLDP)

Length of program: Three years

Geographic location(s) of program: Primarily in Benton Harbor, Mich. Additional assignments could be in any of Whirlpool's manufacturing divisions throughout the United States or around the world.

The HRLDP is a three year, three rotation program that is designed to give the participants training and development through two avenues: on-the-job training and quarterly learning sessions.

First, the participants are assigned to a part of the company that has an open-staffing situation and they are given the responsibilities and objectives attached to that role. The rotational assignments are not project-based jobs. Working for and directly with a senior HR manager/director, participants take what they learned during college and transform that knowledge into practical application.

The second avenue for training is through quarterly learning sessions. Some of these sessions are focused specifically on HR topics, from such as developments in the compensation system to broader business skills such as how to manage change. In addition to these learning opportunities and the feedback each HRLDP receives about their performance, HRLDPs also are assigned a senior HR leader as a mentor.

Whirlpool Technical Excellence Program (WTEP)

Length of program: Three years. Participants are assigned two six-month project assignments during their first year. The second year is based at University of Michigan completing master's degree in engineering and the third year is another series of two six-month assignments.

Geographic location(s) of program: The first and third year of the program can be in any of our technology and manufacturing sites in the United States (and in some cases around the world). Many of the assignments will be at our corporate headquarters in Benton Harbor, MI. The second year of the program is spent at the University of Michigan in Ann Arbor.

Please describe any other educational components of this program (i.e., tuition reimbursement): Full-time enrollment in the University of Michigan's masters of engineering program.

Supply Management Rotational Track (SMART)

Length of program: 18 months

Geographic location(s) of program: Primarily in Benton Harbor, Mich. Additional assignments could be in any of Whirlpool's manufacturing divisions throughout the United States or around the world.

The SMART program is designed to develop Whirlpool's leadership capability in the procurement area. During the two-rotation program participants have the opportunity to learn about the procurement processes, procedures, and across the board activities on-the-job training and quarterly learning sessions.

Besides receiving on-the-job training program participants, also take part in learning programs designed to enhance their skills on a functional basis, as well as develop leadership skills. All program participants are assigned a mentor who is a senior leader in manufacturing, logistics or procurement.

Global Supply Chain Leadership Development Program (GSCLDP)

Length of program: Three years

Geographic location(s) of program: Primarily in Benton Harbor, Mich., but could be at any of Whirlpool's manufacturing divisions throughout the United States.

The GSCLPD is designed to develop Whirlpool's leadership capability in the areas of logistics, procurement and operations (manufacturing). During a series of one-year rotational assignments, program participants have the opportunity to learn about the three key areas of supply-based management at Whirlpool—logistics, manufacturing, and procurement. Besides receiving on-the-job training program participants, also take part in learning programs designed to enhance their skills on a functional basis, as well as develop leadership skills. All program participants are assigned a mentor who is a senior leader in manufacturing, logistics or procurement.

Finance Leadership Development Program (FLDP)

> ***Geographic location(s) of program:*** Primarily in Benton Harbor, Mich., but could be at any of Whirlpool's locations throughout the United States.

The purpose of the Finance Leadership Development Program is to develop future leaders by leveraging the finance and accounting skills learned in college and supplementing that knowledge with opportunities to develop, learn and grow as leaders. All program participants take part in functional and cross-functional training to develop required skills and enhance their current skills.

The program has two different focuses. The first is for accounting majors who will join the Whirlpool internal audit and internal controls team. The second is for finance, accounting and economics majors who will provide financial analysis skills to the company.

Strategic Plan and Diversity Leadership

How does the firm's leadership communicate the importance of diversity to everyone at the firm?

Diversity Organizations are challenged by Whirlpool leaders to take responsiblity for delivering business results to the Whirlpool Corporation through bottom line numbers. They believe this will help all individuals understand the value of diversity in an organization as our consumer base is diverse and who better to reach out to them. In addition, each of these organizations are responsible for providing employee and community benefits for the diversity network being a part of this community, which has been done through community festivals, celebrity speaking engagements, high school and migrant worker mentoring, and general awareness/diversity training sessions.

Leaders have also held an innovation session surrounding breaking down barriers to success. Out of that innovation session came an action plan that has over the course of the last year been executed upon to ensure everyone feels included in our corporate strategy.

We also develop an annual communication plan that is part of the diversity council objectives. Primarily, we communicate through our global employee Intranet portal, on our diversity web sites, through our diversity networks' newsletters, through the annual diversity and inclusion meeting for managers and employees and at our annual diversity and inclusion summit.

Whirlpool encourages diversity and inclusion throughout our global organization because diverse employees reflect our global customer base and help provide a keen understanding of our customers' needs. Simply put, diversity is about being different, while inclusion is about the respectful involvement of all people and making use of everyone's talents. We believe that differences create value. And we practice inclusion throughout our organization, not only because we believe it's the right thing to do, but also because it's a winning strategy that enables us to respond to the diverse needs of our customers.

We have a dedicated diversity web site posted internally that is easy to find by all employees that lists all diversity activities and events of the clubs as well as our overall strategy, accountability and network information. Some of the information included on the site is the following:

By acknowledging our diversity and practicing inclusiveness, we are able to utilize everyone's unique strengths to increase Whirlpool Corporation's productivity, profit and performance.

Our Diversity Strategy:

Build Accountability

- Align with our BFVC strategies and core competencies
- Align performance goals and behaviors
- Improve our Balanced Scorecard results

Connect Diversity and Inclusion to the Business

> • Build the business case around diverse consumers
> • Value ideas from everywhere and everyone

Recruit and Retain Diverse People

> • Recruit and retain great diverse talent at all levels

Drive Understanding, Education and Awareness

> • Communicate the business case, opportunities learning, and networking
> • Provide diversity training and awareness opportunities

Create the Environment

> • Create an environment that leverages and vales each person's unique strengths, allowing everyone to contribute to their fullest potential

Who has primary responsibility for leading diversity initiatives at your firm?

CEO Jeff Fettig, and his Executive Committee along with our Diversity Council made up of our Executive Committee as well as presidents of each of the Diversity Networks.

Does your firm currently have a diversity committee?

Yes.

If yes, please describe how the committee is structured, how often it meets, etc.

The committee is made up of the presidents of each Diversity Network, our three global diversity directors, and nine executive committee members. They meet once a month to discuss on the on-going status of Whirlpool's diversity initiatives to ensure we are mimicking/advancing our consumer base and behavior.

If yes, does the committee's representation include one or more members of the firm's management/executive committee (or the equivalent)?

Yes.

If yes, how many executives are on the committee?

> *Total Executives on Committee:* 12

Does the committee and/or diversity leader establish and set goals or objectives consistent with management's priorities?

Yes. Each year the council reviews and measures objectives against our plan. In addition, the January meeting focuses on setting objectives aligned with our strategic business issues.

Has the firm undertaken a formal or informal diversity program or set of initiatives aimed at increasing the diversity of the firm?

Yes, formal. Each region/function develops action plans and goals for increasing representation at all levels of the organization, but particularly in the feeder groups and leadership ranks. Goals are part of the overall "People Scorecard" that is directly tied to compensation of both the executives that lead the organization as well as its employees. This ensures that everyone within the organization maintains a top of mine approach to diversity.

How often does the firm's management review the firm's diversity progress/results?

Quarterly.

How is the firm's diversity committee and/or firm management held accountable for achieving results?

Each region/function develops actions plans and goals for increasing representation at all levels of the organization, but particularly in the feeder groups and leadership ranks. Goals are part of the overall "People Scorecard" that is directly tied to compensation and end of year rewards. This means that not only are the executives rewarded for increasing diversity within the organization, but that the employees have the focus as well.

Ideally, all employees will feel a personal responsibility for embracing and acting on the concepts described in this brochure. To ensure traction, the company has established clear roles and accountabilities:.

• Overall leadership for the effort resides in the Office of the Chairman.
• The Office of Diversity is responsible for developing the strategy and related initiatives.
• Our regions, business units and global functions are responsible for ensuring that our diversity strategy gets implemented.
• The Diversity Council is responsible for advising leadership on matters pertaining to diversity.
• Diversity networks exist for the purpose of assisting in delivering with diversity commitments.
• Each employee is responsible for understanding and executing our diversity strategy.

"It is no coincidence that corporations, groups, governments and citizens all across the country are focusing on diversity initiatives and methods to make people feel more included. Whirlpool Corporation has made workforce diversity and corporate citizenship top priorities as the company has set out to bring about lasting, systemic change inside and outside of our company.

"For the past 20 years, Whirlpool has worked to make our work culture one that recognizes the benefits of a diverse employee population, as well as one that values and respects those things that make each of us unique. Our company leadership knows that diversity and inclusion are vital to our continued success and competitiveness. We hope that the strategies and high expectations we set for ourselves will truly add value to each employee's experience here."

Corporate Director, Global Diversity

The Stats

Employees

2006: 80,000 (worldwide)
2006: 30,000 salaried roles (worldwide)

Revenue

2005: $19 billion (worldwide)
2004: $13.2 billion (worldwide)

US Employees Demographics

Minorities: 17 percent
Women: 40.19 percent

Retention and Professional Development

How do 2005 minority and female attrition rates generally compare to those experienced in the prior year period?

Attrition rates at Whirlpool are generally extremely low. On average we lose four percent of our general employee populations. Our diverse population attrition rate is still low however, it is around six percent.

Please identify the specific steps you are taking to reduce the attrition rate of minority and women employees.

• Develop and/or support internal employee affinity groups (e.g., minority or women networks within the firm)
• Increase/improve current work/life programs
• Strengthen mentoring program for all employees, including minorities and women
• Targeted diversity summits aimed at breaking down the barriers to inclusion and barriers to success
• Get involved with the many special events, training and activities offered to you at Whirlpool, and you'll find yourself with a new scope of knowledge, experience and networking opportunities. Events such as career workshops, leadership discussions, online learning and specialized training broaden individuals' understanding of the industry, our business and what's going on with the company right now. This page provides you with some basic tools to get involved at Whirlpool
• Partner with established minority clubs to ensure new hires are assigned to a minority buddy from that organization to assist in on-boarding and assimilation

Diversity Mission Statement

The Whirlpool Enterprise Leadership Transformation Agenda Vision: "Building a company of people passionately creating Loyal Customers for life."

Mission: Create and foster an environment that is inclusive and accepting, that allows and encourages diverse employees to be themselves and to participate with equality and dignity in the work environment.

Additional Information

Departments within Whirlpool:

• Communications
• Engineering
• Finance - Corporate (Internal Controls/Audit, Treasury, Tax)
• Finance - North American (Financial Analysis in Brand, Channel, and Product Delivery)
• Finance - Technology
• Human Resources
• Information Systems
• Legal
• Marketing
• Operations
• Sales
• Supply chain

Williams Companies, The

One Williams Center
Tulsa, OK 74102
Phone: (918) 573-2200
Fax: (918) 573-7700
www.williams.com/careers

Locations

Tulsa, OK (HQ)
Denver, CO (Regional)
Houston, TX (Regional)
Salt Lake City, UT (Regional)

Diversity Leadership

Alison Anthony
Manager of Staffing, Diversity, & College
Relations

Employment Contact

Steve Beatie

Recruiting

Please list the schools/types of schools at which you recruit.

• *Private schools:* University of Tulsa, University of Houston
• *Public state schools:* University of Oklahoma, Oklahoma State, Louisiana-Lafayette, Colorado School of Mines, University of Utah, Texas A&M, University of Texas, Penn State, Georgia Tech, University of Maryland
• *Historically Black Colleges and Universities (HBCUs):* Prairie View A&M, Florida A&M (potential)

Do you have any special outreach efforts directed to encourage minority students to consider your firm?

• Sponsor minority student association events
• Outreach to leadership of minority student organizations

Do you use executive recruiting/search firms to seek to identify new diversity hires?

No.

Entry-Level Programs/Full-Time Opportunities/Training Programs

Rotational Program

Length of program: Two to three years
Geographic location(s) of program: Houston; SLC
Please describe the training/training component of this program: Engineering OJT Rotations

Strategic Plan and Diversity Leadership

How does the firm's leadership communicate the importance of diversity to everyone at the firm?

Monthly highlights of diverse populations include e-mails, presentations, and a diversity Intranet site.

Who has primary responsibility for leading diversity initiatives at your firm?

Alison Anthony, manager of staffing, diversity, and college relations, although the primary responsibility rests with all of company leadership.

Does your firm currently have a diversity committee?

Yes.

If yes, please describe how the committee is structured, how often it meets, etc.:

Meets quarterly, made of representatives across the organization.

If yes, does the committee's representation include one or more members of the firm's management/executive committee (or the equivalent)?

Yes.

> *Total Executives on Committee:* CEO is member of committee

Does the committee and/or diversity leader establish and set goals or objectives consistent with management's priorities?

Yes.

Has the firm undertaken a formal or informal diversity program or set of initiatives aimed at increasing the diversity of the firm?

Yes, informal.

How often does the firm's management review the firm's diversity progress/results?

Quarterly and annually.

The Stats

Williams has a 14 percent minority rate and a 25 percent female rate in its workforce.

Retention and Professional Development

How do 2005 minority and female attrition rates generally compare to those experienced in the prior year period?

About the same as in prior years.

Please identify the specific steps you are taking to reduce the attrition rate of minority and women employees.

- Develop and/or support internal employee affinity groups (e.g., minority or women networks within the firm)
- Increase/improve current work/life programs
- Succession plan includes emphasis on diversity

Diversity Mission Statement

At Williams, we foster an environment that attracts a high-performing, diverse workforce. All individuals are respected and valued for their contributions and have the opportunity to achieve their maximum potential.

Wisconsin Public Service Corporation

700 N. Adams St.
Green Bay, WI 54301-9001
Phone: (920) 433-4901
Toll Free: (800) 450-7260
Fax: (920) 433-1526
www.wpsr.com

Diversity Leadership

Ka Youa Kong,
Corporate Recruiter
Phone: (920) 433-2571
E-mail: kykong@wpsr.com

Employment Contact

Laura Charette
Corporate Recruiter
WPS Resources
700 N. Adams St., P.O. Box 19002
Green Bay, WI 54307-9002
Phone: (920)433-4961
Fax: (920)430-6170
E-mail: lkcharette@wpsr.com
www.wpsr.com/career

Recruiting

Please list the schools/types of schools at which you recruit

We recruit at the following schools: St. Norbert College, UW Green Bay, UW Platteville, UW Madison, Michigan Tech, University of Michigan-Ann Arbor, Notre Dame, UW Oshkosh, UW Whitewater, UW Milwaukee, Iowa State, University of Minnesota

Do you have any special outreach efforts directed to encourage minority students to consider your firm?

• Advertise in minority student association publication(s)
• Participate in/host minority student job fair(s)
• Sponsor minority student association events
• Outreach to leadership of minority student organizations
• *Other:* Relationships with multicultural centers

What activities does the firm undertake to attract minority and women employees?

Participate at minority job fairs.

Do you use executive recruiting/search firms to seek to identify new diversity hires?

No.

Internships and Co-ops

Deadline for application: March 1st
Number of interns in the program in summer 2005 (internship) or 2005 (co-op): 38 (internship); two (co-op)
Pay: $9.06-$17.80 per hour

Length of the program: 10-14 weeks

Percentage of interns/co-ops in the program who receive offers of full-time employment: 20 percent

Web site for internship/co-op information: www.wpsr.com

We have an internship program which includes education and social events throughout the summer. We believe our program does a wonderful introduction to the utility industry and allows you to network within and outside of your department. We hire in the following areas for interns: engineering, accounting and finance, IT (computer science and MIS), business management and public affairs.

Scholarships

Business and Technology Scholarships

Deadline for application for the scholarship program: February 1st

Scholarship award amount: $1,500 renewable per year

Web site or other contact information for scholarship: www.wpsr.com

Open to current sophomore and junior college students, and minority or female students.

Strategic Plan and Diversity Leadership

How does the firm's leadership communicate the importance of diversity to everyone at the firm?

Diversity council recruiter that spends 50 percent of her time on diversity efforts.

Who has primary responsibility for leading diversity initiatives at your firm?

Ka Youa Kong, corporate recruiter.

Does your firm currently have a diversity committee?

Yes.

If yes, please describe how the committee is structured, how often it meets, etc.

The committee meets on a monthly basis and discusses and develops new ideas to bring in diverse talent and to recognize existing diverse employees.

If yes, does the committee's representation include one or more members of the firm's management/executive committee (or the equivalent)?

Yes.

Has the firm undertaken a formal or informal diversity program or set of initiatives aimed at increasing the diversity of the firm?

Yes, formal.

Hiring a recruiter to spend 50 percent of her time building these efforts.

How often does the firm's management review the firm's diversity progress/results?

Quarterly.

Retention and Professional Development

How do 2005 minority and female attrition rates generally compare to those experienced in the prior year period?

About the same as in prior years.

Please identify the specific steps you are taking to reduce the attrition rate of minority and women employees.

• Develop and/or support internal employee affinity groups (e.g., minority or women networks within the firm)
• Increase/improve current work/life programs
• Work with minority and women employees to develop career advancement plans
• Strengthen mentoring program for all employees, including minorities and women

Diversity Mission Statement

Diversity is valuing and respecting all the dimensions that make one person different from another. It includes differences in our ethnic heritage, race, gender, language, age and beliefs. It also includes family, financial and educational background as well as life experience, personality type and diversity of thoughts, etc.

Additional Information

Wisconsin Public Service Corporate offers the following programs to help promote diversity within the firm:

• Diversity learning curriculum for all leaders and employees. In addition, a diversity component is woven into all workshops. Diversity lunch sessions scheduled quarterly, with topics ranging from veterans benefits to intercultural communication to Native American organic foods
• Community involvement in all the communities we serve. Events include the Hispanic Fair, Hmong New Year Celebration, and more
• An increased focus on supplier diversity
• To expand the talent pool, ongoing diversity recruiting initiatives in all companies and business units
• Partnerships with local and national diversity organizations
• Utilize fair and consistent processes and practices

Wyeth Pharmaceuticals

500 Arcola Road
Collegeville, PA 19426
Phone: (610) 902-1200
www.wyeth.com

Locations

Over 140 locations in:
Africa • Asia Pacific • Australia • Europe • Middle East • New Zealand • North America • South America

Employment Contact

Marisa Kogan

Recruiting

Please list the schools/types of schools at which you recruit.

- *Ivy League schools:* University of Pennsylvania the Wharton School, Johnson School at Cornell (business school), Amos Tuck School of Business at Dartmouth
- *Other private schools:* Vanderbilt, Purdue, University of Chicago, Graduate School of Business, Northwestern University Kellogg Graduate School of Management, University of Virginia Darden School of Business, Drexel University
- *Public state schools:* University of Maryland, Baltimore County, Old Dominion University, Temple University
- *Historically Black Colleges and Universities (HBCUs):* Clark Atlanta University, Spelman College, Morehouse College, Tuskegee University, Fisk University, Cheyney, Lincoln, Howard, Hampton, Virginia State University, Virginia Polytechnic and State University, Xavier
- *Hispanic Serving Institutions (HSIs):* University of Miami, University of Puerto Rico

Do you have any special outreach efforts directed to encourage minority students to consider your firm?

- *Hold a reception for minority students:* National Black MBA Association Conference
- *Conferences:* SWE, NSBE, NOBCCHE, NSHMBA, NBMBAA, NMA, Urban League, SHPE, Consortium, INROADS, ISPE, United Negro College Fund
- Advertise in minority student association publication
- Participate in/host minority student job fair(s)
- Sponsor minority student association events
- Firm's employees participate on career panels at schools
- Outreach to leadership of minority student organizations
- Scholarships or intern/fellowships for minority students
- *Other.* Participate in INROADS and the Leadership Development Institute; facilitate resume and interview skills workshops in the community; recruit to improve minority access to research careers

What activities does the firm undertake to attract minority and women employees?

- Partner programs with women and minority associations
- *Conferences.* SWE, NSBE, NOBCCHE, NSHMBA, NBMBAA, NMA, Urban League, SHPE, Consortium, INROADS, ISPE, BEYA, UNCF, minorities in research science, HBA
- Participate at minority job fairs
- *Seek referrals from other employees*: Wyeth has a bonus program for internal referrals.
- Utilize online job services

Do you use executive recruiting/search firms to seek to identify new diversity hires?
Yes.

Internships and Co-ops

Wyeth Summer Internship Program and Co-Op Program

Deadline for application: March 15
Pay: Commensurate with year, experience
Length of the program: 12-week internships and six month co-ops
Web site for internship/co-op information: www.wyeth.com or www.INROADS.org

Wyeth's summer internship program provides valuable work experience within a pharmaceutical company to outstanding students ranging from the first year of college through the masters and PhD levels.

Program Objective:

The objective of the program is to provide positive work/training experience in a corporate environment, identify and track potential full-time employees, and establish "ambassadors" for Wyeth on campuses. Interns receive project-focused assignments and challenging objectives consistent with their career goals. Interns are also assigned a mentor in addition to their supervisor/coach.

Interns will receive a broad orientation to Wyeth, the specific business unit and the individual work group to which they will be contributing. Developmental opportunities may include educational workshops, meetings with corporate executives, business unit information exchanges, networking events and facility tours.

Timeline:

Submit your resume before March 15. All offers for our summer internship program will be extended by May 1.

General qualifications:

Overall GPA of 3.0/4.0 or above is required.

Full-time students will be considered from four or five year, accredited U.S. colleges or universities. Interns must be enrolled to return as full-time students following their time at Wyeth.

Wyeth MBA Summer Internship Program

Deadline for application: March 15
Pay: Commensurate with year, experience
Length of the program: 12 weeks
Web site for internship/co-op information: www.wyeth.com

Scholarships

Wyeth Internal Scholarship Program

Deadline for application for the scholarship program: January
Scholarship award amount: $3,000 one-time scholarship
Web site or other contact information for scholarship: Contact a local Wyeth HR representative

This scholarship program is open only to children of Wyeth employees. This program provides $3,000, one-time scholarships for up to 40 undergraduate students who are dependent children of current active full-time and part-time (who work 20 hours or more per week) employees and eligible retirees. The program is administered by the National Merit Scholarship Corporation, an independent nonprofit organization, which selects recipients based on high school academic record, activities and contributions to school and community, test scores, the school's recommendation and a student essay.

Wyeth Scholarship; United Negro College Fund

Deadline for application for the scholarship program: March
Scholarship award amount: $5,000 one-time scholarship
Web site or other contact information for scholarship: www.uncf.org/scholarships

Opportunities for students with scholarships up to $5,000 and a possible eight to 10 week summer internship, who are pursuing health-related careers or business. Applicants must attend an accredited four-year institution.

Affinity Groups

Wyeth supports and encourages its employee networks, voluntary, employee-established groups that meet to support and facilitate professional growth and personal development of participants. Wyeth's diversity department is chartered to support all Wyeth business units in cooperation with division leaders and HR business partners in their efforts to create a more inclusive workplace environment, to attract diverse candidates for employment and to enhance managerial skills for working with an increasingly diverse and global workforce. Wyeth's employee networks help advance the professional and personal growth of all employees through networking forums, career development workshops and community service.

Wyeth Pharmaceutical's employee networks are:

• ADVANCE: African-Americans Dedicated to Adding Value Added Networking & Corporate Excellence
• Wyeth Latin Network
• Rainbow Alliance: Supporting LGBT employees and allies
• Women's Professional Network
• Women in Leadership

To provide senior leadership and guidance to these groups, Wyeth leaders have been named executive sponsors to work closely with each group.

Xcel Energy

414 Nicollet Mall
Minneapolis, MN 55401
Phone: (612) 330-5724
Fax: 612-330-7935
E-mail: mark.w.sauerbrey@xcelenergy.com
www.xcelenergy.com

Locations

Colorado • Kansas • Michigan •
Minnesota • New Mexico • North Dakota
• Oklahoma • South Dakota • Texas •
Wisconsin

Employment Contact

Mark Sauerbrey
Recruitment Consultant

Recruiting

Please list the schools/types of schools at which you recruit.

• Private schools
• Public state schools
• Hispanic Serving Institutions (HSIs)
• Other predominantly minority and/or women's colleges

Do you have any special outreach efforts directed to encourage minority students to consider your firm?

• Hold a reception for minority students
• Conferences
• Advertise in minority student association publication(s)
• Participate in/host minority student job fair(s)
• Sponsor minority student association events
• Firm's employees participate on career panels at schools
• Outreach to leadership of minority student organizations

What activities does the firm undertake to attract minority and women employees?

• Partner programs with women and minority associations
• Conferences
• Participate at minority job fairs
• Utilize online job services

Do you use executive recruiting/search firms to seek to identify new diversity hires?

Yes.

List all women- and/or minority-owned executive search/recruiting firms to which the firm paid a fee for placement services in the past 12 months:

Chandler Group.

Internships and Co-ops

Engineering/business internships are posted per business unit upon approval from hiring managers. The business units run corporation-wide and are open to all students per our EEO policy.

> **Deadline for application:** Varies upon posting
> **Number of interns in the program in summer 2005 (internship) or 2005 (co-op):** 37-40 internship opportunities; summer internships can lead to co-op
> **Pay:** $13.00 to $21.00 per hour
> **Percentage of interns/co-ops in the program who receive offers of full-time employment:** Three to five percent are hired to full-time positions, but they must apply as external candidates
> **Web site for internship/co-op information:** www.xcelenergy.com

Strategic Plan and Diversity Leadership

How does the firm's leadership communicate the importance of diversity to everyone at the firm?

The firm's leadership communicates the importance of diversity through e-mails, the company web site, newsletters, and meetings.

Who has primary responsibility for leading diversity initiatives at your firm?

Paul Moore, director of diversity & staffing.

Does your firm currently have a diversity committee?

Yes.

Has the firm undertaken a formal or informal diversity program or set of initiatives aimed at increasing the diversity of the firm?

Yes, informal, aiming to increase the number of women and minority applicants for 2006.

How often does the firm's management review the firm's diversity progress/results?

Monthly.

The Stats

Employees
2005: 9,781

Revenue
2005: $9.6 billion

Retention and Professional Development

How do 2005 minority and female attrition rates generally compare to those experienced in the prior year period?

About the same as in prior years.

Please identify the specific steps you are taking to reduce the attrition rate of minority and women employees.

• Develop and/or support internal employee affinity groups (e.g., minority or women networks within the firm)
• Increase/improve current work/life programs
• Succession plan includes emphasis on diversity
• Strengthen mentoring program for all employees, including minorities and women
• Professional skills development program, including minority and women employees

Additional Information

One of Xcel Energy's core values is respecting all people. This ranks in importance with doing business in an ethical, honest manner, protecting our environment, working safely and serving our customers to the best of our ability.

When people believe that who they are and what they do is respected, morale and productivity go up. The end result is a workplace where people feel comfortable being who they are, regardless of their individual differences or personal characteristics.

A number of departments and sites will also go through a training program called "M.E.E.T. on Common Ground: Speaking Up for Respect in the Workplace."

Xerox Corporation

1700 Bayberry Court, Suite 200
Richmond, VA 23226
Phone: (804) 289-5493
www.xerox.com

Locations
Stamford, CT

Employment Contact
D. Garvin Byrd
Corporate HR, Manager of College Programs

Recruiting

Please list the schools/types of schools at which you recruit.

• Ivy League schools
• Other private schools
• Public state schools
• Historically Black Colleges and Universities (HBCUs)
• Hispanic Serving Institutions (HSIs)
• Native American Tribal Universities
• Other predominantly minority and/or women's colleges

Do you have any special outreach efforts directed to encourage minority students to consider your firm?

• Advertise in minority student association publication(s)
• Participate in/host minority student job fair(s)
• Sponsor minority student association events
• Firm's employees participate on career panels at schools
• Outreach to leadership of minority student organizations
• Scholarships or intern/fellowships for minority students
• Brand ads in diversity publications

What activities does the firm undertake to attract minority and women employees?

• Partner programs with women and minority associations
• Participate at minority job fairs
• Seek referrals from other employees
• Utilize online job services

Do you use executive recruiting/search firms to seek to identify new diversity hires?

No.

Internships and Co-op

Xerox College Experiential Learning Program

Deadline for application: March
Pay: By week; Varies based on academic classification
Length of the program: Minimum 10 weeks
Percentage of interns/co-ops in the program who receive offers of full-time employment: 63 percent conversion rate
Web site for internship/co-op information: www.xerox.com/employment

The internship/co-op program guidelines require the individual to be a full-time student enrolled in a college program leading to achievement of bachelor's or higher level degree. Must be able to work a minimum of 10 weeks and carry a 3.0 or higher GPA.

Scholarships

Xerox Technical Minority Scholarship Program

Deadline for application for the scholarship program: September 15 of each year
Scholarship award amount: $1,000 to $10,000 once per each year award
Web site or other contact information for scholarship: www.Xerox.com/employment

Guidelines include: Applicant must be Asian, black, Hispanic, or Native American; must be enrolled in a four year technical degree program which, when completed, will result in applicant's obtaining a bachelor's, master's or PhD degree. Applicant must have a 3.0 GPA or higher.

Affinity Groups

ACT — Asians Coming Together

http://www.asianscomingtogether.com/

Provides a voice and forum for education, professional development and interaction, to improve awareness and advocate equitable recognition and advancement opportunities for Asian employees within Xerox.

BWLC — Black Women's Leadership Council

http://www.bwlc.com/

The Black Women's Leadership Council serves as a catalyst to advance professional development and address issues unique to black women in the Xerox work place. The Black Women's Leadership Council forges partnerships with senior management that facilitate the hiring, retention and development of black women and satisfy business needs.

HAPA — The Association for Professional Advancement

http://www.hapa.org/

The HAPA National Leadership Council is the voice to Xerox management representing Xerox Hispanics and HAPA Chapters, promoting Hispanic objectives that enable increased Xerox business results.

GALAXE Pride At Work

http://www.galaxe.org/

Galaxe Pride At Work is a formal organization for Xerox employees who are or who support gay, lesbian, bisexual, or transgendered (GLBT) persons. Galaxe Pride At Work's mission is to offer support and visibility within Xerox and beyond to its members, and to provide an official point of contact between its membership and Xerox Corporation, as well as with other gay, lesbian, bisexual, and transgender organizations external to Xerox.

National Black Employee Association (NBEA)

http://www.nbea.net/

The National Black Employees Association (NBEA) is a national caucus group of African-American Xerox employees. 10 local caucus groups covering the continental United States make-up the NBEA. The NBEA is devoted to the principle that professional abilities and talents are possessed by individuals and that these traits are not the exclusive traits of any one ethnic or racial group. NBEA supports all efforts to eliminate employment and promotion practices that tend to deny this fundamental principle.

TWA — The Women's Alliance

http://www.thewomensalliance.net/

The Women's Alliance (TWA) is a catalyst to increase communications and awareness of women at Xerox, enabling women to attain their personal goals. The vision of TWA is to see that the women of Xerox are recognized and valued by the company for their significant contributions and leadership.

Entry-Level Programs/Full-Time Opportunities/Training Programs

VP Development Program

The VP Development Program provides leadership development for "ready-now" and newly appointed VPs. The content of the program is based on nine priority development objectives for VP candidates:

• Deliver more customer value
• Develop a powerful organizational vision and motivate their team to achieve it
• Explore a wide range of innovative options in the decision-making process
• Hire and retain the right people
• Make personal and organizational growth a priority
• Stay the course, walk the talk and maintain an optimistic outlook even in trying times
• Make the leap from a tactical to a strategic role
• Learn to prioritize more effectively
• Work for the benefit of the entire company

The Emerging Leader Program

This program provides leadership development opportunity for selected employees who have demonstrated the potential to move forward in the company. The program spans two years and involves four five-day face to face participant meetings and independent learning opportunities between meetings.

Tuition Assistance: Another important aspect of some employees' development and work/life balance is educational pursuits. If a Xerox employee or his/her dependent is planning to attend college, Xerox offers three programs to help finance this. The tuition aid program supports an employee's professional development by reimbursing her/him for tuition and fees based upon successful completion of each course (up to $10,000 per year). The ConSern program offers employees the opportunity to apply for low-cost loans ranging from $2,000 to $20,000. The funds can be used for an accredited college or university, private secondary school or pre-approved proprietary or trade school. In addition, Xerox employees have access to an online university on our Intranet of more than 1,000 training courses, which they may pursue on their own or under the guidance of their manager at no cost.

Strategic Plan and Diversity Leadership

How does the firm's leadership communicate the importance of diversity to everyone at the firm?

• Town hall meetings with senior managers
• Quarterly reviews with employee caucus group leadership
• Internal and external diversity web site
• Electronic communication/announcements to all employees
• Electronic communication web board for employee stories

Who has primary responsibility for leading diversity initiatives at your firm?

Chief diversity and employee advocacy officer.

Does your firm currently have a diversity committee?

Yes.

If yes, please describe how the committee is structured, how often it meets, etc.

Xerox Executive Diversity Council.

Purpose: Serve as an executive leadership body and focus group for diversity and work environment initiatives and concerns. Represent the balanced needs and requirements of all employees.

Objectives: Focus efforts on the vital few, for example:

• Workforce representation
• Work environment
• Diverse customer markets
• Review, recommend and advise on Xerox diversity practices
• Support organizational efforts to address the needs of a multicultural workforce

Council composition & operation:

• Members selected by the office of corporate diversity and corporate VP of HR, and supported by the CEO
• Consists of 12 members
• Council meets two to three times per year

If yes, does the committee's representation include one or more members of the firm's management/executive committee (or the equivalent)?

Yes.

Total executives on committee: Six corporate officers.

Does the committee and/or diversity leader establish and set goals or objectives consistent with management's priorities?

Yes.

Has the firm undertaken a formal or informal diversity program or set of initiatives aimed at increasing the diversity of the firm?

Yes, formal. In 1985, Xerox initiated its Balanced Work Force Strategy. The BWF program is intended to be a program of inclusion for all people. It is designed to achieve equitable representation with respect to race and gender at all levels, in all functions, in all disciplines, in all business divisions. All managers need to demonstrate appropriate diverse behaviors, and ensure that their human resource practices are fair and equitable. This strategy has been carefully designed to improve balances in representation in the Xerox workforce and to ensure a balanced workforce is maintained in the event of restructuring initiatives.

Employee Caucus Groups

Primary mission:

• Employee advocacy

• Self-development

• Promoters of change

• Management interface on work environment

Corporate Champions Program

• Voice at corporate level for employee concerns

• Council's and advises caucus leadership

• Serve as a communication linkage in regards to continuous improvement

Succession Planning

• Focuses on all employees

• Ensures diverse supply of talent for key management positions

• Help develops employees to meet their career objectives

• Assist in meeting the long-term business needs of the company

Minority/Female Vendor Program

Demonstrates Xerox's commitment to purchasing products and supplies and services from qualified minority and women owned businesses.

Diversity Training

Two Levels:

• Awareness—introduces concepts, values and policies

• Skill building—leveraging diversity to enhance performance and productivity, E-learning main delivery, limited trainer led sessions

Work Life Programs

• Dependent care fund

• Alternative work schedules

• Life cycle assistance (adoption assistance, mortgage assistance & partial pay replacement for FMLA leaves)

• Child care subsidy, child care resource & referral

• Employee assistance program

• Education assistance

• A matter of choice (benefits programs)

• Domestic partner benefits

How often does the firm's management review the firm's diversity progress/results?

Monthly

Quarterly

Retention and Professional Development

Please identify the specific steps you are taking to reduce the attrition rate of minority and women employees.

• Develop and/or support internal employee affinity groups (e.g., minority or women networks within the firm)
• Increase/review compensation relative to competition
• Increase/improve current work/life programs
• Succession plan includes emphasis on diversity
• Work with minority and women employees to develop career advancement plans
• Professional skills development program, including minority and women employees

Additional Information

Vision

Our vision is for everyone to treat each other with equality, dignity, and respect. As individuals on a team, each member can rely on others' strengths to build on team potential and company productivity.

Goal

Our goal is to promote understanding and inclusion, and to raise awareness of behaviors surrounding all types of "isms", e.g. sexism, racism.

In support of this the company will

• Leverage differences as a competitive advantage
• Develop leadership that values unique perspectives
• Embrace a framework which diverse work groups can consistently perform and improve their work

YMCA of the USA

101 N. Wacker Drive
Chicago, IL 60606
www.ymca.net

Diversity Leadership
Nicole Steels
Senior Human Resources Generalist

Employment Contact
Jim Campbell
Human Resources Assistant
101 N. Wacker Dr., Suite 1400
Chicago, IL 60606
Phone: (312) 977-0031
Fax: (312) 977-3542

Recruiting

What activities does the firm undertake to attract minority and women employees?

• Seek referrals from other employees
• Utilize online job services
• *Other:* Utilize minority job boards

Do you use executive recruiting/search firms to seek to identify new diversity hires?

Yes.

If yes, list all women- and/or minority-owned executive search/recruiting firms to which the firm paid a fee for placement services in the past 12 months.

We make formal written requests to the each of recruiting and search firms whose services we use to seek out diverse candidates for our open positions.

Scholarships

Scholarship Types/Categories:

• Funding limited to participation in YMCA University training
• Funding limited to undergraduate studies (bachelors programs)
• Funding limited to postgraduate studies (masters & PhD programs)
• Other YMCA affiliated scholarships

Primary Eligibility Requirements for all YMCA of the USA Scholarship Funds:

• Applicant's YMCA must be in compliance with Article II, Section 2 of the National Council of YMCAs Constitution (Qualifications for Membership), which may be viewed at www.ymcaexchange.org.
• Applicant must be a full-time or part-time employee of a YMCA within the United States.

Application Process:

• Apply online at www.ymcaexchange.org during the open application period noted for each individual scholarship.

• If further materials are required to be submitted please forward them to the following address:

> Jennifer Flannery
> Scholarship Coordinator—YMCA University
> YMCA of the USA
> 101 North Wacker Drive
> Chicago, IL 60606
> Toll Free: (800) 872-9622 x 8409
> Direct: (312) 419-8409
> E-mail: jennifer.flannery@ymca.net

Award Facts:

All applying applicants will be notified by letter, directed to the applicant's name and address on their application, by June 30th of each year. Please allow 10 days for delivery.

Reimbursement Process:

For scholarships monies that are awarded after completion of training or college courses, student must retain all proof of the completion of said course work. Submission of proof must reach the YMCA of the USA by one year after a scholarship has been awarded. Please submit paperwork to Jennifer Flannery at the above address.

YMCA STAFF SCHOLARSHIP PROGRAMS

Hispanic Staff Scholarship Program

The purpose of the YMCA Hispanic Staff Scholarship Program is to aid Hispanic staff members in obtaining additional training experiences which will impact in a significant and positive way their growth as YMCA professional directors and assist in their potential for upward mobility.

The minimum grant is $200 and the maximum $1,000. Applications must be completed online no later than May 31 and all applicants will be notified in writing by the Scholarship Committee no later than June 30.

Eligibility Criteria

Any currently employed Hispanic full-time exempt YMCA staff member.

Eligible Training Events

Training events for which grants are made must be job/career related and may be offered within or outside the YMCA University training system.

Selection Process

The YMCA University Scholarship Committee will review all applications received and will notify all applicants as to their decisions. Scholarship checks will be made payable to the recipient's local association, after a verification of attendance at approved training.

YMCA Minority Staff Scholarship Program

This program is sponsored by the YMCA of the USA. The purpose is twofold: to assist minority staff members to advance in the YMCA through training experiences that help them grow as YMCA professionals, and to assist them in completing their college education so they can embark on a professional YMCA career.

The scholarships operate from July 1 to June 30. Award monies expire on July 1 the following year. Scholarships are awarded based on need and availability, and are usually, but not necessarily, limited to $1,000 per person per calendar year. Scholarship awards are disbursed on a reimbursement basis only.

Eligibility Criteria

• Applicants must be active staff members of the YMCA: exempt or nonexempt, full-time or part-time.
• Applicants must be Hispanic/Latino, African-American, Asian/Pacific Islander or Native American/Alaskan Native.
• Education and training events must be career-related. They may be offered within or outside the YMCA.
• For education, scholarships are awarded only to those YMCA staff members who have taken some YMCA training towards achieving their YMCA senior director certification.
• Applicants must exhibit determination to continue work with the YMCA.

Application Deadline:

Online application must be completed online at www.ymcaexchange.org by May 31.

William A. Hunton Fellowship Fund

The purpose of the scholarship is to help African-American staff members complete the staff development program of the YMCA of the USA. The scholarship can be awarded for training towards director, professional director or senior director certification or for use towards the completion of college credit if the applicant has the director or professional director certification.

William A. Hunton became the first full-time African-American director of a YMCA in 1888, when he joined the Colored Y of Norfolk, VA., as general secretary. He later joined the national YMCA staff as head of the Colored Works Department.

The scholarship period is from July 1 to June 30. Award monies will expire on July 1 on the following year. Scholarships are awarded based on need and availability, usually, but not necessarily, limited to $1,000 per person per calendar year. Awards are disbursed on a reimbursement basis only.

Eligibility Criteria:

• Applicants must be African-American exempt staff members currently employed at a chartered YMCA.
• Awards will be made on the basis of need, with consideration given to the applicant's tenure, position and previous staff development training.
• Applicants must exhibit determination to continue their work with the YMCA.
• For college credit, the scholarship can be awarded only to those applicants who have completed YMCA training for director certification: group work, volunteerism and principles and practices.

UNDERGRADUATE EDUCATION SCHOLARSHIPS

Armstrong Scholarship

Earl P. Armstrong, retired in June, 1982, following 42 years of professional service to the YMCA. In recognition of Earl's outstanding service, a host of friends elected to pay tribute to him by establishing the Armstrong Scholarship Fund, and made the initial contributions to the former South Field Office of the YMCA of the USA for that purpose.

It was his decision to use these funds for scholarship awards to deserving YMCA professionals. This was especially appropriate, as Earl was the first recipient in the YMCA of a John R. Mott Scholarship. In establishing the Earl P. Armstrong Scholarship Fund, others would benefit, as he did, in furthering their education and enhancing their contributions to the Young Men's Christian Association. The scholarship is available for qualified YMCA Directors throughout the country.

Earl continues to serve YMCAs throughout the country as a professional volunteer, especially in the field of personnel and salary administration. He is the single greatest influence in the YMCA in this field, and in 1983, served as editor of the YMCA's personnel and salary administration manual.

Gratitude is hereby expressed to those many friends whose generosity made possible the Armstrong Scholarship fund. Contributions will be gratefully accepted and will help provide more scholarships for YMCA professionals. Checks should be made to the YMCA of the USA and mailed to the YMCA University, YMCA of the USA, to the attention of Jennifer Flannery. Contributions are tax-exempt.

Eligibility Criteria for the Armstrong Scholarship:

• Must be a current, professional employee of a chartered YMCA, in good standing.
• Must have at least three years of professional YMCA experience.
• Must have completed all requirements for YMCA senior director status.
• Should have positive YMCA career goals which indicate a plan for future YMCA involvement.
• Other factors that will be given consideration include personal commitment to the YMCA's basic Christian purpose, demonstrated leadership ability and scholastic aptitude. All qualified applicants are welcome regardless of age, race or sex.

Yearly award schedule:

• March 15: Online applications available at YMCA of the USA web site, www.ymcaexchange.org .
• May 31: Deadline for applications to be received (via online application process only).
• June 30: Awards announced. Notification occurs by letter, mailed directly to applicant. Please allow 10 days for delivery. Study may begin in the summer, fall or winter semesters (must begin no later than January semester). Award must be used within 12 months of notification.

Other considerations:

• Awards will be given only for study in a recognized formal accredited academic institution.
• Grants will be made to cover tuition, fees and books, not to exceed $1,500, and will normally be paid directly to the educational institution.
• Funding will be granted for one year at a time.
• Being a recipient of any other scholarship or financial aid will not disqualify an applicant for this scholarship.

F.M.M. Richardson Fund

This scholarship was established in 1971 through a bequest by F.M.M. Richardson, general secretary from 1929 to 1939 of the YMCA in Birmingham, AL. In accordance with his wishes, it assists Africa-American senior directors in obtaining training and education toward professional growth and greater upward mobility in the national movement. It also supports development projects at YMCAs serving black communities in the South Field YMCA and throughout the Y system.

> *Amount available:* $600 per person per academic year.
> *Criteria:* Applicants must be African-American certified senior directors of the YMCA.
> *Deadline:* Online applications are accepted year-round.

GRADUATE EDUCATION SCHOLARSHIPS

John R. Mott Scholarship

This scholarship is designed to assist YMCA senior directors in continuing their education through graduate study. It was established in honor of John R. Mott, a major YMCA leader for more than 60 years and winner of the Nobel Peace Prize in 1946. The scholarship period is from July 1 to June 30. The award monies expire on July 1 the following year. The scholarship award is disbursed on a reimbursement basis only. A maximum of $15,000 per person per year is available.

Eligibility Criteria:

• Applicants must have YMCA senior director certification.
•Applicants must exhibit determination to continue work with the YMCA.
•Applicants must be enrolled in an accredited university or college.
• Course of study should be in keeping with current and future YMCA duties.

Application Deadline

• Online application must be completed online at www.ymcaexchange.org by May 31.

OTHER YMCA AFFILIATED SCHOLARSHIPS

Solon B. Cousins YMCA Scholarship

For Springfield College and George Williams College of Aurora University students planning a YMCA career.

Springfield College has, throughout its history, provided education and training for YMCA professionals. George Williams College of Aurora University also has a long history of educating YMCA career professionals. Today, Springfield and George Williams maintain a formal affiliation with the YMCA of the USA as the only Independent Association Colleges.

Capping a rich and varied career in the YMCA and United Way, Solon Cousins retired in 1990 after serving ten years as national executive director of the YMCA of the USA. The scholarship fund was created in his honor by the national board of the YMCA of the USA upon his retirement.

General information:

• Scholarships are available to Springfield College & George Williams College of Aurora University students planning a career in the YMCA.
• Applicants should have a background in YMCA or other human service endeavors.
• Applicants should exemplify the YMCA character values of caring, honesty, respect and responsibility.
• Applications are accepted until May 31 online at www.ymcaexchange.org.
• Scholarship awards announced June 30.

For more information contact:

Paul Katz
Director, YMCA Relations
Springfield College
263 Alden Street
Springfield, MA 01109
E-mail: pkatz@spfldcol.edu
Phone: (413) 748-3914

Dovetta McKee
Associate Professor & Director of YMCA Programs
Aurora University, George Williams College
347 South Gladstone Avenue
Aurora, IL 60506
E-mail: dmckee@aurora.edu
Phone: (630) 844-5229

The Harmon O. DeGraff Memorial Scholarship

The Harmon O. DeGraff Memorial Scholarship Fund was created to assist young men with a strong human relations orientation to pursue graduate study. The selection is made by the three-person Memorial Scholarship Committee. The selection is based upon ability, motivation, objectives and human interests, similar qualifications without regard to race, creed or religion. According to the terms of Dr. DeGraff's will, the scholarship is restricted to males.

Details of Scholarship:

• Deadline is March 31. If scholarship monies are still available, applications may be submitted until May 1.
• Fund is restricted to those pursuing a graduate degrees in sociology, social work, theology, industrial relations or any field in which human relationships is an integral part of the applicant's program.
• Amount varies from $1,000 to $4,000 per year and is renewable for additional periods of time as required by the degree program.
•Full-time course of study is expected.

For more information please see the following link: http://www.akronymca.org/forms/general/degraffscholarship.pdf

Affinity Groups

African-American Alliance diversity group

The purpose of the group is to establish an alliance among African-American staff at YMCA of the USA.

The goal is to develop an agenda that will identify strategies and solutions to create, enhance and promote opportunities for African-American staff, both professionally and personally. The group also aims to work in establishing a more positive environment and working relationship within Y-USA.

SPEAK diversity group

Background and Justification

The YMCA of the USA SPEAK (Serving People with Equality, Acceptance and Kindness) Diversity Group was originally formed in 2002 to address Gay, Lesbian, Bisexual, Transgender and Questioning (GLBTQ) sexuality issues of Y-USA employees and to promote a work environment where all employees—regardless of sexual orientation—are treated equally.

Mission

Our mission is to connect, serve and lead YMCAs in building a diverse culture of inclusion and respect—without discrimination, intimidation or disparate treatment—especially for GLBTQ individuals within Y-USA and throughout the movement.

Purpose

Our purpose is to educate national and local YMCA staff around GLBTQ issues, provide support, foster open discussion and create a welcoming environment for all employees.

Vision

We envision a workplace where sexual orientation plays no role in how an employee is treated, and where each employee feels welcome, important and respected based on his/her own merit, efforts and actions and not on perceptions, beliefs or stereotypes.

Strategic Plan and Diversity Leadership

How does the firm's leadership communicate the importance of diversity to everyone at the firm?

Our CEO takes the time to reinforce his support of our diversity initiatives at key speaking events and in written communication to staff as part of our strategic plan. Additionally, our diversity group has conducted staff focus groups and surveys specifically relating to diversity at YMCA of the USA, then released the results of the survey at a staff lunch presentation. Recently, the diversity group's strategic plan was distributed via our staff Intranet along with an invitation for staff to participate in the group. The strategic plan was also discussed at the all-staff meeting.

Who has primary responsibility for leading diversity initiatives at your firm?

Sam Evans, interim director, YMCA of the USA.

Does your firm currently have a diversity committee?

Yes.

If yes, please describe how the committee is structured, how often it meets, etc.

the group is set to meet at least once per month, but during the development of the strategic plan they have met approximately three to four times per month. The group is structured with a lead change agent for the group, one diversity consultant and the remaining staff members, who represent a cross-section of the organization in terms of position in the company, work location and different characteristics of diversity.

If yes, does the committee's representation include one or more members of the firm's management/executive committee (or the equivalent)?

Yes.

If yes, how many executives are on the committee, and in 2005, what was the total number of hours collectively spent by the committee in furtherance of the firm's diversity initiatives? How many employees are on the committee, and how often does the committee convene in furtherance of the firm's diversity initiatives?

The committee has three executives who are involved with the group's goals and operations. The overall committee is made up of 13 individuals, with Sam Evans serving as the primary change agent. In 2005, it is estimated that the group collectively spent approximately 150 hours to further the diversity initiative at YMCA of the USA.

> *Total Executives on Committee:* Three.

Does the committee and/or diversity leader establish and set goals or objectives consistent with management's priorities?

Yes.

The diversity initiative is one of three primary initiatives for YMCA of the USA. Although the stated priority of the diversity initiative is directed towards making local YMCAs more diverse, we feel as though we need to serve as a model for local YMCA associations, and have given great attention to the issue of diversity at YMCA of the USA.

Has the firm undertaken a formal or informal diversity program or set of initiatives aimed at increasing the diversity of the firm?

Yes, formal. The YMCA of the USA is actively participating in the YMCA diversity initiative. The diversity initiative uses a six-step process for creating systemic change. Y-USA's vision for the diversity initiative is that the YMCA movement will be known for practicing inclusion by valuing the diversity of all people within its associations and the communities it serves. Through training and counsel, Y-USA helps YMCAs increase and support the cultural competence of their staff professionals, volunteers and members.

Diversity is the mosaic of people who bring a variety of backgrounds, styles, perspectives, beliefs and competencies as assets to the YMCA. By practicing inclusion, Ys not only address societal trends and remain relevant to their communities but also remain true to the YMCA mission, goals and values.

How often does the firm's management review the firm's diversity progress/results?

Annually. There will be a diversity team progress evaluation/review component built into the completed strategic plan.

How is the firm's diversity committee and/or firm management held accountable for achieving results?

YMCA of the USA sponsors the national diversity initiative, helping local YMCAs throughout the U.S.A and Canada to initiate their diversity initiatives. In this sense, we are held accountable by local YMCAs who expect us to lead them in diversity efforts.

Furthermore, the national executive director of YMCA of the USA has set out specific directives for his leadership team in regards to actions for their specific departments, and leadership team members are held accountable for achieving these goals as a part of the performance management process.

Additionally, YMCA of the USA has set an organizational performance goal stating that all staff must attend training in one of our three national initiatives, one of which is our diversity initiative. Thus far, over half of our staff have participated in this diversity training.

Finally, the diversity committee is presently finalizing the overall diversity strategic plan, and the plan will explicitly contain an accountability portion within it.

The Stats

	TOTAL (U.S. AND WORLDWIDE).		TOTAL WORLDWIDE	
	2005	2004	2005	2004
Number of employees	332	330	332	330
Revenue	$77.15 million	$79.68 million	$77,151,000	79,684,000

DEMOGRAPHIC PROFILE				
ASIAN	BLACK	HISPANIC	WHITE	FEMALE
4%	17%	4%	75%	59%

Retention and Professional Development

How do 2005 minority and female attrition rates generally compare to those experienced in the prior year period?

About the same as in prior years.

Please identify the specific steps you are taking to reduce the attrition rate of minority and women employees.

• Develop and/or support internal employee affinity groups (e.g., minority or women networks within the firm)
• Increase/improve current work/life programs
• Adopt dispute resolution process
• Professional skills development program, including minority and women employees

Diversity Mission Statement

Vision statements depict the ideal state of an organization 10 or more years in the future. Stated below is the vision for diversity and inclusion at YMCA of the USA. Imagine if we could truthfully and undeniably say this about ourselves here at Y-USA:

YMCA of the USA staff and leadership take pride in living our values of caring, honesty, respect and responsibility. We live out these values by fostering a culture in which we hold each other accountable for making diversity and inclusion integral to our plans, processes, decisions and actions. Together we create a trusting, exciting atmosphere that values the diversity, contribution, and talents of every individual, enabling all to reach their fullest potential. We do this to achieve our highest level of performance, resulting in exceptional leadership and service to YMCAs and the movement.

Goals are the broad targets toward which an organization directs its efforts.

• The YMCA's mission is to build spirit, mind and body for all. Therefore we will value every staff member's diverse talents and help each other develop to our fullest potential.

• Because YMCA of the USA has a role in leading the movement, we will show our commitment to diversity and inclusion by moving forward with our own diversity plan and demonstrating daily policies and practices which fulfill that plan.

- In keeping with YMCA traditions—fun, fellowship, community and values—we will create a vibrant and trusting environment in which all staff feel that they are respected and that they belong.

- Diversity is an essential component of high-performing organizations, so we will build and maintain a diverse staff that reflects the YMCAs and communities we serve.

- Strategies identify the course or path an organization will take—what it needs to do, to be, or to become—in order to attain its goals.

Strategies to achieve our vision and goals include:

- Culture: Create and nurture an environment of respect, trust and inclusion.

- Access and development: Ensure equal access to opportunities and proactive development for all staff, so that we can utilize all staff to their full potential, increasing our capacity to serve YMCAs and the movement.

- Dialogue practices: Actively engage principal stakeholders in meaningful dialogue before making decisions.

- Leadership: Cultivate and reward leaders whose mind-set, vision and behavior foster diversity and inclusion.

- Accountability, evaluation and celebration: Engender ownership (responsibility, accountability and pride) in Y-USA's culture of inclusion.

Additional Information

History of the National Diversity Initiative—Continuing its Priority at the YMCA

Throughout its 154-year history, the YMCA has responded to the demands and shifts of a society being transformed with ever-growing communities. Its quest has been to build strong kids, strong families and strong communities. A new era in fulfilling that mission arose in response to changing demographics and needs in communities served by YMCAs: a comprehensive diversity initiative for the YMCA of the USA was an idea whose time had come. At the heart of this initiative is the voice of communities across the nation that expressed the need for the YMCA to remain a significant, relevant and viable servant leader to our communities and the families in them.

In the late 1990s, the urban group began exploring ways that local associations could become more culturally competent and inclusive in their service areas. They formed a task force that assessed the cultures within YMCAs and brought back recommendations. Begun in 1999, the task force convened a team of 12 people that worked with Dr. Tina Rasmussen, the Y-USA's external diversity consultant, to create a diversity plan and process that could be implemented. Their goal was: To support the YMCA mission by encouraging, facilitating and supporting increased cultural competence in YMCA individuals and organizations and achieving measurable progress on locally defined diversity goals.

The Y-USA's vision for diversity is:

The YMCA will be known for practicing inclusion by valuing the diversity of all people within our associations and the communities we serve.

The Task Force transitioned to a National Diversity Steering Committee comprised of CEOs, heads of leadership development networks (formerly termed "affinity groups"), national Y support staff and the external consultant. Significant accomplishments have been made since the first YMCAs began their association-wide diversity initiatives in January 2000. Principle accomplishments are:

- Championing a diversity initiative workshop, a two-and-a-half day institute was developed. This workshop guides CEOs, their association's change agents, staff and volunteers through the six-step diversity enhancement process. More than 500 individuals representing more than 100 associations (including YMCA of the USA) have graduated from this workshop with numerous Ys experiencing scorecard results as they implement the process.

- Diversity module added to principles and practices training series, ImpactPlus, Teens and other national and mission strategy trainings.

• The Y-USA created the diversity specialty consultant position to guide the initiative nationally and provide support to the Y-USA internal diversity team (2002).

• Creation and preparation of a support network for champions through the designated diversity consultants (2003) and Diversity Initiative Advisory Team (July 2004).

• Inception of an interactive, innovative diversity web site on the YMCA Exchange as of June 2004 where Ys can download tools and share program and other innovative strategies.

• Received and working collaboratively with other Y-USA staff seeking corporate and foundation funding support to sponsor aspects of implementation.

• Enjoyed the first issue of *Discovery Magazine* devoted specifically to the diversity initiative (June 2004).

• Approximately 120 YMCAs have completed the initial workshop and are implementing the strategic model for ensuring that YMCAs serve all. Approximately 1000 YMCA staff, executives and board members have attended the workshop.

• A second level of workshop entitled "Deepening the Diversity Initiative within your YMCA" has been designed and launched in 2004 with tremendous results. In this two-day workshop, branch executives, staff and volunteers become equipped to use the systemic change model in their every-day operations. To date, approximately 10 such workshops have been conducted.

• In its 2005 summer issue, the Association of YMCA Professionals' publication, *Perspective* featured the National Diversity Initiative via its challenging theme, "Is the YMCA Truly for All?"

Yum! Brands, Inc.

1441 Gardiner Lane
Louisville, KY 40213
Phone: (502) 874-8300
Fax: (502) 874-8662
www.yumcareers.com

Locations

Dallas, TX
Irvine, CA
Louisville, KY

Diversity Leadership

Richard-Abraham Rugnao
Public Affairs, Manager, Global Diversity

Recruiting

Please list the schools/types of schools at which you recruit.

• Ivy League schools
• Other private schools
• Public state schools
• Historically Black Colleges and Universities (HBCUs)
• Other predominantly minority and/or women's colleges

Do you have any special outreach efforts directed to encourage minority students to consider your firm?

• *Conferences:* National Society of Hispanic MBAs, National Black MBA Association, INROADS
• Participate in/host minority student job fair(s)

What activities does the firm undertake to attract minority and women employees?

• Partner programs with women and minority associations
• *Conferences:* National Urban League, NAACP, NCLR, LULAC, OCA, INROADS
• Participate at minority job fairs
• Seek referrals from other employees
• Utilize online job services

Do you use executive recruiting/search firms to seek to identify new diversity hires?

No.

Scholarships

Yum! Scholarship Program

The Yum! Scholarship Program offers scholarship money to all U.S.-based restaurant and restaurant support center employees that have worked at the company for at least one year and average at least 20 hours per week. Yum awards the following: $2,500 for any field of study in a four-year or graduate program, $1,000 for any field of study at a two-year or vocational-technical school, and up to 10 "bonus" awards of $1,500 for students pursuing an approved food service/hospitality degree.

In 2004, Yum! awarded more than $500,000 in scholarships for the Yum! Scholarship Program. Approximately 15 percent of the scholarships awarded went to African-American scholars.

KFC United Negro College Fund Scholars

As part of KFC's ongoing commitment to diversity and the development of its employees, KFC provides scholarships to eligible students attending UNCF schools. The KFC/UNCF scholars program is aimed towards employees who are entry-level college freshman pursuing degrees in business management, computer science or liberal arts.

Scholarships for Minorities

Yum! Brands has a number of scholarships for minorities including the American Indian College Fund to increase the number of American Indian graduates, and similar programs for Hispanic-, Asian- and African-Americans.

Taco Bell Glen Bell Scholarship Program

Open to Taco Bell hourly employees, the program awards financial scholarships of up to $2,000 for accredited undergraduate, graduate and vocational-technical educations. In 2004, Taco Bell's Glen Bell awarded $100,000 in scholarships.

Language Class Reimbursement Program

Hourly or salaried employees can receive up to $500 per year for language class tuition, books and materials.

Tuition Reimbursement Program

The company will reimburse full-time, salaried employees up to a maximum of $4,000 per calendar year for graduate and under-graduate courses.

Affinity Groups

Pizza Hut has an African-American, Hispanic and women's group. Each brand is exploring the development of their respective groups.

Strategic Plan and Diversity Leadership

How does the firm's leadership communicate the importance of diversity to everyone at the firm?

Yum! takes a comprehensive approach to communicating its diversity efforts. All means of internal and external communications are utilized.

Who has primary responsibility for leading diversity initiatives at your firm?

Terrian Barnes, director, global diversity.

Does your firm currently have a diversity committee?

Yes.

Does the committee and/or diversity leader establish and set goals or objectives consistent with management's priorities?

Yes.

Has the firm undertaken a formal or informal diversity program or set of initiatives aimed at increasing the diversity of the firm?

Yes, formal.

How often does the firm's management review the firm's diversity progress/results?

Quarterly.

Retention and Professional Development

Please identify the specific steps you are taking to reduce the attrition rate of minority and women employees.

• Develop and/or support internal employee affinity groups (e.g., minority or women networks within the firm)
• Increase/review compensation relative to competition
• Increase/improve current work/life programs
• Adopt dispute resolution process
• Succession plan includes emphasis on diversity
• Work with minority and women employees to develop career advancement plans
• Strengthen mentoring program for all employees, including minorities and women
• Professional skills development program, including minority and women employees

Diversity Mission Statement

Diversity is not a strategy or a program at Yum! Brands. It's a shared commitment by all of us to uphold our founding truths and to live out our "How We Work Together" principles every day.

Additional Information

Yum! Brands, Inc., with more than 33,000 restaurants in over 100 countries, is the parent to A&W Restaurants, KFC, Long John Silver's, Pizza Hut and Taco Bell. As the world's largest restaurant company and the third largest employer in the world with more than 850,000 employees around the globe, our continued success in the marketplace depends on creating an environment where all people are valued, appreciated and have the opportunity to grow and learn. That is why we have built a global culture focused on respect and recognition.

Moreover, Yum! is committed to realizing the business benefits of driving diversity and inclusion by developing current and future business leaders, franchisees and suppliers that reflect the changing demographics of our customers.

Making progress in diversity is a personal priority for our chairman and CEO David Novak and a business priority for our entire organization. David updates the system annually on the progress we are making to reflect the communities in which we operate. Everyone in the company—from our senior leadership team at the Restaurant Support Centers to our team members in the restaurants—is accountable for fostering an inclusive, diverse workplace culture.

"Yum! Brand's commitment to diversity helps drive all aspects of our business," says David C. Novak, chairman and CEO, Yum! Brands, Inc. "It's important that our global culture is actively developing a workforce with a broad mix of backgrounds and viewpoints at all levels of management. Building on our diverse foundation at all of our brands gives us a competitive edge and helps drive 'Customer Mania.'"

For the past two years, Yum! Brands has been nationally recognized by a leading business magazine as one of the 50 Best Companies for Minorities, claiming the number-one spot for managerial diversity. The magazine ranked Yum! among the top 10 companies having the highest percentage of African-American and Native American employees. In 2004, Yum! jumped 20 spots to place 15th out of 50 on the list.

In addition, Yum! also has been named the number-one company for work/life balance in Louisville, one of the Best Places to Work in Kentucky and Pizza Hut has been named the No. 1 Best Place to Work in Dallas. We are very proud of these accomplishments because they reflect Yum!'s commitment to diversity and to making the company a great place to work.

Our goal for 2005 is to continue to embrace and strengthen our diversity effectiveness with customers, franchise partners, suppliers and the community and to continue to build our talent pipeline with an even stronger emphasis on diversity.

Zurich North America

1400 American Lane
Schaumburg, IL 60196
Phone: (877) 847-6593
Fax: (847) 413-5206
E-mail: debbie.jandt@zurichna.com
www.zurichna.com

Locations

Complete listing on web site.

Diversity Leadership

Carol Bullock
Director, Diversity

Employment Contact

Debbie Jandt
Manager, College Relations and Recruiting
1400 American Lane
Schaumburg, IL 60196
Phone: (877) 847-6593
Fax: (847) 413-5206
E-mail: debbie.jandt@zurichna.com

Recruiting

Please list the schools/types of schools at which you recruit.

• Private schools
• Public state schools
• Historically Black Colleges and Universities (HBCUs)

Do you have any special outreach efforts directed to encourage minority students to consider your firm?

• Participate in/host minority student job fair(s)
• Outreach to leadership of minority student organizations

What activities does the firm undertake to attract minority and women employees?

• Partner programs with women and minority associations
• Participate at minority job fairs
• Seek referrals from other employees
• Utilize online job services

Do you use executive recruiting/search firms to seek to identify new diversity hires?

Yes.

Internships and Co-ops

Zurich Internship Program

Deadline for application: February 15th
Number of interns in the program in summer 2005 (internship) or 2005 (co-op): 70
Pay: $10-$25 per hour
Length of the program: 10-12 weeks
Web site for internship/co-op information: www.zurichna.com

The objective of the internship program is to prepare individuals for careers in their field of study. In the end, participants come away with a unique and well-rounded understanding of Zurich in North America—its products, its services, and its customers.

Candidates are recruited for those locations that have determined a need for interns. The program is formalized and structured; it encompasses "real work" assignments. These are formalized program assessments throughout the summer for the intern and assigned mentor. During the course of the summer program, the intern will assume the duties of the job as if it were a permanent position and work alongside the talented individuals who actually perform the roles today.

The internship program is for college sophomores and junior candidates who can demonstrate problem-solving skills in a customer focused environment; a willingness to work hard and to learn; strong written and verbal communication skills; excellent time-management skills; flexibility; the ability to work independently; self-motivated and a minimum cumulative grade point average of 3.0. The program is from May to August and housing is not provided.

INROADS

> *Deadline for application:* April
> *Number of interns in the program in summer 2005:* Four
> *Pay:* $10-$25 per hour
> *Length of program:* Varies
> *Web site for internship/co-op information:* www.zurichna.com

Entry-Level Programs/Full-Time Opportunities/Training Programs

Associate Program

The Zurich Associate Program is a unique learning, mentoring and networking program that provides select individuals with an insurance education, experience in the way we do business and opportunities to build a career.

Associates participate in broad-based training sessions and work directly with experienced underwriters, risk engineers and claims professionals across the U.S. and Canada over the course of 11 months. Rigorous field preparation and comprehensive examinations are also included in the curriculum. Performance is continuously evaluated, and associates advance only when each phase is successfully completed. In addition, associates must be willing to relocate and be available to work in any one of our North American office locations.

Every new Associate Program class kicks off in the North American headquarters in Schaumburg, Ill., just 45 minutes northwest of Chicago. Associates first take part in a series of insurance and general business workshops. The insurance workshops focus on the core disciplines of commercial insurance: claims, risk engineering and underwriting.

To be considered for the Associate Program, you must be a college graduate (graduated no earlier than one year before the next class start date), eligible to work in the U.S. for the duration of the training program and eligible to work in the U.S. after the training program. In addition, you must have a:

• Bachelor's degree
• Minimum 3.0 cumulative GPA
• Valid driver's license and acceptable driving record documents

Strategic Plan and Diversity Leadership

How does the firm's leadership communicate the importance of diversity to everyone at the firm?
Web site, presentations.

Who has primary responsibility for leading diversity initiatives at your firm?

Director—Diversity, Carol Bullock.

Does your firm currently have a diversity committee?

No.

Has the firm undertaken a formal or informal diversity program or set of initiatives aimed at increasing the diversity of the firm?

Yes, formal.

How often does the firm's management review the firm's diversity progress/results?

Annually.

The Stats

Employees

2005: 8,775
2004: 9,011

Additional Information

Zurich Financial Services is an insurance-based financial services provider with a global network that focuses its activities on key markets in North America and Europe. Founded in 1872, Zurich is headquartered in Zurich, Switzerland. Through its offices in more than 50 countries, 57,000 Zurich employees serve customers in more than 120 countries. In North America, Zurich is a leading commercial property-casualty provider serving the global corporate, large corporate, middle market, small business, specialites and program sectors.

Through its diversity and inclusion vision, Zurich is committed to creating a culture of inclusion consistent with Zurich Basics (values); one that attracts top talent and that promotes the development and full contribution of all employees to achieve business goals.

We want an environment where all people are recognized, feel valued, and can go as far as their talent and ambition allow. We want to create an inclusive culture that understands and values diversity in age, ethnic origin, gender, lifestyles, physical abilities, race, religious beliefs, sexual orientation, work background and other perceived differences. We encourage, recognize and reward individuals to work together toward team, company and individual goals; we believe that by leveraging diversity as a competitive advantage we make our organization a better place to work.

About the Authors

About Vault

Vault is the leading media company for career information. The Vault Career Library includes 100+ titles for job seekers, professionals and researchers. Vault's team of industry-focused editors takes a journalistic approach in covering news, employment trends and specific employers in their industries. Vault annually surveys 10,000s of employees to bring readers the inside scoop on industries and specific employers.

Popular Vault career titles include

- *The College Career Bible*
- *Vault Guide to the Top Internships*
- *Vault Career Guide to Accounting*
- *Vault Career Guide to Biotech*
- *Vault Career Guide to Consulting*
- *Vault Career Guide to Human Resources*
- *Vault Career Guide to Investment Banking*
- *Vault Career Guide to Marketing & Brand Management*
- *Vault Career Guide to Media & Entertainment*
- *Vault Career Guide to Pharmaceutical Sales & Marketing*
- *Vault Career Guide to Real Estate*
- *Vault Guide to Technology Careers*
- Many more

For a full list of titles, go to www.vault.com

About INROADS

Since 1970, INROADS has provided leadership and support for the national effort to increase the representation of talented Black, Hispanic/Latino, and Native American Indian women and men in the private sector. The Fortune 500 companies and other organizations that support INROADS recognize that INROADS is a doorway for business – leading to the benefits of early access to the most talented ethnically diverse human capital before the competition.

In the past 34 years, INROADS has trained more than 40,000 high school and undergraduate students in leadership skills and business competencies. With a focus to improve access and build workforce diversity, INROADS provides a talent pipeline of high potential future executives to America's leading businesses by placing these professionally trained students in multi-year internships.